D1481918

DEMCO

Chicago in Story / A Literary History

Chicago

in Story

A Literary History

Clarence A. Andrews

Midwest Heritage Publishing Company

108 Pearl Street
Iowa City, Iowa
52240

For Amy and Alana

Our Chicagoans

And for Lennox Bouton Grey

Who showed the way

And a special thank you to Thomas Kilpatrick and
Patsy-Rose Hoshiko

And *Illinois! Illinois!*

Books by Clarence A. Andrews

A Literary History of Iowa (1972)
Writing: Growth Through Structure (1972)
Technical and Business Writing (1975)
Growing Up in Iowa (editor/contributor) 1978
Christmas in Iowa (editor/publisher) (1979)
Growing Up in the Midwest (editor/contributor) 1981
This Is Iowa (editor/publisher) 1982

Chicago in Story:
A Literary History

Midwest Heritage Publishing Company
Iowa City, Iowa
1982

Library of Congress Cataloguing in Publication Data

Andrews, Clarence A.
Chicago in Story:
A Literary History

Includes index
1. Chicago (Ill.) — 1830-1982
2. Chicago (Ill.) — literature, films, and authors I. Title
82-Library of Congress Catalog Card Number-061136

Requests for permission to make copies of any part of the work should be sent to Permissions Editor: Midwest Heritage Publishing Co., 108 Pearl Street, Iowa City, IA, 52240.

Printed in the United States of America by Julin Printing Company, Monticello, IA.

First edition

Acknowledgments

Harriet Monroe, "Chicago, 1933," *Poetry*, 1933. ©1933 by the Modern Poetry Association. Reprinted by permission of John F. Nims, Editor, *Poetry*.

Quotation from "Starting Out in Chicago" by Saul Bellow, ©1974 by Saul Bellow, reprinted by permission of Harriet Wasserman.

"Chicago," ©1959 by the Fisher Music Company, Inc. reprinted by permission of the Fisher Music Company, Inc.

"Ruby," from *Excerpts,* by Ronald Fair, ©1975, used by permission of Ronald Fair.

Selections from *A Peculiar Treasure* by Edna Ferber, ©1939. Used by permission of Doubleday & Company, Inc.

Selection from "America Remembers" by Paul Engle, ©1933, used by permission of Paul Engle.

Selection from R. V. Cassill's review of "In a Wild Sanctuary," used by permission of Washington Post Book World.

Selections from Lennox Bouton Grey, *Chicago and the Great American Novel: A Critical Approach to the American Epic,* used by permission of Lennox Bouton Grey.

"The Shooting of John Dillinger Outside the Biograph Theater, July 22, 1934," from David Wagoner, *Collected Poems, 1956-1976,©* Indiana University Press, used by permission of David Wagoner.

Selection from John R. Powers, *The Last Catholic in America* used by permission of John R. Powers.

"Evening Song" by Sherwood Anderson from *Mid-America Chants,©* 1945 by Eleanor Copenhaver Anderson, used by permission.

Portrait of Sherwood Anderson by Hyde Man, based on a photograph by Alfred Steiglitz, used by permission of Eleanor Copenhaver Anderson.

Selections from *Chicago Poems* by Carl Sandburg; ©1916 by Holt, Rinehart and Winston, Inc.; ©1944 by Carl Sandburg. Reprinted by permission of Harcourt Brace Jovanovich, Inc.

Selections from *From Scarface to Scarlett: American Films in the 1930s,* ©1979, 1981 by Roger B. Dooley. Reprinted by permission of Harcourt Brace Jovanovich, Inc.

Contents

Introduction

    Why This Book 1

    A Postscript 5

II.   *"Early Day" in the North-West*

    The Indians and the French 6

    The Fort 9

    "The Strange Boy" 17

    How Chicago Got Its Name. 20

    Summary 21

III.   *The Civil War, the Fire, and Crime*

    The City Grows 22

    The Civil War 23

    Literary Magazines. 24

    From Rags to Riches. 26

    The "Urbs in Horto" Becomes the "Urbs Incinerata". 26

    The First Literature of Crime. 30

    Crime and the Short Story 34

    A Miscellany 35

    The "Rube" Comes to Chicago 36

    Summary 37

IV.   *The "Urbs Recondita"*

    Chicago Rebuilds. 38

    Literary Magazines and Chicago Journalists 39

    The Haymarket Affair in Literature. 43

    Chicago Women. 45

    A Congeries 46

    Joseph Kirkland 48

V.   **The White City and the Black**

Variety in the 1890s 52
Spokespersons for the "Lower Half" 53
"The White City"—The World's Columbian Exposition 57
Miscellaneous Novels of the Nineties 64
Postscript 70

VI.   **Chicago Literature Comes of Age**

Chicago's Higher Evolution 71
Chicago's Literary Societies 72
Chicago Opera and Music 74
The Art Institute 74
Hobart Chatfield Chatfield-Taylor 75
The Romantic View of Life 77
The "Veritist" Movement 78
The Chap-Book and Other "Little" Magazines 82
The Little Room 84
Henry Blake Fuller 85
By and About Journalists 89
Summary 94

VII. **"More Than Their Share"**

William Dean Howells 95
Turn of the Century Historical Romances 96
The Romance of Business 96
Politics and the "Boss" 103
The Employed and the Unemployed 105
The Social-Service and Settlement Novel 109
Novels of Love and Romance 110
Novels of College Life 116
Robert Herrick 117
A Miscellany 119
Summary 124

VIII. *"The Literary Capitol of the United States"*

The Studio World 125
Chicago Little Theater 127
Book Publishing in the Second Decade 131
Chicago Journalists 131
Journalistic Criticism 133
Ringgold (Ring) Lardner, Jr. 134
Romanticists and Sentimentalists 137
Edna Ferber in Chicago 140
Henry Kitchell Webster 143
The Chicago Renaissance 145
Carl Sandburg 146
Theodore Dreiser 148
Masters and Lindsay and Anderson 149
Poetry and *The Little Review* 151
Realists and Romanticists 153
Two Contemporaries Look at the Chicago Literary Scene 162

IX. *The Roaring Twenties*

Crime in Chicago Drama 163
The Chicago Gangster in the Chicago Novel 169
Mystery Novels 170
Edna Ferber in the 1920s 171
Edgar Lee Masters in the 1920s 176
Robert Herrick's Third Decade 178
Other College Novels 179
Journalists as Authors 180
"Young-Man-Going-Somewhere" 184
Novels By and About Women 186
Saga and Chronicle Novels 191
Novels of Business 193
Two Children's Novels 195
Farmers Against the City 195
Chicago Ethnic Novels 196
Payne and Webster 198
Utopian Novels 199
A Potpourri 200
Carl Sandburg 207

A Rash of Poets...208
Chicago's Little Magazines 211
"Chicago: An Obituary"....................................212
A Note on Jack Woodford 213
Other Chicago-Based Films of the 1920s 214
A Footnote 217

X.   *The Depression Years*

Overview..219
Gangsters and Fellow Travelers............................220
The "Who-Done-Its'" Big Decade 225
The Century of Progress Exposition 227
The Depression 229
Chicago Industry..232
Chicago Ethnic Novels.....................................233
Chicago's History...238
By and About Women 240
Young Love in Chicago 244
Chicago Families and People 246
Other Chicago People......................................248
Margaret Ayer Barnes 251
Life in the Suburbs.......................................253
Elizabeth Corbett 254
College and University Life 255
James Thomas Farrell (1904-1981) 257
Poets and Playwrights.....................................260
Chicago Little Magazines 261
Esquire 261
Other Chicago Films of the 1930s..........................262
A Final Note 263

XI. *The War Years and After*

Overview..264
The Depression in 1940s Novels 264
World War II in Chicago Literature 265
The Suburbs...267
Chicago History...268

The Entertainers..270
Industry and Labor Problems......................................271
Chicago People 274
Religious and Ethnic Themes......................................277
Three Novels About Chicago Blacks................................279
Crime in Chicago Literature of the 1940s 280
Two Chicago Poets 285
Chicago Little Magazines of the 1940s............................286
Some Sequels...286
A Congeries..287
Summing Up 288

XII.   *The "Grease" Decade*

The "Grease" and "Rock" Generations 289
Historical Novels..290
Immigrants and Ethnic Groups 291
Blacks in Chicago..293
Other Chicago People...294
College Life 300
Willard Motley...300
Chicago Crime in 1950s Novels and Films 302
Solo 304
Gwendolyn Brooks — Poet 304
Saul Bellow — The Fifties and After 305
This Is Chicago 306
City on the Make 306
Chicago-Based Films in the 1950s.................................306
A Summing Up...307

XIII. *Years of Protest*

Harry Mark Petrakis..308
Blacks in Chicago Literature of the 1960s........................309
Ethnic and Historical Novels 312
Chicago People...313
1960s Films Set in Chicago.......................................321
A New Poetic Image...323
David D. Wagoner — Poet..324

XIV. *The Decade of Disbelief*

The Chicago *Daily News* 325
Professional Football 326
Nelson Algren 326
The 1968 Democratic Convention and the
    Streets of Chicago 327
Chicago Blacks 328
Crime and — Sometimes — Punishment 331
The Medical Scene 333
John R. Powers and Chicago Catholics 333
A Final Miscellany 335
Ordinary People 339
Film Treatments of Chicago in the 1970s 339
Chicago in 1970s Drama 341
David Mamet 342
As the 1980s Begin 344
Meyer Levin 344
Looking to the Future 345
Epilogue — The Norwegian Emigrant Novel
    in Chicago 346
Coda 347

Appendix 349

Mystery Novels With a Chicago Setting 349
Dime Novels With a Chicago Setting 354
Footnotes 357
Index 381

A List of Poetry Editors 1913 to Present

1913-1936 Harriet Monroe, founder and editor

1936-1937 Morton Dauwen Zabel

1937-1942 George Dillon

1942-1946 Peter DeVries with Marion Strobel as co-editor
Strobel (Mrs. James Herbert Mitchell) had been Associate Editor for many years.

April 1946 Dillon, Strobel, Margedant Peters and John Frederick Nims are listed as Editors.

April 1949 Hayden Carruth becomes editor.

February 1950 - September 1955 Karl Shapiro

1955-1968. Henry Rago serves as Editor, the second longest tenure of any *Poetry* editor.

1969-1977-78 Darryl Hine was the Editor

From 1978 to the present John Frederick Nims is the Editor.

I.
Introduction

Hog Butcher for the World,
Tool Maker, Stacker of Wheat,
Player with Railroads and the Nation's Freight Handler;
Stormy, husky, brawling,
City of the Big Shoulders; . . .[1]

Why This Book?

Writing in 1947, Horace R. Cayton commented that a hundred thousand books had been written about Chicago, the metropolis of America's Heartland.[2] In 1973, Finis Farr said the library of the Chicago Historical Society contained about 90,000 books, manuscripts and pamphlets.[3] On that basis, Cayton's figure is obviously over-estimated, but the Society's collection of possible items is incomplete.

There have been books and pamphlets about Chicago's history, its people and ethnic groups, its Fairs, its Fires and other disasters, its architecture, its crime and corruption, its politicians, its commerce, its schools, its River... every facet of the *Urbs in Horto.*

But so far one Chicago subject has been as a whole ignored — its literature, its poetry, its drama, its short stories. To be sure, the approximately twelve hundred volumes that contain literature by Chicagoans about Chicago have been partially written about, reviled, praised or even ignored by reviewers, re-appraised in magazine and newspaper stories, critically evaluated in journals, and even treated in part in some books.

The major treatments to date have been:

Grey, Lennox Bouton: *Chicago and the Great American Novel: A Critical Approach to the American Epic.* A 1935 University of Chicago dissertation of over 600 typed pages. For the most part, it ignores short stories, drama and poetry, and obviously doesn't handle the last forty-five years.

Duffey, Bernard. *The Chicago Renaissance in American Letters.* Focuses primarily on the first two decades of this century (1954).

Duncan, Hugh Dalziell. *The Rise of Chicago as a Literary Center from 1885 to 1920: A Sociological Essay in American Culture* (1964).

Williams, Kenny Jackson. *In the City of Men: Another Story of Chicago.* Primarily the 1890s (1974).

Fleming, Robert Edward. *The Chicago Naturalistic Novel 1930-1966.* Unpublished dissertation (1968).

Kramer, Dale. *Chicago Renaissance/The Literary Life in the Midwest/1900-1930* Lively (1966).

Hansen, Harry. *Midwest Portraits; A Book of Friendships and Memories.* Chicago authors, 1911-1920 (1923).

Williams, Kenny Jackson. *Prairie Voices: A Literary History of Chicago from the Frontier to 1893.* Jackson's "voices" include many non-literary writers (1980).

What values accrue to studies of the fiction, drama and poetry about Chicago? Many view such material as mere entertainment, and there's the antiquated Puritan view that such materials are time-wasting and therefore tools of the devil. To such people, here is an answer from one of Chicago's more recent historians, Finis Farr:

[In the 1880s,] the gutter journalist Shang Andrews wrote the sensational novel *Wicked Nell* to portray commercialized vice ... For the [Columbian Exposition] I found a fresh point of view in a novel of the period, *Sweet Clover* ...

The question of how useful fiction may be to a writer of history is an interesting one. I found that many fictional Chicagoans struck me as absolutely real and trustworthy. There were not only Wicked Nell and Mrs. Burnham's Clover, two girls of the South Side, but a gallery of convincing men and women in the works of Theodore Dreiser and George Ade; and Henry Blake Fuller's people have existence for the historian like the New Yorkers of Edith Wharton and Henry James. I believed in the profane truck driver of the Rev. E. P. Roe's *Barriers Burned Away,* the Lake Forest heroine of Hobart C. Chatfield-Taylor's *An American Peeress,* and the grain speculators of *The Pit* by Frank (Benjamin Franklin) Norris, and I saw truth in the picture that was drawn by Arthur Meeker, Jr. in *Prairie Avenue.* The greatest realistic work of fiction about Chicago is, I feel sure, the Studs Lonigan trilogy by James T. Farrell ... The pages of these novels tell even more about Chicago than the studies from the University, which is saying a good deal ... But Studs and his friends and enemies are alive, and whenever an historian can touch life, he has a chance to make of his history something that lives.[4]

We can go further in this vein than Farr has, for in the pages of Chicago literature one will find the whole range of the "Windy City's" history from the days of the Indians and French who traversed the old Portage to Jean Baptiste Point du Sable, to John Kinzie and Gurdon Saltonstall Hubbard, to the Fire and the Columbian Exposition, to Al Capone and Samuel Insull, to Mayor Daley and the Democratic Convention of 1968.

But suppose one asks if Chicago's literature is worth noting at all? Surely, that would have been a proper question in 1855 when Emerson, Thoreau, Melville, Hawthorne, Whitman and Poe were dominating the American literary scene, and Chicago "one of the most miserable and ugly cities yet seen in America, little deserving of its name 'Queen of the Lake.'"[5] Even four decades later a famous English author was to describe the culture he found in Chicago in these lines:

I know thy cunning and thy greed,
Thy hard high lust and willful deed,
And all thy glory loves to tell
Of spacious gifts material.[6]

But by 1899 when these lines were published, Boston had ceased to be the "hub of the universe;" the financial center was New York, the governmental center Washington, and the center of American population was moving westward. The major literary names were now in the middle west: Tarkington, Norris, Herrick, Fuller, Garland, soon to be followed by the "Chicago Renaissance" and H. L. Mencken's pronouncement that Chicago had become the literary capitol of America."[7]

The criteria used for determining what is Chicago literature are:
- The setting is Chicago or its suburbs, or the area that became Chicago;
- The characters are Chicagoans, or were early residents of the area that became Chicago;
- The themes are pertinent to Chicago at some stage of its history;
- With the exception of some utopian or futuristic novels, the incidents are actually those that took place in Chicago, are typical of what took place, or might have happened in Chicago;
- The authors grew up in the Chicago area, or lived in the Chicago area for a significant part of their lives. Where there are exceptions, the reason for the inclusion of the work is made clear.
- With some exceptions, the work to be discussed is a booklength work.
- With a few exceptions, books by Chicagoans which do not meet these criteria either are not included in this history, or else are noted only in passing. Exceptions include such works as Henry Blake Fuller's *The*

Chevalier of Pensi Vani and *The Châtelaine of La Trinité,* which although apparently set in Italy, are obvious satires on Chicago's
materialism; and Janet Ayer Fairbank's *The Cortlands of Washington
Square,* and Lillian Budd's *April Snow,* both first volumes of trilogies
about people who become Chicagoans in later volumes.

• Books which have only a small portion of their action in Chicago are not
included or else noted only in passing.

An added merit of this literary history is that it fills a gap usually found
in other histories of Chicago. For in reporting on the authors who wrote
about Chicago and the books they wrote, it supplies information lacking in
even very detailed histories of the city.

There are those, of course, who object to "Literature of Place," a term
sometimes applied pejoratively to literature similar to much of that described in the following pages. Other terms such as "provincial" or "local
color" are also applied in a pejorative sense. But the location of a work of
literature has nothing to do with its quality, and the real question is
whether or not a work rises above the mere "provincial." As for "local color,"
that kind of literature found excellent expression in Chicago.

A Chicago author, Donald Culross Peattie, who was both a scholar and a
novelist, pointed out the values in this "literature of place:"

> History sums up [the] story [of our forebears]; it detects the great propulsive
> movements to which they were subject as children. [But History] cannot stop
> to listen to individual forgotten heart beats. But [we] shall listen, and [we] will
> claim the poet's right to say he knows what to think and feel who are too
> headlong in life to make a song of it.[8]

Which is not to say, of course, that we claim artistic greatness for all the
authors or all the books we shall discuss. Many of the books described here
are here "for the record" only; a larger number are "the work of authors who
fall just below the standard of distinction which we set for ourselves." Surely
some of us will puzzle, as Joseph Warren Beach did, "over the works of
writers ... who seem to have all the materials for significant fiction —
character, background, feeling and understanding, seriousness and industry
— and yet somehow just fail to ring the bell."[9]

From time to time we shall see the reasons why some Chicagoans wrote
about their city's past, present, and, in some cases, imagined future. Mrs.
Kinzie, for example, wrote *Wau-Bun* because she believed that historians
were presenting a negative image of her father-in-law's role in the Fort
Dearborn disaster, and because she seems to have felt the need to establish
the primacy of her husband's family over claims being made for the role of
Gurdon Saltonstall Hubbard as "the first citizen" of Chicago. But she also
had another reason for writing, a rationale which was to motivate many a

later Chicagoan:

> The march of improvement and prosperity [has] in less than a quarter of a century ... so obliterated the traces of "the first beginning," that a vast and intelligent multitude [is] crying out for information in regard to the early settlement of this portion of our country ... [10]

This feeling, that something important has happened in the founding and continued growth of Chicago, is an implicit theme in many a Chicago novel, play, poem or short story.

Some Chicago writers wrote because of their moral indignation over certain aspects of Chicago growth — its vice and corruption, its materialism, its political scandals, its crime and criminals. In Henry Blake Fuller, the first important Chicago novelist, we shall trace the beginnings of that alienation which so many American artists have felt with respect to their country or their local environment.

Some writers had more meretricious goals. While seemingly protesting, they were actually capitalizing on the gaudier or more morbid aspects of the Chicago scene.

Some writers focused on the giants of Chicago history. Others turned to the humbler people — to the working class, to ethnic groups, to the "dregs of society" — the sparrows of this world.

If all this sounds as if Chicago literature is in effect a microcosm of American literature — well up to a point that is true. But the strong feature of Chicago literature is that Chicago is its subject — and Chicago is unique. North Side, West Side, South Side, the Loop, the galaxy of "neighborhoods" — there is no place anywhere like Chicago.

A Postcript

In addition to the books of fiction, poetry and plays about Chicago, films presenting fictional accounts of Chicago are also discussed. The film is of course a form of drama and as such deserves attention by its own standards. In the following pages, however, films are discussed either in terms of their subject matter (the Chicago Fire), or because they derive from Chicago literature *(The Man With the Golden Arm, Front Page).*

II.
"Early Day" in the Northwest

Chicago has very little respect for the seventeenth century. The seventeenth century has done nothing for Chicago: she does not even know that this is the greatest hog-market in the world.[1]

The Indians and the French

Before the French, the first white men, came to the Chicago area, the Illinois Indians were here, and sometimes others — the Mascoutens, the Potawatamis, the Ojibwe. They did not care for the flat marshy land with its rank odors, referring to it as "Checacqua" or "skunk." They rarely used the portage from Lake Michigan (they called it the Lake of the Illinois) up the south fork of the Chicago, across to the Des Plaines, thence downstream to the Mississippi.

They preferred the other portages — up the Fox to the Wisconsin, then down the Wisconsin. Or up the St. Joseph to the Kankakee, then down the Kankakee. Both routes bypassed the Chicago area by a wide margin.

Although the French explorer LaSalle (for whom LaSalle Street is appropriately named) and Marquette and Joliet used the portage, were it not for Father Marquette, the Chicago portage would scarcely be worth mentioning in Chicago's literary history. Marquette came through the portage only twice, the first time in the spring of 1764, the second time in the later winter of that year.

The earliest literary reference to Marquette's 1764 voyage through the portage is in Joseph Hall's "The Dark Maid of the Illinois," a sketch which is also a very early Illinois literary work. Hall's fictional priest and his entourage leave the lake and pass over the site of the Chicago-to-be:

> ... the waters were high and they floated over the inundated lands, pushing their boats among the trees of the forest, and over the rank herbiage of the low prairies of that region, until they found the current, which had set towards the north, began to flow off in the opposite direction, and floated them into a small stream running toward the south [the Des Plaines].[2]

When Marquette came again to the portage he was a sick man, forced to endure the bitter winter in a "rude cabin ... inland a few leagues" on the South Branch of the River. The incident is noted briefly in Parish's *The Man With the Iron Hand* (1913) and in Ruth Russell's *Lake Front* (1931):

> ... It was time to keep the promise with the Illinois. October leaves were red when [Marquette] and his two *donnés* took the trail again ... November came, and to their right were black trees and white cliffs set between gray sky and gray lake.
>
> "Health of the sick, pray for us."
>
> Chicagou was near. It was a place with a river that led to the portage, and on the river the canoe could lie quiet and he could rest. With hope he looked at the wind-swept sand dunes and the stunted trees along the river banks.
>
> ... All winter they were held to the cabin; outside were the snow on the prairie and the stiff black trees ...[3]

It is easy to see why "Chicago has very little respect for the seventeenth century" other than a few street and place names. The seventeenth century passed Chicago by, concentrating its energies downstate at Fort St. Louis, Fort Crèvecoeur and Kaskaskia.

The largest literary tribute to Marquette is an ironic one in the pages of Jay William Hudson's *Nowhere Else in the World* (1923) with its description of Chicago's monument to the site where the sick Marquette spent that winter of 1674:

> The Marquette Cross is in one of the most dismal parts of the city. To get there, one travels southwest from the Loop, through a wretched poverty-stricken street, which lengthens itself out for dreary mile after dreary mile — a street of second-hand stores, junk shops, cheap lodging houses, restaurants covered with signs in strange languages, and miserable frame dwellings, ramshackle, colorless, bleak ... The trolley car ... can take you only to the foot of Robey Street where it dumps you at the edge of a wilderness of lumber yards ... You make your devious way through an alley, over plank walks set in seas of black mud, until, at last, you come to an open place, where struggling weeds push themselves up amid heaps of cinders and refuse. There, on the very edge of the river, where it stealthily empties its noisome secrets into the Drainage Canal [on the north side between Damien and Canal D] rises the Marquette Cross. It is a large, flat, wooden cross bound at the edges with rusted iron, worn, battered, storm-beaten, corroded by rain and snow and hail

and wind and sun, defaced with countless initials as high as a human hand can reach, above which one reads, "In Memory of Marquette and Joliet, 1673."

The first white men that ever set foot on Chicago's soil built a hut here. Two hundred fifty years ago a dream was born here.

Here is the cradle of Chicago ... The one landmark in all Chicago's boasted bigness that might lend her poetry, romance, and the touch of a dramatic glory is abandoned and forgotten![4]

Recent reports indicate that the Marquette Cross no longer exists. Moreover, a metal plaque, once attached to a nearby bridge and commemorating Marquette's residence in the area, has disappeared.

Elizabeth Farnsworth Means, who concealed her identity under the romantic *nom de plume* of "Nellie Wildwood," wrote a long narrative poem in decasyllabic couplets about *The Voyage of Pere Marquette*. But long narrative poems such as this one fell out of fashion long ago, and with them went Nellie's reputation.

After the English defeated the French in the French-Indian-Indian Wars, the French political, economic and social influence gradually disappeared from the Great Lakes and the Great Valley, leaving isolated pockets here and there and a heritage of place names.

The passing of the French left mixed emotions behind. Joseph Hall's effete French barber, "Madcap" Pierre Blondo, says Lennox Bouton Grey, "is clearly a product of French-British-American frontier rivalries, and is an indirect justification of the rugged Americans who replaced him. . . . Hall saw New France as an alien ambition which had been overcome in the interest of the better [American] culture that was to develop here." Occasional Chicagoan Mary Hartwell Catherwood, who beginning in 1888, and until her death in 1902, wrote a series of historical romances about the French in northern Illinois and on the Lakes, saw the French as representatives of "a gracious culture defeated by the rapacity of a few men ...[5]

In the mid-nineteenth century, a non-literary writer lamented that "French gaiety [was] rapidly ebbing ... the shriek of the steam whistle and the laborious snort of the propeller ... announce ... the age of the practical hard-working, money-getting Yankee is upon us, and that the careless, laughter-loving Frenchman's day is over."[6] In one way or another, that estimate was to appear in a great deal of subsequent Chicago fiction.

In his 1938 *A Prairie Grove,* Donald Culross Peattie, a naturalist as well as a novelist, presents a factual-fictional history of millena of northeastern Illinois history with a sharp focus on a patch of land just north of Chicago. Peattie samples four time-stages: the pre-historic period, the Indian period, the French period, and the coming of the narrator's ancestors. As other novelists of the twentieth century, Peattie avoids the nineteenth-century

Indian stereotypes:

> Here was a species whose talons were arrows, whose speed was in their cunning, whose strength was the prairie fires they lighted that ran without need of breath or water, and so outran the stumbling herd of heaving flanks and lolling tongues. They ate as the beasts ate, ravenous and gorging in hours of abundance; they all knew famine in its season, and like carnivores they had then to eat the memory of old feasts. They took some thought against the morrow, but never enough. Yet in the midst of abundance, they were not wasteful, they were too ignorant to kill for sport. The animals too, they thought, had souls; they must not be insulted or their spirits broken; the herbs were in the earth's keeping, and when they gathered their simples they asked her pardon. "I take these thy hairs, Nokomis, grandmother, and I thank you and ask your pardon."[7]

Peattie's French are fictional: "the names of Father Gabriel Forreste and Father Pierre Prud-homme you will not find in all the seventy-two volumes of the *Jesuit Relations*," the narrator says. Again, "you will find my Robert Du Gay in La Salle, Frontenac, Champlain. You will find the *coureurs du bois* everywhere in frontier history."[8]

In general critics praised *A Prairie Grove*, one calling it an attempt at an epic, another a "nostalgic prose-poem to what was the wilderness of the Middle West."[9] Some, however, were put off by Peattie's style:

> The [novel's] effect is weakened, however, by an idiom that often sacrifices the necessary precision of statement for the sake of a vague lyricism in which description gives way to song. This lyrical mood, carried to booklength, tends to diminish the epic stature of an epic theme.[10]

The Fort

Chicago's first entrepreneur, if not its first citizen, was as the Indians liked to emphasize, a black — Jean Baptiste Point du Saible who about 1770 built the first trading post on the north side of the Chicago River.[11] du Sable sold his property to Jean Lalime, who in turn sold it to John Kinzie. In a quarrel between the latter two, Lalime died. All of these men appear in Chicago literature.

In 1803, Secretary of War General Henry Dearborn ordered a contingent of men to build a fort on the Chicago River at its mouth. The contingent's commander was Captain John Whistler, destined to be the grandfather of the American artist, James Abbott McNeil Whistler. One hundred and thirteen years later, Edgar Lee Masters attempted an epic around Whistler's role as builder of the fort:

"Aeneas" Whistler you shall found a city
You've built Fort Dearborn, that is the beginning.
Imperial Rome could be put in a corner

Of this, the city which you'll found. Fear not
The wooden horse, but have a care for cows ...[12]

About 1850, the Canadian-born Major John Richardson described the
Fort and the surrounding village in his *Hardscrabble; or, The Fall of Chicago:*

> The Fort of Chicago [Fort Dearborn] stood upon a portion of the same
> ground occupied by its successor [built in 1816], and was, in fact, a very
> epitome of a fortress ... Two blockhouses constituted its chief defense while
> on the north, a subterranean passage led from the parade-ground to the river
> . . .
>
> The mouth of the Chicago River was then nearly a half mile more to the
> southward than it is now ... On the same side of the river was the Govern-
> ment Agency House ... Immediately opposite to the Fort [on the site of the
> residence of du Saible] stood the residence and trading post of [John Kinzie]
> ... And close to his abode, lived ... Ouilmette ... About a quarter of a mile
> beyond Ouilmette's, and immediately opposite to the Pottawattamie encamp-
> ment, was another small but neat dwelling. This belonged to Mr. Heywood.[13]

Masters, in his 1916 "epic," projected a scene from military life at the Fort:

> Throw logs upon the fire! Relieve the guard
> At the main gate and the wicket gate! Lieutenant
> Send two men 'round the palisades, perhaps
> They'll find some thirsty Indians loitering
> Who may think there is whisky to be had ...[14]

But when the War of 1812 began further east, the Indians thirst for
whisky changed into a thirst for Yankee blood and the small settlement of
"Garlic Creek" found itself in trouble:

> It was the evening of the 7th of April, 1812. The children of Mrs. [John]
> Kinzie were dancing before the fire to the music of [Kinzie's] violin. The
> teatable was spread, and they were awaiting the return of their mother who
> had gone to visit a sick neighbor about a quarter of a mile up the river.
>
> Suddenly their sport was interrupted. The door was thrown open, and Mrs.
> Kinzie rushed in, pale with terror, and scarcely able to articulate, "The In-
> dians! The Indians!"
>
> "The Indians? What? Where?" eagerly demanded they all.
>
> "Up at Lee's Place, killing and scalping!"[15]

"Lee's Place," about four miles up the South fork of the Chicago River, is
the place Richardson's novel said belonged to "Mr. Heywood." Richardson
also calls the area "Hardscrabble." Jesse Dick, in Edna Ferber's *The Girls*
(1922) is socially unacceptable to the aristocratic Thrift family because he
comes from Hardscrabble. In more recent years the area has become known
as Bridgeport.

Soon, the Indians were at a fever pitch of excitement in the old Northwest.

Tecumseh and the British had stirred them to the boiling point. They were unrestrainedly eager to sink their tomahawks into American scalps:

[The capture of Mackinac on July 17, 1812] on the part of the British completely cut off the post of Chicago at the head of Lake Michigan, leaving it isolated, in what was then a very remote wilderness. Chicago, Mackinac and Detroit were the three grand stations of the Americans on the upper lakes, and here were two of them virtually gone at a blow![16]

On August 9, 1812, Captain Heald, the Fort commandant received orders from General Hull to abandon Fort Dearborn, and to bring the garrison and civilians to Detroit where Hull was. When Heald, as a consequence, began destroying the Fort's ordnance and liquor supply, John Kinzie protested, but Heald insisted he had to carry out his orders. On the morning of August 15, to the tune of "The Dead March," the Fort personnel moved out. In a short time, over half of the party were dead, the victims of an Indian ambush at what is now Prairie Avenue and Eighteenth — the corner where for some years the palatial residence of George M. Pullman stood. The Kinzies were spared because the Indians regarded Kinzie as their "father." Kinzie's daughter, the wife of a garrison officer, was rescued by an Indian named Black Partridge. The moment of rescue is commemorated by an heroic bronze sculpture in the main entrance of the Chicago Historical Society.

The Massacre's place in Chicago's literary history is considerable. It produced Chicago's first serious literary effort, "The Narrative of the Massacre,"[17] by Mrs. John H. Kinzie, John Kinzie's daughter-in-law, as well as a quantity of later books, plays and poems.

"The Narrative" begins with the April 7th incident and continues through the roundup of survivors after the Massacre. It is important both for its lively literary style and for its part in a continuing controversy about the Kinzie family, a controversy carrying well into this century. It is also the main source for all the later literary efforts.

"The Narrative" presents John Kinzie's role in the Massacre in a favorable light, presenting what came to be called the "anti-military view" of the event.[18] Its publication in 1844 — it may have been written as early as 1836 — was without doubt in answer to the rumors floating about the newly-incorporated Chicago of possible improprieties in "John Kinzie's domestic affairs before coming to Chicago, about Kinzie's bitter opposition to [the Fort Commandant] at the time of abandoning the Fort, and the fortuitous escape of the Kinzie family, about the killing of Lalime, and about the sizable Kinzie [land] claims in the Indian treaty of 1833."[19] In particular, the "Narrative" shows Captain Heald, the commandant, as a bumbler whose failure to act wisely or to take Kinzie's advice led to the Massacre.

There was a second reason for the "Narrative's" publication in 1844. The

Kinzies had learned that Judge Henry Brown of Chicago was about to publish his *History of Illinois* (1844), and that his book would present the "anti-Kinzie" view about the Massacre and other Chicago incidents. Judge Brown had seen the "Narrative" in manuscript, and he paraphrased parts of it in his history. But he added conflicting reports of the event taken from the Archives of the War Department in Washington, reports which supported the "anti-Kinzie" view. By including these, and by using Mrs. Kinzie's material without permission, he earned the lady's anger.[20]

Five years later, Elbert H. Smith used the Kinzie material for his ambitious poetic epic treatment of the Massacre in *Me-ka-tai-me-she-kia-kiak, or Black Hawk, and Scenes in the West, a National Poem* (1849). His epic in both rhymed and blank verse, is easily forgettable.

A much greater success was achieved by Major John Richardson, a Canadian. His *Hardscrabble, Or, the Fall of Chicago; A Tale of Indian Warfare* (1850) is limited to the Indian attack on Lee's place, and his *Wau-Nan-Gee; Or, The Massacre at Chicago; A Romance of the American Revolution* (1852) treats the Massacre itself. Lennox Bouton Grey calls *Hardscrabble* ... "the first Chicago novel."[21]

Richardson's novels, incorporating both factual and imaginary romantic details, are the archetypes for later expansions of Mrs. Kinzie's dramatically-compressed narratives through the nineteenth and on into the mid-twentieth century. Setting the precedent for later works, his two books place additional characters at the Fort, add or manipulate details, and change names of characters or places. Often some of the imaginary events and people are more important than actual events or people. A familiar character in these books is the historic Black Partridge; in later books, he ranges all over the area and saves the lives of many of the imaginary characters.

Many of Richardson's romantic touches were not in the first versions of *Hardscrabble* when it was published in *Sartain's Union Magazine of Literature and Art* in 1850. Either Richardson added these to his later paperback book version, or else (and this is more likely) they were deleted by Mrs. Carolyn Kirkland, one of the editors, who made it known that she objected on principle to the "miserable [romantic] trash of which the public have given unequivocal symptoms of disgust."[22]

But Mrs. Kirkland, whose liking for realism was passed on to her son, Joseph, and through him to Hamlin Garland, apparently had misjudged the public's taste on this occasion; Sartain's soon expired. Meanwhile, Richardson's slender books went through edition after edition, and Richardson was touted as the successor to another American author of Indian and pioneer life:

The Author of *Wau-nan-gee,* since the demise of [James Fenimore] Cooper, stands unrivalled as a writer of the romance of Indian warfare. The book now put forth is perhaps the most interesting story of its kind which has ever issued from the American Press.[23]

In presenting the "cultivated military" view as opposed to Mrs. Kinzie's "cultivated civilian" view,[24] Richardson had stolen the spotlight from the Kinzies. Meanwhile, Judge Brown's *History* had made a strong case for the "anti-Kinzie" point of view. And John H. Kinzie had been defeated in his attempt to be the first mayor of the newly-incorporated city by a brash newcomer, William B. Ogden. So John's wife, Mrs. Juliette Kinzie, had several reasons for expanding the "Narrative of the Massacre" into the book-length *Wau-bun, The "Early Days" of the Northwest.*

Juliette Kinzie, says Hugh Dalziell Duncan, "wanted to found a Kinzie dynasty in Chicago. Her own testimony and that of others [shows] that she was ambitious to assume cultural and social leadership in [the burgeoning city]. To achieve a great name on the stage, or in the arts, was possible, but it was not possible for a socially ambitious woman [at that time]. The stage was not respectable, the arts hardly less so. Literature was entirely respectable — and it was the one way in which a woman might become known beyond her own circle."[25]

The Fort Dearborn massacre takes up only two chapters of *Wau-bun.* The book focuses primarily on the frontier life of John H. and Juliette Augusta Magill Kinzie from shortly after their marriage in New York in September 1830 until 1833 when the couple was planning to take up residence in Chicago. It contrasts the events of these three years with the adventures of the elder Kinzie and his wife, Eleanor Lytle McKillip Kinzie. *Wau-bun* had its origins in family anecdotes and legends maintained by Eleanor; John Kinzie had died (in 1826) before his son's marriage:

> "My child," [Eleanor would say to Juliette], "write these things down as I tell them to you. Hereafter our chidren, and even strangers, will feel interested in hearing the story of our lives and early sufferings."[26]

In *Wau-bun,* says Duncan, Juliette "gave the Fort Dearborn legend its accepted form." The book's narrative style has been widely praised, although many of its facts have been questioned. In fact, there have been continuing disagreements as to whether the book is fiction or history. "Chicago fiction, and indeed, Chicago literature begins with . . . *Wau-bun,*" said William Morton Payne in the *Dial.* "It is invaluable as a historical document, and has not a little charm as a piece of literature."[27] Chicago librarians have disagreed about its classification.[28] Novelist Henry Blake Fuller, in 1923, wondered if it was a novel.[29] And historian Milo M. Quaife, while admiring the book in its own terms, said that it was worthless as a work of history.[30]

Lennox Bouton Grey says that *Wau-bun's* motives are primary ones in Chicago literature, "giving impulse and direction to Chicago's concept of itself." In particular he notes the use of "biographical-social interweavings" that could be traced in a hundred Chicago novels.[31]

So, as Henry H. Hurlbut said, "No one ever attempts to write about the history of Chicago without drawing from the pages of Mrs. Kinzie's book."[32] And Joseph Kirkland, though calling the book "a novel," and pointing out its inaccuracies, says, "It should be reprinted [as it has been on several occasions] and have a place in every Chicago library."[33]

Wau-bun's 1856 publication "gave the Fort Dearborn legend its accepted form."[34] Almost immediately, in December, 1856, Chicago's Rice Theatre produced a three-act "afterpiece," *Chicago in 1812: The Massacre of Fort Dearborn.* Although this play owes it plot to *Wau-bun,* it owes some of its details to Richardson's novels.

In 1870, at the end of her life, Mrs. Kinzie finished her last manuscript, *Mark Logan, the Bourgeois;* it was not published until 1887. The further adventures of her family are the basis for this novel.

Fort Dearborn next appears in a poem by Benjamin Franklin Taylor, Chicago editor and poet, and one of the most important literary figures in Chicago at this time. His *Complete Poetical Works* (1886), which no longer commands the respect it once did, includes "Fort Dearborn: Chicago:"

I hear the Block-house gates unbar, the column's solemn tread,
I saw the Tree of a single leaf its splendid foliage shed
To wave awhile that August morn above the column's head;
I heard the moan of muffled drum, the woman's wail of fife,
The Dead March played for Dearborn's men just marching out of life,
The swooping of the savage cloud that burst upon the rank
And struck with its thunderbolt in forehead and in flank,
The spatter of the musket-shot, the rifle's whistling rain —
The sand-hill's drift round hope forlorn that never marched again![35]

The "Tree" referred to above was the "Massacre Tree" which, bearing scars of the battle, long stood in the Prairie Avenue area.

From Taylor on, says Duncan, "Chicago writers . . . created Fort Dearborn in terms of the legends and myths they found stimulating to their own imaginations. Chicago elites and their publics, in turn, accepted these myths in order to gain and sustain the kind of power they wanted."[36] With the turn of the century, says Grey, "time [was to] metamorphose Fort Dearborn into the glamorus stuff of romance, in the mode of [the romantic novelist of the lost French cause] Mary Hartwell Catherwood."[37]

Duncan sees Kinzie's influence in another light — "the power of Mrs. Kinzie's pen to give form to the longings of a new business society for heroes drawn from its own ranks. Mrs. Kinzie's transformation of her father-in-law into a 'cultivated trader' and the founder of a dynasty served as a model for all future Chicago 'lady' writers. Martha J. Lamb, Mary Healy Bigot, Margaret Potter Black, Katherine Keith, Marion Strobel, Janet Ayer Fairbank, Margaret Ayer Barnes, Mary Hastings Bradley, and other Chicago women produced 'dynastic' novels of generations in which the business hero is a central figure." For Duncan "the forms of literature became the forms of life." The legend of Kinzie, the "heroic trader" became the legend of the "founding father;" this legend will remain "as long as Chicago remains a 'commercial city.'"[38]

Thus, says Grey, Myrtle Reed's 1903 *The Shadow of Victory: A Romance of Fort Dearborn*, while written "in the mode of Catherwood," was also written "in response . . . to the general interest in 'business romance' at the turn of the century. On the other hand, the clowning of a Lieutenant Ronald "is an anchronism of college nonsense." Grey attributes the mythical young officer's behavior to a period of anti-collegiate spirit, reflected in such phenomena as the will of a plumbing supplies manufacturer who left a large portion of his estate to improve training in the secondary schools because he felt that college education was wasteful for "self-made men" such as himself.[39]

The most popular of the turn-of-the century Fort Dearborn romances was Randall Parrish's *When Wilderness Was King, a Tale of the Illinois Country* (1904). A paragraph from this novel illustrates how it ties the frontier past to the commercial present:

> What a marvelous change has less than a century witnessed! Once the outermost guard of our western frontier, it is now the site of one of the great cities of two continents. To me, who have seen these events and changes, it possesses more than the wonderment of a dream.[40]

Three juveniles haved used the Massacre as a subject for books in which children play prominent parts: Col. H. R. Gordon's *Black Partridge, or the Fall of Fort Dearborn* (1906) Evelyn Hunt Raymond's *The Sun Maid, a Story of Fort Dearborn* (1900), and Mary Virginia Fox's *Ambush at Fort Dearborn* (1962). "Col. Gordon" was a pseudonym for Edward Sylvester Ellis. Both Ellis and Raymond were authors of a number of "frontier juveniles." Fox's book, like *Wau-bun,* but unlike the romances, tries to treat the Indians sympathetically.

The character of Ensign George Ronald in Reed's *The Shadow of Victory* is an exaggerated treatment of an Ensign Ronan who died gallantly in the Massacre while others about him were panicking in fear. In 1955, Leon E. Burgoyne used young George Ronan as the central character in his story for young people, *Ensign Ronan; A Story of Fort Dearborn.* Burgoyne's story shows Ronan as an impulsive person who angered older soldiers and the Indians, especially one name Pe-so-tum. John Kinzie's step-daughter, however, identified Pe-so-tum as one who helped "The Black Partridge" save her life.

Two twentieth-century poets have used the Dearborn incidents. Francesca Falk Miller's reach exceeded her grasp in *"1812," the Story of the War of 1812 in Song and Story* (1935). The other and earlier was Edgar Lee Masters, who wrote to Harriet Monroe about his adopted city:

> Chicago fascinates me ever and ever. Oh, this is quite a magical place! And what it may yield when the right imagination does La Salle, Marquette, the Green Bay country and Michigan![41]

Masters applied his enthusiasm and his imagination to his third volume of verse, *The Great Valley* (1916), a book of verse largely about Chicago's history. One poem, "Captain John Whistler" (see page 9) attempts to establish Whistler as the "father of Chicago," and, by implication, detract from Kinzie's reputation. Another, "Fort Dearborn," also looks backward from the Chicago of 1916 to the time when "the old fort stood/when the river bent southward," and John Kinzie was a fur-trader:

In the loneliness of the log-cabin,
Across the river,
The fur-trader played his fiddle
When the snows lay
Across the camps of the Pottawatomies
In the great forest.
Now to the music of the Kangaroo Hop,
And Ragging the Scale,
And La Seduccion,
The boys and girls are dancing
In a cafe near Lake Street.[42]

In 1910, the last literary defense of the Kinzies by a member of the family, Eleanor Lytle Kinzie's *John Kinzie, the Father of Chicago* was privately printed. In 1917 *Hearts Undaunted,* by Eleanor Stackhouse Atkinson, Chicago school teacher, popular historian, biographer, *Chicago Tribune* writer, and author of *The Story of Chicago* (1910), is also a defense of the Kinzie family. Concentrating primarily on John Kinzie's wife, Eleanor Lytle McKillip Kinzie, it portrays the Kinzies not as merchants who began the Chicago commercial tradition but as cultured people. Kinzie, Senior's fur trading is de-emphasized; he is most often referred to by the Indian name, "Shaw-nee-aw-kee," the "Silverman" and craftsman. Although the novel portrays Eleanor's history as a child captive of the Indians, it ignores some of the unsavory Chicago rumors about both John and Eleanor before their marriage.

As the centennial of Chicago approached in the late 1920s, a wave of nostalgia for the past swept over those Chicagoans who could free their minds from the boom and bust cycles of the times. A third "Fort Dearborn" was built near the site of the Massacre, and a "Century of Progress" Exposition was built on the nearby lake front. There was an appreciative echo from the book publishing trade which had also fallen upon hard times and needed a spur. In 1933, among the many books celebrating Chicago's history, there was another reprint of *Wau-bun* and the first volume of Mary Hastings Bradley's fictional *Old Chicago*.[43] In *The Fort*, the violence of the Massacre is overshadowed by a romance between an imaginary young Englishman and an Indian woman. The Englishman chooses death in the Lake Michigan dunes to life with the Indians.

The most recent adult novel to use the Massacre, as well as the 1835 Chicago Powwow which formally ended the Indians' presence in Illinois, is Julia Altrocchi's widely-praised *Wolves Against the Moon* (1940). The historical novel traces the struggle between Indians and whites for the Old Northwest through the career of Joseph Bailly from 1794 to 1835. Baillytown, east of Gary, is named for this actual historical person.

"The Strange Boy"

So far we've overlooked the greater rival for Kinzie's imprimatur as "Father" of Chicago than Masters' "Aeneas" Whistler. Though throughout the nineteenth century, Gurdon Saltonstall Hubbard was to be John Kinzie's arch-rival for the title of "Chicago's first citizen,"[44] he lacked a literary champion. Hubbard, who came to Chicago as a boy in 1818, is not mentioned in William H. Bushnell's *Prairie Fire: A Tale of Early Illinois*.[45] Still, this 1864 tale must have recalled to readers in Chicago (where the story was extremely popular[46]) many of the elements of Hubbard's exciting career. The ride of Bushnell's frontiersman for help and the flood-stage of the Vermilion River must have prompted memories of the 1828 Chicago Indian scare when Hubbard (whom the Indians named "Pa-pa-ma-ta-be" or "Swift Walker") in only seven days hiked the 125 miles to Danville and returned with a volunteer garrison.

In *Wau-bun*, Mrs. Kinzie had carefully avoided any reference to Hubbard, even though he was one of the two best known American Fur Company *bourgeois* in Chicago. Her husband was the other![47] In her *Mark Logan, the Bourgeois*, she refers to Hubbard only as "H."[48] Yet by the time she wrote the book, she and Hubbard were among the founders of Chicago's St. James Church, "long the church of Chicago's leading families."[49]

Hubbard outlived both Kinzies, John by six decades and John H. by two. At his death in 1886, he left behind a partial autobiography. Two years later

Chicago's Rand McNally and Company published Henry E. Hamilton's *Incidents and Events in the Life of Gurdon S. Hubbard*. In 1890, the Chicago Historical Society, recovered from its losses in the Fire, published Grant Goodrich's *Gurdon S. Hubbard*. The myth-makers had begun their work.

The first fictional portrayal of Hubbard, though not in this case as a central figure, is in Amanda M. Douglas's *A Little Girl in Old Chicago* (1904). Douglas had ransacked the pages of A. T. Andreas's three-volume *The History of Chicago* (1884-1886) though apparently ignoring the two books on Hubbard.[50]

In 1911, Hubbard's partial autobiography was edited by Caroline M. McIlvaine and privately printed by Chicago's R. R. Donnelly and Sons.

In 1916, Edgar Lee Masters, at work upon his *The Great Valley* turned his attention to Hubbard, paraphrasing in verse Hubbard's own account of his arrival at the second Fort Dearborn in 1818:

> ... And when we came as far
> As thirty-ninth or thirty-first perhaps —
> Just sand hills then — I never can forget it —
> What should I see? Fort Dearborn dazzling bright,
> All newly white-washed right against that sky,
> And the log cabins round it, far away
> The rims of forests, and between a prairie
> With wild flowers in the grasses red and blue —
> Such wild flowers and such grasses, such a sky,
> About where now the Public Library stands
> On Randolph Street ...[51]

There are four full scale fictional treatments of Hubbard's life, none of the quality of *Wau-bun*. In Ada and Julian Street's *Tides* (1926), he is seen as "Zenas Wheelock," an old man trying to recall Chicago's pioneer days, bitter that his earlier family home is now the center of Chicago's red light district.

Harry Raymond Hamilton's *Epic of Chicago* (1932, an obvious echo of James Truslow Adams's 1931 *Epic of America*) was labeled both "romance" and "history" by its publishers.[52] It portrays Hubbard as an heroic type against the background of the early settlement and city. Its motivation, like Henry E. Hamilton's, springs from the same roots of family pride as *Wau-bun*. The two Hamiltons belonged to the Hubbard clan.

Alfred Hubbard Holt (another family member) in his *Hubbard's Trail* (1952) emphasizes Hubbard's pioneer experiences and his "marriage" to Watseka, an Indian woman, which lasted only two years. Hubbard then married a woman of his own race.

Holt's book opens with Hubbard and his second wife surveying the ruins of their business on the morning after the Fire. Hubbard then begins reminiscing about the events which have brought him to that point.

Holt says his book is not "history," and he admits having juggled dates and persons, and inventing incidents. But he pulls no punches in dealing with some of the darker parts of Hubbard's career. In the scene in which an investigating board exonerates Hubbard from any blame in the 1860 sinking of Hubbard's *The Lady Elgin* off Winnetka, Illinois, he shows dissenting board members angrily asking about the lack of lifeboats, and he shows Hubbard's "grim, staring face" as he hears a child sing a stanza from the popular ballad about the tragedy:

Lost on *The Lady Elgin,*
Sleeping to wake no more,
Numbered in that three hundred,
Who failed to reach the shore.[53]

The fourth is Winifred E. Wise's *Swift Walker; A True Story of the American Fur Trade* (1937). This fictionalized biography is based on Hubbard's partial autobiography. Although it covers his life from his birth in 1816 to his death in 1886, its primary emphasis is on his youth and early career as a fur trader, his marriage to Watseka, and the beginning of his own business enterprises after the decline of the fur trade.

Two writers, Mary Hastings Bradley and Louis Zara have brought together members of the Kinzie family and Hubbard. In addition to *The Fort* (above), Hasting's *The Duel* (1933) shows John Kinzie in retrospect, and places a modern emphasis on the relations among these prominent Chicagoans. *The Duel* gives considerable attention to Hubbard — although ignoring, like other novels, his meat-packing enterprise. It took a long time for Chicago authors to recognize any respectabilty in those industrialists who gave the city the name of "Porkopolis!"

Zara's epic, *This Land Is Ours* (1940), narrates the travels of a fictional Benton family from 1775 to 1835. Like other historical novelists, Zara juggles history to suit his novelistic purposes. Andrew Benton accompanies an equally fictitious Commandant Hamtramck to the Portage to survey for a fort; there they encounter the real Point du Saible. Later, Andrew is at the Fort at the time of the Massacre, but, like all those other fictional people who escaped the fate of the real-life people in the ambush, he too escapes. Later the Bentons are at Danville with Gurdon Hubbard and they accompany Hubbard northward along "Hubbard's trail" to save Chicago from the threat of the Winnebagoes.

A late arrival in the Fort Dearborn cavalcade of novels is Regina Z[immerman] Kelly's *Beaver Trail* (1955). Like others before it, this novel presents a fictional young man who arrives at Fort Dearborn at the time of the Massacre and is saved through the efforts of none other than Black Partridge.

How Chicago Got Its Name

There have been numerous attempts to account for the name of "Chicago" as it applies both to the River and to the City. One of the earliest was Rachel G. Heyer's in a December, 1851, *Sartain's Union Magazine* story, "Chikagou and Tonika." Heyer relates that Chikagou, an Indian, was "respected by red and white man alike," and left his name "to be perpetuated by the flourishing city of *Chicago*." This story, says Grey, shows very early "ambitious intent to lift the name to dignified heights."[54]

In *Wau-bun*, Mrs. Kinzie says that the city was named for an Indian chief, Che-cau-go, who had drowned in the River. But her tale smacks of the tourist lore found throughout the midwest.[55]

In *The Story of Chicago* (1892), Joseph Kirkland offers a smorgasbord of sixteen choices; the three most popular theorize that the name is based on Indian words (from several tribes) meaning either "skunk," "skunk weed" or "wild onion" (referring to an odorous plant growing along the Chicago River, from whence is derived the sometimes pejorative, sometimes sentimental "Garlic Creek") or "great" or "strong." Howard Vincent O'Brien wrote that the name could have been derived from any one of similar Indian words, each with a different meaning. Bradford Mitchell found humor in the situation: "Chicago means strong; it means great; it means polecat; it means onion; it means a man standing by a tree; it means a place where there are no trees to stand by." And Grey, in his search for an epic behind every Chicago title, said, "The 'epic' desire to reduce the name from 'great smell' to 'great' [keeps recurring.]"[56]

Although one historian argues for the semantic origin "strong," most accept that Chicago is named for the lowly leek or garlic ("wild onion") which once abounded in the level marshy country along the river. "A little bulb, strong, hardy and wholesome, sustaining the famishing wanderer," said Joseph Kirkland slyly, in the same tone as other Chicago writers who are unwilling to take the "I Will" city too seriously. He recalls the memoirs of "brave, devoted, generous Tonty [LaSalle's lieutenant with the 'iron hand'"] who wrote that the plant sustained him and his comrades through a bitter winter. "A great metropolis, powerful, kindly and gay, feeding the hungry world. ... Chicago [should adopt] the Chi-ca-gou, from root to flower, as her civic emblem ... Touch it who dare!"[57]

Henry G. Alsberg in *The American Guide* (1949) provides the appropriate tone of "boosterism:"

> The name, Chicago, comes from Ind[ian] word for "strong, powerful," applied by the Miami Indians because of pungent garlic beds. Modern metropolis justifies original meaning in its vigor and bigness. City of spectacular sports, mammoth conventions, fabulous fairs, mass demonstrations and riots, it has

also been country's greatest melting-pot, pride of capitalist enterprise and capitol of political corruption, gangsterism and market speculation, literary capitol during the "American Renaissance," hotbed of muckraking and social reform. Century of Progress, 1933-1934, flaunted miracles of science and technology.[58]

Summary

Of the books discussed above, only *Wau-bun* has stood the test of time as its several reprints demonstrate. It is an eminently readable book. Masters' "Chicago poems" are at best second rate. Romantic historic novels, such as Parrish's and Catherwood's, have been moved from the adult shelves to the juvenile shelves and then to the annual fund-raising used book sales. *Wolves Against the Moon* and *A Prairie Grove,* while not major works, are still worth reading at the historical level.

It is somewhat surprising that film makers have found the Fire of use as a film subject, but have ignored the much more complex story in the Fort Dearborn Massacre. The complex Indian-white relationships, the problems of life in a remote frontier outpost, the conflicts between Kinzie and the military, the dark secrets of the Kinzie family, and even the presence of young love all would contribute to a powerful motion picture story.

III.
The Civil War, the Fire, and Crime

One dark night when everybody wuz in bed,
Mrs. O'Larry lit her lamp'n the shed;
Cow kicked it over and winked he's eye 'n' said,
'There'll be a hot time in the ol' town ter-night, Mah baby —
W'en you hear —[1]

The City Grows

Mary Hastings Bradley's *Old Chicago* (1933) was one of a retrospective "old City Fiction Series;" Edith Wharton's *Old New York* (1924) had been the first. *Old Chicago's* second volume, *The Duel* and its third, *Debt of Honor,* feature

> ... push and drive, successive orgies of speculation, the rise of a lawless plutocracy, the accompanying immorality and corruption, the hordes of hangers-on and floaters that picked up crumbs from the great builders and preyed on the small fry; the influx of immigration from Europe in successive waves, the rise of agriculture in the Middle West and its extension beyond the Mississippi; the Erie Canal and the coming of the railroads ...[2]

The fourth volume, *The Metropolis,* begins with the opening of the Crosby Opera House in 1865 and ends with the year of the World's Columbian Exposition in 1893. The four volumes, slender as they are, review in vignettes the eight decades of Chicago's growth from 1812, "when Chicago was the frontier," through the years "when Chicago was a town," and then "became a city," to that time when "the eyes of the world" were on the brash city which had taken the Exposition away from its arch-rivals, New York and St. Louis.

These years were also the years of the Panics of 1857 and 1873, the years of the Lincoln-Douglas debates and the nomination of Lincoln at the Wigwam, the years of the Civil War, the time of the Fire and the rebuilding of the city as it rose Phoenix-like from its ashes, the beginnings of labor troubles, the Haymarket affair and the Pullman strike; the era of the "balloon-frame" houses and the skyscraper ("high-rises"), and of the Spanish-American War.

But it was not a time for very good or very much Chicago literature; the "American Renaissance" which produced *Moby Dick* and *Walden* in the "old northeast" did not permeate the growing metropolis of the "Old Northwest" until near the end of the century, when its first echoes began to be felt.

Still, there were trends. In 1843, John Stephen Wright, a "wordy, ecstatic editor," who made Chicago aware "of the value of super-optimism in business,"[3] founded the *Prairie Farmer, Devoted to Agriculture, Mechanics and Education.* The *Daily Tribune,* later in a phrase Wright would have admired, "The World's Greatest Newspaper," published its opening number on June 10, 1847, the same year the Federal government issued its first postage stamps. In 1856, Rand McNally and Company began publishing maps; seven years later, R. R. Donnelly joined the firm of Church and Goodman, publishers of the *Christian Messenger.*

Chicago, said Lloyd Lewis, became a city not only of merchant princes, railroad kings, gamblers, prostitutes [and] toilers," but also of "art-collectors — not many, but a few — Theodore Thomas and his orchestra, musicians, actors, more bookstores in proportion to population than in any other American city — so it was claimed."[4]

Contemplating such riches from his Michigan newspaper job, Will Carleton turned to rhapsody:

> The rich and voluptuous city,
> The beauty-thronged, mansion-decked city,
> Gay Queen of the North and the West.[5]

The Civil War

Chicago, split between Douglas supporters and those who had nominated Lincoln, between "Copperheads" and staunch loyalists, produced only one booklength fiction on the War during the War years — the anonymously-written *Carl Almendinger's Office; Or, the Mysteries of Chicago, A Story of the Present War.* The novel ran in nine monthly installments in the war-conscious *Knickerbocker Magazine*[6] in 1862-1863. Internal evidence suggests that the author may have been Martha Joan Lamb, who we shall see later.

One scene, unique to this novel, is the death of the popular Colonel Ellsworth, who with his Zouaves, exotically-clad in jaunty caps, red pantaloons, blue jackets and devil-may-care expressions, are seen parading in more than one retrospective Chicago novel:

> The little dapper colonel follows after the Seventh to Washington. His Zouaves [the first in the United States] are gazed at as an earthly edition of Pandemonium. They see the secession flags waving [across the Potomac] in Alexandria, and are impatient to cross the Long Bridge and haul them down. At length the order "Forward March!" is given; the little dapper colonel is in their van; he sees a rebel bunting waving aloft; he leaves his regiment; mounts staircase after staircase; wraps it around his body and descends to his regiment. As he does so his blood distains the flag; he cries "MY GOD," and falls in death.
>
> He is borne back to Washington by his Zouaves on litter of their guns.[7]

The 1857 Panic, German immigration, and the publication of a German-language newspaper (there were two in Chicago at the time) are other themes in the book.

In a second Civil War story linked to Chicago, "The Four-Leafed Clover" (1874),[8] Helen Hunt Jackson used an incident which was to be echoed half a century later in the climactic end of the German *All Quiet on the Western Front*. Karl Reutner, a Chicago Hungarian immigrant, reaches for a four-leafed clover at the top of a Gettysburg trench and suffers a near-fatal bullet wound. He recovers and returns to Chicago where he marries a school-teacher (the first in a long series of fictional Chicago schoolma'ams) despite an early misunderstanding caused by his Teutonic mannerisms.

The third full-length work which connects Chicago with the War was not published until 1890. Elizabeth Winthrop Johnson's *Two Loyal Lovers: A Romance* looks in some detail at the Copperhead-inspired "Northwest Conspiracy" of 1864, a two-pronged plot to release the 8,000 Confederate prisoners held at Camp Douglas on the South Side, and to burn the city at the same time. The last third of the novel is set in "Port Prairie" (Chicago):

> We march on Port Prairie. We send parties to cut the telegraph wires and burn the railroad stations; meanwhile, the rest of our local friends get together in that square before the Court-House ... Our main body joins them and we make a clean sweep of everything."[9]

The fourth novel, Joseph Kirkland's *The Captain of Company K*, will be discussed later.

The Civil War also plays a part in a number of retrospective Twentieth Century Chicago novels, such as Edna Ferber's *The Girls*.

Literary Magazines

Historians tend to stress the Chicago emphasis on industrialism and commercialism — as well they should. But there has always been another side to Chicago — its cultural side, as the modern presence of the Art

Institute, the Auditorium, the Crerar, Public and Newberry Libraries, Orchestra Hall, the Field Museum, the Chicago Historical Society, the several colleges and universities, and other institutions testify.

"Efforts to establish literary magazines and periodicals in Chicago were begun as far back as the early prairie days," Herbert E. Fleming wrote in 1906. "These attempts were the earliest budding of the creative literary desire in this locality ... All told at least 306 magazines and journals [of this type] have sprung up in Chicago."[10]

The *Gem of the Prairie* was founded in 1844 — "the first weekly of predominantly literary character." In 1852, it became the Sunday edition of the *Chicago Daily Tribune*. In 1844, Chicago had only about 12,000 people. The *Gem* and many others like it hoped that eastern readers would want to read a Chicago magazine. Benjamin Franklin Taylor, whom we have seen earlier, "a brilliant literary man ... a genuine poet, a westerner of rare genius" edited the *Lady's Western Magazine* in 1848. *Sloan's Garden City* began as a house organ for a patent medicine company but became a "prowestern literary organ of genuine merit."[11] Its title was taken from Chicago's Latin motto on its charter, *Urbs in Horto*.

Another periodical, *The Literary Budget*, "a journal of truly high standard," sounded the clarion call for many of these early publications:

> The West should have a marked and original literature of its own. Writers of fiction have used up all the incidents of our glorious revolutionary period. The romantic scenery of the East, too, has been made to aid in the construction of some of the best romances ever written ... [Now] a new field is open to authorship ...
>
> THE GREAT WEST, in her undulating prairies, deep-wooded highlands, mighty rivers, and remnants of aboriginal races, presents topics teeming with interest ... and big with beautiful scenes for the artist's eye. The West is full of subject-matter for legend, story, or history. Sublime scenery to inspire the poet is not wanting ...[12]

"Such unqualified sectionalism," says Fleming, "had its roots in the [changing Chicago] economic and political situation," and the growing "population of Chicago and its environs."[13]

The best of these early Chicago-based literary magazines before *The Dial* was the *Lakeside Monthly* (begun as the *Western Monthly*). For five years from 1869 to 1873, surviving both the Fire and the Panic, the magazine was a triumph of literary taste and fine typography. Its original mission was "to explore the fields of [new middlewestern] literature and gather the ripe fruits of her pioneer talent."[14] Founded by H. V. Reed, it soon came under the editorship of one of Chicago's major nineteenth-century literary figures, Francis Fisher Browne. The magazine was successful, reaching a circulation of 14,000, but an attack of cholera forced Browne to stop publication and forsake magazine publishing for a few years.

From Rags to Riches

Three novels of this period focus on the Chicago newsboy, a type that had been "entirely overlooked" according to the anonymous author of *Luke Darrell, the Chicago Newsboy* (1867). This book, in which the author attempts "to portray the fearful rapidity of a downward course from right and good principle," like a great many later, semi-fictional, semi-tract Chicago books, is presented "not as a work of fiction, but as a true tale."[15]

However, the "newsboy type" had not been overlooked — not even in Chicago. Horatio Alger's *Luke Walton or the Chicago Newsboy* (1865, 1867) had appeared two years earlier. This, and Alger's *The Train Boy* (1883) are both "rags-to-riches" formula stories — the poor but fanatically honest boy (modeled on Lincoln legends?) is befriended by a rich benefactor or two, but finds his way to the better life he so obviously deserves temporarily blocked by a dishonest employee of the benefactor and the latter's scalawag nephew. *The Train Boy* is worth noting historically for its early whack at "Porkopolis's" meat-packers, a trade of which Chicago's authors always seems ashamed; the spoiled daughter of a "pork-merchant" is one of the lesser villains. Luke Walton of the first book finds his benefactor in a woman who lives in a Prairie Avenue mansion.

Walter Sherwood's Probation (1897) is the third and last novel Alger set in Chicago. Walter, a college dropout, comes to Chicago with a hundred dollars in his pocket (not a small amount in the 1890s) to look for a job. Like many another emigrant to Chicago, he encounters those who prey on the weak and innocent — ruthless employers, confidence men, thieves and bullies. Walter manages to find employment with a friendly old man who runs a medicine show — another artifact of the American past. Now the typical Alger reversal of fortune takes place, and at the end of one year Sherwood is able to return home with a thousand dollars in his pocket — at a time when possession of that amount was considered the first step on the way to real wealth.

Agnes Leonard Scanlan's *Heights and Depths* (1871) is a "morality tale of a type long persistent in Sunday School magazines." It was, says Lennox Bouton Grey, "published just before the Fire and deserved the oblivion the Fire brought to it."[16]

The "Urbs in Horto" Becomes the "Urbs Incinerata"[17]

After the Massacre and the Lincoln assassination, the third great traumatic event in Chicago's history was the Fire of October 8-9, the blaze that nearly incinerated the city of "shams and shingles," and enshrined the

O'Leary cow in America's folklore.[18] "The burning of Chicago supplied a topic for hundreds of books, articles, lectures and sermons, and preachers told congregations that the fire had been a visitation aroused by the wickedness that flourished in the city."[19]

One minister found more than a sermon topic in the flames — he found a book. E. P. Roe's *Barriers Burned Away* (1872) is, in part at least, a product of that holocaust which overnight converted the *Urbs in Horto* into the *Urbs Incinerata,* and divided Chicago history and social status into two parts, Before the Fire and After the Fire. Roe, subsequently the author of an extended series of East coast romances, began his career as an eastern Presbyterian minister and Civil War chaplain. Still, because of an extreme and anti-Puritan fondness for fiction, he continuously "contemplated a literary life." When he heard that the "city of Chicago was burning and . . . [its] population was becoming homeless," he impulsively entrained for the western metropolis and was soon among the smoking ruins:

> . . . For days and nights I wandered where a city had been, and among the extemporized places of refuge harboring all classes of people. Late one night I sat for a long time on the steps of [a friend's] church and watched the full moon through the roofless walls and shattered steeple. There was not an evidence of life where once had been populous streets . . . The vague outlines of my first story . . . began to take form in my mind.[20]

One critic, however, speculates that the book may have been well underway before the Fire, noting that the Fire does not "break out until page 395 of a 487-page book," and that the Fire had "scarcely cooled before [the] novel appeared."[21]

In any case, and despite the protests from friends, Roe's interest in the Fire and his bent for always creating "mental serials" led to one of the three Fire novels based on first hand experience. It has the most detailed descriptions of the Fire to be found in fiction.

Barriers Burned Away is in the Alger tradition — the young man of sterling moral character rises in the world through strict adherence to his moral code and by hard work. The Fire serves as a catalyst — Roe's thesis is that the Fire wiped out all financial and social differences. (Pre-Fire Chicago Society never accepted that premise.) A new, democratic, Chicago could arise from the ashes of the Garden City, its leaders the fundamental Christians.

The book was one of the nineteenth century's best sellers, although the modern reader, unaccustomed to the nineteenth century moralizing novel, may find *Barriers Burned Away* too sentimental, its dialogue too stilted. But Fred Lewis Pattee points out its historical importance:

> . . . The [American] novel gained its present respectability as a literary

form by what may be called an artifice. It came in disguised as moral instruction, as character-building studies of life, as historical narrative, as reform propaganda ... The period of moralizing fiction culminated with the work of [Roe] ...[22]

In 1925, more than half a century after its publication, *Barriers Burned Away* became a motion picture. Once again the myth that the O'Leary cow was responsible for the fire was offered as fact. Although the period was convincingly done, according to a *New York Times* critic, including faithful representations of such Chicago leaders as Potter Palmer, Alan Pinkerton and Marshall Field, the actual fire scenes were not impressive. It remained for *In Old Chicago* (1938) to render the Fire in all its Technicolor splendor.[23]

Martha Joan Reade Nash Lamb's *Spicy, A Novel* (1873 also makes use of the Fire as a catalyst in resolving the affairs of some of its principals. This "most skillful Chicago novel before Kirkland's *The McVeys*"[24] begins with the Civil War and Chicago's part in it. In those War years, during which Mrs. Lamb resided in Chicago, she was the Secretary of the first of several Chicago Sanitary Fairs, forerunners of the later Worlds' Fairs and Expositions. This first fair which raised one hundred thousand dollars for the War effort and "encouraged the worn veterans on the battle fields" is described in some detail in the novel.[25]

Spicy's treatment of the Fire is journalistically vivid:

> The river looked like a vast stream of blood ... Great lumber-yards disappeared like dissolving views ... The vessels in the river took fire one after another in quick succession, the masts and spars falling like rain drops in a shower, while, at the same time, the fire streamed along eastward, swallowing the great Michigan Central Railroad depot, and innumerable blocks of large and small buildings around it, and the body of flame presented a front of half a semi-circle, behind which was a crackling, raging, roaring hell of half a mile in depth.[26]

Mrs. Lamb was related to Charles Reade the English novelist. Her later biography of George Washington and her two-volume history of New York City led the New York *World* to call her "one of the most advanced women of the century."[27]

About half of journalist John McGovern's *Daniel Trentworthy, A Tale of the Great Fire of Chicago* (1889) is taken up with the Fire. Again the Fire serves as a catalyst, resolving the dilemma which faces Trentworthy after he learns that his ex-sweetheart has murdered a "boodler"[28] for whom she once jilted Trentworthy. And to give the novel an extra fillip, McGovern places Trentworthy at the O'Leary house when the Fire begins:

> We may cast our eyes backward to the early days, forty years before this night of oncoming ruin, and see the trees waving over the stream at the foot of West Taylor Street. We may behold Patrick O'Leary and his wife on the little

cabbage patch up the way [and] see him safe in his cottage beyond the reach of the landlord in [County] Mayo . . .

And now in these later years he needs a shed, at the alley, for the real-estate speculators must invade his cabbage-patch and fight his title, even to the ground under the very house that he lives in! Musha! Yes, he must keep the horse further away from the cottage, for the fresh air is being cut off. [Chicago] is growing, and Halsted Street is no longer at the far west.

He casts his eye across the scattering town. There is but one brick building in sight — the Lake House. He hitches his express wagon and meanders with the road from the trees at Taylor along the bayou to Wolf Point, where he may cross on the drawbridge. The schooners leave lumber there, at Wells and Market, on South Water Street. We may see him whipping the inglorious steed homeward over a bad road with the fagots for a city's pyre. Load after load, it toils over the greasy clay. . . . So good a shebeen had never the O'Learys on the old sod. Throth now!

Here the demon slept for decades.[29]

"Daniel Trentworthy," says a critic, "stands just short of the dividing line between the old melodrama and the new realistic novel . . . [It combines] the theme and problems of a hundred [later] novels . . . the novel of the political boss [coming a decade later], the business baron, the self-made man rising from the streets, the breaking up of the home, the loss of the old faith and the weakening of the church, labor reform, social climbing, graft and crime, American and European social and cultural contrasts."[30] A rich topical package, indeed.

In *Metropolis,* the concluding volume of Mary Hastings Bradley's *Old Chicago* (1933), the Fire provides an opportunity for a *beau geste* on the part of a philanderer. To save the honor of a lady he has seduced, Brent, the philanderer, walks coolly into the blazing inferno.

The Fire also is the climax of Darryl Zanuck's *In Old Chicago* (1938), a film based on a story, "We, the O'Learys" by Niven Busch, with the screen play by Lamar Trotti — although the Fire itself seems based on Roe's Fire. The film makes one of the O'Leary boys a much more prominent Chicago politician than he was, and renews the legend that the Fire began when Mrs. O'Leary's cow kicked over a lantern in the shed at the rear of 137 De Koven Street that Patrick O'Leary hauled the lumber for. Both the O'Learys and historians long ago rejected Mrs. O'Leary's bovine as an accessory before the fact.

In Old Chicago, in the words of one critic, "achieves the lusty amoral quality of the original city, the city of prodigious growing pains, the infant Gargantua of the prairies . . . Vulgar, ostentatious, squalid, exhuberant, bawdy and delightful to contemplate at least, Zanuck's Chicago makes Carl Sandburg's metropolis of bohunks seem as literary and anemic as the

Hamptons."[31]

William Steuber's 1957 novel, *The Landlooker*, uses a fire leitmotif also. A Chicago harness-maker of German origin sends his two sons out to the Wisconsin lumber camps to sell surplus Civil War harness. The disastrous Peshtigo, Wisconsin fire of the same date as the Chicago fire proves climactic in their lives. When the younger son, who survives the fire, returns to Chicago with his orders, he discovers the father's business has gone with the Chicago inferno.

The Time Travelers (1964), most recent item to use the Fire, is a science fantasy film in which two 1960s' scientists are transported back in time to Chicago the day before the Fire. They are seeking a possible cure for a nineteenth-century plague which threatens their own century. The climax of the film as expected is the Fire, which they narrowly escape, although one is forced to leave behind the girl he has fallen in love with. Many of the Fire scenes were actual footage from *In Old Chicago*.

The best nonfiction accounts of the Fire are Robert Allen Cromie's *The Great Chicago Fire* (1938), and Herman Kogan's and Robert Cromie's *The Great Chicago Fire, 1871* (1971), the latter an annotated pictorial history of Chicago before and after the Fire. There are apparently no photographs of the Fire itself.

The First Literature of Crime

One of Chicago's earliest citizens, Pierre Moreau, "The Mole" (fl. 1675), was said to have been a bootlegger. John Kinzie, Sr., the "father of Chicago," stabbed a neighbor, Jean Lalime to death, an act which Kinzie defenders were still rationalizing in the twentieth century. In the year of Chicago's incorporation, its first thief was caught and sold for a quarter to a Negro. By the eighteen-sixties, Chicago was being called the wickedest city in the United States. The *Tribune* of that time said that Cicero was "a more lawless, uncivilized, uncontrollable settlement [than exists anywhere else] in the whole country." Sixty years later Alphonse Capone had brought his own brand of criminality to the area.[32]

Chicago has endured many notorious citizens and incidents: Herman W. Mudgett, the Everleigh sisters, "Big Jim" Colosimo, Johnny Torrio, the Leopold-Loeb-Bobby Franks case, the Jake Lingle shooting, the St. Valentine's Day "massacre," the shooting of John Dillinger in the lobby of the Biograph Theater, "Bathhouse John" and "Hinky Dink," Big Jim O'Leary, C. T. Yerkes and Samuel Insull.

From Eugene Field who once wrote

Things are looking mighty blue, Hinky Dink!
Since the skates lambasted you, Hinky Dink!

'Twas an evil deed they done
When the rats and terriers trun Hinky Dink![33]

to the Chicago *Times* headline writer's "Jerked to Jesus," following an execution, Chicago authors have luxuriated in the opportunities presented by the city's criminal class.

The earliest crime novels of record are those of R. H. "Shang" Andrews, Chicago journalist. His four published novels are undoubtedly the remnant of a much larger number of lurid, melodramatic newspaper novels about Chicago criminal activity in the 1870s and 1880s: *Wicked Nell, a Gay Girl of the Town* (1877); *Cranky-Ann, The Street-Walker, a Tale of Chicago in Chunks* (1877); *Chicago After Dark* (1879); and *Irish Mollie; or a Gambler's Fate, The True Story of a Famous Chicago Tragedy* (based on an actual person, it was also published as *Irish Mollie, the Queen of the Demi-Monde* [1882]). All alike, they all feature "wicked women in the wickedest city in the world," and they point up the alliance between prostitution and big business that William T. Stead was to document a few years later. Modern readers will note the victimizing of women by men.[34]

The hyperbolic quality of the novels seems typical of Chicago — whatever the subject, Chicagoans tend to be hyperbolic about it. Perhaps that explains the more recent sobriquet, "Windy City!"

The theme of reform runs through all the books. The "wicked" prostitute always come to the aid of the innocent girl about to be seduced by an evil man. Murder and attempted murder, kidnapings, druggings, trickery, deceit, gambling, forced seduction and disguises are common incidents. The settings are houses of prostitution and the streets. All are badly written but they seem to have been extremely popular.

Suppressed Sensations by a "Reporter" (1879), reprinted as *Mysteries of Chicago* (1881) apparently in order to trade on the growing popularity of the city's name,[35] pretends to be a reporter's experiences, too "unprintable" for a newspaper's pages. "Chicago has always been notorious for its criminals," says this exposé, "but it is not alone in the lower and brutal grades of crime that Chicago stands preeminent. A certain looseness of morals exists which has no parallel in any other city in the world."[36]

The materials in this not-too-well written book will be treated with much better effect in the work of Fuller, Payne, Norris, Herrick and other later Chicago writers — a corner in wheat, medical malpractice, jail conditions, "Bohemia" and the Chicago ghetto, "rackets," the "forward young woman," and other topical concerns.

The "forward young woman," an adventurous feminine type, which in subsequent books would become the "new" or "modern" woman and a feminist, is also a feature of an incredible story of crime, *Shadowed by Three*

(1880). The novel is purportedly by a Pinkerton detective; the actual author was Emma Murdoch Van Deventer.

Beginning in 1884 and continuing into the twentieth century, a variant of the crime novel entered the Chicago literary scene. These were the so-called "dime novels," printed in a magazine format, usually sixteen to thirty-two pages, by a variety of hands, often anonymously or pseudonomously written. The most famous publisher of these was Beadle and Adams; others appeared in the "Old Cap. Collier" series, the "Fred Fearnot" series, the "Frank Merriwell" series and the "Nick Carter" series. Because these were cheaply printed and because many parents and others considered them objectionable, they were quite perishable and are not easily found today — except at high prices.

Some forty titles with Chicago settings have been identified by researchers.[37] The heros are usually private detectives, such as members of the Pinkerton group, and the most common crime seems to be kidnaping. Most are badly written, obviously dashed off in a hurry. But taken as a group, they offer mute testimony to the prevalence of crime in Chicago (and elsewhere) in the late 1800s, and to the obvious interest among juveniles (and others) in the subject.

Several of these titles have their setting in the World's Columbian Exposition of 1893; they are specifically treated there. Synopses of all the titles were published in *Illinois! Illinois!* in 1979.[38] A complete list is in the Appendix of this book.

Two novels of the 1880s focus on attempts to gain wealth through murder in the business world. Robert H. Cowdrey's *Foiled by a Lawyer, a Story of Chicago* (1885) features a young married couple caught in the evil plots of an older woman and saved by a young lawyer who had had to work his way through Northwestern University. The lawyer's father, reflecting a commonly-held attitude among the self-made men of the times, had not wanted his son to go to college. Martin A. Foran's *The Other Side/A Social Study Based on Fact* (1886) also shows a young man of the white-collar class outwitting criminals of his own social and economic standing. The novel has two story lines: Richard Arbyght's solution of the twenty-year old murder of his father back in Pennsylvania and his reunion with his long lost sister, and the attempt to create more equitable working conditions in Chicago — a theme that also makes this a story of labor.

Symmes M. Jelley, writing under the pseudonym of "Le Jemlys," is the author of two of Chicago's earliest mystery novels, a category that will become very popular in the twentieth century. *Shadowed to Europe; A Chicago Detective on Two Continents* takes up the case of Pauline Barr, a young, beautiful and wealthy Evanston widow whose fortune has been taken from her. *Lawyer Manton of Chicago; A Detective Story of Thrilling Interest* (1891) reports the investigation into the disappearance of one of Chicago's more successful lawyers, and the complications that ensue.

Allan Pinkerton, who had once beaten "Long John" Wentworth, Mayor of Chicago in a street brawl, later a deputy sheriff to Cook County, later Lincoln's guardian on the newly-elected President's journey to Washington, and still later a foe to those who participated in the events leading up to the Haymarket Affair, was the author of *The Burglar's Fate and the Detectives* in 1883 — a barely fictionalized account of a real bank robbery in Geneva and the bringing to justice of the robbers by Allan Pinkerton's Agency. A. Frank Pinkerton (no relation) authored *Dyke Darrel, The Railroad Detective; or, The Crime of the Midnight Express* in 1886; the title tells the story. Edmund C. Strong's *Manacle and Bracelet; or, The Dead Man's Secret* (1886) relates the consequences for an innocent man of a wealthy resident's murder.

The ex-Iowa journalist, Frank Bangs Wilkie, also turned his hand to the criminal novel with *The Gambler/A Story of Chicago Life* (1888), a novel of revenge and poetic justice which introduced Natalie, a Negress, a "Fetich" worshipper, a character so unusual that Wilkie felt the need to document her in an appendix. Like many another novel of Chicago in these growing years, this one features a young immigrant to the city. The novel's den of iniquity where the hero is singed by the "crimson flames" of sin was modeled on a real life Chicago institution, the Owls' Club.[39]

John McGovern's *Burritt Durand* (1887) begins with banditry and horse-stealing in rural Indiana, much like the earlier *Banditti of the Prairies* (1850), then moves to a small Iowa town. The final third of the novel is set in Chicago just before the Fire. Durand, successful at cards, unlike the protagonist of Wilkie's *The Gambler*, clears his father's name of a charge of horse-stealing, saves his employer's fortune, and aids an Iowa girl in achieving success at the doomed Crosby Opera House, which opened just before the Fire and was destroyed by it. The girl becomes the first of several hinterland girls who come to Chicago to advance their operatic careers. But *Burritt Durand* is too melodramatic to be taken seriously.

John W[illiam] Postgate, the author of a trivial 1896 romance, *The Mystery of Paul Chadwick*, was also the author of two crime stories. *The Stolen Laces; An Episode in the History of Chicago Crime* (1889), supposedly taken from the diary of a former Chicago police chief, relates how a lying lawyer and his flirtatious wife become involved in a Chicago burglary ring. *A Woman's Devotion; or, The Mixed Marriage/A Story of the Rival Detectives* (1887) tells of the consequences of a suburban farmer's murder, and the attempts of two competing detectives to solve the crime. Postgate claims that this story is based on fact. The setting of the actual or fictional murder, as the case may be, is now well within Chicago's city limits.

Edith Sessions Tupper's *By a Hair's Breadth* (1889) was a prize story in the Chicago *Tribune* prior to book publication. The murder of a Chicago millionaire is first blamed on an innocent man, but a Chicago news-paperman, turned detective, proves that "the butler did it!"

In that same year of 1889, on the night of May 4, Dr. P. H. Cronin of Chicago, a leader in Irish politics in Chicago and internationally, was called away from the Windsor Theater to attend a patient; he was never seen alive again. The Cronin murder became a cause célébre, and although several persons were convicted for complicity in the case, it is generally agreed the true culprit was never found. "Old Cap. Lee's" dime novel, *Who Killed Doctor Cronin* (1889), distorts the facts somewhat but imitates nature in not identifying a real culprit. "A Chicago Detective's" *The Great Cronin Mystery; or, The Irish Patriot's Fate* (also 1889) also distorts the facts in implicating an unfaithful wife and a jealous husband, but, like the much shorter dime novel, does not identify a real culprit.

Elia W. Peattie's *The Judge* (1891), "the *Detroit Free Press* prize story," is a murder mystery centering on a Chicago judge, his daughter and the daughter's suitors. Although Peattie does her best to conceal the novel's dastardly villain's identify, no one should be surprised at the end to discover the murderer is the judge. Peattie was the mother of Donald Culross Peattie.

W. B. Lawson took advantage of the notoriety of Jesse James, the Missouri train and bank robber, to put him into a novel set in Chicago (where James probably never came), *Jesse James in Chicago* (1898). The Chicago detective in this novel is "Wiliam Lawson;" he is engaged by a Chicago man to break up a love affair between the man's son and a young woman thought to be the son's half sister, and also to solve the mystery of two thousand odd dollars missing from the Chicago man's safe. Interestingly, Jesse James is portrayed as a Robin Hood type.

The story was reprinted in 1901 as *Jesse James in Chicago; or, The Bandit King's Bold Play.*[40]

P[aul] J[ames] Duff's *Side Lights on Darkest Chicago* (1899) may have been produced as a consequence of the popularity of W. T. Stead's *If Christ Came to Chicago!*, for it too contains a list of places where Chicagoans or their out-of-town guests might spend their evenings. The reader is taken on vicarious tours of the House of David, a gambling joint; Gamblers Alley (one of the Chicago settings of Ferber's later *Show Boat*); Chinatown, South Clark Street, Little Africa, and various other night spots

Crime and the Short Story

Israel Kahn Friedman's first book, *The Lucky Number, a Book of Stories of*

Chicago Slums (1896) represents several "firsts" in the Chicago literary tradition: it is the first Chicago collection of short stories to be published in book form; it is the first Chicago book to use as subjects Dreiser's "vast mass writhing in ignorance and poverty;"[41] the form which its several short and long stories took anticipated O. Henry's first collection by eight years. Like Elia W. Peattie, Friedman had his roots in the department of sociology at the University of Chicago — the first large American university with such a department.

The Lucky Number is a literary illustration of the fact that the American dream presented in such Alger titles as "Bound to Rise" did not apply to everyone. Chicago may have served as the base for a successful career for some, but this book shows the city as a gathering place for demoralized people who have turned to petty or serious crime: a beggar, an alcoholic ex-vaudeville performer, a magician, a swindler, a cab driver, a greedy mother, a corrupt father. Poetic justice is often a theme. "The Lucky Number" is an ironic title, referring both to the name of the saloon which serves as the base of operations for most of the book's characters, and to the characters themselves — the only "luck" which they enjoy is bad luck.

A Miscellany

Chicago's first volume of poetry seems to have been William Asbury Kenyon's *Miscellaneous Poems,* published in Chicago in 1845. The book also included several prose essays. Kenyon also published *Poetry of Observations and Other Poems* in 1851.

Louise M. Thurston's *Charley and Eva Roberts Home in the West* (1869) is a sentimental, didactic story for young people about two orphans in Chicago in the 1860s.

Martha Louise Rayne's *Against Fate; A True Story* (1876) tells of three girls who come to Chicago seeking to better themselves, but, like many others who placed themselves in the same situation, they become the victims of the evils awaiting country girls in the rebuilding City.

Mary Hartwell Catherwood's *The Dogberry Bunch* (1879) tells the story of seven children who manage to survive the loss of their parents. The setting is Cincinnati and Chicago.

Helen Dawes Brown's *Two College Girls* (1886) contrasts Boston and Chicago — a favorite theme of the time. Only two chapters are set in Chicago.

LeRoy Armstrong's *Washington Brown, Farmer* (1893) tells a story which Lynn Montross will retell three decades later — the revolt of farmers against the Board of Trade. Armstrong's farmers are Kansans, and a chief interest of the story is the far-reaching effect of Chicago on its hinterlands.

Henry E. Scott's *Beauty's Peril; or, The Girl From Macoupin* (1895; published also in 1894 as *The Girl From Macoupin)* tells a story which O. Henry picked up later: "Pearl Linwood, of Macoupin, goes to Chicago in search of employment and a recreant brother, and finds work in a department store. Her experiences show the trials and temptations to which girls compelled to work in department stores and 'sweat shops' were often subjected."

The "Rube" Comes to Chicago

A variant on the novel of crime, usually featuring a detective trying to catch a criminal or criminals, developed from the theme of confidence men trying to victimize newcomers in Chicago, particularly newcomers from the country, "hicks," "hayseeds," or "rubes," who are supposedly less sophisticated than their city cousins.

Three novels written at the end of the century, two by Indiana humorist Dwight LeRoy Armstrong, capitalize on the problems faced by young men migrating from the rural hinterlands to Chicago — only to be met at the numerous railroad stations and elsewhere by every variety of confidence man — and bring rural humor to Chicago for at least a ten-year stay. (It persisted years longer than that in the "Toby" tent shows which migrated every summer through the small towns of Illinois and Iowa.) The three novels combine "rube comedy" and "shrewd journalistic criticism" in the format of "railroad fiction" (such as that written by Opie Read) — "a type sure to appeal to Chicago visitors."[42]

Byrd Flam in Town; Being a Collection of That Rising Young Author's Letters Written at Chicago (1894) satirizes an epistolary style, all the Chicago institutions of the time, including authors Charles Eugene Banks and Hobart Chatfield Chatfield-Taylor, and Mrs. Potter Palmer, the leader of Chicago society. The novel's protagonist always manages to come out ahead of the sharpers, thus demonstrating that rural folk are smarter than some city folk at least.

Dan Gunn, the Man From Mauston (1898) offers a parody of the "muscular Christian" hero, this one from Iowa, trying to find his lost fiancée. The novel, says one critic, was popular but worthless.[43]

Uncle Ben Morgan of Morganville, N.Y. in John S. Draper's *Shams, or Uncle Ben's Experiences With Hyprocrites ... Shams and Sharpers of the Metropolitan World* (1887?1898) is tutored by sharpers "for good and bad so genially" that he hates to leave Chicago; despite its confidence men, he is "well satisfied" that it is the "greatest city on the American continent."[44] Ben makes the Grand Chicago Tour, taking in everything from the Old Palmer House to the now-lost Panorama of Gettysburg.

The popularity of Chicago as a setting in these books, and the continued repetition of the city's name in book titles demonstrates the continuing attraction the city had for Americans in these years before and after the World's Columbian Exposition. That attraction would bring authors — George Ade, George Barr McCutcheon, Theodore Dreiser and members of "the Chicago Renaissance" — and their creations — "Sister Carrie" is the obvious example — to the city by the lake.

Summary

Most of the nineteenth-century stories of crime in Chicago — Andrews' or Friedman's or any of the others — are low in literary values, and they are too sentimental or too melodramatic for modern tastes. But they show evidence of the corrupting influence of the former "Garden City" on human nature as it becamse a "Metropolis." In addition to showing how people can and do prey upon each other, they also show a relationship among the criminal, the politician and the business man — a relationship which twentieth-century authors of Chicago literature were to emphasize.

The books of this period also show Chicago's growing distance from the rural hinterlands which nourished it and provided the base for its growing industrialism. The writers of the 1880s, in Duncan's words, were measuring the new raw Chicago against the old established countryside with its moral and ethic values.[45] But from 1875 to 1900, several distinct types of Chicago literary models were emerging — the detective, the reporter or journalist, the business man, the new woman, and the city's "lower half."[46]

IV.
The "Urbs Recondita"

Blackened and bleeding, helpless, panting, prone
On the charred fragments of her shattered throne
Lies she who stood but yesterday alone.

Queen of the West! by some enchanter taught
To lift the glory of Aladdin's court
Then lose the spell that all that wonder wrought.

Like her own prairies by some chance seed sown,
Like her own prairies in one brief day grown,
Like her own prairies in one fierce night mown.
                              (Bret Harte)

Just two days after the Fire had burned itself out on the North Side, Joseph Medill of the *Chicago Tribune* got out the first post-Fire issue with this editorial:

"CHEER UP"

"In the midst of a calamity without parallel in the world's history, looking upon the ashes of thirty years accumulations, the people of this once beautiful city have resolved that CHICAGO SHALL RISE AGAIN."[1]

Meanwhile, Medill's partner, William "Deacon" Bross, a journalist with artistic pretensions, had raced for New York "while the city was still smoking." There, surrounded by reporters, he took advantage of public interest in his eye-witness accounts of the Fire to "toot" his "'booster' horn," and "promise . . . the city's rebirth:"

> "I tell you within five years Chicago's business houses will be rebuilt, and by
> the year 1900 the new Chicago will boast a population of a million souls . . .
> She has only to wait a few short years for the sure development of her
> 'Manifest Destiny.'"[2]

Bross, as much of an Anglophile as William "Big Bill" Thompson was later an Anglophobe, was heard in England. There, Thomas Hughes, Alfred Lord Tennyson, Robert Browning, Charles Darwin and Queen Victoria herself, heard his appeal and responded with over 8,000 volumes which became, in 1872, the nucleus for Chicago's first public library.[3]

As Chicago began to rebuild, its writers more and more began to contrast their city with Boston, New York, and even London and Paris.

Literary Magazines and Chicago Journalists

As a group, Chicago literary magazines continued to flourish through the nineteenth century. Individually, however, most lasted but a short time — one, indeed, in which Hamlin Garland had an interest, never got into print. Moreover, there were few of them which are worth mentioning today.

One of these, *The Chicago Ledger*, began in 1873 as an imitation of a successful New York City literary magazine and became the Chicago literary magazine with the second longest run. At first, it made a "leading feature of stories which were literary in the accepted sense of that word [, but] little by little . . . the higher class of well-written fiction was dropped. One reason for this was competition produced by the advent of the [Chicago-based] 'Lakeside Library.'" The *Ledger* lasted until the middle 1930s under the direction of W. D. Boyce.[4]

For the most of the Chicago magazines of the nineteenth century, "literature" was either verse or the essay. But in 1880, a book publishing firm, A. C. McClurg & Co., began the *Dial* as a journal of literary criticism — and a new dimension was added to the term "literature" in Chicago.

McClurg's at the time was one of three booksellers in "Bookseller's Row," immediately south of the Field-Leiter store on Chicago's State Street. These stores were selling books not only in Chicago, but throughout the Middle Border country. To meet competition, McClurg's conceived the *Dial* as a means of bringing information about new books — primarily those it brokered — to ministers, teachers, drug-stores and book-stores. To give the *Dial* a proper critical, didactic and genteel tone, McClurg's retained as editor Francis Fisher Browne, who had recovered from the bout of cholera that had led to the closing of the *Lakeside Monthly*.

The *Dial* was "devoted exclusively to literary criticism and information [about] new books," Fleming wrote. It made no appeal "to the aesthetic interest." The Chicago area was "a section where literary appreciation was much more predominant than the creative literary interest — writing and publishing."[5] In Browne's opinion, Chicagoans were readers, not writers.

In 1892, because of charges of self-interests in its review, McClurg sold the *Dial* to Browne, and he retained William Morton Payne as the editor. Under the direction of these two men, the *Dial* became "the leading journal of literary criticism in the nation." Browne and Payne utilized "experts in special topics" for reviews, it allowed them to express their opinions freely, and it paid them for their work.[6]

Humor was another dimension of the Chicago literary scene. "The early humorous writing of Chicago authors often possessed a frontierlike quality; it was rough and salty," said Albert Halper, thinking particularly of Franc Bangs Wilkie's two books of this period, *Walks About Chicago* (1869, 1881).[7] Wilkie, who signed himself "Poliuto" in his Chicago *Times* column, was a popular journalist in his day, and the forerunner of Field, Ade and Dunne. He was the first of several Davenport, Iowa emigrants who became prominent in Chicago's journalistic and literary history. In his books he wrote about the rich Chicagoans on the South Side, the Germans on the "Nord Seite," and the pretentious middle class on the West Side:

> Every woman in Westside once lived on The Avenue of a place known as Southside. Whenever she goes downtown, she goes to visit a friend on The Avenue. Whenever she has been downtown, she has been to call on a friend who lives on The Avenue. A good many ladies who live in Westside carry the idea, in the cars, that they live in Southside, on The Avenue, and are only in Westside for a visit ...[8]

A novel about Chicago journalists of the 1880s, Henry Francis Keenan's *The Money Makers/A Social Parable* (1885) also uses wealth as a theme. In his book, Keenan quotes the *English Review:* "It may be said that the millionaire is the romantic hero par excellence of the nineteenth century." However, the two newspapermen in this occasionally melodramatic novel are also romantic figures. Once friends, later opponents, both are in love with the daughter of a millionaire who uses his wealth to suppress journalists and to buy elected officials.

The widely-admired Benjamin Franklin Taylor, whom we have already seen as a poet, contributed his one novel at this time. *Theophilus Trent: Old Times in the Oak Openings* (1887) is set in Michigan in the 1840s, but Chicago is the base of reference. There is a spectacular fire, always a "favored Chicago 'diversion,'"[9] and there are ironical comments about Chicago in its second decade:

> She ... went almost to the end of the world to live — Chicago. Of course you know the place; college men are supposed to know everything ... They say

Chicago is on the border of the missionary ground; that may do it some good.[10]

At this time when the Chicago press, with its ten newspapers and thirty magazines, was becoming the liveliest in the nation, [11] Taylor had become literary editor of the *Chicago Evening Journal,* and an early member of a long list of Chicago journalists who were to influence Chicago and American literature. His contemporaries included, among others we shall see, George P. Upton ("Peregrine Pickle"), Charles A. Dana, Melville E. Stone, Joseph Medill, "Deacon" William Bross, Victor F. Lawson and Slason Thompson, destined to become Eugene Field's biographer.[12]

Eugene Field was recruited from Denver, Colorado, and came to Chicago as a special writer for the *News.* Field, who was a humorist, poet, classicist and bibliophile, collected some of his Chicago writings in *Culture's Garland, Being Memoranda of the Gradual Rise of Literature, Art, Music and Society in Chicago, and Other Western Ganglia* (1887). With the brashness of those who were boasting capitalistic conquests for "Porkopolis," he noted:

> "It is universally conceded that Chicago is rapidly achieving world-wide reputation as the great literary center of the United States.[13]

His "garland of culture," however, was a string of sausages!

For all Field's joking, there was a "growing metropolitan consciousness; [its] most interesting expression," according to Fleming, was "the Saints' and Sinners' Corner," "a score of bibliophiles — clergymen, general readers, and literary workers — who held meetings, imaginary for the most part, in the rare-book corner of A. C. McClurg & Co."[14] (From another corner, as we have seen, the *Dial* was being edited.) In actuality, the "Corner" was located in Field's *Daily News* column, "Sharps and Flats:"

> Here in Chicago "a hand well known in literature" is a horny, warty hand which, after years of patient toil at skinning cattle, or at boiling lard, or at cleaning pork, has amassed sufficient [wealth] to admit of its master's reception into the *crème de la crème* of Chicago culture.[15]

Field's last major literary effort, one that remained uncompleted because of his untimely death in 1895, is *The House; An Episode in the Lives of Reuben Baker, Astronomer, and of his Wife Alice.* Despite the fact that it lacked a final chapter, it was published by Charles Scribner's sons in 1896.

The book represents a humorous treatment of Field's actual purchase of a house on the North Shore, the setting for the book. As such, it might be called the *Mr. Blandings Builds His Dream House* (1948) of its time. The first person narration begins as whimsy but shifts to light satire as Baker describes his problems with his wife, his neighbors, a tramp, salespeople, city hall and finances. Dr. Gunsaulus, one of Field's "Saints," and Hamlin Garland appear in the book as Baker's friends.

Because of Field's interest in classical history, he named the actual house

"The Sabine Farm." The materials for *The House* were published first in the "Sharps and Flats" column of the *Daily Record* from May 15, 1895 to August 15. Fields died November 3, 1895.

In the introduction to *The House,* Joel Chandler Harris wrote that "only in [this] story do we find [Field's] humor so gently turned, so deftly put, and so ripe for the purpose of literary expression. It lies deep here ... "[16]

In 1887, the last two of seven railroad lines built into Chicago in the 1880s were completed. In that same year, and directly as a consequence of Chicago's importance as a railway center, Opie Read brought his humorous *Arkansaw Traveler* north to Chicago: Said Read:

> ...Our paper was sold chiefly on railway trains. We moved to Chicago so as to be in position for reaching the largest number of railway passengers daily.[17]

Five years later, Read eased himself out of the *Traveler;* lacking his genius the magazine declined. But Read stayed on in Chicago to author a number of "railroad novels" — romatic, lurid, cheaply-printed paperback books, mostly set in the south, sold in railroad stations and on trains by "news butchers" such as Alger's "train boy" and young Tom Edison.

A friend of Read's was John McGovern, an employee of the Chicago *Tribune* for sixteen years, and a central figure in the Chicago Press Club, the group to which all these journalists belonged. The club members were to play important roles in the building of one of America's great journalistic traditions and in the production of Chicago literature as well.

In *The Colossus* (1893), a novel about a department store empire and a rising young journalist, Read wrote these words about the Press Club and McGovern:

> The Press Club is a democracy. In the Press Club the pulse of the town can be felt. About McGovern's character a whole book might be written. An individual almost wholly distinct from his fellow men; a castigator of human weakness ... a hero-worshipper of the human being whose brain had blazed and lighted the world. Art was to him the soul of literature. He regarded himself simply as a man of talent. [18]

In 1902 McGovern helped Samuel Eberly Gross accumulate the evidence used in convicting the French playwright, Edmund Rostand, of plagiarizing *The Merchant Prince of Cornville* (1896) in *Cyrano De Bergerac* (1897). Gross, a "Chicagoan of leisure" who had made a fortune in real estate, claimed to have written his play at least a score of years before its 1896 publication by R. R. Donnelly, Rand McNally, and Stone and Kimball. McGovern's motivation may have derived from his belief that Sir Gilbert Parker had plagiarized his *The Right of Way* (1900) from McGovern's *David Lockwin; The People's Idol* (1892). McGovern's badly-written novel of dirty politics is set in Chicago and the upper Great Lakes country.[19]

An associate of Read's and McGovern's in the Press Club was Stanley Waterloo, whose *The Story of Ab* (1897), a novel about a cave man, proved to be one of the most popular books ever written by a resident of Chicago. Although not listed as a 'best seller" by either Frank Luther Mott or Alice Payne Hackett, the book went through at least fifteen editions by 1930.

The Haymarket Affair in Literature

"The Railroad Strike of 1877 was the first National strike in America," says Faye M. Blake.[20] On July 26, 1877, police, federal cavalry and armed citizens set upon a throng of 10,000 strikers on the Halsted Street viaduct. Twelve were killed, many wounded. Among those taking notes was an Iowa writer, a friend of Marshall Field and Andrew Carnegie, Octave Thanet (Alice French), whose "Capitalists and Communists; A Sketch From Life" (1878) based on her observations of this affray, and also on a strike in Moline, Illinois, may well have been the first piece of American fiction to use a strike as a subject.[21]

The Railroad Strike and some subsequent strikes were settled, but nine years later, on May 4, 1886, there occurred in Chicago one of those events which become symbolic of a city's and a nation's history. On that evening, a confrontation between strikers and police in the Haymarket just off Des Plaines Street, an open area which served as a market-place for farmers, led to the throwing of a bomb, the killing of seven people, the wounding of 200 others, and, ultimately, the execution of four men, the suicide of another, the imprisonment and eventual pardons of three others — and a decades-long Chicago fixation on the subject of "anarchists."

The "Haymarket Affair," as it came to be called, came to be the subject of more Chicago literature than almost any other Chicago event, including the Fire, the Massacre and the World's Columbian Exposition, with which it is approximately even. At least seventeen novelists and two playwrights have used the Affair in one way or another, and all have reached differing conclusions about it.[22]

H. K. Shackleford's "dime novel," *The Red Flag; or, The Anarchists of Chicago* (August 7, 1886), was the first. Its twenty-eight pages tell about a poor but famous Chicago artist who narrowly escapes being dragged into the "Riot."

Steele MacKaye's *Paul Kovar, or Anarchy* (1887) is the first play and first major work. Although MacKaye was convinced privately that an injustice had been done to the "anarchists," his play "encouraged the usurpation of reason by hysteria." When audiences heard the play's theme "The torch of liberty which should light mankind to progress, if left in madmen's hands, kindles that blaze of Anarchy whose only end is in ashes —" they rose cheering to their feet.[23]

Ninety four years later, a play by Joanne Koch, *Haymarket: Footnote to a Bombing,* was presented October 10, 1981, at the Cultural Center, Randolph and Michigan.

But back to 1887. "At a meeting in the home of Judge Roger A. Pryor, the counsel for the Haymarket defendants, MacKaye caught the eye of . . . William Dean Howells." Because privately MacKaye was "espousing the cause of justice of the anarchists," the meeting between the men was probably a sympathetic one. Howells was determined at whatever cost to his reputation as dean of American letters or even to his position with *Harper's,* to defend the anarchists and to attack "the thing forever damnable before God and abominable to civilized man:"

> The last two months have been full of heartache and horror for me, on account of the civic murder created last Friday at Chicago. You may have seen in the papers that I had taken part in petitioning for clemency for the Anarchists, whom I thought unfairly tried, and most unjustly condemned . . . . It's all been an atrocious piece of frenzy and cruelty, for which we must stand ashamed forever before history. But it's no use. I can't write about it. Some day I hope to do justice to these irreparably wronged men.[24]

Howells best use of this material came in *A Hazard of New Fortunes* (1888), a novel, which, however, is not set in Chicago. "It is clear," says Everett Carter, "that Howells took his enormous personal anguish over the Haymarket Affair and sufficiently objectified it; his novel became more than a personal purgation; it became an imaginative invention."[25]

Robert Herrick, "one of Howells' disciples in realism,"[26] also shaped the Haymarket Affair for his artistic goals in *Memoirs of An American Citizen* (1905) and *One Woman's Life* (1913). In both novels, Herrick, a University of Chicago English professor, demonstrated his sympathies for the convicted men.

Charlotte Teller's *The Cage* (1907), which is not mentioned in the only study of "The Haymarket Affair in Literature,"[27] is less successful in its use of the Affair. Although the major focus of *The Cage* is on labor affairs, Lange, one of the convicted men, appears as a central character.

Frank Harris's *The Bomb* (1908) is the only full-length novel which makes exclusive use of the Affair. Harris, the English biographer of Oscar Wilde and George Bernard Shaw, came to the United States in 1907, researched the newspaper accounts, and produced a book in which the first-person narrator confesses to having made and thrown the bomb. Harris concluded that the other six men "were as innocent as [he] was, and that four of them had been murdered — according to law."[28]

Harris's novel, however, was not widely read in America, and his reputation, based on his lurid autobiography, would not have led to support for his thesis.

Ruth Russell's *Lake Front* (1931) was the next book to make considerable use of the Haymarket Affair. James O'Mara, one of the central characters, reports the strike at the McCormick Works which led to the bombing:

> Nowadays men were turning atheists because of Bob Ingersoll's lectures at the Haverly Opera House. But it was clash like this fighting ["he heard the strikers call for dynamite to throw at the rich, he saw the police club and shoot the strikers, he watched the men on the paper write such things as 'Feed these men out of work — feed 'em strychnine — feed 'em lead'"] for food in a land of plenty that made you doubt.[29]

But O'Mara undergoes a change of heart after viewing Lingg in his cell, and decides to place money-making ahead of every other concern. At the end of the novel he fights his way through a mob at Pullman (1894) with no sympathy for the strikers.

Fifteen years later (1946), Howard Fast's *The American* ostensibly was a fictional biography of John Peter Altgeld, the Illinois governor who angered the people of his state by pardoning the three imprisoned anarchists and shaming his state's citizens for their treatment of all the men. But early in the book, Albert Parsons, one of those hanged, replaced Altgeld as the central character.

Summarizing the "Haymarket Affair in Literature," Grey commented in 1935: "In fifteen ... novels portraying ... the Haymarket theme, the theme has passed from a fearful whisper through violent protest to [a] final balancing of blame in *Lake Front*."[30] In his summary in 1950, Carter, who had also ignored *Lake Front* but who had read *The American,* wrote: "The Haymarket tragedy gave Steele MacKaye the opportunity to satisfy his audience's prejudices and gave Frank Harris and Howard Fast a stick with which to belabor American capitalism; but it gave Robert Herrick material which he absorbed into his fine novels, and it provided William Dean Howells with the impetus to produce his most impressive work."[31]

Chicago Women

Chicago's growing industry and commerce were producing a class of business men who concentrated all their interests and energies on work and the increase of wealth — a frequent theme, by the way, in Chicago novels about businessmen. One result was the growing leisure time of their wives and daughters, left alone by their husbands and further freed from housework by the availability of household "help" from the ranks of immigrants, particularly Germans and Irish. These women began to interest themselves in society (following the lead of Mrs. Potter Palmer), in dilettantish activities such as literary clubs and artistic affairs, and in social work, some of the latter centering around institutions such as Jane Addams's Hull House, established in 1889. A great many Chicago novels focus on these upper middle class women and their various interests. Most were written by women.

An early novel of this type, Lillian Sommers' *For Her Daily Bread* (1887, published under the pen name of "Litere"), satirizes women engaged in charitable works in the teeming Halsted Street ghetto and elsewhere. Other Chicago novelists were also unhappy about these "basket benevolences" or "Christian Milk and Water Benevolences" which seemingly paid only lip service to the real needs of the poor.[32] But Sommers' main theme is the new-woman-in-business, a theme emphasized in the novel's preface by Robert Ingersoll, the notorious "free thinker." Norma Southstone sees Chicago as a city of opportunity, even though she knows from personal experience the perils a woman might face in the city. Like the several heroines of "Shang" Andrews lurid novels, she has narrowly escaped incarceration and involuntary servitude in a brothel.

A decade and half earlier, just two years after the Fire, there appeared the first of many Chicago novels to exploit Chicago-European contrasts. For by this time, wealthy Chicago women, emulating their well-to-do sisters on the eastern seabord, were traveling abroad, although not always happily. In June of 1869, Julia Newberry, sitting in the mansion that became the Newberry Library, wrote in her diary:

> Here I am in the old house where I was born, & where I wish I could always live; it is the dearest place on earth to me, & worth all London, Paris & New York put together.[33]

Lakeville: or Substance and Shadow (1873) was in all likelihood the first novel by a daughter of a prominent Chicago family to exploit her family's social and historical backgrounds — sometimes to the family's unhappiness. The novel's author, Mary Healy, was the daughter of the distinguished portrait painter, George Peter Alexander Healy, and one of the first Chicago society girls to marry a European, thus emphasizing the beginning of the reversal of the westward trek. *Lakeville* is a conventional story of love, courtship and marriage, with settings both in Europe and Chicago.

The novel has a description of the notorious "Sands" district on land north of the River and east of du Saible's former cornfields. It was then an area of "cheap lodging houses, rattle-trap parlors of assignation and prostitution, low saloons, gambling-dens, clustered on land which nobody owned."[34] The area is now the site of Chicago's North Side Miracle Mile.

A Congeries

Alice French claimed that she had gotten the "Thanet" half of her pen name from a sign on a railroad boxcar. Robert C[artwright] Givins acquired his pen name (Snivig C. Trebor) by the simple but awkward expedient of spelling his name in reverse order.

With this bit of information firmly in hand, we are not at all surprised by Givins' campy treatment of his thesis that "the basis of all security is LAND" in *Land Poor; A Chicago Parable* (1884). Barnabee Smith and his family convert native prairie near Naperville into a fertile farm. Because Barnabee dreams of one day being wealthy, he is an easy mark for an unscrupulous land agent who persuades Barnabee to trade his fertile farm for worthless land near Chicago. But lo and behold! Barnabee sells the land for $2,000,000 to a corporation looking for a site for its factory. And that was a deal of money in 1884.

Bessie Albert's *How Bob and I Kept House; A Story of Chicago Hard Times* (1880) is a riches-to-rags story of the daughter of one of Chicago's wealthiest families and her marriage to a real estate broker. But life in the "most beautiful house in Chicago" comes to a sudden end when the financial panic of 1873 ruins them. The couple dismisses all its servants and moves into a six-room house; the husband finds a job at $2,000 a year. The moral of this sad tale, in the author's words, is "Poverty is no disgrace, but then it is just a trifle *inconvenient!*" Unfortunately, says Thomas L. Kilpatrick, she is serious.[35]

William J. Yexter's *Luck in Disguise* (1889) carries this menacing subtitle: "Written in Good Faith, by Wiliam J. Yexter. Revised and Punctuated by L. P. Culter, Sole Proprietor of the Winchester News Depot. A Romance of Love and Travel Into the Far West near Chicago." With a little help from his friend Culter, Yexter tells how the Means family charitably helps a poor family in the ghetto, then tries to steer son Henry away from a life of debauchery by sending him to a farm in Nebraska.[36]

Snivig C. Trebor's *The Unwritten Will; A Romance* (1886) again takes up the theme that someday its protagonist will be wealthy. Henry Norwood, however gets off to a bad start, ending up wrongfully imprisoned and without his fiancee's hand in marriage. Out of prison, a sadder but wiser man, he moves to Chicago, becomes wealthy practicing law and gets the girl. All this in the 1860s.

Edward R[eynolds] Roe's *Dr. Caldwell; or, The Trail of the Serpent* (1893) lets us watch a prominent doctor demonstrate his own thesis that alcohol is a psychological poison by drinking himself to death over a lost romance.

Sarah Davieson's *The Seldens in Chicago; A Domestic Tale* (1889) demonstrates the consequences when Horace Dean marries the wrong Selden girl, the one with money. The jilted sister sets out to get revenge.

Robert C[artwright] Givins, using his rightful name, and the title *Jerry*

Bleeker; or, Is Marriage a Failure?, (1889) shows us the Chicago divorce courts of the 1880s in this tale of an on-again, off-again marriage.

Paul James Duff's *Crimson Love; A Realistic Romance of Guilty Passion* (1895) is an early pulp paper book, which shows what happens when the staff of a Chicago newspaper, the *Gong*, take time off from hard writing and hard drinking to engage in affairs of the heart. In *Woman's Duplicity; A Realistic Novel*, he unloads his anti-feminist venom on two imaginary women who have the ill-fortune to meet a jerk named Vincent Ashley.

Duff was also the author of two very minor items: *Hot Stuff, a Budget of Laughter and Love* (1897); and *Rosa's Confessions, a Realistic Romance of Love and Adventure* (1897).

Wilhelm vom Strande wrote and published three evangelistic Chicago tales in his native German. Robert Edward Gutermann translated these into English and published them as *Chicago in Tears and Smiles* (1893). The book concerns one Brother William who takes over a Chicago church, only to discover that his parishioners are gambling, drinking and otherwise debauching themselves. Rather than convert the sinners, he chooses to minister to their wives and families.

Fani Pusey Gooch's *Miss Mordeck's Father* (1890) tells of Browne Mordeck's discovery that a prominent business man is courting her and an exact double — who turns out to be Browne's half-sister. Then the girls discover they have a common father who maintains two homes, two families and two lives. *The Remarkable Mr. Pennypacker* (1953) handles the same plot in a much livelier, more believable fashion — but it's not a Chicago play.

Harold R[ichard] Vynne's *Love Letters; A Romance in Correspondence* lets us read the lively communications by mail and telegram between Frederick Morton of New York and Helen Merrick of Chicago. The novel tells us more about nineteenth-century courtship manners than it does about Chicago.

Herbert B. Duff's *Chester* (1898), set in Chicago and southern Illinois, relates how a man is saved from the road to ruin by his marriage to a fine woman, and from poverty by the death of his wealthy father.

A world of talent and serious intentions separates this hodgepodge of authors and books from the life and work of the next Chicago author on our list.

Joseph Kirkland

Joseph Kirkland, a pioneer in American literary realism, a major influence on Hamlin Garland, and a probable influence on Stephen Crane's *The Red Badge of Courage* (1895), was the second son of Carolyn Kirkland, that advocate of literary realism we saw in connection with Richardson's *Hardscrabble*. Kirkland had lived in Chicago from about 1868, and had begun practicing law in 1880. From 1889 to 1891 he was the literary editor of the Chicago *Tribune*. Just before the end of his life he published an 1891 *Story of Chicago* which contained this observation:

> The time is not far distant when culture, civilization's chief adornment, will give an added lustre to Chicago's fair fame; and the height of her buildings, the size of her grain elevators and the reports of her slaughter houses will be of secondary importance as compared with the scientists, artists, scholars and musicians she has fostered. Already there is forming here a nucleus of men of letters whose reputation is no longer local. Eugene Field, David Swing, Henry Blake Fuller, all write, not for Chicago or the West, but for the whole country. Dr. W. F. Poole, Elwyn A. Barron, Harriet Monroe, Mary Abbott, Hobart Chatfield Chatfield-Taylor. Harry B. Smith, Clara Doty Bates, Amelia Gere Mason, Opie Read and many others have placed their names on Chicago's literary calendar, which will be a source of pride to us one of these days when we have faith in our own judgment, and no longer wait for the East to set its seal of approbation on our literary and artistic achievements.

Kirkland's literary reputation was made by *Zury: The Meanest Man in Spring County* (1887), and two sequels, *The McVeys* (1888), and *The Captain of Company K* (1891), the latter written for a Detroit newspaper contest in 1888.

His goal as he wrote *Zury* was to write "a novel of Western rural life."[37] His artistic philosophy, he told the readers of *The Dial*, was to "deal no more with the unbridled vagaries of romanticism, webs as foolish and purposeless as the gossamer."[38] *Let only truth be told*, was henceforth to be the battlecry. But this new clarion call was tempered with a disclaimer — *and not all the truth*. He was a true son of his mother.

Yet he wove a sometimes unbelievable romantic plot into the realistic fabric of the account of the rise of Usury ("Zury") Prouder from youthful poverty on the northern Illinois prairie to a state of power, affluence and influence — a rise which spanned a quarter of a century, and which, like the "unbridled vagaries" of the Horatio Alger stories, echoes the rise of men like Abraham Lincoln or Andrew Carnegie. *Zury* focusses on an affair between Zury and Anne Sparrow, a woman whose twin illegitimate children are in fact Zury's. Zury's neighbors and the children themselves believe that one John McVey, whom Anne has married after becoming pregnant, is the father.

Zury ends some years after the marriage of Zury and Anne; by then the twins have grown and struck out for themselves.

In a preface to his novel, Kirkland wrote:

> If a critic shall say —
> "This novel is a palpable imitation of Thomas Hardy's 'Far From the Madding Crowd;' an attempt to reproduce on American soil, the unflinching

realism of the picture given by that remarkable work, of English low life down in actual contact with the soil itself."

Then the writer will be satisfied. He will know that he has hit the mark, or at least come near enough to it to make his aim evident.[39]

Zury was favorably received; it is still regarded as a classic of the realistic tradition. Hamlin Garland praised the book as "absolutely unconventional . . . every character is new and native . . ."[40] As a result of this review the two men met in Chicago, and Kirkland encouraged Garland to write realistic fiction about the rural life he knew — the life of Wisconsin, Iowa and South Dakota, and ultimately, Chicago.

In an early draft of *Zury*, Kirkland had shown the boy, Phil McVey, as an engineer on the *Pioneer*, the first locomotive to run from Chicago to Galena, at that time a town with pretensions of becoming the midwest metropolis. At the end of the draft, Phil had died in a train wreck. But in the novel's published form, the railroad scene and Phil's death were deleted.

Pleased with the reception of *Zury*, Kirkland used the deleted material in a sequel, *The McVeys*. The second book begins with a summary characterization of Zury, still the "meanest man in Spring County," but a man who had become "possessed of a heart and soul fairly typical of the great and generous West in its ideal development."[41] The time is in the early 1840s, some ten years before the end of *Zury*; Phil and his sister, Meg, are still at home with their mother. Phil aids a surveyor in laying out the route of the Galena-to-Chicago railroad, a line which Chicago business men opposed, fearing that Galena would benefit the most by it.[42] Along the right of way, Phil meets a farm girl, Dolly Sanders, and her stepfather, "B'God" Hobbs. The two add several complications to Phil's life, and Hobbs is the cause of the train wreck which kills Phil. Phil's death is the catalyst which results in the marriage of Anne and Zury.

Critics did not like this novel as well as they had liked the first one, saying it lacked the strong character of Zury Prouder and was too loose and episodic. They felt the scene where Zury comes upon the dying Phil was too sentimental and almost ruined the novel.

Two of the characters in *The McVeys* were Ann Marsten, a girl Phil fell in love with in Chicago, and Perry Fenton, a young Chicago merchant also in love with Ann. Changing their names to Sara (Sally) Penrose and Will Farjeon, Kirkland wrote *The Captain of Company K*, one of the four full length novels which directly connects Chicago and the Civil War. When the War comes, Farjeon, in a public-spirited moment, leaves his business to become a Union officer. Home on his first leave and in a fit of depression about the War and business, he sells his mercantile establishment at a loss. He fights at Fort Donnellson and at Shiloh, where he loses a leg. Returned home, he is brevetted a major at Camp Douglas on Chicago's South Side, named for Stephen A. Douglas on whose land the camp had been built. Eventually he marries Sara. Their financial problems are solved when her uncle wills them his estate.

Kirkland's own estimate that the book was a "potboiler" has not been challenged by his critics.[43]

Statistically, the four books linking Chicago with the Civil War are not proportionate to the use of the subject by American authors as a group — despite Chicago's strong interest in the War. From 1862 to 1899, almost 250 novels were published in America on the subject of the War, and there were to be many more in the twentieth century.[44]

Partly, the cause lies in the small number of Chicago authors in the nineteenth century. For example, when in November of 1887, a congress of American literary figures assembled in New York City for a benefit reading, there were no authors from Chicago. Only Edward Eggleston and James Whitcomb Riley, both of Indiana, and Mark Twain, who had long since settled in the East, were listed as midwestern authors.[45] Field's statement that Chicago was becoming a "literary center" cannot be taken very seriously, even if one adds in the newspaper people who were moving to Chicago and becoming authors in their spare time.

For its first fifty-five years, Chicago's principal energies had been expended in commerce and industry, and in building and rebuilding the city. Only one important Chicago book — *Wau-bun* — had been written, and only three important writers — Kinzie, Field and Kirkland — had lived in Chicago. But there were harbingers of a brighter literary future, and indeed the nineties were to mark the real beginnings of a serious Chicago literature. Kirkland had pointed the way for those Chicago realists who were to make Chicago and literary realism synonymous; Garland, Herrick, Fuller, Dreiser, Halper and Farrell among them; a journalist-literateur tradition had begun that was to produce Ade, Sandburg and Hecht; Field had become the first major humorous newspaper columnist (Ade and Dunne were waiting just offstage); the *Dial* was beginning to comment on the state of Chicago authorship; new literary magazines, including the *Chap-Book* were in the wings; the Auditorium had opened for business; several fine literary clubs were meeting regularly; and three major Chicago writers, natives of Chicago, were at the threshhold of their careers. The "White City" in Jackson Park was about to catch the eyes of the world. There were other symptoms, major and minor, of an "uplift" movement, of "Chicago genteelism" as it came to be called.

V.
The White City and the Black

These are the things I used to know:
A book called "Remember the Alamo,"
Written, I think, by Amelia Barr;
And the Cottage Grove cable car —
It was purple, but the State Street car was red
That passed by the bakery of Livingston's bread.
In our yard, near the drying shirts and socks,
I planted nasturtiums and four-o'clocks,
And in winter I often used to glide
On Johnny Cudahy's toboggan slide —
(He had a pair of pants with stripes,
And lived just across from the Conrad Seipps).
And Toots McCormick and Alma Meyer
Yelled when I passed on my Barnes White Flyer,
And a thousand other things I knew
In the sweet Chicago of '92.

Thus in 1943 did Frankin P. Adams, the famed F.P.A., recall his youth in Chicago.[1] It was the decade of the "Gay Nineties," as some have called it, but for Chicago it was to be a decade of both "heights and depths."

In that decade, the rising tide of Chicago literature in the nineteenth century crests in several waves: more examples of the novel of crime; dreams of the Chicago that could be, in "utopian" and tract novels; a flourish of romantic novels, inspired by a new voice in Chicago literature; the movement called "Chicago's higher evolution"[2] or "Chicago genteelism," which finds itself at this point in time somewhat at odds with a new interest in "Western," "realistic," or "veritistic"[3] literature, and which will in a decade and a half be submerged under a new tide of bohemianism; a Midway Plaisance of novels about the "White City," the World's Columbian Exposition of 1893; further developments in literary magazines, this time under the influence of "fin de siecle" bohemianism from Europe; and the evolution of newspaper humor into literature.

Spokespersons for the "Lower Half"

Lillian Sommers' second novel, *Jerome Leaster of Roderick Leaster & Co.* (1890) is dedicated to Robert Ingersoll (who had written the preface to her first book) thus forecasting the author's biases in the book. It contrasts the life of the industrialist, the artist, and the person with religious convictions, and apposes life in the factory, a west side "shanty," and a Chicago mansion. But its good intentions were marred, as were the good intentions of *Spicy* and *Daniel Trentworthy* by a gothic subplot — this one focuses on a mad housewife, once a nun, who, among other actions, has adulterous relations with her priest.

The novel presents an image of Chicago as the "black city:"

> The roofs of adjacent buildings with their chimneys, water tanks and smoke stacks, and the dwarfed or enlarged shadows of these in the dim light, look ... more like the last poor home of a man, a graveyard, well-marked with vaults, tall monuments and tombstones ...[4]

The terms "white city" and "black city" seem to have been coined by Paul Bourget, a French novelist who came to Chicago to see the World's Columbian Exposition, and who wrote that "the White City must disappear, while the Black City, which will endure forever, is only at its commencement."[5] A third term, "the grey city" came to be applied to the new campus of the University of Chicago.

Such utopian novels as Sommers' were an outgrowth of social unrest, labor conditions like those that led to the Haymarket Affair, changing philosophies of life, and external literary influences. America was not turning out to be the land of opportunity except for a few. Poverty was no longer seen as punishment; failure was no longer seen as a "God-given condition, a punishment for sin." Populism was attracting attention as a political theory in the city as well as in the country. The Machine Age had at last reached the middle west but it was a curse as much it was a blessing. "Most factory jobs offered no opportunities for pride or joy ... either in real life or in [fiction]. The work was dirty, backbreaking and dangerous ... repetitive enough to be soul-destroying." Slowly but surely sympathy for the worker was being built up.[6]

Among literary influences, the most influential was Edward Bellamy's 1887 novel, *Looking Backward.* "It introduce[d] the theme of socialism sympathetically and it set the pattern for a flood of Utopian novels to come which contrast a better world of the future with the chaotic society of the present."[7] Among Chicago literary influences might have been G. C. Scott's *Driven From Sea to Sea* (1885) which exposed railroad land thefts in Chicago, and *Daniel Trentworthy,* which showed a western railroad official bribing Chicago aldermen.

The best Chicago utopian novel is Robert H. Cowdrey's *A Tramp in Society* (1891), published in Chicago by the F. H. Schulte Company, a firm which specialized in "radical" books. Schulte also published Hamlin Garland's *A Member of the Third House* (1892) which was concerned with the corrupting influence of the railroads on legislature. The latter book contained this advertisement for Cowdrey's novel:

> One of the most striking features of the times is the fact that so many pens are turned upon finding some solution for the portentuous labor question. Bellamy's ideal has come and gone without [effecting] any great change in the tendencies of the times or the nature of our laws. Ignatius Donnelly has given us a startling view of the next century in "Caesar's Column" (Schulte, 1890) a book which has aroused to serious thought the people of both hemispheres. It remained for Robert Cowdrey to give us the individualistic novel and perhaps no man is better fitted for this task. His address before the Tariff Commission of 1882 attracted widespread attention, and, having been the United Labor Party candidate for President of the United States in 1888, his writings have a prestige and standing with thousands of readers even regardless of their literary merit.[8]

Cowdrey's book has little of the novelistic quality, however. Its basic theme is that of Henry George, the political mentor of Hamlin Garland and Herbert Quick and other Populist authors — the evil of crime and poverty can be laid to private ownership and to rents. The setting is "Freeland," a suburb of Chicago. Cowdrey apparently had George H. Pullman's Pullman in mind, but in Freeland the workers pay no rent. (In Pullman, the workers were forced to pay rent even though the Pullman Company had no jobs for them.)

Under the pseudonym of F. S. Norton, Cowdrey also wrote *Ten Men of Money Island* (1892) also a Schulte book. This utopian novel has no Chicago setting.

In the long severe winter of 1892-1893, work was progressing at an unbelievably fast rate along the beach in Jackson Park. A Boston architect had publicly doubted that the World's Columbian Exposition could be finished on time, but Chicagoans with a spirit later to be labeled "I Will" intended that it should be. Around the globe people watched and wondered, and prepared exhibits which would be shipped to Chicago to catch the eyes of millions. The excitement was contagious, and writers began to speculate — if this wondrous "white city" could be built by the Lake in such a short time, why couldn't the problems of mankind be solved as easily?

Henry L. Everett's *The People's Program: The Twentieth Century is Theirs* (1892) is one product of such speculation, but it is "an utterly disorganized book."[9] The anonymous *The Beginnings: A Romance of Chicago As It Might Be* (1893) is another. It looks forward to a utopian Chicago of 1922 which is like the pre-Fire "Garden City," except for one difference:

> "I expected to see the city full of twenty to thirty story buildings by this time."
>
> "O no ... You remember there were quite a number of those same skyscrapers up when you left, and you would hear people say, 'How we will astonish the foreigners when they come to the World's Fair,' and no doubt it did ... Well, they kept on building them, shutting out the sun and light, till we began to feel we were in the cellar when we were down town, and at last some people began to carry lanterns. Of course ... it had to stop ...[10]

At the World's Columbian Exposition, the Pullman Company, sensing future labor troubles at its model town on Chicago's far South Side, handed out booklets, *The Story of Pullman.* Apparently in answer to this, Charles H. Kerr & Company, another Chicago publisher of "radical" books, brought out Nico Bech-Meyer's *A Story From Pullman-town* (1894). Like *The Beginnings,* it's more a tract than a novel. Anti-capital, pro-workingman, the book focusses on a couple who have had to leave South Dakota because of harsh conditions but find Pullman, with its workers unemployed but its company-owned stores still demanding cash, no better. The book ends as the 1894 Pullman Strike begins.

The major problem of these books is that they have too much of the reformer's zeal, too little literary talent.

The 1894 Pullman Strike is one of the chief topics of Charles King's *A Tame Surrender/A Story of the Chicago Strike* (1896). The "surrender" refers to the other topic, a romance between the Army officer hero and a young typist for a Chicago library, not unlike the Newberry. King, an army officer and the author of a number of popular romances about soldiers in the Great Plains, is an obvious supporter of a strong Federal government (his state officers are soft-headed liberals like Altgeld) and of capital over labor. His villain, a humble hypocrite right out of Charles Dickens, supports labor. Reflecting an attitude in many labor novels of the times, King's union organizers are accused of stirring "tramps and loafers" with "no end but mischief in view."[11]

Henry O. Morris's *Waiting For the Signal* (1897) is another tract novel which is of interest today because of its two chief characters, Chicago newspaper men working for a ficitonal newspaper whose editorial policy is in opposition to all the other Chicago newspapers and particularly the *Chicago Inter-Ocean*, a leading Chicago newspaper in the 1890s.[12]

Perhaps the most interesting of the Chicago-based tract literature of this period was *Coin's Financial School* (1894, reprinted 1963) by William H. "Coin" Harvey. Although the book deals with a very real situation, the 1890s debate over the merits of gold and silver coinage, the method of presentation is fictional. "COIN" was an imaginary character, and his school never existed. And, although real Chicagoans appear and speak — Medill of the *Tribune*, Wilson of *Farm, Field and Fireside* — they utter Harvey's ideas.

Coin's Financial School was one of the four "best sellers" of 1894,[13] and an important book in its time:

> The student who tries to recapture the emotions of [the "Free Silver"] crusade reads [William Jennings] Bryan's [1896] "Cross of Gold" speech as the great document of the silver cause. Yet this speech sums up a case already made; it assumes much and explains little to a reader ignorant of the preceding years of monetary argument. One cannot tell from it how the silver men arrived at their sense of conviction. If Bryan was immediately understood by his audience, it was because he played upon a set of feelings already formed and inflamed by a vast literature of analysis and agitation; and of all this literature, by far the most effective and memorable work was William Hope Harvey's little book of 155 pages ...[14]

In the year of the Columbian Exposition, when Chicago was the focus of writers from all over the globe, William T. Stead, a London reformer, and founder, proprietor, and editor of the British *Review of Reviews,* praised Chicago in "From the Old World to the New, or a Christmas Story of the World's Fair (December, 1893)." He had come to Chicago just in time to see enough of the Fair to gather material for his article. After the "White City" on the Lake had closed, Stead visited the "Black City" to the north. His observations of the hardships of the poor, who gained nothing from the Fair and were hard hit by the consequences of the 1893 Panic, led him to read a paper, "If Christ Came to Chicago" at two mass meetings. In his paper, he praised saloon keepers for feeding the poor, but he castigated others for "political corruption, toleration of vice and the greed of employers."

Successive talks with Jane Addams, who only four years before had founded Hull House in the heart of Chicago's Halsted Street ghetto, led Stead to seek further first-hand experience, the fruits of which were his book, *If Christ Came to Chicago! A Plea for the Union of All Who Love in the Service of All Who Suffer* (1894). At once this became the most popular book in Chicago, selling hundreds of thousands of copies. However the use of cheap sulfite paper and perishable bindings makes the book a rarity today.[15]

In his book Stead talked about vice in Chicago and he documented his statements with a map of the vice district, which may have served in some ways he did not intend! In fact, for all of Stead's good intentions, "the sale of the book was mostly due to his reports on the vices of Chicago. Here he entered Shang Andrews' territory [and] found himself in frequent agreement with that gutter journalist," who by this time was publishing a daily *Chicago Street Gazette* in the city's red-light district. For example, both admired the intelligence and hard work of three of the red-light district's more noted madames, Carrie Watson, Lizzie Allen and Vina Fields.[16]

Many, noting that some of Stead's material was based on hearsay, disagreed with him. Among these was Austyn Granville, a Chicago newspaper man, who wrote a response, *If the Devil Came to Chicago* (1894). The narrator is supposedly Beelzebub I, Prince of Darkness. Curiously Granville, whose other books are too badly written to be worth noting, did not see the irony in his choice of the Devil as a defender of Chicago!

By contrast with Stead's "Christmas Story of Chicago," which complained about the present, Charles O. Boring's *A Christmas Mystery* (1896) looks a half century into Chicago's future on Christmas Eve, 1949. From the book's Utopian viewpoint, Chicago has become a place where poverty no longer exists, there is no use for jails, and all social activity is centered around "The Church of the Redeemer."

Two other futuristic Chicago novels deserve mention. The journalist Stanley Waterloo's *Armageddon* (1898, reprinted 1976) is a story of a Chicago inventor who builds a dirigible and uses it in a war of the worlds. William Thomas Walsh's *The Mirage of the Many* (1910) is a capitalistic answer to the socialist threat, set in the Chicago of 1952. A Chicagoan who has lost his wealth on the Board of Trade shifts to socialism (although he gags at a favorite socialist tenet, "free love") but reforms and wins the daughter of a North Sheridan Road steel manufacturer.

"The White City" — The World's Columbian Exposition

Chicago had begun its efforts to secure the proposed celebration of the 400th anniversary of the coming of Columbus to the New World in the 1880s. But there were many competing cities, chief among them New York City, and at first the "Urbs Recondita"[17] was given hardly a chance. The choice was made after a hearing before a Congressional committee in which Chicago's advocates argued her central location, her lake frontage, her hotel rooms, her wealth, prosperity and enterprise, and above all the enthusiastic confidence of her people.[18] Still, as the time for opening the Fair approached, there was fear and pessimism in the city. "Instead of completing their half-finished city [the people of Chicago] have been amusing themselves in building another over yonder, under pretext of their exhibition," wrote Paul Bourget, the French novelist, half in jest.[19] The negative moods stemmed

partly because of the national economic situation, partly from the anticipated hordes of hoodlums, criminals and others with vicious intent. "I'm
goin' to Chicago to the Fair," said a Marion, Indiana man, "but I'm goin' to
wear nothin' but tights and carry a knife between my teeth and a pistol in
each hand."[20]

But the Fair was built and opened as predicted. "It was because of the
Black City that Chicago built the White City," said one historian. "Out of
industrial warfare, it was a cry for peace and faith."[21] Whatever, the Fair
was responsible for a sizable number of the 100,000 books that are said to
have been written about Chicago.

The poets played a part. At least two "Columbian Odes" were written for
ceremonies that preceded the opening of the Fair, one of them by a woman
who was to play a major role on the Chicago poetry scene for the next four
decades. Miss Harriet Monroe, an art critic for the *Tribune* had originally
attracted public notice as a poet when her "Cantata" was sung at the
opening of the Auditorium in 1889. Eugene Field had recommended she be
given the opportunity to read lines such as these:

> Hail to thee, fair Chicago! On thy brow
> America, thy mother, lays a crown.
> Bravest among thy daughters brave art thou,
> Most strong of all her heirs of high renown.[22]

But later in life Miss Monroe "cancelled the publication" of the "Cantata
. . . for two reasons:

> . . . first, its academic and minor quality as poetry; and second, its anarchy
> strophe, which implies approval of that mass execution of the seven so-called
> anarchists [sic], which my more mature judgment denounces as an hysterical
> public crime and a blot on the city's honor.[23]

The later Columbian Ode was written because Miss Monroe, voicing an
opinion she was again to voice two decades later, argued that all the other
arts were to be represented at the Fair and so poetry should be included as
well. Charles T. Yerkes, the builder of Chicago's transit system, agreed with
her. But as the time approached for the reading and singing of the Ode,
complications intruded. At last, the decision was made in Miss Monroe's
favor, but an actress, with a more powerful voice, read only a portion of the
Ode:

> Lo, clan on clan,
> The embattled nations gather to be one,
> Clasp hands as brothers on Columbia's shield,
> Upraise her banner to the shining sun . . . .[24]

These lines reflect an optimistic Chicago attitude implicit also in the tone
of this Chicago *Tribune* account of the dedication:

Historians yet unborn may date from the dedication of the Columbian Exposition ... the millenium of universal liberty and of the brotherhood of man. ... It stood for the highest aspirations of all men — not for us alone, not alone for our United States. The representatives of all the nations of the earth took part in the ceremonies, and the blood of all nations flowed in the crowd that called itself the American people.[25]

In an "oversanguine" mood, Miss Monroe had printed 5,000 copies of the Ode for sale at the Exposition. Most of these she used as fuel in her study stove the following winter![26] Apparently the multitudes of visitors to the Exposition did not share Miss Monroe's enthusiasm for poetry, nor share with Joseph Kirkland the view that the Ode was "full of grand imagery, clothed in splendid diction well versified ... The Ode cannot die; such words are immmortal."[27]

But "one of the country's most powerful newspapers, the *New York World*, shared Kirkland's and Monroe's enthusiasm:

A *World* reporter had obtained an advance copy of [the] Ode, and had sent the poem to New York in one of the longest press telegrams ever filed from Chicago. It had appeared in full, except for one lost line, on the front page of the *World* for Sunday, October 23. The editors knew that the author had reserved copyright and forbidden publication. Nevertheless, they had ordered their Chicago man to get a copy, telling him they would take their chances with Miss Monroe ... It made them angry, when Harriet's lawyers announced suit for theft of literary property, since Joseph Pulitzer, publisher of the *World*, detested writers who had lawyers. Therefore, the *World* refused to settle out of court...

In the end, the *World*, which might have gotten the New York rights to the Ode for a couple of hundred dollars, was ordered to pay Harriet the sum of $5,000 plus lawyers' fees and court costs.[28]

Later, Exposition authorities announced a contest for a formal "Columbian Ode." The record does not show that the by-now unhappy Miss Monroe submitted an entry, but at least a thousand others did. A non-Chicagoan, a man who became Poet Laureate of Kansas, Thomas Brower Peacock, won, and read his *Columbian Ode/An Ode of Greetings* in the Art Palace on May 24, 1893.[29]

Bernard Isaac Durward, a Scotsman who came to Milwaukee in the 1840s, wrote his epic *Cristofero Columbo* (1893) for the Exposition. It attracted national attention at the time, but like Monroe's and Peacock's odes, it is today forgotten. In 1935, Miss Monroe offered an explanation for the change in literary tastes:

The form and content of the ode may seem academic to the modernist, but in its day it was considered revolutionary ... [The poem] may be said to mark the beginning ... of an epoch, a period full of illusions and comfortable orthodoxies, resting on an apparent stability which was ... to be rudely shaken [by the first World War] ...[30]

Some fifteen novels, all of them contemporary with the Exposition, plus one written in 1900 and one written in 1947, are set in and about the Jackson Park site. Many later novels used the Exposition incidentally. Two novels written at the time of the Century of Progress (1933) have protagonists who had visited the 1893 Exposition (one had visited the 1876 Centennial Exposition) and had returned for the later Fair. Finally, a book written in 1957 for young people comes close to being the best of the lot.

Grey says, "As an expression of [Chicago's mixed feelings of fear, pessimism and 'brave radiance'], the World's Fair novels at once agree with and depart from the [utopian novels]. Where the latter are addressed primarily to city laborers and sympathizers, the World's Fair novels are addressed to farmers, villagers, and middle-class city folk — particularly to women — in need of another sort of reassurance about the city. They are addressed to Henry Adams' 'retarded minds.'"[31]

Of the novels written at the time of the Fair, the best by far is Clara Louise Burnham's *Sweet Clover, A Romance of the White City* (1894) which, says Finis Farr, offers "a fresh point of view" about the Exposition.[32] The characters are from the village of Hyde Park (now a part of Chicago), the first use of this setting in a Chicago novel. Through the eyes of Clover Bryant, Jack Van Tassel, and "Aunt Love" who offers a favorite New England point of view, we visit the Exposition on a number of occasions, and we are present after the Fair, when the Peristyle, with its "heavenly promise ... Ye shall know the truth and the truth shall make you free ... [has] gone back to heaven" in one of the several fires that plagued the Exposition, either during its great summer or later.[33] The detailed setting of the exposition serves as a backdrop for a romance focussing on the triangle of Clover, Van Tassell, and Van Tassell's cousin from Boston, Gorham Page.

Three other novels of urban romance have their settings in and around the Exposition. St. George Rathbone's *The Bachelor of the Midway* (1894, 1896), written under the pseudonym of "Harrison Adams," is a complex mystery-romance, involving a Canadian and a Turk. The setting is "The Streets of Cairo" although "Little Egypt," the legendary belly-dancer does not appear — nor does she appear in any other contemporary Exposition novel. A tenement fire helps resolve the mysteries.

Three Girls in a Flat (1892), an early "bachelor-girl" novel,[34] by Enid Yandell, Jean Loughborough and Laura Hayes, has a strong feminist note; it is dedicated to the Board of Lady Managers of the Exposition. Its three authors appear, slightly disguised, in the novel, one as a sculptress, one as a secretary, one as a jobless journalist. From internal evidence Laura Hayes seems to have written most of the book, and also seems to have secured most of the seventeen pages of advertising in the endpages.

Frances Hodgson Burnett, author of the fanciful, sentimental and popular *Little Lord Fauntleroy* (1886), carried the fancy and sentiment of that novel together with the explicit theme of John Bunyan's *Pilgrim's Progress* into her adult novel of twelve-year-old twins at the Exposition, *Two Little Pilgrims' Progress, A Story of the City Beautiful* (1895, 1897).

The novel has a typical account of Chicago "push:"

> He was quite used to hearing jokes about Chicago. The people in the country around about it were intensely proud of it, and its great scheme and great buildings and multi-millionaires, but those who were given to jokes had the habit of being jocular about it, just as they had the habit of proclaiming upon its rush and wealth and enterprise.[35]

Perhaps the most unusual Exposition novel is Hyland C. Kirk's *The Revolt of the Brutes, A Fantasy of the Chicago Fair* (1893), a book which one critic calls "a modern version of [Chaucer's] *Parlement of Foules*, [of] *The Hind and the Panther, Gullivers' Travels* and *Alice in Wonderland* rolled into one."[36] It is somewhat akin to the utopian novels. Primarily a satire on American politics, the book comments on just about every issue in the minds of Chicagoans of that day.

Two other Chicago mystery stories are set at the Exposition, Emma Murdoch Van DeVenter's ("Laurence L. Lynch") *Against Odds: A Romance of the Midway Plaisance* (1894), and *The Mysterious Disappearance of Helen St. Vincent* (1895) by John J. Flinn, like Van DeVenter an author of "potboilers." *Against Odds* is one of two Chicago novels which use the burning of the faultily-constructed Cold Storage building as an event. In the course of that fire, thousands watched in terror and helplessness as seventeen firemen died, trapped on the roof in full view of the pleasure-seeking crowd.

There were several Exposition novels which are either juveniles or comedies of rural bumpkins at the Exposition, or combinations of both. Charles McClellan Stevens's ("Quondam") *Uncle Jeremiah and Family at the Great Fair: Their Observations* (1893); Tudor Jenk's *Century World's Fair Book for Boys and Girls* (1893); Mary C. Crowley's *The City of Wonders* (1894); and Martha Finley's *Elsie Dinsmore at the World's Fair* (n. d.), one of the popular girls' series.

Hezekiah Butterworth's *Zig Zag Journeys on the Mississippi From Chicago to the Island of Discovery* (1892) and *Zig Zag Journeys in the White City* (1894) are also juveniles, the first designed to "prepare its readers to discuss the meaning of the great World's Fair of 1893 . . . and to talk of the politics of different nations intelligently."[37] The second volume looked at the Exposition in retrospect: "The White City was the prophetic vision of the ages . . . To the American people it will ever be revelation . . ."[38]

The last of these has won some notice from earlier historians. Marieta Holley, author of an earlier work, *Samantha at the Centennial* (1876), about the Philadelphia Exposition, showed the Chicago Fair from the point of view of Samantha Allen of "York State" in *Samantha at the World's Fair* (1893). There is a constant emphasis on the achievement of women at the Fair, ranging from Queen Isabella of Spain, who in a way was responsible for the Fair, to Mrs. Potter Palmer, who managed to give some people the impression that she was running more than just the Board of Lady Managers.

In some seven-hundred pages, Mrs. Holley supplies a mass of information about the Fair and displays an optimistic philosophy as well. "The motive of the Fair, as she sees it, is a Columbus-like search for 'that New World' sought by all prophets who have 'walked the narrow streets of earth . . . in chains and soul-hunger," says Grey.[39]

Weldon J. Cobb's *A World's Fair Mystery* (1892) was actually published the year before the Fair opened, and the story begins several years prior to that. A Chicago lawyer and a broker swindle an orphan out of her inheritance then blame another for the crime. During the Fair, the man falsely accused escapes from jail and suceeds in concealing himself among Fair visitors. All ends well.

Harold Richard Vynne's *The Woman That's Good; A Story of the Undoing of a Dreamer* (1900) is a less than ordinary romance set at the Columbian Exposition. Vynne was also the author of several stories in *Tales From Town Topics* (1897) and *Chicago By Day and Night. The Pleasure Seeker's Guide to the Paris of America* (1892), a guide for World's Fair visitors.

As any one familiar with the "dime novel" genre might suspect, at least a half dozen of these paperback mysteries were set at the Fair. These novels gained some credibility from the repeated predictions that hordes of confidence men, pickpockets, thieves and general scoundrels would descend on Chicago and the Exposition, and later reports that the predictions had proved true.

The Fair was also the subject of dozens of non-fiction books, and two books of journalistic sketches, the latter reprinted from newspaper columns: Martha R. Holden's *A String of Amber Beads* (1893), and Teresa Dean's *White City Chips* (1893).

In 1947, more than a half-century after the Fair had closed, Clara Ingram Judson wrote *The Lost Violin; They Came from Bohemia*. Judson's novel tells of the coming of the Kovec family from Czechoslovakia, and the disappearance of a prized violin on the day the family arrives in Chicago. The real value of the novel lies not in this skimpy plot line but in the images of Bohemian life in the city and of the Columbian Exposition.

In the 1950s, a film and a book looked back at the Exposition. *Little Egypt*

(1951) is a film set at the Columbian Exposition; it features the belly dancer in "The Streets of Cairo" who had all the yokels as wide-eyed as forty years later when Sally Rand came to the Century of Progress with her fans.

Robert Lawson was a fine writer and illustrator of books for children; he won both the Caldecott Award and the Newberry Award. His last book, *The Great Wheel* (1957) may well represent the peak of his career; certainly it is a book which both adults and young people can still enjoy. It relates how Cornelius Terence Kilroy ("Conn") comes from Ireland to America and helps George Washington Gale Ferris build the Columbian Exposition's "great wheel" which Ferris's detractors said could never be finished and would not be safe to ride in any case.

In a number of later Chicago novels there are comments on the Fair. Here is Robert Herrick's *Waste* (1924):

> With the end of the great Fair somehow the city had crumpled exhausted
> ... Thousands of idle starving people prowled the ice-cold streets and slept in
> the filthy alleys. Violence broke forth. Once more Chicago became the frontier
> village, unkempt and unsafe ...[40]

Another is a parody of a song popular during the Fair, and repeated over and over in *Sweet Clover:* "After the Ball:"

> After the Fair is over,
> What will Chicago do
> With all those empty houses,
> Run up with sticks and glue?
> I'd rather live in Brooklyn
> (Somebody'd know me there)
> Than to live in Chicago,
> After — the — Fair.[41]

Two artifacts remained in the Jackson Park area after all the other traces of the Fair had been burned or removed. One was the Museum of Science and Industry, a more permanent stone replica of the original Art Palace where Peacock had read his *Columbian Ode.* The other was a row of scruffy, flimsy, false-front shops which were still around in the early nineteen-sixties. These were to play a prominent part in the Chicago Renaissance movement some twenty years after the Fair. They had been a marginal part of the Exposition, but they would be the new Midway in the later literary movement.

There were of course many other publications which emphasized the Fair. These ranged from the *Chicago Tribune Souvenir Glimpses of the World's Fair, a Selection of Gems of the White City and the Midway Plaisance, (1893, almost more title than book!)* to Hubert H. Bancroft's elephant-size, 2,000-page *The Book of the Fair* (1895). Undoubtedly the most significant of all is *The Education of Henry Adams,* and most particularly the chapter "The

Virgin and the Dynamo." Grey says:

> ... At Chicago Adams found "a matter of study to fill a hundred years, and his education spread over chaos." But there were three things that stood out for him in what he saw. He saw that the Fair brought "retarded minds" out of the past to confront the world of 1893. He saw that the artists "talked as though they worked only for themselves." He saw that the Fair predicted a bewildering shift from "historical sequences" — still dominant — to "mechanical sequences" before which the historian and the average man felt helpless. What did all this mean? Did Adams know? "Certainly not!" he exclaimed. But in time he rationalized it into the symbol of the Dynamo, in contrast with the Virgin at the other extreme.[42]

Miscellaneous Novels of the Nineties

Through the 1890's the first native Chicagoans as well as expatriates from other parts of the country were writing about Chicago. From *Wau-bun* on, women authors have outnumbered the men, however. And more than one writer has come to Chicago, written one book about the city, and then gone on to greener pastures elsewhere.[43]

Edgar R. Beach's *Stranded: A Story of the Garden City* (1890) is set in Chicago from 1836 to 1866. Like other books of an earlier period, it "endeavor[ed] to present facts in the rosy light of fiction" with its moral: "The way of the transgressor is hard."[44] Its cast includes a confidence man-foppish gambler, a little rag-picker and his rich and miserly uncle, a Michigan Boulevard judge and his daughter, a young manufacturer, and, the most interesting of all, one Michael Snoozer, of Spanish-Indian-Negro-Chinese origins, ugly as the sin the book is about, and Lord of the "Sands," the notorious squatter district on the north side of the River where it flows into the Lake.

Carter H. Harrison, "our Carter," who was the only Chicago mayor to write a work of fiction (other than, perhaps, the annual reports of city business!) produced two non-Chicago novellas under the title, *A Summer's Outing* and *The Old Man's Story* (1891). The "outing" or rustic idyll was spent in Yellowstone and Alaska. Grey sees the second story as a "tentative approach to the type of social misfortune which would breed anarchists" of the Haymarket stripe.[45]

Kathryn Donelson's *Rodger Latimer's Mistake* (1891) is set in the twin cities of "Clinton" (Chicago) and "Edgewood" (Evanston). (Realistic writers of this period were sometimes shy about the use of actual names, even when the models were obvious.) Rodger Latimer, like Daniel Trentworthy, comes from Harvard to Chicago; such westward movements were one of the reasons why Chicagio grew so rapidly. In Clinton, Rodger marries a fortune-hunting girl, daughter of an Edgewood professor, and follows the kind of life style which led Thorsten Veblen, University of Chicago sociologist, to coin his term "conspicuous consumption" (*The Theory of the Leisure Class*, 1899). Meanwhile, Rodger's true love, his wife's more conservative sister, engages in social work in a neighborhood of gambling dens, saloons, and "dance houses" (brothels). All ends well as Rodger enters the Chicago profession with the highest status (law), and his wife conveniently dies. Then he marries the sister, whose name — Margaret McVey — is also the name of the heroine of Kirkland's *The McVeys*, published three years earlier.

Lillian Blanche Fearing, another native of Davenport, Iowa, is responsible for three Chicago titles in this decade. *In the City by the Lake* (1892) has two long narrative poems, each in four parts: "The Shadow," and "The Slave Girl." The first contrasts the lives of two neighboring children who grew up in contrasting lives of poverty and affluence. Like Longfellow's *Evangeline*, which the poem suggests, it ends in tear-jerking tragedy. The second deals with slum children, forced to work in sweatshops, but it has a happier romantic ending. Both poems take place over a decade of a time.

Her *Asleep and Awake* (1893), written under the pseudonym of "Raymond Russell," is more of a sermon than a novel, full of melodramatic scenes involving a deserted unwed mother, life in a brothel, the madness of the heroine and her final discovery, one day too late, by the repentant hero.

Roberta (1895) is the lurid tale of the career of Roberta ("Berta") Green from some time after the Fire until about the Fair. There is the omnipresent mortgage on the workingman's home, the sweatshop, the swindler and the embezzler with mysterious designs on the girl, the bastard child, a career as a musical comedy star, the disguise (a popular device in moralistic and melodramatic tales of latter-nineteenth-century Chicago), the trial of the heroine for murder — all obviously designed for the women and rural people who seem to have constituted the largest audience for Chicago books.

A recurring theme in many of these books is the wickedness of Chicago. This theme seems also to have had a great appeal to readers.

Emma Scarr Booth's *A Wilful Heiress* (1892) is related through excerpts from Mercie Freeman's diary and through letters written by her and by her relatives and friends. Mercie is "duped into marriage to a scoundrel" with the somewhat improbable name of Adolphus Pericles Montague; he is aided by a sister with the equally improbable name of Angelina Victoria Muggs. Her husband also manages to acquire control over her fortune. But after he is killed in a brawl, she marries "Sebastian Burness, a poor but honorable gardener." Thomas L. Kilpatrick says "this novel provides a good view of the stringent legal, social, and moral code by which women were bound in the latter half of the nineteenth century."[46]

Fred A. Chappell's *Bill and Brocky; A Story of Boy Life in Chicago, Especially Adapted to the Understanding of Old Boys* brings together a boy from a middle-class Chicago home, and a boy who lives in a packing crate. The boys are involved in such adventures as building a tunnel in a sawdust pile and conflict with a goody-goody boy named Reginald. The novel is more caricature than real.

Bunker Hill to Chicago (1893), by Eloise O. Randall Richberg (the mother of Donald Richberg, who we shall see later) has nothing to do with Boston, or, as its date of publication might suggest, the Columbian Exposition. Its Bunker Hill is a Pennsylvania village, the origins of a Chicago-bound family, brought to the city by the father, a Yankee inventor. His goals for his four daughters are their education, an increase in their self-reliance, and the prospects of better marriages. Recognizing that "God made the country and man made the town,"[47] the author apportions three of her heroines to city roles and one to life in the country. Meanwhile, the father prospers as a manufacturer of bicycles. The Yankee exile from New England as a successful Chicago business man or industrialist will become a familiar figure in Chicago literature.

The virtues and defects of this "railway news-stand literature," says Grey, "are manifestly of a kind with McGovern's and Kirkland's novels ... They are the traits to be expected in novels by writers not native to the city; by writers particularly of rural background, often New England background, striving to adjust themselves to the city. The violence of the Haymarket [Affair], which seems to be [an] unacknowledged reagent behind the flood of novels ... was not a force to quell melodrama. The impulse to escape to the countryside pulls continually against the impulse to fathom and settle this city business."[48]

Preserved Wheeler's *From Side Streets and Boulevards/A Collection of Chicago Stories* (1893) tells in turn of a Chicago girl of 14 who joins a touring theatrical troupe (the first Chicago story to use what will become a familiar theme), a family of Irish immigrants caught up in a Romeo-Juliet type of love affair, and two sons who speculate unwisely in real estate. There is a great deal of moralizing about Demon Rum and land speculation, the latter a subject of continuing interest to Chicago writers. Appended are several poems, one of which looks obliquely at the Columbian Exposition; one about "Rosehill," the northwest Chicago cemetery where a great many of Chicago's personages are interred; and one about "Grandma," which looks back from the time of the Exposition to the Sanitary Fair of 1860 and the Fire.

Although Opie Read's "railroad novels" are largely about life in the south, his *The Colossus* (1893) contrasts the affairs of a great Chicago store merchant with those of a rising young journalist. The complex plot involves a would-be journalist who passes himself off as a man he believes is dead. The ending is predictable.

The Colossus is interesting not only as the first of several Chicago novels about Chicago mercantile people, but also for comments, such as this one on the role and status of the Chicago writer:

"To money [Chicago] gives worship ... but to the writer it gives neglect — the campaign of silence."

"... You forget the difference that exists between new and old cities. A new community worships material things; and if it pays tribute to an idea, it must be that idea which appeals quickest to the eye — the commoner senses. And in this Chicago is no worse than other raw cities. Fifty years from now ..."[49]

[But ninety-years later, Pete Hamill, commenting on the death of Nelson Algren in Sag Harbor, N.Y., wrote:

Algren was a great American writer ... but he didn't belong to Sag Harbor or the East. He belonged to Chicago. That city hurt him into art, praised him, damned him, and finally broke his heart ... [Still] Algren talked about Chicago the way some men talk about women they have loved, not wisely, but too well.

"Chicago's a bust-out whore," he said one night. "Her teeth are gone, she's got varicose veins. She's got nothin' left but the memories." ...][50]

Judge Elbridge (1899) is Read's "second major effort to embrace the city scene."[51] The theme of this novel is that of Wilkie's *The Gambler* — in this case the Judge's foster son is the one caught up in the web of a gambling club. George Bodney, like the "Mephistophelian friend who leads him to moral ruin" is a college graduate. But Read's gambler, unlike Wilkie's, turns out all right.

Judge Elbridge abounds in pungent, epigrammatic statements of a kind that made Read's books extremely popular — especially among his journalistic peers:[52]

"His house in Indiana Avenue, at first far out, was now within easy reach of the city's pile-driving heart."[53]

"Morality without intellectual force is a weakness waiting for temptation."[54]

Read's third novel dealing with Chicago, *The New Mr. Howerson*, although published in 1914 after four years of work, [55] is, like Read's two other Chicago novels, basically a novel of the 1880s when Read first came to Chicago. It treats of an anarchistic plot to murder a Chicago capitalist who keeps, in his luxurious mansion, the log cabin where he was born. The poet selected for the assassination has a change of heart, and joins ranks with the capitalist. Even the girl anarchist ringleader reforms. Read's biographer says of these changes of heart "that Read's affectons were not with the money scramble of his Chicago environment, but that he was forced to write of it to satisfy the taste of the time." He argues that although Read "felt he was at last producing 'the great American novel'" which Chicago journalists were always talking about, "as a matter of fact he was merely writing an empty defense of finance capitalism." The book "was not written from Read's simple romantic heart."[56]

M. Train's *Ray Burton, A Chicago Tale* (1895) is the story of the efforts of a Chicago man to rebuild the family fortune, lost when the father was drowned in the Chicago River by footpad sailors, and the family was subsequently defrauded by the father's business partner. Ray Burton works as a telegraph messenger boy, a clerk for a clothing company, a station master on the Rock Island railroad, a court reporter and a newspaper reporter at the Columbian Exposition. The novel features an explicit portrait of a "boodling" alderman, as well as unscrupulous lawyers; the beginnings of social lines with a consequent deplorable "hint of aristocracy" in the seventies and eighties;[57] the rise of a morality which "depends upon one's condition, surroundings and ambitions;"[58] and increasing emphasis on the business "machine."[59]

Preserved Wheeler's (Ella McDougall) *One Schoolma'am Less* (1895) is the story of two daughters of a genteel Chicago family in financial straits. The parents raise their daughters in as genteel a fashion as circumstances will permit. The older daughter sacrifices her own career as a teacher in order to help the younger girl get a teaching certificate. But the younger girl's chances are lost because she lacks political influence. The novel is one of several over a period of years that attacks the Chicago educational system.

Alwyn M. Thurber is the author of three novels in this decade, two of which are attempts to persuade readers to accept his view of occultism. *"The Hidden Faith: An Occult Story of the Period* (1895) and *Zelma, the Mystic; or, White Magic, Versus Black* (1897) tells us little about Chicago of the 1890s, however. His *Quaint Crippen; Commercial Traveler,* sandwiched in between these two in 1896, is based on the relationships between a star salesman and a woman he meets and befriends.

Edward Waterman Townsend's *Chimmie Fadden* (1895) was a very popular collection of humorous monologues featuring a New York City Bowery lad. Hamlin Garland had said the "Chimmie Fadden" monologues were historical of New York's East Side just as George Ade's *Fables in Slang* were historical of Chicago.[61] In 1896, William A. Phelon, Jr., a reporter for the Chicago *Daily News* brought Fadden to Chicago in *Chimmie Fadden Out West; A Sequel to Chimmie Fadden.* Chimmie Fadden cruises on Lake Michigan, tours Chinatown, ventures onto Chicago's public transportation system, and has other adventures.[62]

Amelia Weed Holbrook's *One of the McIntyres* (1896), purporting to be the story of the seven-year-old son of a wealthy family, is little more than propaganda for the Chicago Waif's Mission.

Henry M[artyn] Blossom's *Checkers; A Hard-Luck Story (1896)* features a down-on-his-luck race track tout at Chicago's Washington Park Race Track and his friendship with a Chicagoan who tries to help him. The first part of the novel is told in Checkers' own voice, the second part in the voice of his friend. The first part is a "brilliant character study," but the second is not nearly so good.[63]

Two novels of this period, one slight and stereotyped and one which "just misses greatness," show a "transition from the old basket-charity ["basket-benevolences"] and the religious mission to the social settlement. Hull House had been founded in 1889 and Jane Addams' famous *Twenty Years at Hull House* was to be written in 1910. But several of the novels discussed here — *For Her Daily Bread, Jerome Leaster of Roderick Leaster & Co., Rodger Latimer's Mistake* — had raised questions of social service long before Miss Addams' book.

Merrick A. Richardson's *Chicago's Black Sheep and Bonnie McClear's Friends* (1898) tests our credibility severely at its very beginning as it asks us to believe (and the even more skeptical Chicago police as well!) that a sweet, virginal girl who conceals her true name behind not one but two aliases is not up to something. But we have read novels like this before and so we read on, knowing that pure Bonnie McClear's innocence will survive any test or accusation — or even a night in an 1890s' Chicago police lockup!

Hervey White's first novel, *Differences* (1899), uses Chicago's "stinking" Goose Island and the ten-year-old Hull House (where White lived from about 1895 to 1900) as its bases of operations. Its hero, John Wade, is based on an Englishman, Ralph Whitehead, who was also at Hull House and who, in 1900, helped White found an artist's colony near Woodstock, New York. Whitehead is also seen in Hutchins Hapgood's *The Spirit of Labor* (1907), and other Chicago novels of this period. There's a young businessman with more interest in *The Dilettante* (read *The Chap Book,* of which more later) than in a business firm or Chicago's craze for dollars. There are several instances of man's compassion for his fellow man. When Wade can't find work in Chicago and goes on a tramp, he is saved from freezing in an open box car by a Negro who uses his own body to warm Wade. Later, a group of "grubbing" Belgian farmers aid Wade. Ironically, the ambition of these men is to leave the farm and go to Chicago to find work.

Although Stanley Waterloo's *The Seekers* (1899, published by Herbert S. Stone & Company of Chicago of whom, also, more later) is set in Chicago, it is not so much a city novel as it is a book about various philosophies of healing. The several characters reject medicine and pursue jingoistic faith healers, pseudo-Eastern mystics and others. The story is not worth the publication care given it by Stone, and it's a bit difficult to perceive from either this novel or *Armageddon* the literary merits Opie Read, John McGovern and his other peers in the Press Club, saw in Waterloo's work.

Margaret Horton Potter [Black[s] first novel, *The Social Lion* (1899, 1901, 1903, written when Margaret was seventeen), although ostensibly an exposé of 1880 Chicago society, is so obviously about a society of Potter's own time that her scandalized family tried to suppress the book and did order the destruction of the plates of the first edition.[64] The central character, Herbert Stagmar, is a novelist of the 1890s realistic school in Chicago, and, as well, a successful operator on the Board of Trade, whose past escapades come back to haunt him. There are a number of thinly disguised Chicagoans in the novel, one of whom was probably looked at again in Fuller's *Under the Skylights* (1901, *infra*).[65]

Grey says that *The Social Lion* "shows that the younger generation on Prairie Avenue," one of Chicago's most elite residential areas in the 1890s, "was explicitly looking into its values 'morally, socially, artistically' at the end of the century, much as Katherine Keith" and Arthur Meeker were to look at the same Prairie Avenue values later.[66]

"The West should have a marked and original literature of its own," *The Literary Budget* had argued in 1854. But most of what had been produced in Chicago up to 1890 — with, perhaps, the exception of Eugene Field's newspaper humor, had been pale imitations of European literature, transmuted through the filter of the New England writers. But as the 1887 literary congress had shown, the day of the New England writers was past. America's literature would have to develop in new places. Field was a bit ahead of the times when he said that Chicago was rapidly becoming the literary center of the United States but only a bit. There were Chicagoans who read his witticism who were about to move Chicago solidly along on the road to a "culture's garland" that would not be a string of sausages![67]

Postscript

George Putnam Upton, a nineteenth century music and art critic for the *Chicago Tribune* and a prolific author of books about music, produced one Chicago title, in 1871: *The Chicago Plant: or Chicago in 1970*. This first of Chicago utopian literary works was a drama "originally performed at the Dearborn Theater" in 1871, apparently before the Fire.[68]

Upton's career lasted until the days of the Chicago Renaissance and the round table at Schlogl's.

VI.
Chicago Literature Comes of Age

"Out in Chicago, the only genuinely civilized city in the New World, they take the fine arts seriously and get into such frets and excitements about them as are raised nowhere else save by baseball, murder, political treachery, foreign wars and romantic lovers."[1]

Chicago's Higher Evolution

In the February, 1893 issue of *The New England Magazine,* William Morton Payne attempted "what should be said of the positive growth of the literary spirit of Chicago, and of the literary productions of the men and women who are identified with this city [where] the arrogant self-assertion and dull philistinism of the American character are more clearly typified than perhaps anywhere else in the land."[2]

Chicago was not entirely hopeless for Payne. It had passed that first of "three well-marked stages" where "literature is regarded with indifference or even with positive contempt." Twenty years earlier, the city had attained the "second stage of dilettantism, characterized by a general awakening of interest in literature, and by the organization of all sorts of societies for intellectual purposes." And the city was now standing "upon the threshold" of the third stage in which "literary production comes to be a distinct factor in the intellectual activity of the community," and the dilettantish stage "begins to bear its natural fruit."[3]

Payne's esssay reveals those curious literary tastes which would eventually lead him to dislike Sandburg. He implies that novels are sub-literary, and he dislikes E. P. Roe, then a very popular novelist. Instead he singles out "Mr. Charles M. Hertig's clever and audacious story of *The Verdendorps*" (18??) which all subsequent Chicago critics have ignored. He praises the Chicago Institute and various "literary" schools which have conducted courses in Dante, Goethe, Homer and Shakespeare. While he approved of the literary clubs of the time, he derogated the Browning clubs; "like the poor they are always with us," he said. He praises James Grant Wilson's *The Chicago Magazine* (the first of several with that title) even though it lasted but six issues and its contents are now forgotten. Among poets, he praises the Rev. F. W. Gunsaulus, one of Field's "Saints;" Benjamin Franklin Taylor; Eugene Field, who was better known in Chicago as a humorist; Harriet Monroe, the laureate of Chicago, "particularly for her Columbian Ode, which, as we have seen, Miss Monroe later retracted; and Blanche Fearing, whose unremarkable work (in this writer's opinion), would "have been still more remarkable if signed by a name of far wider reknown."[4]

Among novelists, Payne praises Mrs. Kinzie for *Wau-bun*; Joseph Kirkland for his three works; Henry Blake Fuller for his *The Chevalier of Pensieri-Vani*, and *The Chatelaine of La Trinité* because they "bind together the various aesthetic interests of the traveller in Italy or Switzerland"; and Clara Louise Burnham for non-Chicago books which preceded the yet-to-come *Sweet Clover.*

Payne closes with the comment that Chicago, which had not had a Public Library before the Fire, was about to become the "second, if not the first, library centre in the United States."[5] As Henry Blake Fuller was to write four years later, "Chicago's Upward Movement" was under way.[6]

Chicago's Literary Societies

Payne's appeal in the *New England Magazine* was to that segment of Chicago society which had organized a cultural revolt against the "arrogant self-assertion and dull philistinism" which had given Chicago its sobriquet of "Porkopolis." Beginning in the years after the Fire, this revolt took form in the organization of literary clubs, and in the promotion of European opera and classical music. This movement was to be called "Chicago's higher evolution," or "Chicago genteelism."[7]

An operational definition of Chicago genteelism was provided by George Putnam Upton:

> Does it not demonstrate that Chicago is not altogether absorbed in material pursuits, but is slowly and steadily caring for those higher things which make for sweetness and light? That grain and lumber and lard and hogs are not our only staples? And that in this city of the boundless prairies, swept with panics, scourged with fire, menaced with the bombs of the alien Anarchist, palled with smoke and grimed with soot, and fighting for the prizes of material competi-

tion, if you will have it so, there are many earnest men and women who have labored all those years for the things in which we should live, and who now see the harvest of fruition in the new Art Institute, the three great libraries, the colossal Chicago University springing forth full-fledged like Minerva, and the great white city at Jackson Park which will set the seal of success upon their endeavors?[8]

The English origins and influences on this genteel movement can be seen in the use of the terms "philistinism," and "sweetness and light," both derived from the essays of Matthew Arnold, the English poet who died in 1888 of a heart attack, as, in quite ungenteel fashion, he was running to catch a street car.

In the spring of 1874, Francis F. Browne, the Rev. J. C. Burroughs, President of the former Chicago University, and several other men formed the Chicago Literary Club to "promote the true sovereignity of letters and culture; to sustain the same by the moral and social virtues; to form and maintain a literary organization fairly representative of the intellectual rank and progress of Chicago; and to cultivate fraternal relationships with other exponents of literature and art.." Its membership of about two-hundred-and-fifty professional and business men with literary interests met weekly.[9]

Its opposite group, the Fortnightly Club, had been formed two years earlier by Mrs. Kate Doggett. For many years her home was "the gathering-place of what was best and most earnest in the culture of Chicago." The Club's membership was limited to one hundred-and-seventy-six women.[10]

Four years later, in 1876, "a number of women seeking a wider field for their work than that afforded by mere reading and discussion of papers, organized the Woman's Club." This group of five or six hundred women discussed not only literary matters, but practical social matters as well and worked diligently at shaping public opinion.[11]

A more select group was the Saracen Club whose eighty female members met but once a month. It drew its name and purpose from the medieval Saracens who "held up the torch of learning at a time when the Dark Ages dimmed the light of the Western World," a theme particularly applicable to a group in a city where the "dull philistinism of the American character is more clearly typified than perhaps anywhere else in the land."[12]

These were the major Chicago clubs among a larger number, all devoted to serious discussion of literary, cultural or scientific studies.

From Payne's point of view, it was easy to praise these examples of "dilettantism." But from a more democratic viewpoint, such activities might appear in a different light. "How paltry, how shrivelled and shrunken does the swallow-tail culture of the literary snob appear," wrote Robert L. Wiggins in 1918.[13]

And only eight years after Payne's essay appeared in the *Dial*, Mrs. Roswell Field in a *Ladies' Home Journal* story, *The Russells in Chicago*, satirized the Chicago Woman's Club so strongly that the editor of the *Journal* was constrained to append a footnote of apology.

After reporting that "a literary woman who would shed so much light on the annals of the club by her literary and social prestige that the members would be dazzled" had withdrawn from the Club because a "colored lady" had been admitted, Field went on to add:

> There were many serious matters, however, that the Woman's Club studied and discussed, such things as "Public Playgrounds for Children," "School Boards," "Civil Service Reform," "Civic Care of the Young, the Poor and the Defective," "Clean Streets and Other Civic Sanitation," "The Non-Legalization of All Forms of Vice," and a lot of other things that made men green with envy. And these same women could talk to men about these earnest and strenuous matters. They were real thinking machines, on earth for a purpose, and that purpose was not to stay at home to be simply mothers and housekeepers. No, indeed, that was quite out of date. The woman of today has to be "up and doing;" up to everything and doing everything — and everybody."[14]

Chicago Opera and Music

From Fuller's "The Upward Movement in Chicago" to the recent "A Robin's Egg Renaissance: Chicago Culture, 1893-1933" and "130 Years of Opera in Chicago," Chicago cultural enthusiasts have found much to praise in Chicago's interest in and emphasis on vocal and orchestral music. Chicago's first European opera was performed in John B. Rice's theatre on July 29, 1850; Crosby's Opera House, built for operatic performances began in 1865 and ended in the Fire; and opera companies continued to perform at several Chicago theatres until The Auditorium Theatre became Chicago's principal home for opera in 1889. In the 1890s, Patti sang there with the Metropolitan Opera Company and Walter Damrosch brought his German Opera Company there.[15]

In 1891, Theodore Thomas, the first conductor of the Chicago Symphony, was persuaded to come to Chicago "to maintain a permanent orchestra of the highest character." From that year until his death in 1905 ("a victim to the dampness and chill of the rooms" of the newly-finished Orchestra Hall) he presented concerts usually focussed on the music of the "three B's — Beethoven, Bach and Brahms — but he also included Wagner, Strauss and solos by the Polish pianist, Ignace Paderewski.[16]

The Art Institute

An academy of Fine Arts had been established in Chicago in 1879; in 1893, under its new title of the Chicago Art Institute, it moved into its present quarters on Michigan Boulevard at Adams. As the years had passed, Chicagoans who had scoured Europe in search of old masters for their private collections began to turn their accumulations over to the Institute; these were to include twenty-two Edouard Manets Bertha Honoré Palmer had bought in the year 1892 alone.[17]

It can be seen from this brief review of artistic activity in Chicago in the 1880s and 1890s that the dramatic upsurge of book production — both in quantity and in quality — took place in an atmosphere of aesthetic and intellectual activity that had begun within the first two or three decades of the city's existence.

It is to that dramatic upsurge — Payne's "third stage" — that we now turn our attention.

Hobart Chatfield Chatfield-Taylor

As Hugh Dalziell Duncan has pointed out, "many Chicago novels and stories describe the relationships between art and society in Chicago," at least a dozen in the two decades of feverish aesthetic activity from 1895 to 1915.[18] The first of these, *Two Women and a Fool*, was by a native Chicagoan, Hobart Chatfield Chatfield-Taylor.

Taylor was born in 1866 (in Dale Kramer's gossipy style) "a true son of the native-born, white, Protestant, aspiring-to-be-gentry society" of Chicago. He had been given the first "Chatfield" at birth in recognition of a branch of his family; in order to claim an inheritance from another branch, he was obligated to assume the second. Friends often referred to him as Hobart Chatfield "Come-Again Taylor;" a fellow author created a character "Hubbard Chattering Chattering-Hunter."[19]

Chatfield-Taylor's literary interests began early. At 22, in 1888, with Slason Thompson, he co-founded *America,* the third of a trio of literary magazines of that period (the other two *Current* and *Literary Life.*) Thompson's interests were in politics and immigration, Chatfield-Taylor's in literature. Thompson was one of Field's "Sinners;" Chatfield-Taylor was just out of Cornell University, a young man of independent means who believed he could "set the world on fire."[20]

They were an "odd couple," but for twenty-three issues and four years they did very well. During that time *America's* contributors included James Russell Lowell (who, according to Payne, was shabbily treated during an 1888 visit to Chicago[21]), Charles Dudley Warner, Nathaniel's son Julian Hawthorne, Frank R. "The Lady or the Tiger" Stockton, Maurice Thompson, Oliver Wendell Holmes, James Whitcomb Riley, Hamlin Garland, Stanley Waterloo, Ella Wheeler Wilcox, Louise Chandler Moulton, and a number of English authors. Eugene Field's "Little Boy Blue," perhaps his most famous "poem of childhood," was written for *America.*[22] For Bret Harte's "Jim," the editors paid $500, a fabulous price for the times.[23]

Chatfield-Taylor's first novel, *With Edge Tools* (1981), was written before he had hyphenated his name; by chance, the book has some fun with one Howard-Jones or "Hyphenated" Jones. A romance, set in Chicago and New York, it focusses on three affairs. The style would seem influenced by Oscar Wilde, but Wilde's first book, *The Picture of Dorian Gray* appeared the same year. And one of the characters' attempts to save a friend's reputation antedates the famous incident in *Lady Windemere's Fan* by a year.

With Edge Tools makes a number of self-conscious points about Chicago. For example, "youthful, growing Chicago" is like a college boy;

> She has left the school of preparation and has taken her place among the great cities of the earth, where, full of energy and life, she is fighting her way to the front. Her mature colleagues of the Old World smile patronizingly at her efforts but doubt her powers; while the cities of the East, seeing in her a young rival, taunt and ridicule her with jealous anger . . . if she is sometimes carried away by the very energy of her youth, she is never daunted, and the older cities of the East have already felt the vigor of her sinewy grasp. Chicago, with her broad avenues and stupendous buildings, her spacious parks and stately homes, her far-reaching railways and towering chimneys, her bustling marts and busy, surging crowds of active men and women is the archetype of American energy — the creation of yesterday and the marvel of today . . . Her people built Chicago and she is the best memorial of their energy.[24]

The book also contrasts "boosterism" of this sort with the culture that the dilettantes were seeking, with an added pointed comment about the number of actual sophisticates in the city in 1890:

> Marion continued, "You don't have to live here nine months in the year, and you don't know all the intricacies and peculiarities of our society."
>
> "Perhaps I don't, but to me the peculiarities are all in Chicago's favor. I love the go-ahead spirit, and I love the lack of affectation among the people one meets."
>
> "The go-ahead spirit you love," Marion replied, "is but an insatiable craving for the 'mighty dollar,' and the lack of affectation resolves itself into a lack of *savoir faire*."
>
> "Why, Marion, how can you say such things, you have friends here with as much knowledge of the world as any one."
>
> "Yes, but how many? Perhaps fifty, or be liberal and say a hundred, and they were all brought up away from Chicago, or, like myself, have lived away from here a good many years of their lives. If they remain here long enough they will stagnate like the natives."
>
> "You unpatriotic rebel. I have almost a mind to denounce you to the people you are slandering."
>
> "I am not slandering them. I am only speaking my convictions. You think I am captious, but I merely understand the subject, and I ought to, for heaven knows I have had long enough experience. One has the choice here between

parvenu vulgarity and Puritanic narrow-mindedness. The one makes us the butt of the comic papers and the other is simply unbearable. I was brought up on the latter, and of course all ancient families, — that is to say, those dating from the Fire, — come under that eminently respectable classification, but I actually believe one would find the pork-packers more distracting."[25]

In time such self-consciousness would disappear from Chicago fiction.

Most of Chatfield-Taylor's next novel, *An American Peeress,* (1894) is set in England. It is the second Chicago novel whose Chicago heroine marries abroad. Though the "Western prairie rose" comes from the place of "pigs and millionaires," she manages to hold her own in English society. As Joseph Hall had pointed out half a century earlier, Americans are adaptable:

> In Americans the instinct which enables them quickly to adopt new manners and modes of life is abnormally developed. Whether this arises from the fact that the nation is still in a formative state with no settled traditions, or results from physical traits peculiar to the race, is perhaps a matter for some future anthropologist to decide.[26]

Two Women and A Fool (1895, Stone & Kimball) takes place in one sleepless Chicago night and reviews an artist's affairs with two women he had met at Northwestern University.

By this time, Chatfield-Taylor seems to have had second thoughts about Chicago and the immigrants coming to the city:

> Those people who passed me, how brutal were their faces; how beast-like their little eyes. But they were the repulsive life of this great city. The character of the people one meets here has changed since I was a boy. There is less vigor and Yankee pluck in their faces, more of the degradation of the European serf.[27]

The Romantic View of Life

In 1887, with tongue firmly in cheek, Eugene Field had written in his "Sharps and Flats" column:

> Chicago has very little respect for the seventeenth century because there is nothing in it. The seventeenth century has done nothing for Chicago; she doesn't even know this is the greatest hog-market in the world.[28]

Still, Field must have been aware that the spirit of entrepreneurship which was the guiding spirit of the City by the Lake had first been brought to the Great Valley in the seventeenth century by Robert Cavelier, sieur de la Salle, and his lieutenant, Henry De Tonti, the "man with the iron hand." Is it purely coincidence that the street named for LaSalle is the heart of the Chicago financial district, while the Marquette cross no longer exists? And surely Lennox Bouton Grey was right when he wrote that Tonti's "artificial hand represents a natural journalistic selection of what is picturesque secondary detail [because] to a mechanical age the 'Medicine Hand' helps to make Tonti immediate as well as romantic."[29]

The first fictional use of La Salle and Tonti's attempts to colonize what became the Chicago area for God and King also marks the beginning of two literary movements: a reincarnation of interest in Chicago's past history as a subject for literature (a reincarnation that was to last for the next eighty years) and the same kind of romantic distortion of historical event and character that we last saw in Richardson's stories of Fort Dearborn.

The guiding spirit in these two movements was Mary Hartwell Catherwood (1847-1902), a resident of several Illinois towns and Chicago. Her *Romance of Dollard* (1888) the first of a number of novels and stories focussing on the French in Canada, the Great Lakes and the Great Valley, was singled out by historian Francis Parkman as "a pioneering departure in American fiction."[30] By virtue of her early work and her championship of her literary philosophies (as we shall presently see), she undoubtedly influenced a great many other writers, both in the Chicago area and elsewhere.

Catherwood's *The Story of Tonty* (1890) and "The Little Renault" (in *The Spirit of an Illinois Town and The Little Renault*, 1897) romanticize the historical accounts of the work of La Salle and his faithful lieutenant. Following Marquette into the Chicago area by five years, they built Fort Crevecoeur and Fort St. Louis as part of an effort to surround the English with a ring of forts, all manned by converts to the Roman church. The 1890 novel celebrates Tonty's "devotion to La Salle and his ill-fated visions of New France;"[31] the 1897 novel converts a shadowy real-life figure in Tonty's company into a girl, who, disguised as a boy, sacrifices her life for Tonty.

The "Veritist" Movement

The three movements in Chicago — the romantic, the uplift or genteel, and the aesthetic, in one way or another came to be focussed in the early 1890s in a fourth man, a newcomer to Chicago; in turn, he was to point the way to a fourth movement, also a literary one.

His name was Hamlin Hannibal Garland and his formative years had been spent on the bleak prairies of northeastern Iowa where he had come to see the rural people there as "peasants," victims of European "landlordism."[32] Seeking something better, he had made his way to Boston in 1884, and was there introduced to a cultured dilettantish world similar to Chicago's club society. In January of 1893, Garland spent several days in Chicago and was impressed by the air of "artistic and intellectual enterprise" which he found there in connection with the building of the Exposition.[33] He had begun to think that Chicago should be the country's new "literary and art center."[34]

Still, as Garland's biographer says, there could not have been much to Garland's liking in May of 1893 in Chicago. Kirkland, with whom he had talked on an earlier visit, had ceased writing fiction, and the few local colorists were mainly journalists who cared little for fiction. One exception was Frank Hutcheson, whose "Barkeep Stories" featuring Chicago street dialect and the dialect of an Irish policeman, were being published in the *Daily News*. (They were published in book form in 1895.)

In mid-summer, Garland returned to Chicago to meet with Francis J. Schulte, the young publisher of two of his recent populist books; the two men began discussing a new western magazine to make literary use of the social problems discussed in B. O. Flower's Boston-based *Arena*. While he was marking time waiting for Schulte to raise the capital for the proposed magazine, Garland managed to get an invitation to speak at the Literary Congress of the Columbian Exposition in early September.

George Washington Cable opened the Congress (held in an auditorium in the Art Institute on Michigan Boulevard) by arguing that the novel at its best "elevates our conception of the heroic and opens our eyes to the presence, actuality, and value of a world of romance that is, and ought to be, in our lives and fates." Mrs. Catherwood, following him, supported his statement. Then it was Garland's turn, and in the words of Harriet Monroe's sister, Lucy, Garland, "with his accustomed felicity of phrasing and intensity of manner [argues] that every novelist should draw his inspiration from the soil, should write of nothing but the country he was bred in and the people most familiar to him." Then it was Joseph Kirkland's turn to support the realistic movement.

But Mrs. Catherwood, who was "definitely committed to the presentation of the ideal and romantic in fiction" had had enough of that kind of talk. She jumped to her feet "to say a few words in defense of the old heroes."[35]

The resulting quarrel, one of the better publicized debates over literature, turned out to be a five-sided affair. Mrs. Catherwood, "a past president and active member of the Western Association of Writers, an organizaion anti-realist in its leadership and position," continued to defend her point of view. Garland, defending his, saw the debate as not only a debate over what authors ought to write, he saw it also as a contest for people's minds and, taking it even further, as a quarrel between East and West, a quarrel over the genteel way of life:

> It really comes down to a contest . . . between sterile culture and creative work, between mere scholarship and wisdom, between conservative criticism and native original literary production. It is a question of *books* versus a literature of life, a struggle between adaptation to new surroundings and conformity to the ancestral type . . . Because there happen to be more conservatives in the East . . . the contest takes on an appearance of a War between the East and the West.[36]

The quarrel moved beyond the walls of the Art Institute. *The Dial*, ever a defendant of genteelism, pitched in, calling Garland a "strong-lunged but untrained product of the Prairies," and also attacking the Hoosier poet, James Whitcomb Riley, and Eugene Field, whom a *Cosmopolitan* magazine critic had said was the only author of what could "properly be called Chicago literature:"[37]

> Skilled in the arts of self-advertisement, these men are quick to enlarge the foothold thus gained; their reputations grow like snowballs; they come to take themselves as seriously as they are taken by others; and the people of real refinement and culture, whose numbers are rapidly increasing in the West, have to endure the humiliation of being represented, in the minds of a large proportion of their fellow-countrymen, by men who are neither cultured or refined.[38]

The fifth side to this debate, an anti-intellectual position, was presented humorously by Eugene Field in his "Sharps and Flats." He called Garland one of the "apostles of realism," then added: "Mrs. Catherwood hath chosen the better part: she loves the fanciful in fiction. . . . Garland's *in hoc signo* is a dung fork or a butter paddle; Mrs. Catherwood's is a lance or an embroidery needle. Give us the lance and its companion every time."[39]

The final word was Garland's in his *Crumbing Idols* (Stone & Kimball, 1894). In his manifesto, he came down hard on the side of local color as a part of his "veritistic" theory. His book followed by some three years the critical theories presented by his friend and mentor, William Dean Howells in *Criticism and Fiction* (1891). The difference between the two men is significant. Garland's biographer, Donald Pizer says:

> *Crumbling Idols* differs from *Criticism and Fiction* in a way quite important for the history of literary ideas in America. To Howells the "truthful treatment of material" was above all a fidelity to average life and experience analogous to the objectivity demanded by science. Garland's impressionistic bias, on the other hand, resulted in a decidedly subjective conception of truth in art. Though separated by only three years, [the two books] were pointing in opposite directions. Howells summed up several of the major tendencies of the last third of the century, whereas Garland . . . "anticipated the subjectivism that was to characterize much modern literature."[40]

The two novel-length results of Garland's stay in Chicago are *Rose of Dutcher's Coolly* (Stone & Kimball, 1895) and *Money Magic* (1907). Rose, a Wisconsin farm girl, matriculates at the University of Wisconsin. She leaves there, a beautiful girl with two intense, apparently irreconcilable desires — for love and marriage, and for a career as a writer. In Chicago she joins a group of artists, writers and professional people. She falls in love with a newspaper man, a would-be writer, and marries him. She discovers that she will be most successful as a writer if she rejects classical English models and writes about her Wisconsin valley.

Carl Van Doren noted that *Rose* is the "first work in American fiction in which a woman's choice between domestic duties and a career is squarely faced."[41]

For its time, the novel was a strong dose of medicine, especially for those of the genteel persuasion. It didn't seem to condemn premarital sex relations and it seemed to support trial marriage. Similar protests were made against the later *Sister Carrie,* with which it is often compared, though Rose and Carrie are cut from unlike bolts of cloth. As a result of the protests, Garland made some revisions in subsequent editions.

The novel contrasts Wisconsin rural life with Chicago life. The Wisconsin section is much the better of the two. The cultural life that Garland argues for comes across as mere dilettantism.

The fault is in Garland, himself, as his friend Henry Blake Fuller's satirical sketch, *Under the Skylights* (1901), implies. In Chicago Garland had become a part of that dilettante life we see in *Rose.* Lorado Taft, the sculptor, whose work is still visible in Chicago, and Fuller became his close friends, and he married Taft's sister, Zulime. Because his realistic fiction was not making him enough money, he turned to romantic fiction. Mrs. Catherwood was not around to see this turnabout — she had died in 1902. By 1912, Garland was an important figure in Chicago's genteel society.

His only other book with a Chicago setting, *Money Magic,* feaures a triangular romance with a Bret Harte ending. The story begins in Colorado, site of many of Garland's books in the early part of the century, with a rough-and-ready heroine who, after leaving her Colorado ranch, quickly attains the sophistication of a woman of the world. In Chicago she and her husband become members of the "true Bohemia — Chicago's artistic society," the world Garland was a part of. If the novel was an attempt to emulate *Rose,* it failed. Its plot is too conventional, its characterization too weak.

Meanwhile, for Garland, his dream of Chicago as a "literary center" was faltering:

> Chicago, rushing toward its two-million mark, had not, alas! lived up to its literary promise of 1894. In music, in painting, in sculpture and architecture it was no longer negligible, but each year its authors appeared more and more like a group of esthetic pioneers heroically maintaining themselves in the midst of an increasing tumult of material upbuilding. One by one its hopeful young publishing houses had failed, and one by one its aspiring periodicals had withered in the keen wind of eastern competition.[42]

The problem was not Chicago but Garland. There were young writers in Chicago, on the newspapers, out at the University, and among the homes on the North Side — but Garland ignored them. And when a new group of rebellious young writers came together in Chicago, he was too much of a romanticist and genteelist to sympathize with them, as we shall see.

The Chap-Book and Other "Little" Magazines

All this time there had been building the beautiful city of white palaces on the lake, and it was now open for the world to see what Chicago had dreamed and created . . . [Now] that it was accomplished, in all its beauty and grandeur, it filled [us] with admiration.

[We] took an electric launch and glided through the lagoons beneath the lofty peristyle out to the lake, which was as quiet as a pond. The long lines of white buildings were ablaze with countless lights; the music from the bands scattered over the grounds floated softly out upon the water; all else was silent and dark. In that lovely hour, soft and gentle as was ever a summer night, the toil and trouble of men, the fear that was gripping men's hearts in the market, fell away from me, and in its place came Faith. The people who could dream this vision and make it real, those people from all parts of the land who thronged here day after day — their sturdy wills and strong hearts would rise above failure, would press on to greater victories than this triumph of beauty — victories greater than the world had yet witnessed![43]

Such inspired dreams of a better future than the "Black City" had offered up to then led in the 1890s to continued attempts to build a more cultured city. One such attempt produced *Halligan's Illustrated World's Fair*, a magazine utilizing the new copper-plate half-tones for its pictorial art. In addition to its exciting photographic reproductions, *Halligan's* also published literary materials which, as Herbert E. Fleming said, were of "more interest from the ideas . . . than from the form of presentation."[44] Among these were poems on the Columbus theme done by Emerson Hough, then with *Forest and Stream*, Evanston business man William S. Lord, and Charles Eugene Banks, a prominent Chicago writer and editor, who, like Hough, was a native Iowan. Opie Read submitted "Old Billy at the World's Fair." There were essays by some of the "Saints" of the "Saints and Sinners." Their opposite number, Robert G. Ingersoll, "the Fighting Atheist" supplied one article.

The ephemeral aesthetic periodicals of the *fin-de-siecle* decade in England, which produced such bibelots as *The Butterfly, The Yellow Book* and *The Studio* had their counterparts in Chicago. Among them was the short-lived *Figaro*, which survives today, if at all, in *Figaro Fiction* (1892), a brief anthology of short stories by long forgotten writers. Although the book and the fifty-two issues of the magazine which preceeded it were by "Chicago authors," the guiding light, J. Percival Pollard, was a product of a small Iowa town.

Much more significant than Pollard were Herbert S. Stone, the son of Melville E. Stone, a prominent Chicago journalist who had brought Eugene

Field from Denver to Chicago, and H. Ingalls Kimball. The reputations of these two were made by the publication of the *Chap-book* (1894-1898), and a number of books which were often more attractive than substantial. The *Chap-Book's* origins were clearly in the English *Yellow Book*, the most famous of all the "little" or fine literary and art magazines. The *Chap-Book* was "a miscellany of curious and interesting songs, ballads, tales, histories, etc. adorned with a variety of pictures ... to which is annexed a large collection of notices of books ...:

> In its earlier days the effort to put the public in touch with the new and curious developments in foreign art and literature brought upon it considerable ridicule and as well won for it much admiration. Its habit of free speech produced a curious movement among the young writers of the country. There was scarcely a village or town which did not have its little individualist pamphlet imitating the form and tone of THE CHAP BOOK.[45]

Gelett Burgess, the San Francisco poet who had lyricized about his dislike for purple cows, said:

> The success of the "Chap Book" incited the little riot of Decadence, and there was a craze for odd sizes and shapes, freak illustrations, wide margins, uncut pages, Janson types, scurrilous abuse and petty jealousies, impossible prose and doggerel rhyme. The movement asserted itself as a revolt against the commonplace; it aimed to overthrow the staid respectability of the larger magazines and to open to younger writers opportunities to be heard before they had obtained recognition from the autocratic editors. It was a wild, haphazard exploration ... When the history of the Nineteenth Century decadence is written, these tiny eruptions of revolt, these pamphleteering amateurs cannot remain unnoticed, for their outbreak was a symptom of the discontent of the times, a wide-felt protest of emancipation from the dictates of the old literary tribunals. Little enough good has come of it that one can see at present, but the sedition is broached, and the next rebellion may have more blood to spill.[46]

The *Chap-Book* was originally intended as a means of advertising Stone and Kimball books, but it carried reviews of other publishers.

During its four-year course, the magazine changed size twice. Its authors included both major and lesser English writers of the time and many major American writers.

The artists and writers of Chicago at once formed a coterie, attracted by *"Chap-Book* teas." These teas led to the formation of an "Attic Club," and influenced the style of the later "Little Room."

Stone and Kimball's biographer says that Hamlin Garland's books were the rock on which the firm was securely founded. These were *Prairie Songs, Crumbling Idols, Rose of Dutcher's Coolly, Main Travelled Roads* and *Prairie Folks.*

Stone and Kimball was liquidated in 1897 and was succeeded by Herbert S. Stone and Company; the latter firm suspended business in 1909. Over a period of about eighteen years these two firms published about three hundred books, most of them by non-Chicago authors. The *Chap-Book* was taken over by *The Dial* in 1898.

A second Chicago publishing firm that responded to the debate over "Who Reads a Chicago Book" in *The Dial* in the early 1890s[47] was Way and Williams, founded by W. Irving Way and Chauncey Williams in 1895. In the next four years, through 1898 (when Herbert S. Stone took over the company's backlist) the firm published a number of handsome examples of the bookmaker's art, showing the obvious influence of William Morris's Kelmscott Press in England, and an enthusiasm for *art noveau* design. Maxfield Parrish, who made "Maxfield Parrish 'blue'" famous, Frank Hazenplug and J. C. Leyendecker were three of the leading American poster artists who produced cover illustrations for the firm's books.

Some of the books produced by the firm were William Allen White's *The Real Issue* (1896), L. Frank Baum's *Mother Goose in Prose* (1897), Stanley Waterloo's *The Story of Ab*, Elia Wilkinson [Peattie's] *Pippins and Cheese* (1897) and Opie Read's *Bolanyo* (1897). White and Baum were Kansans; the other three were Chicagoans. Baum had lived in Chicago; some believe that his *The Wizard of Oz* was conceived as a protest against Chicago materialism.[48]

At the time Way and Williams closed shop, they had just finished printing the sheets of Edgar Lee Masters' first volume, *A Book of Verses*. Masters later had these bound on his own.

The Little Room

One of the books published by Stone and Kimball was Madeline Yale Wynne's *The Little Room* (1895). The title became the label for a group of people who met informally every Friday afternoon after the Theodore Thomas concerts in the Auditorium Theatre. Incidentally, the book, a collection of six short stories, has nothing to do with Chicago.

Anna Morgan describes the group in her *My Chicago* (1918):

> The Little Room, which had its beginning in 1893, is perhaps the most unique of Chicago's organizations. It rose from the ashes of the Attic Club which ... for well-grounded reasons disbanded. The new organization was suggested by Miss Lucy Monroe.[49]

Among the original members, Miss Morgan lists Herbert S. Stone, Melville Stone, Jane Addams of Hull House and Lorado Taft, in whose Athenaeum Building studio the group first met. Later when the group's headquarters had moved to Ralph Clarkson's studio on the tenth floor of the Fine Arts Building, Ralph Fletcher Seymour lists the following Chicago authors as members: Henry Blake Fuller, Hamlin Garland, Floyd Dell, Emerson Hough, Elia W. Peattie, Marjorie Benton Cooke, I. K. Friedman, Roswell Field, Henry Kitchell Webster, Llewellyn Jones, Mary Aldis, Alice Gerstenberg and Charles Frances Browne.

The group continued to meet until 1931.[50]

Henry Blake Fuller

Fuller, Chicago's first major writer, was the son and grandson of men who helped build Chicago. As a boy he had experienced the Fire, and he was to live until 1929, dying eleven years before his friend Garland.

Fuller's first two books, *The Chevalier of Pensieri Vani* (1889, 1890) and *The Chatelaine of LaTrinité* (1891) were misread by his Chicago critics. William Morton Payne correctly saw them "as far as possible removed from the method of realism," but then evaluated them as novels of travel, bound together "by the most tenuous imaginable threads of romance." Actually

the hard core of [*The Chevalier*] is an attack on modern industrialism, modern business, and modern governmental corruption. Without a distinguished past, without concern for nature or beauty, and without any more useful purpose than the acquisition of material goods, life in Chicago, it seemed to Fuller, had little to offer the individual who would not consent to become a mere "money-machine." Admittedly, Italy was not perfect; but it was demonstrably better than Chicago. At least the expatriate in Italy possessed more of the peace, beauty, and dignity of life than the toilers in Chicago's industrial society.[51]

Fuller's dissatisfaction with his native city had been expressed a decade earlier after his return from a tour of Europe, including Italy:

... Pray where should discontent
Grow ranker than just here, 'mongst men intent
On non-essentials, empty, earth-bound, low.
Yet not to them; they have no other life
Than centers in this ganglion of trade.
They make it and they are by it made —
This dashing, slashing, flashing, crashing strife.
They buy and sell; with this you have it all.
They know but debit, credit, owe and owed.
This trading-point with goods all stuffed and stowed,
They name a "city" — a metropolis call.[52]

Fuller had not only rejected his city, he had also rejected his family.

For his literary models, Fuller debated (in an 1885 unpublished essay) the relative merits of William Dean Howells and Henry James.[53] He concluded that Howells was a realist and James an idealist, and that Howells was right in setting his fiction in America, a place to "which the cat ... was about to jump." A year earlier, in a Chicago *Tribune* sketch, "The Romance of a Middle-Aged Merchant and his Female Private Secretary," Fuller had been a realist; in "Pasquale's Picture," published in the Chicago *Current* in 1885, he had been an idealist.[54]

Eight years later, in his third booklength work *The Cliff-Dwellers* (1893), perhaps because of the imagery of "The White City and the Black," he became a realist again, this time focussing indirectly on his home city. "If you can only be big, you don't mind being dirty," he wrote, then took a similar cynical view of a Chicago business man: "He towered and swayed like a rank plant [the "Chi-ca-gou!"] that has sprung rapidly from the earth and has brought the slime and mold on its sheath and stalk."[55]

The "cliff-dwellers" are the businessmen whose offices were in those recent Chicago inventions, the skyscrapers, more specifically the Tacoma, the Monadnock, and Fuller's own invention, the "Clifton:"

> From such conditions ... towers the Clifton. From the beer-hall in its basement to the barber-shop just under its roof the Clifton stands full eighteen stories tall. Its hundreds of windows glitter with multitudinous letterings in gold and in silver, and on summer afternoons its awnings flutter score on score in the tepid breezes that sometimes come up from Indiana. Four ladder-like constructions which rise skyward stage by stage promote the agility of the clambering hordes that swarm within it, and ten elevators — devices unknown to the real, aboriginal inhabitants — ameliorate the daily cliff-climbing for the frail of physique and the pressed for time.
>
> The tribe inhabiting the Clifton is large and rather heterogeneous. All told, it numbers about four thousand souls. It includes bankers, capitalists, lawyers, "promoters"; brokers in bonds, stocks, pork, oil, mortgages; real-estate people and railroad people and insurance people ...; a host of principals, agents, middlemen, clerks, cashiers, stenographers, and errand boys; and the necessary force of engineers, janitors, scrub-women and elevator-hands.[56]

The novel brings together the two worlds of Chicago; the business world and the social world. But the social world suffers by contrast:

> This town of ours labors under one peculiar disadvantage; it is the only great city in the world to which all its citizens have come for the one common, avowed object of making money. There you have its genesis, its growth, its end and object; and there are very few of us who are not attending to that object very strictly.[57]

The Cliff Dwellers is the first Chicago novel which looks squarely at life in the city, and contrasts the values of the city itself. It does not compare Chicago life with rural life; Fuller was, as we have said, a third generation Chicagoan and not a newcomer from the hinterlands. And although Fuller had travelled to the east coast and to Europe, the city is not compared with New England or New York or Europe. It is the first important American novel with city life at its theme. And it was the most important Chicago novel to date; more than one critic has noted that Chicago literature began with this book.

For all that, Chicagoans were taken back by Fuller's attack on his home town — and theirs. Even the distant President of Harvard University, the widely-admired Charles Eliot Norton, objected:

> I do not wonder that you detest the Chicago you have drawn, but I think you should have sympathetic admiration, nay, even affection for the ideal Chicago which exists not only in the brain, but also in the hearts of some of her citizens. I have never seen Americans from whom one could draw happier auguries for the future of America, than some of the men I met at Chicago. The Fair . . . was on the whole a great promise, even a great pledge. It, at least, forbids despair.[58]

Fuller's fourth novel, *With the Procession* (1895, 1896) is also about the business world, this time the world of the department store, another Chicago invention, and the social world to which business men's wives belong. The time is that of the Fair.

"The Procession," in Mark Harris's words, "that principle of American freedom promising opportunity for men formerly without hope, political power for men formerly voiceless; wealth, of course, ascension in a single generation to that social class next above one's own,"[59] is symbolized in this striking scene from the novel:

> The grimy lattice-work of the drawbridge swung too slowly, the steam-tug blackened the dull air and roiled the turbid water as it dragged its schooner on towards the lumber-yards of the South Branch, and a long line of waiting vehicles took up their interrupted course through the smoke and the stench as they filed across the stream into the thick of business beyond: first a yellow streetcar; then a robust truck laden with rattling sheet-iron, or piled high with fresh wooden pails and willow baskets; then a junk-cart bearing a pair of dwarfed and bearded Poles, who bumped in unison with the jars of its clattering springs; then, perhaps, a bespattered buggy, with reins jerked by a pair of sinewy and impatient hands. Then more street-cars; then a butcher's cart loaded with the carcasses of calves — red, black, piebald — or an express wagon with a yellow cur yelping from its rear; then, it may be, an insolently venturesome landau, with crested panel and top-booted coachman. Then drays and omnibuses and more street-cars; then, presently, somewhere in the line, between the tail end of one truck and the menacing tongue of another, a family carry-all — a carry-all loaded with its family driven by a man of all work, drawn by a slight and amiable old mare, and encumbered with luggage which shows the labels of half the hotels of Europe.
>
> It is a very capable and comprehensive vehicle, as conveyances of that kind go. It is not new, it is not precisely in the mode; but it shows material and workmanship of the best grade, and it is washed, oiled, polished with scrupulous care. It advances with some deliberation, and one might fancy hearing in the rattle of its tires, or in the suppressed flapping of its rear curtain, a word of

plaintive protest. "I am not of the great world," it seems to say; "I make no pretence to fashion. We are steady and solid, but we are not precisely in society, and we are very far indeed, from any attempt to cut a great figure. However, do not misunderstand our position; it is not that we are under, nor that we are exactly aside; perhaps we have been left just a little behind. Yes, that might express it — just a little behind."

How are they to catch up again — how to rejoin the great caravan whose fast and furious pace never slackens?[60]

Fuller's realistic description of this Chicago street scene is documented by photographs taken at the time, [61] and by this comment by Hamlin Garland, who called Fuller "the finest of all the Chicago writers of that day:"

Masterly in the precision of its phrase, its characterization, and its humor, *With the Procession,* in my judgment ranks with [William Dean] Howells' *A Modern Instance* and [*The Rise of*] *Silas Lapham.* Cosmopolitan in its technique, it made all other stories of Chicago seem raw and crude ...

I still consider it a delightful historical document. Social Chicago of the nineties lies in these pages, more perfectly preserved than in any other story then or since. It is a transcript of life as Fuller saw and lived it. It has humor, understanding, and a nipping irony. The author not only knew his material; he had shared it. Born in Chicago when it was a small town, just before the Civil War, he had grown up with it, and in this story he had put much that was family history, and something that was intimately autobiographic; how much I have never been able to define.[62]

With the Procession is about an old Chicago family with two daughters, one a debutante who founds a home for working girls, and two sons, one an attorney and one with pretensions of becoming an artist. Its familiar Fuller themes of art, business and society are augmented by a concern for the problems of adapting to a changing Chicago lifestyle.

In *On the Stairs* (1917), Fuller uses a stairway as a symbol for the rise of a coachman's son to a position of power and influence, and the simultaneous decline of a cultured man not unlike Fuller himself, for whom the coachman's father once worked. *With the Procession* had not been as good a novel as *The Cliff-Dwellers,* but this late novel represents a major falling off of Fuller's literary power.

Also in 1917, Fuller published his *Lines Short and Long.* "I am doing a set of 20-25 *vers libre* biographies for a book — each piece about 160-170 lines; many of them condensed short stories, in pseudo-poetic guise," he had told Hamlin Garland the year before. "They touch miscellaneously on art, literature, stage politics, society, sociology, psyches, morals et cetry. I feel that I am escaping the multifarious deadening detail of the conventional short story."[63]

Ralph Fletcher Seymour tells us that "Lines Long and Short" came after

Fuller's "reading Edgar Lee Master's 'Spoon River Anthology.' . . . "Eh, I can do that!" he said."[64]

Fletcher says the book "lampoon[s] quite a number of [Fuller's] friends, holding them up to as severe a brand of ridicule as [Fuller] could manage."[65] The verses also show Fuller's continued antagonism toward marriage, his approval of single life as an alternate lifestyle, his critical attitudes towards the emptiness of business life, and the unhappiness and frustrations of the artist in America. Like the characters in two obviously autobiographical verses, his characters are lonely, defeated, both men and women who have failed to reach their potential or to achieve happiness. A prefatorial stanza probably best summarizes his own career:

That he had lived a futile life.
And that Europe was to blame:
His continual hankering after the Old World
Had made him a failure in the New.[66]

Bertram Cope's Year (1919) is the last of Fuller's Chicago novels. Its setting is a campus like the University of Chicago's, and, to some extent, in the nearby Indiana dunes. Cope is a young instructor working on an English Master of Arts degree, and socially engaged with a young widow, three young women in her menage, and a male friend who dreams of an apartment to be shared with Cope and other young men. There is also a young student from Wisconsin who leaves the University after overdoing an epicene role in a drama in which young men take the roles of young ladies. An overtone of homosexuality permeates the novel. As a consequence, Fuller's publisher turned the book down, and Fuller had to seek the aid of his friend, artist Ralph Fletcher Seymour, to find a publisher. The book was a publishing failure.[67]

By this time, the Chicago Renaissance, already fading away, had shoved Fuller even further in the past, and though his close friend, Hamlin Garland, was now at his peak as a literary lion, Fuller was destined to spend the last dozen years of his life in Chicago alone, poverty-stricken, almost unknown.

He must have had time for that new-fangled entertainment device, the films, for in 1930 he produced *Not on the Screen*, the story of a real-life romance set off, through the use of a frame device against a motion picture romance. The novel is a satirical treatment of the self-made man, the fading Chicago upper class and the hackneyed formulas of the films of the 1920s.

By and About Journalists

In *Rose of Dutcher's Coolly*, we have a major treatment of a Chicago journalist, the editor Mason whom Rose marries. A year later (1896), Will Payne's *Jerry the Dreamer* is the first full novelistic study focussing on a journalist. This one is a "faun-in-the-city," like the later Vance Sterling of *A Wingéd Victory* and Felix Fay of Dell's *Moon-Calf*. Jerry Drew is also an emigrant to Chicago where he marries a Chicago girl. Jerry's real dilemma lies in his employment as an editor for a newspaper which opposes a strike and his off-duty role as a writer for a socialist newspaper which supports the strike. The editorial work provides his financial support, but his sympathies are with the strikers and all of life's underdogs. Ironically, his sympathies cost the life of his newborn son.

Payne, who is not to be confused with William Morton Payne, the *Dial* editor, was in turn financial editor of the *Daily News*, of the *Chronicle*, and of *The Economist*. He was a successful writer of short stories about business for George Horace Lorimer's *Saturday Evening Post*, and the author of other novels we shall discuss later.

The late nineteenth century marked the peak of popularity of newspaper humorists — of Robert Jones Burdette in Illinois and Iowa, Pete Pareau in northern Michigan, Snickelfritz in Ohio, Ellis Parker Butler in Iowa. But although some of these people attained national reputations, the major figures in this tradition were four Chicago newspapermen: Frank Hutcheson and Eugene Field, whom we have already seen, Finley Peter Dunne, and George Ade.

Finley Peter Dunne (1867-1936) began his career as a sportswriter for the *Herald* in the 1880s. In 1889 with other young Chicago journalists, he formed the Whitechapel Club. Its origins stem from the unsolved murder of popular Chicago physician, Dr. Cronin, taken "for a ride" in a cab pulled by a white horse on the night of May 4, 1889, never seen alive again. But the club's name came from the London murderer, Jack-the-Ripper:

> The atmosphere of the club was Bohemian, Rabelaisian, and macabre. The latter was in keeping with the criminal associations of the club's origin, the Cronin and Whitechapel atrocities. The decorations of the club were products of the close association of the reporters with new stories of crime. Weapons used in committing murders and ropes used to hang notorious killers were favorites. Then there was a choice collection of human skulls donated by a doctor at an asylum for the insane. To these ... was added a large coffin-shaped table, which gossip frequently and mistakenly designated as a real burial casket.
>
> Perhaps the height of [the club's escapades] was reached in the cremation of a tramp suicide on the shore of Lake Michigan with a gaudy ceremony which tooks its inspiration from Trelawney's account of the burning of [the English poet] Shelley's body, but which was embroidered ingeniously with a procession of odes, "roundelus," orations, and the like.[68]

Club members included Charles Seymour, the Ohio author Brand Whitlock, Frederick Upham (Grizzly) Adams, George Ade, Alfred Henry Lewis,

John T. McCutcheon and Opie Read.

As time passed, Dunne became an editorial writer for the *Post* and renowned for his wit. During the Columbian Exposition he initiated a weekly column about an "Irish publican" one "Colonel McNeery." When the real life saloon-keeper complained to Dunne's employer, Dunne changed the site of the saloon from Dearborn Street to "Archey Road," changed the name of the saloon as well, and on October 7, 1893 Dunne's immortal Mr. Dooley was born:

> "Did ye ever go to McKenna's? No? Well, sir, of all the places! Ye go down Madison Street to Halsted an' down Halsted to Archey road an' out Archey road past packin' houses an' rollin' mills an' the Healy slew an' potato patches till ye get to McKenna's."

But Dooley's penetrating brogue could be more than lightly satirical. "Anger, and a warm sympathy for the underprivileged underlay almost all the 'Dooley' sketches," said Franklin P. Adams [F.P.A.].[68] Here is Dooley at the time President Grover Cleveland sent in Federal troops to break the strike of the Pullman workers:

> "This here Pullman makes th' sleepin' cars an' th' Constitootion looks afther Pullman. He have a good time iv it. He don't need to look afther himsilf. . . . He calls out George Wash'ngton an' Abraham Lincoln and Gin'ral Miles and [police officer] Mike Brinan. . . . an' thin puts on his hat and lams away. 'Gintlemin',' says he, 'I must be off,' he says. 'Defind the Constitootion,' he says. 'Me own is not iv th' best,' he says, 'an' I think I'll help it be spindin' th' summer,' he says, 'piously,' he says, 'on the shores iv th' Atlantic ocean.'
>
> That's Pullman. He slips out as aisely as a bar iv his own soap. An' the whole wurruld turns in an' shoots an' stabs an' throws couplin' pins, an' sojers march out an' Gin'ral Miles looks up the sthreet for some man to show that he can kill men too."[69]

Dunne's "Mr. Dooley" columns were collected in a number of books: *Mr. Dooley in Peace and War* (1898); *Mr. Dooley in the Hearts of His Countrymen* (1899); *Mr. Dooley's Philosophy* (1900); *Mr. Dooley's Opinions* (1901); *Observations of Mr. Dooley* (1902); *Dissertations by Mr. Dooley* (1905); *Mr. Dooley Says* (1899, 1910); and *Mr. Dooley on Making a Will and Other Necessary Evils* (1919). Of these the best are the earliest; in 1938 Elmer Ellis assembled *Mr. Dooley at His Best*. Ellis is also Dunne's biographer — *Mr. Dooley's America*, (1941).

On the night of the Chicago Fire, George Ade, then a five-year-old northwest Indiana boy, watched the distant glow on the horizon. Nineteen years later, four years out of Purdue, Ade came to Chicago to join John T. McCutcheon, Chicago newspaper artist, as a staffer on the *Morning News*. McCutcheon had been a college classmate and was the brother of George Barr McCutcheon, Chicago novelist.

Two stories, one of a freighter explosion on the Chicago River, and the other a unique interview with the iconoclastic Robert G. Ingersoll, started Ade on the road to fame. As a star reporter, he helped the young Theodore Dreiser keep his job with the *Evening Post*.[70]

In 1893 he began writing his own column, "Stories of the Streets and Town." These were realistic stories "with a compact style and a clean Anglo-Saxon vocabulary" in which he demonstrated his "courage to observe human virtues and frailties as they showed on [his] lens."[71] McCutcheon provided illustrations. They were well received and soon they were running on the same page with Eugene Field's "Sharps and Flats" in the same newspaper's *Evening News*.[72]

In his column Ade experimented with all the literary forms which he later used for his major work: the short story, the fable, dialogue, drama and verse. One of the persons who sent him ideas was Franklin P. Adams, then a student at Chicago's Armour Scientific Academy.[73]

Out of these columns came his first three books: *Artie: A Story of the Streets and the Town* (1896); *Pink Marsh: A Story of the Streets and the Town* (1897); and *Doc Horne: A Story of the Streets and the Town* (1899). All three books were published by Herbert S. Stone.

Artie told the adventures of an amazing youth, Artie Blanchard and his girl, Mamie Carroll. Artie's slang amazed his Chicago readers: "reubs," "con talk," "beauts," "lollypaloozers," "rubber neckin'," "pool sharks," "rah-rah boys," "cheese it." Artie talks boldly but he has anxieties that a "sympathetic eye" would observe.[74]

Artie was based on Charles Williams, a real life protégé of Ade's, who later became famous as a book illustrator.

Pink Marsh is the first successful literary treatment of the Northern negro. William Pinckney Marsh is a black bootblack in a barber shop; his rise to success is marked by his securing a job as a Pullman porter.

Doc' Horne is set in the "informal salon of the Alfalfa European Hotel" in Chicago.[75] Doc' Calvin Horne is an 1890s Baron Munchausen, purveyor of tall tales of Chicago's past and present; he confounds his listeners with several melodramatic performances that leave them wondering if he is a liar or a marvelous person.

From the successes of these books, Ade turned to writing "fables in slang," short parables, featuring a generous use of capital letters in the German manner, which seemed to indicate there was something topsy-turvy in the moral order. These were collected and published in 1899 and 1900 and Ade was on his way to wealth and fame. William Allen White once said that he "would rather have written the *Fables in Slang* than [have] been President." William Dean Howells said that Ade's "portrayal of life is almost absolute in its perfection — you experience something of the bliss of looking at your own photograph."[76]

The first of these "Fables" appeared on September 17, 1897 as "The Fable of Sister Mae Who Did As Well As Could Be Expected." It tells of "hard-working Luella ... short on looks but long on virtue, [who] slaved in a factory for three dollars a week, while her lazy, empty-headed, but shapely sister Mae became cashier of a lunchroom, had practically to fight off her masculine admirers, and landed a wealthy husband and crashed society. But did Mae then forget Luella? Certainly not. She gave Luella a job in her home as assistant cook at five dollars a week. The moral of this tale: 'Industry and Perseverance Bring a Sure Reward.'"[77]

For the *Sunday Record-Herald* of November 24, 1901, Ade wrote a football story that was quickly published as *Grouch at the Game* (1901). More of these stories were collected in *In Babel* in 1903. Many of these stories seem to anticipate the O. Henry stories that were to appear in book form for the first time in 1904.

There is a rich variety of characters: a pick-pocket, or "dip" in underworld slang; a Great Lakes sailor; a book salesman trying to sell a set of Russian books to a Chicago merchant — all Chicago's "little people," with a need to maintain self-respect.[78] Henry L. Mencken, who seemed always to like the work of Chicago writers, said, according to Ade's biographer, that two or three of these stories were among the best American short stories.[79]

Over the next one-third of a century thirteen volumes of his fables and materials derived from them were published.[80] Ade also established himself as a popular dramatist and writer of musical comedies. One of these was *Peggy* from *Paris* (1903), about a girl from a small Illinois town who takes singing lessons in France, then comes to Chicago to masquerade as a French opera singer. Her "hayseed" father accidentally exposes her fraud.

Ade, Field and Dunne were not creators of literature. Their work, though some of it is still in print, was popular rather than major. "[Chicago poet] William Vaughn Moody's [play] *The Great Divide* contains more substance than Ade's complete dramatic production," says Arthur Shumaker.[81]

Field's success lay in his use of satire against contemporary people and events, and in writing sentimental verse for children. Dunne's success was in the creation of a *personna* through whom he was able to express editorial views which sometimes would have been unacceptable to his readers and his employer. Ade created a host of original American literary types from his observations of city and country people. All three writers brought enjoyment to large newspaper audiences, and, as their work was published in book form, they attracted the attention of major literary critics and historians.

Summary

And so ended the first important decade in Chicago's literary history — a decade that had seen Chicago's first major writers develop, along with many lesser ones, a pattern that was to follow in successive decades in the new century ahead.

There are those who see this decade in a different light. "What H. L. Mencken termed the 'pianissimo revolt' of the early nineties, the Populist soap-boxings of Hamlin Garland, and the European transplantings attempted by [Frank] Norris, the flourishings of the 'Chap-Book' and the 'Philistine' amounted to little. It was a rebellion of the Frogs."[82]

But a significant change had taken place. From now on Chicago writers would write about Chicago in its own, and their own, terms. William Dean Howells' "tinkle of the little bell" might be all right for *Harper's*, but it wouldn't do for Chicago.[83] The language of Chicago literature would find stronger influences in the work of Dunne, Ade, Garland (and soon, Ring Lardner, Jr.) than it would find in the effete bluestocking East.

Chicago had become one of the world's major metropolises — the Columbian Exposition had brought it international renown. The rural midwest's influence on the city was diminished — no longer would Chicago writers have to condescend to hicks and rubes, nor, for that matter, to outlanders, and their literary ghosts, from Europe, Boston and New York.

VII.
"More Than Their Share"

... the Janus-faced Chicago of the girls who comes there to work, with its face of allurement and its face of despair:

Chicago had called her with moving pictures and with grand-opera music from a phonograph. "I was called," says Katie, "by the voices that had sung into that box. It proved — I thought — that all the lovely things I had dreamed were true. I had only to go and find them. People were walking upon those streets. Then I could walk on those streets. And those people were laughing and talking to each other. Everybody seemed to have friends. Everybody was so happy! And all of that really was." So she answers the call, and comes to Chicago. Only Chicago doesn't know it has called her. Chicago is indifferent. It finally allows her to become part of the machinery of the telepone exchange, and uses her, as it had neglected her, with an indifferent wastefulness. That, too, is Chicago.[1]

"There is no other group in any other locality which will quite bear comparison with ... the admirable artists" who were then "doing rather more than their share of the best literary work in the country," William Dean Howells, "the dean of American letters" wrote in the distinguished *North American Review* in May of 1903. "As an adoptive New Yorker of recent naturalism ... I am aware that there is every appearance in the writers of ... Chicago ... of being ahead of New York in a direction where none, possibly, would be more surprised than Chicago to find them in the van." Howells was particularly charmed by the work of Ade, Dunne, Fuller, Garland and Payne (among those we have seen) and of Robert Herrick and

Frank Norris whose work we will examine in this chapter.[2]

Turn of the Century Historical Romances

The early years of Chicago's existence as a corporation provide the background for Dubois H. Loux's privately-printed and badly-written *Ongon* (1902). Loux drew substantially from Alfred T. Andreas's three-volume *History of Chicago* (1884-1886), adding to the factual events non-historical romantic elements. "Ongon" is a secret society which follows a cross. It is named for the novel's central character, a southerner permanently bronzed by the Indian's "medicine."

A Little Girl in Old Chicago (1904) by New Yorker Amanda M. Douglas is one of a series of at least nine "little girl" books, each featuring a different girl in a different city. Douglas was a meticulous researcher; the result shows in this novel, which, if not the best of the series, is close. Its anecdotes and language will be familiar to anyone who has read nineteenth century Chicago novels or historical materials.

This is not a juvenile book. Its narrative of the life of Ruth Gaynor from 1837 to 1893, her love for Norman Hayne, her marriage to his half-villain, half-hero brother, Dan ("material in every line ... intellectual in scarcely none"), Dan's infatuation for the widow, Polly, which ends with their drowning in Lake Michigan, and Ruth's eventual marriage to Norman, is adult fare. The book has an unusual narrative pattern — Norman narrates the first three years, Ruth the next ten (both in great detail). The final forty-three years are summarized by Norman in one final chapter.

Clark Ezra Carr's *The Illini* (1904) was a lengthy but popular historical novel; it went through nine printings up to 1920. It opens with the coming of the narrator's family to Illinois in 1850, and continues through the end of the Civil War. The novel is based on the Carr family history during that period. Prominent Illinois people also appear. But Carr chose to overlay actual local and national history with a romantic mystery to provide plot complications. The book is illustrated with photographs of actual people.

The Romance of Business

Duncan has said that "every Chicago writer from 1885 to 1920 concerned himself [and herself] with the Chicago business man," yet no two of them saw the business man in the same light.[3]

One Chicago writer who concerned himself almost exclusively with the business man or business themes was Will Payne who wrote novels and short stories in these modes for over forty years, beginning in 1890. Many of his stories were written for ex-Chicago-meat-packer-employee George Horace Lorimer's *Saturday Evening Post* — a magazine founded on two propositions: "that a man's chief interest in life is the fight for livelihood —

business;" and that "the business world was being misrepresented."[4]

At the turn of the century, Payne produced four books about business in Chicago. The first of these, *The Money Captain* (1898), is also the best. It is set in an era of Chicago expansion which was accompanied by "boodling" — the practice of Chicago politicians of first acquiring city franchises, then selling them for personal gain. The "money captain" is Dexter who is trying to build a gas empire through acquisition of franchises. He is opposed by Leggett, a newspaper man, who is trying to expose Dexter's corrupt transactions. A third man, Nidstrom, Dexter's secretary, must choose between life in Chicago and approval of Dexter's business style or life in the country outside Chicago. After Dexter's death, he elects to remain in Chicago.

This book marked the beginning of an effort by Herbert S. Stone & Company to publish more Chicago authors.

On Fortune's Road (1902) is a collection of Payne's short stories about business. "The Chairman's Politics" features the political activities of the notorious real life Chicago First Ward politician, "Bathhouse John" Coughlin. Three stories are set in the Board of Trade at the time when there were no restraints on market manipulations and men strove to "corner the market" and destroy their competitors. This would become a familiar theme in Chicago fiction.

An element of romance is present in each of the book's stories.

Mr. Salt (1903) tells of a tycoon by that name engaged in a power struggle for control of coal fields, railroads, iron mines and steel mills during the financial depression of 1893-1896.

A slighter tale than any of these is *The Automatic Capitalists* (1909). Two young men first lie to each other and then to business associates as, through a "bucket shop" operation, they attempt to pyramid a single industrial bond into an empire. Their balloon bursts, and at novel's end they face prison terms. The whole thing is done with a light touch which made Payne popular with magazine readers.

Bernard Duffey says Payne's business novels "in their totality form a symbolic record of his own brush with the city — encounter, bewilderment, moral defeat."[5] The bewilderment often shows in Payne's inability or unwillingness in his novels to come down hard at the end on one side or another. He usually resolves his irresolution by adding truncated romantic endings to his tales.

Another "author" of novels about Chicago business was "Merwin-Webster," the name under which Samuel Merwin and Henry Kitchell Webster sometimes combined forces (at other times each wrote independently). Their first effort, *The Short Line War* (1899), was a popular success — it went through at least three printings in its first year. Its story line features involved financial manipulations and physical combat as two groups contest for control of a short railroad line out of Chicago. A love affair joins together two young people who are on opposite sides of the struggle — of course.

The success of this venture led to *The Banker and the Bear/The Story of a Corner in Lard* (1900) by Webster, working alone. In addition to the story of a fictional attempt to corner the lard market, the novel features a "run" on a bank, and one more romance between two young people. The two opponents in the attempt to corner the market are friends on the surface, but one is using deceit in his attempts to destroy the other.

There were to be many more novels, many non-fictional books, and even several films about Chicago Board of Trade market manipulations as time passed. The best fictional study appeared in 1902, Frank Norris's *The Pit*. This second volume in a proposed trilogy dealing with wheat growing (*The Octopus*, 1901, set in California), wheat marketing (*The Pit, a Story of Chicago*) and wheat consumption (*The Wolf*, proposed to discuss the consumption of wheat in Europe) in both a major Chicago novel and a major American novel. *The Octopus* focusses on "the war between the wheat grower and the Railroad Trust." *The Pit* is the "fictitious narrative of a 'deal' in the Chicago wheat pit [the Board of Trade]."[6]

The actual story which was the basis for this novel and for others is told in Edward Jerome Dies *The Plunger/A Tale of the Wheat Pit* (1929), published on the 100th anniversary of the birth of Benjamin P. "Old Hutch" Hutchinson, the "Napoleon of the Pit." The biography also reports on others who tried to corner the market — Phillip D. "Peedy" Armour, of the meat-packing family, and Joseph Leiter, son of a partner in Marshall Field's department store venture.

"Chicago," Frank Norris had once written, "is not a place where stories happen."[7] But in *The Pit*, Floyd Dell said, Norris tried to disprove this statement:

> He came, and saw, and wrote his novel. An astonishing capacity for seeing, he had too. In him the reporting instinct amounted to genius. He sketched the city in broad, powerful strokes, taking in with his amateur vision aspects of life that veteran Chicagoans had felt without being able to express. Never, surely, was a city done so well. Better than in any book written by a real Chicagoan, he gives us in his novel a sense of Chicago's streets and buildings and business — its objectives, localised existence. . . . Intrinsically, of course, as a picture of Chicago life, it simply doesn't stand up beside any of the books written about Chicago by Chicagoans. For Frank Norris, who had the gift of seeing the oustide of things, did not penetrate with his imagination to the heart of the city, to discover there the pretences, at once shallow and cruel, which Chicago's own writers have made it their main business to show up. Is Chicago ever called nowadays the Windy City? It was the Windy City in the

nineties, a city of vast and intangible bluff. The feverish straining of the eighties, with its few flashes of beautiful and futile idealism, culminating in the World's Fair, had passed. Chicago had arrived, commercially and industrially. Its pride in itself, its bigness, its hardness, and its success, knew no bounds. It was an uncritical pride that led directly into the mire of fatuous self-deception, from which Chicago's novelists have ever since, not without some success, been trying to pull it. No lie was too egregious to tell about the new-world, western glory that was Chicago. And Frank Norris, it seems, believed it all.[8]

Dell wrote this evaluation in 1912 from the viewpoint of a recent arrival in what was still "the Windy City," and was to be for many years afterward. Eighteen years later Fred Lewis Pattee saw Norris in a different light:

The Chicago movement [of the eighteen-nineties] failed for want of an adequate leader. As the decade was closing, however, the leader appeared, but not in Chicago. It was young Frank Norris, Chicago-born, but long since removed to San Francisco . . . [It] was a voice from California that precipitated a new period, a voice free from provincial narrowness and Puritanical intolerance . . . [It[was the voice of a leader fitted for leadership.[9]

Forty years later, Finis Farr commented briefly that as "a writer of history," he was able to believe in Norris's "grain speculators."[10]

From 1900 on, George Horace Lorimer had been writing for his *Saturday Evening Post* (the "business man's journal") a series of letters purporting to be from a Chicago meat packer. *Letters From a Self-made Merchant to His Son* (1902) are "letters written by John Graham, head of the house of John Graham & Company, pork-packers in Chicago, and familiarly known on 'change' as 'Old Gorgon Graham,' to his son, Pierrepont, member of the Senior Class of Harvard University, and facetiously known to his fellow students as 'Piggy.'" Although pork-packing had been a Chicago industry since Gurdon Hubbard set up his plant on the River seventy-five years earlier, this is the first Chicago novel to glorify the trade. (Lorimer was a journalist, and not a member of Chicago's genteel society.) It was followed two years later by *Old Gorgon Graham*, the sequel probably owing to the popularity of the first volume — it sold over a hundred thousand copies if publisher's figures are to be trusted.[11]

Curiously, although these volumes were advertised as having an "essentially sound philosophy" and "advice so sound, so genuine, and withal so unforgettable that no better book can be placed in the hands of a young man about to begin his struggle for existence," they were sold as "notable books of American humor," and Lorimer was said to have won "a place among the very highest names in that most distinctive achievement in American literature."[12]

The two novels are a tribute to the "self-made man" school of American idealism, and an attack on the dilettantish young men who infested American colleges, including Harvard, and, it is presumed, Lorimer's own college, Colby. Lorimer, a Boston minister's son, at twenty-two had quit a $5,000 a year job with the Armour packing company to take a two-year journalism course at Colby. Cyrus Curtis then hired him at a thousand dollars a year as editor; Lorimer eventually increased that salary a hundredfold.[13]

Lorimer's volumes did not pass unnoticed through the field of American letters. Between them in time, Charles Eustace Merriman's *Letters From a Son to His Self-Made Father* (1903) appeared. This pseudonymously-written epistolary novel keeps the lines of communication open in the Graham family in spite of the obvious differences of opinion on the issues raised by "Old Gorgon Graham." "Pierrepont Graham's" letters home from Harvard dismay the father with their frivolous accounts of college sprees and antics in the staid Massachusetts college town. After leaving college, Pierrepont, though unhappy about the prospect, enters his father's packing plant as a laborer, then becomes a salesman. He finally becomes the man his father had hoped for.

Following Lorimer's second book, Merriman's second response appeared, *A Self-Made Man's Wife; Her Letters to Her Son, Being the Woman's View of Certain Famous Correspondence* (1905). In part a sequel, but also in part parody, these sixteen letters offer a mother's advice to Pierrepont during his honeymoon and first year of marriage. Thomas L. Kilpatrick says this sequel is as good as Merriman's first volume.[14]

Samuel Merwin's *The Whip Hand; A Tale of the Pine Country* (1903) is set partly in Chicago. The head of an independent Wisconsin logging firm courts a settlement worker in the slums of Chicago as part of the action.

Charles Eugene Banks, one of a number of exiles from Iowa who became journalists and authors in Chicago, published his *John Dorn, Promoter* in 1906. It is a poorly-written book, featuring a typical strong man-hero popular in the fiction of that era, but it is interesting as one of several Chicago novels that looks at the Spanish-American War — a war that brought no credit to Chicago meat packers:

> Were these the heroes they had looked so eagerly to see? Yellow with the poison of Cuban swamps, their khaki uniforms soiled and dusty ... Were these the happy, careless, free-hearted boys who in the fresh springtime had gone gaily forth on their mission of mercy?" ...
>
> "San Juan and Gettysburg," exclaimed Dorn. "Had the United States gone to the succor of Cuba forty years earlier, we should have been saved the Civil War."[15]

In the novel, a Chicago company is formed to log Upper Michigan pines, but it intends to treat the Indian land owners fairly, and to replace harvested trees with seedlings. The girl in the story is a successful business woman, an occasional type in Chicago novels about this time.

Banks' book was no match either in literary quality or in its effect on readers for another Chicago book published that same year, Upton Sinclair's classic *The Jungle*. The story of Jurgis Rudkins, the immigrant packing house worker, with its "inartistic and obtrusive sociology" was written, as Sinclair said, "to touch the hearts of the American people" with the plight of Chicago packing house workers, but "it only affected their stomachs" with its queasy details of packing plant operations.[16]

Arthur Jerome Eddy's *Ganton & Co.: A Story of Chicago Commercial and Social Life* came out in 1908. Anothony R. Grosch says that John Ganton, "who is probably [also] modeled after Philip D. Armour, is a man of gargantuan energy, vision, and competitiveness, and he wants his firm to 'be greater than all other packing companies taken together and to extend his control over the slaughtering and packing industry until the world depended on him for meat.'"[17]

Ganton may well have been intended as an answer to *The Jungle* for it condemns the workers and their unions; the latter are "potent organizations, trying offenders in secret and executing them in alleys, in the streets, even in the street cars — anywhere and everywhere the thug and slugger could reach." Ganton, like the "Duke of Gas" of Payne's *The Money Captain*, bribes city officials and union officials alike.

In 1909, the book was dramatized by J. Hartley Manners as *The Great John Ganton*. The play's story line apparently followed that of the novel: Ganton's son is in love with an estimable young lady (played by Laurette Taylor) whom Ganton dislikes, so like the son of Gorgon Graham, the young man goes his own way, a route which gets him into financial difficulties. When news arrive that the younger Ganton has been injured while haranguing strikers in the stock yards, Ganton has a heart seizure. But the girl nurses him back to health and all ends well.

The *New York Times* reviewer said the "play was not as big as it sounds," but he did like the acting of Miss Taylor and the man who played Ganton.[18]

The business of selling life insurance also drew the attention of journalists and writers early in the century. A 1905 *Atlantic Monthly* article showed American mistrust of the business; newspaper revelations of insurance business wrongdoing also appeared in 1905. As one consequence, Elliott Flower, who usually wrote in the muckracking tradition, authored several magazine stories in 1905: "An Incidental Error;" "An Incidental Courtship;" "An Incidental Tragedy," and so on. One critic called these a "counterblast" to the *Atlantic* and newspaper articles. In 1907, these loosely-related stories were collected in *The Best Policy*. Flower's stories, which have little literary value, catalog the precepts which a reliable insurance salesperson should be guided by, and, as well, emphasize the benefits of insurance to policyholders and argue that the marketing of insurance is a social service.[19]

Margaret Potter's *The Golden Ladder* (1908), an "ineffective novel," is dedicated to the "Wives of American Business Men." Potter's thesis is that "the American of today is a slave in his lust for gold," a thesis that critics of the Chicago scene would find little to quibble about. The novel follows the careers of two people, Roger Kildare, a Wisconsin farm boy who comes to Chicago with his eyes on the "main chance," and who eventually becomes manager of the New York office of a Chicago brokerage house, and Kitty Clephane, daughter of a well-to-do boarding house owner. Roger romances Kitty, but she is a tart with dreams of a theatrical career. Eventually, she becomes the mistress of a wealthy New York business man.

George Barr McCutcheon, who had been at Purdue with his brother, John, the long-time Chicago *Tribune* cartoonist, and George Ade, came to Chicago to become a journalist. In the late 1890s, he tried his hand at a romantic novel about a young Chicago couple stranded by a shipwreck in the South Pacific (later re-published as *Nedra*, 1905). That first novel disappeared from view, but in 1901, McCutcheon's second novel, *Graustark*, appeared and McCutcheon gave up journalism for authorship. *Graustark* soon sold 150,000 copies, led to a successful Broadway version and several sequels about other young Americans of the "all-American boy" type romancing other beautiful Balkan princesses. In 1904 he moved to New York City.

McCutcheon's *Jane Cable* (1906) is set in Chicago. Jane is a young woman who has been adopted by a well-to-do railroad magnate and his wife; in her foundling past there is a hint of bastardy, "the bar sinister." She loves another of those clean-cut All-Americans, whose father, however, is a shyster lawyer. The story follows the unraveling of a number of complications; at one time both Jane and her lover are in the Phillippines during the Spanish-American war — he a dashing soldier, she a beautiful nurse.

Jennette Barbour Lee, an English professor and wife of author Gerald Stanley Lee, described, in *Simeon Tetlow's Shadow* (1909) another railroad magnate, this one fiscally sound but physically crippled:

> The tiny, shriveled figure gave no hint of the power that ticketed carloads of livestock and human beings to their destination and laid its hand upon roads half dead, or dying, or alive and kicking, sweeping them gently into the system, with hardly a gulp.

At forty-two, Simeon Tetlow is president of a railroad but a nervous wreck. Surprisingly, this "toad," as a critic called him, is the protege and puppet of a "marvelous office boy with a dull face and an intuitive knowledge of how to manage Tetlow's affairs."[20]

The Nation, in reviewing this "novel of sentiment," wondered why the "innumerable [fictional] studies" of "men of the hour," American financiers or political bosses, had not produced "any really arresting compelling in-terpretations."

> Is the fault with our literary and dramatic artists, or with their theme? Is it possible that these famous magnates of ours, who so distress us and upon whom we so pride ourselves, simply fail to offer any new material for interpre-tation, or even any old material of the first order?[21]

A Human Note by St. Lawrence Chandler, Marquis of Eckerley [!] (1908) suggests that Chicago's often-noted "Lake effect" may have occasionally produced the kinds of weird results on the human imagination that if often produces in the climate of the shore areas adjacent to the Lake. If one can imagine a son of a Chicago butterine [oleo-margarine] manufacturer travel-ing at his father's expense to Russia on behalf of Chicago's Socialist party, and then further imagine that two Russian noblemen would tattoo a one-hundred-thousand ruble note on the son's bare back, one has a start on this story. The balance of the tale concerns a manhunt for the son after he has returned to Chicago.

This is not so much a story of Chicago business as it is a comedy of manners — most of the emphasis seems to be on social affairs.[22]

Politics and "The Boss"

In the late nineteenth and early twentieth centuries, the political "boss," a person able to deliver political entities (a ward, a city, the Irish vote) at election time, a person often working closely with a "magnate" or "tycoon" (such as Charles T. Yerkes), was able to come into political power and wealth by taking advantage of the confusion caused by the rapid growth of the sort Chicago was experiencing because of immigration, both from the hinter-lands and from Europe.

During these two decades, the boss figured prominently in literature set in Chicago and other growing cities.

Francis Churchill Williams' *J. Devlin—Boss* (1901) was regarded as the prototype by many later writers. Although one critic says this novel of an Irish boss who believes that politics are for profit is set in a "satellite city near Chicago," internal evidence strongly suggests the unnamed setting is either Philadelphia or New York City.[23]

Brand Whitlock, a turn-of-the-century Chicago journalist, later author, and mayor of Toledo, Ohio, wrote four novels and one collection of short stories which focus on politics, occasionally with a fillip of romance added. *The Thirteenth District* (1902) is set in a city near Chicago. *Her Infinite*

Variety (1904) features a romance between an Illinois state senator from Chicago and a beautiful young conventional socialite from the city. She opposes the suffragette bill he espouses. An added theme is the conflicting downstate and Chicago interests.

In *The Happy Average* (1904) Whitlock shows us a young lawyer and his bride from Macochee, Ohio, and the difficulties they face in Chicago; a journalist is also a character. *The Turn of the Balance* (1907) contrasts the lives of two families — one rich, one poor — in a city which seems like a combination of Chicago and Toledo where Whitlock took up the practice of law after he left Chicago. The novel focusses on the operations of a political boss and his criminal allies.

The Gold Brick (1910) is a collection of twelve short stories set in Chicago, and Springfield, Illinois (where Whitlock was a reporter for the Chicago *Herald*, a Democratic newspaper.) Three of the stories, "What Will Become of Annie?", "Reform in the First," and "Malachi Nolan," deal with political warfare in Chicago.[24]

John T. McIntyre's *The Ragged Edge* (1902) tells of an Irish political boss in Chicago; the dialogue attempts literal reporting of the Irish brogue. One chapter features an Irish wake and funeral. The conflict in this novel is between the Irish boss and a young Irish lawyer.

Philip Payne's *The Mills of Man* (1903) has two themes — a Chicago boss trying to take over Chicago street traction opportunities and the conflict between Chicago and "Little Egypt's" political forces. "Free silver" is also an issue.

Elliott Flower was the son of Mrs. Lucy Flower, with Jane Addams an early advocate of reform in the treatment of Chicago's delinquent children, and later an editor of the *Tribune* and the Chicago *Evening Post.* In his *The Spoilsmen* (1903) he shows an affluent young man, member of a social crowd with time on its hands, and a young hardware merchant in a poverty-stricken ward, both of whom run for positions as Chicago aldermen. Darnell wins easily in his "silk-stocking" ward; so does Mason, the merchant, in the poorer ward. But when Mason refuses to support the chicaneries of the "Old Man," the Boss moves to defeat him. Darnell saves Mason, but both resolve to drop out of politics. McIntyre's thesis is clear — the good people want nothing to do with Chicago politics and that is why corruption flourishes.

Flower's *Slaves of Success* (1905) is a collection of short stories, seven of which ran in *Collier's Weekly* in 1904. Each of the stories illustrates ways in which Chicago politicians manipulate their pawns. This was a time when reform movements in Chicago were trying to eliminate the so-called "gray wolves" — corrupt adermen — and one story shows a business man-reformer being outwitted by a party boss. A prominent character in the stories is a downstate farmer, an honest but simple man, who has been elected to the legislature.

The ward boss known as "the Duke" in Henry Kitchell Webster's second novel on his own, *The Duke of Cameron Avenue* (1904) behaves himself after the city's reformers have shown their power, but not before

the warden of a settlement house, deciding to have a go at practical reform-politics, throws a scare into the boss, who then realizes that the screws can be put on him at ensuing elections. The positive creed of the story can be reduced to three points: national-party issues are irrelevant in municipal elections; ward bosses, in general, understand only defeats, and cannot be trusted to rise to the purity of their own accord; and a continuation of present misgovernment of slum areas is bound to produce socialists.[25]

J. W. McConaughy and Edward Brewster Sheldon's *The Boss* (1911) is an account of the rise of a Clancy Street saloonkeeper's son to a role as political and financial boss of his Fourth Precinct.

Michael "Shindy Mike" Regan's romance with the daughter of Chicago's leading wheat dealer introduces the viewpoint of the shipper of wheat — a unique point of view for the Chicago novel.

The Hon. Henry E. Scott's *The Alderman's Wife* (1904) and Edgar Rice Beach's *Hands of Clay; A Great City's Half* — and the Other Half (1904), are both minor works written in the populist spirit of the times.

The Employed and the Unemployed

Give me your tired, young poor —
Your huddled masses yearning to breathe free,
The wretched refuse of your teeming shore.
Send these, the homeless, tempest-tossed to me
And lift my lamp beside the golden door.

So wrote Emma Lazarus, looking toward Europe about 1880. By 1890, so many of these "huddled masses" had come to Chicago and settled in the "two-story wooden dwellings, rear tenements, and jerry-built flats" of the Near West Side that what had once been an old and pleasant place was overrun "by the spreading blight."[26]

In 1889, Jane Addams, a young woman from Rockford, Illinois had settled in this area to "live near the city's poor and discover their problems and tend to their needs." Soon she and her co-workers had taken over the former home of a well-to-do merchants and named it Hull House for him. From this center at 800 South Halsted, Jane looked out over a half-dozen large ethnic populations crammed into the area. "Between Halsted Street and the River live about ten thousand Italians," she wrote. "In the south on Twelfth Street are many Germans, and side streets are given over to Polish and Russian Jews. Still farther south, thin Jewish colonies merge into a huge Bohemian colony, so vast that Chicago ranks as the third Bohemian city in the world."[27]

Beginning at the turn of the century, Chicago writers, some with names that reflected Chicago's Yankee heritage, some with names like those to be found in the ghettoes, began to write about the poor and the friendless who lived around Hull House. Some of these writers were students or faculty members at the newly-founded University of Chicago, the first large American university to have a department of sociology and the first major American university to employ professors who were authors rather than researchers.

Lucy Jane Rider Meyer, "Deaconess by the Grace and the Call of God" authored "dozens of sentimental vignettes illustrating poverty in the slum areas of Chicago;" they were collected in *Deaconess Stories* in 1900. Dwight L. Moody, who had died in 1899, furnished the introduction. Moody, an evangelist, had come to Chicago at mid-century to sell shoes, but soon turned to saving "souls" in those years when Chicago had a church for every two-thousand citizens and a saloon for every two hundred. Moody whom a friend once called "the Sunday-school drummer," was famous for his practice of going from rider to rider in street-cars, asking "Are you a Christian."[28]

Israel Kahn Friedman, whose *The Lucky Number* we have already seen, was a student at Chicago. From 1900 to 1907 he wrote four novels about Chicago's "huddled masses."

Poor People (1900) is about people living in a tenement; they are the bottom layer of the social pyramid. "The people at the top of the pyramid press down on those below." The narrator is a composer of music; his two daughters work at menial tasks. There is Rounds, a carpenter, who founds a successful furniture plant and is able to leave the tenement; Adolph Vogel, an alcoholic playwright; and Vogel's son, a watchmaker. The novel relates the efforts of these people to survive.

By Bread Alone (1901) is a *roman á clef*, its fictional setting obviously George Pullman's model town of Pullman, its *leitmotif* a prolonged struggle between capital and labor. A socialist woman is surely modeled on Emma Goldman.

The hero, who could have taken his place in Chicago's affluent society, chooses a Presbyterian pulpit because he wants to save mankind. He leaves the pulpit later to become a steelworker and plan a Cooperative Commonwealth. Meanwhile, he teeters romantically between the daughter of the steel town owner and a school teacher, the latter a daughter of a steel mill worker, who preaches the capitalistic line. The novel ends with a bloody battle between strikers and militia, a replay of the Chicago summer of 1894. The hero finally decides that his best change to save mankind lies in his becoming a politician.

The Radical (1907), most of which is set in Washington, is about a poverty-stricken young man who drives a delivery wagon in the daytime, pursues an education at night, becomes an attorney and legislator, and seems headed for the White House.

In Friedman's *The Autobiography of a Beggar* (parts of which were published in *The Saturday Evening Post* before book publication in 1903), a beggar describes the operation of "the beggars' club", then continues narrating "the hard road of those who attempt social and economic reform through legislation, whether reform of the saloon or of child labor."[29] Critics, who had previously complained about the "odd expressions and fantastic diction," the "wild" grammar and "the author's method of dealing with the subjunctive," found more grist for their mill in the "local color" spelling of this book.[30]

The theme of the honest man in national politics found in *The Radical*, derives, as Grey says, from the national panic of 1907.[31] Two other novels with this theme, *The Land of the Living* (1908) by Maude Radford Warren, a University of Chicago graduate, and *The Politician* (1910) by Edith Mason both use this theme, and, as well, find some influence in the figure of Abraham Lincoln, the centenary of whose birth drew national attention in 1909.

Warren's novel focusses on young Hugh MacDermott, who is adopted and raised by "Big John" Callahan, a Chicago ward boss, who believes that America "is the land for living people," and poetry is the land of the dead. Although he at first argues that "too much schooling is no help to a boy," he relents when Hugh's teacher tells him that Hugh has the potential to become a state governor.

Callahan's political philosophy is that "you've got to compromise or you'll not count in the world," and that as soon as politicians "can show the people that reform's bad for business, off goes the head of reform."[32]

But Hugh, who is basically good and honest becomes a political success and wins the heart of an Irish princess.

Although the dominant male figure in *The Politician* is a New Yorker, a Princeton graduate, there is a Chicago connection in his unhappy romance with a Chicago merchant's daughter, a Chicago Republican convention, and the use of a Lincoln portrait.

Samuel Merwin and Henry Kitchell Webster came together again in 1905 to co-author *Calumet "K"*, a romance featuring another of those Nietschean superman heroes so popular in the early years of the century. "Calumet 'K'" is a grain elevator under construction along the Calumet River on Chicago's far South Side. It is needed to store two million bushels of wheat scheduled to arrive in Chicago by the end of the year as part of a scheme to defeat a "corner" in wheat. (This novel may also be based on the activities of Phillip D. Armour.) Owners of a railroad who have a vested interest in the "corner," and a union "walking delegate," one of many to be seen in labor novels, attempt to interfere with the construction, but are thwarted by the protagonist, a hard-driving construction superintendent.

The protagonist of Octave Thanet's (Alice French) *Man of the Hour* (1905) comes from the Iowa-Illinois Quad-Cities to support the workers in the Pullman strike (1894). Later, realizing that his efforts have only prolonged the agony of the strikers, he switches to the side of Capital and "Brains." A traitorous "walking delegate" is also a character in the novel. French based her novel on personal observation of the Pullman affair.

Clarence Seward Darrow has no peer as a criminal lawyer in the history of American jurisprudence. He was admitted to the bar in 1875 when he was only eighteen. He became nationally and internationally famous by winning an acquittal for Eugene V. Debs in the American Railway Union Strike case of 1894; in securing freedom for Charles Moyer and "Big Bill" Heywood after they were charged with blowing the governor of Idaho to bits; in the Leopold and Loeb trial of 1924; in the Scopes "monkey" trial in Tennessee in 1925 (his opponent was William Jennings Bryan); and the Scottsboro case in 1932. Darrow was then seventy-five.

Darrow had a parallel career as an author; he wrote literary essays and he wrote legal essays for William Randolph Hearst's Chicago *Evening American*.

Darrow's second novel, *An Eye for an Eye* (1905, reprinted 1969) is in the naturalistic and deterministic mode which Dreiser began in *Sister Carrie* and carried to fruition in *An American Tragedy* (1925). It tells how Hank Clery, a railroad switchman, goes to the Chicago Dearborn Street County Jail to visit his friend, Jim Jackson, who is to hang the next morning for murdering his wife with a stove poker. Through the long night, Jim tells Hank his story — a long bitter tale of poverty which leads eventually to Jim's murdering his wife, his attempt to conceal the crime and his flight to avoid justice.

Charlotte Teller's *The Cage* (1907), which we have already seen in connection with the Haymarket Affair, is based on a real-life "colony of radicals who lived in an apartment house on the West Side not far from Hull House."[33] Among this group were Clarence Darrow, and William English Walling, the latter a model for the "Austrian Socialist" in Miss Teller's novel, and also for characters in several other Chicago novels.

Hutchins Hapgood, a friend of Eugene O'Neill's, and, like Robert Herrick and Robert Morss Lovett, a Harvard man who had come to Chicago to teach (though only for a short time), tried to combine journalistic and academic points of view in two novels dealing with the labor revolt and the Haymarket Affair, *The Spirit of Labor* (1907) and *An Anarchist Woman* (1909). Hapgood said he came to Chicago to find a typical working man:

> It seemed to me that I should be more likely to find such a man in Chicago than anywhere else. In the democratic Middle West of the United States the common man is probably more expressive than anywhere else in the world. Labor, there, is more self-conscious and socially, if not politically, more powerful than elsewhere ...[34]

His hero, Anton, is found in the Briggs House, a small hotel similar to the Hinds hotel where Jurgis Rudkus at last found employment in *The Jungle*.[35] Using Anton as his protagonist, Hapgood builds a novel of ideas; every concept current in the Chicago of the first decade of the century is touched upon. Among those Anton observes are Eugene Debs whom he sees as "premature;" "Hinkydink" Kenna and "Bathhouse John" Coughlin whom he regards as consorts of crooks; Jane Addams, Clarence Darrow, and "young literary men like Herrick and Friedman who dwell with insistent sympathy upon the emotional and aesthetic demands of the people."[36]

Hapgood's second novel is a sociological case study of Chicago which shows strong influences from the novels of Lillian Sommers. (Hapgood's social ideas were in turn to influence the work of O'Neill.) Although its primary focus is on events in the life of a girl who chooses to become a prostitute rather than labor in a factory, the novel is also a novel of ideas, among them that concept of "free love" which was to intrigue the writers of the Chicago Renaissance a decade later:

> [The anarchists] were indeed all "free lovers," and quite naturally so; the rebellious temperament instinctively takes as its object of attack the strongest convention in society. Anarchism in Europe is mainly political; in America it is mainly sexual.[37]

Hapgood, the son of a well-to-do Alton, Illinois plow manufacturer had met and married Neith Boyce Harrison, daughter of an Indiana Civil War general and a Vermont school-teacher while both were staffers for a New York newspaper. Neith had been an editor of Boston's *The Arena* when her father was a co-owner of the magazine. Neith was the author of a number of short stories and four novels, including *The Forerunner* (1903), *The Bond* (1908, both non-Chicago settings) and *Proud Lady* (1923) which we shall discuss later. Hapgood was best known for his two non-Chicago books, *The Spirit of the Ghetto* (1902) and *Autobiography of a Thief* (1903).

The Social Service and Settlement Novel

The attempts of Jane Addams and her co-workers at Hull House to aid the poor, and contemporary practices of "basket philanthropy" on the part of Chicago middle-class women both attracted public attention, and, as well, provided themes for a number of Chicago novels of this period.

The first of these was Merrick A. Richardson's *Chicago's Black Sheep and Bonnie's McClear's Friends* (1898), a novel which Grey says is "a clumsy yet often perceptive story of a Scottish girl who is reclaimed by the Salvation Army, and who exposes a police detective allied with criminals."[38] A second is *Differences* (1899) by Iowan Hervey White, an under-rated novel and the best of this group.

Among others in which Hull House and philanthropy received some attention were: *Mary North* (1903) by Lucy J. Meyer; *A Winged Victory* (1907) by University of Chicago professor Robert Morss Lovett; *The Cage* (1907); *Just Folks* (1910) and *The Penny Philanthropist* (1912) by travel-writer Clara Elizabeth Laughlin; *Mrs. Mahoney of the Tenement* (1912) by Louise Montgomery; *The Precipice* (1914) by Elia Wilkinson Peattie; *The New Mr. Howerson* (1914) by Opie Read; *Those About Trench* (1916) by University of Chicago professor Edwin Herbert Lewis; *Marching Men* (1917) by Sherwood Anderson; and *The Education of Ernest Wilmerding* (1924) by Edward C. Wentworth.

There was also Charles M. Sheldon, a Topeka, Kansas preacher who in 1899 had published a book, *In His Steps*, that sold about six million copies — although others claim as many as thirty million copies.[39] In 1902 he turned to a city like Chicago and a settlement house like Hull House for the setting of a novel, *The Reformer*. John Gordon, the novel's protagonist returns from a tour of Europe to tell his father he has no intention of entering the father's business; instead he plans to devote his life to improving living conditions for the city's indigent. Gordon moves into Hope House, a settlement house in the tenement district, and begins trying to improve housing conditions through enforced housing codes and stricter housing legislation. It takes a disastrous fire, however, to draw public opinion to his side.

The book attracted reviewers for the *New York Times* and *Outlook*, but it did not make its way to any list of best sellers.

Novels of Love and Romance

"There is a major difference between the novels written in the [eighteen-] nineties and those written retrospectively from the 1900s," says Lennox Bouton Grey. "The effort in the eighties and nineties to formulate into crisp white and black the whole panorama of the city . . . is given up as a primary aim . . . and is subordinated to the study of types of men and women and actions which time and repetition have brought forward from secondary roles in the earlier novels."[40]

The statement is true of Mary Moncure Parker's *A Girl of Chicago* (1901) which looks back at the Chicago of the 1880s. The novel begins with the prospect of the forthcoming marriage of the daughter of E. Gordon Allene of Prairie Avenue, an unscrupulous Chicago soap baron, to a bigamous English Lord. But it ends with the girl's marriage to "plain but well-bred Will Porter," whose father had been ruined financially by Allene in an earlier identity as "Lucky Eddie Allen." The father's failure, however, has "made a man" of young Porter, taking him away from the world of rakes and fops of Chicago's affluent society.

Will Payne's *The Story of Eva* (1901) has many similarities to Theodore Dreiser's *Sister Carrie*, published a year earlier. Eva Crawford, like Carrie, comes to Chicago from a small town:

> ...to her, as to hundreds of thousands like her, drawn in from the New West, Chicago was the great city, the Rome, the Paris, the metropolis, the biggest single expression of life which still meant gaining one's bread from the soil, building however rudely, to make a habitation in the wilderness.[41]

Although she is still married to a husband who has deserted her, Eva moves from a cheap rooming house into a luxurious Prairie Avenue apartment with an affluent educated man. The latter part of the novel focuses on the generation problem in Chicago and the melodramatic ending by which Payne resolves Eva's dilemma.

Carrie Meeber, coming to Chicago from a small Wisconsin town, moves in with her married sister, and then seeks employment to support herself:

> Into this important commercial region the timid Carrie went. She walked east along Van Buren Street through a region of lessening importance, until it deteriorated into a mass of shanties and coal-yards, and finally verged upon the river. She walked bravely forward, led by an honest desire to find employment and delayed at every step by the interest of the unfolding scene, and a sense of helplessness amid so much evidence of power and force which she did not understand. These vast buildings, what were they? These strange energies and huge interests, for what purposes were they? She could have understood the meaning of a little stone-cutter's yard at Columbia City, carving little pieces of marble for individual use, but when the yards of some huge stone corporation came into view, filled with spur tracks and flat cars, transpierced by docks from the river and traversed overhead by immense trundling cranes of wood and steel, it lost all significance in her little world.[42]

Carrie, like Eva Crawford, takes up residence with a man, who though not as wealthy as those he serves, is still well-to-do by comparison with her. But whereas Eva comes off well at the end of her story because of the manipulations of her creator, Carrie works out her own destiny.

Floyd Dell echoed Payne's words in discussing *Carrie*:

> There is a Chicago that lives in the minds and imaginations of young people all through the Middle West, a Chicago that exists by virtue of their aspiration and their need, and that begins to die with their first sight of the town.[43]

But Chicago did not die for either Eva or Carrie. Carrie in particular used it and the two Chicago men in her life as stepping stones "in quest of the warmth and light she craved."[44]

Most readers of the time probably thought as Randolph Bourne did that Carrie should either have been redeemed or degraded. To such feelings, Dreiser responded:

> We were not used then in America to calling a spade a spade, particularly in books. We had great admiration for Tolstoi and Flaubert and Balzac and De Maupassant at a distance ... but mostly we had been schooled to the literature of that refined company of English sentimentalists who told us something about life, but not everything.[45]

Dreiser overlooked Joseph Kirkland whose motto had been "to tell the truth — but not all the truth."

Still Bourne liked the novel. "*Sister Carrie* is one of those rare stories that present not only lives but a rudimentary pattern of life itself ... [It] is beautiful, and [has] that inevitable air of almost having written itself."[46]

The debate over the morality of *Sister Carrie* was probably settled with Kazin's statement "that Dreiser had made possible a new frankness in the American novel."[47] But the debate over Dreiser's style (or lack of one) still goes on.

Although *Sister Carrie* endures as one of America's literary classics, going through reprint after reprint, a film version, *Carrie* (1952) does not do the novel justice. It is only an average motion picture, and Jennifer Jones's "Carrie" is too passive.[48]

The Second Generation (1902) by another University of Chicago English professor, James Weber Linn, combines Chicago journalism, corrupt politics, and a romance between the son and daughter of two former friends who had separated and quarreled after the girl's father supported an oil company in the legislature rather than those who had elected him. The novel is almost too full of coincidences to be believable.

Linn was the nephew of Jane Addams, and the author of *Jane Addams, a Biography* (1935), "which he wrote as a labor of love about the saintly woman who was his aunt."[49]

In *Every One His Own Way* (1901), a collection of short stories, and *True Love, a Comedy of the Affections* (1903), Wisconsin-born Edith Wyatt attempted to convert the native ways of a small town named Centreville and of Chicago to a pattern of genteelism. "In the manner of Jane Austen,"[50] Chicagoans are contrasted with the people of Centreville, and sense is set off against sensibility. Several of the characters of the short stories re-appear in the novel, including Fred Hubbard, "black sheep" of the oppressive Hubbard family of Chicago. "Two Citizens," the first story in the first book, "is in general problem and outline an anticipation of" *True Love.*[51]

"True Love" drew the attention of William Dean Howells, and led to his *North American Review* essay "Certain of the Chicago School of Fiction." Here he praised Miss Wyatt and argued that he was "fairly justified in speaking of a Chicago school." Overlooking Theodore Dreiser, whom he might not have known about, he lists as members of the "school" Wyatt, Payne, Herrick, Dunne and Ade, writers working in all of the genres then being used in Chicago — humor, romance, realism and genteelism:

> The peculiar Chicago note . . . is not less perceptible in the writer who came to Chicago full Boston-grown than those to the manner born. The republic of letters is everywhere sufficiently republican; but in the metropolis of the Middle-West, it is so without thinking; it is almost without feeling; and the atmospheric democracy, the ambient equality, is something that seems like the prime effect in literature of what America has been doing and saying in life ever since she first formulated herself in the Declaration.[52]

The Bondage of Ballinger (1903) by Roswell Field, Eugene Field's brother, is a different kind of romance — the tale of a man with an incurable life-long love affair with books, a *Magnificent Obsession* of a bibliophile. Thomas Ballinger and his long-suffering Quaker wife lead a precarious impecunious existence because he can't resist a book; on one occasion when he takes a precious book to town to sell to obtain money for food, he returns with another book — and no food. Eventually Ballinger meets one Bascom, a wealthy grocer-merchant, who is unable to understand that Ballinger only buys for possession, not to resell at a profit. But is is Bascom who provides the romantic solution to Ballinger's pecuniary problems.

Field's *Little Miss Dee* (1904), like Henry James "The Beast in the Jungle," carries the note of some latent event, the potential for which hangs over an Anglo-American family now resident in Chicago. This genteel tale relates how Agatha Dee rejects a suitor, then raises the orphaned son of a friend. The orphan becomes a pretentious lawyer who subsequently loses his savings in the market. Anonymously, Agatha pays his debts, but the young man continues to ignore her. Meanwhile, Miss Dee continues to await the fulfillment of the ages-old prophecy.

George Barr McCutcheon's experiment in tragedy, *The Sherrods* (1903) must have chilled the ardor of those of his fans who were looking to another *Graustark*. A young Indiana man, whose father had committed suicide, marries a neighbor girl. A rich Chicago girl encourages Dudley Sherrod to come to Chicago for art lessons; his wife remains in Indiana, supporting her husband's lessons by her teaching job. Then Dudley marries the rich girl bigamously and goes to Europe with her. His Indiana wife, meanwhile, bears his son. When a newspaper exposes Dudley's bigamy, he kills himself.

One would suspect that McCutcheon had read Ibsen's *Ghosts*.

Philip Payne's *Duchess of Few Clothes* (1904) was the *Grand Hotel* of its day. There is the Duchess, a country girl in Chicago, Ned Hazard, a former Boston blueblood, Quarles, a self-made man, the Pantheon Hotel's owner and his daughter, the hotel barber, the bellhop, hotel patrons. The Duchess, "The Cinderella of Cigars," manages the hotel's tobacco shop.

A reviewer called it "thoroughbred in its force and brilliancy . . . a carefully-written, well-planned, wholly absorbing novel."[53]

Margaret Potter's *The Fire of Spring* (1905) is another romance with a tragic ending. Virginia Merrill, daughter of a bankrupt, is "sold" by her mother to a plow manufacturer. Virginia detests her husband and becomes romantically involved with his cousin. When the husband discovers the affair, he takes his cousin with him on a wild, early-morning buggy ride. A train strikes the buggy and the cousin is killed.

Potter then turned to more exotic subjects for the balance of her career; her later work was not well received.

John Merritte Driver's *Purple Peaks Remote* (1905), subtitled *A Romance of Italy and America*, is set in Rome, Naples and Chicago. It tells of a Chicago lawyer who romances both an Italian woman who dies of shame, and, years later, her daughter. Thomas L. Kilpatrick says the novel, for all its faults, presents "an adequate account of . . . Chicago society during the late 1800s.[54]

Herbert Quick, best known for his 1920s novels of pioneer settlement in his native Iowa, is the author of *The Broken Lance* (1907) which he called "the best sociological novel [he] ever wrote."[55] It begins in the Iowa city of "Lattimore" (probably modeled on Sioux City where Quick was once a reform-minded mayor) and ends in Chicago, the latter setting accounting for about half of the book. In Lattimore, Emerson Courtright is converted to Henry George's philosophy of the single tax. (Both Quick and Garland were followers of George.) When Courtright begins to preach his new economic theory, his parish of wealthy men leaves him and he ends up with a church of working men. Then his plutocrat ex-members force him out of his church, and he becomes an itinerant labor leader, surfacing in Chicago. There, the man who converted him to Georgism is now an "enlightened" newspaper man, and the girl who rejected him after his conversion is an internationally-famous musical comedy star. Sick and beaten, Cartwright is nursed back to health by the girl. But once healthy, Cartwright takes part in a strike, and is shot down by a militia-man who had been a member of Cartwright's Iowa church.

The Broken Lance suggests that Quick, like his contemporary Garland, often used his novels to advocate his economic theories. Quick is cynical about the intentions of the well-to-do and powerful, both in Sioux City (which in the 1890s was thinking of itself as a "little Chicago") and in Chicago. In the end he is pessimistic about the prospects of working men for achieving fair and equitable treatment in their society.

In the early part of this century Bert Leston Taylor as "B. L. T.," was essaying another of those personal journalistic ventures so popular at the time, a daily Chicago *Tribune* column, "A Line o' Type or Two." Begun under the influence of Eugene Field (Taylor and Field were friends), the column has continued down through this century under the direction of a number of hands, the last vestige of one of America's great periods of journalism.

Taylor's *The Charlatans* (1906) is a satirical novel about "The Colossus . . . the largest conservatory of music in this or any other land," and those whom it attracted — the charlatans who came to Chicago for the easy money the city offered, and the sincere people of talent who came to Chicago for pleasure or fame, and who were taken in by the charlatans. Once the confidence men of Chicago's literature had roamed the streets looking for innocent victims — now, according to this novel, they hid behind gilt-lettered signs that suggested reputable business dealings.

Clara E. Laughlin was to write more fully about Chicago than in *Felicity* (1907), a novel which has only one chapter set in Chicago. The novel is one of many to come (and like *The Broken Lance* and *Sister Carrie*) whose subject is in whole or in part the music hall stage or the traveling troupe of actors. *Felicity's* heroine is a member of a traveling troupe.

A similar girl is a character in two of the chapters of newspaperman Joseph Medill Patterson's study of the aristocratic, *A Little Brother of the Rich* (1908). She begins her struggle for existence in a Chicago department store, then goes on the stage and becomes a star performer. Her counterpart in the novel is a Chicago young man who passes up a chance to "rise" gradually in Chicago. He goes to New York to capitalize on his athletic prowess, first displayed at Yale, where he was a "little brother" to his millionaire classmates. Patterson, a grandson of the first *Tribune* editor, was politically a Socialist, and his book received some harsh criticism for that reason. But the book deserved the bad reviews it got.

Marion Foster Washburne's *The House on the North Shore* (1909), a novel for "older girls," accents the theme of what in those years was thought of as "modern love (as distinct from the old love romance.)" Another theme in the novel is the repudiation of the City for the land — a reversal of "the revolt from the village" theme. Both of these themes were to be worked out in other Chicago novels of the time as well as in non-Chicago novels.

A third theme in the novel is that of heredity and suicide, one we have seen earlier in this section in McCutcheon's *The Sherrods*. Washburne probably was looking over her shoulder at Ibsen's *Ghosts* as she wrote this book.

Finally, the heroine is a "bachelor girl," a type which will be exploited by other Chicago and non-Chicago authors.

Novels of College Life

James Weber Linn's *The Chameleon* (1903) relates how a "pickle king," a man of "splendid qualities," plans to give a college a large sum of money and make it a university. But the plans of this "courteous, courageous, gentle, clever man," a born "poseur," run counter to "the desires of the [college] president, whose notion of education has never caught up with the utilitarian, half-romantic, half-cheap conceptions fostered by many captains of industry in the late 1890s." Labor troubles, successfully arbitrated by a "ritualistic" Anglican clergyman, also form a part of the novel.

A critic remarked that the book represented Linn's "protest against the ideals of the present American college [and] his preference for the time when 'Mark Hopkins at one end of a log and a student at the other constituted a college.'"[56]

Susan Glaspell, a native of Davenport, Iowa, enrolled in the University of Chicago in the summer of 1902 for post-graduate work. She used this Chicago background in several early short stories and in three novels. "At the Turn of the Road" is a story of a young Iowa girl studying art in Chicago. Two stories are about lonely people in Chicago who long for home and the clean, fresh air of the West. In "From A-Z," a young man and woman meet while working on a dictionary. The man is an ex-journalist with a drinking problem. In this story, love does not conquer all.[57]

Glaspell set her first novel, *The Glory of the Conquered/The Story of a Great Love* (1909) on the Chicago campus. It tells of the love and marriage of a University of Chicago scientist and a young girl, who again is an artist. When he loses his eyesight, she gives up her own career to become a scientist and further his work. But when he dies, she returns to her own career.

Although Floyd Dell and George Cram Cook, her associates at the time, reacted negatively to the novel, the *New York Times* said: "It is not often that a new writer comes forward with a first book so worthy of serious attention."[58]

In Glaspell's second novel, *The Visioning* (1911), the protagonist comes to Chicago searching for a girl who has fled from Rock Island, Illinois in shame. As Katie Wainwright Jones searches for her friend, she begins "to connect the men who work in the Rock Island Arsenal shops with the hot, tired men she sees coming out of Chicago factories . . . and begins to see a relationship between the girls who work in the Davenport candy factory and the Chicago telephone operators and salesclerks."[59] Through Katie, we see Glaspell's sympathy with the causes of trade unionism and socialism, a sympathy in vivid contrast to that of her fellow Davenport author, Alice French, whose *Man of the Hour* reflected her sympathy for the managerial classes.

William Jacob ("Will") Cuppy's *Maroon Tales* (1909, 1910) are eight short tales or sketches which also have their setting on the Chicago campus — at the time when Glaspell was a student there. There are references to various sports, the "Grand Old Man" (Amos Alonzo Stagg), dances, fraternities, classes from the freshman level to the post-graduate, school spirit and so on. A New York reviewer said that although there was an "artistic instinct" at work, much of the material was "bungling or commonplace."[60]

All Chicago students of those days knew the school song:
Wave the flag of old Chicago,
Maroon the color grand;
Ever shall her team be victors,
Known throughout the land.
With the Grand Old Man to lead them,
Without a peer they'll stand!
Wave again the grand old banner
Of the best school in the land!

Robert Herrick

Although Newton Arvin once wrote that Herrick was the author of "three of the most impressive novels in our literature," and that his was "the most capacious and the most truly critical mind at work since Howells and Norris,"[61] the better estimate is that he was a minor figure in American literature rather than a major one — certainly not up to the level of either Howells or Norris. But from Norris's untimely death in 1902 to the Renaissance, he was the major author writing in and about Chicago, and his work is still worth reading. His reputation was further enhanced by his stature as a University of Chicago English professor.

Four of Herrick's early novels, in part or in total, are set in Chicago. *The Gospel of Freedom* (1898) is set partly in Europe and poses the rewards of aestheticism against the rewards of the mundane world. Adela Anthon chose John Wilbur, upward-bound Chicago entrepreneur, over Simon Erard, a painter-critic. After three years of marriage, Adela leaves John, partially because of his willingness to profit through graft and corruption, partly because their business and marital "partnership" has failed. But after she renews her friendship with Erard in Europe, she discovers she cannot get along with him either.

The novel expresses a bitter attitude toward Chicago:

> Still there is left the city, beaming hotter and fiercer mile by mile. Life spins there; man there is handling existence as you knead bread in a pan. The city is made of man; that is the last word you say of it. Brazen, unequal like all man's work, it stands a stupendous piece of blasphemy against nature. Once within its circle, the heart must forget that the earth is beautiful.[62]

Floyd Dell summarized the story line of Herrick's next novel, *The Web of Life* (1900):

> Mr. Herrick exhibits ... the man who has a civic sense, imagination, honor ideals. This young man is a doctor. He does not like the vulgar pandering to the rich which seemed to be the thing in his profession. He does not like the rich, with their ignorance, their tawdry standards, their fatuous pride. He refuses to do what is expected of him, to 'make good' in the conventional way. He cuts loose. And Chicago breaks him scornfully — mashes him in misery until he is glad to crawl back and surrender, making the best terms he can. That, again, is Mr. Herrick's Chicago.[63]

The third novel, *The Common Lot* (1901) tells of an architect who, disappointed in not receiving an expected inheritance, joins in with a corrupt contractor in building jerry-built housing and a South Side hotel. Because of its shoddy construction, the hotel burns with a tragic loss of life. Although a court frees the architect from responsibility for the tragedy, his wife tells him he must acknowledge his errors and change his ways. Seeking salvation in the countryside he has a vision of himself:

> Greed, greed! The spirit of greed had eaten him through and through, the lust for money, the desire for the fat things of the world, the ambition to ride high among his fellows. In the world where he had lived, this passion had a dignified name; it was called enterprise and ambition. But now he saw it for what it was — greed and lust, nothing more.[64]

"Whatever was there in Chicago in 1877 to live for but Success?" asked Floyd Dell as he reviewed the best one of the four novels. *The Memoirs of an American Citizen* (1905) is a first-person account by "Van Harrington" of his rise to a U. S. Senate seat — although he has to buy that from the Illinois legislature. Like many another, Harrington came from elsewhere, from Indiana, looking for work. As a resident of a boarding-house, he is one of the "strugglers on the outside of prosperity, trying hard to climb up somewhere in the bread-and-butter order of life, and to hold on tight to what [he] had got." "What else are we here for except to make money?" another boarder asks.[65]

Harrington serves on the jury which convicts the Haymarket conspirators. "And then back to business. I suppose the world seemed to me so good a place to hustle in that I couldn't rightly appreciate the complaint of these rebels against society."[66]

When the Columbian Exposition — "the one dream that Chicago had it in her soul to dream" — is being built, Harrington is unhappy about his employer's interest in it. "It made me impatient to have Mr. Dround spend on it his energy that was needed in his own business."[67]

Van Harrington rises evenly toward success in Chicago's meat-packing industry, until finally, as Duffey says, "he is nothing but success. The man has died."[68]

Both Dell and Duffey are in agreement as to the nature of Herrick's attack on Chicago: "Chicago was boring, Chicago was vulgar. Chicago was ugly. Chicago was cruel."[69] Both agree on Herrick's extensive use of the city: "Chicago is in each case a moving force in the action and represents a dynamic principle."[70] And Duffey adds; "though in later stories he occasionally used the city for a *mise en scene*, it never again became a principal theme" for Herrick.[71]

Duffey adds a major point:

> In this sense one may say that Herrick's realistic novels all took shape in the world of genteel standards. In his work the method of realism is but a logical extension of the genteel position to make it a critique of the raw and threatening American life symbolized by Chicago. And hence, one may conclude, the forces of the genteel tradition and of realism, so often opposed in American intellectual history, were on occasion made complementary to each other.[72]

Love's Dilemmas (1898) is an anthology of six Herrick short stories which analyze romantic relationships in unconventional ways not found in the popular fiction of the day. One story, set in Europe, has a lesbian relationship as part of its triangle. Secondary themes in the stories concern Chicago politics, justice and journalism.

Herrick's colleague in the Chicago English department, Robert Morss Lovett, is the author of *A Wingéd Victory* (1907), a novel about a strong woman who seems fated to take care of the weak at the expense of her own career. Dora Glenn first aids her "not right" brother; when he dies, she goes to [North] Western University to study medicine so that she can serve children. Then, taking pity on a young poet, she marries him. Finally, after the ever-weakening poet has killed himself, Dora marries a childhood friend who needs no sympathy.

Lovett wrote one other book, *Roger Gresham* (1904), then gave up whatever career he might have had as an author of fiction, and became a literary critic, historian, and a writer of essays of social protest for the *New Republic*.

A Miscellany

Chicago novelists of this decade focussed on a great many other themes — prohibition, policemen, crime, blacks, young marriage, religion, politicians,

Chicago's underworld, newsboys, utopianism, disasters, medicine and women's club work. Some of these, of course, were to become major themes for Chicago writers in later decades.

Bernie Babcock's *The Daughter of a Republican* (1900) is the first of two tract novels by this writer on the evils of liquor. Jean Thorn and her father, a Republican judge (who favors the non-committal position of the Republican Party in the late 1890s) take up opposite sides on the matter of drink.

Father Thomas McGrady's *Beyond the Black Ocean* (1901) is essentially a reprise of utopian novels and tracts of the 1890s. It features a newspaper editor who rails out at all abuses.

Emily [Mrs. Roswell Field] Wheaton's *The Russells in Chicago* (1902) appeared serially in the *Ladies Home Journal* from December 1901 to April 1902. The young Russells — he's a lawyer — create consternation among their friends by their decision to move to Chicago. In the Windy City, Alice Russell finds dirt, democracy and energetic activities; as a consequence she constantly compares Chicago with her former home, Boston: "when one is dining out, a Chicago woman, in a fit of absent-mindedness, is liable to begin blowing over the table in pursuit of soot."

After debating about the best place to live in Chicago, the Russells choose a Lake Shore home and move into proper North Shore society. One Nebraska newly-rich lady is denied similar entrance because "she doesn't know how to spend her money." Alice is finally won over to Chicago by the music of the Theodore Thomas orchestra and the luxuriousness and comfort of the Auditorium. But a meeting with Jane Addams at Hull House leads to her real reformation. She now sees all her mannered social world as a sham.

In the first two installments of *The Russells*, Mrs. Field came down hard on her home town:

> From all Alice could hear there was only one part of Chicago that was at all habitable and that was the North Side. She was told that one might as well go and live among "the submerged tenth," or in the slums, as to live on the West Side; that nobody lived there or ever had been known to live there.

Later Alice discovered that, although she had been told "the South Side was almost as hopeless as the West," the "South Side had many advantages over the North Side, socially and every other way:"

> It might really be called the literary side of Chicago. Literature may or may not count for much in the making of a city, but, like ancestors, it's a good thing to have in the family.[73]

Apparently fearing that such attacks on the city might irritate readers, the Editor appended this note to the first two installments:

> It is perhaps only just to the author to say that her aim in this serial is to show the different phases of her city exactly as they are — not with malice as

she is too good a Chicago woman for that ... In the next installment the author's purpose will be apparent with her good-natured raillery [and her] eminent fairness.[74]

George Horton's *The Long Straight Road* (1902) explores the marital relationships of two Chicago men who grew up together. One, a lawyer, married to a sensible woman, is incorruptible and on his way to Congress. The other, a real estate clerk, nephew of a congressman, is on his way to the lower depths, married to a silly, fatuous girl. The girl becomes involved with a magnate who is obviously based on Charles T. Yerkes, and with an artist. The novel satirizes clubwomen and poetry readings.

Elliott Flower's *Policeman Flynn* (1902) is a fictional account of a Mr. Dooley-like Irish policeman, but the prototype was a member of the Chicago Police department at the time. Policeman Flynn is compassionate, with a wit and dialect like Mr. Dooley, but at the same time he knows evil when he sees it.

Wesley Stanger's *Rescued From Fiery Death* (1903) is the only Chicago novel to make substantial use of a major Chicago disaster, the Iroquois Theater Fire of December 30, 1903, in which 602 people died while watching the comic Eddie Foy. Like Roe's *Barriers Burned Away*, this book uses the disaster as a catalyst to resolve the novel's romance.

James David Corrothers' *The Black Cat Club* (1902) is a collection of Negro humor and folklore, developing from the activities of "the Black Cat Club," whose roster consists of nine blacks and a cat named "Mesmerizer." The group inhabited Chicago's "Levee," the largest vice district in Chicago at the turn of the century. It was bounded by Clark Street, Wabash Avenue, and Eighteenth and Twenty-Second streets.[75]

The image projected by the book is one that Black Americans today would like to forget. Nevertheless, it "is a record of a culture that is changing rapidly and a lore that is fast disappearing."[76]

Frank Hamilton Spearman's *Dr. Bryson* (1902) is the first Chicago novel to deal substantially with medical matters. Here an ophthalmologist romances a married woman whose daughter's eyesight he has saved.

Spearman's *The Close of the Day* (1904) tells of a romance between a twenty-year-old Chicago girl with ambitions to be an opera singer and a forty-year-old bachelor millionaire. The novel's theme is similar to that of F. Scott Fitzgerald's *Tender is the Night* (1934) which also has a Chicago girl as one of its protagonists. Like Fitzgerald's Nicole Warren [Diver], Katharine Sims grows throughout the novel; like Fitzgerald's Dick Diver, George Durant declines to poverty and loss of status.

Wardon Allan Curtis's *The Strange Adventures of Mr. Middleton* (published by Herbert S. Stone & Company in 1903) is a collection of tales modeled on *The Thousand and One Nights*. Edward Middleton, a simple law clerk and a devout Methodist encounters Achmed Ben Daoud, Emir of Al-Yam one evening on South Clark Street. The Emir is looking for someone to try out a new collection of tales on before taking them back to the exotic Middle East. Middleton not only hears the tales but, as well, he has a series of strange adventures that make him wonder "about his Middleton banality and lackluster conventionalism."[77]

Agnes Surbridge's *The Confessions of a Club Woman* (1904) tells of a Kansas woman, who, knowing her only career is marriage, weds a Chicago grocer. While living with her husband in an apartment over his store, she decides her only opportunity for upward mobility is through club work. She joins a club and rises socially; eventually she and her family move to a North Shore Lake front home. She also romances a European nobleman she meets through her club.

Frances Worchester Doughty's *The Brady's Chicago Clew; or, Exposing the Board of Trade Crooks* (1904) is the next to the last of a genre of stories of crimes which were solved by Alan Pinkerton and his agents, or by fictional detectives such as "Nick Carter" and "Old Cap Collier." In the coming century these were to be replaced by new forms of the genre that were to have wide appeal and produce a major share of Chicago fiction in the next half century and beyond. In this novel the failure of the Pinkertons to solve the disappearance of several members of the Board of Trade leads them to employ a private detective, Old King Brady, whose work had been featured in a great many paperback books of the "dime novel" variety.

The last of these to have its setting in Chicago is *The Compact of Death; or, Nick Carter's Singed Hair Clew*, by the Author of "Nick Carter." This twenty-eight page book has the Chicago Mafia as its criminal element.

Marie Graham's *A Devout Bluebeard* (1900) is "a biting satire of organized religion" in which three wives of an evangelist come to untimely deaths as a consequence of their devotion to religious beliefs.[78]

Forrest Crissey's *Tattlings of a Retired Politician; Being the letter (non-partisan) of Hon. William Bradley, Ex-Governor and former veteran of practical politics, written to his friend and protege Ned, who is still busy "carving a career back in the old state,"* with illustrations by John T. McCutcheon (1904) doesn't need much more description than given in the title. Governor John P. Altgeld and Clarence Darrow are thinly disguised characters in the letters.

Grant Eugene Stevens' *Wicked City* (1906) is two books in one, *Wicked City* and *Wicked City Redeemed*. The former is fictional and tells the story of two half-brothers, one legitimate and heir to the family wealth, the other illegitimate with apparently no chances of inheritance. In the course of the story, the illegitimate brother engages in all manner of crime and debauchery. The latter book is reminiscent in its mishmash of factual material of Stead's *If Christ Came to Chicago* and anticipates some of Jack Lait's productions a decade or two later.

The anonymous *Shifting for Himself; or, The Wonderful Luck of a Street Arab* (1906) tries to do in twenty-eight pages what Horatio Alger usually took three hundred or more pages to do. It succeeds about as well as Alger did, with a diamond robbery, more good luck for the central character, and the death of his crippled friend.

Richard R. Montgomery's *That Boy Bob; or, The Diamond That Came by Express* (1909) is also a twenty-six page Horatio Alger-type story of a boy wrongly accused and finally exonerated.

In *The Mills of Mammon* (1909), James H. Brower, "an outspoken advocate of social reform," utilizes the family of a mythical steel industrialist as his means for attacking liquor, "charity, religious fanaticism, socialism, labor unions, white slavery, police corruption, politics and industrialization." Horace Holdon concentrates on making money in his steel mill, exploiting his employees at every opportunity. His wealth enables his daughter to work in the slums, helping the disadvantaged; meanwhile, his son debauches himself.[79]

Families have always enjoyed holidays in Chicago — visiting the Loop and its stores, riding the "L," viewing the Lake, touring the zoos, taking in the Fairs, spending a Sunday at the amusement parks, inspecting the exhibits at the Art Institute or the Chicago Historical Library, enjoying a baseball game or a football game. They've also enjoyed reading about such visits. That's why Wilber Herschel Williams *Uncle Bob and Aunt Becky's Strange Adventures at the World's Great Exposition* [the St. Louis World's Fair] (1904) was a popular book at the time. For all its title, the Springers, from Skowhegan, Maine, spend most of the book in Chicago. They find adventure at the Board of Trade, the stockyards, and the University of Chicago, then a dozen years old or so.

In the chronicles of baseball, the phrase "Tinker to Evers to Chance" is engraved in stone. Frank L. Chance, at first base, the third man in that phrase denoting successful "double-plays," was manager of the Chicago "Cubs" baseball team in 1910 when he wrote *The Bride and the Pennant: The Greatest Story in the History of America's National Game, True to Life, Intensely Interesting*. Charles A. Comiskey, the White Sox President wrote the preface and a Chicago book publishing firm, Laird and Lee, published the book. The novel tells of the star pitcher for the University of Chicago baseball team who flunks out of school in his senior year and is hired by a New Orleans baseball team. However, much of the action takes place in Chicago where the deciding games for the league pennant are played.

Baseball fans, familiar with today's baseball, will find the 1910 version fascinatingly different.

Gale Richards' *Link Rover in Chicago; or, Making Things Fairly Hum* (1905) is a paperback account of a young man, the family "black sheep," who, while on a vist to Chicago, is offered a job as an entertainer. In twenty-eight pages, he becomes the star of the show and has several adventures as well.

Jack London's *The Iron Heel* (1907) is a tract-like expression of the adventure novelist's socialist philosophies. It is a utopian novel set six hundred years into the next millenium. The story is about two revolts, planned in California and carried out, in the latter part of the book, in Chicago.

Summary

And so the decade ended, having produced the beginnings of a "Chicago school of fiction" which was to become more homogeneous and important in the second decade of the new century. The philosophy of genteelism had not only protested against the crass moneymaking interests of Chicago, but had also contested with the philosophies of realism and romanticism for the public's attention. Romanticism had garnered the lion's share of the public attention and purse, genteelism had endured, and realism had gotten a "corner" on the attention of the major literary figures. As well, a new kind of author, the university English teacher had appeared; he was to be a constant in the century and was ultimately to influence the style and subject matter of serious fiction.

In the next, perhaps Chicago's greatest literary decade, a new concept, bohemianism, which had been making its way westward from Europe for some time, and which had already had a slight impact on Chicago, was to become a major philosophy in the "Windy City," and was to help Chicago earn the title of "the literary capitol of the United States." The westward literary movement was about to establish itself as a major force in American literature.

The catalyst for this new movement may well have been an emigrant from Ireland, Francis Hackett.

VIII.
The Literary Capitol of the United States

"Oh, Paul," she exclaimed after a silence, "I am very proud of you — not because you are tall and strong and straight, not because of your mere envelope, but because you, yourself, the inside of you, is fine and purposeful and inspiring. The body after all is but the hired carriage in which the spirit is transferred across the City of Today from the station Past, to the station Future."[1]

The Studio World

Ralph Fletcher Seymour says that after the Auditorium was opened in 1889, to the north in the Fine Arts Building, and in the new Art Institute across "Boul Mich, the finest street in the world," there was created "a district wherein the musicians, artists, book lovers, actors, dancers and craftsmen gathered and established themselves." The Athenaeum to the west, "a plain five story brick building . . . was filled with [more] studios" as well as "art schools, shops, and one of the significant, old art clubs, the Palette and Chisel. The *Dial* . . . moved its quarters there."[2]

Although artists and dilettantes continued to meet on occasion in Gold Coast homes such as those of the Aldises and the Gerstenbergs, there came about a lessening of interest in the old literary clubs, and a rise in the growth of activities centered around performances, exhibits and studio activities. Contributing to this movement to Michigan Avenue may have been the fact that although artists and performers had been invited to homes of Chicago society people, they had not been permitted to become part of the society — they were always outsiders, entertainers.[3]

In these studios, the aesthetic aspect of the Chicago genteel movement was to crescendo in the second decade of the twentieth century.

One of these studios, where W. W. Denslow had drawn the illustrations for Baum's *Father Goose, His Book* and *The Wizard of Oz*, became a rendezvous for George Ade, Franke Holme and Ade's Indiana college-days friends, John and George McCutcheon. An attraction was the free lunch served almost daily by Mrs. Denslow.

Frank Holme was suffering from tuberculosis, and Ade and John McCutcheon created the Bandarlog Press as a means of assisting him financially. Mark Twain was another supporter. Holme designed, illustrated, printed and bound fine editions of "little books." George Ade's Chicago *Record* columns supplied the text for three of a proposed seven volumes of "The Strenuous Lad's Library." The material was written for adults, not boys, and poked fun at Ade's contemporaries.

The slender volumes, *Handsome Cyril; or, the Messenger Boy With the Warm Feet, Clarence Allen, the Hypnotic Boy Journalist; or, The Mysterious Disappearance of the United States Government Bonds,* and *Rollo Johnson, the Boy Inventor; or, The Demon Bicycle and Its Demon Rider* were published in 1903 in Phoenix, Arizona, where Holme had gone in hopes of improving his health.

The social groups which met occasionally in some of the Michigan Avenue and adjacent studios were named for books written by Chicagoans: "The Little Room," and "The Cliff-dwellers."

Francis Hackett, a "brash young Irishman," who had become literary editor of the Chicago *Evening Post's Friday Literary Review* in 1905, recalled that when he arrived in Chicago, "the Little Room" was a polite islet in brawling Chicago . . . and Miss Clara Laughlin, literature shimmering for her afar, bright across black water, officiated:

> A tame, leonine veteran, Franklin Head, received court from his juniors. Lorado Taft, the sculptor, inclined attentively, his profile mournful and sublime. Henry Fuller fluttered about, a white moth, even his wispy beard evasive, but from under his deprecating dots and dashes, his deploring submission to the juggernaut, he shot incriminating darts of intelligence, gently absolute in his perceptiveness, half-dissenting, half-purring. Hamlin Garland was pacific and benign. An equable presence, he had known the rolling prairie and had enough of it, another kind of juggernaut, but his aquiline dignity and keen glance from under bushy brows had not been impaired. Emerson Hough glinted his ax, swinging it around as briskly as "Fifty-four Forty or Fight," letting the chips hit you in the eye.[4]

In 1907, Garland, who claimed to have founded the Little Room, a claim not supported by some, had organized the Cliff Dweller's Club from among the male members of the Little Room. Its name came not only from Fuller's novel, but also from its lofty location on the top floor of Orchestra Hall, at the heart of the Michigan Avenue cultural complex.* Fuller, incidentally, had refused to join.

The Club's purpose was to increase the status of writers and artists. But it became, as it is today, a "comfortable urban club," not unlike the Chicago Club a block and a half away.

With one exception, that is. That exception came once when Garland was absent from the club rooms. His "austere views" about serving cocktails and wines in the club rooms forced imbibers to procure their refreshments in a bar in an adjacent building, a sanctuary reached by a bridge from the top floor of the Hall. On the day that Garland failed to appear as scheduled, some of the rowdier members ordered a serving cart brought to the club from the bar. Then one, holding a cocktail in his hand, jumped to a table top, removed Garland's portrait from the wall, and replaced it with a hastily-lettered sign proclaiming: THIS PLACE UNDER NEW MANAGEMENT![6]

The Little Room lost *its* usefulness long before its 1931 closing. Its only artifacts today, in addition to the printed memoirs of many of its literate members, are old issues of its quasi-official publication, titled *Art* from 1912 to 1914 and the *Trimmed Lamp* untils its suspension in May of 1916. Edited by Howard Vincent O'Brien and others, both published poetry by Vachel Lindsay, Mary Aldis, Helen Hoyt, Margaret Widdemer, and Amy Lowell, and some criticism by John Gould Fletcher.

There are major treatments of this studio world in *Under the Skylights* and *The Charlatans*. Lesser treatments are in *The Long Straight Road, The Pit, The Common Lot, Waste, The Sherrods, John Dorn, Promoter, A Winged Victory, The Girl Who Lived in the Woods, The "Genius"*, and *The Song of the Lark*. A good non-fictional account is in Ralph Fletcher Seymour's *Some Went This Way* (1945).

Chicago Little Theater

The Little Theater movement in Chicago and in all likelihood in America began, not among the aesthetes and dilettantes of the Gold Coast or the studio world, but in the much more unlikely Hull House which had been founded to "uplift" residents of the Chicago ghetto. "It is nearly half a generation since Laura Dainty Pelham established the Hull House Players and laid the first foundation of what is known as the Little Theater," Maurice Browne wrote in 1913. "Our future dramatic historian ... will certainly record the fact that Chicago was the first city in America where the movement came into active being, not only with the work of Mrs.

*Emmet Dedmon says that the club was named, not for Fuller's novel, but for "the cliff-dwelling Indians in the Southwest."[5]

Pelham, but also, a few years later, with the plucky and thorough pioneering of Donald Robertson and the earliest experiments of the Chicago Theater Society."[7]

It was the Hull House Theater which introduced Francis Hackett and his assistant literary editor, Floyd Dell to Chicago. It produced plays which were intellectual rather than "arty," plays by Galsworthy, Masefield and St. John Irvine. It has continued through the years; in the late 1960s, its members were experimenting with improvisational theater.

In 1900, Anna Morgan was using her Michigan Avenue studio to teach "elocution" and dramatic art, and to rehearse production of plays by Shaw, Ibsen and Maeterlinck. Her group was the first in America to produce *Candida*. William Archer's praise of this production led to a friendship between Morgan and Shaw, and to the Chicago staging of Shaw's *Caesar and Cleopatra*. Henry Blake Fuller's Maeterlinck-like fantasy, *The Puppet Booth*, (1896) was also staged. Harriet Monroe wrote five verse plays for Morgan's troupe and published them in *The Passing Show* (1903). One of them, "It Passes By," is set in Chicago.

Duffey says that Morgan's "activities were among the earliest in America to suggest the nature of the later little theater movement."[8] Actually, as Duffey and others have shown, Morgan's theater, with its emphasis on the "artiness" of playwrights such as Maeterlinck, tended more in the direction of the art theater.

What little theaters were attempting is indicated by Susan Glaspell's remarks in *The Road to the Temple* (1926) about the commercial theater of that time:

> We went to the theater, and for the most part we came away wishing we had gone somewhere else. Those were the days when Broadway flourished almost unchallenged. Plays, like magazine stories, were patterned. They might be pretty good within themselves, seldom did they open out to — where it surprised or thrilled your spirit to follow. They didn't ask much of you, those plays. Having paid for your seat, the thing was all done for you, and your mind went out where it came in, only tireder. An audience . . . had imagination. What was this "Broadway," which could make a thing as interesting as life into a thing as dull as a Broadway play?[9]

The Little Theater movement was to continue to flourish in Chicago, its participants changing with the generations. At Hull House, plays were less "arty," more in the "realistic" tradition. Plays were produced there by Oren Taft, Jr.; by Mary Aldis (who also had a theater at her Gold Coast home); by Kenneth Sawyer Goodman (for whom the Goodman Theater at the Art Institute is named); by Ben Hecht; and by Martyn Johnson.

Meanwhile, in 1911, Maurice Browne, an impecunious Englishman with a European Don Juan reputation, came to Chicago in search of money and Ellen Van Volkenburg, a Chicago girl he had met overseas. He became engaged to Ellen and for a while posed as an expert on poetry. But when Ellen took an interest in drama, Browne founded a Little Theatre. Soon, with an amateur cast and borrowed funds he produced the classic *The Trojan Women*. The production was to have far-reaching influences, particularly on Susan Glaspell and George Cram Cook who had followed Floyd Dell to Chicago, and the Washington Square Players of New York City. Glaspell and Cook went east to form the Provincetown Players, to write, produce and act in plays, and to help change the course of American theater.

Browne also brought the famed Irish Players to Chicago. "There were excitements in Chicago just then," said Glaspell. "The Irish Players. Quite possibly there would have been no Provincetown Players had there been no Irish Players."[10]

Two of the better original plays produced for Browne's troupe were Marjorie Seiffert's *The Old Woman* and Cloyd Head's *Grotesques*, the latter, according to Harriet Monroe "the Chicago Little Theater's finest and most original production."[11] But there were not enough good playwrights in Chicago, so Browne turned to European plays, including plays written by Synge and Strindberg.

Theodore Dreiser had seen one of the performances of *The Trojan Women* with Edgar Lee Masters and Floyd Dell. Dell praised the production for its "sheer beauty of scene and gesture and voice."[12] Dreiser became infatuated with Elaine Hyman, playing Andromache, and wrote her into *The Titan* as Stephanie Platow, a Russian Jewess-South American. In the novel, Stephanie is a member of a Chicago little theater group performing Greek drama, and in love with a "young, smug, handsome" theater critic, a character based on Floyd Dell. The troupe's director, modeled after Browne, is a "smooth-faced, pasty-souled artist, a rake at heart, a subtle seducer of women." Dreiser, himself, appears as an aspiring journalist — "tall, fair, passionate" — at the moment making his living as a collector of furniture installments. Chicagoans who were theater *aficionados* had great fun unmasking *The Titan's* characters.[13]

"It was good to know Maurice Browne and the people of the Little Theatre who were putting on Greek plays," said Susan Glaspell, "pleasant to hear the good stories of Sherwood Anderson, who had a trunkful of novels somebody might one day publish, agreeable [to be invited to] dinners at the Dells', [and have] all-night talks with Theodore Dreiser and Arthur Ficke."[14]

In 1916, another "high-aiming" theater venture, the Players' Workshop, was formed in one of the 57th Street studios left over from the Columbian

Exposition. Supervised by Elizabeth Bingham, it produced plays by members of the "Chicago Renaissance" group — Maxwell Bodenheim, Ben Hecht, Kenneth Sawyer Goodman, Elisha Cook and Alice Gerstenberg. Hecht's play, "Dregs," drew the wrath of Chicago clergy who somehow found out about it.[15]

There were little theaters all over Chicago. Gerstenberg's "The Unseen" was produced at the Playshop Theater in the Edgewater Beach Hotel; her "The Buffer" at Grace Hickox's Studios; her "Hearts" at Anna Morgan's studio; her "The Pot Boiler" at the Players' Workshop. "The Menu" was done at the Romany Club, "Upstage" at the Ravinia Workshop and at the Jack and Jill Theatre. Her "Latchkeys" was played on the staircase of the Gerstenberg home at 1120 Lakeshore Drive.

Gerstenberg's plays were collected in *Ten One-Act Plays* (1921) and *Comedies All* (1930); Goodman's in *Quick Curtains* (1923) and *More Quick Curtains* (1923).

Goodman and Hecht collaborated on five plays (collected just after Goodman's death [in 1918 in World War I] in *The Wonder Hat and Other One Act Plays* [1925], with a prefatory note by Thomas Wood Stevens of the Drama Department at the Art Institute). Of these, "An Idyll of the Shops" was Hecht's at least in its inception, and the only one of the five set in Chicago.

The play takes place in a small garment factory loft on the Chicago West Side. It concentrates on a romantic interlude during which Louis Mendelsohn, a sewing machine operator asks Yetta Labowsky, a second operator to marry him. But a few minutes later, the factory owner discharges Louis because Louis has spoiled a garment on which he should have been focussing his attention. Louis leaves, his romance destroyed; Yetta and Sadie, a skirt finisher who is obviously dying of tuberculosis, return to their work.

Stevens' preface anticipates the performance of this play and the others in the just-then-newly-opened Goodman Memorial Theater, attached to the rear of the Art Institute. Funds for the building had been provided by Goodman's father, a millionaire Chicago lumberman.

But the Little Theatre movement in Chicago produced no great plays, primarily because, aside from Goodman, in his "Back of the Yards," the playwrights attempted no great subjects. And "Back of the Yards" suffers because its theme deserved more space than the one act Goodman gave it.

The play has a distinctive Chicago setting, the slum area (sometimes called "Canaryville") adjacent to the west side of the Chicago Union stockyards and packing house district which had also been the setting for *The Jungle*.

A policeman has come to a slum house to arrest a boy for complicity in an attempted hold-up which led to the murder of a victim. A priest has come with him to break the news to the boy's mother. In the home, during the absence of the unsuspecting mother, the policeman and the priest debate the causes for the boy's delinquency. Each comments about the failure of the other's institution to prevent juvenile delinquencies. Neither has a good solution to the problem.

Secondly, the little theatre groups were more interested in production and acting than in writing, a characteristic of other later little theater groups other than the Provincetown and Washington Square Players, both of which preferred to write their own plays. In the 1920s, only Ben Hecht, of the Chicago Little Theater movement would write a major play — and he would have the help of a fellow journalist, also destined to become a major figure in American drama and films.

Thirdly, a great many of the people who took part in theatrical activities were busy with other affairs. Anna Morgan, for example, reports that seven of the nine characters in one performance were either writers or artists, and that sixteen of the thirty-four characters in another performance were either artists, editors or writers.[16]

Finally, it is obvious that most of these people were dilettantes rather than serious professionals. The records they left behind of the social life in the Attic Club, the Little Room, the Cliff-Dwellers and the Whitechapel Club describe the intensive social relationships among these people. There must have been little energy left for the work of writing, acting, directing, painting, drawing, or whatever.

With the exception of Lorado Taft and perhaps one or two others, the serious work done during this studio period of Chicago cultural history was done by writers.

Book Publishing in the Second Decade

"In Washington Street between Clark and LaSalle," says Ben Hecht, "was a large store window reading 'Covici—McGee—Booksellers.'" Because Pascal Covici, "a tall shapely man with a Punchinello handsomeness," and Billy McGee, "a gentle and scholarly man," were also book publishers, operating the latter business from a solitary desk "wedged into the basement catacombs," their bookstore became a "Mecca of the arts." Any Chicago writer of any consequence could be found there, and Covici-McGee published many of their books, becoming for a time a major Chicago book publisher, along with Herbert S. Stone. The Covici-McGee firm later moved to New York City. Stone died in the *Lusitania* sinking in 1915.[17]

Chicago Journalists

Many journalists who became writers as well came to Chicago in these years. Some of them stayed: Henry Kitchell Webster, a native of Evanston;

Will Payne, Howard Vincent O'Brien, Henry Justin Smith, Richard Henry Little, Fanny Butcher, Lloyd Lewis. Others moved on: Hecht, Charles MacArthur, John Gunther, George Cram Cook, Harry Hansen, Henry Blackman Sell, Hackett, Dell, Glaspell, Ferber, Garland and Sandburg.

"Generally speaking," said Kenny Jackson Williams, "the artist in Chicago recognized the futility of remaining in the city . . .

> Like Garland, most of the writers eventually moved to sections of the country supposedly more hospitable to the artist and his creativity. Their answer to the . . . materialism of Chicago was to get away as soon as they discovered that the cultural promise of the city had . . . declined into perpetual bigger and better business weeks. Others unhappily remained. Robert Herrick sank into the direst pessimism and hated the city . . . Others moved in for a short while, like Upton Sinclair, picked one aspect of Chicago's life and held it up with microscopic precision while they, too, ranted about the cancerous growths being fostered on American Society.[18]

Some of the journalists wrote about life as a journalist, some did not. Joseph Medill Patterson's *Rebellion* (1911) is a novel about the failure of a Catholic marriage, owing to the husband's alcoholism, and the problems the wife faces because she feels bound to the Catholic doctrine about divorce. At novel's end, however, she divorces her husband and marries a young Indiana insurance executive. "It is Chicago, the great city, the focus of modernity, which takes hold of [the wife] and makes her marry the man she loves," said Floyd Dell, "[Chicago] that makes her discard the religion in which she has been reared, and all the customs of her people, in order to do it."[19]

Howard Vincent O'Brien, author of a column "All Things Considered," and a book by the same title, had two books in this decade, one about labor and one about journalism. *New Men for Old* (1914) apparently suffered a similar fate to that of *Sister Carrie;* its publisher, after printing and binding the sheets, decided not to issue the book because of its "attitude toward Labor." That attitude plainly favors collective bargaining on the part of a humanitarian management and a responsible union, although it opposes "chaps . . . who belong to the I.W.W. and stick monkey wrenches in the wheels, and ain't never satisfied." "The whole purpose of the story," one critic noted, "is to show that the only real satisfaction in life lies in work." He thought the book might better have been published with its original title, *The Joy of Working.*[20] However that may be, the person who finds the most joy in working, in the novel, is the hero, who, within a few months after leaving an art studio in Paris, has become the successful manager of a Chicago food products company.

O'Brien's *Thirty* (1915), as the title implies, is a novel about newspaper work. Brent Good of *The Workman's World* comes to the home of Judith and

Roger Wynrod to ask what Judith plans to do about the deaths of twenty-two women and children in an Illinois coal mine strike. Judith's response is to buy a Chicago newspaper and install Brent as editor and Roger as business manager. When the paper prints a story about a strike of department store salesgirls, the store withdraws its advertising — but changes its mind because unless it advertises its business falls off. Good finally leaves the newspaper, and Judith, a wealthy heiress, plans to marry the vicar of an Episcopal church. The novel is poorly structured and depends too much on coincidence.

Jack Lait, a Chicago journalist, was a twentieth century successor to "Shang" Andrews, writing often-lurid accounts of Chicago's underworld. Like Ade and Finley Peter Dunne, he put books together by reprinting his newspaper columns. Like the early Edna Ferber, he employs a formula similar to that used by O. Henry.

The merit of his *Beef, Iron and Wine* (1916) is that it suggests that Chicago has a rich heritage of unwritten stories. Lait's characters are cub reporters, taxi drivers, chorus girls, ex-convicts, and detectives.

Gus the Bus and Evelyn, The Exquisite Checker (1917) is a collection unified by its focus on two people: a cafe busboy from Schleswig-Holstein, torn between his sympathies for his native land and his new land as World War I unfolds. Like other Chicago novels of this period, Lait's book shows the process of Americanization and the problems faced by recent Chicago immigrants from Germany.

Henry Justin Smith was for fifty years the distinguished editor of the Chicago *Daily News* (1886-1936) and an historian as well, but when he came to write novels, his ambitions, according to one of his critics, were "in excess of his ability."[21] In his *The Other Side of the Wall* (1919), he attempts to deal with two groups of people — those who inhabit the fashionable eight-room-three-bathroom apartments in the "Fannington," and those who dwell on the other side of a separating wall in the shabby "Fannington Annex." Smith uses an embezzlement, a suicide, a fistful of scandals, and the military discipline consequent to World War I to translift some of the Annex's residents to the Fannington — from a mean life to a life of great comfort. Smith's critics found the tale unbelievable. But Smith must have known something of military life — the training camp chapters set in nearby Fort Sheridan are the best part of the book. The setting is "the City of Deadly Ambitions" — but it's obviously Chicago.

Journalistic Criticism

The solid literary accomplishment of Chicago journalists in this decade came in the area of literary criticism. On March 5, 1909, the publishers of the Chicago *Evening Post,* a newspaper appealing primarily to business men, almost doubled the number of the pages of their daily paper with a literary supplement, the *Friday Literary Review.* The *Review's* editor was Francis Hackett, a young Irish emigré, then just newly-arrived in Chicago. His assistant was an even younger migrant from Iowa who had recently come to Chicago looking for some sort of writing job — Floyd Dell. The two men were destined to make a reputation as writers of literary criticism.

"Criticism was indeed dreary in those days," said Susan Glaspell,[22] but even in a livelier critical period Hackett would have become recognized as a leading book critic. For one thing, he refused to be bought off by expense-paid tours of Eastern publishing establishments. As he himself said, he wrote reviews without reference to anything but the merits of the books in question. "If commercial pressure should by any chance endanger his job, he would rather dig ditches than compromise his integrity."[23]

But Hackett was not entirely objective. "As a point of honor," said Dale Kramer, an historian of the Chicago Renaissance, "Hackett praised the novelists who lambasted Chicago's rulers to the hilt, and then, lest he might seem to be pulling his punches, drove the knife deeper."[24] Among those Chicago novelist-critics Hackett praised was Robert Herrick.

After three years, Hackett went back east to New York City, and Dell became the *Review* editor. Dell promptly sent to Davenport for his former employer on an Iowa vegetable farm, George Cram Cook, and appointed him his assistant. Later, Harry Hansen, also of Davenport, who had replaced Sell as critic for the *Daily News,* replaced Dell.

They were an odd couple, the twenty-five year old Dell and Cook, the vegetable farmer, who is today buried at Delphi on Mount Parnassus. When the older Cook had first seen the poems of the seventeen-year old Dell, he had asked the librarian who showed them to him: "How do you explain the fact that you have this morning neglected to run the flag up over the public library?"[25]

Cook had himself once said, "I sometimes wonder if literary critics aren't as solemn a fraud as the United States Supreme Court," but, says his biographer, Cook "himself was not a solemn fraud as literary critic, nor was the *Friday Literary Review* ... solemn or a fraud."[26]

Cook's criticism was often a report of the spiritual experience he had had reading a book: "The rising from the earth into the air of the various types of aircraft is like the rising of the various types of winged creatures — flying-fish, flying-lizard, old tooth-jawed bird, and the flying-squirrel, which does not fly with wings but on its membraneous spread planes glides."[27]

Dell wrote about these Chicago years in his fictional autobiography, *Moon-Calf* (1920) and his actual autobiography, *Homecoming* (1933):

To Felix Fay (the fictional hero of *Moon-Calf*) as surely as for Dell, Chicago was symbol of new-found freedom and of the "real world." To go there was to stop being 'Felix Fay, the fool, the poet, the theorist.' It was to become a 'young man of action,' to test one's ability to confront the hard facts of life, to discover its meaning, if any, and to come to grips with it ... Flexi faces Chicago with a clean slate, armed with only a 'paper sword' of introduction. Once in the city, he finds that 'the points of the compass seemed ... to have got strangely twisted,' but in this geographical meandering, Felix not only experiences a growing awareness of self and expanding sensibilities, but he also achieves success both as dramatic critic and in marriage. With a background that unites staunch individualism and social purpose, Felix dreams of reform: in Chicago perhaps he will be 'destined to help bring back to English fiction its lost candour, the candour of the Elizabethans and Defoe and Fielding.' To a moon-calf idealist Chicago was neither escape or retreat; it was a unique and genuine experience, even if sometimes very painful. Bohemian villages have always had posers and fakes, but for some it was a true way of life.[28]

In 1916, the leadership in journalistic reviewing passed to the *Daily News*, whose news editor, Henry Justin Smith, often evaluated his reporters on the basis of the books he saw them reading at their desks. Henry Blackman Sell, "a personable, somewhat brash young man, an ex-furniture promoter" persuaded Charles H. Dennis, the editor, to let him edit a book section, provided young Sell could sell enough advertising to make the venture pay. Sell, an entrepreneur as well as a cogent reviewer, lived up to his name and in time the *News* book section would carry as many as ten pages of copy.

The books sent to Sell by publishers were parceled out among *News* staffers, each of whom got a thirty-five cent lunch at Schlogl's, a nearby restaurant, in payment for his review. The noon luncheons at which staffers discussed the books they were reading became the basis for the famed round-table which in time began to attract literati from throughout the Chicago area and from points east and west. The "regulars" included Keith Preston, a Northwestern University professor, who translated "dirty poems of the old Romans;" Burton Rascoe; Harry Hansen, who in 1919 replaced Sell; Lew Sarett, Sherwood Anderson, Edgar Lee Masters, Carl Sandburg, Ben Hecht, Henry Justin Smith, John T. McCutcheon.

One of Sell's innovatons was the "multiple review." If those at the Friday luncheons thought highly of a book, several reviews would follow, each with a different slant.[29]

Ringgold (Ring) Lardner, Jr.

A more significant figure on the American literary scene was Ring Lardner, Jr. Reared in Niles, Michigan, the son of a family of wealth and comfort, he developed two interests — baseball and writing. In 1907, following the trail of his two loves, he got a job as sports-writer for the Chicago *Inter-Ocean,* where he met the immortal Walter Eckersall, the first of the great sports writers of this century. A year later he went to the *Tribune,* the largest of Chicago's eight dailies. Soon, Lardner's by-line appeared on the *Tribune's* sports page alongside those of Eckersall, Jim Corbett, the world's heavyweight boxing champ and Battling Nelson, another fighter. The city editor was Walter Howey, later to be immortalized in Ben Hecht's and Charles MacArthur's *The Front Page;* Lucian Cary, Marquis James, James O'Donnell Bennett, Floyd Gibbons and Edward J. Doherty were writers. "B.L.T." was there, and Finley Peter Dunne was writing a Sunday "Mr. Dooley" piece. Robert Burns Peattie, whose wife was Elia W. Peattie, was literary editor, to be succeeded by Burton Rascoe, who discarded reviews of Peattie's romantic favorites (Harold Bell Wright, Gene Stratton Porter, Eleanor H. Porter) in favor of reviews of the good young new writers. Richard Henry Little was another writer, Percy Hammond and Burns Mantle the drama critics. Harriet Monroe was writing a column on art; Lillian Russell and Laura Jean Libbey were other columnists. The organizer and guiding genius for all this was Joseph Medill Patterson, father of "Cissy" Patterson, socialite and occasional author of autobiographical fiction.

Lardner's *Own Your Own Home* (1916) was a series of four stories originally written for *Red Book.* The stories are told through a series of letters from one Fred Gross, a Chicago detective, to his brother Charley. The world of the stories is that of the ambitious new middle class which came in the nineteen-twenties, here foreseen by Lardner — the social climbing, the attempts to outdo one's neighbors.

The same character traits are shown in *Gullible's Travels* (1916), but here the central characters are seen through the eyes of a sardonic narrator who comments on the action and characters, and is contemptuous of the social life of the middle class:

> Carmen ain't no regular musical show where a couple o' Yids comes out and pulls a few lines o' dialogue and then a girl and a he-flirt sings a song that ain't got nothin' to do with it. *Carmen's* a regular play, only instead o' them sayin' the lines, they sing them, and in for'n languages so's the actors can pick up some loose change offen the sale o' the liberettos. The music was wrote by George S. Busy, and it must of kept him that way about two months . . . The first act opens up somewhere in Spain, about the corner o' Chicago Avenue and Wells. On one side o' the stage they's a pill mill where the employees is all girls, or was girls a few years ago.[30]

You Know Me Al (1916) and "Alibi Ike" (1915) are Lardner's best baseball stories. The novel, consisting of letters written by Jack Keefe to a friend back in his home town, originally ran serially in Lorimer's *Saturday Eve-*

ning Post. In *Treat 'Em Rough; Letters From Jack the Kaiser Killer* (1918), Keefe is at Camp Grant, Illinois. From there he writes letters about army life to his friend, Al.

"Alibi Ike" features a Chicago Cubs player who rationalizes every experience. Eventually this habit almost costs him his fiancee.

Alibi Ike was filmed in 1935 with Joe E. Brown as "Ike" and Olivia De Havilland as his girl. Leonard Maltin calls it an "ingratiating film, Joe E. Brown's best," but other critics wished the scriptwriters hadn't tried to improve on Lardner's story.[31]

Lardner, the subject of several biographies, is the model for Abe North in F. Scott Fitzgerald's *Tender Is the Night* (1934).

Romanticists and Sentimentalists

The world of the Chicago journalist was that of the newspaper editorial rooms, the streets outside congested with traffic, and, when day's work was done, a favorite bar. A mile or so north on Lake Shore drive fronting the Lake north of Oak Street was the "Gold Coast" where the "mansions of millionaires" and "homes of the great merchants formed an uninterrupted line of sumptuous dwellings."[32] In 1910, Janet Ayer "Birdie" Fairbank, daughter of one of these mercantile aristocrats and wife of Kellogg "Ked" Fairbank, another, brought these two worlds together with a series of sketches in the *Record-Herald.* The Chicago poet, bookstore owner and publisher, A. C. McClurg, brought out these sentimental glances at a life few Chicagoans had ever known in "a pleasingly printed and illustrated book" with the title *In Town, and Other Conversations.* "She showed us the way," her sister, Margaret Ayer Barnes was to comment twenty years later after Margaret's novel, *Years of Grace* had won a Pulitzer Prize.[33]

In the same year, a quite different world, that of the "sparrows" of Chicago at the very bottom of the social, economic and cultural society, was described by Clara Elizabeth Laughlin in her *Just Folks.* This book and *The Penny Philanthropist* (1912), are more than the books of "good cheer" she had written earlier, but they still have a sentimental quality. The first novel tells about Beth Tully, a probation officer of the Juvenile Court (founded only a decade earlier), a young woman of 25, a "sentimentalist." Around her are Poles, Irish, laborers, a labor organizer. It is a world of almost unbelievable poverty, ignorance and superstition. Dorothy Dondore calls this novel the earliest (if not the only one) which deals with the work of a probation officer in the ghetto of West Halsted and Maxwell Avenues.[34]

Peggy, the heroine of the second book, lives in the same neighborhood. She runs a news emporium, and as a good deed, sets aside a penny a day from her slender means (she is the sole support of her family) to help someone in more serious straits.

Donald Richberg's *The Shadow Men* (1911) shows a young man who "possesses neither the strength of character to shun wrongdoing nor the tragic flaw necessary to impel him into a life of crime."[35] He is expelled from college when he attempts to ameliorate the consequences of a friend's prank. Later, in the world of business, he again and again is used as a pawn by associates. A slight romance does little to make the story more believable.

Richberg's *In the Dark* (1912) is a mystery-romance which mixes nineteenth-century characters, affairs and social concerns and twentieth-century setting of automobiles, extension phones and electric lights. The protagonist is a Chicago bondsman who becomes involved in the affairs of a young lady in distress.[36]

Jennette Barbour Perry Lee's *Mr. Achilles* (1912) is a sentimental tale relating the consequences of a chance meeting between Achilles Alexandrakis, a Clark Street fruit store owner, only six months from Greece, and the affluent Harrises of North Shore Drive.

When the Harris's small daughter is kidnapped, the Harrises refuse to pay the ransom sum on the grounds they want to discourage other kidnappings of children of the well-to-do! Although the girl is held almost a month, Achilles, who has learned to drive an automobile in this age of transition to the horseless carriage, manages to rescue her. The novel is a far distance from Meyer Levin's *Compulsion,* a novel of a later Chicago kidnapping.

The hero of John T. McCutcheon's *Dawson '11 — Fortune Hunter* (1913, but first appearing serially in the *Tribune*) is a college graduate who is trying to make his way in Chicago by working hard and avoiding the temptations set before him by his fellow-workers. The somewhat sentimental book avoids the polarized evil-and-good structures of the Alger novels. At the end, Dawson is heading back to the small town from which he came.

Dawson '11 is another epistolary novel, written in the form of letters home, and illustrated by McCutcheon, one of America's great newspaper cartoonists. The pictures, as one critic noted, almost tell the stories in themselves.[37]

In Maude Radford Warren's *The Main Road* (1913) another Wisconsin girl follows Carrie and Rose to Chicago from a farm. But Janet Bellamy, who knows little of the world except what she has read in novels, comes to the University of Chicago. An intelligent girl who quickly adapts to a variety of situations, she has an unhappy love affair, spends a season in Chicago society, becomes an active suffragette for a brief period, then an activist in the labor movement, followed by life in a settlement house. Except for factory work or a role as a department store clerk, Janet experiences about every opportunity open to a woman in Chicago in the first decade of the new century.

Elia Wilkinson Peattie, a *Tribune* reporter and Margaret Anderson's nemesis under the *nom de plume* of "Sade Iverson"[38] has several book publications in this decade. *The Precipice* (1914) tells of a girl graduate from the University of Chicago who leaves her small town existence to become a settlement worker in Chicago. There she discovers just how downtrodden the American woman was.

Lotta Embury of Peattie's *Lotta Embury's Career* (1915), a book "written expressly for girls," is the daughter of a small town Iowa storekeeper who comes to Chicago to pursue a career in music. Realizing that her reach has exceeded her grasp, she returns to Iowa.

Ralph Fletcher Seymour, the Chicago artist, book designer and printer, published Peattie's short story *The Angel With a Broom* (1915) in book form. The setting is a street of small shops during the early part of World War I; the "angel" is a social worker who cares for a handicapped young man. Only 700 copies were printed of this now rare and beautiful book.

Clara Louise [Root] Burnham was the daughter of Dr. George F. Root, the author of the popular war song, "Tramp, tramp, tramp, the boys are marching." From 1881 to 1925 she wrote twenty-five novels, only two of which are set in Chicago. *Instead of the Thorn* (1916) was the second of these. It is a romance between the pampered daughter of a Chicago banker who loses his wealth and a young business man. It is, says a critic, "a good portrayal of Chicago's carefree and mobile rich during the early twentieth century."[39]

Herman Gastrell Seely's *A Son of the City; A Story of Boy Life* (1917) is another of those novels of a boy's existence at a time when "to be young was very heaven." Seely's lad is a fortunate fourth-grader in a turn-of-the-century Chicago residential area.

Emerson Hough, an Iowa author of historical romances, set his *The Man Next Door* (1917) on the Gold Coast. "Pyramus and Thisbe without the lion," said one critic of this romance resulting from the transplanting of a millionaire Wyoming ranch couple to Lake Shore Drive. The family, with an attractive daughter, moves into one of those crenellated, turreted Tudor castles next door to an old Chicago family which resents the intrusion of this gauche troupe. The resentment, however, is not shared by the older family's "hired man" — who, of course, turns out to be the handsome son with the usual consequences. "Untrue, insignificant, and generally uninteresting," concluded the critic.[40]

Mary Hastings Bradley's *The Wine of Astonishment* (1919) is as timely as the War with Germany which had just ended; a sub-plot relates a romance between a Chicago girl and a German-American boy and allows the author to present both sides of the German debate. In the main plot, a young man from Chicago's deteriorating West Side meets a girl from the affluent North

Side. Through a series of coincidences he loses her, almost gets her again, loses her, finally wins her. During the interval, the girl enters into a "companionate marriage" with the Other Man.

Edwin Balmer's *Ruth of the U.S.A.* (1919) tells how a Chicago office worker fulfilled her wish to do something for the Allied effort in World War I. She gets a lot of help from her creator.

Katharine Reynolds' *Green Valley* utilizes a western surburban setting which is probably Lombard. This ultra-sweet romance is in part a prohibition tract, particularly appropriate to its year of publication, 1919.

Florence [Jeannette Baier] Ward was to be a prolific but minor Chicago author in the next few years. Her first Chicago book, *The Singing Heart* (1919) is a simple-minded romance whose central character is the non-talented member of a very talented family. Her one ambition seems to be wrapped up in the frequently-uttered "when I marry." Then a young man shows up and shows her that she also has some fine qualities. This book also is set in a Chicago suburb — a second indication of the outward growth of Chicago at this time.

Edna Ferber in Chicago

In 1911, there appeared what seemed at first a modest talent in a midwestern Jewish girl's novel, *Dawn O'Hara: The Girl Who Laughed,* written while its author, Edna Ferber, was employed as a reporter for *The Milwaukee Journal*. Ferber had been born in Kalamazoo, Michigan and had lived in Ottumwa, Iowa (where she experienced religious bigotry she never forgot) and in Appleton, Wisconsin, where in 1904 at age seventeen she became a reporter for the *Daily Crescent*. From Milwaukee, Ferber went to Chicago (one more Eva or Carrie or Rose), coming to the city in search of something seemingly unobtainable in the hinterland's small towns.

Even as she made her move, her short stories, showing "the O. Henry influence" [as she acknowledged] with their formulas, their surprise endings, their sentimentality and ironies, their ordinary people, were appearing in several magazines and becoming intensely popular. Her work, said the *American Magazine* editors, was "novel and refreshing." Soon they were being anthologized.[41]

Chicago, Ferber soon discovered, was not Kalamazoo or Ottumwa or Appleton. It was not only the vastness of the city; Chicago had an attraction the smaller towns did not:

> There were writers of distinction in Chicago; I met some of them, but I saw them rarely. Carl Sandburg was writing his powerful lusty Chicago poems. Ben Hecht was living there, trying hard to be Rabelaisian, sliding his eyes around in a leer, thinking to hide his warmhearted conventional soul; Charlie MacArthur, brought up as a missionary's son, showing his rebellion by a series

of puckish pranks; Floyd Dell, living his moon-calf days; Susan Glaspell, Llewellyn Jones, Sherwood Anderson; and Harriet Monroe with the face of a New England school teacher; Maxwell "Bogie" Bodenheim, striding along Michigan Avenue [the 'Boule Miche'] in beret and smock, looking like a Weber and Fields version of an artist. Over in Evanston Henry Kitchell Webster wrote with a promise which he never fulfilled. Bert Leston Taylor, signing B.L.T. to his *Chicago Tribune* column, was a journalistic fad threatening to become a fetish. A *Tribune* sport column by a chap named Ring Lardner didn't get a tenth the attention. They were sometimes referred to as the Chicago School of Writing as one would say the Barbizon School of Painting.[42]

Three of the stories in her first anthology, *Buttered Side Down* (1912) are set in Chicago. Sophie, the State Street shoe clerk, stops wearing low-cut blouses when she learns they displease her Iowa boy friend. A hungry girl discovers she can get free food samples in a department store. A man from London, England and a burlesque dancer from Wisconsin meet twice — at a one-year interval — at a newspaper stand on Clark street which handles out-of-town peridocials.

Five other stores have some relationship to Chicago.

Ferber's second collection, *Roast Beef Medium* (1913) features the adventures of Emma McChesney, a traveling saleswoman, obviously modeled after Ferber's mother, but only one of the stories is set in Chicago. Her next book, *Personality Plus* (1914), has no Chicago referents.

But eight of the twelve stories in *Cheerful by Request* (1918) are Chicago-based. The title story portrays an Iowa girl who dreams of becoming an actress, an obvious projection of Ferber's own fantasies. "The Gay Old Dog," a Cinderella story in reverse, features a man who supports his three sisters in turn until each of them has married. Then, to his family's disgust, he becomes an aging roué, a "Loophound:"

> The Loop is a clamorous, smoke-infested district embraced by the iron arms
> of the elevated tracks. In a city boasting fewer millions, it would be known
> familiarly as downtown. From Congress to Lake Street, from Wabash almost
> to the river, those thunderous tracks make a complete circle, or loop. Within it
> lie the retail shops, the commercial hotels, the theaters, the restaurants. It is
> the Fifth Avenue and Broadway of Chicago. And he who frequents it by night
> in search of amusement and cheer is known, vulgarly, as a Loophound.[43]

"The Eldest" is Rose, a girl slaving for her careless family in a West Side slum and giving up her lover as a consequence. Fifteen years later he comes to the family's apartment to pick up her youngest sister. "That's Marriage" tells how Terry Sheehan, wearied by Wisconsin life, runs off to Chicago. But enlightened by a chance meeting, she returns home where her traveling-salesman husband has not missed her. "The Girl Who Went Right" is Rachel Willetsky, salesgirl at a chic Chicago department store who is not taken in by all the superficial glamour around her. "Sophy-As-She-Might-Have-Been," a buyer in Paris for Schiffs of Chicago, is certainly another glance at Ferber's mother.

"The Gay Old Dog" was selected by Edward J. O'Brien for his *Best American Short Stories of 1917.* "I gave my consent so that I might legitimately protest against the title and publication of these volumes," said Ferber. "I didn't want anyone to cry sour grapes." But she never again allowed O'Brien to publish one of her stories. "Sometimes the [selected] stories are the worst short stories, not only of that particular year, but of any year in the history of writing."[44] In 1919, "The Gay Old Doy" became *Gay Old Dog,* a Pathe film, the first of Ferber's work to be filmed. "The Eldest" became a play as we shall later see.

Of her life and work in Chicago during these early years of her career, Ferber later wrote: "I've written a lot about Chicago, really, [but] I'm practically never thought of as having written anything about Chicago. Strange."[45]

Albert Halper commented that although "Ferber's reputation rests upon her full-length books ... her early short stories, which are really entire novels crammed into five thousand words, comprise her best work."[46]

And one of the first critics to take Ferber seriously wrote that her work "is full of the perfect human — humorously human — quality which lifts so many of [her] short stories into high place ... [Her characters] are brushed in with a firmness of touch, a fidelity of detail, a humorous artist eye that is, as we say, 'taking' or 'fetching' and wholly delightful."[47]

Ferber's first novel to have a setting in Chicago was *Fanny Herself* (1917). This is another Ferber novel with a woman heroine. After her husband's death in "Winnebago," Wisconsin, Molly Brandeis takes over his variety store and makes a success of it by dealing with men in their own terms — a familiar theme in Ferber's fiction, one reflecting her own experiences in establishing a career as short story writer, novelist and playwright. Molly sacrifices herself and her daughter Fanny's future to send Fanny's violinist brother to Europe. (Sacrifice for another is a familiar theme in Ferber's work.) After Molly's death, Fanny goes to Chicago and a successful career in the mail-order business — one of several uses of this setting in Chicago fiction:

The firm described in the novel might well have been the Montgomery-Ward plant on the North Branch of the River:

> You must have visited it, this Gargantuan thing that sprawls its very length in the center of Chicago. It is one of the city's show places, like the stockyards, the Art Institute, and Marshall Field's. It had been built large and roomy, with plenty of seams, planned amply, it was thought, to allow it to grow. It would do

for twenty-five years, surely. In ten years it was bursting its seams. In twelve it was shamelessly naked, its arms and legs sticking out of its inadequate garments. New red brick buildings — another — another. Five stories added to this one, six stories to that, a new fifteen story merchandise building.

The firm began to talk in tens of millions.[48]

The novel shows "the chaotic aimlessness of Chicago" as producing a "romantic, neo-psychological allure" familiar to "every Chicagoan:"

There are people who have a penchant for cities — more than that . . . a gift of sensing them, of feeling their rhythm. And Chicago was a huge polyglot orchestra . . . leaderless, terrifyingly discordant, yet with an occasional strain, exquisite and poignant, to be heard throughout the clamor and din.[49]

In her autobiography, *A Peculiar Treasure* (1939), Ferber said that "a good deal of [*Fanny Herself*] was real, a good deal imaginary. Certainly my mother, idealized, went to make up Molly Brandeis. Bits and pieces of myself crept into the character of Fanny. A dozen [Appleton people] formed the real basis of the book's people."[50]

Before book publication, *Fanny Herself* was serialized in the *American Magazine*. It was adapted for the films as *No Woman Knows* (1921), the second Ferber fiction to become a film.

Henry Kitchell Webster

Edna Ferber seems to have been one of those Chicago authors of this decade who were neither part of the Genteel tradition nor of the bohemian movement which became the Chicago Renaissance. One who was a part of the Genteel tradition and the studio crowd was Henry Kitchell Webster. He was also one of those writers whose work and popularity helped make fortunes for Cyrus Curtis and George Horace Lorimer of the *Saturday Evening Post*. He was one of America's most prolific writers of the first three decades of this century. But his work attracted serious criticism also; his books were reviewed favorably in *The Dial, The New York Times, The Boston Transcript, The Bookman, The Literary Digest, The Nation* and *The New Republic*. "If you have read any of . . . Webster's magazine stories, you know what real flesh-and-blood creatures his women characters are," said one critic.[51]

The theme of "the woman in revolt" drew readers and critics alike to his 1916 *The Real Adventure*. Rose Stanton and Rodney Aldrich, the latter one of those handsome muscular types so popular in fiction of the time, meet romantically in the rain after he has helped rescue her from a brutal street car conductor. But their subsequent marriage turns out to be a disappointment for Rose, even though she has had twins. So she leaves her husband and family and sets out anonymously to make a career for herself in the theater. She succeeds, and eventually she and her husband are able to build a better relationship.

Webster's *The Painted Scene* (also 1916) has ten short stories set in Chicago's "Globe" theater — a part of the city's commercial theater world. The stories center on the production of a musical comedy, written especially for the "Globe." The characters are an old costume maker, an iron-tongued director, a young stage manager, the leads, the comedy team, the ingenue, the soubrette, the stage door Johnnies, the "ponies," the "mediums," the show girls. Except for their common note of pathos, the stories might have been written by Ferber. Each builds to a dilemma for one character; the dilemma is then resolved by a catalyst.

The Real Adventure and *The Painted Scene* show an obvious familiarity with the commercial theater of Chicago's pre-World War I loop district.

An American Family (1918) is an early example of the three-generation novel, soon to become a popular genre with Chicago writers, among them Edna Ferber and Webster's close friends, the Gold Coast Ayer sisters. The novel uses World War I as a catalyst to spur the hero to action. His family is in manufacturing, something this third generation family member doesn't care much for. He is the misfit in his family; he marries outside his social class. His wife is a socialist, a daughter of an anarchist. (Chicago has never really gotten over the Haymarket Affair.) The novel echoes Alice French's *Man of the Hour,* both in the woman socialist and in the strike which makes it possible for the hero to marry the right girl.

Webster's *The Thoroughbred* (1917) is set in the Chicago of early World War I. It begins with the bankruptcy of a well-to-do couple who live in a luxurious North Side suburban home. After a quarrel over money, each takes a low-paying menial job, and they move into a cheap West Side flat. Their romance warms anew as they face a lifestyle neither is prepared for. Gradually, their income rises, and once again they are affluent. But this time they decide to live a more sensible life on an acreage where they can be small-time farmers and raise their children in a more congenial atmosphere.

Meanwhile, Samuel Merwin, occasional co-author with Webster, was writing a series of novels which plainly have their origins in Booth Tarkington's novels about Penrod and his friends. In *Temperamental Henry* (1917), *Henry is Twenty* (1918), and *The Passionate Pilgrim* (1919) Merwin follows the adventures and romances of Henry Calverly. Although Henry lives in Sunbury (Evanston?), a lakeside town with a university, he drops out of school because he can't stick to anything very long. In this trait, he is much like the hero of Webster's *An American Family.* But Henry does manage a successful production of *Iolanthe,* writes successful short stories, and finally becomes a newspaper reporter. He also writes a successful novel. The series may or may not be autobiographical, but the novels have overtones of coyness which suggest autobiography.

The Chicago Renaissance

While all this writing was taking place in Chicago, a more significant literary activity was underway, one which has attracted the attention of several major literary historians.[52]

"For a short time, a half century ago the Second City became the first city of American literature," said Robert Sklar. "By the time people began to talk about it the moment, as often happens, had already passed. Thereafter nostalgia and local pride combined to give those years the name 'Chicago Renaissance.' . . . that moment marked a new beginning, not simply for Chicago, but for the literary culture of the whole United States."[53]

"Was there something about Chicago, as it then was, that gave [the writers] their special exuberance, even those who ended up in dark places?" asked John K. Hutchens. "One must believe so. For that was the Chicago of Sandburg's poem, the muscular Tool-maker, the Stacker of Wheat. It was still the gateway to the frontier, and rang with the frontier's echoes. It roared with vulgarity and romance. It *lived.* The aspiring writers who came to it, usually from small towns, also had lived. Some of them had ridden the rails, worked with their hands, acquired a rough-and-ready socialism in hobo jungles. By the time they reached Chicago, they had something to sing, say, or shout about."[54]

Llewellyn Jones, who followed Dell and Lucian Cary in the editorship of the *Friday Literary Review* likened what he called the "Literary Renaissance" to a camera tripod:

> The first of the legs on which the cultural life of the town was supported, namely the *Friday Literary Review* . . . was set up in 1909 by Francis Hackett . . . Harriet Monroe set up the second leg in 1912 when her anger at the cavalier treatment of poets by publishers and the public took the constructive form of founding *Poetry: A Magazine of Verse.* The third leg was set up in the same year: Maurice Browne's Little Theater.[55]

But it was the migration of people with literary talent into Chicago, for whatever reasons, that ultimately made Chicago something more than a center for dilettantes and, in H. L. Mencken's words, "the literary capitol of the United States."[56] True, Mary Aldis, Margery Currey, Monroe, Fuller, Garland, Chatfield-Taylor, Dreiser were already there. But Dell, Cook, Glaspell, Hansen, Arthur Davison Ficke and Marjorie Seiffert had to come from the Quad-Cities; Vachel Lindsay and Edgar Lee Masters had to come from downstate Illinois; Sandburg had to give up his tramping around the country and settle in Chicago; Sherwood Anderson had to come from Ohio and Maxwell Bodenheim had to come from the East.

Rejecting the established Michigan Avenue studio society, they set up their own studio society in a row of coldwater shops on Stony Island Avenue, left behind from the World's Columbian Exposition. Uptown they frequented Covici-McGee's bookshop. They opposed genteelism, romanticism and realism with the new concept of "arts for art's sake," a concept that had taken a long time to come from Europe. They practiced what some called "pagan love," others simply "free love." They taunted Chicago with the radicalism, the anarchism, the socialism that many had learned in their home towns. They wrote verse with new patterns, new rhythms, new sounds, new subjects, the patterns, rhythms, sounds and subjects of a more democratic, less aristocratic America. They espoused new philosophies of art — cubism, imagism, dadism. They discarded old American values for their own. They wrote about the provinces and regions from which they came and they wrote about Chicago. They dreamed of a new American theater.

And they moved on. By 1930 Renaissance was past.

Carl Sandburg

Carl Sandburg came from Galesburg, Illinois, where at 14 he had been "recruited" by the money reformer, William H. ("Coin") Harvey, and at 26 had published his first book of verse, *In Reckless Ecstasy*.[57] A couple of years later he took a job in Chicago, writing news of the "platform world" for *The Lyceumite*. In 1908 he married Lillian Steichen, sister of photographer Edward Steichen; she was working for Chicago Socialist publisher Charles H. Kerr. For a couple of years he worked for newspapers in Milwaukee, then came back to Chicago. And there, starting in the March, 1914 issue of *Poetry*, some of his *Chicago Poems* were published, starting off with "Chicago" itself:

Hog Butcher for the World,
Tool Maker, Stacker of Wheat,
Player with Railroads and the Nation's Freight Handler
Stormy, husky, brawling,
City of the Big Shoulders.

Said Harriet Monroe: "*Poetry* had never pleased *The Dial* and [these poems] caused an explosion of academic wrath:"

> The typographical arrangement for this jargon creates a suspicion that it is intended to be taken as some form of poetry, and this suspicion is confirmed by the fact that it stands in the forefront of the latest of a futile little periodical described as a "magazine of verse."...
>
> We think that [this] effusion is nothing less than impudent affront to the poetry-loving public.

To this the Chicago *Record-Herald* responded:

> Clearly it is impossible that *Poetry* and *The Dial* should lie down together. *The Dial* recoils from the "hog-butcher" school [of literature].[58]

Poetry's response was to award Sandburg the Helen Levinson *Poetry* prize for the poems. Levinson's husband, Salmon O. Levinson, was one of those Chicago businessmen who responded as a "guarantor" to Monroe's pleas for support of her magazine.

Strangely enough, although other Chicago writers had found little to like in the Windy City, Sandburg found plenty he liked: subjects, language, the city itself:

And having answered so I turn once more to those who sneer at this my city, and I give them back the sneer and say to them:

Come and show me another city with lifted head singing so proud to be alive and coarse and strong and cunning.

Flinging magnetic curses amid the toil of piling job on job, here is a tall bold slugger set vivid against the little soft cities;

Fierce as a dog with tongue lapping for action, cunning as a savage pitted against the wilderness...

By day the skyscraper looms in the smoke and sun and has a soul.

Prairie and valley, streets of the city, pour people into it and they mingle among its twenty floors and are poured out again to the streets, prairie and valleys.

It is the men and women, boys and girls so poured in and out all day that give the building a soul of dreams and thoughts and memories.

(Dumped in the sea or fixed in a desert, who would care for the building or speak its name or ask a policeman the way to it?)[59]

In "Mamie," Sandburg contributed his share to the Carrie-Rose theme of small town girls coming to the big city:

Mamie beat her head against the bars of a little Indiana town and dreamed of romance and big things off somewhere the way the railroad trains all ran.

She could see the smoke of the engines get lost down where the streaks of steel flashed in the sun and when the newspapers came in on the morning mail she knew there was a big Chicago far off, where all the trains ran.

She got tired of the barber shop boys and the post office chatter and the church gossip and the old pieces the band played on the Fourth of July and Decoration Day.

And sobbed at her fate and beat her head against the bars and was going to kill herself.

When the thought came to her that if she was going to die she might as well die struggling for a clutch of romance among the streets of Chicago.

She has a job now at six dollars a week in the basement of the Boston store.

And even now she beats her head against the bars in the same old way and wonders if there's a bigger place the railroads run to from Chicago where maybe there is romance

and big things

and real dreams

that never go smash.[60]

But Sandburg also found things he didn't like about Chicago:

Of my city the worst that men will ever say is this:
You took little children away from the sun and the dew,
And the glimmers that played in the grass under the great sky,
And the reckless rain; you put them between walls
To work, broken and smothered, for bread and wages,
To eat dust in their throats and die empty-hearted
For a little handful of pay on Saturday nights.[61]

In 1919, the resentment that James T. Farrell's fictional Lonigan family and its real-life South Side prototypes felt toward the growing Black Chicago population exploded into a two-day riot at the end of July. Sandburg, who had been in the "Bronzeville" neighborhood since July 13, doing a series for the Chicago *Daily News,* had predicted the riots on the basis of quotations from a white realtor and a Black Y.M.C.A. secretary. His columns were published as *The Chicago Race Riots* (1919). A young journalist, Walter Lippman, wrote the book's introduction.[62]

Theodore Dreiser

Dreiser's second novel, set partly in Chicago, *Jennie Gerhardt* (1911), is, as Dreiser himself said, "the life story of a woman who craved affection."[63] Initially, Jennie, an Ohio girl, is much like Carrie at the beginning of her story, a victim of misfortune and weakness. Both start out in a life of work and both yield to temptation. From there on the girls' characters follow divergent paths. Carrie is one who takes; Jennie is one who gives.

Jennie Gerhardt was filmed under that title in 1933 in a "meticulously produced version."[64]

With *The Financier* (1912), the first volume of a proposed "trilogy of desire," Dreiser turned away from women to the power structure of Chicago for his subject and his chief character. Frank Algernon Cowperwood, however, does not arrive in Chicago until the second volume, *The Titan* (1914). He is plainly modeled on Charles Tyson Yerkes who came to Chicago (from a Philadelphia jail) in 1876 to build street railways and a fortune for himself, and who, by the end of the century had become one of the half-dozen men who dominated Chicago. Yerkes was the man who, as a member of the Columbian Exposition Committee on Ceremonies had seen to it that Harriet Monroe had received a commission to write a "Columbian Ode." He was also the model for Will Payne's "The Duke of Gas" in *The Money Captain.*[65]

In chapter 35 of *The Titan,* Dreiser introduces two characters who were based on the two most powerful politicians of the time when Chicago aldermen were fattening their own purses by "selling the streets of Chicago."

In the first and second ward of Chicago at this time there were two men . . .

who for picturesqueness of character and sordidness of atmosphere could not be equaled elsewhere in the city, if in the nation at large.

Dreiser's real-life models were "Bathhouse John" Coughlin and "Hinky Dink" Kenna, long-time "boodlers," and overloads of the vice district in the infamous First Ward. Their careers are documented in Herbert Asbury's *Gem of the Prairie* (1940) which reports other examples of Chicago criminal activity, Finis Farr's *Chicago* (1973, a popular history of the city), and Lloyd Wendt's and Herman Kogan's *Lords of the Levee* (1943; reprinted in 1971 as *Bosses in Lusty Chicago*).

"The Bath" had his own moment of literary fame with his "Dear Midnight of Love," at once one of Chicago's most famous and most banal verses, unveiled to an anxious world at the Chicago Opera House:

When silence reigns supreme and midnight love foretells
If heart's love could be seen, there kindest thoughts do dwell,
In darkness fancies gleam, true loving hearts do swell;
So far beyond a dream, true friendship never sell.[66]

Only the first one hundred pages of *The "Genius"* (1925) were set in Illinois and Chicago, the last fictional use Dreiser was to make of the area. Eugene Witla from a small Illinois city enrolls in the Art Institute, finds employment as a newspaper artist, then feeling constricted by Chicago moves on to New York City; there he enters upon a successful artistic career.

Masters and Lindsay and Anderson

Vachel Lindsay, a vagabond poet whose home was in Springfield, Illinois, was never more than an occasional visitor to Chicago, undoubtedly attracted there by the bohemian atmosphere and the rash of writers. Edgar Lee Masters came to Chicago to practice law, but fell in with the writers because of his burgeoning fame as the once-anonymous poet of *The Spoon River Anthology*. In Chicago he was "discovered" by *Poetry* editors.

Masters' first poems about Chicago appeared in *Songs and Satires* (1916), a volume also containing some poems that Harriet Monroe had advised him to forget, and *The Great Valley* (1916), a volume of poems largely about Chicago's history, including the poems "Captain John Whistler" and "Fort Dearborn."

Sherwood Anderson, whom Dale Kramer was to call Chicago's "great unpublished author," came to Chicago, ostensibly to work in an advertising agency and also because his brother Karl, an artist, was there. Through Karl and Margery Currey Dell, Floyd Dell's first wife, Anderson came to the bohemian setlement at 57th Street and Stony Island Avenue — and there he met Floyd Dell. Floyd had reviewed one of Anderson's books in the *Friday Literary Review:*

"Why how exciting. There I was, as Dell was saying in print, in a newspaper read as I presumed by thousands, an unknown man (I do not now remember whether or not he mentioned my name) doing, in obscurity, this wonderful thing. And with what eagerness I read. If he had not printed my name at least he had given an outline of my novel. There could be no mistake. It's me. It's me.[67]

Ever afterward Anderson called Dell his "literary father." At the time Dell was 27, Anderson 38.[68]

Anderson's two novels of this decade, *Windy McPherson's Son* (1916) and *Marching Men* (1917) "are concerned respectively with the characteristic themes of the ruthless money magnate, a marching movement akin to the [19th century Chicago] *Lehr und Wehr Verein* and the 'Knights of Labor' and with a rural inventive genius defeated by an urban-industrial civilization."[69] Both are set in Chicago in the 1890s. The protagonist of the first novel is Sam McPherson, "Caxton, Iowa newsboy and son of the town drunk, who makes his fortune in Chicago. Following the advice of John Telfer to 'Make money! Cheat! Lie! Be one of the men of the big world,' Sam claws his way to prominence . . . [But] wealthy and influential, Sam begins to puzzle over the meaning of his success. . ."[70]

In *Windy McPherson's Son*, says Thomas L. Kilpatrick, "the Chicago setting is beautifully drawn, and the historical aspects of the novel are quite accurate, making this [novel] an excellent reflection on a small segment of Chicago's history."[71]

In *Marching Men*, says Grey, Anderson "interprets in a single mystical movement [a] sense of solidarity, of social pattern, of destination. It is an astonishing exposition of the spirit which will subsequently weld together the Fascists, on the one hand, and the Nazis on the other — an effort to bring form to 'formless' modern Society."[72]

In *Marching Men*, Beaut McGregor, a young man from a coal mining town in Pennsylvania, comes to Chicago "to seek his fortune . . . he finds the city suffering from an over-abundance of able-bodied men and a grave shortage of jobs." While working as a foreman in a warehouse, Beaut learns the lawyer's skills, becomes famous by brilliantly defending a man charged with a crime, and begins to get rich. Then he begins to "organize the Chicago labor force into a unified army" with a common goal.[73]

In a third novel, *Poor White* (1920) Hugh McVey, a boy from Missouri pauses briefly in Chicago:

> [Hugh] was not tempted to become a city man. The huge commercial city at the foot of Lake Michigan, because of its commanding position in the very center of a vast farming empire, had already become gigantic. . . . It was evening when he came into the roaring, clanging place. On the long wide plains west of the city he saw farmers at work with their spring plowing. Presently the farms grew small and the whole prairie dotted with towns. In

these the train did not stop but ran into a crowded network of streets filled with multitudes of people. When he got into the big dark station Hugh saw thousands of people rushing about like disturbed insects ... like distraught cattle, over a bridge and into the station.[74]

In his *Mid-American Chants* (1918), Anderson viewed Chicago in its relationship to its western hinterlands:

Back of Chicago the open fields — were you ever there?
Trains coming toward you out of the West —
Streaks of light on the long gray plains? — many a song —
Aching to sing.

I've got a gray and ragged brother in my breast —
That's a fact —

Back of Chicago the open fields — were you ever there?
Trains going from you into the West —
Clouds of dust on the long gray plain.
Long trains go West too — in the silence
Always the song —
Aching to sing.[75]

Fenton Johnson was a Black poet writing in Chicago during the Renaissance but his name does not appear in any of the histories of the period. He was born in Chicago in 1888 and educated at the University of Chicago and Northwestern. He wrote short stories, dramas and poems of Negro life — some in a formal, cultured English, some in the "corrupted" language of the American Black, and at least one in Yiddish. None of the poetry is set specifically in Chicago. His titles are: *Visions of the Dusk* (1915), *Songs of the Soil* (1916) and *Tales of Darkest America* (1920) and *A Little Dreaming* (1913).

Poetry and The Little Review

"It was on the eleventh of January, 1911, that I finished circling the world at the Santa Fe station in Chicago," said Harriet Monroe in *A Poet's Life* (1938). "I found the city surging with activities and aspirations beneath its commercial surface. The 'Chicago Plan' was being matured under the enthusiastic leadership of. D. H. Burnham — the first of the now numerous 'city plans;' and the twenty-year litigation to put through its first important feature — the two-story Michigan Avenue Bridge, with Wacker Drive to replace the old produce market along the river — was going on quietly to a triumph. The small park movement — another Chicago idea — was progressing, and the Illinois Central Railroad was being disciplined along the shining shore of beautiful Lake Michigan. The Orchestra was firmly established. The Art Institute was increasing its prestige and its collections. The dramatic activities ... were going on toward their 1912 climax in Maurice

Browne's Little Theatre."[76]

In fact, to Harriet Monroe's eyes, everything seemed to be going well in Chicago — except poetry. She discussed the problem with Hobart Chatfield Chatfield-Taylor — "novelist, lover of the arts, man of culture, wealth, and social prominence" and created a prospectus for a magazine of poetry.

Taking Chatfield-Taylor's advice, she solicited over a hundred five-year pledges to support the new magazine, one which, however, was to have its roots in the former *Chap-Book* and the *Chap-Book* imitators.

Miss Monroe's argument was along these lines:

> The average magazine editor's conception of good verse is verse that will fill out a page. No editor is looking for long poems; he wants something light and convenient. Consequently a Milton might be living in Chicago today and be unable to find an outlet...
>
> Painting, sculpture, music are endowed with museums, exhibitions, opera houses, orchestras, prizes and scholarships. Poetry alone receives no assistance, no encouragement ... the modern English-speaking world says "Shut up! to its poets...[77]

Her financial base secured, Miss Monroe's next task was the necessity of "stirring up" present day poets. Mrs. William Vaughn Moody, widow of the University of Chicago poet-dramatist, had been one of her guarantors but Monroe felt that Moody's poetry leaned too much on the past. What she wanted was poetry that was "leading forward," poetry which experimented with "modern themes and characters [perhaps] done in free verse" as in her own "The Hotel," "or in conversational blank verse." "It was this indifference [to innovations] that [she] started out to combat, this dry conservatism that [she] wished to refresh with living waters from a new spring."[78]

As her publisher, Monroe chose Ralph Fletcher Seymour:

> It was on a summer's morning in the year 1912 that a thin, quiet mannered, bespectacled lady, Harriet Monroe ... walked into my office and placed a bulky bundle of manuscript on my desk. Looking sharply at me through shining glasses she said, "Here are the poems and editorials for the first issue of *Poetry Magazine*. Give it your most careful consideration. It is my child and I have brought it to you to dress and help care for." Then her enthusiasm for her child swept her reticence away. She leaned closer, looked hard into my face, with a characteristic, nervous gesture put her hand on my arm and exclaimed; "Oh, Ralph, you will do your best for our magazine? It will mean so much for all of us! We must have it here, in this city, but there is no reason why it should not stand for the best thing of its sort in the world."[79]

Thus Fletcher became the publisher of the "incorruptible magazine" for its first four years; Monroe, Henry Blake Fuller and Eunice Tietjens did most of the editorial and proof-reading work. "Fuller loved to lose himself in proof-reading and in the indexing," said Seymour.[80]

Poetry: A Magazine of Verse appeared on September 23, 1912. In spite of Monroe's attitude toward Moody's verse, some of it was in the thirty-two pages. And Arthur Davison Ficke was represented by two traditional sonnets. The second number was more to Monroe's liking; it had a poem by William Butler Yeats, an anti-social poem by the radical-minded John Reed, and Vachel Lindsay's "General William Booth Enters Heaven."[81]

The first number sold out and so did the second. Soon Yeats was in Chicago, speaking at the Cliff-Dwellers and praising Lindsay. Lindsay responded with "The Congo."[82]

The success of *Poetry* sent ripples through Chicago. Llewellyn Jones says that "a group of some twenty University of Chicago undergraduates, stimulated by [Poetry], formed a poetry club and for a time published their own magazine, *The Forge*. From that group ... there emerged Yvor Winters, Janet Lewis, George Dillon, Glenway Westcott, Sterling North, Jessica Nelson North, Bertha Ten Eyck James, Elder Olson, Gladys Campbell, and Elizabeth Madox Roberts."[83]

As we know, the Chicago Renaissance became history. But *Poetry,* which may well have been the strongest leg of the tripod on which the Renaissance was based, has remained. Its editors have come and gone; some have been brilliant and some not so brilliant; the magazine has published great poetry and poetry not so great. But it goes on.

Margaret Anderson's *Little Review* was a product of both the Renaissance and the wave of progressive views of such Chicago intellectuals as Clarence Darrow and Demarest Lloyd.[84] But during its short tenure in Chicago, in the course of which its publisher embraced both aesthetic innovations in content and design, and Emma Goldman and her anarchistic policies as well, it provided a Chicago "dateline" for James Joyce's *Ulysses*.[85]

The Dial also continued to publish during the Renaissance years, under the editorship of Francis Fisher Browne and his son, Waldo, but always as the voice of the fading Uplift movement, its tastes and its philosophies in opposition to the bohemianism and innovations of the writers and poets living on 57th Street. In 1918 it moved to New York.[86]

Realists and Romanticists

Robert Herrick, operating from his base in the English Department of the University of Chicago, wrote four novels in this decade. Three (*A Life for a Life* (1910), *The Healer* (1911), and *Clark's Field* 1914) are set outside Chicago.

One Woman's Life (1913) takes place on Chicago's West Side in the last two decades of the nineteenth century. Its heroine is Milly Ridge, "an average young woman, born with the instinct of a 'social climber,' and aided by a magnetic personality."[87] Herrick conceived Milly as "an American

Madame Bovary, though against Sentimentalism."[88] Other critics thought Milly was derived from H. G. Wells or Elinor Glyn.[89a]

In 1902, Herbert S. Stone had told the *Record-Herald* that although Chicago writers were "doing honest practical work," their books were not popular because "they have been tinged by pessimism."[89] The *Dial's* criticism of *One Woman's Life* picked up that note:

> Mr. Herrick has now lived in Chicago for the greater part of twenty years, and all the time he has been pouring forth a stream of caustic comment upon the many phases of its ilfe. He does not like the place, and assumes toward it invariably the offensive attitude of the superior person. And to him the West Side, with its church-going habits, its *naive* domesticities, and its feeble gropings after culture, is simply "impossible." Yet the West Side is preëminently that part of Chicago in which the wholesome life of the home is most in evidence, and in which the simple virtues which lie at the basis of American civilization are most generally practiced. But to Mr. Herrick it is, even more than Chicago as a whole, the quintessence of meanness, sordidness and vulgarity.[90]

Marjorie Benton Cooke, University of Chicago graduate, suffragist, magazine writer, and Little Theatre actor, set two novels, *The Girl Who Lived in the Woods* (1910), and *The Threshold* (1917), in the manufacturing towns of Gary and Whiting, and on the north shore. "The Girl" is a young outcast from society, living in the woods near Lake Forest. There is a coincidental connection with labor unrest in distant Gary, then, unlike Lake Forest, an almost new town which had sprung "from a zero of sand dunes and scrub oaks."[91] The novel displays overtones of Chicago's fear of anarchists, lingering on from the Haymarket Affair.

The heroine of *The Threshold,* a girl from the Whiting steel mill district, graduates from the University of Chicago, marries an eastern manufacturer, and inspires a utopian labor scheme based on distribution of "excess profits."

Both of Cooke's novels reflect the themes of utopian books, novels and tracts of the 1890s, but both are much more pragmatic in their attitudes toward these themes. Both feature unconventional romances.

Charles Tenney Jackson's *My Brother's Keeper* (1910), set in Chicago, "the crucible of America," has a very similar theme to *The Girl Who Lived in the Woods.* As in Cooke's novel, an anarchist killer comes in contact with members of Chicago's upper class society. Jackson's novel involves a University of Chicago sociologist whose liberal support of labor movements is severely tested by the presence of the anarchist. A reviewer detected the influences of the English authors George Bernard Shaw and George Meredith on the central character, a radical philosopher whose ideas have angered his socially-prominent father.[92]

Mrs. Bernie (Smade) Babcock, the author of the later *The Soul of Anne Rutledge; Abraham Lincoln's Romance* (1919), turned away from the sentimentalism of much of her work to write, in *Claw and Fang; A Fact Story in a Chicago Setting* (1911), what Thomas Kilpatrick calls "an impassioned diatribe against liquor." The story is set in "That Sodom of America — Chicago;" its protagonist is Ulig Golzoch, a Russian immigrant who takes part in the Haymarket Riot — and dies for his beliefs.

Alice Gerstenberg's *Unquenched Desire* (1912) is undoubtedly a *roman á clef*, based on Gerstenberg's activities in the Chicago dilettante society and the Little Theater. It tells of the daughter of a wealthy Chicago manufacturer who takes part in Chicago amateur theatricals and then seeks a career on the commercial stage. There is a deliciously satirical account of the Chicago of 1910-1912 in the first third of the novel. The balance of the book, relating the girl's success, is quite uneven, seemingly beyond Gerstenberg's experience and her abilities to project.

Mary Austin is usually thought of as a southwestern writer, but in one novel, *A Woman of Genius* (1912), she used Chicago for a part of the setting; her theme is a frequent Chicago theme as well:

> The story of the "new woman" who rises to full stature as an actress or opera singer, sketched with increasing force in McGovern's *Burritt Durand* ([1887] 1890), Lillian Sommer's *Jerome Leaster* (1890) and Dreiser's *Sister Carrie* (1900), now reaches its most studious expression in Mary Austin's *A Woman of Genius* and Willa Cather's *The Song of the Lark* (1915). Though they are a part of the larger movement which included explicit Feminism, these novels should not be indiscriminately catalogued as Feminist. Their heroines are not feminists; they are not average types. They are women of genius, whom the city can educate but cannot down. They correspond to the business barons in their self-realization. They are sublimations of the strongest in this new way of life and in the old combined, freed from ignorance and narrow tradition, and freed ultimately, like Hapgood's *An Anarchist Woman* from the spirit of revolt itself, and from its less Olympian agents.[93]

In Austin's novel, Olivia May Lattimer progresses from Taylorville, "Ohianna" through Chicago to New York City in her search for a career as an actress. Along the way, she divorces a husband and decides not to marry a second man.

Her reaction to Chicago is like Harriet Monroe's:

> Though here in Chicago there was money for every sort of adventure that stirred the imagination of man, there was none for that particular sort of investment I represented. At least not the price I was prepared to pay.[94]

Samuel Merwin's *The Citadel; A Romance of Unrest* (1912) is another novel about the political boss in Chicago. The novel begins in Washington where John Garwood, a member of the House, angers his supporters with an attack on the Constitution. Back home, a girl, Margaret Lansing, encourages him to form a new progressive movement. The novel echoes the political divisions of the 1912 national elections.

The year 1913 brought the first fictional attempt to deal with the "race problem" in Chicago, just six years before the 1919 race riots on the near South Side. Although the first Chicago resident had been black, [95] and although by 1870 there was a small black settlement "south of Harrison," and blacks constituted nearly the whole staff of the elegant Palmer House that opened that year, blacks had rarely appeared in Chicago fiction until Ade's *Pink Marsh* and some other stories. In one of his early stories, Ade depicted a "ragged [white] man" who had in his pocket a copy of Henry George's *Progress and Poverty* and a pair of "brass 'knucks.'" "I'm savin' that for the coon [Black]," he said.[96] But nevertheless, as Duncan says, most Chicagoans could laugh at Pink Marsh, the "shiftless, worthless, lovable black darling,"[97] because it was thought that the race problem would work itself out and the black would be grateful for the 'opportunities' the city offered, and be satisfied with a low status.[98]

The Strange Case of Eric Marotte, a Modern Historical Problem-Romance of Chicago by John Irving Pearce, dealt not only with the black problem but also, as had Jennette Lee's *Mr. Achilles* the year before, with intellectual misfits. Both Lee's Achilles Alexandrakis, a Greek, and Pearce's Eric Marotte, a talented educated Negro, find places in the Chicago sun, but with difficulty. Their successes are aided by the fact their creators treat them as puppets, not as real people.

Edwin Baird's improbable picaresque *The City of Purple Dreams* (1913) pictures the rise of a tramp to millionaire status through sheer brassiness and effrontery. Daniel Randolph Fitzhugh, a potential blackmailer and anarchist, romances with light-haired Kathleen Symington, daughter of a millionaire, and with black-haired Esther Strom, a Russian Jewess. Using money won in a poker game, Daniel gambles successfully in the Chicago wheat market.

Under the same title, a film was produced in 1928. In the film Daniel is seen as a mill worker who realizes his dream of becoming a financial power in the wheat market while winning the love of a social worker whose father is Chicago's Wheat King.

Hollywood's use of a Chicago book for a film was not an extraordinary matter as this history will demonstrate. Through the twentieth century the film industry was to turn and return to Chicago stories, novels and plays or else Chicago settings, incidents and characters as the basis for films. In the seventy-year long history of the American film, only New York, Hollywood, and San Francisco were to be used more often.

One of the early motion pictures which is still extant is the eleven-minute long *A Corner in Wheat* (1909). In its brief run through the projector, the film details the rise and fall of a callous manipulator and the social consequences of his actions. The film was directed by David Wark Griffith.

In *The Losing Game* (1910), Will Payne, by now "one of our serious pragmatic novelists,"[100] singles out the "bucketshop," a type of corrupt Chicago business which since has been legislated out of existence. Payne focusses on a scoundrelly telegraph operator who tries wire-tapping as a means of gaining an advantage in the trading of stocks and bonds. He's also a scoundrel in his marital relationships and gets his come-uppance on both scores.

Edwin Balmer and William MacHarg began long writing careers (either in partnership or singly) with *The Achievement of Luther Trant* (1910), a volume of short stories about a young Professor of Experimental Psychology in a Chicago college who uses various scientific instruments (including, for the first time in fiction, the lie detector) for solving various crimes associated with "business." Although the stories vary in quality, the volume has been singled out for praise for its introduction of scientific equipment to the fiction of detection.

Chicago is the setting because it is a place where violent crime is commonplace (at least in the novel!) and because it provides a diversity of criminal activities.

Balmer and MacHarg again joined talents for *The Blind Man's Eyes,* a novel of mystery and business (1916). The novel begins in Seattle where a prominent business man is murdered. The story continues on a Chicago-bound "special train." Along the way, another prominent business man, traveling anonymously, is murderously attacked. The novel concludes in the latter's suburban Chicago home. Although the principal characters are in the business world, violence is the principal theme, and we learn very little about Chicago business.

Lake Michigan has always been a backdrop for the settings of Chicago fiction, but up to now it had played an active part in only two of them. Both *Rose of Dutcher's Coolly* and *John Dorn, Promoter* had used the December, 1895 storm as an incident; that storm appears again in one of the two novels which in this decade linked Chicago and its fortunes with Lake Michigan.

MacHarg's and Balmer's *The Indian Drum* (1917) uses a mystery based on a superstition that an unseen (but heard) Indian drum beats every time a Lake Michigan ship sinks — one beat for each drowned or missing person. The novel has a romance between two persons involved in the mystery, but its central figure, a lake man, is one of those romantic Chicago entrepreneurs:

There are in every city a few individuals who from their fullness of experience in an epoch of the city's life come to epitomize that epoch in the general mind ... others of his rivals ... may be actually more powerful [or wealthier] than he; but he is the personality; he represents to the outsiders the romance and mystery of the secrets and early, naked adventures of the great achievement. Thus to think of the great mercantile establishments of State Street is to think immediately of one man; another very vivid and picturesque personality stands for the stockyards; another rises from the wheat pit; one more from the banks; one from the steel works.[101]

The Indian Drum was a popular book and ran through a number of editions. It is a combination of the adventure tale, the romantic love story and the increasingly-popular mystery novel. Moreover, it linked twentieth-century Chicago to its Indian past.

MacHarg (1872-1951) and Balmer (1883-1959) were both educated in the Chicago public schools and both worked for the Chicago *Daily Tribune* for a short period, MacHarg as an editor in 1899. MacHarg graduated from the University of Michigan, Balmer from Northwestern. In 1909 Balmer married MacHarg's sister, Katharine. Both men wrote short stories for magazines, and the work of both men was often dramatized. From 1927 to 1949 Balmer served as the editor of the Chicago-based magazine of fiction, *Red Book*. His first screenplay was *The Breath of Scandal* (1924). MacHarg's *The Price of a Party* was also filmed that year.

Louise Kennedy Mabie's *The Lights are Bright* (1914) features a woman industrialist, the owner of a steel mill which depends on the ore boats from the Minnesota and Michigan iron ranges for its ore. She is opposed by two villainous rivals from another steel mill. In their efforts to defeat her, they isolate her on a Lake Michigan boat, but she is able to overcome their strategies.

A number of women novelists who were to be successful authors for several decades were coming into prominence in this decade in Chicago. We have already seen Janet Ayer Fairbank (whose sister Margaret Ayer Barnes was to come along in the 1920s), Susan Glaspell, Mary Austin and Edna Ferber, all of whose work had focussed on women, as had the work of a number of male authors of this time.

Now in mid-decade came two more women, one of whom, appearing surprisingly in Chicago, was to win world-wide fame for her books set in the west. Willa Cather's *Song of the Lark* (1915) begins in "Moonstone," Colorado, but Thea Kronborg's musical aspirations bring her to Chicago in the days of the great Theodore Thomas; Thea is seen as a musical student in a Michigan Avenue studio. Later Thea goes to New York as many of her real life contemporaries were to do.

"When [Ibsen's] Nora slammed the door," a New York reviewer wrote in 1916, "the sound reverberated through the house of literature, and each year we hear new echoes. Last year [Henry Kitchell] Webster published *The Real Adventure* and now we have *Cecily and the Wide World*."[102]

This novel, set in Chicago and a nearby city on the North Shore, was the first of fifty-two novels and several magazine stories by Elizabeth Corbett, a native of Aurora. It was not well done, as reviewers were quick to point out, but its characters with whom her readers could identify (particularly Carrie Eaton Meigs, the subject of several novels) were to win her a host of readers.

Indiana author Booth Tarkington's *The Turmoil* (1915) is a novel set in what is obviously Chicago, the "ugly duckling" tale translated to the Windy City's business world.

Bibbs Sheridan, the "ugly duckling," suffering from nervous exhaustion is sent off to an asylum by his family, which would like to pretend he doesn't exist. Because Bibbs wants to become a poet, his business-man father places his hopes in a second son. Meanwhile the Sheridans have built a huge new house next to the Vertrees, a down and out old Chicago family. To save her parents, Mary Vertrees decides to make herself available to one of the Sheridan sons. Her younger sister, Edie, elopes with a despicable young man, much to the Sheridans' grief. In the end, Bibbs takes over the family business as the other sons prove to be less than worthy. And Mary gets Bibbs.

Elias Tobenkin's *Witte Arrives* (1916) is the first Chicago novel whose theme is the Americanization of the Jew from Europe — in this case Russia. Aaron Witkowski remains a peddler all his life, but his Emil Witte becomes a Chicago journalist, later, like real life counterparts, going to New York. As *The Jungle* of a decade before, it focusses on the helplessness of the average individual in contemporary life. But this novel stresses the need for such individuals to assert themselves, and to find new values and social structures by and in which they can live.

As a potential writer, Emil Witte sees a need for an *Uncle Tom's Cabin* of the industrial worker:

> He began making plans for a book, a novel that should portray the Great Fear — the Fear for the Job — that hovered over the masses, that should depict the caste lines that divide American society. He would paint the helplessness of the modern factory worker, the horror and despair of worklessness. He would make these poor people so palpable that no one would mistake them, that once seen they could not be forgotten.[103]

Witte Arrives was praised by *The Dial* — but it is not the book Witte planned. It is, rather, a success story, of sorts, of a Chicago journalist, and, it seems in part at least, also a *roman á clef*.

Edwin Herbert Lewis's *Those About Trench* (1916) is set on South Halsted Street, but the society of Dr. Isham Trench's boarding house is not the world of Clara Laughlin's "Penny Philanthropist" — although that world is close by. Trench is a pediatrician and teacher, and his boarders are foreign students in Chicago to learn from him. Trench is an agnostic as well as a scientist, and his philosophies, particularly his philosophy of scientific determinism, almost overwhelm the incidents of the novel and its slight romantic plot.

Katherine Keith's *The Girl* (1917) is another novel which deals in part with the world of the Chicago artist of the first two decades. Marian Crosby, a perverse child in school, tells her own story of her life through college, and her love affair with an artist, a friend of her father. In contrast with *Witte Arrives, The Girl* describes Chicago's upper class of the same time. Katherine Keith was the wife of David Adler, designer of elegant moderate-sized houses.

Newton A. Fuessle's *The Flail* (1919) is set in another ethnic neighborhood in Chicago, this one the German community of Chicago's northwest side. Rudolf Dohmer is seen first as a Chicago schoolboy, then as a journalism student at the University of Chicago. He writes in turn for the *Maroon,* the college newspaper, then for the *Inter-Ocean,* a leading Chicago newspaper at the time. He then becomes a business man.

"In [showing] the transition from the timid, dreaming public-school boy to the successful man of business," said a *Dial* reviewer, "the author had the opportunity to show how the demands of contemporary business technique may develop a personality whose native endowments run to softness and sentimentalism, into the triumphant, self-assertive model of the Economic Man." But Fuessle had failed, the reviewer concluded. "The Hun is the scapegoat upon which the sins of the American business regime are fastened."[104]

Charles David Stewart's *Buck, Being Some Account of His Rise in the Great City of Chicago* (1919) is also a story of the upward mobility of a young man in Chicago, but it's old-fashioned for its time. Buck's college days are spent at the University of Wisconsin, a situation which gives his creator, a one-time executive secretary to the Wisconsin governor, a chance to take the usual digs at the value of an education — not unusual for that era when "self-made" men were held up as role models. The novel — and critics wondered if it were a novel — also is one of the last books to report the contemporary use of the horse in Chicago transportation. The automobile had long before appeared in the Chicago novel, and, although there are photographs showing automobiles and horse-drawn vehicles both in Chicago about 1915, by 1920, the horse was almost a thing of the past.[105]

Ella Wood Dean's "badly named but perceptive" *Love's Purple* (1911) is one of many novels about the "new Woman" which had begun with Herrick's *The Gospel of Freedom* (1898) and which featured such themes as "bold experiments with the old sex-morality, ... the Strong Woman in politics and in feminist work ..., the Woman in Business ... the Woman in the Professions," and, most frequently as in Dean's novel, the theme of 'careers' or projects involving temperamental departures from accepted social patterns" (Grey 617-618).

The core of the woman's problem was most explicitly presented in Joseph Medill Patterson's *Rebellion:*

> Her belief was orthodox, but it did not hold her as vividly as it held the old folk in the old days. Had she lived nearer to the miracles of the sun going down in darkness and coming up in light; or thunderstorms and young oats springing green out of black ... she would perhaps have lived nearer to the miracles of bread and wine, of Christ sleeping that the world may wake.
>
> But she lived in a place of obvious cause and effect. When the sun went down, the footlights came up for you if you had a ticket, and man's miracle banished God's ... Thunderstorms meant that it was reckless to telephone; oats, wheat and corn, something they controlled on the board of trade; the melting of the snows showed the city hall weak on the sewer side — what else could you expect of politicians? — the dying leaves presaged the end of the Riverview season and young Al's excitement over the world's series.
>
> Living in the country puts a God in one's thoughts, for man did not make the country and its changes, yet they are there ... Man built his own city of steel and steam and stone, unhelped, did he not?
>
> God may have made the pansies, but he did not make "the Loop ..."
>
> Never had Georgia questioned her faith ... She had consciously yielded no part of her creed. But its living quality was infected by the daily realism of her life (105-107).
> . . . .
> She took pride in her big city ... It followed no rules but its own, and did not always follow them. It ruled the future in fee and pitied the past. It said, not "Ought I?" but "I will." It was modern, just as she was modern. She was more characteristically the offspring of her city than of her mother. For she was new, like Chicago; and her mother was old, like the Church (157-158).

M. H. Hedges *Iron City* (1919) completes this decade of Chicago novels. "Iron City" is a manufacturing city on the periphery of Chicago, one of those which came into existence because of the construction of the Chicago Outer Belt Line (Elgin, Joliet and Eastern Railroad) in 1887. The hero is an instructor in a small non-denominational college, a situation which permits his creator a chance to contrast the aims of higher education with those of industry. Randolph Bourne called this "the finest first novel he had ever read, and one of the few great American novels,"[106] but another reviewer said "we grow weary of these youthful remoulders of the universe."[107]

Two Contemporaries Look at the Chicago Literary Scene

Meredith Nicholson, at the time one of Indiana's and America's best known novelists, wrote a 1918 essay about Chicago in which he waxed lyrical about Chicago's enterprise and stockyards, but mentioned merely in passing only five literary figures. Two of these — H. G. Wells and Rudyard Kipling — were English, and the other three — Field, Ade and Bert Leston Taylor — were primarily journalists. Somehow he managed to overlook the writers of the Uplift or Genteel movement, the bohemians of the Renaissance, the numerous writers in the realist and realist-romantic modes — and H. L. Mencken.

For just a year earlier, Henry L. Mencken, scion of a beer-brewing Baltimore tribe, in a New York *Evening World* story (later picked up in London) had commented on the passing of New York City as a literary center, and had crowned Chicago the new "literary capitol of the United States:"

> It is indeed amazing how steadily a Chicago influence shows itself when the literary ancestry and training of present-day American writers are investigated. The brand of the sugar-cured ham seems to be upon them all. With two exceptions there is not a single novelist of the younger generation — that is a serious novelist deserving a civilized reader's notice — who has not sprung from the Chicago palatinate; Dreiser, Anderson, Miss Cather, Mrs. Watts [Wyatt?], Tarkington, Wilson, Herrick, Patterson, even [Winston] Churchill. It was Chicago that produced Henry B. Fuller, the packer of the modern American novel. It was Chicago that developed Frank Norris, its first practitioner of genius. And it was Chicago that produced Dreiser, undoubtedly the greatest artist of them all...
>
> The new poetry movement is thoroughly Chicagoan; the majority of its chief poets are from the Middle West; *Poetry,* The organ of the movement, is published in Chicago. So with the Little Theater movement. Long before it was heard of in New York, it was firmly on its legs in Chicago. And to support these various reforms and revolts, some of them already of great influence, there is in Chicago a body of critical opinion that is unsurpassed for discretion and intelligence in Chicago.[108]

Mencken's enthusiasm was to last for about a decade, as we shall see, then faded away.

Nation-wide prohibition of the sale of liquor and beer had gone into effect just as the decade ended — and it was to lead to the rise of a new literary figure who would replace the business man as the center of interest — the gangster. It is to that character and his affects on Chicago literature and drama that we now turn.

IX.
The Roaring Twenties

Chicago! Gerald smiled. What his relatives [in England] thought of Chicago was a whole comic paper in itself. They believed him to be living in one maze of excitement and adventure, shot at on every corner, dodging bullets and hi-jackers as part of his daily dozen, pursued from safety island to safety island by determined motorists and probably wearing a coat of chain mail to business as a protective measure. In point of fact, Gerald had never even seen a gangster. Sometimes he wished he had. Life in America was dull.[1]

Crime in Chicago Drama

When the Volstead Act became a Constitutional amendment on January 17, 1920, "Prohibition closed the spigots, as *Chicago* said. The event led "Bathhouse John" Coughlin to pen another of his colorful lyrics and send it to the Women's Christian Temperance Union in Evanston, attached to an eight-inch tall beer schooner from Coughlin and McKenna's Workingmen's Exchange Bar:

Dear gentle, gracious, efficient president of the WCTU.
This souvenir of pre-Volsteadian days I beg to present to you.
My sentiments go with it and as you gaze upon it filled with flowers sweet,
I prithee remember that it oft contained Manhattan suds on Clark Street.[2]

Actually, the spigots barely closed at all in Chicago; in no time, it seemed, "beer-hustling" was supplying the Windy City's bars and taverns. Then a new note was sounded. On May 11, 1920, "Big Jim" Colosimo, a man with close connections with Bath House John and Hinkey Dink, was shot down in the front entrance of his luxurious South Wabash Avenue restaurant. Soon names like Johnny Torrio, Al Capone and Dian O'Banion were appearing in Chicago newspapers. The age of gangsterdom had arrived.

Although it took Chicago novelists half of the decade to discover the literary gold in gang wars and gangsters, and the motion pictures even longer (Josef von Sternberg's *Underworld* [1927] with script by Ben Hecht is claimed by some to be the first gangster film), Chicago playwrights saw the dramatic possibilities as early as 1920.

In that year, Jack Lait, author of a crime exposé column in the Chicago *Herald*, and Jo Swerling, apparently one of his staff, co-authored *One of Us*, a three-act play. The play's heroine was based on an Australian musical comedy star, Dale Winter, who had been engaged by Colosimo in his cabaret. Soon Colosimo had managed to divorce his wife and marry Winter. His murder followed shortly afterward. Within ten days Winter had left Chicago after voluntarily relinquishing all claims to her husband's million dollar estate. Within a month she was the star of the Broadway play, *Irene*, a role which she played for three years. It is part of that story, at least, which was the subject of *One of Us*.[3]

Swerling and Lait had a falling-out over the play and Swerling moved on to Hollywood where she became a screen-writer for at least a score of films including several Bing Crosby musicals and the film version of *Guys and Dolls*.

About 1925, Logan "Steve" Trumbull's three-act *The Promised Land*, also about the Chicago gangster scene according to reports, was produced in a store-front theater on North Clark Street.

Neither Lait's or Trumbull's play scripts seem to have survived. Theater critics of *The Chicago Tribune* did not mention either play in "The Season in Chicago" in the appropriate editions of Burns Mantle's *Best Plays*. Nor is either listed in the index to *The New York Times* anthology of play reviews.[4]

In 1926, the first of a trio of stage comedies took a satirical look at the three estates of Chicago power in the 1920s — the gangster, the police and the press. Maurine Watkins' *Chicago*, "a satirical comedy on the administration of justice through the fetid channels of newspaper publicity," rocked the city despite a police denunciation.[5]

In the play's brief prologue, Roxie shoots her married lover because he is leaving her. Although Amos, her husband, tries to take the blame for the murder, Roxie confesses and is locked up in the Cook County jail. There her cellmates tell her no jury will convict a girl with a "baby face" like hers. And Roxie basks in the press spotlight.

A jury frees her, but just as the newspaper reporters crowd around her for her final moment of glory, another woman shoots *her* husband and the latter's paramour just outside the courtroom. The curtain falls on a deserted Roxie.

Early in 1927, A. A. Knopf published the play with an introduction by George Jean Nathan. Later that year, *Chicago* appeared in its first film version with Phyllis Haver as Roxie. However, the story line was modified considerably; the focus was on Roxie's husband who has stolen money from the safe of Roxie's lawyer.

In 1942, hewing closer to the original plot line, the play was filmed as *Roxie Hart* with Ginger Rogers in the title role and Adolphe Menjou as her attorney. Writing about this production in *Chicago*, Dave Kehr says:

> When William Wellman dusted off Maurine Watkins' old stage play, turning it into a very Hechtian comedy of shopgirls, shyster lawyers, and cynical reporters, the strain of transporting one decade's comedy to another showed fatally — the shrewd, grasping characters no longer seemed funny and charming but simply grotesque.[6]

But Leonard Maltin saw the film as a "fast-moving spoof of the Roaring 20s," with some "dry spots."[7]

In 1976, once again as *Chicago*, the play was set to music by Bob Fosse and Fred Ebb. "Lust and chicanery in the Windy City, circa 1925," a reviewer wrote.[8] With Gwen Verdon and Chiquita Rivera in starring roles, the musical played on into 1977.

Maurine Watkins was an Indiana girl who had attended Radcliffe College. At Butler University she began writing plays and sold one to Leo Ditrichsen of Chicago. He asked her to collaborate with him on a second play while he was acting in *The Business Widow* in a Chicago theater. She worked a while for the *Tribune*, then joined Professor George Pierce Baker's famed drama class at Yale. She wrote *Chicago* in his class, got a grade of 98 on it — and the rest is history.[9]

Bartlett Cormack's *The Racket* (1928) also hangs on the balance of power among gangsters, police and the press. It is set in a far Southwest Side police station with Nick Scarsi's booze trucks rolling by outside, the time just two days before an election over whose results Nick seemingly has control. There is an honest cop who has been shipped out to this Chicago police Siberia, and a night club singer who is probably also modeled on Dale Winter.

New York critics liked the play, but Chicago authorities did not. "Chicago bars *The Racket*," read a *New York Times* headline on January 5, 1928. "If Bartlet [sic] Cormack's play *The Racket*, which is said to be an exposé of tieups between gangland and a State's Attorney's Office, is brought to Chicago, State's Attorney Crowe (who had once been a guest of honor at a lavish feast given by a prominent Chicago gangster) will take steps against the play and those producing it . . ."[10]

And although the next day's edition of the *Times* carried a defiant statement from the play's producer that "the play would be acted in Chicago regardless of the State's Attorney's attitude," the record does not show that it ever appeared there. But it was played in San Francisco and Los Angeles.[11]

The Racket was published in book form in 1928.

Like Maurine Watkins, Cormack was from Indiana. He graduated from the University of Chicago with Honors and a membership in Phi Beta Kappa. While in school, he wrote a pair of college shows and was associated for a time with Maurice Browne's Little Theatre. After school he worked for the *Chicago American* and also as a playwright.[12]

Burns Mantle in his *Best Plays of 1927-28* listed *The Racket* as the second best play of 1927 behind *Strange Interlude*.[13]

In the New York play, Edward G. Robinson acted Scarsi so capably that he was the obvious choice for the title role in the film *Little Caesar* in 1931. *The Racket* has been filmed twice. In 1928, Thomas Meighan played the police captain, Louis Wolheim the gangster and "Skeets" Gallagher a reporter. In 1951, the screen adaptation was done in part by W. R. Burnett, author of the novel *Little Caesar*. Robert Mitchum and Robert Ryan played the leads.

The best of this late 1920s series of plays came next. *The Front Page* (1928) was written by the "Katzenjammer Kids of the theater," Ben Hecht and Charles MacArthur:[14]

> Both Hecht and MacArthur owe their literary origins to the newspapers of Chicago. Famous crime reporters, their talents were first cradled in the recounting of great exploits in arson, rape, murder, gang war and municipal politics. Out of a welter of jail-breaks, hangings, floods and whore-house raidings, they have gathered the rich, savory characters [of the play].[15]

"All the underworld is divided into three parts," said *The New Republic's* reviewer. "In Chicago the newspapers are more aggressive and powerful . . . in part because of the close connection of government with crime. The newspapers have the lowdown on both partners . . . it is naturally in their interest [since news is their chief commodity] to maintain a balance of power . . ."[16]

The Front Page shows some Chicago politicians determined to execute a white man who has killed a Negro policeman in self-defense, because the politicians need the black vote in next day's election. The newsmen, seen in a press room in the court house, constantly needle the politicians over their motives while at the same time recognizing the story's value to their readers. A second story line concerns Walter Burns, a hard-bitten Chicago editor trying to keep Hildy Johnson, his star reporter on the story. Hildy has plans to depart for New York with his fiancee. Burns, as corrupt in his own way as the politicians, is determined to use any skullduggery to keep Johnson in Chicago.

Apparently the play exaggerated reality but slightly. Playgoers of the time recognized in Burns and Johnson two well known Chicago newspaper men, Walter Howey, Burton Rascoe's editor on the *Tribune*, and Hilding Johnson, a reporter. Says Pauline Kael of Howey:

> At one time or another, just about all the Hollywood writers had worked for Walter Howey and/or spent their drinking hours with friends who had. He was the legend: the classic model of the amoral, irresponsible newsman who cares about nothing but scoops and circulation. . . .[17]

Still, a reader of Hecht's autobiographies, *A Child of the Century* (1954) and *Gaily, Gaily* (1963), may well wonder if there isn't at least a heaping spoonful of Hecht, MacArthur, and Gene Markey, another Chicagoan who became a film scriptwriter, in the play.

Roger Dooley says that if it "seems incredible that a nation . . . could be so much concerned about a relatively minor problem as an irresponsible press, it should be kept in mind that [the play was] reflecting the world of the '20s . . . a decade that had seen tabloid sensationalism pushed to unparalleled depths of garish tastelessness."[18] But Dooley overlooks the parallel theme of corruption and stupidity on the part of the police and petty politicians in the play — a theme Chicagoans had no trouble in accepting at all.

New York reviewers found the play "vulgar;" Brooks Atkinson said the langugage was offensive.[19] Time have changed; the play seems less vulgar today and one hardly notices the language; but the play is as lively and pertinent as ever.

Dave Kehr says that Hecht's other "great contribution" to Chicago mythology were his "wise-cracking, street-cynical newspapermen; if anything, they were even tougher and more egocentric than [his] gangsters, but they did have the decency to perform their assassinations with withering one-liners rather than machine guns, which made them more acceptable to the censors. Hecht's Hildy Johnson and Walter Burns operated in much the same moral and social void as did Scarface: The newspaper brotherhood closed around them as tightly as the society of the underworld, and for all their efforts to represent themselves to the faceless public as lofty seekers after truth, no crime was too heinous to commit in pursuit of a story that might sell a few extra papers to the suckers."[20]

The play has been filmed three times. *The Front Page* (1931) with Adolphe Menjou as the irascible editor and a young Pat O'Brien as Hildy, was "a faithful adaptation of Hecht and MacArthur's sardonic comedy."[21]

In January 1940, as the 1930s ended, *His Girl Friday*, the second film version of the play appeared — a somewhat different treatment. Hildy Johnson is played by Rosalind Russell; she is recently divorced from Walter Burns, played by Cary Grant. Although the director, Howard Hawks, later contrived an apocryphal anecdote about his accidental discovery that Hildy Johnson's lines read even better for an actress than for an actor, Pauline Kael says that this second version was strongly influenced by the tough editor — smart girl reporter — square fiance trio in a 1936 film, *Wedding Present*. [22] But Roger Dooley argues that it was influenced by the 1938 film, *Four's A Crowd*, which also featured Rosalind Russell as a girl reporter.

In any case, this version is a "brilliant success, crackling with dialogue at the fastest pace ever heard on the screen." In the *New Yorker's* words, the version is "a hectic re-make ... directed by Howard Hawks with a kind of terrific verbal slam-bang that has vanished from current film-making.[23]

Billy Wilder's 1974 version used the original title and a 1920s setting comes off as third-best. Walter Matthau and Jack Lemmon are far too old and jaded, and Carol Burnett is unbelievable as the convicted murderer's girl friend.

Covici-Friede (who had once been Covici-McGee in Chicago, but who were now in New York) published the play in book form in 1928 with an introduction by theatrical entrepreneur Jed Harris and an epilogue by "The Authors," who called the play "a romantic and rather doting tale of our old friends — the reporters of Chicago."[24]

And Harris commented that "in an age when the theatre seems imprisoned in a vise of superficial and literal realism, a paradise for the hacks and journeymen who infest the Authors League of America, and in a day when the successful portrayal of a newspaper reporter is accomplished by attaching to the person of an actor a hip-flask and a copy of the *American Mercury*, it is soothing and reassuring to stumble on a stage reporter who begins an interview in this innocent fashion:

"Is it true, Madame, that you were the victim of a Peeping Tom?"[25]

In 1942, a radio adaptation by Charles Newton was broadcast over WJZ on March 29.[26]

A film, *Chicago After Midnight*, featuring bootleggers, night clubs, and the murder of a Chicago gangster, was produced in 1928. It seems to have had no literary or dramatic origins. However, a New York *Times* critic said it was reminiscent of the play *Broadway*, a mid-1920s hit.

A musical play, *Happy End,* with book by Bertold Brecht and score by Kurt Weill, was a 1929 satirical treatment of guys, dolls and gangsters in Chicago in the 1880s. The setting was a Chicago dance hall. The play was based on a story, "Under the Mistletoe," by Dorothy Lane. The play was revived at Yale University in the 1960s, and played again at Broadway's Martin Beck Theater in 1976.

One other play of the period, *Harvest*, (1925) by Kate Horton, avoided the omnipresence of Chicago crime by using a setting in the sand dunes of southwest Michigan. Its central characters were a wealthy business man from Chicago and his college boy son. The play's message was that rustic rural life is preferable to life in the city. There seemed to be no notable rush of people either for tickets to the play or for trains out of Chicago.

The Chicago Gangster in the Chicago Novel

Edwin Balmer's *That Royle Girl* (1925), although it does not focus primarily on gangsters, introduces the theme of Chicago gangsterdom with its tribal murders, its fringe-of-the-city nightclubs, and is ability to avoid prosecution. Moreover, Joan Daisy Royle, a Chicago girl of 20 has a drunkard father and a drug-addict mother. The male love interest is an honest member of the Cook County Attorney's office. The chief villain is another Italian mobster.

"That Royle Girl" was filmed in 1925, following Balmer's story line carefully. In his second film role, W. C. Fields plays Joan Daisy Royle's hard-drinking father!

Diversey (1928) was Iowa author MacKinlay Kantor's first published novel, and Chicago's second gangster novel.

Marshall Javlynn, like his creator, was an Iowan transplanted to the Windy City in search of a career. Unlike his creator, he is involved with two women, a gangster, a double-crossing Prohibition agent, a newspaper columnist, and several others. All of this on the Northwest Side around Diversey.

Albert Bein's *Love in Chicago* (1929, written under the pseudonym of Charles Walt) is more about Chicago's gangland than about love. There is a love triangle involving a gangster chief, the daughter of an ambitious politician indebted to the gangster, and her lover, a young truck driver. The novel ends tragically with the imprisonment of the truck driver on a false charge and the girl's suicide.

In a prefatory note, Bein said that he was encouraged by Clarence Darrow, Chicago attorney and novelist, and by Zona Gale, Wisconsin novelist and playwright, to write the book.[27]

The American image of the Chicago gangster of the 1920s derives a great deal from William R. Burnett's *Little Caesar* (1929, filmed in 1931), published when Al Capone was already in a Pennsylvania jail. The novel dramatizes the brief rise and fall in Chicago of Cesare Enrico ("Little Rico")

Bandello. Most critics praised the book. Herbert Asbury, author of *Gem of the Prairie: An Informal History of the Chicago Underworld* (1940) said "a better story of this type may appear at some time in the future, and a more accurate portrait of a gang chieftain may be drawn, but is is a matter of grave doubt."[28]

What, other than a good story line and good writing, made the gangster novel (and the gangster film) so interesting to the American public — an interest that has continued for the last sixty years? Roger Dooley offers this explanation:

> Of all the . . . heroes defined by their occupations, none cut a wider swath across the [the] '30s than the gangster . . . Curiosity about those living outside the law seems a perennial human trait by no means confined to the gallant Robin Hood tradition. Morbid fascination with more lurid crime has had an equally long history — witness the bloodier Greek myths [and plays], folk ballads like "Edward, Edward," the gory Elizabethan and Jacobean revenge tragedies, the later Gothic tales of terror and their echoes in the criminal characters and violent scenes in many classic nineteenth-century novels.
>
> Gangsters by definition operated in packs — hence such phrases as "the mob," the "syndicate" and "organized crime" — all expanded by Prohibition into a multimillion-dollar enterprise. Just as war has been defined as the continuation of foreign policy by other means, so the cold-blooded gang vendettas, ambushes and massacres, purely to eliminate rivals, seize power and increase profits, seemed in effect the extension of the methods of big business to their logical extreme — cutthroat capitalism without hypocritical pretense.
>
> Thus some of the best gangster [stories] at least subliminally invited the [public] to identify with a hero who had, however outrageously, beaten the system and made it pay off in possessions that weaker man could only envy: beautiful women, fine clothes, big cars, lavish apartments.[29]

Mystery Novels

The books, plays and films discussed above had their real life antecedents in the gang wars, hijackings and assassinations in the streets of Chicago. The genre described in this section as often as not had its antecedents in the imaginations of its authors.

Randall Parrish was an historical novelist whose books about Chicago's beginnings we have seen earlier. In *The Case and the Girl* (1922) he turned to intrigue — the supposed scheme to defraud an imaginary Chicago heiress of her inheritance. A reviewer said the book featured "many a hair-raising adventure."[30]

Paul and Mabel Thorne's *The Sheridan Road Mystery* (1922) relied on a Chicago police detective for its sleuthing, while their *The Secret Toll* (1922) utilized a potential extortion-murder victim to foil the criminal. On his own, Paul Thorne authored *Spiderweb Clues* (1928), an abduction case, and

Murder in the Fog (1929), a case involving a derelict Great Lakes freighter with a mutilated corpse aboard.

The ubiquitous Edwin Balmer's *Keeban* (1923) featured a dissolute twin impersonating his unknowing brother, a man of good character, to the latter's grief. Time, 1920.

In Kirby Williams' *The C. V. C. Murders* (1929), the Citizens' Vigilante Committee finds a rotten apple in its midst. *The Opera Murders* (1933) is self-descriptive.

Edna Ferber in the 1920s

When Susan Glaspell and George Cram Cook had gone east from Chicago, they made their way to New York's Greenwich Village and its bohemian lifestyle, and, in the summers, Provincetown, Massachusetts. In Provincetown with Floyd Dell, Eugene O'Neill and others, they founded the Provincetown Theater in an old shed on a wharf. Here O'Neill's plays were first produced, as well as plays by the former Iowa trio and their associates. In the winters the group headquartered in an old store building, renamed the McDougall Street Theater.

There, on January 9, 1920, far from Chicago and Chicago's theatrical district, the Players presented Edna Ferber's own dramatization of her short story "The Eldest" (from *Cheerful by Request*, 1918). It was Ferber's first play. Somehow Ferber had learned that the Players planned a production of this realistic Chicago play. Looking into the matter, she learned that someone else had written a crude adaptation of her story. Quickly she sat down and wrote her own dramatic version. The Players liked it better.

The Eldest had exactly the kind of regional realism the Players desired, with its Cinderella-in-reverse slavery drudging for her family on Chicago's poverty-stricken West Side. *The Eldest* was published in book form in 1928.

The one-act play was also a harbinger of new directions for Ferber. Drama on the stage and on the silver screen was to be an important part of her highly successful career.

She continued, however, to write short stories, and soon a new volume of these appeared as *Half Portions* (1920). Of its nine stories, four are set in an imaginary Chippewa, Wisconsin and three in Chicago. Six of them are set in the first World War; one of these is about a Chicago soldier whose recovery from battle wounds is miraculously abetted by a letter from his Chicago sweetheart.

Another, "Farmer in the Dell," is the seed from which grew the later *So Big*. Ben Westerveld, a Dutch farmer, has moved to Chicago during the war to please his shrewish wife. In the city, Ben begins to go to seed; then one day at the old Water Market, on the south bank of the Chicago River (later the location of Wacker Drive) he sees the girl he had given up for his wife twenty-five years before. She is Selina Peake, a produce grower who has learned how to deal with the tough male habitues of the Market. So Ben goes back to the farm; farm life has triumphed over city life.

Because this short story "about a horny-handed old tiller of the soil" marked a significant step toward a later Ferber publication, Ferber's comments on its origin are worthwhile reporting:

> Walking or driving about Chicago's streets I had seen many of these trans- planted farmers withering and dying under a life of ease in the city. The down- state prairies yielded up hundreds of these forlorn creatures. You saw them clumping along the asphalt or sitting, vacant-eyed, in the porch swings of their bungalows on the far South or West Side of Chicago, their great hands lying inert and open on their knees. One of these lonely souls I depicted as prowling around South Water Street, at that time the produce market which fed Chica- go's millions. What I really encountered in that world of market gardeners, produce men, wholesale grocers and commission men was a woman whose face so impressed me that it made an indelible picture in my mind. She was a small quiet woman in blue serge. I don't know what she was doing there among the boxes, barrels and crates of potatoes, chickens, tomatoes, beans, turnips, squash. I never talked to her, I never talked to her again. But somehow I connected her with that truck-garden region south of Chicago where families of Dutch descent worked their plots of ground and drove daily to market with their laden wagons. I had seen the loads, horse-drawn, plodding toward the city in the evening twilight.
>
> So truck gardens and wagons, South Water Market and little wrenlike woman were tucked away in my mind in 1919 to grown and ferment and twist and turn until finally they emerged. . . .[31]

Although Ferber thought that writing a novel was "a long pull" compared to writing plays or short stories, she turned next to a novel of three genera- tions of "Chicago old maids," *The Girls* (1921). She began composing the book "in the bizarre background of Hollywood" where she had personally sold *Fanny Herself* to Irving Thalberg, then "a wisp of a boy, twenty-one-so slight as to appear actually frail."[32]

As she began the first draft of *The Girls*, "all the varied aspects of the Chicago [she] had seen in the past ten years, and all the dramatic and absurd stories [she] had read and heard about its brief past came floating back to [her] mind. The Old Fort Dearborn days; the Civil War; the Chicago Fire; the shocking performance of *The Black Crook*, with women actually wearing tights; Potter Palmer, the dry-goods merchant, and his wife [Bertha Honoré] who became queen of midwest society; the high rickety sidewalks above the mud wallows of the streets of 1875; picnicking in the groves around Twenty-Ninth Street." When memories were not enough, she researched in the Chicago Historical Library.[33]

"At one time it looked as if nothing could drag Chicago into the focus of the novelist," said Francis Hackett, reviewing the book. "Chicago didn't want to sit in all its sprawling horror . . . [moreover] the artist shrank from touching Chicago . . . [Other] artists roped the beast and yanked him forward, but there was felt resistance and a not quite happy conquest. The sitter and the artist both remained, if not uncomfortable, certainly heroically strained."

Ferber and Ferber's novel demonstrated a new direction. "Chicago to her is one of the richest, most natural, most established of themes ... The city permeates her book. Not only that, it permeates the three generations of Chicagoans with whom she so buoyantly and glowingly deals."[34]

The Girls is a landmark novel in the history of Chicago literature for it is the first to encompass nearly all of the city's history, and it is the prototype of the three-generation novels which followed. Great-Aunt Charlotte Thrift was born in the early 1840s. Charley, her grand-niece is twenty at the novel's end. Other women in the novel are Charlotte's sister, Carrie Payson, Belle, Carrie's daughter, and Lottie, Belle's sister.

Charlotte tries to rebel against the social pressures of her family and their aristocratic neighbors, but yields to the social pressure and remains a spinster. Carrie marries, but after her husband leaves her for another woman, she becomes a "managerial philistine" and keeps his real estate business going. Lottie become a perpetual servant to her mother. Just at the end, however, she rebels in a too-sentimental moment — a moment when Ferber lets her own guard down. Belle, Lottie's sister, marries.

It is Charley, Belle's daughter, who is the only rebel in the family, rebellious from her childhood on. But, as Robert Nathan pointed out, her rebellion does her "no good in this life."[35]

Nathan, Hackett, and other reviewers said that Ferber was at last reaching her rightful state as a novelist.

In *The Girls*, Ferber is obviously sympathetic to the "Hardscrabble Dicks" of this world — the opposite side of Chicago's social coin. Her sympathies may well have derived from her own nomadic life in Kalamazoo, Ottumwa, Iowa, Appleton and Chicago, particularly from her reaction to the sniggerings of small-town street loungers who seemed, as one critic said, "to have anticipated the manners of the Nazis."[36]

In *Gigolo* (1922), a set of stories which had been published in magazines between 1920 and 1922, the Payson theme from *The Girls* appears in a story "The Sudden Sixties" with a twist — Hannah Winter tries to make her children independent of her. She succeeds with her son, but not with her daughter. "Home Girl" (an ironic title) shows how the twelve-year-old marriage which began in a $28.25-a-month flat and continued on into a $250-a-month apartment is destroyed by the ever increasing demands of the wife for a better "home." This "morality tale" was typical of many appearing in women's magazines of the time.

"Old Man Minick," the fourth Chicago story (the third was about a young garage mechanic) helped change the course of Ferber's authorial career and start her toward her real success as a writer. The plot is simple enough — an old man of seventy comes from a Chicago suburb to live with his son and his son's wife. They treat him as if he were helpless although he is quite capable of caring for himself. One day in a Chicago park he meets some Chicagoans his own age. Gradually he breaks away from his children and eventually he moves into an apartment with his new friends.

The story came to the attention of George M. Kaufman, a New York playwright, and co-author of several popular plays with Marc Connelly. Kaufman wrote to Ferber telling her there was a play in the story. Ferber didn't agree with him. In fact she never did, but she was unable to resist the opportunity to co-author a play with a celebrated New York playwright. "It would be enchanting," she told herself.[37]

But in New York, Ferber learned that making a three-act play from her short story would require changes in both the story and the title. She acquiesced, and in 1924, under the title *Minick*, the play was produced in New York (but not in Chicago).[38] Although most of the critics agreed with Ferber's original evaluation, the play was a popular success and an "also-ran" in the Pultizer Prize competition that year. However its real importance was that it had introduced Ferber and the Broadway stage to each other.

"Old Man Minick" was filmed as *The Expert* in 1931. The film, said Roger Dooley, was "the rarest of all variants" on stories of family life, one that focussed on people "as they normally appear in life, trying to adjust to failing powers and reduced income while fitting into the busy lives of indifferent grown children."[39] Chic Sale, who had made his reputation with a slight book about outdoor "privies," played the role of Minick. With only a few changes, the story was again filmed in 1939 as *No Place to Go*, with Fred Stone as Minick.

Meanwhile, as Ferber later said in her 1939 autobiography, *A Peculiar Treasure*, her short story "Farmer in the Dell" continued to haunt her. "It was the most important single influence in my writing life." Also haunting her was

"a woman whose face so impressed me that it made an indelible picture in my mind ... a small quiet woman in blue serge, once seen among the boxes, barrels, and crates of potatoes, chickens, tomatoes, beans, turnips, squash" on the old South Water Market. There was also the image of American youth of the 1920s, the "Lost Generation," who "really were only playing hide-and-seek with life ... No generation of American boys and girls ever had so much money."[40]

Ferber didn't note the ghost of something else that may also have been haunting her, Robert Morss Lovett's *A Winged Victory*. Lovett's 1907 novel was set in the same period of time (1876-1890) that Ferber was to use in her new novel; Lovett's central character was a Miss *Peaker* who taught at Prairie Grove School. His central theme was that of a strong woman who gives up her own career to make a great artist of her man.

In Ferber's new novel, *So Big* (1924), "the small quiet woman in blue serge" became Selina Peake, who taught at High Prairie school in the pleistocene beach ridge area of far south Chicago — the area that became the small Dutch farming community of Roseland. She marries Pervus DeJong, a stolid Dutch truck farmer. When he dies, leaving her with her small son, Dirk, Selina takes over his truck farm and begins marketing her produce in Chicago. As the novel progresses and she becomes successful, her life centers on her son. Still, unlike "Farmer in the Dell" which is a man's story, *So Big* is a woman's story.

The Girls had been serialized by *The Woman's Home Companion*. Gertrude Battles Lane, the long-time editor-in-chief of that now-extinct magazine, had objected not at all to the novel's ending with Lottie bringing her illegitimate baby back from France — a daring subject for a woman's magazine in the early 1920s. Now Mrs. Lane agreed to serialize *So Big*, even though the "high point" was a woman driving in to Chicago with a load of vegetables.[41] But she thought the novel would do better in her magazine if it were titled with the heroine's name — "Selina."

There had been no Pulitzer Prize in 1907, but there was one in 1924, and *So Big* won, the first Chicago novel to do so. Although there were the usual complaints from critics over the award, reviewers of the time praised the book, and one compared Ferber to Sinclair Lewis and Willa Cather.[42]

So Big was filmed in 1925 with Colleen Moore, a star of the silent films, in 1932 in a "talking" version with Barbara Stanwyck, and in 1953 with Jane Wyman, the first Mrs. Ronald Reagan. Although critics have liked all three versions, the 1932 film is considered the best.[43]

Like *The Girls*, Ferber's next novel, *Show Boat* (magazine serial and novel both 1926) is a three-generation novel, also called the *roman â fleuve* or chronicle novel, a French genre which became popular in the United States in the 1920s and 1930s. *Show Boat* begins in the 1860s on the Mississippi River, but about one-fourth of it is set in the notorious "Gambler's Alley of the Chicago of the 1890s. (Selina Peake's father had also been a

Chicago gambler.) This setting allowed Ferber to fictionalize the colorful nether world of "Bath House' John Coughlin and "Hinky Dink" Michael Kenna, of the Everleigh Sisters and Chicago's plushest house of prostitution, and of gamblers, hoodlums, politicians and Chicago show people.

Show Boat was immensely popular, not only as a novel, but also as a musical play on the Broadway stage and in the films. Florenz Ziegfeld, (a native of Chicago, where his father had been a prominent musical figure) produced the first stage version in New York in 1927 with Helen Morgan as the tragic Julie and Charles Winninger as Captain Andy Hawks. (Winninger, co-incidentally, had been a vaudeville favorite of Ferber's back in Appleton.) Successive revivals have been staged in New York in 1932, 1946, 1948, 1954 and 1961. Its first film production was begun as a silent film with Laura La Plante, a star of the time, in the lead. But the advent of the sound film just then led the producers to tack on a singing-talking prologue and a singing epilogue; in the latter, non-singer LaPlante seemingly sang "Old Man River." The definitive film version was produced in 1936 with Allan Jones and Irene Dunne in the leads. Kathryn Grayson and Howard Keel recreated the leads in a 1951 film with Ava Gardner as Julie.

Show Boat was also the basis for "a sustained radio program lasting over six years."[44]

The initial success of *Show Boat* demonstrated to Ferber exactly where her future lay — in "gorgeously romanticized" tales of the American past.[45] But she set no more of her books in Chicago.

Looking back five years later, Lennox Bouton Grey said that "no writer in the last twenty years has surpassed Ferber in the profitable talent for catching the current fluttering of the American pulse, as the swift adaptation of her novels to stage and screen will suggest — a sign of timeliness that is her strength and weakness."[46] But Grey is not altogether right about Ferber; *So Big* and other Ferber books remain in print, and *Show Boat* has become an American classic. Ferber has managed to catch more than the "current fluttering" of the American pulse.

Ferber did set two of her later short stories in Chicago — both collected in *Mother Knows Best* (1927). "Consider the Lilies" uses the Hungarian ("Hunkies") neighborhood of Clybourn, North and Halsted from 1903 to 1923. "Blue Blood" is about an Irish family in Canaryville in the Back of the Yards District. There is a romance between a third-generation boy and girl who live and work in the Yards, but who want to get out of the area. The title story was filmed in 1928.

Edgar Lee Masters in the 1920s

In the early years of this decade, Masters, always restless in his search for vocation and for feminine companionship, turned to a new guiding light — the novel. His decision got mixed responses: one critic wondered "whether Mr. Masters is not more successful as a novelist than as a poet;"[47] another said that "in Mr. Masters the critic and the novelist are at war."[48]

Two of his three novels, *Mitch Miller* (1920) and *Skeeters Kirby* (1923) are autobiographical. The first takes Kirby (based on Masters) and his friend Mitch Miller through the first twelve years of their lives in an Illinois town, up to the point where Miller dies. The second is a novel of revolt, of Kirby's "inarticulate struggle for self-expression and freedom under the compulsion of a social system which has room only for conformity and suppression."[49] The novel has its obvious origins in the English author Samuel Butler's *The Way of All Flesh* (1903). Like Masters, Kirby studies law because of his father's insistence. After the death of a sweetheart, he goes to Chicago to enter the legal profession.

In Chicago, Kirby is successful as a lawyer and as a lover. At the end of the novel he is writing verse under a pseudonym for a St. Louis magazine publisher — just as Masters wrote *The Spoon River Anthology* for William Marion Reedy's *Mirror* under the guise of "Webster Ford." Kirby's image of himself is always as an author.

"Skeeters Kirby is assuredly both real and interesting, distinctly human both in his virtues and in his shortcomings," said the *New York Times*. "The entire book, moreover, is decidedly entertaining; it is written with a trained and capable hand and gives one illuminating glimpses of life in Chicago and in the smaller Midwest towns."[50]

Masters' *Mirage* (1924) carries on the story of Skeeter Kirby for the next decade when Kirby is 42. Most critics, including Robert Herrick and Burton Rascoe, were unhappy with the book.

Masters' next novel, *Nuptial Flight* (1923) is the story of a marriage mismatch and the subsequent divorce on three generations of an Illinois family. "The book is Masters' most considerable performance since *The Spoon River Anthology* and places him, in that shabby but useful phrase, in the front rank of American novelists," said the *Nation*.[51]

There have always been two points of view in Chicago and Illinois about the relative merits of Abraham Lincoln and Stephen A. Douglas, a debate which began with the first political competition between the two. In *Children of the Market Place* (1922), Masters came down firmly on the side of Douglas, portraying him in the novel as the greater.

Masters, however, places Douglas off-center in the novel. His first-person narrator is an Englishman, James Miles (1815-1900). Miles, born and reared in the empire-building tradition of nineteenth-century England, can thus admire Douglas in a manner that an American narrator, influenced by popular American portrayals, could not.

Masters added an additional story line with the introduction of Miles' discovery that in the new land he has an octaroon half-sister. This led at least one reviewer to relate the book to the race problem in America rather than to the treatment of Douglas.[52]

Robert Herrick's Third Decade

After a lapse of seven years, Herrick returned in 1923 to the novel with *Homely Lilla*. Herrick's skill had improved so much that Robert Morss Lovett commented that Herrick had "gained rather than lost in mastery of his vehicle."[53] And Joseph Wood Krutch, perhaps thinking of the opening scene in which Lilla's father is mangled by a power saw, said that the novelist had a "new grasp on fundamental things."[54]

Lilla, at twelve, is taken to Chicago from the Wyoming ranch where she would rather be. Although she wonders at the Columbian Exposition's marvels, she dislikes her Chicago suburb because it has sidewalks. Atypical of her time but typical of novels of the 1920s, Lilla is a sexually-liberated heroine; seduced by a cousin, she doesn't take the matter as seriously as he does.

Lilla becomes a teacher and marries a teacher — which gives Herrick another opportunity to attack education. Dr. Gordon F. James, the husband, believes in the work ethic, and is a cold fish, perhaps like Herrick himself, who, we are told, seemed to have a distaste for teaching and students.[55] He also is one of those educators with an eye always out for the main chance and he is promoted again and again. He and Lilla quarrel over the subject of children, and they differ over the German question in World War I. Lilla begins to wonder why a wife must accept her husband as sole arbiter of her destiny. Finally, rejecting her husband's values and those of the city, she returns to the agrarian traditions of the West.

In a book review of this period, Herrick had repeated what he had written on another occasion — that "the 'enduring' province of the 'real novel' is 'social history' because men cannot understand themselves apart from their times." But he also thought that his art had "romantic and realistic elements."[56] "Habitually," said a contemporary, "he chooses as subject some aspect of the national life either disturbing to his conscience or repugnant to his intelligence, and interprets it from the critical point of view dictated by these conditions of choice."[57]

In *Waste* (1924) Herrick recurred "to a theme implicit in several of his earlier novels, the depredations suffered by the integrity of [an] individual [Jarvis Thornton, architect-engineer-teacher] as a consequence of the material organization of our national life."[58] The novel is set in the years from

1880 to 1920; "forty years in the wilderness," said a critic. [59] The action takes place in Minnesota, Massachusetts, Idaho, New York and elsewhere; part of the novel finds Thornton in Chicago at the time of the Columbian Exposition, and for a few years afterward.

Waste was praised by the major critics of the time — Joseph Wood Krutch, Harry Hansen, Henry Seidel Canby, Lloyd Morris, Allan Nevins and Carl Van Doren.

In 1923 at 55, Herrick resigned his University of Chicago professorship. He could have stayed on for another fifteen years, but he was not feeling good. Three years later his *Chimes* appeared — a *roman â clef* of sorts, based on his career at Chicago. The novel opens with the beginning of "Eureka" University in 1893 and follows it through the administration of two presidents. Unlike *This Side of Paradise* and other novels of college life appearing about this time, *Chimes* avoids students in favor of the teachers and the administration.

Eureka "had been founded with the stroke of a pen slashed across the foot of a colossal check" — the product of a lumberman's millions. It was "founded on the fruits of industrialism, and dedicated, as the author sees it, to the interests of industrialism." Its architecture is a "vulgar imitation;" its graduate program "pretentious." It became an educational treadmill. In World War I it took up the national mood; its "chimes" played militant tunes while reserve officers deployed about the campus. *Chimes* was, in other words, an exhibition of Herrick in the act of biting the hand that had fed him.[60]

At the end of the first quarter of this century, Herrick's literary reputation reached its high water mark. "When the history of the American novel for the first quarter of this century shall have been written, the name of Robert Herrick will loom large," said Percy A. Hutchison. Others of that time would have agreed with him.[61] But today, although some of his work is still taught in survey courses in American literature, he is seen as a minor figure, dwarfed by Dreiser, Anderson, Fitzgerald, Hemingway and Lewis, among his contemporaries.

Other College Novels

There were four other college novels set in Chicago in this decade. Zoe Flanigan said that her *Grey Towers* (published anonymously in 1923) was "not a photograph but an interpretation."[62] Whichever, it is a sardonic study of a recently-built University on the shores of a lake in the middle west — either Northwestern or Chicago served as the model. The school had been built as a monument to Humanism and Democracy by its "Founder." But the novel portrays a University which loses its humanism and democracy as it turns into a graduate college whose goal is research.

A parallel story line shows a bohemian group (the Bohemiennes) who produce plays under the style of The Attic Theater, and whose members often trade mates with each other (in the fashion of the Renaissance bohemians in their cold-water store fronts on 57th Street). Joan Burroughs is the Victorian heroine who avoids the oft-tendered male contact on every occasion. Meanwhile, the marriage of Joan's sister flounders under the strain of the husband's ever-changing romantic interests.

The novel was not well received by critics.

Edwin Balmer's *Fidelia* (1924) is set on the campus of Northwestern University in the early 1920s. Other than the depiction of life on the Evanston campus in these years, the novel's portrayal of a college girl with a secret in her past is not worth much.

Neither is Florence [Jeannette Baier] Ward's *The Flame of Happiness* (1924). It tells of a co-ed whose rearing by a maiden aunt and education at an all-girls' boarding school has ill-prepared her for a co-educational campus.

By far the best of these Chicago college novels (including Herrick's) is Willa Cather's *The Professor's House* (1925), set in a hypothetical college town somewhere north of Chicago. An English reviewer noted that it is scarcely a story in which place matters: "it is a study of an interior, for though we are shown the professor going about his work outside, in the university town and in Chicago, we always see him as if we were looking out through the windows of his house"[63]

Cather's novel seems to have confused most of its contemporary reviewers. Henry Seidel Canby came close, seeing the story "as slow discovery by Professor Godfrey St. Peter — of himself."[64] Most reviewers could not comprehend the inclusion of the Tom Outland material, even though some of them commented that the story was well done.[65]

Journalists as Authors

The *Chicago Daily News* was founded as a penny daily newspaper in 1875 by Melville E. Stone. A year later he sold the struggling newspaper to a young friend, Victor F. Lawson. Lawson ran the newspaper until 1926.

Under Lawson's management, the *News* hired Finley Peter Dunne, whose Mr. Dooley once advised: "Dont't thrust anybody but your mither — and even then cut th' ca-ards;" Eugene Field, whose "Little Boy Blue" and "Wynken, Blynken and Nod" appeared in the paper; George Ade, and then at the turn of the century, as its editor, Henry Justin Smith.

Smith, in turn, hired Ben Hecht, who in turn "sweet-talked" Smith into hiring Carl Sandburg; John T. McCutcheon, the cartoonist and brother of George Barr McCutcheon, the novelist; John Gunther; Howard Vincent

O'Brien; Robert J. Casey; and Robert Hardy Andrews. Other *Daily News* authors were Meyer Levin, Vincent Sheean, Vincent Starrett, Harry Hansen, Henry Blackman Sell, Lloyd Lewis and Sterling North.[65]

By any standards, Smith is one of the more important figures in the history of Chicago journalism and literature. "Such reporters as get to Heaven," said Ben Hecht, "are given a desk in Editor Smith's Local Room."[67]

One wonders if any other American newspaper can match the book-publishing output of those who have reported for the *Daily News* in its 102-year history?

Smith added to the list with three books about Chicago journalism. *Josslyn* (1924) is subtitled "the story of an incorrigible dreamer;" the title fits the hero of this novel perfectly. Although his adopted city (Josslyn is from a Chicago suburb) becomes ugly and foul, Josslyn sees it always through the eyes of an idealist. Later, in Paris, he weighs his religious and aesthetic values and Chicago as well against Europe.

Smith's *Poor Devil* (1929) is the story of Bruce Warren who brings his bride from a small town to Chicago. He is, in the words of a reviewer, one of thousands of "poor devils for whom life will never hold anything but a calendar of petty problems with here and there a red-letter disaster."[68] The best part of the novel tells of Warren's work for the "Faith Publishing Company," and one Gowdy, its chief. Gowdy plagiarizes, and his company publishes, those flimsy tracts of faith, good hope and presumed knowledge which attract the gullible and unthinking.

Smith's *Deadlines: being the quaint, the amusing, the tragic memoirs of a newsroom* (1922) is a fictional series of sketches of life in the big city newsroom:

> Only the atmosphere of a certain news-room is authentic. There is a full description of a day in a newspaper office, beginning with the morning twilight among the deserted desks and waste-baskets, presaging boredom but growing more tense as the hours wear, becoming suddenly hectic when a piece of important news flashes over the wires, then slackening till at last the room is deserted and sad-faced old men with large sacks come to clear away the debris of the day's task. Then there is the "cave of tongues," the cigar-store below the office — noon-hour haunt of the gang. There follow pen pictures of the star reporter, the drunkard, the "young-man-going-somewhere" and several other types, not the least of which is the poet to whom the desk of city editor becomes a Golgotha.[69]

The poet, of course, was Carl Sandburg, the "young-man-going-somewhere," Ben Hecht.

Howard Vincent O'Brien's *The Terms of Conquest* (1923) surveys big business conditions in Chicago for almost a quarter of a century, from about the time of the Pullman strike (1894) until the end of World War I. The conquest of the title is achieved by a self-made man who might have inspired an Ayn Rand novel. Restlessly ambitious, he leaves his wife behind in Michigan to come to Chicago. He works first as a printer, then as a salesman, and then displaces the head of a book publishing firm, the husband of a woman he has fallen in love with. In Michigan, his wife becomes an invalid. His children turn out disappointingly, one of them marrying a radical University of Chicago professor.

O'Brien's *Trodden Gold* (also 1923) is also not about the newspaper world he knew, but about people with money and about people without money who have money problems but don't mind them. The novel contrasts the unhappiness in the marriage of Lyman and Constance Wainwright (who begin by having money problems, and end by having too much money) with the happiness in the marriage of Norris and Deborah Sears (Constance's sister). Norris is an impoverished lecturer in chemistry at the University of Chicago, interested only in "pure" research. He has no interest in a larger salary or advancement. When Sears discovers Searite, a useful plastic with great prospects, he loses his chance for wealth because he tells an unscrupulous associate of his discovery. Eventually, however the associate uses his gains to set up a Research Foundation and Sears is installed as its head.

O'Brien's third 1923 novel, *The Thunderbolt,* tries to show that success belongs to the man who asserts himself. Barnaby Lamb, once likable, easy going, a failure alters his view of life, acquires business savvy, becomes socially prominent and enters into a romance. The story, however, is oversimplified, unrealistic.

O'Brien's last novel, *An Abandoned Woman* (1930) is the first Chicago novel to use the stock market crash of 1929 as an important plot element. The theme of this novel about well-to-do sophisticated North Shore residents, whose grandparents made their fortunes with their hands in Chicago, is that the institution of marriage doesn't work very well. There's a lot of wife and husband swapping. Steve Hilliard is wrapped up in business and money-making; his wife in art and ennui. The children are sent off to school. Joan follows an artist to Paris. Steve loses all in the crash and shoots himself. Joan returns home to help him recover. The artist stays in France.

Like Smith, O'Brien was a better journalist than novelist. O'Brien depends too much on coincidence, and elements of his narrative are confusing. His characters are simply cardboard cutouts, not the real people he wrote about in his news stories and columns.

A second of Smith's star reporters was to become far more famous than either Smith or O'Brien. John Gunther, a Chicago native with a University of Chicago Ph. B. degree, was a *Daily News* reporter before he became a world-wide correspondent and the creator of the famous "Inside" books.

His 1926 *The Red Pavilion* reports a week in the lives of several Chicago young people, living together in a tenuous relationship: a poet in the Dostoievsky tradition, seeking death, and dying under the wheels of a bus; a girl who anxiously tells everyone she has just lost her chastity in a routine affair; a widow of a college professor who is being courted by a professor while at the same time one of his students is trying to seduce him in an effort to get a better grade in French.

Gunther overloads his narrative with diagrams, footnotes, a passage in Russian, and catalogs of words. He seems to be imitating Carl Van Vechten whose novels were in vogue at the time. Critics liked the novel, although one said he "looked forward to seeing [Gunther] without the crutches used in this book."[70]

Two of the characters in *The Red Pavilion,* Shirley and Richard Northway, divorced but living together, appear in Gunther's next novel, *The Golden Fleece* (1929). Joan Tilford, daughter of a very early Chicago family, has difficulty making up her mind about love. For a while she dates a young reporter, then enters into several affairs, some with older men and one which seems like an incestuous relationship with her father. At the end of the novel she still seems to be looking for a compatible male.

At one point, Joan visits the Loeb-Leopold trial with the reporter:

> These were the two boys then. Joan sat in the press box and watched them. They were sitting in a little depression on wicker chairs; both sallow, extremely well dressed, sullen, smiling.
>
> [Darrow, the defense] attorney strolled back and forth, round and about, shaking his mane of gray hair off his forehead, twiddling his suspenders at the trousers. It was hot. Even the judge was in shirt sleeves. The prosecutor was a sandy-haired man with a ringing, metallic voice and a permanent sneer to his lips; his nose splashed over his face like confused disaster ...
>
> "We'll get the dirty bastards, hang 'em," said the prosecutor.[71]

Among those who watched the "trial of the century" in the hot summer of 1924 was a University of Chicago student who had known the defendants as fellow classmates. Out of college, Meyer Levin became a reporter for Hearst's *Chicago Evening American* and began planning the Great American novel. A staff reduction cost him his job; soon he was working for the young *Esquire* and writing in his spare time.

His first novel, *Reporter* (1929) was not the Great American novel; it was not even a very good novel.

> Consternation gripped the mighty gods of the city desk. In the same moment had come two flashes: Manfredi, king of bootleggers, ambushed and filled full of slugs; the President of the University of Chicago dead after an operation for

gallstones.

Should the streamer be:

GANG LEADER SHOT, DIES
OR
U. OF C. PRESIDENT DEAD

Although the book's publisher says the book went through three editions, Levin himself says the book was withdrawn soon after publication because a woman reporter threatened suit on grounds she was libelled.[72]

In 1929, Henry Justin Smith and Lloyd Lewis, one of his better editors, co-authored a popular, literary *Chicago/The History of Its Reputation.*

"Young-Man-Going-Somewhere"[73]

In the 1920s, Ben Hecht, a third star reporter for Smith began to acquire a journalistic and literary fame that eventually rivalled Edna Ferber's. In June, 1921, he became a columnist in the *Daily News* with his "One Thousand and One Afternoons." The column's thesis was that "just under the edge of the news as commonly understood, the news often flatly and unimaginatively told, lay life; that in this urban life there dwelt the stuff of literature, not hidden in remote places either, but walking the downtown streets, peering from the windows of skyscrapers, sunning itself in city parks ...[74]

A year later, with a sentimental preface by Smith, *One Thousand and One Afternoons in Chicago* appeared in book form. It sketches were "dramatic studies often intensely subjective ... comedies, dialogues, homilies, one-act tragedies, storiettes, sepia panels, word-etchings, satires, tone poems, fugues, bourrees ..."[75]

Whether "fluff" or tragedy, these sketches were immensely popular; the book went through a number of editions and was still in print a dozen years later. Its success led eventually to sequels: *Broken Necks, Containing More 1001 Afternoons* (1926), and *1001 Afternoons in New York* (1941), written after Hecht had moved from Chicago.

Also in 1922, Hecht published *Gargoyles,* a novel set in Chicago from 1900 to 1918. It featured a poet who seems very much like Hecht's friend, Carl Sandburg. The central character is a college graduate who is elected to the United States Senate on the basis of several "witch-hunts," and becomes chairman of the Vice Investigation Commission. He conducts an investigation of department store owners who hire girls at such low salaries that the girls are forced into lives of prostitution in order to survive. But he ignores the "Bath House" Johns and "Hinky Dink" Kennas who prosper on prostitution.

Erik Dorn (1921) is a more serious attempt to show the efforts of two people to find themselves in their work and love affairs, and the failures that follow. Erik Dorn, a newspaper and magazine editor, modeled on Henry Justin Smith, leaves his wife of seven years to live with Rachel Laskin, an artist. Then he and Rachel go their separate ways to disillusionment.

The novel provides glimpses of the Chicago Hecht knew — a newspaper office, the Renaissance bohemians, anarchists, the law courts. We see Hecht's usual fascination with crowds (as in *Gargoyles*), and there is an excellent description of the city:

> In the evening when women stand washing dishes in the kitchens of the city, men light their tobacco and open newspapers. Later, the women gather up the crumpled sheets and read . . . Tick, say the words and tock say the juries. Tick-tock, the cell door and the scaffold drop. Streets and windows, paintings of the Virgin Mary, beds of the fifty-cent prostitutes, cannon at Verdun and police whistles on crossings; the Pope in Rome, the President in Washington, the man hunting the alleys for a handout, the langorous women breeding in ornamental beds — all say a tick-tock.[77]

And, says Nelson Algren, "in no other American novel is the relationship between the book's hero and the novelist revealed so lucidly."[77]

Humpty Dumpty (1924) seems like a second *Erik Dorn* and very much like an autobiographical novel. Kent Savaron comes from a small Wisconsin town (Hecht came from Racine) to Chicago to be a writer. But Hecht reverses his own situation — Stella Winkleberg, the girl, is Jewish. Despite some parental opposition, Kent and Stella wed; after the birth of a child they separate. Kent seems on the way to writing success with one novel in print and a second on the way. Then, apparently suffering from Hodgkin's disease, he kills himself, leaving Stella to wonder why.

From 1924 to 1927, Haldeman-Julius Publications of Girard, Kansas, publishers of the popular five-cents-a-copy "Little Blue Books," published six collections of Hecht stories: *Tales of Chicago Streets* (1924); *Jazz; and Other Stories of Young Love* (1927); *The Policeman's Love-Hungry Daughter; And Other Stories* (1927); *The Sinister Sex; And Other Stories of Marriage* (1927); *The Unlovely Sin; And Other Stories of Desire's Pawns* (1927); *Infatuation; And Other Stories of Love's Misfits* (1927). Not all of these stories were set in Chicago.

Together with his then-close friend, Maxwell Bodenheim, Hecht privately printed *Cutie: A Warm Mama* (1924), a scorching satire of literary critics who assailed Bodenheim for his allegedly obscene work.

Bodenheim was the author of *Blackguard* (1923), an autobiographical novel based on the author's early life; *Sixty Seconds* (1929), in which a condemned criminal reviews his life; and *Duke Herring* (1931), a bitter attack on Hecht in retaliation for a Hecht caricature of Bodenheim.

Hecht and Charles MacArthur left Chicago to write for New York news-papers. But soon their attention was attracted to the burgeoning film scene on the west coast, and it wasn't long before both were adapting, writing, editing and producing for the film industry. Hecht directed eight films, produced nine, was the original author of twenty-three, and the screenwri-ter for thirty-four, including the magnificent *Wuthering Heights* (1939), *It's A Wonderful World* (1939), *Spellbound* (1945), and his final film, *Gaily, Gaily* (1969), based on his penultimate and autobiographical 1963 book.

Novels By and About Women

The first Chicago author of consequence had been a woman (Mrs. Kinzie), and women had played an important part in her *Wau-bun*. Women had been prominent in the Chicago literary scene ever since, both as authors and as subjects:

> It is not merely that [male authors] take men for their central characters, and that women take women ... It is that the men tend toward a sharp epochal form, set between prologue and epilogue and emphasizing the changes in total social pattern from period to period, even as the men of business see the city in boom and depression, with faces on the street changing en masse. In contrast the woman novelist stresses a domestic continuity, divided into less sharp epochs by the stages of growth of children or by growth or decline of social relationships.[78]

When Lennox Bouton Grey made that comparison he was writing about Chicago novels prior to the early 1930s, and he was particularly familiar with the novels of the 1920s.

The first of these, Mary Borden's *The Romantic Woman* (1920), a not-too-well-written book, sets out to compare "the rawness and the childishness of the ultra rich of Chicago" to certain titled specimens of English society. The heroine, like Borden a Chicagoan, is disillusioned by Chicago and English life. Borden, not too incidentally, had taken her BA at Vassar and her second husband was a British army general who took her to London to live.

Jake (1921) by Eunice Tietjens (Mrs. Eunice Strong Hammond) is by a woman who was one of the lesser poets of the Renaissance and one of the early *Poetry* clique. Her subject is a triangle involving her hero, his second wife Carla, and his domineering paranoid mother. Although Jake draws cartoons for the *Inter-Ocean* (an important Chicago newspaper in the first years of this century), this book is not, in the words of a critic, "a study in place; it is a study in man."[79] The character of Jake unfolds subtly, even poetically, through the words of his fictional biographer, Ruth, the fourth woman in his life and the only one who seems to understand him. It possesses, said the critic, "the rare virtue of originality," but it would prove a "disturbing book" to the ordinary reader.[80]

Isabella Holt's *The Mariotts and the Powells* (1921) is, according to a reviewer of that time, one more of the "Canaan begat Aaron" school of fiction which began with John Galsworthy's *Man of Property* (1906).[81] To help the reader sort out the cast, the author includes a family tree of the fictional tribe.

The important members are old Joshua, a Civil War veteran who made his money in a foundry (sometimes it seems as if all Chicago millionaires made their fortunes in foundries), his three children, and the three cousins, Danning and Eddie Marriott, and Diantha Powell. The novel mixes romance, politics, banking, a radical newspaper, and relationships among well-off and not-so-well-off-but-scheming relatives.

Peggy Shane, who married novelist Thomas Boyd, and who used the pseudonym "Woodward Boyd," has three novels in this decade, *The Love Legend* (1922), *Lazy Laughter* (1923) and *The Unpaid Piper* (1927). The first novel follows four girls of Lakeshore, just south of Hyde Park, who have been taught since their father's death to trust in the "love legend of the prince who was to come and change the world with a magic kiss." The prince, however, never comes, as each girl's life takes a different route. Two of the girls become socialists, like their dead father, a former University of Chicago English professor. The other two marry rather conventionally.

Lazy Laughter follows its heroine from St. Paul's Summit Avenue to Chicago and a career as a visitor to Chicago schools for a philanthropic organization. Along the way, Dagmar Hallowell, a lazy, indifferent girl romances a high school principal afflicted with flights of imagination and a tendency for hyperbolic language, but marries a man much older than she. Critics called the novel an "indifferent" one.

The Unpaid Piper is one woman's life story from childhood to maturity. She longs for love, but she falls in with a bounder and suffers tragically.

Essentially, in these three novels, Boyd, who was not in her husband's class as an author, is saying that the "love legend" or any romantic dream just doesn't work out.

Samuel Merwin's *Goldie Green* (1922) is the story of "the new breed of girl" in Chicago. The time is the 1920s; "good girls are still courted in the front parlor, attend social functions escorted by their mothers, and wait patiently to be discovered by boys of suitably marriageable age and financial status." But Marigold Green looks at the "new America, luxuriously pagan, given to jazz dancing and pocket flasks and continuous aimless motion," and decides to be a part of the active scene. She sells automobile insurance, becoming the first businesswoman in the fictional Chicago suburb of Sunbury, then turns to theater management.[82]

Florence [Jeanette Baier] Ward's *Phyllis Anne* (1921) is the story of a girl whose father is a star of the stage. Phyllis Anne disguises herself as an older sister to leave the convent where she is a student and go to Chicago for several days. Later, she again leaves the convent and takes a part in one of her father's plays. As a result she becomes a professional actress. One of Ward's conventional, somewhat trivial romances follows.[83]

Neith Boyce's (Mrs. Hutchins Hapgood) first novel since *The Bond* fifteen years before, *Proud Lady* (1923), is only partly a Chicago novel. It begins in the late 1860s in a small town close to Chicago (refugees from the Fire stream in at one point) and some of its events take place in Chicago. The heart of the novel is a nineteenth-century four-cornered love affair, involving a married couple, the wife's continuing affection for a minister she had known before her marriage, and the husband's affair with his Chicago mistress.

In the years from 1903 to 1923, the Hapgoods had been occasional American expatriates in Italy and Europe, seeking liberation, culture, opportunities to live well and cheaply. Their friends included O'Neill, Dreiser, Max Eastman, Walter Lippman, John Reed, and Margaret Sanger.

Ellen Du Pois Taylor was a South Dakota author of a prairie novel, *Towers Along the Grass* (1928). In her *One Crystal and a Mother* (1927), a South Dakota woman becomes a Chicago newspaper reporter and falls in love with her editor. The "Crystal" of the story is a young lady whose escapades are constantly being reported to the newspaper by her mother — who had poisoned her own husband.

Maude Lavinia Radford Warren, a prolific Chicago author, set her second Chicago novel, *Never Give All* (1927) in Chicago's South Side Chelsea Park, near the University of Chicago in 1901; the University plays a prominent part in the novel. Teresa Santley Lane, daughter of a University professor and mismatched with an impecunious, arbitrary English teacher, thinks of herself as an "independent woman" and wants to become an author. Through an affluential North Side girl "slumming" at the University, the Lanes are introduced to North Shore society, and Teresa's step-sister marries a North Shore man.

During World War I the scene shifts to France, where both Teresa and her husband serve. Although Teresa happens upon her husband and her step-sister in a hotel room, the marriage survives. The novel ends in 1925.

Floyd Dell has two novels of boy-girl relationships in this period, both at least in part autobiographical. *An Unmarried Father* (1927) is an unusual tale for its times, one seemingly more appropriate for the 1970s and 1980s. A young law graduate of Harvard returns to Vickley, Illinois (Dell had lived at Alton) and becomes engaged to a girl there — seemingly headed for a routine middle-class middle-west existence. Then he learns that he has fathered a child out of wedlock in Chicago, and that the mother does not want him or the child. So the lawyer gives up his life in Vickley and moves to Chicago to take over the chore of rearing the child. As usual, Dell's characters, like Dell himself, are incurable romantics.

In *Love Without Money* (1931), another tale as appropriate to the 1970s and 1980s as it was perhaps inappropriate to the late 1920s, Dell shows us pair of teen-agers who defy parental authority and small-town morality by moving to Chicago, finding jobs, and settling down in a flat to live together until the time when they can decide whether to marry or to live apart. Gretchen Cedarbloom and Pete Carr are universal characters, and a modern reader will find their story as poignant as readers of 1931 found it.[84]

Negley Farson's *Daphne's in Love* (1927) presents a view of male-female relationships probably inconceivable to the author of *True Love*. Daphne Howard, who works in the Chicago office of the Eureka Motor Truck Company, knows that a "petting party lay at the end of every drive in the country," and that "decent girls didn't have much fun." She is, however, "willing to pay the fare," provided that she can retain her virtue until the right man comes along. Her affairs are complicated when she falls in love with two men, one of whom a bit later turns out to have a crippled wife. The whole affair, with even more complications involving an office mate and *her* romances, is resolved in a suburban night club shootout.

Farson's *Fugitive Love* (1928, originally in the *Chicago Daily News*) begins in one of those backwaters of the Chicago River, Corey's Wharf. The chief characters are Hickey Cain, a Chicago contractor not above paying off to win a lucrative contract, and Chauncy O'Malley, a politician, who's willing to help Cain get contracts. The "fugitive love" concerns Jenny Cain, whom Hickley is willing to award to O'Malley, and Torsten Aberg, a truck mechanic wanted elsewhere for murder. All ends well.

Margaret Weymouth Jackson's *Beggars Can Choose* (1928) narrates the consequences of the marriage of a wealthy girl to the son of a family servant, and their resulting fortunes. Two somewhat unusual subplots are featured in this tale of cyclical marital fortunes — a character's creation of a cartoon of a cat and its sale to the films — the time is about that of the creation of "Mickey Mouse" — and the unwitting, unwilling involvement of the family in a gang murder which leads to the loss of the family savings. But all ends well — for "beggars can choose" where the affluent cannot.

Henry Channon was the son of one of Chicago's early citizens but he preferred to live in England where he achieved a position in English society. These circumstances led to his *Joan Kennedy* (1929), the story of an English country girl who married the son of the second richest man in "El Dorado,

U. S. A." — another pseudonym for Chicago. The novel thus reverses the situations of Mary Bigot Healy's *Lakeville* and Mary Borden's *The Romantic Woman,* and permits an outsider's view:

> Chicago and Chicagoans were never more sharply seen than through the eyes of Joan Kennedy. Their absurdities, their loyalties, their insularity, their almost gargantuan self-satisfaction are as incomprehensible to her as her coldness, her dowdiness, and her class prejudices are to them.
>
> . . . The tremendous force of the city is more impressive to her than it is to the native sons and daughters for she sees it in perspective and to them it is something they merely accept.
>
> Channon has made Chicago a strangely different place from the Chicago we know, and he has done it by seeing it through the eyes of someone rooted in an entirely different culture.[85]

Mary Synon's *The Good Red Bricks* (1929) brings together the world of the musical entertainer and the world of the pugilist. The story is set on Chicago's West Side amidst the red brick houses at Harrison Street and in the downtown district from 1895 to New Year's Eve, 1899. During these years Sally Burt's father is in Stateville Prison — a term he could have avoided by telling the truth. Sally is married to Joe Gates, would-be doctor and prize fighter. She becomes a musical star, singing Paul Dresser's "On the Banks of the Wabash." Meanwhile, Joe hits the skids and dies of tuberculosis.

Synon writes in a "flaunting, flaring, sentimental and pretentious prose:"

> Static crowds, men and women shivering down Harrison Street in the gray cold of winter mornings on their way to work in factories to the eastward, those great, grim fortresses of toil outposting the sluggish river; chunky girls in bulky coats and knitted hoods, jabbering in strange tongues as their heavy shoes crunched through the snow; dark-skinned boys from sun-baked deserts of Syria and Palestine, from blue-shadowed hills of Italy and Greece huddling against icy winds from the southwestern prairies; sharp-voiced traders from Balkan bazaars and Russian ghettoes; Sicilians, Armenians, Lithuanians, Slovaks, Finns, Norse, spilling from polyglot colonies into arterial highways, seeking the labor that had lured them out on the world's course of empire . . .[86]

The Trespasser (1929) is an unusual Chicago literary work. It began as a film, featuring Gloria Swanson in her first talking and singing role. She plays the part of Mary O'Donnell, a Chicago girl from "back of the yards," who changes her name to Marion O'Donnell, when she becomes a private secretary to an industrialist.

Secretly she marries the third-generation son of a wealthy Chicago industrialist; when the father learns of the marriage he has it annulled. But by this time Marion is pregnant. Later, her ex-husband marries a Chicago debutante in Paris. But through an automobile accident and some other circumstances, the young couple are rejoined with their baby.

The film was "wildly acclaimed" in its first showing in London, and then was shown in New York to "a notable gathering," some of whom were no doubt attracted by Miss Swanson's presence at the American premiere.[87]

The film's success led to its novelization by Harry Sinclair Drago, author of some seventy "western" novels. Drago worked from the "scenario" (shooting script) by Edmund Goulding, the film's director. The book was published in 1929 by A. L. Burt Co., a New York publisher of inexpensive popular books. It got no reviews.

Emily Calvin Blake's *The Third Weaver* (1929) is set only partially in Chicago; its other settings are England, New York City, and Portland, Oregon. Its heroine acquires conflicting values and personality traits from an aristocratic father and a lower-class mother. Her husband is a writer and publisher with socialist ideals who has consequential problems in finding a secure lifestyle. The novel presents a picture of the bohemian life style of the World War I era.[88]

Saga and Chronicle Novels

"Chicago history, it seems to me, is more fictional than the tale of any other American city," Franklin P. Adams said in 1943. "For one thing thousands of Chicagoans still living have heard their grandparents tell of Tecumseh and Black Partridge, and their parents talk about General Logan and General Phil Sheridan." He listed those "whose early memories are ... of listening to the stories of the Fire; of the Ellsworth Zouaves at Camp Douglas, and even of Fort Dearborn ... [of] Fernando Jones, who was born in 1820 and came to Chicago in 1835, and who, still in 1900, could speak the Pottawattamie language that he learned from the [last Chicago] Indians in the [eighteen-]thirties ... [of] the opening of Crosby's Opera House, postponed to April 20, 1865, on account of the assassination of Abraham Lincoln on the 14th ..."[89]

It was fortuitous for Chicago writers and literature that such oral histories were available, for much of the written history of early Chicago, including all of the materials of the Chicago Historical Society had gone with the fire storm of October 8-9, 1871. It was equally fortuitous that Andreas and Kirkland and others had mined the memories of pioneer Chicagoans, men or women with first- or second-hand accounts going back to the Fort. The availability of these resources plus the post-Fire written and photographed records made such fictional history as Ferber's *The Girls* possible.

A dozen years after her *In Town and Other Conversations,* Janet Ayer Fairbank turned to her own upper-class background for three novels about a fictional family and the building of Chicago. She (and her sister, Margaret

Ayer) had been born to the Chicago mercantile aristocracy. Her husband was Kellogg "Ked" Fairbank, son of a merchant and soapmaker. On the first Sunday of each January, " 'everybody in Chicago' came to the Fairbank's home at 1244 North State Parkway; by all accounts, the host and hostess were two of the world's most charming and agreeable people."[90]

The Cortlandts of Washington Square (1922) is the story of Ann Cortlandt, ward of a New York Knickerbocker, a fictional character who must have been much like her creator. Ann experiences the Battle of Gettysburg first hand and meets Lincoln. At Antietam, she nurses a wounded soldier, Peter Smith, to health and then elopes with him. At the novel's end, we see her surprise as her train enters Chicago — the city is more metropolitan than she had expected.

But Chicago is not New York and Peter Smith is not a Knickerbocker. In *The Smiths* (1925) Peter Smith must start at the bottom in the booming iron business, and the Smiths must make their home in a lower-class neighborhood. As his business prospers — despite such trials as the Fire, which levels his plant, and the 1873 Financial Panic — Peter concentrates more and more on his work, thus demonstrating a trait found often in Chicago literary males — for the male, the only activity that mattters is work, whether it be in industry, commerce, the professions, banking or speculation. His counterpart in the novel is an attorney representing the best of transmitted New England culture in Chicago.

Ann, unhappy that Peter has not kept his original promise to share his life with her, still maintains her marriage vows, although there is one "pastel-tinted romance" with an opera singer in Paris. She survives Peter to become a great-grandmother.

"I have read all the chronicle novels dealing with Chicago, including one or two of my own fabrication," said Henry Blake Fuller, "and I incline to believe that [*The Smiths*] is the best of the lot ... Mrs. Fairbank writes out of a nature richly endowed to begin with, and endowed by many contacts with the world of men and affairs."[91]

Rich Man, Poor Man (1936) completed Mrs. Fairbank's saga of the Smith family, running from 1912 to 1929, and ending just before the Depression. The book begins with the formation of the Bull Moose Party and Hendricks Smith's desertion of the Republican Party for the Progressives. Out west in Kansas, Hendricks meets a bobbed-hair suffragette and marries her instead of the girl his family had intended. Back in Chicago he becomes a newspaper reporter, and is wounded in World War I. When he returns home after an affair with the other girl in Paris, his wife leaves him and moves to Greenwich Village — where many of the Chicago Renaissance bohemians were moving at this time. Hendricks becomes a banker; as the novel ends we see his "vague discontent" stiffening.

The Smiths is the best of the trilogy. Although the third novel is a lively book and demonstrates that Mrs. Fairbank knew politics, it represents a falling-off of her talents.[92]

Idle Hands, a collection of her short stories, had been published in 1927. With one exception, these stories are not up to the level of her longer works.

Edith Franklin Wyatt's *The Invisible Gods* (1923), "a slice of American life," is a novel set mostly in Chicago, 1882 to 1921. We see the descendants of old General Marshfield (he dies in 1921): Hetherington and his son Hancock; Judge Elijah and his three children, Louise, Joseph Winthrop and Maisie, and Enos Marshfield, a peripatetic onithologist. The story follows the children until Hancock is 45; he becomes a successful free-lance writer of essays, married for a while to the daughter of his and his sibling's music teacher. Jo becomes a successful Chicago surgeon and head of Chicago City Hospital. He dies of pneumonia at 36, however, after a bitter struggle over the hospital with Chicago politicians. Maisie marries an artist, only to discover he has married her for her money.

Most critics of the time thought, as one critic said, that the book was "a notable achievement" for all that it had attempted so much.[93]

Novels of Business

Newton Fuessle's second novel, *Gold Shod* (1921), developed, according to Robert Morss Lovett, "the two chief interests of American fiction [of the time], business and sex. [It is] a biography of a hero."[94]

Gold Shod follows the career of Fielding Glidden from a Chicago clerkship to the control of a Detroit automobile factory and to a role as an industrial dictator in World War I. Along the way he has more love affairs than Masters "Skeeter's Kirby." Although covering the same ground as Charles G. Norris's better-known *Brass*, published at the same time, it is one third the length of Norris's novel and moves at a much more rapid pace. Fuessle's thesis, actually developed through a story of three generations, is that a man will sacrifice what he truly desires rather than make the effort to find himself. Or, in Lovett's words, "one comes to feel that *Gold Shod* is America, and Fielding Glidden its soul."

Like Fairbank's *The Smiths,* Fuessle's novel also shows a Chicago business man who willingly gives everything else up for his work.

The prolific Edwin Balmer's next book about Chicago, *The Breath of Scandal* (1922), tells of the attempts of several people and a corrupt lawyer to hush a scandal and protect a Chicago corporation. The better portions of this novel show Chicago as a city of neighborhoods and the changes in the city in the post-World War I years. Another theme is the frustrations of women in a society dominated by the ambitions and work of men.

Balmer's *Dangerous Business* (1927) introduces a new motif — the use of "party girls" to persuade business men to switch their purchases from competitors. In a secondary plot, the hero marries a girl whose reputation has been tarnished by one of his friends. Reflecting Balmer's interest in Lake Michigan, the novel features a yacht race from Chicago to Mackinac and a rescue during a storm on the Lake.

In 1926 Ada and Julian Street's *Tides* fictionalized the career of Gurdon S. Hubbard, pioneer Chicago businessman from the morning after the Fire — October 10, 1871 — until 1900. In this chronicle of a Chicago family

> three generations of the Wheelocks (Hubbard) — the pioneer grandfather who wrests a moderate fortune from the development of the Northwest; the dilettante son; and the earnest, hard-working grandson — constitute the center of a long and loose narrative. The first chapter shows us that Chicago which is just decisively outstripping St. Louis as the western metropolis: a Chicago in which the Union stockyards are but a decade old, the Pullman car is a novelty, the river tunnels and lake crib are new, long streets still have to be raised from the primeval marsh, and Jackson Park is being built far out in the country. The later chapters show us the Chicago which found itself a real city after the [Columbian Exposition]; a Chicago with the first steel skyscrapers, with William Rainey Harper's new university, with David Burnham's dreams of a city plan, with long rows of millionaires' residences on the North Side, with Eugene Field and Hamlin Garland, with the rush and roar of the new century. The intervening years have carried the eldest Wheelock from middle age to death and the youngest from infancy to manhood.

The Saturday Review of Literature concluded that *Tides* was not "watered-down history; the novel succeeded in making Chicago an actuality without labored scene-setting, and in creating three persons, who, in varying degree are vivid, real and interesting."[95]

Felix Riesenberg's *Red Horses* (1928) is a revision of a 1925 novel, *P. A. L., A Novel of the American Scene,* the first treatments of the advertising business in Chicago. "P. A. L. Tangerman is blood-brother to the man who invented the slogan for Listerine, the advertisements that commence 'And when I turned to him and said in perfect French . . .' Riesenberg has created a synthesis of the masterminds behind everything from the Haldeman-Julius Blue Books to the International Correspondence School."

And, concluded the reviewer, as "befits a Chicago career, P. A. L. ends up a murdered man "shot by a young and beautiful widow." Shades of Roxie Hart![96]

In two novels, *Sweepings* (1926) and *The Great Bear* (1927), Lester Cohen traced the fictional histories of two brothers, Daniel Pardway, who builds a great department store, and Thane Pardway, who sets out to be the Great Bear of the Chicago Board of Trade. Their story begins with the Pardway's grandfather at the end of the Revolutionary War, thus connecting Chicago's growth to the original impetus that built this country. Daniel raises a family, but an employee succeeds him in his store. Thane never marries, but he does have an affair with a young secretary he keeps in his home.

Ernest Sutherland Bates said that *Sweepings* is a novel which doesn't fight shy of industry or the realism of business. He compared the book to *Buddenbrooks,* rated it equal to Balzac's second best work, and called it better than George Gissing's best. Lillian Hellman was not as impressed with the second novel. "Where *Sweepings* was fresh and important," she said, "*the Great Bear* is stale stuff, overdone."[97]

Sweepings was filmed twice, the first time in 1933 with Lionel Barrymore as Daniel and Alan Dinehart as Thane, the second time under the title *Three Sons* (1939). Critics were inclined to like the first version more.

Two Children's Novels

While 1920s adults were reading the books described in this section, their children were probably acquiring a juvenile view of Chicago through Wilbur Herschel Williams' *The Merrymakers in Chicago and Their Adventures in That Great City* (1920) and Clara Ingram Judson's *Alice Ann* (1928). Ned, the oldest of the Merrymakers, reports the Republican National Convention for a New York newspaper while his younger siblings visit their widowed aunt and participate in several adventures, all contrived to hold the attention of the less sophisticated youth of that time.

Alice Ann focusses on the summer activities of a group of middle-class Chicago lakeshore surburban children who encounter obstacles in their plans for the use of a neighborhood vacant lot for recreational activities. So they shift their focus and begin planning a city-wide summer program for young people. Unfortunately, the book seems scarcely relevent to the problems of young people in the Chicago of the 1980s.

Farmers Against the City

John Tinney McCutcheon is better known as a Chicago *Tribune* cartoonist, and particulary for his "Indian Summer." But in *The Restless Age* (1921) he portrays the growing disillusionment with city life of a farm boy who thought he has seen greener pastures in the city's concrete. Wiser, the boy returns to the land.

Lynn Montross, whose wife Lois was also an author, published his *East of Eden* in 1925, an account of the farmers' side of the consequence of gambling in grain futures on the Chicago Board of Trade, the other side of the subject of *The Great Bear.* Although most of the novel is set in a rural area one-hundred miles southwest of Chicago, Chicago dominates the novel. When farmers form a Grain Marketing Association for their own protection, they are opposed by a major trader in the Pit, as well as other farmers. The Association farmers are defeated by the passage of the Lantz bill in the Illinois State Legislature. Bankrupted, Fred Derring, the chief organizer of the Association, commits suicide with his automobile, and his son and daughter go off to Chicago to work.

In *Profane Earth* (1927) Holger Cahill tells the story of the son of impoverished dirt farmers. When his mother dies and his father disappears, Ivor (we never learn his family's name) makes his way by freight train to Chicago. For awhile he is a deckhand on a Lakes oreboat, dividing his off duty time between brawls in port hellhouses and tours of art galleries. A marriage to an artist's model ends in divorce. He also fails in an attempt to be an artist and is last seen as a journalist of sorts.

"There are Babbitts in the arts as well as in real estate," one critic wrote. "The subjective tempests arising in the souls of distraught young intellectuals will [some day] be relegated to their proper place — the teapot. ... An all around and objective treatment of artistic failure within the profane earth of America might be an excellent undertaking. But we will never get it until aspiring artists cease reading *Jean Christophe*."[98]

Chicago Ethnic Novels

Elias Tobenkin's *God of Might* (1925) is a tale of a Russian Jew who changes his name to Samuel Waterman and migrates to Lincoln, Illinois, where he gets a job as a store clerk, learns English and married a *goy* girl. He fails to find work in Chicago where we get occasional glimpses of the wholesale trade with its Jewish element. Eventually a Jewish colony forms in Lincoln; as a result the Jews become social outcasts. This is not a Chicago novel except for its occasional scenes of Jewish life in the city. It was written by a Chicago Jewish author, and, according to Zona Gale, a Wisconsin author, "presents a protagonist new to fiction: The Hebrew in America with a Christian wife, and with a Christianized family circle, which, together with his social and business Gentile associates, secretly reveals him as an outsider." Gale found the book to be "an honest and significant performance, a vivid contribution to the long and dramatic story of ethnic conflict."[99]

Norman Matson's *Day of Fortune* (1928) begins in Norway and follows Mary Aasen and Knut (Kjösnaes) Chezness to Chicago where they are married after the Fire, and where their son is born just before the Columbian Exposition. From Chicago, the family, always in search of their "day of fortune" move westward, their search in Chicago a failure. Matson was married to Susan Glaspell at the time he wrote this book.

The first seventy pages of Vera Caspary's popular first novel, *The White Girl* (1929) are set in Chicago. Solaria Cox is the twenty-year old daughter of a black gentleman janitor and his heavy-set wife, both of whom can look back to distinguished ancestors, the Dunbars of Mississippi and the Coxes of North Carolina. Solaria works in a stock room of a dress manufacturer — and dreams of wealth. Her Jewish boss won't let her model clothes even though she looks like a white girl. Still he lusts for her. She rejects a proposal of marriage from a black pianist-composer, and another from a wealthy Negro banker — she doesn't want to marry a black. When she and her mother are forced to move to a black slum after her father's death, she quits her job and goes to New York City. There, eventually, she commits suicide because she has fallen in love with a white man who wants to marry her — but she knows her children will be black.

"Among the problems confronting these United States there is none more difficult than that of the color line," wrote a reviewer of the time. "And it is one which is not growing less perplexing with the advance of time. It is easy to construct theories as to the relations which should exist between the races; it is far from easy to deal with a concrete case such as Vera Caspary sets before us in her very interesting and apparently authentic novel, *The White Girl*."[100]

The reviewer might have had in mind also William Edward Burghardt DuBois's *Dark Princess: a romance* (1928), a story set in New York, Berlin, Chicago and again in New York. The narrative develops the melodramatic, sometimes incredibly coincidental adventures of Matthew Towns, a black "of brilliant promise," who leaves a New York medical college because of discrimination. In Berlin he finds an international racism as strong as in America. He joins a black movement led by an Himalayan princess, and comes to Chicago to promote the movement. He works for a time as a railroad porter until he is jailed after a train wreck. Finally he becomes involved in politics.

The novel got mixed reviews; one critic argued that "DuBois [was] not a novelist at all." Noticeably, the critics reflected the racial prejudices of their time.[101]

Nella Larson's *Passing* (1929) begins in Chicago and ends in Harlem. It is the story of two light-skinned girls who are able for a while to pass themselves off as black. But Clara's feeling for her own race leads to the discovery of her duplicity and her apparent suicide — although critics think she is more likely a murder victim.

The novel, says Lennox Bouton Grey, "touches with psychological criticism the miscegenation which has appeared as a romantic fear in Carr's *The Illini* (1904) and as a symbolic fact in Masters' *Children of the Market Place* (1922):

> "It's funny about 'passing.' We [Blacks] disapprove of it and at the same time condone it. It excites our contempt and yet we rather admire it. We shy away

from it with an odd kind of revulsion, but we protect it."

"Hugh Wentworth," a character in the novel seems to be modeled on the Iowa writer, Carl Van Vechten.[101a]

Critics were mixed in their opinions of the novel, but the *Saturday Review of Literature* reviewer took a firm stand in favor of it: "Mrs. Larson has produced a work so fine, so sensitive and distinguished that it rises above race categories and becomes that rare object, a good novel."[101b]

Payne and Webster

In a mystery novel, *The Scarred Chin* (1920), Will Payne used a complex plot based on blackmail, a love triangle and a 1912 setting. A Black is also featured. The blackmailers are a reporter, a shyster lawyer and a dectective.

In *Mary Wollaston* (1920) and *Joseph Greer and His Daughter* (1922), another long-time Chicago novelist, Henry Kitchell Webster, told what is essentially one story of two families. The two books are linked by a music critic and other characters who appear in both novels.

Mary Wollaston was a "modern" story for its time. It features the effort of a young Chicago woman (a friend of Mary Wollaston's) to make a success of an opera career at the Ravinia Summer Opera Festival on Chicago's far North Side. She fails.

The second novel is a complexly-plotted tale of a Chicago businessman and his daughter. Joseph Greer "is a rugged, self-confident, aggressive man, with the soul of an adventurer and the daring of a pathfinder; he is one of those nondescript individuals who are too big for mediocrity and too small for greatness, and so find themselves dangling precariously between success and failure ... [102] His daughter is very much like her father.

It may well be Webster's best book; still, critics complained of the mass of irrelevant detail which helped build the plot, and to the lack of a real style. In general, however, they felt the book was worth reading and thinking about.

Webster's *The Other Story* (1923) is an anthology of short stories. "The Other Story" is about a Kentucky girl who wins a ten-thousand dollar prize in a contest sponsored by a Chicago newspaper. In "Inside and Out," a Chicago man buys a deluxe automobile and disguises it as an old car as a joke on his wife and brother-in-law. In "The Shower," a Chicago girl is caught in a rain shower with a stranger, a soldier in World War I. Although she is engaged to an older man, she accompanies the soldier to a movie theater. Watching the film, she learns both about the film process and herself. She decides to reject the older man (who is never seen) for the soldier.

In *The Innocents* (1924) and *The Beginners* (1927) Webster wrote what is obviously two-thirds of a planned trilogy. Both novels are set in "Lakeside," a suburb of Chicago. The "innocents" of the first novel are Edward Patterson, Sr. and Edward Patterson, Jr., 18, who has a sister, Edith.

The Innocents probably owes a lot to Booth Tarkington's *Penrod* stories. Edward is interested in radio-telephony — he invents a device for attaching a radio to a phonograph — but he never seems aware of what is going on around him. His parents of course misunderstand him.

Edward does manage to discover something of the wonders of sex during the summer of this story. At the same time his father is much more interested in Ruth Ingraham, a widow who lives next door, and for a time it appears as if the Patterson marriage may end because of his interest.

In *The Beginners,* however, Edward, Sr. gives up the widow and quits his job to enter into a manufacturing partnership. Edward, Jr. goes off to college, and the novel turns its focus on Edith. At the end of the novel, Edward, Jr. is still at college and Edith's romantic prospects are beginning to shape up. At the same time the father is in New York City hoping to arrange a large contract for the manufacture of automobile carburetors.

Neither book is up to Webster's previous standards, and perhaps for that reason he did not finish the trilogy. Both novels, incidentally, like much of Webster's work, ran serially in *The Pictorial Review,* a national magazine.

The potential in the confusion of identities of identical twins has served as a catalyst for numerous works of fiction. Webster's *Philopena* (1927), a Chicago-based romance, shows the consequences when Cynthia substitutes for her identical twin, Celia. Celia, however, is married — in fact, twice. The complicated plot unravels satisfactorily. Chicago itself is of little importance in the story — it might have happened anywhere.

The novel was dramatized "ineptly and futilely" by Louis E. Laflin, under the title *Mixed Doubles.* It was played in early 1928 at the Kenneth Sawyer Goodman Memorial Theater.[103]

Webster's *Rhoda* was serialized in *Good Housekeeping* from September 1928 until April 1929. A small town college professor resigns from his professorship because of some mysterious allegations. His daughter goes to Chicago to find a job so that she can support him. Various mysterious happenings take place around her; little by little she is able to see that her father was the victim of a conspiracy in which a tyrant of an uncle is also involved. The story did not reach book form.

Utopian Novels

In this decade, the novel which looked at Chicago in some more glorious possible existence almost disappeared. But there were two.

Edward Chichester Wentworth, a Chicago poet-dramatist, is the author of

The Education of Ernest Wilmerding (1924), an ineptly-written novel which may contain a great many autobiographical elements. Most of the story is set in the years 1879 to 1886; one of Wilmerding's romantic interests is shot and killed in the Haymarket Affair. An epilogue looks at Wilmerding in a Utopian Chicago in 1959, a century after his birth in the year of the publication of Darwin's *Origin of the Species* — a work which had some influence on this book.

T. S. Stribling's *Christ in Chicago,* "a complete novelette," which echoed Stead's title, was published in *Adventure* for April 8, 1926. The Chicago of this story has a population of fourteen million and the loop is dominated by 60-story "behemoths of ferro-concrete." The story features a conflict between medicine and faith-healing; a mysterious doctor seems bent on wiping out Chicago; his antagonist is a latter-day Messiah. An editor of the *Tribune* is sacrificed in the fray.

A Potpourri

This section features a variety of books: a Chicago novel by Edgar Rice Burroughs; a second roman á clef by Floyd Dell, a fictional biography of Governor Altgeld and a "flapper's" story.

To those acquainted with the popular fantasies of jungle life, featuring Tarzan the Ape Man (first seen in 1912), or of his fantasies of life on Mars, it may seem strange to find Burroughs in this catalog of novels about Chicago. But Burroughs was a native of Chicago as was his illustrator James Allen St. John. (Johnny Weismuller who played Tarzan for seventeen years was also a Chicagoan.)

In *The Mucker* (1921), Burroughs turns aside from the jungle and outer space to narrate the uneven career of Billy Byrne of Chicago, raised on the city's West Side streets, and becoming a gang member in the Lake, Halsted, Grand and Robery area. Although an armed robber living outside the law, he comes to the aid of a policeman facing three hoodlums and is accidentally shot. When later he is falsely accused of murder, the policeman warns him, and Billy flees to the far East where a series of typical Burroughs fantasy adventures await him. Back in New York City, Billy becomes a champion boxer and a girl from Riverside Drive falls in love with him despite some conversations along these lines:

> "Youse ain't agoin' to double-cross Billy Byrne. I gotta good notion to han' youse wot's comin' to you. Youse is de cause of all de trouble. Wot youse oughta get is croaked. You and your bunch of kale give me a swift pain. For half a cent I'd soak you a wallop to de solar plexus, dat would put youse to sleep for de long count you — you — "[104]

Billy tells the girl her social station is too far above his and he resolves to clear his reputation in Chicago. For his pains he is sentenced to life imprisonment in Stateville. Enroute to the prison, he escapes from a guard and flees to the American southwest for another round of incredible adventures and another chance meeting with the girl. At last a Chicago confession clears him and all ends 'well for Billy Byrne, now redeemed and, as a consequence, on the same social level with the girl.

Edwin Balmer's *Resurrection Rock* (1920) is named for a Northern Michigan landmark, but most of this novel takes place in Chicago. Like many of Balmer's novels, it is both melodrama and mystery. Its heroine is a rag-to-riches case; its hero a young World War I veteran whose parentage is shrouded in mystery. And that's for starters.

Donald Richberg's *A Man of Purpose* (1922) has a protagonist whose career somewhat parallels that of Governor Altgeld — but at a slightly later time. Richberg's "man of purpose" is, like Richberg himself, a "child prodigy, a university student, a young Chicago lawyer who becomes a politician."[105] The novel also focusses on the women who influence the central character. The time is from the late 1800s to the early 1900s.

Floyd Dell's *The Briary-Bush* (1921) is also a *roman á clef*, continuing the life of the faun-like Felix Fay first seen the previous year in *Moon-Calf*, the novelistic treatment of Dell's artistic beginnings in Davenport, Iowa. Disappointed in his Iowa love affair, Felix moves to Chicago where he becomes a reporter for a Chicago newspaper, then, later, a dramatic critic. A major portion of the book depicts the efforts of Felix and his wife, Rose-Ann, from Springfield, Illinois, to define what love and marriage ought to be for two people caught up in the marital and romantic mixups of Chicago's bohemian society.

One of the novel's themes is one which troubled the minds of other writers of the time, the so-called "revolt from the village:" the rejection of village values and a movement, on the part of intellectuals, back to the cities. By 1890 the westward trek to the open "virgin lands" had taken up all the land available. Thereafter the trek turned back in its tracks for some, back to the East. One version of the theme is in Sinclair Lewis's *Main Street* and all its imitators; another is in *The Spoon River Anthology;* still others are seen in *Sister Carrie,* in Susan Glaspell's *The Visioning,* in Edna Ferber's *Fanny Herself.* The central characters of these latter novels leave the small towns of the Chicago hinterlands and move to the city for better or for worse.

Peewee (1922), a novel of an orphaned newsboy in Chicago, is by William MacHarg, who occasionally collaborated with Edwin Balmer on stories of the Great Lakes. Peewee, an apparent orphan, escapes from an orphanage and supports himself by selling flowers and newspapers. Meanwhile, the mystery of his parentage deepens; MacHarg withholds information from the reader. Gradually we learn that Peewee's family has something to do with an ex-truck driver, one of the families which built Chicago, and a family which once had a corner on wheat. If we stick with this narrative, despite our unwillingess to suspend disbelief, we will probably wonder why Chicago newspapermen wrote such fantastic tales when the real world of Chicago offered much better story lines.

Clara Palmer Goetzinger's *Smouldering Flames* purports to be the diary of a "flapper"-type girl from sixteen and a half years to twenty-three. Our first impression is that either Goetzinger was a bad writer, or she just possibly has caught the style of a girl of this type during this time. Whichever, the novel was published in 1923 and 1928, each time by a different publisher.

Nan Livingstone lives with her widowed mother on "Lake Shore Drive, Chicago, in one of the most expensive and exclusive 'apotments,' where on every floor the private front entrance to each separate apartment is ornamented with some ornery 'Coat [of Arms[' on a fancy-doodle doorknocker . . ."106

> I smoke, take a nip when I think the party needs it, or I do; adore wild experiences; dance every minute I get a chance; and pet when or where I sense the fever rising.[107]

The novel is a modern *Pamela*. Nan gets what she wants, even a young man with money enough to afford a private railroad car — but she never "goes the limit;" she gets what she wants without sacrificing her virtue.

Three of the stories in Sherwood Anderson's *Horses and Men* (1923) are set in Chicago, but they are not set on the Gold Coast Nan Livingstone knew, nor are their characters likely even to know what a private railroad car is:

> At times all Chicagoans grow weary of the almost universal ugliness of Chicago and everyone sags. One feels it in the street, in the stores, in the homes. The bodies of the people sag and a cry seems to go up out of a million throats, — "we are set down here in this continual noise, dirt and ugliness. Why did you ever put us down here? There is no rest. We are always being hurried about from place to place, to no end. Millions of us live on the vast Chicago West Side, where all streets are equally ugly and where the streets go on and on forever out of nowhere into nothing.[108]

And yet, the characters in "A Chicago Hamlet," "Milk Bottles," and "A Man's Story" are not Chicagoans, but people who have come to Chicago from Wisconsin and Ohio and Kansas, because they have "revolted from their villages:"

> In those dead flat Kansas towns lives have a way of getting ugly and messy without anything very definite having happened to make them go on.[109]

But in Chicago, whether a character becomes a wardrobe mistress in a blowzy theater or an advertising man who needs whiskey to stand up against Chicago's ugliness, life is also flat and messy except, perhaps for those girls like Nan Livingstone, daughters "of a man who owns a soap factory," who are likely to be "very pretty girls:

> I saw [one] once. She is nineteen now but soon she will be out of college and if her father makes a great deal of money it will profoundly affect her life . . . "110

Still, the narrator of "Milk Bottles" has a low opinion of those who join Chicago's commercial world:

> "You're all right, Ed. You're great. You've knocked out a regular sock-dolager of a masterpiece here. Why you sound as good as Henry Mencken writing about Chicago as the literary centre of America, and you've lived in Chicago and he never did. The only thing I can see you've missed is a little something about the stockyards, and you can put that in later."111

Anderson dedicated his book to "Theodore Dreiser in whose presence I have sometimes had the same refreshed feeling as when in the presence of a thoroughbred horse."

And he acknowledged his own obligation to Dreiser, in spite of Dreiser's "heavy prose" and "heavy feet:"

> The feet of Dreiser are making a path, the heavy brutal feet. They are tramping through the wilderness of lies, making a path.112

Anderson's *Dark Laughter* (1925) which begins in the 57th Street cold-water flats (although Anderson calls it "47th Street") is a novel of revolt: against the old moral standards with respect to marriage and divorce, in protest against the Bohemian enervation in these same studios; and against typical newspaper practices of that time, the government "bunk shooting" through the newspapers during World War I, the practice of having some "smart Jew" rewrite a journalist's story in newspaper jargon. Bruce Dudley, the young journalist finally leaves Chicago because there "any little smart newspaper scribbler can turn [one] out a cynic, and where newspapers are a necessary part of modern life. They weave the loose ends of life into a pattern. Everyone interested in Leopold and Loeb, the young murderers. All people thinking alike. Leopold and Loeb become the nation's pets . . . Dance Life! Awake and dance . . . (65).

"Nowhere Else in the World [1923] places [its author, Jay William] Hudson definitely in the ranks of the new novelists who have appeared in America since the War," said one critic of this novel.113 Hudson at the time was a professor of Philosophy at the University of Missouri, and part of the novel is set at a middle western school called "Athens."

Hudson's hero, Stephen Kent, is a young man who, after publishing his first novel in Paris, returns to Chicago where he unwillingly enters his father's construction business. In Chicago, however, he has a new vision of the city and writes a second and successful novel about the city:

> He had called it ugly. Perhaps it was ugly. Yet here was the terrible beauty of chaos in conflict as it must look to God when he fashions a world — the beauty that yearns, throbs, pulses through life with infinite passion, fights endless battles, achieves impossible valors.[114]

A vision of Chicago that neither Robert Herrick, another professor or Sherwood Anderson seemed willing to put on paper.

In 1923, University of Chicago professor Edwin Herbert Lewis published his second novel, *White Lightning*. The book reflects Lewis's strong interest in science; its chapters, for instance, are titled consecutively in the atomic order beginning with hydrogen and ending with uranium; each element is brought into its chapter in some fashion. The novel's central character is Marvin Mahan, who, from his twelfth birthday on, is insatiably curious about chemistry. The settings are in and near Chicago, and in Michigan's Upper Peninsula. Trench's elliptic, ambiguous style may turn away even some dedicated chemists.

Justin Sturm's *The Bad Samaritan* (1926) has been called a "fantasy" or a novel of the "Freudian wish." Dick Farr, a Nebraska boy, sees Barbara Stewart twice, both times by chance: on Armistice Day in France, and in a church the day she marries a wealthy young Chicago merchant. When they meet again by chance, they fall in love — Barbara is being neglected by her husband who works all week and golfs on Sunday. In the end, Dick's "wish" for Barbara is "fulfilled;" he wins her. This improbable plot is presented in a tongue-in-cheek tone that makes it impossible for the reader to take the tale very seriously.

Ring Lardner's "Mr. and Mrs. Fixit" (in *The Love Nest and Other Stories* (1926) tells caustically of a Chicago couple who constantly meddle in the affairs of another Chicago couple they've met by chance. It's not necessarily a story limited to Chicago, and it tells us very little about the city itself.

Walter Leslie River's *The Death of a Young Man* (1927) is the erstwhile journal of David Bloch, a University of Chicago student who has been told he has a year to live. Bloch's acquaintances include M., a girl to whom he is attracted, R., an affluent male, perhaps a teacher, Polly Carr, who seems to tease David with the possibilities of seduction, Fuqua, a morbid psychologist, Dr. Mies, a sociologist who studies slum families and Fuqua's slum-dwelling family. These characters are seen on a number of disconnected occasions, one of which is set in a "black and tan" cabaret. The novel seemingly echoes the philosophies of Walter Pater, the *fine-de-siecle* English writer.

David O. Tomlinson says that the "life-style of Kenneth Flexner Fearing [born in Oak Park] was colorful enough to cause at least three Chicago novelists to model characters on him:" W. L. River, in *The Death of a Young Man;* Margery Latimer (Mrs. Jean Toomer), in *This Is My Body* (1930); and Albert Halper, in *Union Square* (1933).[115]

Fearing took a B.A. at Wisconsin in 1924 and then moved to New York City where he became a poet and novelist. His first book, *Angel Arms* (1929) has sixteen poems on the rigors of city life.

In *Are You Decent?* (1927), Wallace Smith used the same formula earlier seen in Webster's *The Painted Scene*. These ten short stories originally appeared in *Hearst's Cosmopolitan*. Each story focusses on a member or members of a theatrical or circus act, all of whom live, when not performing out of town, in a Chicago theatrical boarding house. Each story, like those of Webster's, catches its central character at some moment of crisis. The stories have an O. Henry quality without the surprise endings.

James Marshall's *Ordeal by Glory* (1927) is a fictionalized novel of the life of John Peter Altgeld, the Illinois governor who pardoned the surviving members of the Haymarket group, who was a populist, and, in the eyes of many, a radical. There was a particular timeliness in the publication of this novel — it came at a time when the governor of Massachusetts was being petitioned to pardon Sacco and Vanzetti for their alleged roles in a payroll robbery. The same issues were at stake in both cases — a populace inflamed by charges of anarchy and socialism demanding a scapegoat.

Why Marshall, a lawyer, chose to use a fictional name for a character whose life is exactly like that of Altgeld puzzled critics who said that it was time a biography was written. His decision does, however, permit him to paint his hero, not as a firebrand or reformer, but as "a straight-thinking, simple-minded man" who was conscious of his strengths and weaknesses, and disliked injustice. Marshall summarizes his view of Altgeld in a final passage:

> He had been Governor, and so they placed his casket in a public place. And all day long, out of the drizzling rain, there moved a line of care-worn, sad-faced people to look upon his sad and care-worn face. All day long they passed with wet feet and dripping coats. The drops made puddles where they fell from the men's doffed hats, from their umbrellas, and the hems of skirts, upon the marble floor. A woman, weeping, said: "There's them as says he was a fire-brand — because his heart was warm." Someone beside her turned to say: "There ain't much difference between a firebrand and a torchlight. He may have singed them here and there, but it was a torchlight he held for all that."[116]

Edward Shenton's *Lean Twilight* (1928) is, as a reviewer said, "a book of futilities." Its heroine is a girl who relates her search for peace and security in a stream-of-consciousness fashion, as her search takes her from a married lover in New Jersey to an employer in Chicago to a single young man in Europe. Camar O'Neill is "a wax slate on which [is] written impressions in unfinished sentences." Married at last, "she becomes just like thousands of other women in the lean twilight of middle age."

"The book," concluded the reviewer, "is worth reading."[117]

Lucian Cary's *The Duke Steps Out* (1929) is a not-to-be-taken-too-seriously romance between Duke Wellington, a North Clark Street prize fighter and a Chicago girl. When Susan Corbin goes away to "Minnewaska" (the University of Wisconsin?) to become a "collidge" girl, the Duke follows her and becomes a student also. There, while wooing the girl (handicapped by detectives the girl's father has put on the Duke's trail), Wellington conceals his role as a boxer. The novel was so popular that a sequel was called for. The second book has very little to do with Chicago.

Thyra Samter Winslow, a popular short story writer of the time, set most of a 1920s novel and a 1923 collection of short stories in Chicago. *Picture Frames'* collection of eleven stories presents

> a series of pictures of types from various walks and times of life. There is the thoroughly sophisticated country girl from Iowa, coming to Chicago with the intent of capturing a millionaire. But not until she has been taught by a city girl how to be really simple does she succeed in making an impression. There is the grandmother who divides the year equally among her three married children — to be overworked in one place, politely tolerated in the other and the target of all the family ill-humors in the third — and who feels herself a personality only while she is between families. There is the immigrant Jewish family who pass through the entire cycle from abject poverty to great wealth with the gradual changes in their name: Rosenheimer, Rosenheim, Rosen, Rose and finally Ross.[118]

Edna Ferber had been presented as the patron of Mrs. Winslow, but her review of the collection was not wholeheartedly enthusiastic:

> The fault to be found with these stories of Winslow's is, perhaps, that she takes these people and makes them interesting, not in spite of themselves, but in spite of herself. They interest her, but only clinically. She cuts, dissects, lays open, and says, 'There you are. Observe that dark reddish mass. You will notice that it pulses, or beats. The heart. Interesting organ.' So she presents them, starkly, weaving no words of shining fabric to cover their nakedness. There are whole pages of writing that make the reader wish for just one graceful phrase, one lovely word, one fluid paragraph. Hard, tough, common, little Anglo-Saxon words about hard, tough, common, little American people.
> 119

Winslow's *Show Business* (1926) tells

> how Helen Taylor went on the road with the 'Silver Slipper' company, how she learned to graft dinners and suppers and perfumes and cold cream, how she

went back to Chicago and learned to be beautiful by having her hair touched up, how she went into the chorus of 'Happy Days,' and learned about suppers with lobster in huge chafing dishes and champagne in magnums.[120]

Eventually Helen Taylor weds a young and handsome millionaire. Reviewers had mixed opinions about the novel:

The book is technicaly competent, consistently conceived, and with at least one character who comes alive out of the pages. As a whole, however, the novel hardly lives up in poignancy or philosophy to the promise of Winslow's short stories, and leaves this reader at least with the feeling that her genuine and important talent should continue to apply itself in the other field.[121]

Carl Sandburg

By the early 1920s Carl Sandburg had become, in Harry Hansen's estimation "a figure of national importance." He had won a Doctorate of Literature from Knox College in his home town of Galesburg; he had begun reading and singing his verses on college campuses across the land and reciting his *Rootabaga Stories* to ever-increasing audiences.

In the 1920s Sandburg was attempting "the longer epic, the descriptive poem of several hundred lines that portrayed a wide canvas." One of these poems was "The Windy City" in his *Slabs of the Sunburnt West:*

Forgive us if the monotonous houses go mile on mile
Along monotonous streets out to the prairies ...

If a boy and a girl hunt the sun
With a sieve for sifting smoke ...

Forgive us if the jazz timebeats
Of these clumsy mass shadows
Moan in saxophone undertones,
And the footsteps of the jungle
The fang cry, the rip claw hiss,
The sneakup and the still watch,
The slant of the slit eyes waiting —
If these bother respectable people
    with the right crimp in their napkins
    reading breakfast menu cards
    forgive us — let it pass — let it be.
Forgive us
If boys steal coal in a railroad yard
And run with humped gunnysacks
While a bull picks off one of the kids
And the kid wriggles with an ear in the cinders
And a mother come to carry home
A bundle, a limp bundle
To have his faced washed, for the last time,

Forgive us if it happens — and happens again
And happens again ...

The poem, said Harry Hansen in his *Midwest Portraits* (1923), "is a monument that shows the futility of portraying the city as a woman in a coat of mail with the words "I Will" across her breast; it heaps irony on statues of "civic virtue" and other outcroppings of municipal vanity."[122]

Midwest Portraits is, on its own merits, a work of art. It begins with the moody retrospective of Schlogl's, the "ancient tavern" where Chicago writers had hung out, and whose menu offered "partridges and mallards in season" and "owls to order." It then digresses to the row of one-story frame buildings on Stony Island Avenue once occupied by Columbian Exposition vendors and later by the Renaissance bohemians. One of these — once occupied by Thorsten Veblen — was the residence of Margery Currey, Floyd Dell's ex-wife. Here in the years of the Renaissance came Arthur Davison Ficke and Witter Bynner, *vers libre* poets and imagists; Maurice and Ellen Van Volkenburg Browne with talk of their Little Theater; Edgar Lee Masters, bearing a manuscript of a poem; Sherwood Anderson, always reading from one of his "unpublished books;" Floyd Dell, George Cram Cook, Carl Sandburg, Ben Hecht and "Bogie" Bodenheim," always in a spirited controversy over a play or a poem; Dreiser, Edna Kenton, and Margaret Anderson, the latter planning her *Little Review;* Vachel Lindsay, "booming his *Congo*," Clarence Darrow, Eunice Tietjens, Harriet Monroe, Clara Laughlin, Vincent Starrett, Marion Strobel, Llewellyn Jones.

Hansen's book relives those golden days of Chicago's history through his recollections of days just past in which he, also, had played an important part.

A Rash of Poets

Never again in the next half century or longer would Chicago be home to such a fine group of poets as it had during the Renaissance. But although Margaret Anderson and the *Little Review* had gone east, *Poetry* stayed in Chicago, and poets continued to abound — if of lesser stature.

Some verse was set to music in this decade and became better known than any non-musical verse. Harry von Tilzer had written his "Only a Bird in a Gilded Cage" in a Chicago roadhouse; it was appropriate to Chicago with its story of a pretty girl whose

beauty was sold for an old man's gold.
Just a bird in a gilded cage ...[123]

But the song that became Chicago's trademark was "Chicago, Chicago," written in 1922 by Fred Fisher, who wrote a thousand other popular songs

— but it was this song that set Chicago toes tapping:

Chicago, Chicago, that toddlin' town, toddlin' town —
Chicago, Chicago, I'll show you aroun' —
   You'll love it.
Bet your bottom dollar you lose the blues in
         Chicago, Chicago
The town that Billy Sunday could not shut down.
On State Street, that great street
I just want to say, just want to say,
They do things they don't do on Broadway —
      Say —
They have the time, the time of their life,
I saw a man who danced with his wife,
In Chicago, Chicago, my home town.[124]

Edward Chichester Wentworth's *The Valley of Enna and Other Poems and Plays of 1922* (1923) included the three-act *The Growing Dawn,* and *The Spirit of the Lower North Side.* The first brings together an unlikely group — an affluent Chicago business man and his wife, their son and his bohemian friends, a tutor named Richard Mansfield, and two artists. The son is obsessed by the idea of the Pre-Raphaelite Brotherhood — hardly a magnificent obsession.

The second play, set in 1917, features a group of pacifists and war resisters.

Lois Seyster Montross, whose husband's novel we have seen earlier, published her *The Crimson Cloak* in 1924. This first volume of lyrical and dramatic verse attracted reviewers in all the major reviews. "[The poems] are better at the first than at the second reading," said Mark Van Doren. Their note is an intense one and their inspiration is undoubtedly true; but a certain over-neatness robs them of their full effect."[125] "An obviously youthful, yet not uncompromising first book of verse," said Arthur Guiterman.[126]

In 1927, Montross published a volume of short stories, *Among Those Present.* "Near a Park" tells of a young couple forced to move by economic conditions. "Rickard's Daughter" is about an affluent middle-aged Chicago alderman who passes off a young ex-chorus girl as his daughter. "Georgy Porgy, Prodigy," is about a young man, son of a college professor, who comes to a moment of realization following a brief flirtation with a married woman.

Dorothy Dow, from Chicago's "Black Belt" was the author of *Black Babylon* in 1924 and *Will-O-the-Wisp* in 1926. The black "Babylon" is south of 22nd and all along State Street in the Chicago of the 1920s; the specific reference is to night life and the world of the demi-monde. "The Great Grim Lincoln" is pictured watching this world from Heaven with a heavy and chill heart. He tells Jesus his children need him. Jesus and Lincoln go down to earth to "see." After observing a night of carousal and sin, Lincoln weeps and prays in agony. But Jesus says: "Be not uncomforted. It was so men sinned in Babylon ages ago ..." But when "Babylon falls, their souls ... shall all come home to me ..."[127]

The meters seem at times to be influenced by Edna St. Vincent Millay, at times by Vachel Lindsay:

> Early in the night,
> About half past eight
> South of Twenty-second
> And all along State,
> The music started,
> And the lights flared up
> In a flame on the dregs
> Of the City's cup.[128]

A newspaper article of the time linked the names of Dow and Edgar Lee Masters, then recently divorced. The writer quoted a couplet of Masters':

> There near the Luxembourg when their waging kiss
> Caught between lips the rapture of a bird ...

and said it referred to Dow and Masters.[129]

Dow did not publish a book of verse again until 1947. "Dorothy Dow enjoyed a brief flare of popularity in the 1920s," a Chicago critic wrote, "and was a sort of minor rival of Dorothy Parker's, although her verses were not so bitter. Wonder if anyone reads her things today?"[130]

Marion Strobel, whom we shall see later as a novelist, and who was associated with *Poetry* about this time, published her *Once in a Blue Moon* in 1925, a collection of some seventy-five lyrical verses. Some had first been published in *Poetry*, *The Bookman* and *Good Housekeeping*.

Edwin Herbert Lewis, author of two Chicago novels, published his *University of Chicago Poems* in 1923. "To call them university verses would sound like a play on words," he said.[131] Many were topical items he had been called on to compose and read at various University affairs. "The Ballad of Ryerson," for instance, marked the retirement of Martin Antoine Ryerson, Chicago business man, art collector, patron of the Art Institute, and President of the Board of Trustees of the University:

> But what of the day when the planet is full and breeding constrained?
> When the last black fern is a ghost and the last of the coral drained?
> Will the sword bite harder than ever? Will the grade and glory be done?
> These grave halls are the query, and the gravest is Ryerson.
> For the man is become a tower ...[132]

In the late 1920s and early 1930s, Jean Toomer, another black Chicagoan, published two volumes of verse and two collections of short stories under the name of Margery Latimer. Many of the poems have Chicago settings, others are out of the midwest: *We Are Incredible* (1928); *Nellie Bloom and other stories* (1929); *This Is My Body* (1930); *Guardian Angel and other stories* (1932).

At twenty-one, in 1927, George Dillon was associate editor of *Poetry* and author of *Boy in the Wind,* a collection of verse which had previously appeared in *Poetry, The Dial, The New Republic* and *The Saturday Review of Literature.* He wrote, said Ruth Lechlitner, "in sweeping gestures of wind, rain, and flame:"[133]

> Finding the city below me like a flame
> In the last sunshine, I said to autumn, "Blow on!
> We are building a beautiful spring you cannot claim
> In this country of stone."

> And seeing so many march in a thousand ways
> The old ways of hunger and thirst, I thought,
> They are going somewhere, somewhere their dream is waiting,
> Whether they know it or not.[134]

Dillon's second volume, *The Flowering Stone* (1931) was the first Chicago book of verse to win the Pulitzer Prize.

Dillon's work was reminiscent of Tennyson in its verses, of Shakespeare in its themes of love, death, life and nature. "I like [Dillon's] poetry the better because it reminds me of . . . poets of the past," said Robert Morss Lovett, his teacher and critic. "George Dillon is beyond question a poet."[135]

Dillon, one of the youngest poets to win the Pulitzer Prize for Poetry was born in Florida and educated at the University of Chicago where his poetry won several awards. He was the president of the University of Chicago Poetry Club; its members included Maurice Lesemann, Glenway Westcott, Elizabeth Madox Roberts and Vincent Sheean. He founded the *Forge,* a magazine of verse. In 1932, the year he won the Pulitzer, he also won the Guggenheim Award which enabled him to spend two years in France.[136]

Marion Strobel (Mrs. James Herbert Mitchell) whom we have seen as the author of several novels, and who, in the 1920s was active in the editing of *Poetry,* in 1928 published a volume of her own poems, *Lost City.* The book has four sections: "Lost City," "Women," "Spring Hat," and "Fair Weather and Nursery." Some of the latter verses are about her daughter, Sally. Several of the verses had appeared in *Poetry* and *The Saturday Review of Literature.*

Chicago's Little Magazines

The *Dial,* long out of sympathy with much of Chicago writing, moved to New York City in 1918, there to become, in the hands of new owners, "a showcase of avant-garde literature."[137] It published Anderson's post-*Winesburg* stories, for example.

In the 1920s, continuing a decades-long tradition, new literary and art magazines appeared, trying to fill the vacancy left by the *Dial,* and back-stopping *Poetry* which remained in Chicago through the decade. Newspaper commentator Vincent Starrett's *The Wave* persisted from 1922 to 1924; Steen Hinrichsen's *The Mediator* began in 1923 and simply faded away.

The Dill Pickler was the organ of the Dill Pickle Club, an organization for the promotion of the arts, crafts, literature and sciences, from 1922 to 1924. Dale Kramer said "the bacchic revels" of this group took place in a "Tooker's Alley speakeasy where pseudo-bohemians, including slummers from the Gold Coast, met for Al Capone's hootch, poetry readings, one-act drama shockers by Ben Hecht and Maxwell Bodenheim with no extra charge for a sight of the authors and sex 'lectures.' "[138]

The Forge made a more valiant effort under the editorship of author-poet Sterling North; it ran from June of 1924 to the Fall of 1929.

In one of its final efforts, Covicic-McGee published Ben Hecht's *Fantazius Mallare,* "a dark and wayward book ... affectionately dedicated to [his] enemies" by Hecht. The Federal government charged him, his artists and his publishers with obscenity and the *Daily News* fired him. Hecht's response, with the aid of Maxwell Bodenheim, was the *Chicago Literary Times,* published from March 1, 1923 until June 1, 1924. It was a four page tabloid which parodied the Chicago Renaissance and various literary magazines. Chicago, said the initial issue, was "the jazz baby ... reeking, cinder-ridded ... bleating, slant-headed rendezvous of half-witted newspapers, sociopaths and pants makers ..." "Raffish nihilism," commented Dale Kramer.[139]

The *Times* labeled Sherwood Anderson "a phlegmatic, practical-minded con man" with the "mellow garrulity of a small-town barber." Even Sandburg, Hecht's erstwhile friend, got his lumps. "A certain manic megalomania characterizes nearly all his remarks ... The ten years that have witnessed his ascent brought about a change in his manner ... His sense of importance would embarrass the Pope of Rome. A formidable wariness lurks in his eyes. A sense of vast injury and vast defiance animate his simplest remark."[140]

"Chicago: An Obituary"

With the passing of the Renaissance, H. L. Mencken's enthusiasm for Chicago as "the literary capitol of the United States" passed also. In 1926, his and Nathan's *American Mercury* published a funeral sermon for Chicago's literary reputation, "Chicago: An Obituary." It was writtten by Samuel Putnam, who had been a Chicago journalist for over half a century and was one of the regulars at Schlogl's famed round table.

After World War I in Chicago, what? he asked. The literary reviews of the *Evening Post* no longer mattered — Dell, Hackett and Cook had gone on to Greenwich Village and Provincetown, taking Susan Glaspell with them. There were no critics left in Chicago. As for literature: "Chicago ... keeps up the illusion that it is producing literature," even though Masters, the two Andersons, Dreiser, William Morton Payne, Ade, Dunne, Lardner and George Barr McCutcheon had moved east. Even Garland had given up on Chicago and was now mining his past for his new books. Putnam granted that there were the Bookfellows, the Friends of American Writers, the Poetry Lovers of America, the Book and Play Club, the Greater English Club, and the Society of Midland Authors. Still, as Putnam reviewed the scene, all he was able to find were a feeble Fuller, a dreaming Opie Read, Lew Sarett and his "Cigar Store Indians." "The Little Theatre [was] dead from an overdose of war tax. *Poetry* still carried on but it was not the *Poetry* of old." It needed great poets and there were none left in Chicago.

Putnam's estimate was as understated as Mencken's had perhaps been overstated. A decade which had produced *The Girls, So Big, Little Caesar, The Racket,* and *The Front Page* presaged something for the future; and Monroe, Marion Strobel, Ferber, Webster, Balmer, Herrick, the Norths, Janet Ayer Fairbank and Margaret Ayer Barnes were still on hand. There were, in other words, intimations of some future immortality for Chicago literature.

Chicago is dead! said Putnam. Long live Chicago! says history

A Note on Jack Woodford

His real name was Josiah Pitts Woolfolk. He was reared on Chicago's Near North Side by his grandmother who lived only a short distance from his parents. Although his name never appears in any of the histories of the time, he knew all the Chicago writers — Clarence Darrow (about whom he once wrote a novel, *Find the Motive* [1932]), Maxwell "Bogie" Bodenheim, Louis Zara, Sherwood Anderson, Theodore Dreiser, Vincent Starrett, Meyer Levin, John Gunther, Henry Justin Smith, Ben Hecht. As a young reporter, he managed to "scoop" all the other Chicago reporters on the *Eastland* disaster in 1915.

Under such pseudonyms as Gordon Sayre, Jack Woodford, Sappho Henderson Britt and Howard Hogue Kennedy, he wrote short stories for "sex magazines," and seventy-seven romantic novels (he called them "sex novels"). Some of these have Chicago settings. Their titles are in the National Union Catalog.

And the literary critics and historians ignore him.

Other Chicago-Based Films of the 1920s

In the early years of this century, says Emmett Dedmon, "young George Spoor and Maxwell Anderson ... had formed the nucleus of a film colony ... in their Essanay (S and A) studios on the North Side." Essanay "brought to the screen Wallace Beery, Gloria Swanson, Lewis Stone, Colleen .Moore [whose dollhouse is still on view at the Museum of Science and Industry], Edward Arnold and Tom Mix. By 1910, one-fifth of [the world's movies] were being made in Chicago. Carl Laemmle, hearing of the opportunities in the young film industry, sold his clothing business in Oshkosh, Wisconsin to open a Chicago movie theater. Adolph Zukor gave up the fur business he established in Chicago after the World's Columbian Exposition" to get into the film business.[141] But even though the industry soon moved to California to get away from Chicago's harsh winters and to take advantage of the sunlight, the film industry never forgot Chicago. The city has been used more often as a setting for films than any American metropolis except New York, Los Angeles and San Francisco.

In 1921, Chicago and the copper country of Michigan were the settings for *Rainbow*, a film based on attempts to gain ownership of a copper mine. "Rainbow" was the heroine.

Environment (December, 1922) is the story of "Chicago Sal," a lady crook who is sent to a country home for rehabilitation. After being attracted to a young farmer, she returns to the city to take up her life of crime. When the farmer comes to Chicago to help her reform, he is arrested on a charge of vagrancy. "Sal" returns to the farm to await the release of the young man.

The novels of Indiana author Booth Tarkington (a close friend of Ade and the McCutcheons) were filmed as rapidly as they were published in the early 1920s. Among these was *Gentle Julia* (1922, filmed 1923), a story about an Indiana girl with many suitors who is lured to Chicago by an older man. In Chicago, Julia discovers he is already married and she returns home.

The first film version of Eugene O'Neill's *Anna Christie* (1923) (but not the play itself or later film versions) shows Anna leaving her Minnesota home to become a Chicago street walker before moving on east to see her father.

The first *Adam's Rib* (February, 1923) is the story of Mrs. Michael Ramsay, who, neglected by her Chicago wheatbroker husband and her daughter, romances the deposed King of "Moravia." Meanwhile the daughter romances a University of Chicago professor. The broker buys up Moravia's wheat crop; when America's wheat crop fails, he reaps a fortune. (The later *Adam's Rib* [1949] uses an entirely different story line.)

The Little Girl Next Door (1923) shows a Harmony, Illinois boy who, in

Chicago to seek his fortune, is forced into a drug-running operation. He is rescued with the aid of his hometown girl friend who has come to Chicago looking for him. The film's incidents are based on an Illinois State Vice Commission report of 1916.

The hero of *Lightning* (1925) is a boy from down state Illinois who has his heart broken by a Chicago gold-digger.

Life's Greatest Game (1924) focusses on a Chicago Cubs' pitcher who refuses to "throw" a game for a gambler. The gambler, in retaliation, breaks up the ballplayer's home.

Hell's Highroad (1925, based on a novel of the same year) shows a poor Chicago secretary who falls in love with a struggling young engineer. But she opts for a lonely life of poverty rather than marriage, and moves on to New York where the balance of the film is set.

In the Name of Love (1925) is based on a novel by Lord Bulwer-Lytton, an English novelist. A Chicago business man goes back to the French town where he was born to seek out his childhood sweetheart. She rejects him when she discovers his business connections, but true love wins out.

In *Sweet Adeline* (1926), a country boy, bullied by his older brother, writes a song about Adeline, a girl he and his brother are courting. When he sings the song in a Chicago cabaret (the film is a silent film!) he becomes famous, and he wins the girl.

Emil Jannings' famous *The Way of All Flesh* (1927) begins in Milwaukee with the home life of a bank teller, his wife and his children. But on a trip to Chicago he becomes infatuated with a woman named Mame, an adventurous woman, whose lover is a criminal. Like Dreiser's Hurstwood, in *Sister Carrie,* the teller comes to a tragic end.

The Chicago of these "melodramas," says Dave Kehr, was the archetypal Sin City, consisting of little but bars and dance halls, populated mainly by chorus girls and con men with their shifty eyes focussed on the proceeds on the family wheat crop . . . It was profoundly an outsider's view of the city, though it was aimed at the people who lived within it — the new residents who had not yet adjusted to the rhythm, who found themselves surrounded by multitudes of an exotic new creature they had never known before — the stranger. The city was a threat to stability, morality, security, a place of surprises and frightening new possibilities — new freedoms that were seen as new evils, new threats. The happy endings of these melodramas consisted not in adapting to the city, in becoming a comfortable, successful citizen of it, but in conquering the city — stealing away its prize of money and success and returning home. The Chicago of this early image was a place of evil, only a step removed from folktale — a cave of treasure, guarded by dragons — and it loomed as large and vague and black as legend.[143]

"When this hazy, almost supernatural myth of Chicago finally coalesced into something close and specific, it was largely through the influence of Ben Hecht, who had been lured to Hollywood by the unforgettable invitation of his friend Herman J. Mankiewicz: 'There are millions to be grabbed out here, and your only competition is idiots.' "[144]

In his first week in Hollywood, Hecht "knocked out" an 18-page treatment, "rooted in the low-life milieu" he had known as a Chicago journalist. He got $10,000 for his work and, later, an Academy Award. His treatment was filmed as *Underworld*, "the first significant gangster film and a tremendous world-wide success."[145]

Hecht's "uneasy balance of often naive romanticism and bitter, comic cynicism" came together in his central character, "Bull" Weed, the protagonist of the film:

> Only a cynical, street-wise reporter like Hecht would dare to elevate a thuggish common criminal over the fine-browed, noble-souled protagonists who then dominated melodrama, and only a feverish romantic like Hecht could have granted this lowbrow hero his fine and tragic destiny — to sacrifice himself so that the woman he loves may live on with the man *she* loves.[146]

Dave Kehr sees a mythic quality in Hecht's achievement:

> This figure of a man who both lives beneath the contempt of society and, in his lofty ideals, soars above it, probably dates back in American literature as far as James Fenimore Cooper's Leatherstocking Tales. It was Hecht's contribution — and a crucial one — to find a living contemporary equivalent of the Noble Savage. As Hecht created him, the gangster is both a rebuke to society — an outsider, in some sense even a revolutionary — and society's sacrificial victim; his inevitable defeat tested the strength of society's laws and assumptions, and found them strong. The mythic role of the gangster, like that of the Indian who preceded him in fiction, is to rebel and fail. He challenges the established order from above and below, giving vent to our frustrations, discontents and fantasies. And when he is brought low, he is like the heroes of Greek tragedy . . . a strangely comforting figure. He tells us that we are better off for not rebelling, that the system — be it fate or society — is unbeatable in the end.[147]

Like the later *The Widow From Chicago, The Girl From Chicago* (1927) also shows a Chicago girl involved with criminal elements in New York City where most of the action takes place. "It seems as though the background of this film had been Chicago," says Mordaunt Hall in his *New York Times* review, "and that the author or scenario writer decided to transfer the plot to New York, perhaps because Chicago had already manifested a dislike for unpleasant propaganda as the city that invariably afford a menace."[148]

For all that, the producers of *Yellow Contraband* (1928) didn't hesitate to show a Chicago gangster involved in an international drug-running scheme. Nor did the producers of *Chicago After Midnight* (1928) hesitate to show an ex-convict coming to Chicago seeking revenge on a fellow crook who had double-crossed him. There, the ex-convict unwittingly falls in love with the double-crosser's daughter, a night club entertainer. However, she is in love with the club's orchestra leader. When the ex-convict kills the crook, the orchestra leader is blamed. But the girl helps prove his innocence and the ex-convict dies in a shootout with police.

The final Chicago-based film of the 1920s was a western! Hoot Gibson, leading western film star is The Montana Kid, a character Gibson played in several films. The Kid brings his horse to Chicago for a rodeo, and, once there, falls in love with a Chicago girl. The obligatory chase scene, in which The Kid runs down and captures a fleeing bandit, takes place in Loop traffic with the horse unerringly threading his way through taxicabs, trucks and street cars.

A Footnote

An interesting variation of popular literature, the comic strip, has at least one representative clearly set in Chicago. *Gasoline Alley,* begun in 1919 as a comic strip reflecting the growing American interest in automobiles, changed its theme in 1921 to a narrative about the suburban family life of Walt Wallett ["Uncle Walt"], his wife Phyllis, and their adopted son "Skeezix" — who had been left as a foundling on the Wallett's doorstep. The cartoon became America's longest-running comic strip with an ongoing story line. Children grew up and adults aged. "Skeezix" served in World War II and his son in Viet Nam.

Photos Reproduced with permission of the Chicago Historical Society

Reconstructed Fort Dearborn at 1933 Century of Progress

Black Partridge saves Mrs. Helm from death

Carl Sandburg and bust of Abraham Lincoln

George Washington Ferris's gigantic Ferris Wheel

Robert Lawson's *Big Wheel*

Eugene Field at the desk where he composed Sharps and Flats

Bust of Henry Blake Fuller by Lorado Taft, Garland's brother-in-law

Hobart Chatfield Chatfield-Taylor

Sherwood Anderson in Chicago

(from top left) Fannie Butcher, Harriet Monroe, Carl Sandburg

Ben Hecht, Daily News correspondent, ca. 1915

Schlogl's Round Table — at left Henry Justin Smith

Margaret Ayer Barnes (Mrs. Cecil Barnes)

Janet Ayer Fairbank, January 1933 (at right)

Nelson Algren, 1950

Mark Smith, author of *Death of the Detective*

John R. Powers, author of *Do Black Patent Leather Shoes Really Reflect Up?*

SHERWOOD ANDERSON
Drawn from a Photograph by Alfred Stieglitz.

X.
The Depression Years

It was one of those tense moments in a newspaper's local room when the paper has been put to bed and the presses are rumbling out the first edition.

The city editor, pacing restlessly, paused at my desk. "What are you going to do now?" he asked ... I had just received notice that the staff was being reduced and women's news no longer seemed of sufficient importance to require a reporter of my sex.

"Star in a one-woman act — from the deadline to the breadline," I ad-libbed with attempted bravado.

"I envy you," he shot back. "You'll be in the thick of the greatest experience of our generation. The war wasn't a picayune to the gigantic upheaval that is taking place today. You may go hungry, but I don't believe you'll starve. I hope that you'll turn out a story of what is going on today — and you can't do that unless you've lived it."[1]

The Decade of the Great Depression, for a number of reasons, not all of which pertained to Chicago alone, produced the greatest outpouring of regional books in America's literary history. This was particularly true of the midwest — Ohio to Nebraska, Missouri to Michigan's Upper Peninsula — and of Chicago. The number of regional book titles is even more significant when one realizes the total number of book titles in print in that decade — some seven thousand titles in 1934 as compared with over forty thousand in any one year in the late nineteen-seventies.[2]

In Chicago, the Centennial of Chicago's charter, and the two-year Century of Progress Exposition (1933-1934) helped produce a great many recapitulations, fictional and non-fictional, of Chicago's past.

The Depression caused a new category of books — books about business failures, the loss of family wealth, the proletariat point of view, the plight of the laborer in the technocratic and push-button machine age.

There were few books of Chicago poetry and few plays about Chicago. The major playwrights — Ade, Hecht, Ferber, MacArthur, and Lardner — had gone on to New York or else to Hollywood.

Gangsters and Fellow-Travelers

By far the largest number of Chicago titles of this decade pertained to gangsterism, criminal activities and hoodlumism. Although authors had been slow to pick up journalists' interest in the subject, by the beginning of the 1930s, both groups were in full cry, hot after the underworld and its affiliates.

Two Chicagoans, among others, have commented on the relationships between Chicago crime and the city's best citizens. Al Capone, 1920s gang lord, once said: "My customers include some of the finest people in the city, or in the world, for that matter. But I'm just a bootlegger. I violate the prohibition law. All right, so do they."[3]

To which a later Chicago writer appended: "But that's Chicago ... The question has never been how you made it, but if you made it. The city was built by great men who demanded that drunkards and harlots be arrested, while charging them rent until the cops arrived:"[4]

> The Chicago of the gangster films is a city without a social structure, without classes — everything has been swept into the general desolation and the streets are empty ... The disappearance of the crowd, the ordinary people who make the city work, is the defining omission of the gangster films ... All that remains is the gangster in primal conflict with the police, their battle self-contained and touching no one else.[5]

Two Chicago novels of the early 1930s, W. R. Burnett's *The Silver Eagle* (1931) and Clifford Samuel Raymond's *Our Very Best People* (1931), are among several which explore this sometimes implicit, sometimes explicit relationship between Chicago gangsters and the well-to-do and powerful. Burnett's Frank Harworth has two ambitions, to become a member of Chicago's society and to make a lot of money in the entertainment business. The former leads to his engagement to a beautiful blonde society girl, the latter to an association with a gangster chief who is modeled on Capone. Unfortunately Harworth becomes so involved with the gangsters he has to be "rubbed out."

Raymond's novel is a tongue-in-cheek look at a powerful Chicago family, descendants of an itinerant peddler of the 1830s. (Like the author of *The Marriotts and the Powells,* Raymond provides an end-paper genealogy.)

Fifty-five-year-old Hubert Trotter Howeling, scion of the family, becomes involved, unwittingly and unwillingly, with Pasquale "Con" Amore, the man who killed Bugs Moran and Al Capone. (Al Capone?) But Hubert, about to become Sir Hubert over in jolly old England, is saved from death when his clerk, Podex, sprays Con and ten other gangsters with machine gun fire after they had threatened his fiancee.

Burnett's *Protection,* a novel about Chicago gangsters and society people, ran in *Collier's Weekly* during the ten weeks from May 2, 1931 to July 4.

Walter Noble Burns' *The One Way Ride* was another 1931 novel about Chicago gangsterdom.

The decade of the 1930s started with two crime films, *The Widow From Chicago* (1930) and *Roadhouse Nights* (1930). In *The Widow,* anticipating his role in *Little Caesar,* Edward G. Robinson played a gang leader, this one agreeably despicable but stupid, who satisfied the requirements of poetic justice and the Hayes office by falling into a police trap at the end of the film. In the second film, based on a story by Ben Hecht, the police chief of "Moran," a fictitious Chicago suburb moonlights as a rum runner:

Percival Christopher Wren was an English author whose *Mysterious Waye/The Story of the "Unsetting Sun"* (1930) is about a huge diamond owned by an "Englishman" with a strange accent and a country house staffed with attractive female servants. Eventually we learn that the "Englishman," his servants and almost everyone else in the complex tale, either is a Chicago gangster or has gangster connections. Before the devious tale is finished a number of the characters die violent deaths and Waye himself commits suicide.

Loren Carroll's *Wild Onion* (1930) is one more attempt to cash in on the obvious popularity of books about Chicago gangsters, but in this tale of a man who begins as a waiter in a "speakeasy" and becomes a beer baron, Carroll does make an attempt to understand the behavior of Joe Dulac, his protagonist.

More lurid than literary are Jack Lait's *Put on the Spot* (1930)* and Edgar Wallace's *On the Spot* (1931). According to a glossary in Lait's book, "put on the spot" means "lured or betrayed to a place where one or more may be murdered with a degree of safety and favorable chance of getaway for the murderers."[6] That, and the words of one of Wallace's gangsters to the Chicago Chief of Police — "we save the state a lot of money by rubbing each other out" probably say all that is necessary about these novels. Lait's glossary may be a useful item for students of the language. Lait was also the author of a script for a forgettable film, *Gangster Girl* (1930).

---

* Dramatized as *On the Spot* (Broadway, Fall, 1930) with Anna May Wong. The theme was Chicago racketeering.

Elias Tobenkin's *In the Dark* (1931) is a poorly-constructed novel which adds to the theme with two more points: criminal activity is a part of the economic life in a big city — insurance companies, for example, thrive on it; and the inexperienced and innocent young person doesn't always have a choice about the business of making a living. With particular reference to the second point, Tobenkin shows us the "dead end" to which many of those who "revolted against the village," and migrated to the city came:

> It was a world of dead-end jobs and second-hand lives; a world of elevator operators, of laundry workers, of doormen; of cooks, dish-washers, bus boys; of porters and night watchmen; of women who cleaned offices, of chambermaids, "madonnas of the washtub;" of girls who pasted labels, who worked in wire-frame factories or sorted pen points nine hours a day. Some of the denizens of this world ... had their roots elsewhere and still cherished an occasional memory of brooks and trees; of country roads, the glitter of the moon through the treetops...
>
> It was a world of drab rooming houses, of assignation hotels, of poorly dissembled vice resorts; a world of crap, pool, bowling; of speakeasies, of cheap night clubs, of tough cabarets.
>
> All about were men and women for whom the grandiose and thrilling promises of the city had largely vanished.[7]

The three best all-time gangster films, says Roger Dooley,[8] appeared successively in 1931 and 1932: *Little Caesar,* with a script by W. R. Burnett, who had written the novel; *The Public Enemy* (1931, not entirely a Chicago film); and *Scarface* (1932, like Burnett's novel based on the career of Al "Scarface" Capone). At least thirty other gangster films appeared in 1931, a much smaller number in 1932.

Caesar Rico Bandello — who calls himself "Rico" (the "Little Caesar" sobriquet comes from the newspaper reporters) — is seen as a man driven by a desperate hunger for recognition. He moves up the power ladder by superior cleverness. In the end it is his love for his young protégé that leads to his downfall, and that memorable final line, "Mother of Mercy, is this the end of Rico?"

The Public Enemy, with James Cagney in a role modeled on that of an early Chicago bootlegger, was unusual in that it established childhood behavior as a prime source for later delinquency. It was also the first film to link World War I, Prohibition, and the rise of the beer racket.

Scarface was based even more closely on Capone's life and career than *Little Caesar.* Its significance lies in showing how easily innocent citizens could become victims of racketeering and accompanying gang wars and that Capone was not only a nation's shame but also the shame of respectable Italian-Americans.

Ben Hecht wrote the script for *Scarface* (its subtitle, decreed by the New York censors was *The Shame of a Nation* — they held the film up for a year and Chicago authorities banned it for another); Paul Muni was a powerful "Scarface:"[9]

> As the Depression [had] deepened, so did the ferocity of the gangster films ... Ben Hecht's Noble Savage gradually lost his obvious nobility. The gangster became a brutal killer, his heroism (for he was still very much a hero) defined only by the act of his revolt, his sheer ability to make himself an individual ... *Scarface* is at once the most violent and most joyous of gangster films ... The Chicago of *Scarface* belonged to the gangsters.[10]

A 1931 film, *Dance Fools Dance,* with Clark Gable as a gangster chieftain and Joan Crawford as a "cub" newspaper reporter, used the 1929 St. Valentine's Day "massacre" and the 1930 slaying of Jake Lingle, *Tribune* reporter and vice chief as events.

Another 1931 film of crime, *The Secret Six,* was published simultaneously as a novel, written by Francis Marion. It is set in "Centro" (Cicero?), a new town built up by industrial plants and the stockyards. The story, featuring several gang killings and two Chicago newspaper reporters, runs from 1921 to 1924.

McKinley Bryant's *Sporting Youth* (1931) tells of the rise of a young Chicago boxer under the patronage of Giorgio Fabrizzi, a Chicago gangster. An average novel, the book still presents vivid images of the 1920s gang wars. The funeral of Big Jim Colosimo and the murder of Dion O'Banion are two events.

Two novels by Arthur Dorman Welton, *The 27th Ride* (1932) and *The Line Between* (1933) continue the exploitation of the gangster world, adding, for novelty's sake, a character named Tony Boloney and the theme of clairvoyancy. Henry Justin Smith's last novel, written three years before he died, *Young Phillips, Reporter* (1933) is a melodramatic novel about a young reporter working for a big city newspaper which is fighting corruption. Its principal targets are a gangster and the mayor. Through the efforts of young Phillips, the goal is accomplished.

The Song of the Eagle (1933, originally *The Beer Baron*) is set in Chicago during the Prohibition year of 1926. An honest German-American brewer loses one son in World War I, then is forced out of business by Prohibition. Although gangsters want him to produce illegal beer he refuses and, as a consequence, is murdered by one of his former drivers. Then his surviving son gathers together some of his World War I buddies and, after a showdown battle with the gangsters, restores law and order. At its end the film boldly predicted that the end of Prohibition in the year the film was made would mean the end of the gangster era.[11]

Paul Hutchens' *Romance of Fire* (1934) combines mystery-fiction, reliance on the heroine's faith in God, and relationships with Chicago gangsters, an unusual mixture for a Chicago-based novel.

A 1935 film, *The Chicago Kid,* based on an original story by Karl Brown, features a crime-does-not-pay theme, the operations of a black market gang, and a son's revenge against those who embezzled his late father's fortune.

Brock Williams' *The Earl of Chicago* (1937) is the second novel of this decade to send Chicago gangsters to England. "The Kid," a Chicago gang leader, just out of Stateville Prison, is discovered to be the Ninth Earl of Gorley. Meanwhile, he is involved in a deadly feud with a Chicago rival who has just blown the Kid's Chicago nightclub to bits on the eve of a homecoming party.

Ultimately the gang rivalry is transferred to England where it turns out that the English blokes, are just as capable of vicious gang rivalry as Chicago gangsters. All ends well for the "Kid," however; he triumphs over his English and Chicago foes, wins the girl, and assumes his rightful name of "Clarence."

The "Kid's" description reads as if Williams had both Hollywood and James Cagney in mind. Hollywood got the message; *The Earl of Chicago* was filmed in 1940, but with Robert Montgomery attempting the part of "The Kid."

Clarence Darrow figured in a 1919 trial resulting from an attack of "red"-baiting hysteria which swept over an Illinois town as a consequence of World War I. Alice Beal Parsons' *The Trial of Helen McCleod* (1938) fictionalizes Darrow and his role in the court case, which actually took place in Rockford, Illinois. As in the Leopold-Loeb case, the trial defendant was socially prominent, but here the defendant and nine others are charged with sedition. The atmosphere was prejudicial to Darrow's clients as was often the case in defenses he undertook; it was a time when the "hundred per cent American" slogan covered every sin of prejudice, threat and venom, in the words of one critic.[12]

Darrow dominates the book; it comes to life after his introduction under his fictitious name. Parsons' picture of the attorney is a powerful one. He's a man "rugged as the hills, uncouth as a frontiersman, careless in dress and speech, but edged as a fine blade when it came to cutting denunciations of those who forgot the meaning of American liberty."[13]

William Jourdan Rapp's *Poolroom* (1938) is just another mediocre gangster-romance, but it does present an interesting picture of horse racing at Arlington and the wagering clearinghouse which is located in Chicago.

Two Chicago novels of this decade feature prostitutes. Wallace Smith's *Bessie Cotter* (1936) is a whore with a heart of gold who is capable of entertaining up to twenty-five men on a Saturday night when *both* the Cubs and the White Sox are out of town. The time is 1901, the setting "Hinky Dink's" and "The Bath's" notorious vice district.

Jim Tully's *Ladies in the Parlor* (1935) is set in a much more deluxe house in the mid 1930s; the charge for a "lady's" affections has risen from two dollars to fifty, liquor extra, and that's during the Depression, whether the baseball teams are in town or not. Tully is better known for his non-Chicago novels of tramp and circus life written during this era.

The "Who-Done-Its" Big Decade

"Mystery stories . . . are plentiful in Chicago," Lennox Bouton Grey wrote in 1935. "Chicago is not so notable for the solution of its crimes as for the bold ingenuity of its criminals, and it is this which finds the most exploitation . . . The popularity of these murder mysteries lies in the fact they offer a clear and certain chain of causes and effects and solution in a nervous world where such clarity and solution are often lacking."[14]

Henry Kitchell Webster finished out his three-decade long career with a half dozen or so romantic mystery novels. *Who Is the Next* (1931), set in a Chicago suburb, features a Norwegian immigrant who came to Chicago the night of the Fire and who later built a luxurious estate on the bank of the north branch of the Chicago River. When he is murdered, along with his secretary, his ward, a young girl who keeps her own airplane on the estate, is suspected. The real killer is found by a surburban police chief using all the newfangled police methodology.

Webster's last book effort, *The Alleged Great-Aunt* (1935) was begun in "the last year of his life and was partially written when he learned that he had not long to live." After his death, his widow gave the unfinished manuscript to his longtime friends, Janet Ayer Fairbank and Margaret Ayer Barnes, with a request that the sisters complete the book if they could. "The story [had] ended abruptly in the middle of a sentence where Webster had dropped his pen . . . The greatest 'mystery' that Webster had left behind him was the mystery of what he had intended to do with his last story."[15]

Webster, however, had not used a Chicago setting for the book.

Lennox Bouton Grey particularly admired Webster's work; he also singled out the mystery stories of [Charles] Vincent [Emerson] Starrett for praise. Starrett, a *Daily News* commentator who had once said that Sherwood Anderson's suits always seemed one size too big and his hats one size too small,[16] who had been a friend of Harriet Monroe's and Margaret Anderson's, and who had been the editor of *The Wave* for its two years (1922-1924), published three collections of short stories and four novels from 1924 to 1944, all in this vein and nearly all set in Chicago; *The Blue Door* (1930); *The Case Book of Jimmie Lavender* (1944); *Coffins for Two* (1924); *Dead Man*

Inside (1931); *The End of Mr. Garment* (1932); *The Great Hotel Murder* (1935); and *Midnight and Percy Jones* (1936).

A friend of Starrett's at the *Daily News,* Robert J. Casey, "a pudgy leprechaun with steely insides," set a "prize-winning" mystery novel, *The Third Owl* (1934) in a family mansion in the Fox River valley on the wesern edge of Chicago. Several murders occur as part of the family's complex inter-relationships. Although a poorly-written novel, hardly deserving of any award, it was reprinted at least once.

Mignon G[ood]. Eberhart set eight of her more than forty crime novels and one novelette in Chicago from 1933 (she began writing in 1929) to 1949. Of these, the best is probably *The Dark Garden* (1933) set in an old Chicago mansion.

Among the more interesting novels in this category are those of Harry Stephen Keeler — some twenty-five in all. Of these, five at least depend on "three or more plots and sub-plots, Wabash Avenue auction rooms, University of Chicago professors, black and tan cafes and Chicago police."[17] Of particular interest is Keeler's use of Chicago's small Chinatown, in the vicinity of Wentworth and Cermak Road, as a setting — a setting rarely used by Chicago authors. These five titles are: *The Voice of the Seven Sparrows* (1928); *The Green Jade Hand* (1930); *The Riddle of the Yellow Zuri* (1930); *The Fourth King* (1930); *The Amazing Web* (1930). Keeler's novels are dated from 1927 to 1944. He sometimes reworked plots and on one occasion even repeated the chapters from one book in another. Many of his books are lengthy, ranging from 250 to over 700 pages — very long for this genre.

The prolific Edwin Balmer co-authored *The Shield of Silence* in 1936 with another well-known writer, Philip Wylie. The central characer is a Joliet prisoner serving a life sentence for a murder he refuses to discuss — until a second murder is committed.

Clyde B. Clason authored three Chicago mystery novels; Martin Joseph Freeman two; Oscar Jerome Friend two; Jonathan [Wyatt] Latimore four; Lewis Herman and William Targ one; James William MacQueen, writing as James G. Edwards, M.D. over a dozen, and, as Jay McHugh, one more, *Sex Is Such Fun* (1937); Mary Plum, wrote three, including one we shall see in the discussion on the Century of Progress; Charlotte Murray Russell wrote four; and Tiffany Thayer set one, *One Woman,* (1933) in Chicago.

Thus, more than seventy-five titles testify to the popularity of this genre, and to the popularity of Chicago as a setting as well. These seventy-five titles represent somewhat over five percent of all Chicago titles; taken in conjunction with other crime novels being written at the same time, they represent a large percentage of books in print. A list of titles and authors not included here is in the Appendix.

The Century of Progress Exposition

In 1933, on the fortieth anniversary of the World's Columbian Exposition, Chicago staged its second world's fair — this one named "the Century of Progress." It was built, and it opened, in the depths of a severe economic depression. Perhaps for that reason fewer Chicago writers found inspiration in this Exposition. Whatever the reason, it produced only a handful of books, nowhere near the number of titles produced by the earlier Exposition.

Still, some found themes in the congeries of buildings on the Lake just south of Grant Park. Two writers in particular picked the same romantic theme — a visitor to the Columbian Exposition returns to Chicago to marvel at the new Fair.

In 1893, Mattie, a farm girl from southern Illinois, met Henry, a farm boy from Wisconsin at the Columbian Exposition. For a week they toured the Fair, made love, and planned to marry. But circumstances intervened, and each married another. In 1933, now widow and widower, they met by chance again at the Fair; again they toured the grounds, again they planned marriage. But Mattie's common sense intervened this time, and at the end of the week each one went back home.

That's the story of Minnie Hite Moody's *Once Again in Chicago* (1933), a novel which critics found timely and satisfying.

Michigan author Mildred Walker titled her *Light From Arcturus* (1935) from the formal opening of the Century of Progress which utilized a light ray from a distant star. Julia Hauser, a seventeen-year-old bride, honeymoons at the 1876 Centennial Exposition in Philadelphia. The brief glimpse of a world beyond her ability to conceive stays with her through fourteen years of marriage in a small Nebraska town. In 1890, she persuades her Main Street merchant husband to move to Chicago in order that the four children can grow up in a more cosmopolitan atmosphere. The venture proves disastrous for Max Hauser; he loses his savings in Chicago and is forced to take a clerk's job in an old South Water Market produce house. Meanwhile, Julia is hired by no less a personage than Mrs. Potter Palmer to work in the Woman's Building at the Columbian Exposition.

Forty years later, Julia and her children, now themselves parents, visit the new Fair. Max is long since dead, but the footloose Julia, at seventy-four, is planning an airplane trip to California.

Critics found the book pleasant, but unremarkable, not as satisfying a novel as Walker's earlier book about life in Michigan, *Fireweed* (1933).

Fanny Butcher, the Chicago *Tribune* critic, called her friend Dorothy Aldis's *Their Own Apartment* (1935), with its detailed description of social life at the Century of Progress, a novel "for a summer weekend . . . comfortably easy to read . . . [but] distinctly worth reading."[18] Aside from the scenes at the Fair, this is a story about a woman who gave up her "tidy, careful and attractive life" to marry a husband with an "overwhelming family." One gets some notion of the McIlvaine family when one learns the mother is named "Pussy!"

Mrs. Aldis, wife of a Lake Forest real estate executive, an active member of the Chicago Little Theater movement, and a young Chicago poet in the Renaissance, also set one of her juvenile books, *Magic City* (1933), at the Fair.

Two mystery novels complete the catalog of Century of Progress fiction: John M. Ashenhurst's *World's Fair Murders* (1933) and Iowan Mary Plum's *Murder at the World's Fair* (1933). Plum was also the author of two mysteries set in Chicago, *The Killing of Judge MacFarlane* (1930) and *Dead Man's Secret* (1931).

In 1893, Harriet Monroe had been selected to write an official Columbian Exposition ode. Even though her subsequent experience with the ode made her quite unhappy, in 1933, through her *Poetry* magazine, she announced a contest for poems about the forthcoming Century of Progress. The contest and a hundred-dollars from the Friday Club of Chicago, were won by Paul Engle, a young man from the cornfields of Iowa since distinguished for his overseeing of the University of Iowa's far-famed Writers' Workshop and International Writers' Workshop.

The poem, "America Remembers," was published in the "Century of Progress" number of *Poetry* in June of 1933:

Here by this midland lake, this sand-shore
Water that pulses with no sea-tide heart,
Where the grain of a nation pauses on its golden
Way to the world's belly, and the long trains plunge—

. . .

Here at the Windy City
The long trains whistle by the sun-loud lake.
I shall remember these men in my land.[19]

Engle was invited to read his poem at the Fair's opening ceremonies and was introduced by Harriet Monroe.

"America Remembers" was published in Engle's 1934 volume, *American Song*. Response to the poem was mixed. J. Donald Adams and Leon Whipple found much to praise in Engle's "fullest expression of his Americanism."[20] Jesse Stuart, Allen Tate and Malcolm Cowley found much to dispraise, both in the quality of the poetry and in the "eagle oratory" of the poem's message. "This long declamation . . . richly deserved to win . . . the prize," said

Cowley. "Here was a subject that would have embarrassed most poets."[21]

But Stephen Vincent Benét concluded, "Here is somebody walking in America in proud shoes."[22]

The division between Cowley, Tate and Stuart on the one hand, and Adams, Whipple and Benét on the other, was as much political as it was aesthetic.

Although she did not enter it in the *Poetry* contest, Miss Monroe also wrote a Century of Progress poem, Chicago "Chicago, 1933:"

My city, keep the faith you found
When huts rose on the marshy bar!
Lift up your banners from the ground
Whence Lincoln marched, led by his star!
Hear the new song of man's desire
The wireless winds of dream shall bring
When bold Arcturus lights your fire
And the bright towers leap up to sing.[23]

The Depression

The ostentatious display of prosperity of the "bright towers" and other buildings at the Century of Progess was not matched in the streets of Chicago. Among the many expedients which were tried in the 1930s as a means of helping people were several Federally-funded programs in the Arts. In Chicago, offices of the Federal Theater program and the Federal Writers' Program were established, the latter under the direction of Iowan John Towner Frederick. The main thrust of the Theater program seems to have been play production, providing work for unemployed actors; there was less emphasis on play writing. Because of directives from Washington, the main thrust of the Writers' program was the production of state and regional guides. Some important young writers worked for Frederick on these projects, among them Richard Wright and Nelson Algren.

Frederick had brought his *Midland* literary magazine to Chicago in 1930. *Midland* had been published since 1915 in Iowa, Minnesota and Michigan as a means of advancing the careers of beginning midwestern writers; among Chicago writers were Farrell, Halper, Kantor, Sarett, Seiffert and Starrett. In Chicago, Frederick hoped he would find enough readers and writers to keep the magazine going. But he was forced to suspend publication in 1933.[24]

Of the three hundred and eighty four stories set in *The Midland* in its eighteen years existence, only forty-six of these were set in cities. Of these forty-six, however, half were set in a city which is recognizably Chicago. One of the best of these is "Cinemania" by Cyril John Clarke. It relates one day in the career of the manager of one of the numerous "Byzantine" film palaces in Chicago. Several thousand people come to the theatre, many of them drawn by Lou Montrose, an orchestra leader who performs during intervals between films. But although most of the theater's patrons are enjoying their day at the theater, the manager himself is unhappy for he is aware that this is probably his last day on the job — the management of the chain of which the theater is a part plans to discharge him.

Frederick stayed on in Chicago as a teacher, a book reviewer for Chicago newspapers, a literary columnist, the producer of a weekly book review program on radio, and as director of the Chicago Writer's program.

Although Edwin Balmer was editing the Chicago-based *Redbook,* he was still finding time to write novels. His 1934 *Dragons Drive You* covers the years from 1929 to 1933 — the years of "boom and bust" in Chicago. Martin Cathal O'Mara's grandfather died with sixteen others in the flames atop the cold storage building at the Columbian Exposition; Martin, like Clarence Darrow, is a lawyer who is always on the defendant's side. Judson E. Braddon is a supporter of Samuel Insull. The girl in the case is Agnes Gleneith, whose father at the story's beginning, is making millions on the market. When the crash comes, Braddon, Agnes's father and others either kill themselves or else come to the despised O'Mara for help.

Nelson Algren, a machinist's son, grew up in Chicago blue-collar ethnic neighborhoods and graduated from a journalism program at the University of Illinois in 1931. For a time he was a drifter in New Orleans and Texas where he served a jail term for stealing a typewriter. Back in Chicago he began writing short stories and poems. Some of these appeared in "radical" magazines: Balmer's O'Mara and Algren were one in their sympathy for the underdog. In 1935, his first novel, *Somebody in Boots,* appeared. It was scarcely noticed, although an English critic said it had an "insipid title." The book is based on Algren's experiences as a derelict in the South. It was republished in paperback in 1956 as *A Walk on the Wild Side,* and filmed under the latter title in 1962.

Somebody in Boots is dedicated to "those innumerable thousands, the Homeless Boys of America," about whom a film, *Wild Boys of the Road* had been made in 1933. The book contains an arraignment of Chicago's Century of Progress phase. Its hero, Cass McKay, is a young man to whose fate society is indifferent.

Critics saw a potential in the young Algren but there were reservations. Algren "was bred in a literary generation that identifies reticence and suppression, and begins to attach a ritual value to the vernacular of obscenity and fetor ... [H]e takes that view of the under dog which involves a denial of any virtue whatever to the upper dog. Solvency and authority as they appear in this narrative, are invariably cruel, arbitrary and corrupt."[25]

Constance Casady's and Ruth Cardwell's *Even in Laughter* (1935) is about two sisters, Alix, married to Herbert Dodd, a printing company owner whose business fails, and Elinor, married to Stanley Grayce, son of Professor and Mrs. Henry Grayce of Hyde Park and the University of Chicago. Alix is selfish, demanding, wasteful; Elinor is thrifty, hardworking. Alix is a parasite; Elinor a case worker for Cook County. Both their marriages fail. Herbert's mistress and a Chicago gangster also have roles. In all, the novel shows the effect of the depression on four Chicago families.

The collapse of Samuel Insull's utilities empire in the 1930s touched millions of Chicagoans and others. In Louise Redfield Peattie's *Fugitive* (1935) we see the effect of a similar crash — Howard Gorman's travel and transport empire. Gorman flees to Corsica but is extradited. His wife, Viola, who once tried to kill herself, is stoned to death by rock-throwing socialist fanatics. A girl named Rose and an art critic survive to provide a somewhat happy ending.

The Insull empire collapse was also the subject of a 1933 film, *I Loved A Woman*, with Edward G. Robinson playing the role of a "sensitive art-loving heir" to a Chicago meat-packing fortune who sells tainted meat to the Government both during the Spanish-American War and World War I. He sponsors the career of an opera singer, with whom he is infatuated, at the Chicago Opera House and dies in lonely exile in Greece. Although the protagonist is shown as a meat-packer, the Insull parallel is obvious.

"Why is it that some people seem to take hold of life and make it do their bidding, while others have to be carried along?" asks Marcia Ellsworth, the do-it-yourself heroine of Louise Andrus's *Though Time Be Fleet* (1937). Marcia's promising career as an actress ends when she must help her ailing Chicago parents. But she becomes a successful newspaper reporter (like her creator), and marries a shell-shocked World War I veteran. He loses their savings gambling on the stock market and once again it is up to Marcia. Through her initiative they begin a surburban newspaper and succeed in exposing a corrupt county official.

Edward Anderson's thousand-dollar prize winning *Hungry Men* (1935) is akin to Algren's *Somebody in Boots;* it's about homeless, unemployed drifters on the road in the America of the 1930s. Like Algren's novel, Anderson's novel is based on personal experience. "He has bummed with the restless and hungry from frontier to frontier," said his publishers. But there the resemblance ends. "The American," said Anderson, "wasn't going to turn Socialist or Communist . . . America is rich. There is plenty and nobody is actually die of hunger."[26] Critics of his book were unhappy with this forecast; one suggested that if Anderson really wanted to "study the shift in American economic thinking . . . he would be well advised to turn his inquiring eye away from the road and towards the universities, the newspaper offices, the magazines, business houses and factories. Revolutions are never made by down-and-outers."[27]

Anderson's novel ends in Chicago where his hero finds economic salvation by organizing a German band that plays on street corners.

Chicago Industry

Albert Halper was a native Chicagoan[28] and most of his work is set in Chicago. *The Foundry* (1934) is the story of a fictional Chicago foundry in the twelve months leading up to the stock market crash of 1929. *The Chute* (1937) is the story of a Chicago mail order house, also fictional, in the 1930s. Both novels, like his 1933 *Union Square,* are proletariat novels. Halpert doesn't develop major characters — he writes of groups of people, brought together by some common interest, such as family or work. He might also be labeled a Jewish writer, particularly in his novels of family life where he presents a clear picture of what it was like to be a member of a Jewish immigrant family in Chicago.

Halper's image of the promised land is pessimistic. His "little people" have come to America to find that promised land — but the promised land can provide only a marginal living through long hours in small shops or in factories which, concentrating on the profit motive and the work ethic, provide little if any sustenance for the human spirit.

Moreover, for those who fled Europe to avoid its political entanglements, America offers little hope. It was sucked into World War I and will be sucked into World War II. Halper sees America's entanglements as coming from the operation of a vast propaganda machine which has its basis in an American refusal to consider all sides of the political spectrum, and from its failure to heed its first President's advice to avoid foreign entanglement.

In *The Chute,* the "chute" itself (a device for moving parcels from upper floors to the lowest floor) becomes a symbol of the manner in which the "speed up" of modern industry literally devours a worker. That incident echoes the scene in Sinclair's *The Jungle* where a worker becomes a part of packages of Durham's pure leaf lard.

At the end of *The Foundry,* one of the three entrepreneurs who owns the plant leaves a suicide note: "You will find my carcass in the privy, folks." And that, said a critic for *The New Republic,* was "a good enough curtain for the Coolidge era" in American politics.[29]

Halper's *The Chute* provides an interesting contrast to Ferber's study of the mail order business in *Fanny Herself.* One of Fanny Brandeis's first suggestions to her employer is to put the order fillers on roller skates to save time in filling orders. A second suggestion has to do with packaging infant clothes to make them more attractive and to sell more merchandise. Fanny, we are told, "fits into the scheme of things" that helps her firm "talk in tens of millions, its stock become gilt-edged, unattainable." Halper shows us the other side of the mail order company's gold coins.

Halper's 1932 *Chicago Side-Show* contains his recollections of the city for the four seasons of one year. "The raw slangy Chicago of his youth" is fashioned "into a collage forming as perfect a description of the city as has ever been written."[30]

Chicago Ethnic Novels

For the first time in nearly half a century, there were no Utopian novels by Chicagoans. Replacing them in the canon in this decade were a large number of novels about Chicago immigrants — the only category with more entrants was that of crime and mystery novels.

Before he was thirty, Langston Hughes had distinguished himself with several volumes of poetry. In 1930, he turned to the novel for the first time, producing an autobiographical novel based on his childhood in Kansas and his young manhood in Chicago. *Not Without Laughter* (1930) is the first major novel about the black experience in Chicago. It was not to be the last one.

"Here," said a reviewer for *The Nation* . . .

is the Negro in his most picturesque form — the blues-loving Negro, the spiritual-singing Negro, the exuberant, the impassioned, the irresponsible Negro, the Negro of ancient folk-lore and romantic legend. "Good-natured, guitar playing Jim Boy;" Anjee Rogers, loving Jim Boy no matter where he goes or whom he lives with; Aunt Hager, the old mammy of a dead generation, "whirling round in front of the altar at revival meetings . . . her face shining with light, arms outstretched as though all the cares of the world had been cast away;" Harriet, "beautiful as a jungle princess," singing and jazzing her life away, sneering at sin as a white man's bogy, and burying beneath peals of laughter "a white man's war for democracy;" and Sandy, seeing his people as a "band of black dancers captured in a white world," and resolving to free them from themselves as well as from their white dictators — these are the Negroes of this novel, these the people who make it live with that quick and intimate reality which is seldom seen in American fiction.[31]

George Davis's *The Opening of a Door* (1931) is about a Canadian family which had migrated to Chicago from Ontario, and about the gradual deterioration of that family in Chicago. Reviewers compared the novel to Stern's *The Matriarch* (1925) and to Wisconsin novelist Glenway Westcott's *The Applie of the Eye* (1924). Derivative or not, critics praised it, and it was the runner-up for nomination as the Harper Prize Novel for 1931-1932. "This novel is a high achievement in creative literature," said the *New York*

Times. "It is a work of beauty, in pattern, finish in style, and maturity in thought, one no less distinguished for its craftmanship than for its power."[32]

Vera Caspary was a Chicago-born writer who worked for a while in a shellac and varnish factory, then studied dramatic criticism at Northwestern University for three months, followed by six months at the Chicago Art Institute. Wanting to write, she got a job in an advertising agency where she produced her masterpiece "Rat Bites Sleeping Child." Later she had various editorial and writing jobs. After *White Girl,* she wrote *Ladies and Gents* (1929), the story of a girl who becomes a celebrated dancer; *Music in the Streets* (1930), an average romance; and, in collaboration with Winifred Lenihan, a play with an all-woman cast, *Blind Mice* (1930).

These were very light fare, compared to her *Thicker Than Water* (1932), a saga novel of a Jewish family which can trace its ancestry back four hundred years in Portugal. The time is 1885 to 1931, the central character the matriarchal Rosala Piera. In Chicago, the aristocratic Pieras from necessity must intermarry with Germans (second class Jews) and Polacks (despised Jews).

The family is in trade — millinery and stocks and bonds — and is financially well off. As time passes, its orthodox beliefs change, thin out or are simply rejected. The focus comes to rest more and more on the children of the several marriages, and the events of *their* lives. Rosalia is replaced as a central character by her daughter, Beatrice, who marries a Gentile.

Albert Halper's *On the Shore* (1934) is a collection of short stories, all set in Chicago, and featuring Jewish immigrants in the late nineteenth and early twentieth centuries. "A Herring for my Uncle" (compare Faulkner's title, "A Rose For Emily") recalls a young man's family's past history. "My Aunt Daisy" vividly depicts the Chicago tenement life on hot summer nights when everyone is outdoors and the men sing songs of their native lands. Both stories emphasize the closeness of family units, and the relatively hard life which these immigrants face. "The Penny Divers" are young West Side Chicago kids who dive in the Union Park lagoon for coins tossed by passersby. "The Race" takes place on the same lagoon on a winter day. "Going to Market" takes place in the Randolph Street market at Ogden Avenue. Waiting for his grocer father to pick up merchandise, a boy watches two white laborers knife a Negro co-worker. The story is based on an actual knifing Halper saw during the 1919 race riots. On a "Winter Evening" the family grocery, near Lake Street on Chicago's West Side, is robbed by a gunman. The father is unable to report the crime — he has no telephone and the son cannot find a policeman on the snowy streets. "Farm Hand" is the report of an encounter between a Chicago tough and a migrant worker, whom the tough attempts to rob.

In contrast with Caspary's novel of upper-class Jews adapting to a new cultural mix, Halper's short stories show an immigrant lower class Jewish family also adapting to a new cultural mix. The two books thus provide an overview of the whole problem faced by European Jews emigrating to the Windy City.

Louis Zara, a New York publishing executive who got his college education in Chicago, wrote two novels about Chicago immigrant families, one Russian-Jewish, the other from Brittany.

Blessed is the Man (1935) follows the career of Jake Krakauer, who came to Chicago from Russia, from 1880 to 1920. In those forty years Jake rises from cleaning stables and peddling produce door to door to sole ownership of a commission enterprise and State Street's biggest store. At the same time his brother prospers with girls, women, junk and politics and becomes a ward heeler. Jake has only two problems that he cannot overcome with hard work and thrift — he is snubbed by his neighbors after he builds a magnificent home on the far Northwest Side, and he can't get along with his children and his relatives.

Zara's *Give Us This Day* (1936) covers the entrepreneuristic Brabants from 1900 to 1935. The Brabants are bakers by inheritance; they live in a Chicago neighborhood which is like a small town business district. Some members of the family branch out into printing, dentistry, saloon ownership and politics. At the end of the story the Brabants are forced out of the bakery business by the advent of factory-type operations. But the saloon owner has learned how to buy enough votes to become an Illinois state senator.

"Mr. Zara," said Alfred Kazin, "happens to be one of those fresh, exhilarating young talents who come on the scene without personal fireworks; a writer who is deeply responsive to the unpleasant facts of life, but who has so sharp an ear and so droll and tender a flavor that his sensibility seems unique."[33]

Rose Basile Green in *The Italian-American Novel* (1974) lists only one Italian-American novel with a Chicago setting — Bernard DeVoto's *We Accept With Pleasure,* written by an Italian-American but with no reference to Italians in America. Green overlooked all the Chicago novels about Italian-American gangsters, and she missed Grace D. Hall's and Ernesto G. Merlanti's *Honor Divided* (1935).

Mario and Albert are the two sons of honest, God-fearing Sicilian immigrants living in Chicago's Little Italy. Mario becomes a leading Chicago racketeer and sends Albert to law school. Albert becomes a judge; Mario is brought before him on a murder charge. This Cain-Abel story line may well have had its antecedents in the 1934 film, *Manhattan Melodrama* with Clark Gable as the criminal and William Powell as an attorney. This was the film John Dillinger had seen on the night he was shot down in Chicago.

Meyer Levin graduated from the University of Chicago in 1924; he was a classmate of Nathan Leopold, Jr., and Richard Loeb, about whose infamous "experiment" in crime he was later to write *Compulsion*. As a reporter on the *Daily News,* it appeared for a while that he was being groomed to replace Ben Hecht, but he was soon fired. By 1937 he had written several novels, had been to Europe and to Palestine (a place which later in his life took up much of his time and energy). As a member of the Federal Theater Project in Chicago, he wrote a play which was banned as it was about to be produced. By late 1937, he was an editor and motion picture critic for the then Chicago-based *Esquire.*

His 1937 novel, *The Old Bunch,* examines the lives of a dozen men and women from 1921 (when they were "flappers and jellybeans") until 1934. All Jews, some siblings, they formed a club on Chicago's West Side. The novel follows them as they grow older, go to college or choose careers, love and marry. Some of the action takes place in Europe and the Middle East. These are second generation Jews, children of lower class families like those in Halper's short stories, and small business-people. Some are upwardly mobile, some are not. There is no central character.

"The Old Bunch is not only [Levin's] most serious piece of work," said James T. Farrell, "it is also one of the most ambitious novels yet attempted by any fiction writer of his generation, a work which demands a discipline and intelligence that are as yet unmatched by most novelists of his age."[34]

At his death in 1981, the book remained Levin's best novel.

Beatrice Bisno was also a Chicagoan by birth. She was educated at Columbia and New York Universities. As a journalist she traveled widely. In the 1930s, she worked in the Home Relief Bureau as Personnel Director, and in the Amalgamated Clothing Workers of America with Sidney Hillman. Thus, before writing *Tomorrow's Bread* (1938), she had had a long and intimate experience with the kinds of labor problems she wrote about in the novel.

Tomorrow's Bread is set mostly in Chicago from 1880 to post World War I. Sam Karenski, a fourteen-year-old, with his family, fugitives from Russian pogroms, comes to Chicago. Working in a family sweatshop in the Maxwell Street ghetto, he becomes indoctrinated with Marxist-Socialist philosophy. As a consequence, he subordinates his own and his family's welfare to his idealistic goals for Jewish sweatshop workers in Chicago and New York. He marries twice, but he is a constant philanderer, his moral code deriving from his socialism. Ultimately he achieves a kind of prosperity by becoming a business man, but his years of fatiguing work and poverty cause a fatal heart attack.

"There is a fierce white light that beats not upon a throne but upon prize awards," said a reviewer of Bisno's novel. "It is in such radiance that [*Tomorrow's Bread*] comes to us, after having been selected by Dorothy Canfield Fisher, Fannie Hurst, and Edwin Wolf, 2nd, as the winner of the $2,500 prize offered by the Jewish Publication Society of America for the best fiction of Jewish interest submitted during 1937."[35]

Waters E. Turpin's *O, Canaan!* (1939) begins in 1916 in Mississippi; crops are bad and a black boy has just been lynched. Joe Benson persuades Sam the barber to join the Benson family and forty other blacks in taking advantage of a special group train fare to emigrate to Chicago where, because of World War I, there is work. In Chicago they join the waves of blacks up from the South on Chicago's South Side — a rural culture transplanted to urban life. Aside from the brief interlude of hate during the 1919 Race Riots, most of the blacks live like other middle-class Chicago families — their sons go off to the War, the children to school, the men to work in the packing plants. Joe, a storekeeper in the South, opens a store, Sam, a barbershop. Some blacks become pimps, prostitutes, pool hall loafers, hoodlums. Others become church stalwarts.

Soon Joe is able to move his family from a State Street shack to a house on Prairie Avenue vacated by a wealthy white family moving to the North Side. With the advent of Prohibition, he becomes a bootlegger and enters into a restaurant partnership. His Jewish friend, Nick, is murdered in a gang war. As the prosperity of the 1920s reaches the blacks, Joe and his wife spend too much money; like the whites they lose everything in the 1929 stock market crash. Joe, suffering from a heart ailment, takes a job as a Pullman porter. In one way or another the blacks survive, endure.

The novel suffers from a poor structure and conventional touches. Moreover, Joe Benson comes off as a black Babbitt. "It is not the whole truth," said Alfred Kazin.[36]

There is an interesting connection between Waters Turpin and Edna Ferber. Here it is in Ferber's own words:

> It was at this time (the spring of 1925) that there walked into my life [by way of an employment service] that amazing and dimensional human being, Mrs. Rebecca Henry. Hailing from Maryland, she was — and is — a superb example of the Negro race. For almost fifteen years she has been a working member of my household. I think no one in my life has brought me more comfort and happiness. Anyone who has known me these past fourteen or fifteen years has known Rebecca. A person of taste and distinction — and what a hand with chicken and lobster and banana cake and meringue and lemon chiffon pie and clear soup (simmered two days). My friends, seeing me after an absence always say, "How are you? How's your mother? How's your sister?

How's Rebecca?" Her people in Maryland and Washington are physicians, teachers, civil-service employees. When Rebecca says of a new hat or dress, "Oh, Miss Edna, that's good-looking!" I know it's right. A widow, she has a son, Waters Turpin, by her first marriage, whose first novel [*O, Canaan!*] got reviews that would have made me jealous if I hadn't been so pleased...[37]

Scott Nearing's *Free Born*, subtitled "An unpublishable novel," was written when Nearing was almost fifty and published in 1933. Thomas L. Kilpatrick calls this an "unpleaant novel" of "persecution in its vilest forms." The story line utilizes lynching, rape and murder, life in Chicago's negro ghettos, and a race riot. The Chicago stockyards are a prominent part of the setting, and there are vivid descriptions of "the internal struggle in the labor unions of the 1920s."[38]

Chicago's History

Three unusual items begin this section. Herma Naomi Clark, a writer for the *Tribune*, was contributing a column "When Chicago Was Young" to the Sunday edition. In 1933, twenty-seven of the columns were published as *"Dear Julia*—, Letters from Martha Freeman Esmond to her friend Julia Boyd of New York in the days — When Chicago was Young." The letters are dated from October 27, 1854 to August 14, 1879. In 1941, a second selection, *The Elegant Eighties*, picked up from the previous book and continued through 1889. A third selection, *When Mother Wore a Bell Skirt and Father, a Derby Hat*, was published in 1943. This selection focussed on the history of Henrici's, a famous Chicago restaurant, from 1868 to 1943, the first seventy-five years of the restaurant's operation.

Some novels written in this decade about Chicago's history have been reviewed in the second chapter.

Ruth Russell's *Lake Front* (1931) carries a disclaimer that "since this is a story of a city, truth to the lives of individuals has been subordinated to truth to the life of the city." *Lake Front* opens with a prologue showing the young Pere Marquette's dream of becoming a Jesuit priest and "missioner" to New France; it ends with an epilogue in which a 1920s gangster dies in his florist shop as he hands a floral piece to a rival gangster — across the street from a "yellow stone cathedral." The ironic contrast between the death of Marquette, dying to save the souls of barbaric Indians, and the death of a gangster in a commercial act is intentional.

The novel itself focusses — like so many Chicago novels of this period written by women — on three generations: a woman who comes to Chicago looking for wealth and finds it; a daughter who admires Chicago's democracy; a son who would rather take the case of a dissolute, cheated investor for nothing than the case of a railroad tycoon who had done the cheating; and a grandson, son of the lawyer, who, as a newspaper man watching strikers die in Chicago's streets, decides he can do better, and in ten years becomes a powerful, affluent attorney representing the railroad interests his father scorned.

Lake Front's theme is that youthful idealism doesn't pay in Chicago where power resides in the hands of those who take it either with money or a gun. The novel has large aims, but in the words of one critic, "it represents a victorious retreat from the ambitious success it sets out to achieve."[39]

In her *The Bright Land* (1932) Janet Ayer Fairbank went even further back in time than her *The Cortlandts of Washington Square*. The novel tells of a young eastern lady who in 1845 elopes with a young man from Galena, Illinois. At that time it appeared that Galena, rather than Chicago, would be the "Queen City" of the West. Abby-Delight Flagg spends her life in Galena with occasional trips to Chicago whose rising sun always hovers in the east.

Mary Hastings Bradley's *Old Chicago* (1933), although it begins with the grim Fort Dearborn massacre, was written and published as part of an effort by several Chicago writers to take Chicagoan's minds away from the grim reality of the Depression and the problems of financing the Century of Progress, and to focus them on a vision of a more cheerful future by reviewing the accomplishments of the past.

A native Chicagoan, and "the most skillful of retrospective Chicago writers in introducing the familiar Chicago stories," Mary Hastings Bradley wrote with affection of the city she grew up in, even if she did not produce "the great Chicago novel."[40]

Edgar Lee Masters' *The Tale of Chicago* (1933) is as much a reflection of Masters' personality as it is a popular history of Chicago from its French past to its 1930s present. It seems obviously written to coincide with the Century of Progress Exposition. Masters' prejudices are clear: he dislikes Chicago, he sets Douglas above Lincoln as a political figure and person, he favors populism and the cause of labor, he seems to dislike the newspapers. He ignores the Chicago Renaissance of which he was a part, and he gives Samuel Insull much more attention than he gives to Chicago authors. He ignores "Hinky Dink" and "The Bath." And he dislikes war, seeing it as a tool of the capitalists.

"There is a Chicago spirit," Masters writes, "which proceeds from its inner life and is not immediately related to the careers of defaulting officials and to greedy business. There is a Chicago which sensitive observers are readily aware of in the city if they cannot very definitely describe what their intuitions realize."[41]

In general critics liked the book.

Earl Chapin May's *The Prairie Pirates* (1932) is a written-for-juveniles fictional tale of the settlement of northern Illinois and the beginnings of Chicago. Critics liked this tale of "the little mudhole called Chicago which most of the settlers passed by to take up residence in Galena."[42]

Pere Marquett's last fictional appearance as a Chicago-area personage came in this decade in Charles Corcoran's romantic novel, *Blackrobe* (1938). The most recent biography is *Jacques Marquette S. J. 1637-1675* (1969) by Joseph P. Donnelly.

By and About Women

Maxwell Bodenheim, who had come from Hermanville, Mississippi to become a part of the Chicago Renaissance and a collaborator with Hecht in the *Literary Times,* had gone on east to Greenwich Village where he took part in the dadaistic and nihilistic aesthetic movements. He wrote poetry, and at least two novels, *Georgie May* (1928) and *A Virtuous Girl* (1930) in which he demonstrated his sympathy for the good girl gone wrong. (Rumor had it that Bodenheim might have known a few.)[43] The time of the second novel is 1900; Emily Luise Filkins is accidentally seduced by a Jewish boy, and, as a consequence, is sent to spend the summer with a relative. The novel traces her through a series of sexual encounters as the summer passes.

"Bodenheim believes that virtue resides in the free heart," said a critic, "that convention is an obscene stupidity; that sex is noble; that middle age visits the frustrations of its youth upon the lives of its children; that the moral code flings us from hyprocrisy to coarseness and back again."[44]

Big Business Girl (1930) "by one of them" was actually the work of two people, H. W. Swanson and Patricia Reilly. It is the story of Claire MacIntyre, "Mac," and Johnny Goodman, musician and band leader; of her career in the dry cleaning business, of his career as an entertainer, and of their marriage which is kept secret for a while — even from the reader. Claire is independent not only in seeking a career and subordinating her marriage to it, but also in insisting on romantic alliances, particularly with one of her employers. Settings include the University of Chicago and Chicago night clubs during the prohibition years. The operations of Chicago racketeers also play a part.

Big Business Girl was filmed in 1931 with Loretta Young as Claire and Joan Blondell as a divorce co-respondent.

[Charles] Robert Douglas [Hardy] Andrews began with Henry Justin Smith at the *Chicago Daily News* in 1928, another "young man going somewhere." Although in his autobiographical *A Corner of Chicago* (1963), Andrews says that he had trouble getting his first stories accepted by Smith, by 1930 he was churning out books about as fast as he was writing stories about the daily news.

The first of these, *Three Girls Lost* (1930) is about three girls, from Oregon, South Dakota and Nebraska respectively, who meet on a train to Chicago and take up residence together in the Windy City. Two become involved in murders and one faces the anger of a wife seeking revenge. It was filmed in 1931; Andrews was the scriptwriter.

The ink was hardly dry on this one when its sequel, *One Girl Found* (1930) appeared. Marcia Talent, the Oregon girl loses her savings to a swindler, then tries to organize a modeling school. She becomes involved with illicit liquor traffic and the Chicago underworld, and two lovers.

The Stolen Husband (1931) was also billed as "A Chicago Novel." A stenographer, discovering that her husband of a year has been unfaithful, leaves him and returns to employment in Chicago. She becomes involved with an older woman with a like marital problem, a gangster who is marked to be "put on the spot," and her husband — who now is about to be arrested for fraud. Andrews was obviously here practicing for the radio and television soap operas he would write later in his career.

Marion Strobel has three novels in this decade about young Chicago women. *Saturday Afternoon* (1930) reprises the Chicago Renaissance in which Strobel, a friend of Harriet Monroe's, played a part. Susannah Pease, a Chicago publisher, is trying to encourage two young men to write, respectively, poetry and a novel. With them on a picnic in Grant Park she mysteriously disappears and is presumed drowned in the Lake. But while the young men and others search for her, Susannah is back at her office enjoying all of the uproar over her "drowning." Late in the afternoon, Susannah kills herself.

The first edition of the book included a "literary supplement" described in the book. It contained essays about Susannah by John Farrar, Kenneth Horan, Llewellyn Jones, Harriet Monroe, Howard Vincent O'Brien, Harry Hansen and Fanny Butcher, and sympathy telegrams from Floyd Dell, Burton Rascoe and Alta May Coleman. The book must be read with the same tongue-in-cheek attitude with which it was obviously written.

In all three of these Strobel novels, including the second, *A Woman of Fashion* (1931), a woman is the catalyst that sets off a chain of social reactions. In this novel, Strobel used the North Shore neighborhood she knew intimately as a background for a study in narcissism. The first time Eric Wesley met Della Nash, he seduced her; the second time they meet, they are married. He is an impecunious Chicago architect who loses his job in the stocket market crash; she loses her inheritance when she marries him. To support the two of them, Della becomes a fashion model. The novel is brilliantly written, smartly facile, with an overthick patina of glamour. Still it rings true.

Sylvia Fox of *Sylvia's in Town* (1933) is the social agent in the third novel; her reappearance among Chicago suburbanites set "everything off like firecrackers," in the words of one character in this slickly-written superficial story about a group of women with too much thyroid and to little to do as the consequence of marriage to men who work too hard, make too much money, and in general ignore their wives.

Alan Breuer Schultz's *The Rise of Elsa Potter* (1932) is the story of a woman whose motivations for becoming a magazine writer fade when an editor offers to trade her a publication opportunity for a sexual affair. In Chicago, she becomes "Madama Elsa" of a dress emporium, then opens a cosmetic business. She uses her physical attractions to enhance her opportunities. As one critic said, "Elsa's career is likely to convince anti-feminists that they have been right all along."[45]

Sterling North's *Tiger* (1933) seems to ape the earlier *Big Business Girl*. A private secretary is subject to all sorts of blandishments from her boss, who, ostensibly a radio producer, is actually involved with the Chicago underworld. But Jerry Hartford is too naive, and her boss to charming and debonair. *Pussycat* might have been a better title. The book lacks all the qualities of North's other work.

The time was 1901, the setting Chicago's Northwest Side near Avondale and the Swedish settlement there. Margaret Weymouth Jackson's *Sarah Thornton* (1933) is seventeen, attracted to Kurt Mueller, a German boy, son of a possessive mother. Sarah's father is a doctor whose large family shares the same building which houses his office. Thornton is an idealist; contrasted with him, his sons are shallow, reactionary, intent on success, prestige, money. Sarah becomes engaged, but because of Kurt's mother, the engagement drags on until after Kurt has returned from fighting on Germany's side in World War I. The characters of Sarah and Dr. Thornton are especially well done.

Jackson was also the author of *Jennie Fowler* (1930).

John Patrick Lally's *Anne Herrick* (1934) is a Chicago schoolteacher in those Depression years when the Chicago Board of Education was unable to pay its teachers' salaries except in scrip or warrants payable at some later date. A portion of the story tells of the attempts of her husband to start a business manufacturing and selling small portable radios.

Undoubtedly the best of the lot of these novels about women in Chicago is Willa Cather's *Lucy Gayheart* (1935), which begins and ends in a small Nebraska town. The plot is slight, but as Howard Mumford Jones said, no one reads Cather for her plots.[46] A young and impulsive music teacher from Nebraska falls in love with a middle-aged male singer in Chicago. She repulses the home-town banker's son with the lie that she has gone "all the way" with the singer. The banker's son marries someone else; the singer drowns; and the girl returns home with a sense that her life has been enriched by the Chicago experience. Then she drowns also. Too late the banker's son realizes what he has missed.

"A novelist less skilled would have created [of this] a sentimental romance," said Jones. "A novelist less wise would have satirized the singer, the heroine, and the stuffy little town [in the manner of Sinclair Lewis?]; a novelist less humane would have denounced bourgeois morals and sent his heroine off on a career of hard-boiled episodes."[47]

The scene of William Charles Lengel's *Candles in the Wind* (1937) is the Chicago of the turn of the century, the Chicago of the "bustling small business men, the business men who were just beginning, in the early Nineteen Hundreds, to talk about efficiency, to introduce typewriters into their offices and to hire pretty girls to run them — thus unintentionally starting a social revolution." As a result, "America was developing a new and distinct type of womanhood — a girl who desired to be daring yét who was shy; a timid yet ruthless invader in a man's world. All in all, she was becoming the most provocative type of woman in the world."[48]

Lengel's heroine is Jane Owain who left an illegitimate baby behind in Wales and came to Chicago to live and work with her aunt, a servant in the home of a man who owns a wholesale millinery business. From there, given Jane's natural charms, it is but a short step to a role as a model. And from there it is yet another short step to a series of entanglements with a man and two women rivals.

Unfortunately for Lengel's thesis, the story drifts off into romantic nonsense and melodrama.

Dorothy Aldis's *Time at Her Heels* (1937) relates in Aldis's "calm, ladylike style one hectic day in the life of" the novel's central character. Although the novel is set in Chicago during the Depression, it overlooks that larger social concern to follow a woman in her several roles as wife, mother, lover, friend and nursemaid. In the words of one critic, this novel is "an absolute joy to read."[49]

Lois Montross's next Chicago novel, *No Stranger to My Heart* (1937) was also designed to take reader's thoughts away from the Depression. It is slick magazine fiction, summery fluff, of a type not to be taken too seriously. Still, its heroine, daughter of a radical Methodist minister and a professional dancer, is an interesting person. In Chicago she marries into an orthodox family and her troubles begin. Her problem — will romance survive the joining of two incompatible persons in wedlock?

In 1931, Eleanor Blake [Atkinson Pratt] had written a mystery, *The Jade Green Cats*, featuring a Chicago doctor, an Evanston professor, and a quantity of stolen radium. In 1938, she turned to a much different type of literary effort in *Wherever I Choose.* Bergit Martison begins life with her Norwegian parents on a northern Michigan farm. She is seduced by a young man whose parents are summer residents in the area. When he leaves her, she moves to Chicago where she marries a middle-aged part owner of an advertising agency. Caught in the movement of suburban social life, she finds herself involved in bridge, parties, too much drinking and a relationship with the husband of a friend.

Bergit's problem is her rootlessness; Blake had found her title and her theme in these lines from Whitman:

> Afoot and light-hearted, I take to the open road,
> Healthy, free, the world before me,
> The long brown path before me, leading
> > wherever I choose.

Allis McKay's *Woman About Town* (1938) has its setting also in the Chicago advertising business, but also in the near North Side world of the affluent young people engaged in that business. Leila Garsten, separated from her husband, is a "completely indifferent woman," except that she yearns for a male script writer in her agency. The focus is on Leila and two female friends in the world of agencies, artists, clients and writers, and the constant chatter of work, men, and after-hours pleasures. In the years of 1928-1929 covered by the novel, the theme of woman's place in a man's world is constantly reworked.

Kenneth [O'Donnell] Horan's *It's Not My Problem* (1938) relates, in diary form, one year in the life of a young Chicago matron whose writing wins a literary prize and an offer to continue her work in Hollywood. But the narrator chooses to remain in Chicago with her husband and family. A critic calls this a "rollicking domestic comedy."[50]

Mrs. Horan relates in her autobiography, *Remember the Day* (1937) that she was named "Kenneth" because her Michigan parents wanted a boy. She was a Chicago literary critic and the author of several books, most of them set in Michigan.

Dorothea [Thompson] Brande's *My Invincible Aunt* (1938) tells of a recluse living in a Chicago flat, whose life style is completely turned about by her teen-aged ward. Kit Willow develops a complexion cream and promotes it across the nation. She amasses a fortune and becomes spiritual leader of a "Smile-and-Love cult."[51]

Dorothy [Keeley] Aldis's *All the Year Round* (1938) features a woman who falls back from city life for a year to regroup.

Young Love in Chicago

Meyer Levin's *Frankie and Johnny* (1930) has nothing to do with a well-known song by the same title. It's a novel of a love affair between two lower-class Chicago kids — he a shipping clerk, she a high school girl. The affair, never consummated in anything more physical than "necking" or "petting," ends in disillusionment for both. Levin maintains the language and tone at the level of his protagonists. Most critics thought that the novel was point-less.

Levin's *I, Jerry, Take Thee, Joan* (1931) tells of the marriage of Joan Prentice, at 21 heir to millions, who bypassed the logical candidate for her heart and hand to wed Jerry Corbett, 32, newspaper drama critic, a confirm-ed alcoholic. Jerry was drunk for the engagement party, drunk for his wedding, and he is still drunk after Joan's death from pneumonia following her attempt to drown herself in Lake Michigan.

The novel was selected for the *College Humor* — Doubleday, Doran Prize for 1931, perhaps, as Muriel Rukeyser said, because "the book will be true as long as people who live on lakefronts throw open parties, as long as people like Jerry give away fraternity pins, or forget names and remember tele-phone numbers, or find it impossible to stand up under the sixth beer."[52]

There was nothing in either of these two early Levin novels to indicate his potential for writing *The Old Bunch*.

University of Chicago professor Carl Grabo's *A Man and a Woman* (1931) features a Chicago girl who attempts "to carry feminism and the teaching of birth-control into the [downstate] Illinois valley, and who remains as the wife of a farmer."[53] It is, said an historian, one of several novels of this time which repudiate the city, seeing "no fit solution for" its problems:

> ... the return to the land by city dwellers who believe that "only ideas are
> life" involves a conquest as real as that of the countryman who believes that
> "Chicago is an absurd place ... [all] cities are," and that the machine age "will
> go to pieces of its own momentum."[54]

Of the novel, a Chicago *Tribune* reviewer said that "Grabo is more skillful in his choice of material than he is in working it out."[55]

Florence Ward, the author of a baker's half-dozen of books set in and near Chicago in the 1920s and 1930s, has two 1930s novels in this category. *Wild Wine* (1932) relates the decade-long delayed romance between a couple who are teen-agers as the novel begins. In the background is the Chicago construction boom of the 1920s and the beginnings of the Depression.

Women May Learn (1933) is set in a fictional Chicago suburb; it's about one woman and the three men who fall in love with her.

After a lapse of several years, Robert Herrick returned to writing with *The End of Desire* (1932). Herrick's protagonists are two doctors, one a widow, one a widower. His thesis was:

> My field is the ironic transposition of the ancient sexual values, at least

those parts conventionally attributed to either sex for untold generations. . . .
Thus the two sexes meet in the eternal conflict on a new ground, which
provides a tragi-conflict failure in mutual misunderstanding.[56]

Herrick's "new ground" consisted of the couple's grownup children "with
their mistaken loves and marriages [which] reflected the views of their
parents on masculine and feminine relationships."[57]

Herrick's final book, published five years before his death in 1938, was
Sometime (1933).

Rosamond Neal DuJardin's *Only Love Lasts* (1937) tells of a rural Illinois
girl who comes to Chicago because of her dislike of a cruel stepfather. The
heroine is pictured as a typical virtuous and unselfish heroine who has
several unhappy experiences with males until she meets a young man from
her home community.

Joseph McCord's slight *The Piper's Tune* (1938) also has a heroine who
comes to Chicago — this one from Oklahoma.

Chicago Families and People

Although the dominating theme in each of the eight novels explored in
this section is that of relationships within and between Chicago families,
other themes previously treated are also present — romance, the Depression, college years, gangsters, and the like.

Katherine Keith, whose husband was David Adler, the Chicago architect
of townhouses, uses her novel *The Crystal Icycle* (1930) to focus on a somewhat unusual triangle — a cartoonist for a Chicago newspaper, his wife ("A
Catholic puritan"), and an artist who is the oversexed wife of a University of
Chicago professor. Keith, whose first novel had been published twelve years
before, handled the situation with enough charm and skill to satisfy Chicago critics.[58]

MacKinlay Kantor's *El Goes South* (1930) is set in Rogers Park, a quiet
far north side suburb linked by the screeching elevated trains to the roaring
life of the city to the south. A department store employee and a widower
comes to the aid of a younger woman whose husband has been murdered by
a gangster. Complications ensue when he marries her and brings her home
to Rogers Park. Two of his children dislike her, two others get into a quarrel
over her and a shooting follows. The affair is hushed up, and life in Rogers
Park moves on quietly once more. The novel begins in garish fashion:

> It's a tomcat, squawling north on Sheridan, wrenching along through the
> blackness on four rubber legs, rubbing the icy asphalt into smooth streaks
> behind it. Sometimes there are red tomcats; they run in the day, also, and the
> white cats run too, and it's all hell when they run together.

After some ten pages of that "perfectly terrible" style, the novel settles
down into a "tender and understanding story of a middle-class family in

Chicago . . .[59]

"This story of Chicago is an authentic picture of our time," said a critic, although she noted some unnecessary coincidences, the latter a characteristic of Kantor's later work.[61]

Henry Channon's *Paradise City* (E. P. Dutton's "prize novel" for January, 1931) was written in London and Venice, so it's not surprising that some of the novel's scenes take place in those two cities. "Paradise City" seems to be modeled on Oconomowoc, Wisconsin, a summer resort where Chicago people come in the 1880s.

One of the four sections, essentially a novelette, tells of a hack driver who goes to Chicago with a nest egg of $400 and a wife whose father is a legislator. He works at the Columbian Exposition, gambles on wheat at a time when an attempt is being made to corner the market, almost loses his wife in the Iroquois fire, engages in manufacturing and becomes wealthy. His wife, a brash woman, pushes and worms her way into society. During World War I she almost forces her husband into bankruptcy.

In David Burnham's Hemingwayish *This Our Exile* (1931) the twenty-three-year-old author writes of two near North Side affluent families, two of whose children marry and go off to Paris to collect material for a "little" magazine. The families have summer homes in Winnetka and belong to the best clubs. We see these families in Chicago, just before the 1929 crash, trying to live through the crises resulting from a death in one family and the breakup of the children's marriage. This is a novel about people whose wealth enables their children to pursue lives of leisurely dilettantism. One wonders what happened to these people in the Depression.

Marion Strobel's *Fellow Mortals* (1935) features a similar North Side family from 1916 to 1931, the World War I years, the boom years of the 1920s, and the first years of the Depression. Unlike Burnham's families, the Newton Ambler fortunes suffer in the crash. A death and a bank failure leave the Ambler's penniless, Isobel Ambler's tearoom venture fails as does the son's marriage. Critics found the book dull.

William Churchill and his wife were members of the North Shore Country Club in the 1920s. Following Mrs. Churchill's suicide, Churchill used the pseudonym of Arthur Walcott to publish an angry, thinly-veiled attack on the Club's social life, *Uncertain Voyage* (1936). In the novel, a married woman of twenty years becomes the lover of another man. After publication people who identified themselves in the book persuaded the author to destroy all but a few, now rare copies.[62]

Mary Hastings Bradley's *Pattern of Three* (1937) is a love triangle set in the early 1930s in Chicago. A daughter of a Chicago banker who has lost his money because of the Insull crash, her employer, a Chicago lawyer, and his wife are the threesome. It is, said a critic, "an honest attempt to depict fairly one of those situations so frequent in real life, when right and wrong merge into one another and become inextricably entangled."[63]

For twenty years, the Albert Scherers and the Tom Lundmarks of Mary Jane Ward's *The Wax Apple* (1938) had been neighbors. The Scherers and their three children have the upper half of a duplex; their tenants and their two children live downstairs. Donald Scherer had once been engaged to Aggie, but she broke off the affair and now sports mink and expensive clothes. When Aggie decides to have one last fling with Donald, he murders her and commits suicide.

A wax apple, with an accidental bite out of it, in a bowl on the Scherer dining table symbolizes the drabness of life on a South Side Chicago street. For such an existence, Albert Scherer's terminal cancer comes almost as a release.

There were two "Converse beauties" in Detroit; Isabella Holt's *A Visit to Pay* (1939) dwells on the events of their marriages, and the affairs in which their resulting families are involved. The Chicago portion of this novel is set in Lake Forest (where "Towny" Abercrombie is a debutante), and in the Chicago Loop, where Martin Sadler, in love, works as a radio script writer. From a modern viewpoint, the novel's greatest interest may lie in its descriptions of early-day radio broadcasting in the Windy City.

Other Chicago People

William Riley Burnett followed up the success of *Little Caesar* with a novel about another Chicagoan, *Iron Man* (1930). Burnett's protagonist is Coke Mason, who got his start as a "palooka" in professional boxing, and became the middleweight champion. As he progesses, he has problems with his manager, largely because of the meddling of Coke's wife, Rose. Regan, the manager, is the best-developed of these three. "What we have here," said a critic, "is one more contribution to the literary gallery of what Malcolm Cowley called the New Primitives. Hard-boiled characters are presented in hard-boiled words. Not, in this instance, dangerously hard-boiled words [meaning profanity or obscenity] — the Iron Man and his associates swear, but they swear oaths long familiar to the printed page. The book offers an entertaining, safely-conducted voyage through rough country."[64]

Iron Man was filmed in 1931 with Lew Ayres as Coke and Jean Harlow as his "gold-digging" wife. In 1951 it was filmed with Jeff Chandler and Evelyn Keyes.

In *Dark Hazard*, Burnett turned to another world that polite Chicago society saw only from a distance, if at all — dog racing. This Book-of-the-Month selection for August, 1933, has only its opening pages in Chicago.

J[oseph]. P[atrick]. McEvoy, the creator of "Dixie Dugan," a comic strip featuring a showgirl who later became a career girl, set two of his books in Chicago. *Denny and the Dumb Cluck* (1930) is a collection of eight short stories about the greeting card industry, a star greeting card salesman, and a Chicago shop girl, "the dumb cluck," whom he finally marries. *Mister Noodle, An Extravaganza* (1931) is about an apple picker from Southern Illinois who attends classes in the Art Institute, then becomes a star cartoonist for a Chicago newspaper.

Robert Andrews' *Windfall; a novel about ten million dollars* (1931) relates what happens to ten people when a diabolical millionaire gives each of them a million dollars from his deathbed. The unsuspecting but happy heirs are a prostitute, a child, a housewife, a business man, a blind prizefighter, a poet, a stock broker, a shoe manufacturer, a convict and a secretary.[65]

Andrews' "Cinderella" story was filmed in 1932 as *If I Had a Million* — "the ultimate in wish fulfillment to countless viewers who didn't know where their next meal was coming from." The ten people, picked at random, are a forger who cannot cash his check without being arrested; a condemned criminal for whom the check comes too late; a man who thinks the check is a joke and uses it to pay a restaurant check; a prostitute whose dream is a warm bed by herself. These are ironic situations; the funniest episode of the ten (each directed by a different director) shows Alison Skipworth and W. C. Fields as a couple whose precious new car has been wrecked by a "road hog." Their first expenditure is for a fleet of old "tin lizzies" with which they spend a day gleefully wrecking the automobiles of other road hogs they encounter on the highway.[66]

Jack Tuthill's *Sideshows of a Big City: Tales of Yesterday and Today* (1932) consists of twenty-four tales about young married couples, elderly, immigrants, hustlers, blacks, and teen-agers in Chicago. One of the stories is set in Chinatown, another in an "opium den." The stories are in the tradition established by George Ade.

Arthur D. Welton's *Mr. Weld Retires* (1933) recalls Ferber's "Old Man Minick." Weld is pushed out of his business, which he had founded and run for forty years, by his sons. So, like Ferber's Minick, he heads for a Chicago park bench. There he finds soap-box orators, street gamins, ex-crooks and struggling artists. Trying to help these people solve their problems, he is involved in robbery, burglary and murder — but all ends well for him.

Harry Hansen was another Davenport, Iowa newspaperman who came to work for a Chicago newspaper, and who, in 1923, wrote his *Midwest Portraits* about his memories of the writers who had sat around Schlogl's famous roundtable. His *Your Life Lies Before You* (1935) is about an Iowa journalist with ambitions also to become a concert musician who comes to Chicago in the early years of this century — a *roman à clef* of the same period as Floyd Dell's autobiographical novels set in Chicago in part. Dell and Hansen had been friends in Davenport.

Edna Ferber's sister, Fanny Ferber Fox, had many of Ferber's qualities — vitality, inventiveness, warmth, an eye for detail, a keen interest in what people ate! In *Chocolate or Vanilla* (1935) Mrs. Fox brought together a collection of short stories about people in Chicago and small midwestern towns in which these qualities are demonstrated.

Chicagoan Elisa (Bialk) Krautter took courses in journalism at Northwestern and then worked as a newspaper reporter and columnist. She turned to writing some 200 short stories and plays for young people. Eleven of her twelve books were mostly about young people who like horses. One play, *The Sainted Sisters*, was filmed in 1948. It is set in Maine.

There are seven people in her twelfth book, *On What Strange Stuff* (1935): Gracie Rose, who takes her first job at fifteen as a fan club secretary and at seventeen becomes a publicity agent for a downtown Chicago hotel; Ben Adler, whose wife leaves him just as he gets his first big break in vaudeville; Ed Dossinger, whose marriage gives him the money and entry he needs to get into Chicago bootlegging and politics; Julia Nagodna, of Chicago's Polish "Bucktown" who changes her name to "Yorke Morrow" and becomes a writer; Peter Van Heusen, dissipating himself in hedonism; Philip Gregory, son of a wealthy meat packer, who goes to the University of Chicago to become a violinist, and eventually romances Yorke Morrow; James O'Donnell, who moves from the state's attorney's office to become Dossinger's attorney. The novel traces these people's interlocking affairs for about three years in the late 1920s.

The Reverend Doctor Lloyd C. Douglas was the author of a number of books of warm philosophy. *Green Light* (1935) is set "in a city never quite identified as Chicago."[67] The central character, Dean Harcourt, is custodian of a large midwestern cathedral and the mouthpiece for Douglas's message "that all that happens is somehow for the best."[68] This book with its Pygmalion-Galatea theme was the number one best seller in 1935 — 854,000 copies were sold. It was filmed in 1937 with Errol Flynn in the role of the doctor who is aided by the Dean.

Harold [Augustus] Sinclair was the author of a number of fine midwestern historical novels. His *Journey Home* (1936), however, was a contemporary story of a young man who at twenty-nine had lost his wife in a divorce court and his savings in the 1929 stock market crash. On a hobo trip from the east coast to his home on the west coast, he stops off in Chicago for six months of Bohemian living, involving a girl, music and books.

[Earl] Jerome Ellison set two novels in the Chicago area at this time. The first one, *The Prisoner Ate a Hearty Breakfast* (1939) is a story of self-destruction in contrast with *The Dam* (1941). An optimistic young man works for a college education with dreams of becoming an artist. But the death of his girlfriend following an abortion sets him on a downward path. Part of the novel is set in New York.

Manuel Komroff is not ordinarily identified with Chicago, but his *Coronet* (1930), a chronicle of the wanderings of an inanimate object, a medieval Florentine golden crown, concludes in Chicago where the crown finally comes to rest in the vaults of a Chicago pork packer, next to a golden cast of a hog's head.

Margaret Ayer Barnes

Margaret Ayer Barnes (Mrs. Cecil Barnes) was Janet Ayer Fairbank's younger sister, and like her older sibling, had been reared in that lifestyle Janet had pictured in *In Town, and Other Conversations.* Her home was on North Dearborn Parkway and she had summer homes at Bar Harbor and on the Des Plaines River. She began writing literally by accident — an automobile accident invalided her for six months, and she used her enforced leisure time to write short stories for magazines. These were collected in *Prevailing Winds* (1932). "Janet showed us the way," Barnes wrote in the preface.

Not all of the stories are about Chicago. "Home Fire" tells of a Chicago banker who divorced his wife and went to New York with an actress, there becoming a playwright. "Shirtsleeves to Shirtsleeves" tells of Hiram Baxter who came to Chicago at twenty-one, succeeded, and built a home on Prairie Avenue. He longs for an heir, but only one appears — a granddaughter. At the end of the story she has opened her own shop as her grandfather once did. The story reads like the outline for Barnes' later *Within This Present.*

In "The Dinner Party" a North Shore woman relives a dinner party of nineteen years before with the man she had fallen in love with on that earlier occasion. But meanwhile she has married another man.

Barnes first novel, *Years of Grace* (1930), is also her best; it won the 1931 Pulitzer Prize for fiction. It is, said Fanny Butcher, "a long leisurely record of manners as well as morals, a colorful picture of the rapidly shifting background of a Chicago emerging from the self-consciousness of the days just before the World's Fair of 1893 to the even greater self-consciousness of the front pages of 1930."[69]

Jane Ward was seventeen the year of the Columbian Exposition and in love with a French boy, but her parents asked her to postpone marriage until she was twenty-one. By then, the young man was embarked on a career as a sculptor, so Jane married Stephen Carver. At thirty-five she fell in love with her best friend's husband; this affair led her to a moment of truth:

Sex was a loaded pistol . . . thrust into the hand of humanity. Her mother's generation had carried it carefully, fearful of a sudden explosion . . . Her generation . . . waved it nonchalantly about, but after all with their carelessness, they didn't fire if off any oftener than their parents had. What if the next generation should take to shooting? Shooting straight regardless of [its] target.[70]

Jane had to face the situation again when her daughter fell in love with a friend's husband — the third repetition of this motif. The first two situations ended tragically, but the daughter's generation was able to cope.

Years of Grace makes an interesting comment about those Chicago business men who devoted their lives to their careers:

Stephen didn't have much fun, thought Jane. With a sudden pang she realized he looked his forty-four years. His curly blond hair had receded over his temples and was grey above the ears. The temples were rather shiny and the hair was growing perilously thin in a small circular area at the top of his head. His grey slack suit was just a little wrinkled after a hot afternoon in a suburban train. Yes, Stephen looked just like what he was — the forty-four year-old first-vice-president of the Midland Loan and Trust Company, badly in need of his summer vacation.

Men drew the short straw in life, reflected Jane. Men like Stephen at least. If it was a man-made world, men had certainly made it with a curious disregard of their own comfort and convenience. How terrible to be a first-vice-president of a bank and work eight hours a day for forty years at a mahogany desk and never have more than three weeks' holiday. Why did men do it? When the world was so wide and so full of a number of things and they didn't really *have* to marry to — to enjoy themselves. (244-245)

Like others of the three-generation Chicago novels, the book continually glances at the Chicago cavalcade:

"We'll jump off the Michigan Boulevard Bridge together. Some early spring afternoon when the ice is just out of the river and the first sea-gulls have come and the water's running very clear and green. We'll climb up on the parapet together and take a last look down the boulevard, thinking of how it was once just Pine Street. We'll shut our eyes and remember the old square houses and the wide green yards and the elm trees meeting over the cedar-block pavement. We'll remember the yellow ice-wagons and the Furnesses four-in-hand, and the bicycles, and the hurdy-gurdies and sitting out on our front steps in the summer evenings. (458)

"In an interesting way," said Rebecca Lowrie, *Years of Grace* paralleled Caspary's *Thicker Than Water* (published two years later). "It is Chicago of practically the same period, and of the same social group [but] in another [ethnic group]. Both are novels of prejudices and possessions and the effect of time and growth on each."[71]

Barnes' next novel, *Westward Passage* (1931), tells of a woman meeting her first husband on a voyage home from Europe, and almost deciding to give up her second husband, a staid Chicago business man, to return to the more romantic first one. But a day with her first husband in a New England farmhouse persuades her to leave well enough alone. The book was filmed in 1932 with Laurence Olivier and Ann Harding.

In *Within This Present* (1933), Barnes left the present and returned to a "shirtsleeves to shirtsleeves" family chronicle. Although set in the years from 1914 to 1931, the novel retrospectively cuts back to the Chicago founder of the family, a pre-Fire banker. He manages to save the bank's assets and build a fortune. In 1933, his widow watches the bank fail — one of numerous bank failures of that period.

The novel's events are seen through the character of a granddaughter through her school days back east, her marriage to a philanderer, her love affair with a poet, and the stock market crash.

The book's conclusion marks the end of an epoch — the epoch of the "years of grace" which the families of Barnes' two novels had been fortunate to experience. Still, Barnes leaves the reader with an optimistic sense of more "years of grace" in the future.

All of these first three novels were "best sellers," each going through several printings.

In *Edna His Wife* (1935) Barnes turned to a commonplace woman, the daughter of a railroad depot agent, who instead of marrying the railroad man she might have, weds an upwardly-mobile lawyer. The novel's time is 1900 to 1935. During this time the husband becomes a part of upper-class social groups and takes on a mistress. Meanwhile the wife is reduced to seeking vicarious romance in movie matinees — while her chauffeur waits outside.

In her next novel, *Wisdom's Gate* (1938), Barnes again left the romantic novel for a return to the family chronicle — again the families last seen in *Years of Grace*. This time it's the current generation and their marital mixups, and the problems of living in a small social community with close-knit family ties. A sidelight shows one character producing one-minute advertising films to be shown on motion picture screens.

Wisdom's Gate was one of the last Chicago novels to focus on families in the mode of romantic realism. Meanwhile, as we shall see presently, another Chicago writer had begun writing the chronicle of a Chicago family — but using the mode of literary naturalism.

Life in the Suburbs

Jessica Nelson North was a poet, an associate editor of *Poetry* and wife of Sterling North, Chicago journalist and author. Her *Arden Acres* (1935) shows "the backwash of the depression" over a settlement of families living on acreages southwest of Chicago. The Chapins, "Gram," Tim and Loretta, and their five children, live in a one-room shack on one of these plots. Tim ekes out a living for the brood, selling stolen automobiles. Loretta and her oldest daughter have a romantic interest in an artist. Tim's neighbors report him to the police. He is set free, but is shot down by a gangster. And life goes on in "Arden Acres."

American Acres (1936) was written by Louise Redfield Peattie, wife of Donald Culross Peattie. It shows the same love for the Illinois land that Peattie's *A Prairie Grove* shows. *American Acres* is a family saga, beginning with old Adironam Honeywell who built a log cabin on the Grand Portage between the South Fork of the Chicago and the Des Plaines River, now on the southwest edge of Chicago proper. Most of the novel is set in the present with flashbacks to old sin. The two modern protagonists plan to restore Grand Portage to its rightful estate.

In *Dalesacres* (1939), Florence Jeannette [Baier] Ward wrote about a family dynasty which had begun on a two-thousand acre farm on the west outskirts of Chicago. Like a Greek tragedy, this novel unravels ancient crime and sin, and shows their effects on the present-day members of the family.

Elizabeth Corbett

Since writing *Cecily and the Wide World* (1916), a novel about a girl's life on the distant edges of Chicago, Elizabeth Corbett had been attracting readers with novels about a fictional Carrie Meigs of Ohio. In 1934, she set off on a new track, creating the Chicago suburb of "Mount Royal," and writing the first of nearly a dozen books about the place, *The House Across the River*. Some others were: *Mount Royal* 1936); *The Langworthy Family* (1937); *Light of Other Days* (1938); *Charley Manning* (1939); and *The Far Down* (1939). In the first novel, she called her town "Hillport," and showed the boredom and tedium of Hillport wives left behind by the five-day-a-week exodus of their husbands to Chicago. In the "Mount Royal" titles, Corbett examined the whole social structure of the town; the "far down," Irish Catholics at the bottom of the social ladder, the Langworthys near the top of society, the lower-middle-class Reillys, Charley Manning the wealthiest man in the town and a born philanderer. Each novel focusses on a different family group or character but the social relationships overlap. There is both upward and downward mobility in the town as the years pass from the town's founding in 1846 to the late 1930s.

In *Golden Grain* (1943), Corbett placed the heroine of two non-Mount Royal stories in Mount Royal. *The Richer Harvest* (1952) is a better story. It tells of a self-sacrificing man who finally achieves some happiness for himself. In *The Head of Apollo,* a Mount Royal music teacher finds only unhappiness. Corbett's final novel, *The Old Callahan Place* (1966) is set in Helios, another mythical western Chicago suburb. Like *The Far Down,* it too is about an Irish-American family but the focus here is on the eldest daughter who endures a long spinsterhood in order to help her family and earn professional success.

Corbett's contribution to Chicago literature is the most extensive study of suburban life of any Chicago author. This serious-minded author has never gained the literary esteem awarded to others, such as Farrell, but she has *earned* more attention than she has gotten so far.

College and University Life

From the founding of the University of Chicago in the early 1890s to the present, Chicago authors have concentrated some of their energies on novels of college life: Herrick, Farrell, DeVoto, Vardis Fisher, Linn and Fuller are the most prominent names in the list. This decade produced nine college novels set in the Chicago area.

John Hawley Roberts, an English teacher, portrayed a modern Narcissus in his study of a Chicago school youth, *Narcissus,* 1930. Through private and prep school and two years of college, Millwater Crane, whose father is dead, admires himself too much and as a result cannot relate to others. An uncle, discovering his problem, offers to help Crane. The result is an ill-fated tryst with a University of Chicago girl graduate student.

The novel should be compared with the later *Behold a Cry* (1947).

"Life has taught me three things," says a sorority girl in Betty White's *I Lived This Story* (1930, a Doubleday Doran — *College Humor* prize novel), "holding drinks, a distrust of blondes and birth control." However, this opinion is not shared by Dorinda Clark, the novel's heroine, who, as time goes by, loses her romantic dreams of what a college ought to be, and begins attacking her school's false qualities in student-newspaper editorials.

"This is the only good novel that has ever been written about a co-educational university," said Bernard DeVoto, American scholar and historian. "It is the only good college novel written from the co-ed's point of view."[72] DeVoto should have praised the novel, for he appears in it as young Professor Lewis Ford who influences Dorinda's (Betty White?) change of heart. DeVoto was a teacher at Northwestern University, the obvious model for the book's "Colossus U."

Like Dorinda, DeVoto got himself in trouble at Northwestern for *his* radical notions; he was forced to leave the school. In his *We Accept With Pleasure* (1934), DeVoto used the same period of time and his own experiences at Northwestern as a basis for a novel. DeVoto is seen as Ted Graysson, a young assistant professor of History at Northwestern who is fired for supporting the League of Nations.

"*We Accept With Pleasure* catches almost to perfection the remoteness, the troubled aloofness, the bewildered idealism and cautious radicalism of the people with whom it deals," said Fred T. Marsh. "Or better, perhaps, it catches the present puzzled and disturbed approach of Harvard, Boston, New England and the higher American 'Academy' towards the swift and indecorous destruction of the old tenets anent the good, the liberal life."[73]

Idahoan Vardis Fisher set part of the third book of a tetralogy, *We Are Betrayed* (1935) in the graduate college of the University of Chicago from 1920 to 1923. "The novel examines in detail the exigencies of existence for a brilliant but troubled mind."[74] Fisher was a Chicago Ph.D. graduate.

In 1936, James Weber Linn, who had been teaching for at least three decades at the University of Chicago, and who had been relatively silent for some time (except for his biography of Jane Addams), published two novels of campus life.

This Was Life covers one year at the beginning of the University of Chicago's history. Its central character is a minister's son, freshman, would-be football hero, university correspondent for a Chicago newspaper and conspirator in a plot to keep a co-ed's marriage secret. Except that his grades improve from "C" to "A," nothing ever happens to Jerome, but everything happens to his friends.

Winds Over the Campus shows us these same people forty years later. Jerome Grant is now a Chicago professor. The "wind over the campus" is radicalism. Walgreen, the drug store chain king, who actually withdrew his niece from Chicago because she was asked to parse a sentence from a Soviet primer, appears in the novel as Borgman, the synthetic butter king.

Although critics thought that Linn provided an excellent picture of a university at all its levels from freshman to Ph.D. candidates, they concluded that this was not the great college novel.[75]

In Mary Jane Ward's complex *The Tree Has Roots* (1937), the emphasis is on the non-academic employees — those who make it possible for teacher and student to have the leisure to conduct the learning processes. The scene is Elm University in Elmgate, Illinois, a college town, close to steelmills, with big buildings, wealthy society people and a hard core of Puritanism.

Critics liked this first novel of Ward's much better than Minnie Hite Moody's college novel, *Towers With Ivy,* which appeared at the same time.

Marjorie Hill Allee's *The Great Tradition,* also in 1937, reads as though it were written for secondary school girls; it is about a group of young women, all in the Biology Department at the University of Chicago. The "tradition" is the heritage of scholarship at the school, a tradition to which the novel's characters adhere. There's another theme in the novel — the place of blacks on a campus and the problems they face as, ill-prepared in preparatory school, they try to compete with better prepared whites.

Sterling North's *Seven Against the Years* (1939) begins with the 1929 graduation ceremonies of the University of Chicago and ends with the tenth anniversary reunion of seven of the 1929 graduates, whose careers have been traced in the novel. Seen are a factory worker/union organizer, a meat packing heir, a newspaper man (who didn't graduate), a social worker, a Greek entrepreneur and promoter, a socialist, and a critic/novelist. North's sympathies are with Maloney, the radical, with Gundarson, the union organizer, and with Harbord, the journalist, who seemingly speaks for North: "[I am] bewildered and ashamed for the whole generation, the youth in which America had such hope." But North makes it clear these three had accomplished something with *their* lives.

North's novel should be compared with Susan Glaspell's *Norma Ashe* (1942), a novel covering about the same period of time with much the same theme of disillusionment in young American college graduates of promise.

North got a BA from Chicago in 1926, then became a Chicago journalist and eastern establishment literary editor.

James Thomas Farrell, (1904-1981)

James T. Farrell is one of Chicago's major literary figures and certainly its most prolific one. He was born in Chicago in 1904 and published his first short stories in his prep school magazine in 1929. The book that made him a major American literary figure, *Young Lonigan: A Boyhood in Chicago Streets,* set in the South side Irish-Catholic neighborhood of his own youth, was published in 1932. From that time on he published almost twenty-five novels, over fifteen collections of short stories, two volumes of poetry, and a half-dozen or so collections of essays, prose pieces and at least one play.

This output was not accidental; in college he conceived a "life-plan" to write twenty-five novels. "What I want to do in this whole series of at least twenty-five books," he told a Vanguard Press editor in 1942, "is to drive toward a feeling about life, a thorough and exhaustive account of a way of life, a period, of endless and complicated tendencies pressing for action."[76]

Readers will agree that Farrell's output is "thorough and exhaustive." By the time one is through the Lonigan-O'Neil-Carr novels, one is sure that he or she could travel through Chicago's South Side and identify all the landmarks and recognize a great many familiar faces.

His Studs Lonigan — Danny O'Neill novels are his best work. Studs' story is related from June 16, 1916, when Studs was 14, until his death of a heart attack on August 15, 1931. His story is related in *Young Lonigan, The Young*

Manhood of Studs Lonigan (1934) and *Judgement Day* (1935).

An early reaction to these novels came from the pen of a major critic of the time, Henry Seidel Canby:

> I wonder whether these naturalists in fiction of the thirties are not lagging behind the development of the other arts. While Mr. Farrell's material is fresh and convincing, the setting reminds me of the now almost forgotten and once so influential [David] Belasco who saw to it that his stage had real milk bottles, a real clock with a crack on the dial, real dirt, real smells, if necessary, a real cow. The stage has long since got beyond all that. The novel, or at least the naturalistic novel, dealing frankly, honestly with the dirt, the disorder, the viciousness of low-class American life is still at the Belasco level. It depends upon a massed description, upon every detail, to the color of a girl's drawers and the most minute indecency of a boy's conversaton. Mr. Farrell's artistic integrity is impeccable, but while his conscientious inclusiveness would be admirable in a sociologist doing case histories, it is old-fashioned and bad-fashioned in art, though alas, too common in the quasi-art of naturalistic fiction.[77]

The story of Danny O'Neill, in what Farrell called the O'Neill-Flaherty series (Flaherty was Mrs. O'Neill's maiden name) was told in *A World I Never Made* (1936); *No Star is Lost* (1938); *Father and Son* (1940); *My Days of Anger* (1943); and *The Face of Time* (1953). They take Danny from 1909 (he enters school in 1911) to the time when Danny leaves home, and his studies at the University of Chicago, to become a writer in New York City.

Of the last book in this series, Nelson Algren wrote:

> The present saga is easily the best written of Farrell's many novels. There is nothing faked here; every line of dialogue rings true. If the book takes a deal of ploughing to get through, it is still worth the ploughing — though it could have been cut in half without losing a thing.

But Algren thought that the novel failed "in affording that convulsive sense of life we discover in a Conrad, a Poe, a Stephen Crane or a Scott Fitzgerald."[78]

Farrell next turned to a new series and a new central character whom he called "Bernard Clare" in the book with that title (1946), and "Bernard Carr" in the second novel in the series, *The Road Between* (1949), and in the third and final book, *Yet Other Waters* (1952). Farrell changed his protagonist's name because of a libel suit by a man named Bernard Clare.

The second and third novels, at least, are *romans á clef*. Edward Branch says: "From a working-class family, Bernard illustrates Chekhov's statement used as the epigraph to *Bernard Clare:* 'What writers belonging to the upper class have received for nothing, plebeians acquire at the cost of their youth.'"[79]

Farrell's other books of the 1930s are:

Gas-House McGinty (1933) is a portrait of men at work in a Chicago express office. Danny O'Neill and his father are characters. Farrell, as a young man, worked in such an office.

Calico Shoes (1934) collects sixteen stories in which "Farrell is still considerably pre-occupied with the biological urge — the love lorn to the sex-starved, with perverts, aging prostitutes, young tarts and drugstore cowboys..."[80]

Guillotine Party (1935) collects sixteen Chicago short stories and three others. More social realism.

Can All This Grandeur Perish? (1937) contains sixteen stories set in Chicago and one other. Better writing than in earlier stories.

Farrell's other books of the 1940s are:

Ellen Rogers (1941). A spoiled, willful Chicago flapper of the mid-1920s encounters more than she can handle in the unscrupulous Ed Lanson and she drowns herself in Lake Michigan. Two of Farrell's more memorable characters.

Farrell's other 1940s works are all volumes of short stories: *$1,000 a Week* (1942); *To Whom It May Concern* (1944); *Twelve Great Stories* (1945); *When Boyhood Dreams Come True* (1946); *The Life Adventure* (1947) and *Yesterday's Love* (1948). Over half of these stories are set in Chicago.

Farrell's work in the 1950s and later years:

An American Dream Girl (1950). Seven of the twenty-one stories in this gloomy, cynical collection are set in Chicago.

A Dangerous Woman and other stories (1957). At least five of these stories are set in Chicago.

Boarding House Blues (1961). Farrell takes a long look back to Chicago's near North Side in the Depression years. The bohemian colony is shown. Ed Lanson and Danny O'Neill, and a boarding house run by an Irish woman.

Sound of a City (1962). Eight of these twenty-four short stories are set in Chicago's decadence and glory.

The Silence of History (1963); *Lonely for the Future* (1966), *What Time Collects* (1964); *When Time Was Born* (1966); *A Brand New Life* (1968); and *Judith* (1969) are the finished novels Farrell envisioned as part of a new series *A Universe of Time*. Farrell foresaw some thirty novels in this series (he was fifty-nine when the first one was published!) organized into four divisions: *When Time Was Young* (1924-31); *Paris Was Another Time* (1931-32); *When Time Was Running Red* (1932-37); and *A Universe of Time* (1937 to the present). Actually the time covered goes back as far as Chicago of the 1870s.

The central character in this series is Farrell-like Eddie Ryan. In the first novel he is seen as a mid-1920s student at the University of Chicago. In the second novel Eddie is seen with two friends, George and Alec McGonigle, who Farrell planned to make major characters in later novels in the series. A major setting for this novel is the Bohemian Forum, a night spot on the near South Side frequented by young people on the make.

What Time Collects features a young girl in her twenties, Anne Duncan Daniels, a resident of a midwestern town called Valley City. At the end of the novel, divorced, Anne will move to Chicago. The time is the 1870s.

A novel not in The Universe of Time series, *New Year's Eve/1929* (1967) picks up Danny O'Neill and his girl from *Boarding House Blues* and places them in a bohemian area near the University of Chicago campus. The central character is an ex-nurse, dying of tuberculosis.

In *A Brand New Life*, Anne Duncan Daniels is seen in Chicago in 1928. There she becomes involved with two men.

The Dunne Family (1976) focusses on Eddie Ryan's grandmother, Grace Hogan Dunne, an 1860s immigrant from Ireland to Chicago. In the 1930s, an invalid, she recalls the good times and the bad of her past and contemplates her present family and its problems.

Now that Farrell is dead, his work complete, the scholars and historians will begin work in earnest on his life and work. Meanwhile, the best study to date is Edgar M. Branch's *James T. Farrell* (1971), a study of his work to that time. The book includes bibliographies of Farrell's work and essays about it, and notes about Farrell's critics.

Poets and Playwrights

Earlier we have seen Herma Clarke's series of imaginary letters written for the Chicago *Sunday Tribune* under the general heading of "When Chicago Was Young." A play based on this material was presented at the Goodman Theater, atttached to the Chicago Art Institute, in 1933.

Meyer Levin's first attempt at drama, *Let's Re-elect FDR*, subtitled "The Good Old Days," or "The Good Old Nineteen-Thirties," is a musical comedy set in Chicago in early 1936. Most of the characters are college students, one of whom thinks he has discovered a birth control pill, but subsequent events prove him wrong. There is also Gusick, a labor organizer, who seems more interested in making passes at college girls than at industrial tycoons. In its emphasis on free love, the play was probably simply echoing the sentiments of the long-past members of the Renaissance. Except for some dated references to Franklin Delano Roosevelt, the play still reads well.

Margaret Ayer Barnes had three plays produced at the beginning of the decade: *Dishonored Lady, Jenny,* and *The Age of Innocence.*

Harriet Monroe's *A Poet's Life* (1938) is mostly autobiography, except for the years 1922-1936 which were covered by Morton Dauwen Zabel, a later editor of *Poetry*. The book is also a biography of the magazine from 1912 to 1936.

Because Monroe was 52 when she founded *Poetry*, much of the book is taken up with the record of a poet's life from the post-Fire years until 1912; there's a long narrative about her experiences with the Columbian ode. And because Monroe's sister, Lucy, married an architect, Monroe also discusses architecture and the arts in Chicago.

A list of *Poetry* editors from 1912 to 1938 is appended, and places of publication are listed.

Chicago Little Magazines

There are only a few of these on record. *Earth* (subsequently *A Midwestern Expression*) ran from April, 1930 to January, 1932; its issues reflected interests in literature. Sterling North and James T. Farrell were two contributors. *Contemporary Poetry* lasted six issues in late 1932. *Left Front* (June 1933-June 1934) was dedicated to the "proletarian culture front;" one of its poets was Richard Wright.

Adamant, a quarterly of beautiful verse began in the winter of 1933/34 and ended with the Winter issue of 1935, a total of five issues. *The New Anvil*, succeeded *The Anvil* when that publication merged with *The Partisan Review*. It lasted from March, 1939 to July/August 1940 under the editorship of the well-known proletarian novelist, Jack Conroy. It was a leftist publication.

These publications were usually personal expressions, appealing to limited audiences. They were ephemeral, usually lasting as long as the printer would carry the bill. Now and then they gave a major new writer a chance to try his or her wings.

Esquire

In August of 1933, a time when "there were very few rich people left," a new magazine appeared in Chicago — at fifty cents a copy. It was *Esquire*, and it had been founded in Chicago by a man from the West Side. Its headquarters from the beginning was in the penthouse of the then Palmolive Building (now the Playboy Building), up under the Lindbergh Beacon. It would be easy to argue that the figurative beacon of the new magazine shone more brightly than the actual one above.

The founder/publisher was David A. Smart, and his editor was the immortal Arnold Gingrich, in 1933 a recent Phi Beta Kappa graduate of the University of Michigan. Meyer Levin, not long out of the University of Chicago, worked over the slush pile, the unsolicited manuscripts, looking for nuggets in the garbage. Levin also was the motion picture reviewer, and on weekends, he slipped away to a shack in the center of a nudist colony where he wrote unnoticed. Clarence Darrow was one of the writers, McKinlay Kantor an occasional war correspondent. Gingrich found a 25-year-old Chicagoan, son of a Chicago minister, Peter DeVries; DeVries told him "I do nothing and writing." Gingrich also got some poems from a young West Sider named Nelson Algren.

Esquire left Chicago in the early 1950s, moving on to New York.[81]

Other Chicago Films of the 1930s

In 1931, following their triumphs in *Little Caesar* and *Public Enemy*, Edward G. Robinson and James Cagney made *Smart Money*, the only film in which the two appeared together. Robinson is a small-town barber whose skill with dice and cards takes him to Chicago where he becomes "the ace of gamblers." In a quarrel with Cagney, Robinson accidentally kills him and Robinson is sent off to prison charged with manslaughter.

The Man Who Dared (1933) is a sympathetic biography of Anton (Tony) Cermak who became Chicago's mayor, succeeding "Big Bill" Thompson in April of 1931, and who, in May of 1933 at Miami was killed by a bullet that Cermak and others believed was intended for President Roosevelt.

Although some historians claim that Cermak brought to office a machine as corrupt as his predecessor's, the film sees him as an admirable man from a Bohemian background in Chicago, solidly detailed in the film. The story begins just after the Fire when Cermak (Jan Novak in the film) is nine and follows his political progress from that time until, as he lies dying, he tells the President: "I'm glad it was me and not you."

Heroes For Sale (1933) deals with the problems faced by a World War I veteran during the Depression. A Chicago laundry worker, he leads other workers in an attack on the machines which have displaced them and cost them their jobs. He is sent to prison for inciting a riot (even though his wife was killed in it); when he returns home, "Red Squads" brand him as a dangerous agitator and force him to flee from the city.

The World Changes (1933), like *The Man Who Dared*, also covers some seven decades of time. The son of sturdy Swedish immigrants in South Dakota becomes the partner of a Chicago meat packer and marries the packer's socially ambitious daughter. Like other Hollywood films of the time, the plot was familiar: such films show "the rise and fall of a tycoon, preferably self made, who claws his way to the top, usually in Chicago . . ., along the way ruthlessly disposing of rivals and, if necessary, friends, driving his neglected wife to insanity and/or suicide, become entangled with a younger woman, always with disastrous results, and, of course, finally getting his come-uppance."

The historian who wrote these words then asked "why so many of these sagas were set in Chicago rather than in New York, where the greatest fortunes were made and spent." "One possible reason," he thought, was "that the studios ... were controlled from New York by banks still owned by the descendants of the city's leading Robber Baron families, whereas their Chicago counterparts, like the Fields, Swifts, Armours and McCormicks, seemed safe targets."[82]

The World Changes followed *I Loved A Woman* into the theaters so quickly that film critics also wondered what Warner Brothers, the producers of both, had against Chicago meat packers!

The Power and the Glory (1933) dramatized the life of a lowly railroad trackwalker who becomes president of the Chicago and Southwestern Railroad. His first wife helps make him a success but he drives her to suicide; his second wife turns out to be a faithless woman, and he commits suicide.

The Woman in Red (1935) is a professional horsewoman who marries into the snobbish society of Chicago's North Shore, then risks her marriage to save a friend wrongly accused of murder.

In Old Chicago has been reviewed in the section on the Chicago Fire.

A Final Note

Thus the decade which had begun with the economic chaos resulting from the turbulent twenties and their aftermath closed with the onset of World War II. It had been a glorious decade for Chicago authors — although the number of fiction titles produced annually in America was to double in the next forty years, never again would any decade produce so many novels, plays and short stories set in Chicago. The golden days of regional writing were past.

And although the decade may not have been as significant as the decade from 1910 to 1920, it had seen several major figures — Halper, Levin, Barnes, Kantor, Farrell, Burnett, Caspary, Fairbank, and Corbett. All but two of these would be writing about Chicago for the next twenty or thirty years.

Meanwhile, unknown to just about everybody, the writer who was to become Chicago's most honored writer — Saul Bellow — was just beginning to write.

XI.
The War Years and After

It isn't hard to love a town for its broad and bending boulevards, its lamplit parks and its endowed opera. But you never truly love a place till you love it for its alleys, too. For the horse-and-wagon, cat-and-ash-can alleys below the thousand-girded El.[1]

The 1940s were to be the last years in which any sizable number of Chicago novels were to be produced. The old guard had all but disappeared — only James Farrell, W. R. Burnett, Elizabeth Corbett, Meyer Levin, Albert Halper and Marion Strobel would continue to publish in this decade. But localized regional literature of place would not again be published in the quantities of titles or copies that the last four decades had seen.

In these years in which the nation's attention was turned away from itself to Europe and Asia, there would still be some interest in the Depression, and there would be some novels dealing with the impact of the War. A few new names would appear — notably Saul Bellow, Richard Wright, Gwendolyn Brooks, Willard Motley, and Arthur Meeker. The themes of family, people, ethnic groups, suburbs, business, history and crime would still be utilized.

The biggest surprise for the 1940s is the appearance of some four dozen titles in the mystery novel category — all with Chicago settings.

As for poetry — Samuel Putnam's mid-1920s prophecy could now be engraved in stone.

The Depression in 1940s Chicago Novels

A major concern of the Roosevelt administration during the 1930s was the creation of new jobs for the vast numbers of unemployed — usually on public construction. Jerome Ellison's *The Dam* (1941) is about one such project. "The dam" was on the Chicago Sanitary Ship Canal at Stony Ridge (Summit), an old "bear-trap" type which John Storm, an ex-farm boy turned engineer, had helped build at the start of his career. Now, in 1937, seven years into the Depression, it needs replacing; its collapse would siphon the waters of the Great Lakes and flood the Des Plaines valley.

Storm had been a successful engineer, but his business had collapsed with the Depression. He turns to selling housewares door-to-door, even to stealing coal on occasion. For a time, his pride prevents him for applying to the federal Works Progress Administration for employment. He changes his mind when he learns that the engineer in charge of the dam's rebuilding is to be replaced because of his alcoholism. Storm completes the work, despite some obstacles. Just as Ellison's *The Prisoner Ate a Hearty Breakfast* had echoed the work of John O'Hara, this novel echoes John Steinbeck's *Grapes of Wrath* (1939).

The hero of Peter DeVries' third novel, *Angels Can't Do Better* (1944), is a young college instructor who runs for alderman of Chicago's eighteenth ward in the 1930s — though he gets no support from his father, his fellow teachers or the voters. DeVries' method is to introduce zany characters and ridiculous situations and to make light comedy of matters others were taking far more seriously.[2]

World War II in Chicago Literature

LaMar Warwick's *Yesterday's Children* (1943) uses a thinly-disguised Evanston as its setting and the early years of the War as its time. Jim and Doris Weaver listen to the nightly radio news and worry about the consequences of the war in Europe on their ancestral British Isles. But they also worry about their son, Randy, a high school student — about his grades, his inability to win acceptance to membership in a prestigious high school club, his choice of summer work in an industrial plant rather than on their country club's tennis courts, his cross-country automobile jaunt with two other youths.

But when the Japanese attack Pearl Harbor, Randy decides not to finish his senior year, and he enlists, with his parents' consent, in the Army Air Corps.

Reviewers for the New York *Times* and the New York *Herald Book Review* agreed that *Yesterday's Children* was "a grand book."[3]

In Saul Bellow's *Dangling Man* (1944), a new, major Chicago writer appeared. Like Robert Herrick, Robert Morss Lovett, James Weber Linn, and many others before him, Bellow was also writing from the University of

Chicago campus. But times had changed in the 1940s — journalists were becoming reporters instead of writers, and in the next few years a great deal of serious writing would originate on college and university campuses.

"What was it, in the thirties, that drew an adolescent in Chicago to the writing of books?" Saul Bellow asked in 1974.

"How did a young American of the depression period decide that he was, of all things, a literary artist? I use the pretentious term literary artist simply to emphasize the contrast between such ambition and the external facts. A colossal industrial and business center, knocked flat by unemployment, its factories and even its schools closing, decided to hold a World's Fair on the shores of Lake Michigan, with towers, high rides, exhibits, Chinese rickshaws, a midget village in which there was a midget wedding every day and other lively attractions, including whores and con men and fan dancers. There was a bit of gaiety, there was quite a lot of amoebic dysentery. Prosperity did not come back. Several millions of dollars were invested in vain by business men and politicians. If they could be quixotic, there was no reason why college students shouldn't be impractical too. And what was the most impractical of choices in somber, heavy, growling, low-brow Chicago? Why, it was to be the representative of beauty, the interpreter of the human heart, the hero of ingenuity, playfullness, personal freedom, generosity, and love. I cannot even now say that this was a bad sort of crackpot to be."[4]

Dangling Man is told in diary form by a young Jewish boy (Bellow says he thinks of himself "as a midwesterner and not a Jew"[5]) who gives up his job in a Chicago travel bureau because he expects to be inducted into the army. But the army keeps him "dangling" for a year. Because the young man cannot get his job back, "there is nothing to do but wait, or dangle, and grow more and more dispirited."[6]

The *New Yorker* reviewer said that the novel was "one of the most honest pieces of testimony on the psychology of a whole generation who have grown up during the Depression and the war."[7] John W. Aldridge says the book appears to have been "strongly influenced by Sartre's *Nausea.*"[8] But critics agree it is not his best work.

Two Chicago women, Jane Mayer and Clara Spiegel, used the pseudonym of Clare Jaynes for *These Are the Times* (1944), a World War II novel. Doctors at a Lake Shore hospital near the Chicago River are preparing to form a medical unit for service overseas. But Dr. John Kenyon is married to a possessive wife who tries to keep him at home. Her attempts lead to the death of his young protégé.

Catharine Lawrence's *The Narrowing Wind* (1944) tells of a farm girl who takes a job in a Chicago war materials plant. Her ambitions and hard work anger others in the plant. The author, however, is not attempting a feminist novel, but simply a story of a Chicago industrial plant and an Illinois farm girl caught up in the war effort.

The novel was the winner of the third Dodd, Meade Intercollegiate Literary Fellowship.

Josephine Herbst was one of the proletariat novelists of the 1930s; her proletariat sympathies and method are reflected in her novel set in Chicago during the War, *Somewhere the Tempest Fell* (1944). But to call this a novel of wartime Chicago is misleading to one who has, perhaps, Harriette Arnow's *The Dollmaker* (1954) in mind as a novel of wartime Detroit and Willow Run.

Adam Snow, a writer of mystery novels, returns to Chicago from Italy where he has been living. He believes that he has unwittingly betrayed a friend, a member of the anti-fascist underground. In Chicago, his daughter has a romance with a member of a jazz group. Some family relationships are explored. That's essentially the story.

Critics were concerned about Herbst's narrative abilities. "There is no question that her novel would have been better for vigorous rewriting," said Diana Trilling:

> "If the dangling ends of narrative had been caught up, if there had been a sounder proportion between important events and trivialities, if the characters had been better projected, if — even — its mad punctuation had been corrected." Trilling was also concerned that Herbst failed to develop the potential of the jazz world with "both its decent and disturbing political overtones, the marijuana route it travels toward criminality, the personal and artistic idealism it both satisfies and frustrates."[9]

The Suburbs

Elizabeth Corbett's *Faye's Folly* (1941) is set in her Mount Royal area, but no connection is made with that town. The "Folly" is a huge farm home; the time is the late Civil War and after; the characters are members of the Faye family, particularly the daughter Sheba Faye, and one Pierce Bigelow, a southern sympathizer in the North, trying to build up support for his cause. The story features romantic complications but is chiefly of interest for its picture of people trying to cope during the Civil War.

Sheba's life as a married woman in "Syracuse, Illinois," and as a widow of thirty-eight in Syracuse and Mount Royal is continued in *Early Summer* (1942) and *Golden Grain* (1943).

Virginia Dale, author of *Honeyfogling Time* (1946) and *Nan Thursday* (1944) was a Chicagoan, but set the first novel in a suburb about fifty miles north. "Honeyfogling" is defined as "courting, coercing with sweet words." The novel deals with relationships among men and women, and the dominance of men, particularly in politics. Still, the major figure in the novel is a woman so ignorant that she deliberately exposes her child to a fatal illness.

For all that, the tale is a humorous, even at times hilarious one.

Nan Thursday features a popular female singing team on Chicago radio in the early 1940s. When her partner falls to death from the balcony of a Chicago hotel suite, Nan Thursday turns detective to find out what really happened. The story, while a mystery story, echoes many soap operas being produced in Chicago in the early 1940s.

Chicago History

Julia Cooley Altrocchi's lengthy (572 pages) *Wolves Against the Moon* (1940) and Louis Zara's even lengthier (750 pages) *This Land Is Ours* (1940) have already been discussed in chapter 2. Zara, a New Yorker who moved to Chicago in 1917, was also the author of *Ruth Middleton* (1946), a story of the first fourteen years of life of a girl whose father was an iconoclast laborer and whose mother was the daughter of a well-to-do Chicago family. Ruth grows up a poor girl on the fringe of prosperity in the Chicago of gas lights, cable cars and the Bryan campaign of 1896.

Elizabeth Howard's popular *Dorinda* (1944), a novel for "older girls," looks back at post-Fire Chicago and a girl from rural Indiana who comes to Chicago to live. Eventually, however, Dorinda decides that life back on an Indiana farm with the man she loves is better than life in the expanding metropolis.

In a much different type of novel and with a much different audience in mind, Howard Fast, who just a few years later was to be "blackballed" from Hollywood as one of the "Unfriendly Ten," looked back at the life of former Illinois Governor John Peter Altgeld — the second fictionalized version of Altgeld's life in two decades — *The American* (1946). Critics and readers were puzzled by Fast's use of fiction as a medium, by his omission of important aspects of Altgeld's early career, by his placement of Altgeld's origins in Iowa rather than Missouri, and by his tampering with other facts of Altgeld's history.

Clifford [Samuel] Raymond's *The Honorable John Hale; A Comedy of American Politics* (1946) relates "the political careers of a wealthy young man from Chicago's fashionable North Side." After becoming a lawyer in the early part of the century, Hale stands for the Illinois State Legislature. Later he becomes involved with Chicago strikers, is nearly nominated for the Presidency and participates in various family crises. The treatment is largely satirical.[10]

Irving Stone's *Adversary in the House* (1947) is a close-to-the-truth fictional biography of Eugene V. Debs, the radical American labor leader who served a prison term for his role in the 1894 Pullman Strike. The "adversary" is Debs' wife, Kate Metzel, here rather imaginatively treated since little is known about her.[11]

Fredrika Shumway Smith's *Rose and the Ogre* (1948) is the story of a sixteen-year-old Chicago girl in the 1890s. The "ogre" is her step-grandfather. The girl's story is set against the background of the Columbian Exposition, the Pullman Strike and an 1890s prohibition movement.

"The odd thing about Arthur Meeker is that he should ever have become an author at all," wrote Alson J. Smith, Jr., in his *The Left Bank of Chicago* (1953). "His father was a wealthy meatpacker, an official of Armour and Company who expected that when Arthur was old enough he would come into the packing business. But young Meeker perversely got a job as a newspaper reporter and with the money grubbed from that dismal occupation took a trip to Europe. It was there that he decided that he wanted to become a novelist, a decision that always seemed a little strange to Arthur Meeker, Sr."[12]

When one of his [non-Chicago books] was selected by the Book of the Month Club, young Arthur rushed to tell his father the news; the latter's only comment was a gloomy "Is that good?" Later, Arthur's father reconciled himself to the idea that his son was a writer and would never become a meat-packer, and in time even took a considerable amount of pride in being pointed out as "Arthur Meeker's father."[13]

The Meekers lived in a Prairie Avenue mansion in the heyday of that thoroughfare, and so Arthur Meeker, who was a meticulous researcher, knew what he was talking about when he wrote *Prairie Avenue* (1949). The novel is a realistic slice of the life on the near South Side Chicago residence street from 1880 to 1918. The early years was a period of growth where newly and very rich Chicagoans built an assortment of mansions that aped assorted European architectural practices. In the later years, as the families of these Chicagoans began moving to the North Side to escape the noise and dirt of the Illinois Central, and to join the others who followed Potter Palmer there, decay and destruction set in on the glamorous Avenue until it reached the state it is in today where a slight turnaround is taking place.

The novel focusses on four periods of the fictional Ned Ramsay's life: when he was twelve in 1885-1886; 1895-1896; 1904; and 1918, just after the end of World War I. We see people who started life in a very ordinary way, then became immensely wealthy because they were in the right place at the right time as lumbermen, provisioners, railroad builders, and merchants in the fast-growing Chicago. The women and children are thrust into lifestyles for which they are ill-prepared. They don't know how to cope with their newly-acquired affluence, and their lives are directed by the demands of others, particularly by those attempting to live by Eastern manners. The main emphasis of the novel, in other words, is on the Prairie Avenue family, not the men.

Ned Ramsay's career is apparently modeled after that of his creator. He becomes first a music critic for a Chicago newspaper, then an author. At the end of the book he is about to write a novel that is obviously *Prairie Avenue*.

A critic of the time looked back to Dreiser's *Sister Carrie* for a comparable novel and commented that Dreiser's work had more depth but that Meeker's book had more polish.[14]

In *The Sands* (1948), Francesca Falk Miller created a fictionalized history of what had been known as "Streeterville," the area north of the Chicago River, east of Rush Street, and south Oak Park Beach — now the area around the Water Tower Plaza. The novel runs from about 1856 to World War II when the last of the old fishermen's shanties were bulldozed by the Navy. Sulie West, a rather well-to-do Wabash Avenue girl moves into a fisherman's shack with Jack Hannon, a ne'er-do-well, in pre-Streeter days. As the years pass, the novel shifts its focus to Streeter and his scrapes with those trying to evict him, then to his niece, Nonie Holst and her young husband, Herman. In the background are the Fire, the Columbian Exposition, the deaths of Jack and Sulie and the coming of the new century. By the time "Cap" Streeter dies, Herman has become a successful merchant. At the end Nonie watches as the last shack disappears. *The Sands* seems very much like an attempt to emulate Ferber's *The Girls* but Miller is no Ferber.

The Entertainers

The story is told that on July 8, 1922, Louis "Satchmo" Armstrong in New Orleans got a telegram from King Oliver, a black orchestra leader in Chicago:

> Come Immediately Lincoln Gardens Chicago Job For You Thirty Dollars a Week[15]

Whatever, when Jazz came north up the Great Valley of the Mississippi, it came to Chicago where it found fertile ground on 22nd Street and 35th Street. It also found talented midwesterners, including Bix Beiderbecke of Davenport and Chicago's own Gene Krupa.

And just as Chicago literature had dealt previously with both popular and serious music, now Chicago writers found subjects in jazz.

Annamarie Ewing's *Little Gate* (1947), like Josephine Herbst's *Somewhere the Tempest Fell* of three years before and Standord Whitmore's later *Solo* (1955) shows the Chicago jazz scene. Joe Geddes, a white youth, the "Little Gate" of the novel, perhaps modeled on "Bix," is fascinated by the jazz he hears played by Negroes in the black district of Muscatine, Iowa, and on the campus at the University of Iowa, and he grows up wanting to be a jazz saxophone player. With an unpaid-for instrument, he flees to Chicago and its black jazz district where he finds a job as a musician. Later, because of trouble with a girl and her gangster friend, Joe goes on to New York City. The novel's description of the Chicago jazz scene, while somewhat melodramatic in its treatment of Joe's love affair, presents a more interesting study than Herbst's novel; at the same time its hero is far less of an existentialist then the Virgil Jones of *Solo*. Joe wants to live to play; Jones seems hell-bent on self-destruction.

The 1959 *Gene Krupa Story* is too trite a film; it could have done a much better job of presenting the setting in which Krupa became a great jazz drummer.

John O'Hara's *Pal Joey* (1940), written as a series of letters from "the self-serving jerk" whose name provides the title, is an almost plotless confessional in which Joey brags about his monetary and feminine conquests. Joey sings in a Chicago night-spot in the book; in the later Rodgers and Hart musical (1940), Joey becomes a Broadway heel. In the film, Joey, played by Frank Sinatra, lives on the West Coast. The short stories which were collected for the novel originally ran in *The New Yorker*.

Two 1949 books, both written by successful Chicago "soap opera" script writers, are about radio in Chicago in the years before television. Robert Hardy Andrews, whose novels we have seen earlier, left newspaper journalism and fiction writing to become one of radio's and television's most prolific writers of soap operas. In *Legend of a Lady; The Story of Rita Martin*, Hardy takes the reader "behind the scenes" in an "exposé of the commercial advertising business which makes the soap opera possible."[16] Rita Martin joins a Chicago-based advertising agency during the Depression hoping only for success. Ultimately she is forced to re-evaluate her situation in an effort to find personal salvation.

Mona Kent was one of the early authors of radio soap operas, including the long-running *Portia Faces Life*. In *Mirror, Mirror, on the Wall* (1949) she tells of an Indiana girl who bluffs her way into a Chicago advertising agency, then discovers the secret of writing soap operas — they must mirror the life of the average housewife listener. The novel tells of her success with the new genre, and her success and failure with marriage.

Industry and Labor Problems

As we have seen, since the days of the Haymarket Affair, Chicago novels had reflected the growing unrest of working people with working conditions. The novels did not have to exaggerate; although there were places where workers were happy with their employment, too often the situations mirrored were unpleasant, and workers did not receive a fair return for their labor. Octave Thanet's "Communists and Capitalists; A Sketch From Life" (1878) shows the interior of a worker's "hideous shanty" with rats poking their heads out of rat-holes. The laborer whose home it is is told that

"Capital is brain and labor muscle," and "muscle cannot do without brain."[17]

In the 1930s under the Roosevelt administration new laws were passed that revolutionized the status of labor. These laws, however, did not come in time to prevent some serious labor strife.

Meyer Levin's *Citizens* (1940) begins with one of the more serious labor incidents, the Republic Steel "Massacre" on Chicago's far South Side on Memorial Day, 1937. Levin, through his central character, traces the affair socially and psychologically back to the Haymarket Affair.

In his *In Search* (1950) Levin has told how he came to write *Citizens*. He was an eyewitness to the event, and when he came to write the book, he took an apartment in a steelworkers' residential area so he could talk with the steelworkers themselves, and, as well, capture the atmosphere of the environment.[18]

"Meyer Levin has done a remarkable thing," said a critic: "[S]inglehanded, and without forewarning in his previous work, he has struck the shackles of photographic realism from the strike novel ... Perhaps the most notable characteristic of this novel is that it is not a call to arms to one side or the other. There is no special pleading, no propaganda. It is a humble, earnest and successful attempt to understand those things that lead to violence, that set man against man and brother against brother ..."[19]

Writing in 1953, Alson J. Smith said there were two "Chicago expatriates ... who have provided modern literature with its sharpest and most penetrating documentation of the tough life of the city's streets —" Farrell and Albert Halper:

In *The Chute, The Foundry, Little People,* and *Sons of the Fathers,* Halper dissected lower-middle-class Chicago pitilessly. A so-called "proletariat novelist," Halper mellowed considerably after [he left Chicago] ...[20]

The Little People (1942) is set in a State Street hatter-furrier shop and in the homes and recreational places of its employees — the little people who work out of sight in a high-fashion boutique. There are no true central characters; the novel's focus is on the group, a method typical of proletariat novels such as this one. The genre developed in the 1930s, and disappeared in the days of World War II.

Critics who had liked earlier novels by Halper but had disliked the implicit anger in them, found this Halper's best novel to date with no anger in the narrator's voice.[21]

Edward J. Nichols set his *Danger, Keep Out* (1943) two decades earlier in an oil refinery in Whiting, Indiana, just south of Chicago. The refinery itself, hard pressed to keep up with the demands of a nation turning away from horse-drawn vehicles to piston-engined vehicles, is the "protagonist" of the novel; little attempt is made to get beneath the skins of the various individuals. Critics found the story interesting but faulted it for the failure to develop its characters as had Pietro di Donato's *Christ in Concrete* (1939), Halper's *The Foundry,* and William Rollins *The Shadow Before* (1934).[22]

Ward Moore's picaresque *Breathe The Air Again* (1942) ranges from Los Angeles to Chicago and back to Los Angeles again in the late 1920s. In Chicago, Simon Epstein, the picaresque hero, works for a while in a foundry and is jailed for his part in a strike which is part of an effort to organize women household workers in a North Side suburb. Max Eastman praised this "magnificent novel," setting its "erotic experiences" above those described by Hemingway, and calling its style better than Steinbeck's.

Alexander Plaisted Saxton's *Grand Crossing* (1943) was a popular success which ignored the War and looked back at social conditions in the 1930s. Its hero is Michael Reed, a cub reporter who in typical Depression fashion worked his way across country with a friend. Back at Harvard and among his socialite friends, he finds himself ill at ease in the thick atmosphere of culture, snobbery and anti-Semitism (a New York editor had asked Meyer Levin to change the central characer in *Citizens* to a non-Jewish type). In Chicago, at the University, he falls in with a group with socialist leanings and meets William Christmas, a southern black communist. The scene shifts to Halsted and Maxwell where Christmas lives among criminals and alcoholics. Michael goes to work as a railroad switchman at Chicago's South Side "Grand Crossing." At novel's end, he and his girl decide to take a honeymoon with their marriage to come some time later.

Critics thought this first novel showed great promise for Saxton's career as a writer.[24]

There are three strands in Saxton's second book, *The Great Midland* (1948). "The Great Midland" is a Chicago-based railroad; the novel centers on the car repair shops of the imaginary rail line, and the attempt to organize all the shop and yard workers into one union. A second strand concerns the attempts of Pledger McAdams to secure equitable treatment for blacks. The third looks at the marital relationships of Stephanie Koviak and Dave Spaas, and at the Koviak family. Stephanie is seen first as an undergraduate at the University of Chicago and then as a graduate who earns a Ph.D. She, Dave and Pledger are card-carrying Communists. The time of the novel is from the start of World War I to the end of World War II.

Critics praised Saxton for his choice of unpopular characters (for the late 1940s) but found fault with him for shunting the broader labor struggle off to one side and emphasizing Stephanie's "tearful soul-searching" as she tries to choose between "bourgeois security" offered by her University professor husband, and the "precarious existence of a Red agitator's wife offered by" Spaas.[25]

Chicago People

Edith [Elizabeth Kneiple] Roberts' *This Marriage* (1941), set against the gathering war clouds, is the story of what happens to the marriage of two people, intelligent, progressive and idealistic, who entered into a pre-marriage contract "promising personal freedom, free love, free action, and equal sharing of the responsibility of marriage."[26] Unfortunately, the wife finds herself trapped by family responsibilities while the husband is free to do as he pleases.

Roberts' second novel, *Little Hell — Big Heaven* (1942) tells what happens when the pampered son of a Chicago industrialist, while drunk, hits a woman with his car and maims her for life. Attempting to make amends, Philip Meade personally involves himself in helping ghetto young people, and, at the same time, falls in love with his victim. Meanwhile, his pampered sister falls in love with a settlement worker. In the background of this novel are Chicago's slums, resorts, affluent areas, police courts, night life, crooked politicians, influential business men, and playboys. But, says a critic, the author's skills are not equal to the task she has set for herself, and the result is more "of a caricature than a serious portrait."[27]

Clare Jaynes' [Clara Spiegel and Jane Mayer] 1942 novel, *Instruct My Sorrows,* is the story of Jessica Drummond, the widow of an affluent surburban husband. Her problem is not financial but social, primarily of having to cope with her husband's male social acquaintances who assume she must crave amorous relationships with men. ERA was a long time in the future.

Isabella Holt's *Aunt Jessie* (1942) is set in Chicago from 1912, early in the Chicago Renaissance, to 1942, when the Renaissance was ancient history for all but a few people, one of whom is the narrator of this story, Theodosia Kendall, daughter of a wealthy Erie Street couple — Walter Kendall, whose inherited wealth makes it possible for him to be a dilettante artist, and Ann, his wife, whose wealth makes it possible for her to flirt with Renaissance bohemians, and later, to divorce Walter, leave Theodosia and the latter's brothers, Alastair and Benjy, domicile herself with a Swiss poet, then, as a Russian Marxist sympathizer, disappear from the scene.

The children are taken over by Aunt Jessie, a "personnel administrator," victim of an unfortunate love affair, a determined Victorian moralist whose staff of life consists of "quotations," some inherited wealth, and her Presbyterian faith. Her influence on the children is the theme of the novel. Alastair becomes a poet and a radical, Benjy a Princeton graduate and a banker, and Theodosia a sculptor. Theodosia first tries love with a novelist, then marries the boy next door. The whole story is presented as a flashback, beginning with Aunt Jessie's death and funeral.

Louise Maunsell Field noted that this was one of the first novels to deal with the artistic and social effects of the years preceding the first World War. Other critics found the novel "a true and moving story of a time, a place, and a family," a family like that of *Life With Father* (1935, 1940) but with one significant difference — the Kendall children had to live with divorce.[28]

Martin Flavin's *Journey in the Dark* (1943), 1944 Harper and Pulitzer prize novel, begins and ends in an Iowa-side Mississippi River town, but amidships its setting is Chicago. Sam Braden is another of those émigrés to the Windy City, a lonely man going nowhere. As a boy he discovers the meaning of poverty and he resolves to amount to something. Over a period of sixty years he succeeds in the way that many Chicagoans understood — as a paper salesman, partner in a wallpaper factory, as sole owner, and as a business man astute enough to unload just before the crash. Yet all of this is for Sam Braden a hollow triumph; he remains lonely and uneasy for reasons he never understands but which his narrator succeeds in explaining to the novel's readers.

William Maxwell's *The Folded Leaf* (1945) was an immensely successful book; it went through a number of English and foreign language editions, and is still held by a great many American libraries. This "sustained piece of extraordinary good writing" tells of the passage of two boys into manhood, and of life in a small Indiana college town in the mid-1920s. The boys are not homosexuals but "normal boys drawn together by the mutual magnetism of opposites."[29]

Arthur Meeker's *The Far Away Music* (1945) is also based, Meeker says in a foreword, on his own family history. Chicago and a farm near Naperville, used as a station on the Underground Railroad, are the settings for this story of life from 1844 to 1856. Jonathan Trigg marches to a different drummer; during the twelve years of the narrative, he is in either California or Naperville most of the time. There's no problem for his wife and three daughters; they have the Bascomb money and the Bascomb way of life to keep them going. Trigg does try to persuade his eldest daughter, Sissy, to forsake her engagement to Bascomb-like Aaron, and to marry a young man she meets during one summer at the farm. But Sissy is too much a Bascomb, too conventional. However, Nancy, the middle sister, fails to show up for her own nuptials. Possessing, it seems, a character like her father's, she has eloped with another young man.

On that same night the restless Jonathan left on the night boat for Buffalo and an uncertain future as a writer.

The novel may have been intended as a fable of Meeker's own career, for he too seems to have been a restless type. Alson J. Smith wrote that Meeker should be included as a Chicago writer "only by a large measure of courtesy, for while he is a Chicagoan born and bred, he spends most of his time in

Switzerland."[30]

Margaret Culkin Banning was a native of Duluth, and most of her many novels of marriage, divorce, and Catholic family relationships are set in a city like Duluth. But she set *The Clever Sister* (1946), a story about a single career woman in a Chicago insurance office. The office needs a new manager — will Nell Evans, the "clever sister," get the job? Nell is also helping to elect an Illinois governor. Nell's "unclever sister," Hester Savery, is married to an indifferent man who takes his frustrations out in alcohol. So Hester competes with Nell for Bernard Munro, a rising young lawyer.

Mrs. Banning's "basic concerns [in her other books have] been with marriage, money and moral standards," said Lisle Bell. "Now and then her thesis has overbalanced the human equation. No such reservations apply to [this novel] . . . it is her best performance.[31]

Robert Harkness Parrish's *My Uncle and Miss Elizabeth* (1948) is a tale of several people in Chicago, also told, like *Journey in the Dark,* within an Iowa frame. Parrish's narrator recalls his Mason City, Iowa boyhood with his grandmother, and his Chicago life with a bachelor-physical culturist uncle (who may be based on Bernard McFadden). Other characters are a boarder in the uncle's home whose interests are "advertising, the technique of the short story, and the invention of a non-crumbling cracker;" the uncle's fraternity brothers from his college days; and some seedy University of Chicago professors. Miss Elizabeth is the boarder's occasional mistress, lost, drunken, yet indestructible. Like Proust, the narrator searches through his contacts with these people, seeking for some significance in his own life.

In the mid-1930s, Robert Parrish's Mason City, Iowa high school classmates single out Parrish and Martin Yoseloff as the two most likely to succeed as authors. This is Parrish's only novel, but Yoseloff has written several.

Francis Sill Wickware's *Tuesday to Bed* (1948) is a sentimental romance. An architect about to leave for Chicago to receive an award for his design for a model city learns that his wife is about to be identified as a correspondent in a divorce case. At the meeting of architects and designers, he attacks Chicago for its ugliness and its citizens for their decadence. But "an attractive and sympathetic young war widow who interviews him for *Life* helps him straighten out his life."[32]

Edith Roberts' third novel, *The Divorce of Marcia Moore* (1948) is set in Chicago, but this study of the traumatic effects of an unwanted divorce is only a Chicago novel for that reason. The novel focusses on the woman's side of divorce.

Sherman Baker's *Bradford Masters* (1949) is a character study of a young Wisconsin man who travels frequently to Chicago for entertainment.

Reginald Lemming, Sr., the protagonist of Jane [Ball] Eklund's *The Only*

Gift (1949) got control of his wife's family's iron and steel business by marrying her and fathering the first grandson of the founder. The retrospective novel is set in a post-World War II year from Lemming's sixtieth to sixty-first birthdays. During the course of that year we see how Lemming has always dominated and tyrannized his family, setting up conventions which become deep ruts, and demanding that his ideas and values be followed. His wife is a perfect "lemming," and Reginald, Jr. is thoroughly conditioned. But Reginald, Jr.'s wife leaves her husband, and the other children reject their father. Tragedy follows. Lemming is a good example of those fictional Chicago business men who are slaves to work and who discount all values except their own.

Religious and Ethnic Themes

Albert Halper wrote in the preface to his 1940 *Sons of the Fathers* that the book is a novel, not a tract. Nevertheless the book's thesis must have been intended to have some bearing on the growing international tensions during the time Halper was writing the novel.

Halper's "father" is Saul Bergman, the sons Milton and Benjamin. There is also a daughter, Ruth, and other children. With his friend, Aaron, Saul fled Europe to avoid conscription, going to South America first, then coming to the United States, where he at first earned a precarious living peddling wares from door to door. By 1914, married to Etta, living above a Kedzie Avenue store, he has prospered. Milton, who had wanted to become a doctor, has become instead a successful traveling salesman for men's clothing. Ben is a successful debater and class historian.

Saul is against American participation in World War I. The tailor next door who makes uniforms for military officers is for involvement. When war comes, the Bergman's prosper on an even larger scale. Milton, to avoid the draft, volunteers for the Ordnance Corps. Ben finds a draft-free federal job. On the day before the war ends, Milton is killed in France.

The novel, even if it had not included Washington's Farewell Address counseling against foreign entanglements, made Halper's stand clear. He was arguing that America was being dragged into World War II through foreign propaganda. To take that stand was for Halper a courageous action, considering what was happening to the Jews in Germany, and considering the methods Halper's Jewish counterparts in the American film industry were utilizing to build up sympathy for the Jewish position.

Quentin Morrow Phillip's *We Who Died Last Night* (1941) is a fictional case history of a Catholic businessman who lost his affluent status and his wife because of the inroads of the Depression. His staunch Catholic faith supports him as he begins his upward climb from the gutter. But his faith also threatens to interfere with a second chance at marital happiness because of Catholic views about divorce. The novel, says a critic, "presents an accurate picture of the Catholic Church in the 1930s."[33]

Isaac Rosenfeld's *Passage From Home* (1946) details a fourteen-year-old Chicago Jewish boy's search for identity following a family quarrel in his Orthodox home. For a while he lives with his non-Orthodox aunt and her lover in a North Side flat. But the problems he faces there lead him to return home.

Edward J. Nichols' *Hunky Johnny* (1946), a story of South Side Slovaks and University of Chicago people, is set in the 1930s. "Hunky Johnny" is Johnny Opalko; we see one week of his life. The Opalkos are from Gary; Johnny's father owns a saloon in Gary over which the Opalkos live. Johnny's brother is a minor-league Chicago gangster.

Jean, Johnny's girl, whom the Opalkos think of as "white," lives on Woodlawn Avenue, south of the University of Chicago. Johnny worries about the difference between himself and Jean. During the week of the story, we see Johnny's and Jean's attempts to get along. He plays semi-pro baseball, dates another girl of his own heritage, and interviews for a teaching assistantship at the University of Chicago.

A critic wondered whether this was "the drama of the emotionally uncertain first-generation American or merely the old sad story of being young in a mixed-up world." But he acknowledged that Nichols had written "a live, moving book about being young in Chicago in a hot, gone, Chicago summertime."[34]

But Jack Conroy, a lifelong proletariat writer and critic was negative about the book:

> Despite Nichols' laudable flair for recreating the "feel" of a bygone period, it is hard to work oneself into a lather of concern over "Hunky Johnny's" success and failure when there are titanic forces and issues to engage the attention of most of us.[35]

Cecily Schiller's *Maybe Next Year* (1947) is also a novel about Chicago Jews at the time of World War I. Rose Weber has met a nice Jewish boy, Carl, and plans to marry him. They have one moment together as Carl's troop train passes through Chicago, and then Carl dies in France.

The novel traces Rose's moral decline from the later night when she is first casually picked up and then allows the man to seduce her. Rose gives her favors away at first, then learns they can be traded for presents. Three affairs are more serious. One is ended by an accident; the second is with Tony Terrasso, a bootlegger; the third with an affluent and influential business man. Rose's life becomes an example of the hedonistic and existential life, always conditioned by the behavior of others. At novel's end she is contemplating suicide.

Schiller, a Cook County employee at the time she wrote this novel, got a favorable review only from her home town newspaper. Other reviewers were unimpressed.[36]

Sam Ross's *Someday, Boy* (1948) is the story of Benny Garden, a restless youth from the slums and settlement-house playing fields of Chicago who attempts to jet-propel himself to success — but he is no match for the harsh verities of Chicago in the pre-Depression years of business expansion.

Three Novels About Chicago Blacks

The year 1940 saw the first important novel written by one of the new wave of black authors then coming into their own in America. Richard Wright had survived in the Depression years by writing in the Illinois Federal Writers Project for a man who had discovered many promising midwest writers, John Towner Frederick. Now at the start of the decade, newspaper reviewers hailed "the new American Tragedy," *Native Son* (1940). Peter Munro Jack pointed out that both Dreiser's *An American Tragedy* (1925) and *Native Son* dealt "seriously and powerfully with the problem of social maladjustment and individual behavior, and subsequently with crime and punishment," and the protagonists of both novels are executed for being "social misfits," not criminals. But Bigger Thomas's "tragedy" was that he was born "into a black and immutable minority race, literally, in his own words, 'whipped before you were born.' "[37]

Native Son was an immediate popular success, a Book-of-the-Month-Club selection; its sales reached a quarter of a million within a month. But with the coming of World War II, it passed from the public consciousness, and, because it did not accord with the literary theories of the academic critics who in recent years have dominated the literary scene, it quickly passed from the view of serious readers as well. It took the black explosion of the 1960s and the introduction of "Afro-American studies" into campus curricula to bring the book back into public view.

Native Son (The Biography of a Young American) was produced in 1941 as a play in ten scenes, written by Wright and Paul Green, Black American playwright. The play is made up of cuttings from the novel. Bigger Thomas is seen at home and on the street before being offered a chauffeur's and gardener's job by the Dalton's, well-to-do residents of Chicago's Drexel Avenue, just ten blocks from Bigger's home in the black ghetto. On his first day on the job Bigger takes Mary Dalton to a radical meeting and then on a drinking spree — at her orders. Home, he tries to help her to her room because she is too drunk to make it on her own. When her blind mother comes in to check on Mary, Bigger covers her head with a pillow to keep her quiet. Then, discovering she has suffocated, he panics and stuffs her body into the furnace. Later, with a girl friend, he plans to make Mary's disappearance seem like a kidnapping in order to get $10,000 from the family. But a newspaper man discovers what Bigger is up to, and Bigger flees to a tenement. There, his girl friend is shot by police and Bigger is blamed for her death. Bigger is sentenced to death; in the play's final scene he is seen in the death chamber.

By contrast, Lewis A. H. Caldwell's *The Policy King*, published as a book in 1946 by a Chicago magazine publisher, garnered very little critical attention, if any. It tells of a South Side Negro minister's son who is sentenced to six months in an Illinois reformatory, then told by his parents he is not welcome at their home. He joins a gambling ring and becomes Chicago's "policy king." His younger brother and sister are unhappy about his occupation, but they use his money to attend college and try to become respectable people.

Alden Bland's *Behold a Cry* (1947) looks at the arrival of black migrants to Chicago from the early days of World War I (which brought them to Chicago) until after the 1919 race riots. The setting is the South Side, around State and Thirty-fifth Streets. Most of the men find jobs in the packing-houses. The race riots result as the blacks try to move eastward across Wentworth Avenue and to swim at Lake Michigan beaches east of the old Prairie Avenue residential area. Later the blacks split amongst themselves on the question of organized labor.

Bland's novel preceded Saxton's *The Great Midland* in its treatment of the urban black worker in the North and the accompanying personal and social tensions. Critics liked it, although some complained that the author focussed too much attention on sexual relationships and not enough on the larger issues.[39]

Crime in Chicago Literature of the 1940s

Two types of criminal stories persisted in the 1940s: the murder mystery (of which there were about four dozen examples) usually featuring crime solution by "private eyes," some of whom appeared in title after title, and novels more closely related to the actual Chicago street scene. Predictably, with memories of the organized gangs of the 1920s and the 1930s fading into Chicago's lurid past, the realistic novel found new subjects — and two important authors.

Among the mystery novels worth noting were two by a woman with roots back to the Chicago Renaissance and *Poetry* magazine. Marion Strobel's novels had heretofore dealt mainly with women in Chicago society; in *Ice Before Killing* (1943) she continued to use the Chicago social world, this time the affluent and decadent people of the near North Side. The novel is set around an ice-skating rink and features two world champion skaters. Aside from the reader's curiosity about "who done it," the novel's interest lies in its portrayal of a society with too much money for its needs, too much leisure time, and a rather generous icing of snobbery, hate, jealousy and lack of morals.

Strobel followed it with another, *Kiss and Kill,* in 1946.

Mystery novels with a Chicago background that might be of interest are: Franklin James' (pseudonym of Robert Godley) *Killer in the Kitchen* (1947), the Chicago underworld; Sidney Marshall's *Some Like It Hot* (1941), Chicago radio personality; Frank Gruber's *The Leather Duke* (1949), the Italian neighborhood; James William McQueen's (pseudonym for James D. Edwards, M.D.) *But the Patient Died* (1948) hospital setting. Four novels are set in Chicago department stores: Phyllis A[yame] Whitney's *Red Is For Murder* (1943, also published as *The Red Carnelian,* 1943); and three by Margaret Lucile Paine Rea: *Compare These Dead!* (1941); *A Curtain for Crime* (1941); *Death For An Angel* (1943).

Four mystery novels involve reporters or the Chicago publishing business: John K. Vedder's *The Last Doorbell* (1941); Alan Pruitt's (pseudonym for Alvin Emanuel Rose) *The Restless Corpse,* (1947); William P[eter] McGivern's *But Death Runs Faster* (1948); and Frederic Brown's *The Screaming Mimi* (1949). Other Chicago-based mystery novels are listed in the Appendix.

Chicago's most precocious mystery story writer was Georgianna Ann Randolph Walker Craig Lipton who took her pen name of Craig Rice from the second of five husbands. (She also used the names of Michael Venney and Daphne Sanders.) Although her obituaries state she was born in Chicago on June 5, 1908, one authority says she was born in a small Wisconsin town.[40] She had no formal education but at nine she was writing verse, at eighteen news stories, and, at nineteen, radio scripts.

Her real forte, however, turned out to be mystery novels — her fourteen titles in this genre sold some three and a quarter million copies in hardback and paperback.

Nine of these were set in Chicago: *Knocked For a Loop* (1957, published posthumously); *The Lucky Stiff* (1945); *My Kingdom For a Hearse* (1957); *The Big Midget Murders* (1942); *The Corpse Steps Out* (1940); *8 Faces at 3* (1939); *The Fourth Postman* (1948); *The Right Murder* (1941); *The Wrong Murder* (1940).

The central characters are Jake Justus, a reformed gambler, his wife, Helene, and attorney John J. Malone, like his creator, a confirmed hard drinker.

"Rice's Chicago," says Peggy Moran, "was a place Chicagoans knew and loved. Her most memorable books are set in Chicago:

Joe the Angel's City Hall Bar was small and far from ornate, but it was handy. One longish, narrow room, the bar running from end to end, the extra space occupied by the 26-Game table, a few small tables and chairs, and a telephone booth — that was all. But it was located in the very heart of Chicago's Loop, and you couldn't toss a stone in any direction from its doorway without hitting a politician who deserved it. If you wanted to bet on a horse, cash a check, get an interview with the mayor, meet the buxom red-haired girl in the Rialto chorus, or just buy a drink, Joe the Angel could fix you up.

Even when her characters go to places like New York City or Bermuda, they are anxious to get back to Chicago."[41]

At least four of her books were filmed. Of these, three got negative reviews. "The Underworld Story," said Bosley Crother, "offered an alarmingly low opinion of newspaper publishers and newspaper men."[42] But the fourth, *Mrs. O'Malley and Mr. Malone* (1951) was reviewed favorably. At their best, the *New York Times* reviewer said, "Rice's detective tomes are stirred with an icepick," and he cautioned the author to keep the icepick in her work.[43]

Three years after her death, Laurence Mark Jenifer, a close friend, authored *The Pickled Poodles,* featuring Malone and the Justuses. This book is also set in Chicago.

Moving along from the mystery novel, we find Lieutenant Tom McGrath's quasi-factual *Copper* (1941), a story of a man who became a Chicago policeman in the 1920s — a period "when crime runs rampant, through the city, police officers are expected to take bribes, and an honest judge seems nonexistent." When a new mayor is elected in Chicago (Anton Cermak replaced William Hale Thompson in 1931), Mike Casey is put in charge of a cleanup squad called [The Mayor's] Cossacks, and ordered to clean up Chicago. A critic commented that "one could hope that Mike Casey is not a representative of Chicago's Boys in Blue."[44]

Sam Ross's second novel, *He Ran All the Way* (1947) is the story of Nick Robey who took part in a holdup in which a policeman was killed, then took refuge on a Lake Michigan beach. Here he met a girl, Peggy Dobbs, who took him to her home because she wanted to help him — she thought he was an emotionally disturbed veteran. Nick, seeing her as a means of avoiding the police, went along. Nick was an evil young man who could not understand goodness; the Dobbs' were good people who could not comprehend evil. Soon, Nick was using his gun to hold the family hostage, confronting each family member in turn. Eventually, Peggy resolved the Dobbs' situation by killing Nick.

Ross wrote the film adaptation for *He Ran All the Way* (1951). John Garfield played Nick.

Call Northside 777 was a 1948 film, photographed in Chicago and at Stateville Prison outside of Joliet. It featured James Stewart as a Chicago newspaperman who answered a classified advertisement placed there by a scrubwoman who was convinced that her convicted son was innocent of the crime with which he had been charged. The film was based on an article by Chicago newspaperman Jack McPhaul.

"In itself," said Dave Kehr,

> *Call Northside 777* is a solid, not particularly memorable newspaper yarn about a reporter who works to free an innocent man convicted for the killing of a policeman eleven years before. But from the perspective of Chicago, the film is fascinating: It seems to be an almost conscious attempt to rehabilitate the city's image, replacing all of the elements — moral and social — whose absence helped define the Chicago of the gangster films. "Chicago is a city of brick, bronze, concrete and guts, with a short history of violence beating in its pulse." ... The film places ... a strong emphasis on the social context of the crime, portraying the Back of the Yards as a neighborhood of honest, hard-working immigrants, the antithesis of the gangster archetype. The reporter seems designed as a deliberate revoke to the Hecht idea of newspaperman.[45]

Another big difference was that *Call Northside 777* was filmed in actual Chicago locations: the Wrigley Building, the Loop, the Back of the Yards District. Older films, supposedly set in Chicago might feature a few stock shots at film's opening; the balance would be shot in Hollywood studio's, using projected backgrounds where necessary. At Warner Brothers, a back lot set, called "New York Street," was used interchangeably for any big city, including Chicago.[46] Location shooting has become common in recent years.

Willard Motley's highly-acclaimed *Knock on Any Door* (1947) introduced a new Chicago literary talent. The novel was set in the "wino"district of West Madison Street:

> West Madison Street hides many things. Night and West Madison hide them all. Jackroller ... crooked cop ... dope fiend ... thief ... West Madison puts them all to bed and blankets them over with dope and secrecy. [47]

Motley tells the story of Nick Romano who began life as an altar boy in Denver, then moved to Chicago where he eventually died in the electric chair. If the novel needed documentation, it would have been found in the pages of Louis Wirth's *The Ghetto* (1928), Harvey W. Zorbaugh's *The Gold Coast and the Slum* (1920), or Clifford Shaw's *The Jackroller* (1930).

> Chicago has great literary tradition [said Horace R. Clayton]. From this midwest metropolis come men who have written directly and realistically — Sandburg, Anderson, Masters, Dreiser, Farrell, Meyer Levin, Nelson Algren, Jack Conroy and Richard Wright. Now in this same school (though this term is used with the knowledge that it has been much abused), Willard Motley has written of Chicago's great teeming West Side — of an Italian youth who lives a crushed, frightened brutalized life. One cannot refrain from comparing Mot-ley's work with others of the Chicago school — Farrell's blundering but

powerful description of the half-life of the Irish immigrants of two decades ago; Levin's depiction of the Jews' stumbling steps toward integration into the main stream of the culture of the city; Algren's sensitive and delicate analysis of the Poles, or ... the city jungles of the Near North Side.[48]

Knock on Any Door was the consequence of Motley's 1939 move to the Chicago slums. He was encouraged to write by Alexander Saxton who was then completing *Grand Crossing*. The two men founded and published *Hull-House Magazine* (1939-1940). From 1940 to 1942 Motley was employed by the Chicago WPA Writers Project. He began *Knock on Any Door* in 1940; in 1943 he sent his first draft, about 600,000 words to Harper's who rejected it. Cut to 237,000 words and extensively revised, it was acepted by Macmillan. But Macmillan had second thoughts (among other things, it was too "sexually explicit") and sent it back. Appleton-Century finally published it. It remained on the best-seller list for ten months.

Motley used some of the omitted material from *Knock* in his later *Let No Man Write My Epitaph*.

Nelson Algren's novel of Polish life, *Never Come Morning,* was published in 1942, his second novel following upon *Somebody in Boots*. The first novel had dealt only in part with Chicago — in the Depression years.

The hero of this second book, Bruno Bicek, had first been seen in a short story, "A Bottle of Milk for Mother," a story collected in the 1941 O. Henry anthology. Bruno was a Near North Side boy with dreams, and some needed skills, of becoming a professional boxing champion. But he drifted into minor crime, then into betrayal of his girl, Steffi, and then to murder. Steffi, as the result of a gang rape by Bruno's gang, became a prostitute. Bruno won a prize fight and seemed on his way toward his dream, but he was arrested for murder and sentenced to die in the electric chair.

Critics liked the novel and compared Algren to Farrell and Wright. Malcolm Cowley spoke of a new "Chicago school" of fiction, writers who said "chapter after chapter that Chicago slums and factories are producing stunted lives." But he concluded that Algren "is not by instinct a novelist. He is a poet of the Chicago slums, and he might well be Sandburg's successor."[49]

Algren's next book, *The Neon Wilderness* (1947) was a collection of short stories about the "people of the abyss."[50] Some of these twenty-four stories, all but eight of which were set in Chicago, had been published in the 1930s in magazines such as *The Anvil* and *Story*. Several of the stories reflected Algren's experiences in Europe in World War II.

Algren's people, said John Woodburn,

are the ones who came to the end of the road and did not stop, and are now too damaged to return. Outlawed and lost, their lives, if they may be said to be alive, have become feral and instinctual, and their acts seem more the convulsive reflexes of dangling men than gestures of volition.[51]

The Man With the Golden Arm (1949), Algren's novel of life in the saloons of West Division Street, is his best book. The story of Frankie Machine, the "dealer" with the "golden arm," of his crippled wife, Sophie, of his girl friend, Molly-O, of Blind Piggy, of Nifty Louis Fomorowski, and of the other denizens of Chicago's West Division Street is a powerful novel, told sometimes in a fine poetic style, sometimes with almost grisly humor.

Motley's *Knock on Any Door* was filmed in 1949 with John Derek as Nick Romano and Humphrey Bogart as his attorney. *The Man With the Golden Arm* was filmed in 1955 with Frank Sinatra as Frankie Machine and Kim Novak as Molly-O. Algren was not happy with the film. He protested that his story, which had "sustained the anti-legalistic tradition toward society which had distinguished Chicago writers since the early years of this century" became "confused, in the public mind, with a cheap biography of Frank Sinatra."[52]

In the 1930s, film companies were prohibited from referring to John Dillinger, the midwestern hoodlum who was shot down in the lobby of Chicago's near North Side Biograph theater in the summer of 1934. So it wasn't until 1945 that the first film on the life of the man who in the 1930s took over the headlines from "Scarface" Al appeared. It was followed in 1965 by *Young Dillinger.* Neither film was well made.

Roger Touhy, Gangster (1944) is not as much of a biography of a 1920s Chicago gangster as the title implies.

As the gangster era faded into the past, films about gangsters tended to become whimsical comedies. *Tall, Dark, and Handsome,* (1941) a film about a Chicago gangster who adopted a street waif, falls in this category.

Two Chicago Poets

When John Frederick Nims' *The Iron Pastoral* appeared in 1947, critics compared Nims with an earlier Chicago poet:

> Since Carl Sandburg's *Chicago Poems* appeared in 1916, there has been no volume of city poetry that compared favorably with Nims' "The Iron Pastoral." ... he is a more penetrating and disciplined Sandburg, a poet who sees the complexity of modern urban-industrial civilization more clearly than the earlier Chicago poet ever did and who expresses his vision in a more orderly, eloquent manner.[53]

For all this praise of Nims, a more important Chicago poet was at work writing about Chicago. But Gwendolyn Brooks' locale was *A Street in Bronzeville* (1945) and her subjects Chicago blacks. This book, as one critic said, was "both a work of art and a poignant social document."[54] Her idiom was a local one (one reviewer entirely missed the meaning of the word "gay") but her themes were universal.

Her next volume, *Annie Allen* (1949) won the 1950 Pulitzer Prize for Poetry. In this volume, Brooks portrayed the experiences of one Chicago black woman — "poverty, loneliness, brief fantasies of escape, loss, the 'over and all' finality of death."[55]

Chicago Little Magazines of the 1940s

Although nothing like the ongoing *Poetry* magazine was established in Chicago in this decade, a few hands managed to continue the tradition of literary magazines in Chicago. One thing was certain; the twentieth century would not produce the number of titles that Fleming had recorded in his 1906 study of nineteenth century Chicago magazines.

Creative Writing, later *New Horizons,* was published from November 1938 to April, 1941, under the editorship of Robert and Margaret Williams, printing both short fiction and poetry. The name change reflected a growing opposition to World War II.

Trend, a University of Chicago magazine, edited by John W. Barnes, began in 1942, attempting to "publish the writers who are doing new things in verse and prose."

The *Kapustkans,* named modestly for its editors, began in May, 1940.

Decade of Short Stories (1939 +) was not anticipating the future; it was looking backward at the 1930s, and those who had experienced "ten years of depression, turmoil, years of struggle, ... a return to normalcy." Among those it published was Louis Zara.

Another University of Chicago publication (reflecting the growing intrusion of the academies upon the literary scene, and the growing tendency of writers to find snug harbors on campuses) was the *Chicago Review* (1946 +). Its goal was to encourage creative writing among student-writers all over the country. Among its early contributors were James T. Farrell and John F. Nims.

Although the first four titles ran only for short periods, *Chicago Review* was continuing on into the 1980s.

Some Sequels

The popular success of some Chicago-based books and films of the 1930s led their creators to write sequels featuring the same characters or similar incidents and settings.

Lloyd C. Douglas' *Invitation to Live* (1940) featured the same Dean Harcourt of *Green Light,* the same Pygmalion and Galatea theme, and the same optimistic philosophy. The novel is set in Hollywood, on a Nebraska wheat farm, and in Chicago. Unlike other Douglas books, it was not filmed.

Margaret Hill Allee's *The House* (1944) returned to Merritt Lane of *The Great Tradition* and the University of Chicago campus. Again the theme of racial prejudice on the campus is examined. "The House" is an experiment in cooperative living involving several men and women during the early years of World War II.

Edna Ferber's *One Basket* (1947), an anthology, recapitulating the author's career as a writer of short fiction, offered in one volume examples of her best work. It included "The Gay Old Dog," which both Albert Halper and Ferber regarded as her best story, and which was the first of her stories to be filmed (1919); "Classified," the second of her stories to be filmed (1925); "Old Man Minick," "Gigolo," and "Mother Knows Best," all of which had been filmed (1932, 1926 and 1928, respectively). Also included was "Farmer in the Dell," the story which had been the prototype or seed of *So Big.*

Ferber died in 1968.

A 1949 film, *Chicago Deadline,* featuring Alan Ladd as a Chicago reporter and Donna Reed as a very mild love interest, might have been better had it not used so many clichés from earlier films about Chicago and reporters. The film was remade for television under the title *Fame Is the Name of the Game* (1966) with Tony Franciosa and Jill St. John, and if that weren't sequel enough, the television film spawned a television series.

A Congeries

Peter DeVries' *But Who Wakes the Bugler* (1940) is "more nonsense than novel," said a critic. George Thwing runs a Chicago boardinghouse. A kind-hearted man, he is pursued by a woman he doesn't want to marry and imposed upon by friends and acquaintances. Those around him constitute the "zaniest group of crackpots ever to occupy the pages of a novel."[57]

His *The Handsome Heart* also features a lunatic, but this one is an escapee from a mental hospital. In Chicago, Brian Carston encounters his brother. From there on the novel illuminates the narrow gap between sanity and insanity by contrasting Brian, ingenious, uninhibited but legally insane, with his successful older brother, malicious and grasping. At times the novel's voice is that of tongue-in-check satire, at times, serious psychological discourse, with occasional flights of fancy, the latter DeVries' hallmark.[58]

Clyde Brion Davis's *Sullivan* (1940) tells of a man hitchhiking west through Arizona to get as far away from Chicago as he can, but continuing to daydream of his career as a struggling art student in the "Windy City." As a consequence, much of the novel's action is set in Chicago.[59]

Phyllis A[yame]. Whitney, whom we have seen earlier as the author of mystery novels, also wrote *The Silver Inkwell,* (1945), a novel about a Chicago girl who aspires to be an author.

Barbara Hunt's *A Little Night Music* (1947) has little action but lots of philosophy. Two Chicagoans, one facing imminent death, the other just returned from service in World War II, discuss the meaning of world and being.

Summing Up

"When Fred B. Millett compiled his exhaustive critical survey of *Contemporary American Authors* in 1940, he did not list a single novelist, short-story writer, critic or historian who was then resident in Chicago," said Alson J. Smith in 1953. "Of course, there *were* some," said Smith, "but Mr. Millett just didn't think they were important enough."[60]

Then Smith added, "Today any such survey which omitted the names of Nelson Algren, Willard Motley, Mary Jane Ward, Arthur Meeker, Paul Angle [historian], Herman Kogan and Lloyd Wendt [historians], Meyer Levin, Louis Zara and Karl Shapiro (Editor of *Poetry*) — to mention only a few — would be ridiculous. It may be debatable that these people constitute a 'school' or that *their* [italics mine] period is a 'Golden Age;' what is not debatable is the fact that they are significant writers working in Chicago, and that there are more of them than at any time since 1924.

"There is a literary ferment in Chicago today. The place is yeasty with good writing . . ."[61]

Significantly in that summary, Smith omitted the name of the brightest star of the lot, Saul Bellow.

And there were other stars coming on in the not-so-fashionable Fifties, as we shall see.

XII.
The "Grease" Decade

Through the criss-crossing branches, Stephanie looked at the lighted windows of the other houses. If I were making a New Year's wish, she thought, I would wish that all Chicago were bright warm windows like those, that trees grew in all the back yards of Chicago . . . I would wish for a city with wide streets and trees, and houses for people to live in; where no one would ever again wait at daybreak in the lines before the relief stations. God, that wouldn't be wishing for much, would it? For a city that people could live in, for houses with windows, for trees in the back yard?

The simpleness of the wish she had thought of, the sudden vision of what the city might be, held her for a moment, transfixed . . . But in the instant . . . the wish and the vision faded. She had seen too often the streets in the bleak lamplight, and the other houses, drab and bleak and ramshackled, stepping away one after another into the shadows. The railroad embankments, the glow of neon signs at distant corners; too often, Stephanie whispered, too often. And the sound of last year's sunflower stalks which thrust up stiffly through the rubble of vacant lots, she had heard the sound of them, rattling in the wind.

Beyond this small oasis of pleasant houses and streets . . . began those other streets, the streets of wooden houses backed against the railroad embankments . . .[1]

The "Grease" and "Rock" Generations

In 1971, on Lincoln Avenue in Chicago, an unusual event took place —

the production of a musical comedy set in the mythical Rydell High School of Chicago in the early rock years of the 1950s. *Grease* with its flamboyant high school guys in leather jackets, greasy ducktails and "hot rods," and its girls in saddle shoes, beehive hairdos and boys' windbreakers, its "caustic nostalgia," and its primitive rock soon moved on to Broadway, then came back to Chicago's Blackstone Theater in the fall of 1973.*

But by and large Chicago authors continued to follow the traditional patterns set decades before. Only one novel, *Rock,* which we shall look at later, utilized the "grease" generation, the cynical youth of the 1950s turning its back on music, manners, morals of the past and initiating lifestyles that were to shake America to its cultural roots in the 1960s and 1970s.

Meanwhile, Chicago authors continued to write historical novels, novels about ethnic groups and immigrants, novels about personal and family relationships, novels about crime, and mystery novels — though there were far fewer of this last category than in the peak years of the 1940s. The Chicago business man, as he had for decades, continued to fascinate Chicago writers; the Depression and World War II were continuing themes. There was a small increase in the number of books about Blacks, and there were also novels with a stronger psychological interest.

James T. Farrell continued to use Chicago as a setting, even though he was domiciled in New York City and other exotic places. The major figure in this decade was Saul Bellow.

Historical Novels

Two novels about Robert Cavelier, Sieur de la Salle, the primary early explorer of the Chicago and Illinois territory, revived, in part at least, the romantic tradition of Mary Hartwell Catherwood: John Tebbel's *Touched With Fire* (1952) and Iola Fuller's *The Gilded Torch* (1957). Tebbel's novel uses a young Parisian as its first-person narrator. Phillipe Brisson follows La Salle from Paris to Nouvelle Francaise, back to Paris, then to the ultimate fatal ending at the mouth of the Mississippi. Fuller, author of the earlier *Loon Feather* and *Shining Trail,* focusses her story on the imaginary twin sons of the Marquis de Lorrenes who supposedly accompany La Salle and his faithful lieutenant, Tonti. Fuller's version ends with La Salle at a high point of his achievement; it concludes before his murder.

For those looking for a non-fictional biography of the man for whom La Salle Street is named, there is John Upton Terrell's *La Salle: the Life and Times of an Explorer* (1969).

Robert Carse's *The Beckoning Waters* (1953) combines the themes of immigration and the development of Great Lakes shipping during the years

* *Grease* was filmed in 1978 and quickly became a "cult" film for the 1970's equivalent of the 1950's "grease" generation; it was followed by *Grease II* in 1982.

from 1876 to 1932. Unfortunately, Carse's grasp of his themes was better than his novelistic skills.

Leonard Dubkin's *Wolf Point; An Adventure in History* (1953) received mixed reviews from critics. August Derleth, for example, said that Dubkin's novel about a mystic experience on the point of land at the junction of the North and South branches of the Chicago River was not up to the level of Donald Culross Peattie's work, but still it would "command the respect of those who enjoy good nature writing."[2]

Dubkin's thesis in this "disappointing book" is that the Point has a psychic quality because others had earlier had similar mystic experiences, and he traced the "psychic quality" back to the Indians who had been in the area before the whites came.

Max Sklovsky's *Dynasty; A Novel of Chicago's Industrial Evolution* (1958) is a slight novel, unnoticed by critics, focussing on a financial tycoon, a girl social worker, and an immigrant union organizer, at the turn of the century.[3]

Immigrants and Ethnic Groups

In the 1950s, Lillian Budd, who had been born in Chicago to Swedish immigrants, completed a trilogy of novels about Swedish immigrants to Chicago: *April Snow* (1951), *Land of Strangers* (1953) and *April Harvest* (1959). In the first novel, Sigrid Eliasdotter and Peter Kristiansson are seen on an island farm in their native Sweden. Though almost unnoticed by critics, this book sold a quarter of a million copies.

In the second novel, set in the early 1890s, the Kristiansson's son, Karl, disappointed in the failure of a childhood dream, comes to Chicago looking for a land of wealth and freedom, but instead finds poverty and hard work. He marries Elin, a girl he had known in Sweden but whom he could not marry there because she was of an aristocratic class. Karl, a dreamer, is never able to make a very good living for Elin and their daughter, Sigrid. Elin dies of tuberculosis contracted while working and aggravated by continued hard work and substandard living conditions. Karl too dies, trying to save a small boy from a runaway team of horses, and Sigrid, orphaned at seventeen, must make her way on her own. The third novel is her story.

Although the three novels form a continuous tale, each stands on its own, each a record not so much of immigrants in general as of individuals.

In *The Sidewalks Are Free* (1959) Sam Ross's third and best novel, we are introduced to a Northwest Side immigrant family just after World War I. The Melov family has come to Chicago from the Russian Ukraine. Largely this is young Hershel Melov's story; we watch him move into adolescence while the family struggles to maintain its cultural identity.

But an unexpected bequest of money produces tragic consequences for the family and a somewhat melodramatic ending for the novel.

One paragraph stands out in the book: "Measure a man by the work he does, the love he has for his family, his not hurting people, his respect for people, his being content with what he has, not by his ambitions, his cruelty, the rock in his heart. Can't a man be a success without gaining an empire?"[4]

Lucile Stern's *The Midas Touch* (1957) is about a young second-generation Jewish Chicagoan who renounces his orthodoxy to avoid the anti-Semitism directed toward him, marries a Gentile girl, and amasses a fortune through the years of the Depression and World War II. Unfortunately the ruthless tactics he has used cost him his friends and create problems for him at home. Eventually he reforms.

The novel was ignored by critics.

Joseph Dever's *Three Priests* (1958) are assigned to a Chicago parish in the 1930s. Each adopts a different role, one fighting corruption in Chicago's government, one editing an archdiocese newspaper, and one active in church politics.

Elsie Reif Ziegler's *The Face in the Stone* (1959) tells of Dushan Lukovich, a Serbian youth who comes to Chicago in 1849 to avenge his father's murder. In Chicago he becomes a stonecutter, working on one of Chicago's early "cliff-dwellings." Gradually he becomes involved in labor problems. A major theme is the conflict of old world tradition with the culture of the New World.[5]

In *Lion at My Heart* (1959) Chicago saw a novelistic interpretation of a hitherto undescribed ethnic group by a native son. Harry Mark Petrakis in this, his first novel, fictionalized his Chicago Greek heritage. The setting is far South Side Chicago in the shadow of the steel mills where Angelo (Pa) Verinakis and his son, Mike, work, and where Anthony (Tony) works part time and goes to college. Mike wants to marry an Irish girl but Pa wants him to marry a Greek girl. When Mike marries Sheila he becomes an outcast from his family.

People who like to dramatize the statistics of demographics today say that Chicago is "the third largest Greek city in the world, and they point to the 30,000 Greek residents of "New Greek Town" centered within a radius of half a mile of the intersections of Chicago's Lincoln, Western and Lawrence Avenues.

But Harry Mark Petrakis, in his Chicago novels and in his short stories, one of which won an *Atlantic First Award,* writes of Greeks on the far South Side where he was reared, and in the "Old Greek Town" just west of Chicago's Loop. "If you want to know about Greeks in these old neighborhoods," says an authority, "you could do worse than to read the books of Harry Mark Petrakis."[6]

The conflict between a Greek immigrant father and his Winnetka son is dramatized by Tom T. Chamales in *Go Naked in the World* (1959). But an old man, also from Greece, helps Major Nick Stratton, a World War II veteran, straighten matters out.

Blacks in Chicago

A larger proportion of Chicago literature in this decade is by and about Blacks. Richard Wright contributed *The Outsider* (1953), a story of a Chicago post office worker with money and women problems who is listed as dead in a subway accident. Damon Cross, however, is unhurt and, moreover, has $800 he had just borrowed from the credit union.

Rather than reveal the identification error, Cross decides to solve his problems by taking up a new identity. When he is accidentally discovered by a friend, Cross murders the man and goes to New York City where his involvement with the Communists eventually lead to his murder.

Frank London Brown was a social worker and an *Ebony* editor when he wrote *Trumbull Park* (1959), a novel about a black family that the Federal government moved into Trumbull Park, a far South Side housing development. Louis "Buggy" Martin and his family were happy at first to discover they could leave the rotting, rat-infested tenement which had been their home since childhood. But in Trumbull Park the family found an atmosphere of hate and bigotry for which they were not prepared. At least in the tenement they had had friends; their new home was clean, but it exposed them to harassment and violence that fell just short of actual personal injury. Even the police seemed more concerned that the Blacks might hurt the whites. However the Martins survive and in the end "Buggy" re-established his manhood by walking through the housing district.*

Gwendolyn Brooks, the poet, told in *Maud Martha* (1953), her only novel, about a Black Chicagoan, from her fifth birthday (about 1920) to the end of World War II. In a series of short anecdotal chapters, Maud Martha grows up, leaves her fairly comfortable home to marry a ne-er-do-well young man who wishes that Maud Martha had a lighter skin. When Paul loses his inconsequential job, Maud Martha takes a job as a servant in a North Side white home. Meanwhile she has had one child and becomes pregnant a second time.

Mark Kennedy's *The Pecking Order* (1953) narrates one day in the life of eleven-year-old Bruce ("B.J.") Freeman, a South Side Black boy, and members of his gang, the Warriors: Snag, Henry, and Johnny Martin. B. J., the leader, indoctrinates the gang with his code of behavior: "We, our gang, is *awways* right! And if ya didn see what happened, say ya did anyhow, that is if it's good for *us*. And if it's bad for *our* side, swear up and down it didn happen."[7]

In that one day, the boys have a rock battle with a marijuana peddler, have

---

* In 1960, Brown told *Library Journal* (84:507) that the novel was based on his personal experience.

run-ins with other juvenile gangs and the police, take part in the murders of two boys, steal cookies and a car. The day ends with B. J.'s death in a struggle on a rooftop.

Lorraine Hansberry's *A Raisin in the Sun* (1959), set on Chicago's South Side, has its origins in a verse of Langston Hughes:

What happens to a dream deferred

Does it dry up

Like a raisin in the sun?[8]

The drama revolves around the sum of $10,000 that the mother of two grown children receives from her husband's life insurance. The son (played on both the stage and in the subsequent film by Sidney Poitier) wants to invest the money in a liquor store so he can quit his chauffeur's job and become a big shot in the Black community. The mother, tired of living in the ghetto, wants to buy a house for herself and her family. There is a daughter also, a belligerent racist, who is attending college, and, to the amusement of a student from Africa, doesn't know the difference between Liberia and Nigeria.

In the white neighborhood to which the family moves, the mother is forced into a debate with a spokesman for the whites. She resolves the situation, not in terms of social justice, as Brown was trying to do in *Trumbull Park,* but in terms of a family pride in the subject of ethical standards.

Lorraine Hansberry also wrote the shooting script for the 1961 film version. In addition to Poitier, Claudia McNeil and Ruby Dee appeared in the film in the roles which had won them high praise on the New York stage. The play won the 1969 New York Drama Critics Circle Award, the first time this award had been won by a Black playwright.

Both the play and the film were praised by all the critics.

Other Chicago People

Christopher Clark was a factory hand when he wrote *Good is for Angels* (1950), a novel in the James T. Farrell tradition of detailed realism. The novel begins and ends in a Chicago cemetery. Except for one moment of high tragedy, it follows the day-to-day affairs of a good but ordinary woman, Lizz Litke, and her family, including her blowsy niece, Ella. The tragedy follows upon the coming of Billie, Ella's son, a Dillinger-like creature of evil who casts a fatal shadow on Joe, Ella's newly-acquired husband.

Calder Willingham's *Geraldine Bradshaw* (1950) is a novel about Southern people who have come to Chicago. The book is a comic tale of an incredible heroine, and two young men she meets, one of them a hotel bellhop, the other a copy boy for a Chicago newspaper. Geraldine, the novel's protagonist, is a pathological liar; Beau St. John, a copy boy whose equal probably would have been difficult to find on a Chicago newspaper. Willingham was a writer whom some critics thought had a genuine talent, whom others thought was a "verbose smut writer." His screen credits include *The Graduate* and *Little Big Man*.

Forest Rosaire's *Uneasy Years* (1950), like Ross's *Sidewalks Are Free,* deals with the consequences of an unexpected legacy. Rosaire, who had once been a student of Robert Herrick's and who had written *East of Midnight* in 1945, shows us a family whose father is a mail-order clerk and wouldbe Salvador Dali, and a mother who must as a consequence work to help support their three children, one of whom is a Ph.D. candidate, one of whom is an undergraduate, and one of whom is in high school. The mother learns of the legacy at about the same time she discovers her husband is a smalltime embezzler, and she resolves to rid herself and her family of him. But she is forced to reconsider when she unexpectedly discovers that the children have a strong loyalty toward their father.

Edward Wagenknecht, a Chicago University classmate of Rosaire's, said that the novel was not one "to miss."[9]

Diana Gaines *Tasker Martin* (1950) is a tale, told in flashbacks, of the rise of a successful Chicago business man (in produce, trucking and railroading) who was equally successful in his amours. The novel has strong overtones of the career of Howard Hughes, a rags-to-riches chronicle; its hero's ruthlessness, his maniac will to succeed, his insatiable restlessness, are in strong contrast to the milk-soppy politeness of Alger's heroes, or the characteristics of the heroes of earlier novels of Chicago business such as *The Pit* or *The Smiths.*

Gaines, said a critic, "paints a brilliant portrait of Chicago during the gangster era when fortunes could be made or destroyed at the whims of a half-dozen men."[10]

Gaines' *Marry in Anger* (1958) deals with an unusual version of the novel of marital relationships. It begins with a Cinderella romance between the daughter of a poor but socially prominent family and the heir to a Chicago department store fortune. On the night before the wedding (the time is the mid-1930s) he tries to call the wedding off because he's romantically involved with his brother's wife. But his fiancee forces him into a compromise; they will marry as planned and then pretend to live together for one year, giving the appearance of a happily married couple during that time.[11]

Malcolm Stuart Boylan's *Tin Sword* (1950) is a success story of another sort than *Tasker Martin.* His Joshua Doty (rhymes with Don Quixote) starts at 13 with a shipboard romance with a married woman. By 19, he has become a Chicago National Guard lieutenant colonel. The fanciful narrative is told in a style somewhere between that of Corey Ford's parodies and the novels of James Branch Cabell.

William Sanborn Ballinger, was the author of *Portrait in Smoke* (1950). It tells of a private detective who traces an old girl friend from her stepmother's apartment in a tenement near the stockyards to the North Side to Oak Park and finally to Lake Shore Drive.

John dos Passos is not usually thought of as a Chicago writer, but he did use Chicago as part of the setting for *Chosen Country* (1951). The novel attempts to explore the ancestry of Jay Pignatelli, a young Chicagoan, Dos Passos' thesis being that everyone is emotionally the sum of his or her ancestors. The novel covers the period from 1848 to 1930. Jay is the son of Jim Pignatelli, a colorful lawyer and railroad man who came to Chicago after the Civil War, and of his mistress. After a chapter about the father, the novel ranges through Europe, the Far East, Ohio, Wisconsin, New York City and Denver, as it follows Jay's adventures. Eventually Jay comes back to Chicago to the girl he marries. Dos Passos knew Chicago quite well, but he uses little of the Chicago setting in this book.

Keith Wheeler's *The Reef* (1951) is set in 1946. Nickerson "Nick" Cotten is haunted by a decision he made during World War II on the island of Tarawa. So he returns to the Pacific Island that had been the scene of some of World War II's bloodiest fighting. The island and Chicago are the settings for this story of a Chicagoan who managed to resolve a problem he carried home from the War.

Vera Caspary's fourth Chicago novel, *Thelma,* (1952) tells of a woman and her daughter from the early 1900s to a time after World War II. Thelma had been embarrassed by her family circumstances, and she resolved to do better for herself and, after her marriage, for her daughter. The daughter's marriage runs into trouble, but the daughter manages, through her innate good sense, to preserve the marriage. *Thelma* is a not-too-well-told sermon on the evils of materialism.[12]

Roswell G[ray]. Ham, Jr.'s *The Gifted* (1952, published also a year later as *Account Overdue*) is about a group of Chicagoans, each of whom is dissatisfied with some aspect of his or her married life. "Embarrassment, degradation and death" follow.[13]

For many years, Chicago novelists had seemed deliberately to overlook Chicago's reputation as "Porkopolis." Early in the century *Letters From a Self-Made Merchant to His Son, Memoirs of an American Citizen* and *Ganton & Co.* had used the meat packing industry as settings, but Gurdon Saltonstall Hubbard had been derogated as a Chicago builder because he had begun as a meat packer. In 1952, Ira Morris, himself a third generation member of a Chicago meat packing family, glorified the packing industry in *The Chicago*

Story, a novel in which the Swifts, the Armours, the Wilsons and the Cudahys are all too thinly disguised.

The first part of the family chronicle is set in 1905 with the founding of Adolph Konrad & Sons. It was a period when building a business and a fortune required a great deal of ruthlessness and pugnaciousness, and often produced melodrama:

> The mass killing and mass preparation of meat had about it something satisfying, almost grandiose. After all, man was a carnivorous creature. Here in the Chicago Stock Yards the process of turning beasts into food ... was raised to a science, if not to an art: here was the quintessence of butchery...[14]

Parts two and three of the book are set in 1920 and 1950 respectively. There are two themes: the unhappiness of old Konrad with the inability and unwillingness of his sons to follow in his footsteps, and the introduction of the technocrat, representing disinterested ownership and managership.

With the exception of Nelson Algren, who never seemed to like anything done outside of Chicago's slums, critics liked the book, although they pointed out that it was not *the* story of Chicago but *a* story of Chicago. "The Chicago story," said aptly-named Fanny Butcher in the *Tribune,* "is [finally] emerging from gossip and journalism into literature. It is a story filled with pioneer vigor, ruthlessness, tenderness, and cruelty as well as beauty of dreams in which ironies of human relationships are jerked apart by heady successes or merged into grim intimacies."[15]

Mary Jane Ward, one of those singled out by Alson J. Smith as a superior Chicago writer, and whose *The Snake Pit* (1948) had been a best selling successful book and source of a powerful film, turned, in *It's Different for a Woman* (1952), to Chicago suburban North Shore society for her subject matter, and to the Garden of Eden story for her plot. The story develops the consequences of a "snake" (an "old flame" of Sally Cutter's Ph.D. husband) coming into the North Shore Garden of Eden — which turns out, through a final revelation by Sally's grandmother, not to have been such a strait-laced place after all.

Rosamond DuJardin set three more "Tobey Heydon" novels *Practically Seventeen* (1949), *Class Ring* (1951), and *Boy Trouble* (1953) in a Chicago suburb. Written for teenage girls, the three books tell of some critical years in the life of Tobey Heydon, a middle-class girl whose problems are typical teenage girl problems, primarily those relating to boys. There is little to indicate in these novels that Tobey and her companions had any forewarning of the forthcoming "grease" generation.

It is useful to compare these novels with Albert Halper's *The Golden Watch* (1953), a novel of Jewish boyhood just after World War I. The chapters in this volume were originally published as short stories or sketches. Each chapter focusses on an incident in a family's life which produces some slight crisis: the arrival of a well-to-do former boyfriend of the mother, now dying of tuberculosis; the first date for an older sister; the high school prom and graduation; business troubles in a not-too-successful West Side family grocery. Perhaps the superficiality of the DuJardin books stems from the superficiality of the suburban society, a society in which family groups are not as tightly integrated as they are in the society Halper writes about, a society which lacks the cultural and religious roots of an older generation closer to its old-world origins.

James Yaffe's *What's the Big Hurry* (1954) tells of a "gusty, combustible Chicagoan" who, orphaned at 17 in 1903, comes to Chicago to live with a cousin, a hat, gloves and accessories merchant. But Dan Waxman is too ambitious for such prosaic undertakings; he becomes an accountant for Martin Drexell (read Samuel Insull, even to the opera singer!), builder of a powerful utilities empire. When Drexell's bubble bursts, causing losses for Dan's friends who have followed his advice and invested in Drexell, Dan is forced to give up his social life in Chicago and move elsewhere — to New York, to Paris, to Ohio. After years of a life of rage, he at last returns to find contentment among his Chicago friends.

Critics liked the book, but they wondered why such an able narrator as Yaffe had proved to be in two earlier books, had chosen to tell Dan's story through the voice of Dan's young nephew.

Sherman Baker's second novel, *Hidden Fire* (1955) is about a Chicago business man who commutes daily from Winnetka where he has an attractive wife, two small children and a home with a mortgage. There's a snake in this Garden of Eden also — a woman named Martha Brown who decides to rescue Max Ferguson from the rut he's in. As a consequence the Ferguson marriage is wrecked and Max is faced with economic ruin. Then Martha sends Max back to his loyal, understanding wife.

David Wagoner was a new light on the Chicago scene in the second half of this decade with three novels and two volumes of verse. Although his biography shows no formal residence in Chicago, he chose the Windy City for the setting of all three novels.*

Money, Money, Money (1955) has a protagonist much like Faulkner's in *The Sound and the Fury* (1929). But Willy Grier is a moron, not an idiot, and he has some sense of good and evil — although others must manage the small legacy which supports him. Grier's present adventures begin with his discovery of a corpse one night while swimming in Lake Michigan near Calumet City. As a consequence, he becomes involved with a nymphomaniac, a gangster or two, and some highly placed Chicago politicians. Falling in love with the woman after she has seduced him, Willy tries to buy her away from one of the gangsters but his money buys him only misery and, perhaps, death.

In *Rock* (1958), Wagoner turns to a different type of protagonist, a young man, recently divorced, who returns to his far South Side Chicago home to try to re-establish himself. There Max Fallon encounters, in addition to a younger sister and his parents, a younger brother who is becoming part of the rock generation — "loose-lipped, defiant, a hip-talker, a youngster rattling around in the iron vacuum of his generation."[16] Although Max is an intelligent person, he has difficulty in communicating with the members of his family. Through his father's political connections he finds a job as a beach lifeguard. There he meets a divorced woman and a teen-age girl. Before he can finally establish relationships with the woman, his relations with the girl make him the target for the pent-up hatred of the members of the rock generation who use the beach as a hangout.

Curiously enough, one of the book's reviewers defined "rock" as a "proto-juvenile delinquent," a second defined it as a kind of motion, a third as the "juke-box idiom by which our currently youngest generation identifies — or rather, masks — its chronic fear of individuality."[17]

"How do you find yourself, then?" a reviewer asked. "You rock a little, roll a little, glockenspiel and rule a little. You get with, not it, but yourself."[18]

Leon Phillips' *When the Wind Blows* (1956) is set in Chicago during the Depression. The son of a wealthy Chicago business man marries a Swedish girl of a different social and economic background, despite his family's opposition. When the marriage falters, it is Helga Bjornson Dawson who keeps things going.

Winifred E[sther]. Wise's two novels, *Frances a la Mode* (1956) and *Frances by Starlight* (1958) focusses on Frances "Franny" Cochrane who goes to work in the fashion coordinator's office of a large Chicago department store. The time is the 1950's. In the sequel, Franny takes a vacation from her boyfriend and studies at the Chicago Art Institute before deciding to try Hollywood. After a stint in the costume department of a studio, she decides that the grass was greener where she came from and she returns to Chicago.

Roger Treat's *The Endless Road* (1959) contrasts the postwar lives of two Chicago men who served together during World War II. Both were alcoholics but one turns to Alcoholics Anonymous, makes a recovery and becomes a successful newspaperman. The other stays on the downward path. The book reads more like a tract or AA propaganda than like a novel.[19]

Up to this time, Jane Mayer and Clara Spiegel had written several books under the pen name of "Clare Jaynes." In 1959, on her own, Jane Mayer (Mrs. Jane Rothschild) wrote *The Year of the White Trees*, a story of the romantic

---

*Wagoner spent several formative years in Hammond, IN.

relationship between Anneira Veck, a 25-year-old teacher in a Chicago private school and Ellis Springbok, a virtuoso violinist who comes to Chicago. Anneira meets Springbok through the affluent members of her social world. He is contemplating divorce; she has been having an affair with a married teacher at her school. In the end, Springbok goes back to his wife, and Anneira is left, as one critic commented, in a "new freedom."[20]

Since the days of the Civil War, there have been military establishments of some sort in the Chicago area, and these places — Camp Douglas, Fort Sheridan, Navy Pier, among them — have occasionally appeared in Chicago fiction. In Ben Masselink's *The Crackerjack Marines* (1959), the military personnel are Marine recruiters in Chicago during World War II. For Masselink, "crackerjack" is a derogatory term, and his novel is a lightweight one which relies on the stereotyped concepts of Marines as hard drinkers and women-chasers.

Pearl S[ydenstricker]. Buck, better known for her novels about China, wrote one novel which also deals with World War II in Chicago. *Command the Morning,* however, focusses on the scientists who research the atomic bomb under the seats of the stadium at the University of Chicago which had once resounded to cheers for the "Grand Old Man" and his football teams.

College Life

Helen R[owland]. Sattey's *Shadow Across the Campus* (1957, the Dodd, Mead Librarian Prize winner) deals with the subject of anti-Semitism in a sorority on the Northwestern University campus at Evanston. Three girls who have grown up together hope they will be accepted by a sorority but one is rejected because she is Jewish. A second one then refuses to join the sorority; the third one becomes a member, hoping to change the sorority's policies from within. The time is the 1950s.

Williard Motley

In *We Fished All Night* (1951), Willard Motley returned to the Chicago he knew so well: the parks, the Gold Coast, the slums, Bughouse Square, Thompson's Restaurants, Soldier's Field, Riverview Park, Michigan Boulevard night clubs. The time is 1937 to 1950, the primary focus on the consequences of the post-war world for three Chicago veterans and a great many others. "The new world was being born, in blood and pain and afterbirth," Motley wrote. "The world was something raw and bloody."[21] The central character is Chet Kosinski who tries to conceal his Polish origins by changing his name to Lockwood. He earns a local reputation in amateur theatricals before the War, loses a leg in battle, takes a job as a supervisor in a mail-order house owned by an arch-conservative, becomes, with the help of a corrupt political backer, a powerful politician married to the daughter of a millionaire.

But his success leads to nothing: "Lord, we fished all night and caught nothing" is the biblical quotation from which the book's title is taken.

The novel is cynical about the means by which Lockwood becomes upwardly mobile:

> And this [stealing an elective office by buying, selling and destroying votes] was the democratic process. This was the foundation of government. This decided city, state, federal rule. Decided the fate of the poor, the slum dweller, the laborer, the great masses of the middle class, housing, health, the young, and the old. This, the democratic process that led from city and town government to the White House itself. This was what decided national policy. And international policy. War or peace.
>
> This was the free democratic process. This was what [Lockwood] had lost his leg for . . .[22]

"The paradoxical truth is that while realistic novels like Motley's have a superficial correspondence to the facts of American life," said Harvey Swados, novelist and critic, "in actuality they express too little of the inner quality of our existence and seem like the troubled utterances of writers who feel that they should have something strong and polemical to say about the ugliness of the post-war world but do not quite know what it is they must say, or even how it should be said."[23] "Its subject matter, dealing with everything from adultery to Zeitgheist, embraces too much," said J. Saunders Redding, novelist and English professor. "Apply the test of realism to it, and you come up with the conclusion that Motley has a grasp of life-like conditions, but that these do not add up to the truth. Apply the test of truth, and you must see that realism is a point of view which the author has mistaken for a method. [It] is as if it were written out of a desperate testing of experience and talent; dredged up from deep, muddied pits of emotion and dumped into an intellectual stream neither swift enough to dissolve it nor deep enough to absorb it."[24]

Motley had spent five years writing this 560-page novel with its "two-hundred-odd ticketed and named characters."[25] Typical of much post-war writing, its writing had been funded by fellowships from The Rosenwald Fund and The Newberry Library. Paradoxically, the fortunes that Chicago tycoons had amassed were being used, in part, to attack the institutions of the city they had helped build.

In *Let No Man Write My Epitaph* (1958), Motley narrowed his focus to Chicago's Skid Row, "a crazy, numbing, neon-lighted world bounded on the north by Nelson Algren, on the west by Saul Bellow and on the south by James T. Farrell"[26] and continued the history of Nick Romano's family — Nick's illegitimate son and Nellie, the boy's mother. Nick II is enslaved by drugs for a time but manages to reform owing largely to the attentions of a sentimental bunch of North Clark Street denizens who seem to have come out of the pages of a Bret Harte story rather than the area between the Newberry Library and the Marina Towers. Although Motley's book drew some major critics because of his previous reputation — Maxwell Geismar, Granville Hicks, Nelson Algren — none of them liked the book.[27]

However, Hollywood did; the film was produced in 1960 under the direction of Philip Leacock, with Burl Ives, Shelley Winters and James Darren in the principal roles. As a film, Motley's story was more successful than as a novel.

Chicago Crime in 1950s Novels and Films

Motley's third novel had skirted the edge of Chicago criminal activity; Nelson Algren insisted that the addict needed medical aid rather than a police court, and he pointed out how much of the legitimate world of business profited by drug addiction.[28]

Similarly, Jack Lait's and Lee Mortimer's best-selling *Chicago Confidential* (1950) ranged along the borderline between crime and legitimacy with its purported exposé of the seamy, underworld, demi-monde life of Chicago, concentrating on gangsters, whores, pimps, B-girls and their ilk. The book emphasizes the "shocking" but factual aspects of this life. Added to it is a lexicon of slang and underworld tems, and a "gazetteer" of places where presumably excitement seekers might be able to view this Chicago zoo life. Aside from the book's demonstration that nothing much had changed in Chicago since Shang Andrews, the Everleigh Sisters, and the old Levee, this book's greatest usefulness may be as a catalog of what was what and who was who in this shadow world of Chicago's post-war years.

A film, *Chicago Confidential* (1957) focussed on an attempt by crusaders to clean up corruption and crime among the labor unions of the Windy City.

The City That Never Sleeps, a 1953 film, featured a Chicago policeman, a married man, who becomes involved with a tawdry cafe singer. *Chicago Syndicate* (1955) featured Xavier Cugat and Abbe Lane, two musical entertainers in a film exposé focussing on attempts to clean up Chicago rackets.

After *Little Caesar,* W. R. Burnett produced a baker's dozen of books on non-Chicago subjects. Then, in *Little Men, Big World* (1951), he returned to Chicago for a story about organized crime. But, as reviewers noted, Burnett relied on a formula long established in silent Western films, and the end was predictable to everyone except the newspapermen who were the book's protagonists.[29]

David Wagoner's *The Man in the Middle* (1954) is anti-hero Charlie Bell, railroad crossing tender, who like Wagoner's Willie Grier, is accidentally involved in adventures he didn't want. The site is apparently East Chicago, a place where the chief of police can "barely talk English," and the "cops" can be bought for a "quarter apiece." When a girl political reporter is killed because she knows too much about a Senator's attempt to blackmail a Chicago newspaper editor, and her corpse is "planted" in Charlie's room, Charlie is forced to flee for his life. The chase — he is pursued by the actual murderer and the Chicago police — take Charlie into a variety of Chicago's "nooks and crannies" before its final "ironical ending." But critics thought "midway in the novel" the author "misplaced his story."[30]

"It was just an experiment," Nathan Leopold, Jr. said about the murder of young Bobby Franks in 1924. "It was as easy for us [his accomplice was Richard Loeb] to justify as an entomologist in impaling a beetle on a pin." But the "experiment" became the "crime of the century" and led to Chicago's most sensational court room trial, a trial in which attorney-author Clarence Darrow outwitted the Illinois State's Attorney by pleading his clients guilty of murder and then arguing "mitigating circumstances," a plea which won his clients a trial before a so-called "friendly judge."

In 1924, Meyer Levin was a classmate of Leopold and Loeb at the University of Chicago, a student of Robert Herrick's, and a wouldbe journalist and author. In 1956, his *The Old Bunch* long behind him, Levin turned the Loeb-Leopold-Franks case into *Compulsion,* a fictional recreation of events before the crime, the crime itself, and the trial. His technique, he pointed out, was accurate personal and reportorial recollection, buttressed with fanciful fiction — the formula for historical novels.[31]

Readers of the mid-1950s were shocked by the "pornographic prose" — homosexuality was a taboo subject then — but were enthralled as Levin ably maintained suspense in a narrative where everyone knew the outcome.

In 1957, a dramatization of *Compulsion* in two acts and twenty-four scenes was produced on Broadway. But in the production process of rehearsal and revision, Levin became angered with the play's producers and withdrew. The program notes for the play, therefore, call it a "producer's version." Whatever the authorship (Levin accused one Robert Thom of being the rewriter) Brooks Atkinson did not like the dramatized version — it was as "odious" as the original crime, he said.[32]

The dramatization was published by Simon and Schuster in 1959, with Levin's version of the New York incidents in a foreword.[33]

Compulsion was also filmed in 1959 in an apparently much more successful dramatization featuring Orson Welles.

James Yaffe's *Nothing But the Night* (1957) also uses the Leopold-Loeb case as the basis for its story; it is similar, says one reviewer, to Meyer Levin's *Compulsion,* at least in theme, though its less brutal, less intense.

In comparison with Levin's current best-seller, this novel is more tightly written and neatly patterned. Levin, however, rummages more freely and imaginatively among the debris and spotlights Leopold and Loeb as intellectu-ally-confused super-hoodlums rather than the misdirected goal-seekers of Yaf-fe's version. With its toned-down approach, *Nothing But the Night* is not quite as effective dramatically as *Compulsion;* moreover, Yaffe lays too much stress on the guilt of affectionate parents. In both novels, [however], one misses the "old-fashioned" point of view that the individual should be held primarily accountable for anti-social self-indulgence.

The Chicago *Daily News* had the final literary word about this case. "Nathan Leopold ended his 33-year prison sentence with a reformation," it reported. "[But] Richard Loeb, who was a master of the English language, today ended a sentence with a proposition." The reference was to Loeb's murder by a fellow convict to whom Loeb had made a sexual advance.[34]

The 1920s Chicago gangster, Al Capone, was also recalled, in three productions, in 1959. Maurice Coons' *Scarface,* written pseudonymously by "Armitage Trail," is about a fictitious Tony Guarino and his rise to power in Chicago gangdom. The events closely follow the activities of the actual Capone — whose nickname was "Scarface."

John Roeburt's *Al Capone* followed closely on the heels of the 1959 film with the same title featuring Rod Steiger as Capone — an obvious coopera-tive operation. The book begins with Capone's arrival in Chicago and his first job as a bouncer at Johnny Torrio's cafe. Events such as the coming of Prohibition on January 1, 1919, the murder of Big Jim Colosimo, the organization of a syndicate with its concomitant division of Chicago among three gangs, the headquarters in Cicero, the St. Valentine's Day massacre and Capone's death in 1947 are events in the film, all lightly rehearsed.

Sixteen mystery novels, usually featuring "private-eyes" — non-official detectives — complete this gory record for this decade. A list is in the Appendix.

Solo

Stanford Whitmore's novel *Solo* (1955) is the story of a great jazz pianist in Chicago. Virgil Jones who wants to play just for himself and who is about as intransigent a hero as Chicago literature has produced, is confronted by Ross Jaeger, another jazz pianist, who is consumed by morbid jealousy; by Helen Kostakos, who loves Jaeger but who splits her loyalties because of her respect for Jones' ability; by an all-powerful agent; and by a puppet disc jockey. These unwanted entanglements lead to trouble for Jones who tries to maintain his integrity and his privacy against the often-overly-persuasive efforts of those who worship the bitch goddess success and see Jones as their "open sesame."

Gwendolyn Brooks, Poet

In the years since 1944 when she published her first poems, Gwendolyn

Brooks has become a major figure both on the Black scene and on the larger American scene with her teaching, her lectures and her volumes of verses, many of which have a Chicago setting: *Bronzeville Boys and Girls* (children's verse, 1956); *Bean Eaters* (1960); *Selected Poems* (1963); *In the Mecca* (1968); *Riot* (1969); *Family Pictures* (1970); *Aloneness* (1971); *Report From Part One* (autobiography, 1972).

Brooks won the Anisfield-Wolf Award in 1969, and in that same year was selected as Poet Laureate of Illinois to succeed the late Carl Sandburg.

Brooks often quotes Karl Shapiro, formerly editor of *Poetry:* "Poetry as we know it, remains the most lily-white of the arts." Then Brooks adds, "From now on, let Whitey have his lily-white garden, and the Black poets will have their own garden."[35]

Saul Bellow — The Fifties and After

Saul Bellow moved to Chicago when he was nine. He was educated in Chicago public schools, the University of Chicago and Northwestern University. From 1938 to 1942 he wrote biographies of midwestern novelists and poets under the aegis of the Works Progress Administration. He then taught at the Pestalozzi-Froebel Teachers College in Chicago. Since 1962 he has taught at the University of Chicago.

He is almost certainly the most famous writer who has lived and worked in Chicago (though he has not attracted the audiences that Ferber has), but he is not a Chicago novelist in the sense I have used the term in this book. It is true that Joseph, the diarist of *Dangling Man* lives in Chicago, but, as critics have pointed out, the book is neither about Chicago nor, for that matter, about World War II. Augie March in the light-hearted *The Adventures of Augie March* (1953) begins life in the slums of Chicago, but this picaresque novel, set in the flapper, Depression and World War II times, is about Augie, not Chicago. *Herzog* (1964,) considered by many to be Bellow's best work, is set in New York City, Massachusetts, and Chicago, but it is neither a Jewish novel or a Chicago novel — rather it "concerns the laboring of the intellectual mind under stress."[36] *Humboldt's Gift* (1975) comes the closest to being a Chicago novel; the book's protagonist, Charles Citrine, is a Chicago Jew with many of the characteristics of his creator. Still, the focus in the novel is on Citrine's "meditations".

John W. Aldridge's "Saul Bellow at 60" (*Saturday Review,* September 6, 1975, pp. 22 ff.) is a good short statement on Bellow. Bellow's own "Starting Out in Chicago" (*American Scholar,* Winter, 1974-75, XLIV, 1, pp. 71 ff.) presents Bellows comments on the beginnings of his career, and is apparently the first chapter in an autobiography. R. L. Dutton's *Saul Bellow* (1971) is obviously incomplete.

This is Chicago

Albert Halper's *This is Chicago* (1952) is an anthology of poems, essays, newspaper stories, short fiction, sketches, and cuttings from novels and other books, all about Chicago, and ranging in time from 1836 to 1950. Subjects include the Fort Dearborn Massacre, the Chicago Fire, the Haymarket Riot, the Columbian Exposition, sports, gangsters, crime and politics. Authors represented include Ferber, Algren, Levin, Wright, Sandburg, Farrell, Zara, Halper, Meeker, Masters, Brooks, Lardner, Anderson, Hecht, Jane Addams, Darrow, Kipling, and Mrs. John H. Kinzie.

City on the Make

That Nelson Algren both loved Chicago and hated Chicago is made obvious in his 1951 prose poem, *Chicago: City on the Make:* "Chicago has progressed culturally from being The Second City to being the Second-Hand City. The vital cog in our culture now is not the artist, but the middleman whose commercial status lends art the aura of status when he acquires a collection of originals."[37]

There was nothing new in this, actually; similar concerns had led to the development of Chicago genteelism.

But that Chicago could react in kind was made clear by the Chicago *Daily News'* review of the book:

> A more partial, distorted, unenviable slant was never taken by a man pretending to cover the Chicago story — a book unlikely to please anyone but masochists — definitely a highly-scented object."[38]

But Algren was capable of another view of his city:

> And never once, on any midnight whatsoever, will you take off from here without a pang. Without forever feeling something priceless is being left behind in the forest of furnished rooms, lost forever down below, beneath the miles and miles of lights and lights... With the smoke blowing compassionately across them like smoke across the spectrum of the heart. As smoky rainbows dreaming, and fading as they dream, across those big fancy Southside jukes forever inviting you to put another nickel in, put another nickel in whether the music is playing or not.[39]

Algren died on May 9, 1981.

Chicago-Based Films in the Fifties

Chicago Calling (1951) with Dan Duryea, a film about a man whose estranged family has been injured in an automobile accident.

Wabash Avenue (1951), a period-piece remake of *Coney Island,* with scoundrelly but likable Victor Mature trying to break up a romance between a saloon owner, Phil Harris, and a musical star, Betty Grable. It's a better film than this brief statement might indicate.

Last of the Badmen (1950). The title seems to call for a Dodge City, Kansas setting and John Wayne as the hero, but this is a story of Chicago in the 1880s.

Machine Gun Kelly (1958). Charles Bronson in a gangster chronicle focussing on one of the notorious figures of the 1920s.

Party Girl (1958). Robert Taylor, Cyd Charisse, in a trite 1920s cop-vs.-gangster film.

A Summing Up

There had been fewer novels set in Chicago in this decade, no plays, and very little poetry of note. Major writers were at work — Motley, Farrell, Brooks, Bellow and Algren. Some names — Meeker, Halper — had been seen for the last time. In the two decades ahead, most of the names would be those of new writers — but some of them would do very good work.

XIII.
Years of Protest

It's not a bad town for writers. It was never a bad town for writers. At this moment there must be a new young crop of them, totally unknown, writing painfully in family parlors and bedrooms, on the North, South and West sides. It was always a good place for a writer to be born in, or to grow up in. And after a Chicago writer reaches adulthood it doesn't matter where he lives, in New York, Paris or Rome. The silver cord is never cut, he never really gets away.[1]

There is no room left for the serious writer to stand up in good old Yahoo Chicago.[2]

Over a century had passed since the first major book about Chicago had appeared. More than a thousand titles set in Chicago had been published since then. And still Chicago, like Cleopatra to Shakespeare's Mark Anthony, was a fascination to writers, something to conjecture about and to spill ink, if not blood, over.

As we have seen, Saul Bellow and James T. Farrell continued producing books during this decade.

Harry Mark Petrakis

Next to Farrell, the most prolific writer of this decade was Harry Mark Petrakis, who continued to write about South and West Side Greeks. *The Odyssey of Kostas Volakis* (1963) covers the years from 1919 to past mid-century, and tells of the hardships faced by a young immigrant couple who come to Chicago to live and work in a cousin's restaurant. Despite seven eighteen-hour-a-day work days every week, a squalid room for a home, and one tragedy after another they remain. A priest and an atheistic doctor are also important characters.

Most of the sixteen short stories in *Pericles on 31st Street* (1965) are set in Chicago's Greek community, as are most of the eleven short stories in *The Waves of Night and Other Stories* (1969). Some of these are O. Henry-type stories with ironic twists of fate and surprise endings.

A Dream of Kings (1966) is a powerful novel of a man's dream to raise enough money to take his sick son back to Greece before his death. Leonidas Matsoukas is both a comic and a tragic man for all seasons with his pretensions of learning, his weakness for gambling on horses, and his fondness for his wife as a bedtime partner.

A Dream of Kings was filmed in 1969 with Irene Pappas and Anthony Quinn in lead roles.

In the Land of the Morning (1973) tells of a young man who returns from the Viet Nam battlefields to his home in the deteriorating Greek community, only to find his father dead, his sister on the verge of insanity, and his mother having an affair with his dead father's bitterest enemy. He finds sympathy in a young woman whose husband had been killed in Viet Nam. Although this is not Petrakis's best work, it deals powerfully with 1970s themes — youthful alienation, re-adjustment to civilian life, parent-child-conflicts, changing traditions, changing sexual mores and family unity.

A characteristic of Petrakis's fiction is its freedom from Puritanism or puritan restraints. Another is the closeness of the link of these Greeks, even in their deteriorating neighborhoods, to their Eurasian culture.

In addition to an *Atlantic* First Award, Petrakis has been awarded a Benjamin Franklin Citation for his stories. His work has twice been nominated for the National Book Award. He has won the annual award of the Chicago-based Friends of American Writers, the Friends of Literature, and the Society of Midland Authors. He has an L.H.D. from his alma mater, the University of Illinois.

In *Stelmark/A Family Recollection* (1970), the St. Louis born/Chicago/raised Petrakis writes a lyrically-styled autobiography of the first forty-seven years of his life. The book ends on the note of *Atlantic's* acceptance of his first short story after ten years of futile effort. Petrakis's Chicago home was near the home of James T. Farrell.

Blacks in Chicago Literature of the 1960s

Paul Crump's *Burn, Killer, Burn* (1962) starts off this decade with a story of the journey of a black youth from the ghetto to the electric chair. Guy Morgan's itinerant preacher father deserted his mother for another woman after Guy's mother was crippled in an automobile accident. Hating his father, Guy takes his vengeance out on others. The setting is Morgan Park.

Richard Wright's *Lawd Today* (1963) tells of one day in the life of Jake Jackson, a Chicago postal worker, a day which is also the anniversary of the birthday of the Great Emancipator. Jake and his wife, Lil, are having marital problems. Jake wants her to have an abortion. He drinks too much and is in danger of losing his postoffice job for that reason, but also because of his debts and his wife's complaints to the postal inspector. Jake borrows a hundred dollars to pay for the abortion, but, like Gypo Nolan of the film *The Informer* (1935) wastes his money in a night of whoring and drinking. He goes home determined to kill his wife but he doesn't succeed. The time is the Depression.

Wright's style in this first novel (but one which was not published until after his death in 1960) was undoubtedly influenced by John Dos Passos' USA trilogy.

It is not as good a book as *Native Son*.

S. W. Edwards *Go Now in Darkness* (1964), written when Edwards was twenty-four, is a story of a young black couple trying to work out their individual identities and at the same time establish a compatible relationship. The time is the early 1960s, the place Chicago's Old Town.

Ronald L. Fair's *Hog Butcher* (1966) has nothing to do with the meat packing industry; rather the title is drawn from Sandburg's "Chicago." Cornbread Hamilton, a star black high school athlete who has been recruited by an all-black college, is shot to death as he runs along a street in a black Chicago neighborhood one rainy afternoon by two policemen, one black, one white. Two ten-year-old black boys, Wilford Robinson and Earl Carter, witness the shooting. In the two inquests which follow, a black store owner is coerced by the police into lying about the incident and Earl is coerced into remaining silent. But Wilford insists on telling the truth and is eventually supported by the black policeman, even though the latter knows what his testimony will cost him. Interpolated in the novel are chapters of background with particular reference to the unemployment caused by the removal of meat packing plants from Chicago, and to the wave of tough new blacks moving into the city.

Bernard Brunner's *The Face of Night* (1967) uses Chicago's skid row as its setting, the death of a young Negro woman as its catalyst. Two detectives, one white, one black set out to arrest the head of the dope ring responsible for the girl's death. One dies, one resigns.

Melvin Van Peebles *A Bear for the FBI* (1968), written in the form of a memoir, reports firsthand accounts of the "trauma of growing up black in Chicago during and after World War II." Says a critic, "It is a beautiful reminiscence for those [Chicagoans] who remember Riverview Amusement Park, the jitterbug, and streetcars ... [it offers] an offbeat view of Negro life for those who equate black literature with hate and violence."[3] (The novel was first published in French.)

Gunard Solberg's *Shelia* (1969) tells of one night in the lives of Shelia Smith, daughter of an affluent black Chicago suburban doctor, and Wayne Divine, son of a somewhat less affluent white Chicago family. The novel is narrated by Wayne, and he tells how he is attracted to the "cool" Shelia, whom he calls "a so-called Negro." Although one critic praised Solberg, a Chicago-area school teacher, because he understood "youth as few of today's teachers and parents can," another critic said the characters were "phoney," and the story line incredible.[4]

In any case, the novel was filmed in 1972 as *Honky.* In the film a "white 'all-American' boy falls for a drug-pushing black swinger." Critics said the film was "lurid and mundane," dismal and hopelessly bad.[5]

Rose Robinson's *Eagle in the Air* (1969) tells about a black girl who is expelled from a large Chicago university for her (non-violent) role in a campus protest; she moves in with a boyfriend because she has no money and nowhere else to live. Later, she goes to Iowa to live with a half-sister. When that arrangement doesn't work, she starts hitchhiking to California and is rescued from an attempted rape. Her rescuer, a white Indiana Hoosier, helps restore some of her lost faith in humanity.[6]

Sam Greenlee's *The Spook Who Sat by the Door* (1969, 1970) relates the consequences of a United States Senator's demand that the CIA be integrated. The Senator's action is cynical — he needs the black vote in a closely-contested election. Only Dan Freeman, a black Chicago social worker is hired, and he becomes a token "visible" black. But Dan has plans to lead all blacks in a revolution against "Whitey," and he goes back to Chicago to implement his plans. Under the pretense of reforming black street gangs, Dan actually trains them as guerrilas, using money from a bank robbery and weapons heisted from the National Guard. The novel ends with Dan killing a friend, a black policeman who has come to arrest him.

Shortly after the publication of *Trumbull Park,* Frank London Brown died of leukemia, leaving behind, like Wright, an unpublished novel. Seven years later in 1969, Brown's *The Myth Maker* was published with an appreciative note by Sterling Stuckey. Brown had experienced the trauma of *Trumbull Park,* and that novel therefore had an immediacy that is missing from *The Myth Maker.* But Brown did know the grinding, dehumanizing world of 58th Street, and so this novel of Ernest Day's wanton murder of an old black man (an act surely influenced by Brown's reading of *Crime and Punishment*) had a believable reality to it.

Brown was also the author of two short fictions, the first "McDougall," the story of a young and suffering white trumpet player married to a black woman:

> McDougall's eyes were closed and he did not see the dark woman with the dark cotton suit that ballooned away from the great bulge of her stomach. He didn't see her ease into a chair at the back of the dark smoky room. He did not see the smile on her face or the sweat upon her flat nose.[7]

"A Matter of Time" is about a black mill hand who knows that he is dying and that life will go on as usual without him. There is little doubt but that the story is about Brown himself.

"It seems to me that to be a Negro writer today must be a tremendously stimulating thing," Eugene O'Neill had written in the late 1920s. "They have within them an untouched world of deep reality. What greater boon can an artist ask of fate?" To read Brown's two books and his two stories is to come in touch with that untouched world in a very personal way not found in other Chicago black writers.

Ethnics and Historical Novels

Three of the four Chicago novels about immigrants written in this decade are also historical novels in that they are all set in the nineteenth century for the most part. The fourth one introduces characters whose ancestors had been a part of Chicago's history.

Ann Kurtz' *Pendy* (1960) is set in Russia, Minneapolis, and Chicago in the last decade of the nineteenth century. Pendy, at seven, is forced to take care of her Russian family when the father abandons them and goes to America to try to recoup a lost fortune. Later, when she is ten and in America herself, the cares of the family again fall upon her youthful shoulders. Finally, to solve the family's problems for once and for all, she marries a wealthy industrialist even though she loves someone else.

The novel was not reviewed. The exaggerated emphasis on the abilities of a child of such tender years mars this one of the few novels about Russians in Chicago.

Camille Layer Ebel's *The Land of Plenty* (1960) is the second novel of recent years to focus on Czech immigrants to Chicago. Nita Kucer comes with her family to Chicago in 1865, just at the end of the Civil War. She quickly adapts to the new life, but adaptation is not as easy for her parents.

Events in the novel include the Fire, the Columbian Exposition and the Spanish-American War; the novel ends at that time.

Reviewers overlooked this book also.

Melanie Pflaum's *The Gentle Tyrants* (1969) tells of a Frenchman who comes to Chicago at the time of the Fire, hoping to make a fortune and then return to his native country to live a life of ease. He begins by collecting scrap metal from the Fire ruins.

He makes a fortune as he had hoped, but he makes it as a Chicago industrialist.

The novel follows the adventures of three generations of the Pierre de Pres family as the city rebuilds, experiences the agony of the Haymarket Riots, gets involved in the women's movements and World War I, suffers the trials of the Depression and finally faces up to World War II.

For the first time since duBois H. Loux's *Ongon* (1902), Indians again become a major part of a Chicago novel in Barbara C[laassen]. Smucker's *Wigwam in the City* (1966). The novels tells in an understanding way the problems faced by a Chippewa Indian family which moves from the northern Wisconsin lake country to a Chicago tenement. The focus is on the family's young daughter.

Rosamond [Neal] Du Jardin's *Young & Fair* (1963) is set in the Chicago of the 1880s. An orphaned girl goes to work for a department store like Marshall Field's in size and importance. Unlike other girls of that time who are reported to have turned to prostitution to supplement their meager shopgirl earnings, the heroine of this novel finds financial independence and romance.

Helen Tann Aschmann's *Connie Bell, M.D.* (1963) is the story of a girl who persists in her determination to become a doctor. She becomes one of the first graduates of the Chicago Women's Medical College in 1871, and then crusades to improve the status of women in the medical profession.[9]

Julia Cooley Altrocchi, whose *Wolves Against the Moon* we have reviewed earlier, set a narrative poem in Chicago: *Chicago: Narrative of a City* (1969?). The poem was selected for the Stephen Vincent Benét Narrative Poetry Award in 1969.

Chicago People

For her final novel set in Chicago, *Evvie* (1960), Vera Caspary returned to Chicago of the 1920s for her setting. Her tale is about two girls who share an apartment. Louise, the narrator, writes clever advertising copy and tells her story in a jargon resembling that of the 1960s beatniks. Evvie, her roommate is "footloose, fancy and bodyfree." When she is murdered, a scandal develops.

Caspary will always be best-known for her non-Chicago novel, *Laura,* particularly because of the very fine motion picture that was based on it.

Karl Stern's *Through Dooms of Love,* written when the author was 54 (1960) features a North Shore suburban girl who supports her father and who is forced to turn to others for help after he suffers a disabling stroke. Her employer suggests an affair, a psychiatrist is too wrapped up in himself to help, while a third friend suggests social work and Catholicism.

Elsie Reif Ziegler's 1961 *Light a Little Lamp* was a fictional biography of Mary McDowell, "the Angel of the Stockyards" as a girl of 20 at the time of the Fire. For the next sixty years, Miss McDowell continued to work for the "lower half." In the winter of 1902-1903, for example, during another of those occasional attempts to "clean up" the "Windy City," she (a member of the then five-year old University of Chicago Settlement), Jane Addams, and others organized to protect fallen women from Chicago's underworld who had testified to "police shakedowns."

Edward Everett Tanner, the author of the celebrated *Auntie Mame* (1956, produced as *Mame* on the musical stage and in a film), wrote *Love and Mrs. Sargent* (1961), a slightly malicious sketch of one Sheila Sargent, widow of a World War II correspondent, and mother of Dicky, 20, and Allison, 18, the latter about to have her "Chicago Season." Sheila, who is closely monitoring the lives of her children, is about to be featured in a *Life* story, about to become Mother of the Year, and is obviously modeled on the Chicago columnist, Ann Landers (whose name is not mentioned in the novel, although her sister's is). The novel ends with Sheila's realization that her children do not need her and are in fact better off without her. So she goes off to a second husband, a man who has been her puppeteer all along.

Peter DeVries *Blood of the Lamb* (1961) begins in Chicago in the early years of the twentieth century and follows the Wanderhope family until the 1950s. Ben Wanderhope, like DeVries, is the son of a Chicago Dutch Calvinist immigrant. The novel was one which puzzled critics; it reports several deaths in the family, those of Ben's older brother, his wife and a daughter, but it was written in DeVries' usual comic manner. However, one critic called it "an angry autobiographical striking out at God and man."[10]

Eda Lord's *Childsplay* (1961) is narrated as a recollection from a child's point of view of a young girl's life in Missouri, Oklahoma, and Evanston, where the novel both begins and ends. Along the way the girl has a number of adventures with a stepbrother only a year older.[11]

Don[ald Elmer] Lawson's *A Brand for the Burning* (1961) is the story of a boy growing up in a west Chicago suburb from just after World War I until the end of World War II. Mark Erikson experiences the prosperity of the Harding-Coolidge years with its accompanying frivolity, the Depression of the 1930s, and "the strong feeling of nationalism brought on by World War II."[12] The point of view is not always well maintained.

Laurene Chinn's *Believe My Love* (1962) is a story of the problems facing a couple who contemplate inter-racial marriage in the 1920s and 1930s.

J[ames]. E[arl]. Powers *Morte D'Urban* (1962) tells of a Catholic priest who is transferred from his Chicago parish to a parish in a remote area of Minnesota. Most of the novel is concerned with his problems there. At novel's end he is returned to head a Chicago religious order. The novel is reminiscent of some of those fictions and plays which deal with Chicago police captains being transferred to remote suburbs.

Diane Gaines' *The Knife and the Needle* (1962), althogh ostensibly set in Chicago, seems to have been based on a disastrous Cleveland hospital fire which claimed over a hundred lives. The novel's course runs for a few days during which Kay Quimby once again meets — and has an affair with — Salvador Scotti, once a colleague of her husband, Dr. Orrin Quimby. Meanwhile, Quimby is having an affair with his nurse. Quimby's clinic burns with a large loss of lives and Scotti seems responsible for the fire. But, like Roe's *Barriers Burned Away,* the fire proves to be the catalyst that leads to a happy ending.

Philip Roth's *Letting Go* (1962) has its first third in Iowa City (where Roth was a participant in the famed Writers' Workshop), its second part in Chicago, and its third part in New York and Paris. Gabe Wallach, the narrator, is first seen as a graduate student at the University of Iowa where he meets Libby and Paul Herz. Gabe and Paul are Jewish, Libby is Catholic. Gabe is well-to-do, the Herz's are not. Gabe is attracted to Libby, but although Paul, in a cynical action, makes it possible for Gabe to seduce Libby, Gabe does not take advantage of the opportunity. After Gabe becomes a teacher at the University of Chicago, he helps Paul get a job there. In Chicago, Gabe has an affair with Martha Reaganhart, a divorcee. Finally, Gabe leaves the University.

Gabe's problem is that he likes neither himself or the world he lives in, a familiar pattern for twentieth century writers. The twentieth century's grey plague, said a *Time* reviewer, is a paralysis of the apparatus that detects meaning in life.[13]

Critics thought the elaborately chronicled-book was at its best in the Iowa setting when Libby was prominent; they felt that it should have been her book. They did not think the novel was as good as Roth's earlier *Goodbye, Columbus.* Neither did Hollywood, which made a fine production of the earlier book but passed up the second.

Hayden Carruth's *Appendix A* (1963) is a novel in autobiographical form. The other man in a lover's triangle recalls the affair as he recuperates in a hospital. "The plot is tired and the writing disjointed and irregular," said a critic, "but the author's gift for observing and recording detail, coupled with his command of the English language, has produced descriptions of Chicago and Chicago society which have seldom been equaled."[14]

Convention (1964) by Fletcher Knebel and Charles W. Bailey II, is not a Chicago novel in itself but it is set in Chicago in August of 1964 in the first McCormick Hall and some downtown hotels. What we get is a journalistically-detailed behind-the-scenes account of the kind of maneuvering that leads to the nomination of a Presidential candidate.

Paul Molloy's *A Pennant for the Kremlin* (1964) is a fantasy about the possible relationships among the sport of baseball, big business and international relations in the 1960s. Angered by the United States' inability to get along well with the Kremlin, a wealthy Chicagoan wills his fortune and the Chicago White Sox (which he owns) to the Soviets.

Given the consequences to the White Sox, the moral of this book might be that Phil Wrigley should have sold the Cubs to *Pravda* instead of the Chicago *Tribune*.

Molloy was a Chicago sports writer.

The events of *The Higher Animals/A romance* by H. E. F. Donohue (1965) take up one day in the life of Dan Conn, a clerk in Gahagan's book store on the University of Chicago campus. The novel explores the relationships among two sets of characters: a man, his wife and her brother from the Cumberland Mountains, and a group of Dan's friends and acquaintances — Philip Hanley, a literature professor; his promiscuous wife, Helen; Wolf Tone Larsen, a reporter; Naomi Morris, a sixteen-year-old nymphomaniac, and a sailor, Herman Morris, whom she has picked up; Timothy White, who tries to commit suicide; Louis Vincent Mosler and John Wright who run Lou's Place, a campus bar; Professor Stuart Wagner and Emil Russell.

After asking Conn for directions to the airport, the Cumberland group robs a filling station, shooting to death the attendant, then murder a policeman who is trying to ticket them for illegal parking. Conn, Hanley and Larsen are involved in a house fire in which three elderly people burn to death. After Hanley fails to save one, he develops a guilt complex. Conn recalls at length the night when he and Helen Hanley seduced each other while her husband was away interviewing for a job.

The novel ends with as much fireworks as a Grant Park Fourth of July celebration. The bandits take hostages and command of the 12th Street Illinois Central Coffee Shop; Hanley and White are the hostages. In the siege by police, all three bandits die as does Helen Hanley trying to rescue her husband.

"The gradual metamorphosis of the characters is not an especially exciting one to witness," said Alexander Coleman. "The novel is concerned with the subtle adjustment of sensibilities to the various unwelcome intrusions of reality. Since they bear only a negative capability at first, the characters are initially of only passing interest, but no matter; the meticulously calculated onrush of events ends by enmeshing the reader into this arresting conflict between violence and reason. Conn and his friends slowly acquire their sense of humanity only as they descend, in a telling reversal of Darwin's description of man's ascent, to the level (once again) of warring natures."[15]

The novel's style seems to be influenced by the work of James Joyce and William Faulkner.

H. E. F. Donohue, a University of Chicago graduate and a former bookstore manager, had been a *Ladies Home Journal* fiction editor. He had earlier produced *Conversations With Nelson Algren* (1964).

Like DeVries' *The Blood of the Lamb,* John Stewart Carter's *Full Fathom Five* (1962-1965) received a great deal more critical attention than most Chicago novels of this period. In a work which is simultaneously a novel, three long stories, and fictionalized biography, Tom Scott, the narrator, seeks to trace his relationship with a beloved but dead physician-father. Tom's grandfather had been a Chicago "robber baron," father of ten sons. Through gossip, remembrance, dream, and the recollections of two uncles, Tom finally secures the revelation he seeks.

"The Keyhole Eye," one of the three stories, focusses on the affluent literate class of present-day Chicago.

Adela Rogers St. John, nearing the end of a long journalistic career, set the first part of *Tell No Man* (1965) in Chicago. The protagonist of this lengthy, badly-written novel, young Henry Angus Gavin, is a successful stock broker and a member of the North Shore social set until he gives up his business career (partly because of a friend's suicide) and sets out to be a second Messiah in Southern California.

Eleanor Medill Patterson, a member of the McCormick and Medill families that had published the *Chicago Tribune* almost since its founding, and who in the 1940s was publisher of the *Washington Times Herald* was also a novelist. In 1966 she authored a somewhat autobiographical novel, *Girlhood in Chicago.* It ran headon into competition: Paul F. Healy's *Cissy, the Biography of Eleanor M. "Cissy" Patterson* published the same year, and Alice Albright Hoge's *Cissy Patterson* (also 1966). Ralph G. Martin's *Cissy* followed in 1979.

William Richert's *Aren't You Even Gonna Kiss Me Goodby?* (1966) features an eighteen-year-old, Jimmy Reardon, who, having paid for a girlfriend's abortion out of his college fund, is told by his father he must replace the money. Jimmy sets out at first as might have Samuel Merwin's *Temperamental Henry* of pre-World War I days. But when the methods Henry Calverley III might have used produce only half the needed money, Jimmy then turns to a means Henry III never would have thought of — he offers to sell his services as a partner in sex to a number of people, including a friend of his mother's. The setting is an affluent Chicago suburb.

Shirley Seifert, a Missouri novelist who had written a number of novels about doctors, and who had a reputation as an author of careful historical fictions, produced *The Senator's Lady* (1967), a fictional biography of Addie Cutts, the wife of Senator Stephen A. Douglas. The novel focusses as well on

Douglas.

In James Purdy's *Eustace Chisholm and the Works* (1967), the time is the early 1930s but the atmosphere is the late 1960s. The location is Chicago's South Side near the University. The characters (the term is also intended in a slangy sense) are Eustace (Ace) Chisholm, a wouldbe poet living in an attic garret; his wife, Carla, who has just returned from a six-months long adulterous affair with a young Chicago graduate to whom she has transmitted syphilis acquired from Ace; Daniel Haws, an ex-coal miner, who is having a homosexual relationship with Ace and others; Amos (Rat) Ratcliffe, a brilliant young Chicago graduate who cannot find a job or become a welfare case because of his youthfulness; Maurine O'Dell, a nymphomaniac painter, and Reuben Masterson, a millionaire.

Amos and Haws love each other but the affair is not consummated. Maureen marries Reuben. Daniel returns to the army where he is murdered by a homosexual captain who then kills himself. Amos also comes to a tragic ending. Ace concludes he is not a poet, and continues his unsatisfactory relationship with Carla.

The novel is an ofttimes brutal narrative of the darker side of the human comedy, an area explored to a lesser degree by Donohue in *The Higher Animals*.

In *The Heart of Silence* (1967), Bentz Plagemann explores the lifelong sibling relationships of the grandsons of a Chicago entrepreneur, sons of a successful Chicago lawyer who had married Dolly Riley, daughter of Senator Tom Riley. James Carstairs, the older, follows a conventional life style. Paul from the beginning is an extremist, either in following the flamboyant Catholic practices of his grandmother, or in his general life style. In the Jack Kerouac tradition, he becomes a dropout from college and family, a World War II army deserter, and finally a hermit practicing strange rituals in a remote corner of Mexico. James, fortified with the family's wealth, tries to persuade Paul to return to the family and a conventional life style. When he realizes he cannot change Paul's ways, he attempts suicide.

Like Willie Grier of *Money, Money, Money* James has come to a tragic end because of his discovery that money cannot buy satisfactory human relationships — at least not in his generation.

Thornton Wilder's most ambitious novel, *The Eighth Day* (1967) is a philosophical study, a sociological study and an exciting mystery-adventure story. Philosophically, it discourses on the meaning of life and the universe; sociologically, it examines Chicago, a coal mining town in southern Illinois, and a mining area in the Chilean Andes. The time is 1902 to 1905, and John Ashley has been falsely accused of murdering his friend and supervisor. Sentenced to death, Ashley escapes and flees to South America where he resumes his career as a mining engineer, unaware that his sentence has been reversed.

While his wife and daughter remain in Coaltown, Ashley's son becomes a successful Chicago newspaper man.

The book was Wilder's first novel since 1948.

Sam Siegel's *Hey, Jewboy* (1967), a novel in the form of a memoir, traces the life of a Jewish boy from the Chicago streets from the time he is orphaned at eleven until he is jailed at twenty on a charge of armed robbery.

Peter DeVries' *The Vale of Laughter* (1967) is told in two parts, the first by Joe Sandwich, a neurotic Chicago stockbroker who downs pills about as often as he trades stocks, and the second by one of his former college professors. Whichever narrator is telling the tale, the manner is DeVries' well-known satirical one.

Judith Barnard Papier's *The Past and Present of Solomon Sorge* (1967) tells of the consequences for an Evanston professor, political scientist and respectable citizen when his wife of twenty-nine years disappears, and he is called upon to rationalize her act.

Arthur Hailey's *Airport* (1968) is set at "Lincoln International Airport" (obviously O'Hare International Airport) during a blizzard which recalls the blizzard of 1967, the worst in Chicago history (at least until 1979). Hailey's exploration of the consequences of everything going wrong which possibly can in a complex social-technological institution could, however, have been as easily set at other northern international airports. In fact, when *Airport* was filmed in 1970, it was filmed at the Detroit International Airport.

Leonard Lamensdorf's *Kane's World* (1968) is quickly described — it relates how a man makes a fortune in Chicago real estate with all the obvious side shows that would accompany a tale of such a three-ring circus.

The three novels by Papier, Haley and Lamensdorf were all listed as "best sellers" in the publication of that title. Haley, of course, has established himself as a blockbusting author with novels similar to *Airport*. His formula is always the same.

Thomas Roger's *The Pursuit of Happiness* (1968) tells of a couple who are University of Chicago seniors who, in a fashion all too familiar and all too disconcerting to thousands of American middle class families were living *en famille* sans license and sans ritual. William, however, is for marriage; it's Jane who is uncertain. Their debate and the concerns of those who know them are made more complicated when William is imprisoned following a series of unhappy circumstances.

Saul Maloff's *Happy Families* (1968) tells of a man of middle age who is, as we would say today, "burned out." He's divorced, he's unhappy with his work, he's discontented with the world in general and himself in particular — and obsessed with sex. But when his seventeen-year-old daughter becomes another statistic as a runaway, and he sets out to search for her, Robert Kalb discovers he has lots of company in his misery. Says a critic "*Happy Families* is a brilliant representation of American popular culture, late 1960s variety, displaying the hostility, cynicism, despondency, and disorientation which typified the times."[16]

The theme would be picked up again by Judith Guest in *Ordinary People.*

Sterling Quinlan had been a major figure in the Chicago broadcasting scene before he wrote *The Merger* (1968), a *roman á clef* which, according to a *Tribune* reviewer, probably helped "clarify some of the recent and strange goings-on in certain [broadcasting] stations."[17] The novel traces the power struggle which results when one of America's largest corporations and a major TV network are merged. Most of the action takes place in Chicago, focussing on Les Madigan, ex-program manager of the closed station, KPRT, his boss, Herb Powell and their wives; Elliott Kimball, president of the old network and one of those axed in the power struggle; and H. B. Ferguson, president of the corporation. Although Ferguson treats the network as a plaything, he demands profits.

Unlike such novels as *The Pit* and *The Titan,* which pictured Chicago power struggles as contests or games which men deliberately entered knowing they might win or lose, *The Merger* depicts the new world of the often-impersonal corporation, a world of a jungle in which the fittest survive because they have the most brutal temperaments. Like the loser in any jungle struggle, the loser in these corporate battles faces death or expulsion from the herd.

Reviewing William Harrison's 1969 novel, *In a Wild Sanctuary,* R. Verlin Cassill wrote:

> Suicide is for the young, as Kay Boyle once put it, stressing not only its romantic appeal but [also] its towering pathos, its irreconcilability with all the norms on which we depend collectively for faith and life. Suicide is the mad objective of the race, warn the political and social moralists, citing . . . how we tax ourselves to multiply threats of military extinction from without and the death of feeling or identity from within . . . [T]he young who die by their own hands have internalized the ills and paradoxes we bequeathed them and are literally murdered by the inadequacies of our love.[18]

Harrison's novel is a study of a suicide pact among four students on the University of Chicago campus but more of an explication of Cassill's thesis than it is a story of Chicago or the University. The prime mover in the pact, however, is a young Chicago black whose Iago-like manipulations of the other three undoubtedly derive from his family background in the Chicago black ghetto. In its existentialist themes, the novel has overtones of the

YEARS OF PROTEST 321

French authors, Gide and Camus. Unhappily for the reader, the most interesting of the young men is the first to die in the pact. Shades of *Romeo and Juliet!*

Alexandra Jane Benchly's *If the Heart Be Hasty* (1969) is a "love story as frustrating as it is unrealistic."[19] Its two characters are two young people who grow up on Chicago's South Side in the late 1930s. Although they care for each other, when Mike enlists in the Army, Jennie marries. And so on for two decades.

Catherine B. Osborn and Margaret Waterman joined forces in 1969 to write a parody of a French classic, using the same title as the original, *Pere Goriot.* The novel has some interest as a commentary on Chicago society of the 1960s, but it would be more fruitful to take French 100 and 101 and read the original.

Marge Piercy's *Going Down Fast* (1969) seems to be the first Chicago novel that has its origins in the urban renewal of the last few years — everything from the magnificent Garrick Theater to the notorious South Federal Street. This book focusses on urban renewal in the University of Chicago area, and the consequences of building-bulldozing on the lives of the residents.

Mary Jane Ward's *Counterclockwise* (1969) continues the interest of this author in the internal affairs of patients and caretakers in a mental hospital, earlier demonstrated in Ward's *The Snake Pit* (1946). In this novel, the protagonist is the author of a best seller about the horrors of life in a mental hospital who later becomes a mental hospital patient.

This novel was also a best seller.

Hoke Norris' oddly-titled *It's Not Far, But I Don't Know the Way* (1969) is a tale of two lovers who meet after years of separation.

Another tale of baseball is Marvin Karlins' 1969 *Last Man In Is Out.* The novel is a futuristic novel as well, relating what occurs when a college professor inherits a baseball team in 2002.

1960s Films Set in Chicago

As the century passed on, Chicago continued to be an important setting for films, both those made for motion picture screens and those made for television.

The 1961 *Tomboy and the Champ* featured a thirteen-year-old Texas ranch girl who exhibited the prize bull at Chicago's International Exposition with the usual teen-age complications.

The Scarface Mob (1962), a two-part segment from the television series, *The Untouchables,* offered Robert Stack as FBI agent Elliott Ness closing in on the Capone gang. Walter Winchell was the narrator.

An Elvis Presley film, *Girl Happy* (1965) opens in Chicago with Presley as a member of a combo playing in a night club owned by a Chicago gangster. The combo and the gangster's daughter move on to Fort Lauderdale during the annual Easter Week Hegira of the college crowd. The usual romantic complications ensue.

Mickey One (1965) was filmed on location in Chicago. A Detroit night club comedian flees to Chicago because of threats from gangsters. In the Windy City he finds employment at a posh West Side club and some complex experiences.

In *Goldstein* (1965), a young sculptor searches the city for an old man he has seen and whom he believes to be the Old Testament prophet Elijah! Novelist Nelson Algren picked up a few quick bucks by appearing as himself in a cameo scene.

The Young Runaways (1968) exhibits some melodramatic adventures of three teenagers who find refuge in the Chicago hippie district.

A 1969 film, *30,* was a hackneyed scenery-chewing attempt to depict a night in the city room of a Chicago newspaper. *Medium Cool* was produced by Haskell Wexler who also wrote the script, basing it loosely on Jack Couffer's 1967 *The Concrete Wilderness.* Wexler used actual footage from events in Chicago's downtown streets during the 1968 Democratic convention, from the assassination of Robert Kennedy and from Resurrection City in Washington, D.C. The resulting ultra-realistic film was warmly praised by critics. It was a fine demonstration of the method by which the camera, rather than the pen or typewriter, might be used as an instrument for creating a film narrative or drama based on actual or imaginary circumstances and characters, and thus, in a sense, producing a new literary genre.

The 1969 *Brandy in the Wilderness* is only partially set in Chicago. *Finney* (also 1969) features a thirteen-year veteran of the Chicago Bears who tries to find a new career as an artist but who becomes a bartender.

Ben Hecht's long literary career came to an end in 1969 with the film, *Gaily, Gaily* of his 1963 autobiography. The time is 1910; a Galena, Illinois boy sets out for Chicago to seek his destiny. He is taken in by a prominent brothel madam and given a room on the top floor of the house. He becomes a newspaperman. There follows a complicated search for a missing ledger which contains a record of civic corruption.

Something went wrong, however. Leonard Maltin said the script (Hecht's last) was "silly, hollow."[20] It was an unfortunate ending to a long and successful Hollywood career.

The Fabulous Bastard From Chicago (1969, also titled *The Fabulous Kid From Chicago, The Chicago Kid* and *The Bastard Wench From Chicago*) was set in Chicago. An East Side Chicago garage is seen as the front for

Chicago's biggest bootlegging operation. Complicated intrigues result from a shooting in the garage (the St. Valentine's "massacre" is the obvious source for this idea).

Two other 1960s films looked back at the gangster period. *The St. Valentine's Day Massacre* (1967) featured Jason Robards as Al Capone, and George Segal doing an imitation of Jimmy Cagney imitating a gangster. There is so much shooting throughout the film that the final cold-blooded machine gunning of seven unarmed men in a Clark Street garage is anti-climatical.

A much more lavish film was *Robin and the Seven Hoods* (1964), featuring Frank Sinatra, the "Rat Pack," and Bing Crosby in a technicolor musical parody of Chicago gangster films. The jokes wear thin long before the film ends.

That film was done in Hollywood, but Robert Altman's *Nightmare in Chicago* (1960) was filmed in Chicago. A pyschotic killer who calls himself Georgie-Porgie terrorizes the Chicago area in "a mad murder spree" for 72 hours. Leonard Maltin called this made-for-TV film "above average."[21]

A New Poetic Image

In September of 1964, poet Ogden Nash, furious over a burglary of his Boston home, wrote this verse:

I'd expect to be robbed in Chicago
But not in the home of the cod.
So I hope that the Cabots and Lowells
Will mention the matter to God.

Soon the Chicago *Sun Times* was reporting the objections of Chicago letter writers to this "routine contumely." "What a poet says about a city can be very important," William W. West says, citing cities that had perished because poets had ignored them:

They had no poet and they died.

Chicago, of course, had not been ignored by poets; in fact, Carl Sandburg had carried the city's fame far and wide with his stanza:

Hog Butcher for the World,
Tool Maker, Stacker of Wheat,
Player with Railroads and the Nation's Freight Handler;
Stormy, husky, brawling,
City of the Big Shoulders.

But, thought Van Allen Bradley, literary editor of the *Chicago Daily News,* perhaps the changes that had taken place in Chicago over half a century warranted a new poetical image of Chicago. So on July 14, 1962, the newspaper announced a contest for a poem that, while not replacing Sandburg's, might at least stand beside it, and offered a $1,000 first prize — a magnificent sum to most poets. The judges were Gwendolyn Brooks, Henry Rago, current editor of *Poetry,* and Paul Engle, Director of the University of Iowa's Writers' Workshop — whose own poem had won the Century of Progress Prize thirty years earlier.

After looking at over two thousand poems, all identified only by code numbers, the judges decided that three poems were equally well done: "A Sheaf for Chicago" by Lucien Stryk, born and reared in Chicago; "Michigan Water" by Hayden Carruth, a former *Poetry* editor (whose novel *Appendix A* is discussed elsewhere) and "The Other Chicago" by John Berryman, a former University of Chicago teacher. The poems were published in the *Chicago Daily News* of August 3, 1963.

David D. Wagoner, Poet

We have seen several novels by David D. Wagoner, a University of Washington professor. His poetry is collected in *A Place to Stand* (1958), *The Nesting Ground* (1963), and *Staying Alive* (1966). In 1969, poems from these volumes and some uncollected poems were combined in *New and Selected Poems.* Among them are several that are set in Chicago or might have been, including this one with a title that would never fit on a theatre marquee: "The Shooting of John Dillinger Outside the Biograph Theater, July 22, 1934:"

> Where was Johnny headed?
> Under the Biograph Theater sign that said, "Our Air
> is Refrigerated."
> Past seventeen FBI men and four policemen who stood
> in doorways and sweated.
> Johnny sat down in a cold seat to watch Clark Gable
> get electrocuted . . .[22]

And so the 1960s ended in Chicago with real blood in the streets, not the imaginary blood of fiction or the motion pictures. Farrell and Bellow were the obvious stars of this decade, a decade which had seen fewer crime novels and far fewer mystery novels (a total of nine) set in Chicago. Aside from Farrell, Bellow, Petrakis and DeVries, most of the writers of this decade were one-novel people, and that pattern was to hold true in the next decade.

XIV.
The Decade of Disbelief

The World's Fair. How could one believe it would ever end? And yet it must: the lights would flicker and die tonight; all the little lives gathered here would flicker and die in their own time. The modern miracles would merge with the past marvels. Soon it would be nothing but ancient history, as remote as the reality of Columbus himself. What had this land looked like four hundred years ago? Nothing but swampy meadow, lightless and lifeless. Perhaps it would be like that again four hundred years from now. God, how quickly we all go down to dust.

"Wuxtry! wuxtry! Read alla bout it!"[1]

The surprise in this final Chicago decade of our history of Chicago literature is the number of novels in which Blacks are the central characters in proportion to the total output for this decade and the number of novels written about professional football in Chicago — four, more in one decade than had ever been written about baseball in Chicago.

Mystery and crime novels continued to be of interest to Chicago writers and readers, but some of them became rather gruesome, and one looked back at a celebrated criminal of Chicago's nineteenth century history. For the first time in some years, two futuristic novels appeared.

And on the Chicago theatrical scene, a new playwright appeared, a writer with a great deal of promise for the future.

The Chicago Daily News

On Saturday, March 4, 1978, the 102-year-old *Chicago Daily News*, a newspaper which had spawned more *writers* (in contrast with *reporters*) and more books by its writers than any other American newspaper,* issued its last edition. In its years of service to the City by the Lake, it had two great Chicago journalists — Victor F. Lawson, its long-time publisher and Henry Justin Smith. It had been founded by Melville Stone, later creator of the Associated Press, and two of its final owners were John S. Knight and Marshall Field IV.

Henry Justin Smith had once expressed the paper's writing philosophy:

> Some of us, so long as we live, will never abandon the old-fashioned but thrilling idea that good writing . . . is worthwhile. We shall wag our gray beards furiously at every fancied opponent. We shall break our lances against every windmill.
>
> We love fine, sincere, exceptional work, and we despise mediocrity. We hate with all our power of hatred every sort of easy, imitative, complacent, patented, bunk-filled, pseudo-literature, and we loathe equally the conditions responsible and the men who teach that sort of writing.[2]

Professional Football

The four novels about professional football are not the traditional "Win-for-old-Siwash" or "star-quarterback-scores-winning-touchdown-in-last-second" type. Noel Bertram Gerson's *The Sunday Heroes* (1972) passes up the playing field for the behind-the-scenes management activities. William Campbell Gault's *Wild Willie, Wide Receiver* (1974) focusses on the conflict between a team owner and the coach over the talents of a black player the owner has hired over the coach's objection. Jack Jones' *The Animal* (1975) is about a man who lacks the killer instinct to be a good pro player, and the talent to become a good artist. Part of this novel is set in the Watts area of Los Angeles.

The best of this lot is Bernard Brunner's *Six Days to Sunday* (1975), a best selling account of the last playing days of a former star quarterback, and of the consequences of his struggle to hold his position against a younger man. The novel, said a critic, "is an engrossing novel of pro football, as tough and as brutal as the game and the men who play it."[3]

Nelson Algren

In the academic year of 1965-1966, Nelson Algren went to Iowa City to teach in the Writers' Workshop there. He did not get along well with other writers there, telling one "If I wrote like you, I'd cut my throat." He is best remembered at Iowa, however, because "he was the most terrible poker player" others had ever seen. He lost several thousand dollars that he had planned to use to take his wife on a honeymoon trip to Europe; she divorced him shortly after.[4]

* It was a reportorial staff half daft with literary dreams," said Ben Hecht.

In the 1970s he produced only one book, and this one, *The Last Carousel* (1973) was an anthology of previous work — poems, essays and short stories. Fourteen of the pieces are set in Illinois.

At the end of his life he had finished *The Devil's Stocking,* a book based on the life of black boxer Rubin "Hurricane" Carter. The book was being published in Germany.

Algren was to be inducted on May 20, 1981 as a fellow of The American Academy-Institute of Arts and Letters, but he died just ten days before on Saturday, May 9.

Kurt Vonnegut said of Algren that his short stories were "often as good as Chekhov's."[5] Ernest Hemingway had once said that Algren was the next best writer of his day after William Faulkner. "Algren can hit with both hands and move around, and he will kill you if you're not awfully careful."[6]

The writers liked him, but the "smug and the righteous did not." Nor did he always love Chicago. "Chicago's a bustout whore," he said once:

Nor all your piety nor all your preaching, nor all your crusades nor all your threats can stop one girl from going on the turf, can stop one mugging, can keep one promising youth from becoming a drug addict, so long as the force that drives the owners of our civilization is away from those who own nothing at all."[7]

Algren died in Sag Harbor, New York, a long ways from the city he both despised and loved. "They buried Nelson Algren very fast," said Pete Hamill. "And I looked down into the open grave, where fresh dogwood blossoms lay on the coffin, and I wished there had been enough time to take him home to Chicago."

In Chicago, Hamill added, "they should have closed the schools and lowered the flags to half-mast, and had one of those old-time gangster funerals [and] Studs Terkel and Mike Royko should have helped carry the coffin, and later they should have read one of his favorite poems ... by Francois Villon:

In my own country I am in a far-off land...
I win all, yet remain a loser...[8]

The 1968 Democratic Convention and the Streets of Chicago

Four novels and a play of the 1970s look back (in anger as often as not) at what have to be the blackest days in Chicago's history since the Haymarket Affair. (The two events are similar in many respects and it can be argued that the second Affair would never have happened had it not been for the paranoia inherited from the first.)

The dramatic experience was provided by *Chicago 70,* a "topical play" (1970), based on the Chicago trial of Bobby Seale, Mark Lane, Allen Ginsberg, Country Joe [McDonald], Linda Morse, Arlo Guthrie and Abbie Hoffman. Produced in New York City by the Toronto Workshop Company, and in a one-night performance in London by a cast featuring author William Burroughs as Judge Hoffman, the play was praised by critics, although, as one emphasized, "the so-called 'Chicago Conspiracy' was the purest form of theater rather than politics [, s]tarring Julius Hoffman, the well-known judge from Chicago, and Abbie Hoffman, the well-known Yippie from Woodstock Nation."[9]

John William Corrington's *The Bombardier* (1970) began with five men — a Jew, a Black, a Pole, a southern aristocrat, and a New York musician — who became friends in a United States Army Air Force bombardier training school, and who, a third of a century after the end of their World War II combat experiences, came together again, with their former Air Force commanding officer, at the 1968 National Democratic Convention. Each reports his reaction to the conflict in the streets of Chicago in his own way in this bitter book.

Ed Sanders *Shards of God* (1970) focusses on the Yippie Movement in 1967 and 1968, culminating with the demonstrations in Chicago. Jerry Rubin, Abbie Hoffman, Keith Lampe and Alan Ginsberg are seen in their own roles; others in the motley cast are Oral Annie, Madame Bun Doctor, and She-Who-Sucks-in-a-Skirt-of-Snakes.

Al[bert Edward] Morgan's *The Whole World is Watching* (1972) "makes the riots during the 1968 Democratic National Convention even more vivid than they were on the television news reports," says a critic.[10] Morgan, as producer of television's popular *Today* show, had had the equivalent of a front row seat at the demonstrations, as had his staff. This best selling novel features the effects of the demonstrations and the consequent police brutality on a fictional television producer and his staff.

James Sherburne's *Rivers Run Together* (1974) singles out several unknowns who did not participate in the demonstrations or the Convention but whose lives were altered by the events of Convention week. They were simply people attracted to the convention area as spectators and who found themselves unwilling participants in the subsequent activities. This novel was also a best seller.

Chicago Blacks
Ronald L. Fair continued writing about Chicago blacks in this decade. *World of Nothing* (1970) includes two novellas, "Jerome," a narrative of a "Black Jesus" with overtones of voodooism and witchcraft, and "World of Nothing," a narrative about "Nothing," one of Chicago's neighborhoods:

> This city is being divided up into little neighborhoods the way it is, it's interesting to see people of like customs getting on at the same stop. And even

more interesting to see the people from the different neighborhoods look down their noses at them. It's a strange city: the Irish hate the Poles; the Poles hate the Italians; the Italians hate the Germans; the German hate the Puerto Ricans; the Puerto Ricans hate the Spaniards; the Spaniards hate the Jews and they all join together to hate the blacks. It's a god-fearing city.

The elevated streaks along the city of hate — through the fat dirty melting pot that never seems to jell; through the unassimilated groups of monsters clawing their way to the top of the pot; through the millions of people who conform to a pattern of life because it's too difficult to think, it's too costly to be oneself; through millions of sheep following the lead sheep over the side of a cliff![11]

Fair's *We Can't Breathe* (1972) "is a novel of what it was like for us [the blacks] to be born in the thirties ... born in the place [our parents] had escaped to — Chicago."[12]

Ernie, the narrator, tells about his gang — Good Ole Sam, Willie, George Washington Benjamin Brown — who come together when Ernie first moves into a South Side neighborhood at ten. At first life is fun — in a year or two there are girls, then all kinds of games, the Lake in summer or winter, stealing from the dime stores. Then life becomes violent — blacks fight whites and other blacks. Always there is the growing anger against the white man's world; the police are enemies.

With the aid of a teacher, Ernie resolves to become a writer. Willie and George become "junkies," and George is shot to death by the police. Willie disappears. Sam dies in World War II. With the coming of the War, blacks find jobs in defense plants — they no longer need to be on welfare where the whites want them.

Fair's *Excerpts* (1975, Volume 26 in the Heritage Series published by Paul Breman, London) is a collection of seventeen poems about the black experience. One is "Ruby:"

a child up from 'sip
with child husband, her man
   ain't nevah goin' back to 'sip

job at the yards
plenty of meat
   chicago's a good place to eat
   ain't nevah goin' back to 'sip...

But Ruby's children bring her disgrace and death;

ruby ran for help, from
even the police
but her heart just quit
on the chicago street...[13]

Bernard Brunner's next novel, *The Golden Children* (1970) is a story of inter-racial marriage in a previously all-white suburb of Chicago. Clare Simmons, whose father is a minister in the suburb marries Marcus Coleman, a Negro boys' club worker, and is subsequently rejected by both her father and her white friends.

David Quammen's *To Walk the Line* (1970) is a novel set "in the heart of Knox," the center of the black ghetto during the years of protest in the 1960s. John Scully, white, comes there to join Dan, a Jesuit seminarian; Kooch; Frank Rapp, and Sr. Margaret, SND (who calls herself Meg Pedretti). These whites have formed an "Operation" to harass Chicago real estate dealers. A frequent visitor is Tyrone Williams, a black schoolboy, head of a Chicago gang, who, while appearing friendly, intends to "burn" all whites including the members of the Operation. A rival black gang occasionally harasses the white members of the Operation. Then the two black gangs get together to plan an elaborate scheme to burn "whitey," but Tyrone goes "square" and does not take part.

The novel is notable for its black "hip" speech.

Cyrus Coulter, a black Chicago lawyer, turned to writing short fiction in the late 1960s, and succeeded in winning the 1970 Iowa School of Letters Award for his first book-length collection of his stories. *The Beach Umbrella's* fourteen stories focus on the Chicago middle-class affluent black rather than the ghetto dweller who is the central figure in the other books discussed here.

Coulter then turned to the novel and produced *The Rivers of Eros* (1972), a story of Eugene and Clotilda Pilgrim who came to Chicago in 1935 when he was forty-two and she was thirty-five. He soon found a fatiguing job in a laundry. Clotilda envied her sister Pearlie, her children and her pregnancy so she seduced Ches, Pearlie's husband. A daughter, Ruby, was born of this affair. Ruby subsequently had two children, Adeline and Lester. Zack Parker, her husband, who ran a garage, became unfairly jealous of Ruby and murdered her. Clotilda took over the raising of the children, supporting them by operating a rooming house. When grown-up Adeline began to associate with a married man, Clotilda, guilt-ridden, murdered her. The novel seems to have more of its origins in Coulter's reading of Greek mythology than it has in black relationships.

Leon Forrest's *There Is a Tree More Ancient Than Eden* (1973) is, says a critic, "more image than plot."[14] Its central focus is on a young black living on Chicago's South Side and formulating "a kind of philosophy for his own life and redemption."

Charles [Richard] Johnson's *Faith and the Good Thing* (1974) begins and ends in Georgia. But its center is set in Chicago where Faith Cross, following the advice of her dying mother and a Hatten County, Georgia "Swamp

Woman," has gone searching for "the good thing," not knowing what she is looking for. In Chicago, Faith endures "poverty, rape, prostitution, love, marriage, childbirth, desertion, hate and misery" without finding what she is looking for. This novel, says a critic, "is a rare enigma in modern fiction, for it combines the idealism of a metaphysical quest, the stark realities of modern day Chicago, the ethereal forces of southern backwoods superstition and magic, and the quality of superior intellectualism in a somewhat less-than-perfect, but very distinguished first novel by a young black author."[15]

James and Geneva Allen's *God Bless This Child* (1975) follows step by step a thirteen year old black youth on Chicago's South Side as he becomes a heroin addict and dies of a drug overdose at twenty-one. This poorly-written book was published by a subsidy press and not reviewed.

The protagonist of Joseph L. Haas's *Vendetta* (1975) is white, formerly a member of a guerrilla group in South Africa which was murdering members of the Mau Mau. He becomes a newspaper reporter in Chicago, then discovers that he is next on a "hit list," marked for execution. In the novel's gory climax, he and a black man, both bent on vengeance seek each other out in the midst of racial strife and a hot Chicago summer.[16]

Harvey Hanson's *Game Time* (1975) looks back to 1957 and a black boy who is an outstanding student in school. But Skip Howard's speech on "Why I'm Proud to be an American" is censored by his teacher, and he remembers that he once threw a strawberry milkshake in a white boy's face because the latter called him "nigger." But he also has problems with members of his own race because he is "sarcastic, sassy and rude."[17]

Robert Beck, who used the pseudonym of "Iceberg Slim," is probably the only "pimp" (procurer) ever to become a published author. He is the author of *Pimp, the Story of My Life* (1970), *Mama Black Widow* (1969), and *The Naked Soul of Iceberg Slim* (1972), all of which detail the world of a Black Chicago pimp of the pre-1970 period, and "Brother Slim's self-cure from pimphood."

A 1975 film was *Cooley High,* the adventures of a group of black Chicago high school buddies in 1964. The setting was the fictitious Edwin G. Cooley Vocational High School. Critics noticed the resemblance to *American Graffiti* and *The Lords of Flatbush* with one significant difference. Where *Graffiti* ended with a boy going off to college, and *Flatbush* ended with an enforced wedding, *Cooley High* concluded with a death, thus, said Dan Rottenberg, "symbolizing perhaps the main difference between black and white adolescence."

Crime and — Sometimes — Punishment

Terrence Lore Smith was the author of two mystery novels set in Chicago. Under his own name, he tells in *The Thief Who Came to Dinner* (1971) of a rising young Chicago executive who quit his job and then began on a dual career, pulling off daring jewel robberies in the Lake Forest, Winnetka-Kenilworth area, and at the same time becoming a member of the same social set he was stealing from.

Disguised as Phillips Lore, Smith next wrote *Who Killed the Pie Man?* (1975). The story line begins with the murder of a Northwestern University professor and a wealthy coed, and an attorney takes it from there.

The next two novels of Chicago crime both have an historical basis. John Cashman's *The Gentleman From Chicago; Being an Account of the Doings of Thomas Neill Cream, M.D. (M'Gill), 1850-1892* (1973) is about a psychopathic killer who poisoned women in Toronto, Chicago and London, where he was finally caught and executed. Cashman said the novel, based on research in Chicago and England was 80 percent fictitious. The novel was a best seller.[18]

William Rayner's *Seth & Bell & Mr. Quarles and Me* (1972), subtitled "The Bloody Affair at Lakeside Drive," is a parody of an old Hollywood cliche — the reluctant gunfighter. The story is set in Chicago and the far west in the late 1800s.

For *American Gothic* (1974) Robert Bloch returned to approximately the same period in Chicago history, but his novel of the years when the Columbian Exposition was being planned and built, and then opened to the public, depicts a world that is a far remove from the world of Clara Burnham's *Sweet Clover* or Robert Lawson's *The Big Wheel*. Bloch's protagonist is "Dr." G. Gordon Gregg who began life with another name, and is, as Bloch says in his postscript, closely modeled on "Dr." Herman W. Mudgett, notorious Chicago mass murderer, who, like his fictional counterpart, built a "castle" near the Exposition grounds and proceeded to entice no one knows how many male and female victims into the building — where most of them disappeared from view for all time. This "novel of mystery and suspense" concludes with the Fair, the castle burning to the ground as the Fair expires in a blaze of fireworks. The other central figure in the novel is a girl reporter for a Chicago newspaper who is ultimately the cause of Gregg's undoing, although (and this should come as no surprise) she almost loses her own life in the process — and inside the castle.

Mark Smith's *The Death of the Detective* (1974) is set in Chicago during the Korean War years. Its 596 pages are packed with "crowded inventiveness," "shouldering complications" and "looping exfoliations of plot."[19] Magnuson, the detective follows a mass-murderer, Helenowski, into every corner of Chicago trying to catch him — Bughouse Square, Chicago gangsterdom, a Chicago North Side mansion, the black ghetto, the Polish West Side. Ironically, Magnuson thinks Helenowski was the murderer's first victim. Eventually, Helenowski, having murdered a dozen victims, drowns himself in Lake Michigan. Magnuson dies of a massive coronary attack while fishing in Lake

Michigan.

If any novel of the 1970s may be said to be a "Chicago novel," this is it.

Mark Smith, was a native of Michigan but a graduate of Northwestern — where his fascination with Chicago began. Earlier he had written two relatively unnoticed novels — *Toyland* (1965) and *The Middleman* (1967), and had received both a Guggenheim Fellowship and a Rockefeller Grant for Writing. At the time the novel was published he was an associate professor of English at the University of New Hampshire where he lived with his wife and four daughters.

William Brashler's *City Dogs* (1976) returns us to Motley and Algren's world of winos, bums, hookers, punks, thieves, punks, hillbillies, derelicts, con-men, fences and the poor. The novel's protagonist is Harry Lum, a 57-year-old Polish derelict, welfare recipient, Cub fan, and wino who plans a heist with two young hoods. The plan misfires, Harry is nabbed by the police, and then released but only after he has identified his accomplices. The consequence is that he becomes the object of a deadly manhunt.

Even the *New Yorker* liked this one.

J. Bradford Olesker's *No Place Like Home* (1976) pitted the staff of the Chicago Police Homicide Division against a sports hero who had become a psychopathic killer, roaming the halls of a North Shore high rise building.

At least a half a dozen other mystery novels used Chicago as a setting in this decade. See the list in the Appendix.

The Medical Scene

Frances Rickett's *An Affair of Doctors* (1975) manages to achieve in only three hundred pages what Arthur Hailey would have taken another hundred or so pages to accomplish — a report of all the professional and personal complications that might ensue when a Chicago university hospital and a suburban hospital plan a one-year experimental affiliation. As any student of the popularity of television soap operas would guess, this book hit the best seller list.

Dr. Geoffrey S. Simmons' set his *The Z-Papers* (1976) in Chicago's Presbyterian-St. Luke's Hospital. A government official who hopes to become the next Vice-President becomes a hostage for the delivery of an antidote to save him from supposed poisoning in exchange for the freedom of six life-term convicts.

John R. Powers and Chicago Catholics

Although John R. Powers graduated in the bottom twentieth of his South Side Chicago parochial school class, and was the only student in the school's history to flunk music appreciation, he managed in the next dozen years to earn a Ph.D. from Northwestern University, to become a professor of speech at Northeastern Illinois University, to publish four books and to convert the material in his books into a Broadway musical comedy.

In *The Last Catholic in America,* Power's *personna,* Eddie Ryan, reminisces about his first eight years at St. Bastion's School, a South Side Catholic boy's school in the "Seven Holy Tombs" neighborhood, so-called because it is surrounded by seven cemeteries. Eddie tosses his slings and arrows at everyone in the school:

> Many people think of a nun as a shy, petite little thing with a sunshine face pushing out of a habit, playing opposite Bing Crosy in a 1940s movie. In fact, nuns are generally sullen, suspicious cynics with a strong streak of savagery. They aren't at all human. At least not any of the nuns I knew at St. Bastion School.
>
> The St. Bastion nuns couldn't have been human. In my eight years of grammar school, I never saw a nun take a drink of water, go into a washroom except maybe to chase after some kid but never for her own satisfaction, or eat something. As far as I could tell, the nuns were totally devoid of biological functions.
>
> The nuns at St. Bastion school had one goal in life: to get out of it and into Heaven. When they first became nuns, they took three vows that were designed to accomplish this goal: the vows of Poverty, Chastity, and Obedience.[20]

In *Do Black Patent Leather Shoes Really Reflect Up?* (1975), Powers returned to Eddie Ryan in a new crime scene — a Catholic high school. The title of this first person narrative of misadventures on the parochial secondary school scene reflects the nuns' warnings to girls not to wear black patent leather shoes because the shoes served as mirrors in which voyeuristic Catholic boys might observe the colors of the girls' undergarments.

In some ways, Powers' humor recalls the less urbane drolleries of an earlier Chicago humorist who once wrote: "Well, I don't know how it is now but in those days practically all the teachers in high school was members of the fair sex. Some of them was charter members." Literary critics of the future can argue over which was the funnier — Ring Lardner or John F. Powers.

Powers' fourth book, *The Unoriginal Sinner and the Ice Cream God* (1977), focusses on the college training of a Chicago South Side Catholic in a near North Side College. It doesn't seem as much a *roman á clef* as the novels of public school life and its humor is more sardonic.

Tim Conroy, the college student-narrator of this book, is a grownup Eddie Ryan who sandwiches four love affairs between slices of education and finds more guidance in Caepan, a filling-station owner, than he does in his teachers. Caepan is the "God" of the novel's title, and he and Conroy constantly exchange notes:

Dear God:
   I didn't go to mass last Sunday morning.

Signed: Conroy

Conroy:
   Don't worry about it. It was a nice day. I don't know who built the church but I made the sunshine.

Signed: God

Powers's three novels have all been reprinted in paperback editions and remain in the book stores. In addition, Powers wrote a musical comedy version of *Do Black Patent Leather Shoes Really Reflect Up?*. It began an extended run in Chicago's Forum Theater in 1979, and in 1980 moved on to Broadway.

So far, Powers' needling of American institutions — the Catholic Church and its schools, college education, and even the Cub Scouts of America — has not led to excommunication, expulsion, or other form of retribution. Higher education has made him a part of the institution. *The Catholic Sentinel* has praised him, saying that "John Powers does for Catholics what Erma Bombeck does for housewives."[22] And *Scouting,* the official organ of the Boy Scouts of America, spread his essay "Some Great Moments in Sloppy Scouting" over its centerfold.

A Final Miscellany

Joyce Carol Oates is not a Chicago writer, but she set a part of her *Wonderland* (1971) in Chicago. It tells of the development of a boy whose father has murdered his mother, sisters and brother, a fate the boy narrowly escaped. In adulthood, the boy becomes a neurosurgeon who is determined to preserve the lives of those who seek his help.

In 1966, Charles [Hamilton] Newman had published a series of short stories in novel form, *New Axis; or the "Little Ed" Stories, An Exhibition.* Little Ed D is a member of a suburban Chicago family; the book is "auto-biographical in tone [and] spans a generation ... The stories deal with a variety of topics ranging from an uneventful free day at home for Mrs. D to a highly charged conversation between Little Ed and a former girl friend, concerning an occasion during their adolescence when they had slept together."[23]

Newman's next book had a title almost as long as some of the "Little Ed" stories: *The Promise Keeper, A Tephramancy ... Divers Narratives on the Economics of Current Morals in Lieu of a Psychology, Here Embodied in an Approved Text Often Working in Spite of Itself, Certain Profane Stoical Paradoxes Explained, Literary Amusements Liberally Interspersed, Partitioned with Documents & Conditioned by Imagoes, Hearty Family-Type Fare, Modern Decor, Free Parking* (1971).

If you managed your way through that semantic jungle, you will probably be interested in knowing that this "acidly satirical novel" is about a "promising young" Chicago broker trying "to make sense out of a senseless world." A critic says that the book improves past the half-way point, but it's "non-family type fare."[24]

Adam Kennedy's *The Scaffold* (1971) has, at least, the merits of a title a reader can remember, and flashbacks set in Chicago, Mexico City, New York and other points north, east, west and south. Floyd Lucas, the adventure story's chief adventurer is involved in two marriages, numberless affairs which produce two illegitimate children, two divorces and two suicides — none of which turns Floyd on.

Peter DeVries produced two of his typical humorous books in this decade. *Into Your Tent I'll Creep* (1971, is the story of the courtship and subsequent marriage (on her terms) of Al Banghart, a philanderer and Miss Piano, a French teacher in a Chicago high school. DeVries has fun with marriage, organized religion, women's liberation, rock and roll and traditional education. In *The Glory of the Hummingbird* (1974) DeVries tells of a Wabash, Indiana boy who leaves home for greater opportunities in Chicago. Jim Tickler dabbles in marriage, business, politics and television but the book's greater interest is in the fun DeVries has with language.

Walter Schwimmer's *It Happened on Rush Street* (1971) has two parts; a collection of short stories and a short section labeled "The Rush Street Philosopher." The setting is the mile-long street which parallels Michigan Avenue from the River to the Water Tower and then angles northwestward to its junction with State Street near the Newberry Library. The time is the thirty-year span from before World War I to the date of publication.

Richard Peck's *Don't Look and It Won't Hurt* (1972) is set in "Claypits" in central Illinois and in Chicago, and tells of the middle daughter in a family of three girls who always seems to catch it from both sides, particularly when her elder sister goes to a home for unwed mothers.

In 1928, McKinlay Kantor, then new in Chicago, had written one of the first, if not the first, Chicago gangster novel, *Diversey*. In 1972, five years before his death, and at the age when most authors get involved in remembrances of things past, he wrote *I Love You, Irene,* a somewhat fictionalized autobiography, telling of those early years when he and his wife came to Chicago to further Kantor's writing career. In the meantime, most of Kantor's books had been set in either Iowa, his native state, or the Civil War, including the Pulitzer-prize winning *Andersonville* (1955).

Fred [Steven] Howard's *Charlie Flowers & the Melody Gardens* (1972) is a fictional biography of a young man's life between World Wars I and II. Flowers becomes a vaudeville performer as a child but after that bad luck sets in, through the Depression years when he has to live with an unsympathetic mother, and through a marriage which ends in divorce and the death of an infant son. The novel ends with Charlie's enlistment in the war effort.

Steve Allen's *The Wake* (1972) is also a look backward, this time at an Irish first- and second-generation family in the Depression. The glances backward in time are triggered by the death of the Irish grandmother.

Stanley Elkin's *Searches and Seizures* (1973) contains three novellas written in the "black comedy" vein. Only the third, "The Condominium," a story about a 37-year-old male virgin trying to make it in a Chicago Jewish housing complex, is set in the Windy City.

When we think of F. Scott Fitzgerald outside the East and New York City, we generally think of St. Paul, Minnesota. But five of his so-called "Josephine" short stories, about a girl named Josephine Perry, are set in Chicago and deal with the problems of an adolescent girl. These were collected in *The Basil and Josephine Stories* in 1973 by John Kuehl and Jackson R. Bryer.

Susan Fromberg Schaeffer's *Falling* (1973) tells of a thirty-year-old Jewish female graduate student at the University of Chicago who tries to kill herself, and then undergoes psychoanalysis which leads to a happy ending.

In 1970, Tillie Olsen dug into her trunk of unfinished work and assembled scraps and fragments of a novel she had tried to write in the 1930s. *Yonnondio From the Thirties, A Fragment of a Novel,* (1974), is the result. The novel begins in Wyoming in the 1920s and moves from there to the slums of Chicago close to and actually on a city dump. The narrative depicts, in a naturalistic style, the terrible degradation, because of Depression-influenced poverty, of the Anna Holbrook family. The dreary book is obviously a leftover from the long-deceased proletariat tradition of the 1930s. As a 1970s book, it was in many ways an anachronism, until one compared the life of the Holbrook family with the lives of black families on Chicago's South Side.

Adam Kennedy's next novel, *Somebody Else's Wife* (1974) relates the consequences of a Chicago businessman's decision to hire an unemployed mentally unstable ex-newspaperman to write a corporation's history. Chet Rector becomes emotionally involved with Helen Bostwick, the corporation executive's wife and the two run off to the Virgin Islands. There they explore each other's past and Chet learns that his paramour has been a kept woman, has gone through several marriages and has stolen $200,000. The novel was another best seller.

Ned Calmer's *Late Show,* written in 1974 when Calmer, a former CBS-TV anchorman was sixty-seven and retired, is a somewhat vindictive fictional biography of a man who succeeds first as a disc jockey for a Chicago radio station, then goes on to greater success as the host of television's most popular late night talk show. But his personal life is less successful.

Iowan Curt Johnson, whose 1959 novel *Hobbledehoy's Hero* had been banned in his home town, and who was also associated with *December,* a literary magazine begun in Iowa and moved to Chicago, authored *Nobody's Perfect* (1974). The novel presents a cynical view of the literary establishment in America and of the country's publishing industry, well in keeping with the iconoclastic bohemianism of its author.

Bruce Dobler's *Icepick: A* Novel About Life and Death in a Maximum Security Prison (1974) is a long documentary novel set entirely within the confines of the Illinois State Penitentiary in Chicago.

Vincent Canby's *Living Quarters* (1975) is about a woman who is charming, beautiful and psychotic, who gets into trouble in Los Angeles, in New York and elsewhere, and who finds a stabilizing influence and occasional lover in a man from Lake Forest. All of which seems to demonstrate that the northern Chicago suburb has something more going for it than just a lovely location on the Lake shore and a great many attractive mansions.

Jerrold [J] Mundis's *Gerhardt's Children* (1976) is the latest in the long series of Chicago generation novels, this one covering five generations which began with a German-Catholic matriarch. The narrative technique is much more complex in this novel than in the novels of the 1920s and 1930s, representing the influence of more sophisticated storytelling methods and, perhaps, the influence of television with its cutting back and forth from narrative to commercials.

Donald Lloyd More's 1976 *Zipline, River Park* is perhaps more interesting as a series of anecdotal recollections of the experiences of a mail carrier in River Forest, Illinois than it is as a work of fiction. The great fictional work about a mail carrier in the Chicago area, beset by mad dogs and Englishmen who never get a letter from bloody old London, remains to be written.

It had to come — a book titled *Chicago* — even though, when it arrived at last in 1976, it was only in Pocket Book format. But Charles Carroll's novel, featuring a thinly-disguised Mayor Daley and Illinois Secretary of State Paul Powell makes up for its-less-than-formidable package by showing the reader graft, double-dealing, bribery, blackmail, murder, newspaper exposure, and income tax invasion, all revolving around the office of the mayor.

Although Bette Howland's *Blue in Chicago* (1978) was labeled by one critic as an anthology of six short-stories of Chicago working class Jewish people, it is a non-fictional autobiography of life in Chicago. It drew flattering reviews from both the *New York Times Review of Books* and the *Nation;* these two reviewers were not confused about the book's subject matter.

Sam Ross returned to Chicago in the 1970s with his *Windy City* (1979), a novel somewhat resembling Bellow's *Augie March*. Ross's Jake Davidson is a swimming star in college in the 1930s and subsequently "bulls his way through life with his native Chicago as his bullring."

He falls in as easily among gangsters as among Communist girls free with their favors; rich Jewish bankers put him through Northwestern and provide him access to gin mills, posh cathouses and Capone-run gambling dens.[25]

Out of college Davidson aspires to be a writer; after a stint on the *Daily Worker*, he joins the Chicago WPA Writers' Project. Later he writes radio dramas, marries and serves in the Navy during World War II. Out of the service, he finally publishes a novel.

The novel is autobiographical and has no obvious organization.

Ross had earlier written *The Fortune Machine* (1970) and *Solomon's Palace* (1973), neither with Chicago settings.

Ordinary People

Judith Guest's uncle by marriage was Eddie Guest, one of the most popular poets who ever lived, because, he said, he attempted to "find in poetry, for the great mass of readers ..., the mirror of themselves."[26] In *Ordinary People* (1976), Judith Guest accomplished that goal for her first novel. For five months the book was on the New York *Times* bestseller list; critics everywhere praised it; it was a Book-of-the-Month-Club selection; it became a best selling paperback; and transliterated to the screen, it became an Academy-Award winning film (1981).

The "ordinary people" of this story are the Jarretts of the Chicago suburb of Lake Forest (where the film was made): Calvin, successful enough to afford a Lake Forest home; Beth, his wife of twenty years; Buck, the older son; Conrad, the younger.

Buck's death by drowning in Lake Michigan triggers a case of severe depression for Conrad; after an attempted suicide, he spends several months in a mental hospital undergoing psychoanalysis and shock therapy. Back home, he tries to take up his life again, but he has problems: his father is over-solicitous, his mother can't forgive him, his grandparents can't understand him, his friends won't forget. But he finds help in an able, humane psychoanalyst, and eventually he is able to challenge his old friend, Joe Lazenby, to a round of golf.

Guest relates the whole tale in the present tense.

Film Treatments of Chicago in the 1970s

The Grape Dealer's Daughter (1970) presents a Chicago photographer who is seeking a nubile woman to play "grape dealer's daughter" to his own sexagenarian Bacchus. As the flower children of that time would have said,

"It's like weird, man!"

The Golden Box (1970) follows a cross-country, East to West search for a hidden box of treasure. The cast stops off in Chicago en route.

A 1970 Canadian film, *Prologue,* deals in part with the events at the 1968 Democratic National Convention.

In *T. R. Baskin* (1970) Candice Bergen plays an attractive small-town girl, alienated from her mother, who takes up apartment life in Chicago and finds problems with a young man her own age and a somewhat older man. The film is uneven in quality but has some good Chicago settings.

Cutter (1972), a play produced for television, used location shooting in Chicago as the setting for a tale of a private detective searching for a missing professional-football quarterback. The show received low ratings.

Stanley Lawrence Elkin's 1973 film, *Searches and Seizures,* consists of three "novellas." The third one, *The Condominium,* is set in Chicago. It was based on Elkin's 1973 book.

The Sting (1973) was an Oscar-winning motion picture featuring Robert Redford. Johnny Hooker, a small-time gambler-pickpocket-con man and his partner, Luther, choose the wrong victim, and Luther is murdered by a syndicate killer. Johnny sets out to get even. In alliance with Henry Gondorff, one of Chicago's best confidence men, Johnny plans and executes a scheme which nets them a million dollars, a tidy sum for the Depression year of 1937 in which the film is set. In 1974, Bantam Books brought out a paperback version of the film's story. The film script was by David S. Ward, the book by Robert Weverka.

My Bodyguard was filmed in Chicago in 1979.

Other films set in Chicago or using Chicago footage were *Looking For Mr. Goodbar* (1977); *The Fury* (1978); *A Wedding* (1978); *Damien: Omen II* (1978); *The Blues Brothers* (1980), featuring Chicago-reared John Belushi; *Thief* (1980), featuring Jim Belushi; *Continental Divide* (1981) featuring John Belushi (a large share of this picture was filmed in the Rocky Mountains); and *Four Friends* (1981) in which Glenne Headly, a Chicago actress "dies" in a West Side car crash.

Some scenes in *Continental Divide* were shot in the *Chicago Sun-Times* news room with Belushi playing a Mike-Royko-type columnist. A jewelry store break-in in *Thief* was filmed in an alley between Michigan and Monroe and Wabash near Monroe Street. A later scene in which actor James Caan's "home" burns was filmed in Budlong Woods. For *The Blues Brothers,* Lake Shore Drive was closed off for an auto chase scene; later the car was crashed into the Daley Center. *Four Friends* was also filmed in South Chicago.

In 1981, a TV film, *The Marva Collins Story,* featured a Chicago school teacher who gained national fame when she abandoned the traditional school system and worked with students previously labeled "unteachable."

Chicago in 1970s Drama

Boss, a musical satire about Mayor Daley, his wife, and assorted others was "half fun, half dull" in its 1973 opening at the Forum Theater, Summit. It was based on Chicagoan Mike Royko's *Boss* (1971); the book and lyrics for the musical version were by Frank Galati.

Daley was presented as "a clown spouting malaprops and mispronunciations, and tripping the light fantastic while boasting about 'the greatest city in the world,'" but he did not appear during scenes of "ghetto riots and policemen whacking hippies over their long-haired heads."[27]

In the summer of 1976, a daily installment of a light-hearted fictional serial, "Bagtime," began appearing in the Chicago *Sun-Times,* written by Bob Greene and Paul Galloway. The hero was Mike Holiday; the story line was set on Chicago's Near Northside. Holiday and his singles lifestyle were enriched by comical companions, his job as a supermarket bagboy and fictional encounters with real life celebrities.

The column later moved to the Chicago *Tribune;* in 1978, it was collected in a paperback, *Bagtime.* The following year, a musical play, *Bagtime* with book by Alan Rosen, a former University of Illinois student, achieved some success.

A year earlier, the Dinglefest Theater Company, which got its start at Northern Illinois University at DeKalb, produced a musical comedy, *Streeter* at its theater on West Belmont Avenue. The musical looked back at Chicago's colorful George Wellington "Cap" Streeter who, beginning in 1886, when he ran his boat aground off what later became the Gold Coast, fought continuing attempts to evict him from "Streeterville" in the "Deestrict of Lake Michigan." Streeter held off until 1918, a far longer run than the play's "kornpone kulture" was able to manage. Robert Fiddler was the script author.

In the spring of 1978, the Organic Theater of Chicago performed a new musical play, *Bleacher Bums* at the Performing Garage. The setting was Wrigley Field, the Chicago Cubs were playing the St. Louis Cardinals, and the audience saw the action through the "eyes," words and antics of eight frenetic fans, one of whom kept massaging her oversized bosom throughout the game, and another of whom, though blind, kept describing the play-by-action — he was picking up the details through an earphone attached to a small radio. The play was as long as a double-header, said the *New York Times* reviewer, a double stretched into a triple with unhappy consequences.

In January of 1979, John Dillinger, the Depression bandit, who had died in a shootout in the foyer of the Biograph Theater on Chicago's North Side on July 22, 1934, was resurrected once more — this time in *Dillinger,* a play acted at the Chicago Victory Gardens Theater. In the play, written by William L.

Norris, the spirit of Dillinger (which has been haunting the Feds for twenty-six years) shows up to torment Dillinger's killer, FBI Agent Melvin Purvis, once more. *Chicago Tribune* critic Linda Winer said that although the production was "solid" and "imaginative," the total effect was "rough, tough, [and] empty."[28]

All around Chicago theatrical activity was continuing. In September of 1980 Second City was unveiling its sixtieth satiric review, and making a special presentation, "Live From the Second City" at the Chicago Public Library. In the early summer of 1982, its sixty-second revue, *Glenna Loved It! Or If You Knew Sushi* satirized video games, gun control, drugs, suburban families, politics and President Ronald Reagan's policies.

In 1979 and 1980 Ramino Carvillo's *Latino Chicago* offfered in dramatic form "a rousing tribute to local Hispanic culture." In October of 1980 Kathleen Thompson's *Nobody Ever Stands on the Evening Express* offered "a series of scenes about life in Chicago."

A much-longer running play, one that seemed likely to last as long as its concurrent city administration, was *Byrne, Baby, Byrne* by Kingsley Day and Ken LaZebnik. As the title suggests, it was a topical satiric review which took on City Hall and its inhabitants. Through its run the play was constantly being rewritten to keep it timely.

Shelly Goldstein's and Jerry Hasimaier's *Body Politic* (1980) focussed on four young actresses struggling to make it in Chicago.

Theater was alive and well in Chicago.

David Mamet

Meanwhile, a new major talent was making theatrical history in Chicago with occasional alarums and excursions to Broadway, the campus of Yale University, Televisionland, Hollywood and back to Waukegan, Illinois.

David Mamet, the son of a South Side Chicago lawyer, attended Chicago schools, then got a Bachelor of Arts degree at Vermont's Goddard College (1969) where he later served as artist-in-residence. In the 1970s, Mamet and some of his former Goddard students formed the St. Nicholas Theater Company, and opened a theater on North Halsted Avenue. Since then Mamet has written eight to ten plays; these have been produced in Chicago, in New York City and on the campus of Yale University where Hamet had a CBS Fellowship.

His plays included: *Squirrels* (1974); *The Duck Variations* (1972); *Sexual Perversity in Chicago* (1974); *The Poet and the Rent* (a children's play) (1975); *American Buffalo* (1975); *The Woods* (1977); *The Water Engine* (1977); *A Life in the Theater* (1977); *The Revenge of the Space Pandas, or, Binky Rudich and the Two-Speed Clock* (1977); *Reunion* and *Lone Canoe* (both 1979).

Some of these plays appeared in revised variations in New York City (both off and on Broadway) and back in Chicago.

Not all are set in Chicago; indeed a *New York Times* critic once said that Mamet was not a Chicago playwright because "his characters are not rooted anywhere in particular."[29]

His *The Duck Variations,* a one-act play, is a dialogue between two old men on a park bench facing Lake Michigan. *Sexual Perversity* focusses on a Chicago girl and boy who have had "vaguely homosexual alliances with . . . botchy and boorish friends," and who are trying but failing "to make a permanent relationship of a love affair." This was at first a one-act play, later a full length presentation.

American Buffalo shows two men planning to rob a coin collector of a valuable "buffalo nickel" collection.

Reunion (1979) shows an alcoholic father coming together again with his daughter.

The Water Engine is set in Chicago of the 1930s; it features a young man who has invented an energy-producing machine, and the attempts of representatives of big business to do away with the machine. The young inventor is murdered by the representatives.

Mamet's plays are usually short, and have in the past depended on language rather than on action. John Simon, reviewing the non-Chicago *The Woods,* says that "as usual Mamet seems to mean his play to be about language — language that under its banalities or eccentricities conceals desperate urgencies."[30] Linda Winder wrote in the *Tribune* that

> The sound is part myth, part game, and the best is great fun to hear. Mamet likes the incongruities — a strict, almost musical sense of form, juxtaposed with dirty talk, third-generation Jewish syntax, kid fantasies, and demons. The talent comes in short phrases, twisting from the poetic to the mundane, sometimes grabbing onto one of his outlandish tangents, or sailing into a whole new topic.[31]

But as this material was being written, there was evidence that Mamet thought he had done as much as he could with an emphasis on language, and that in the future he would move in other directions.

Mamet has been called "the most promising American playwright since Arthur Miller,"[32] and he has won several awards: two Jefferson awards, an "Obie" from the *Village Voice,* and the New York Drama Critics Circle Award for Best American Play of 1977 — both for *American Buffalo.*

In 1978-1979 Mamet was Playwright-in-Residence and Associate Artistic Director at the Goodman Theater. Among the plays scheduled for production that year was the first presentation of the play *Native Son* since 1941.

As the 1980s Begin

Cyrus Coulter showed his intentions of continuing writing with a vast (800 pages) novel of black and white relationships, *Night Studies* (1980). It is only partly set in Chicago.

A new talent, Stuart Dybek, produced a volume of short stories, *Childhood and Other Neighborhoods* (1980) about Chicago Slavic Catholics:

> There are eleven stories in this collection with the age-old neighborhood experiences of growing up (both street-wise and, for the emerging artist, compassionate); the conflicts of family, faith, friendship ... the loneliness, the pain, the fear of this fragile time we have all experienced, but which Dybek heightens with a clarity of image and depth of feeling we will not soon forget...
>
> In the best of these stories there is a double-edged blade of hopelessness sharpened by despair...[33]

Dybek is also a poet. His *Brass Knuckles* (1980) also offers an interpretation of Chicago life

> strong from start to finish and dense with meaning the way that poetry that moves from the real to the surreal can be. It is not only the book's title and the themes of his poems that are tough; the very method, fiercely concentrated, eliminates extras...[34]

The poetry of another contemporary, Richard Friedman, "treats urban experience more personally (*Physical Culture* 1980, for instance.)" In his first book, *Straight* (1975) he had announced that he couldn't "write about anything except" himself. Still, his "Winter Solstice" ranged from the death of Mayor Richard Daley to memories of Friedman's father. In "Chicago to Nemakagon Lake," he says that he has learned "through fear to play it cool, 'Always saving the pure nugget of life force for myself, 'cause it won't keep anyone else going.'"[35]

Other contemporary Chicago poets were: John Dickson (*Victoria Hotel,* 1980); Paul Hoover (*Letter to Einstein Beginning Dear Albert,* 1980) and Maxine Chernoff (*Utopia TV Store,* 1980).

A Lake Forest poet, Lisel Mueller, won a 1981 American Book Award for her 1980 volume *The Need to Hold Still.*

Meyer Levin

Meyer Levin died on July 9, 1981. In the last years of his life, he produced three lengthy novels. Two *The Settlers* (1972) and *The Harvest* (1978) constitute an epic treatment of the settlement of Palestine and related incidents in Jewish history in this century. All but a hundred-odd pages of these two novels are set in Palestine, in Germany or in Russia. The first hundred pages of *The Harvest* are set in Chicago in 1927; a young member of the Chaimovitch family comes to the University of Chicago. There he meets a member of the Straus family, a fictional family seen in Levin's *Compulsion.* But there is little of Chicago in this novel. Mati Chaimovitch's main interests are a little theater group near the campus and romancing two girls, one of whom he eventually marries.

Six months after his death, Levin's final novel, *The Architect,* appeared. This "nonfiction novel" — a label Levin attached to *Compulsion* — focusses on the life and work of Frank Lloyd Wright, the one-time Chicago architect, called Andrew Lane in the book. The book, however, ends in 1914 — a date by which Wright had already achieved a reputation as one of the great architects of his time.

The Architect, says a critic, offers a "who's who of Chicago" during its time period, with numerous "cameo appearances" — Darrow, Louis Sullivan, Jane Addams, Theodore Dreiser, Ernest Hemingway. But, adds the critic, although this technique worked in Doctorow's *Ragtime,* it fails in Levin's book because the "period pastiche follows weakly in the wake of the movements" of the central character.

Although *The Architect* "is a good story and classical in its scope," it's much too long with too "little humor and lightness; Levin's touch is heavy and direct." Moreover, "stylistically it is weak. Levin loved words, but perhaps he should have feared them."

The Architect was Levin's twenty-seventh book. He had produced "film scripts, plays, collections of Hassidic tales and Jewish-American literature, two autobiographies, and sixteen novels." For most of his life he had been "a working journalist and an activist who was involved in every major issue of his time."[36]

Looking to the Future

In the early 1970s, two Chicago futuristic novels appeared — the first since the turn of the century. Allan W. Eckert, whose *Wild Season* (1967) and *The Dreaming Tree* (1968) had been set in the Lakes region northwest of Chicago, set his *The HAB Theory* (1976) in New York, Washington, Kenya, and Chicago in the last decade of the twentieth century. A "celebrated Skokie author, John Grant" and the President of the United States set out to determine the validity of a theory that most of the Earth's surface will soon be devastated, and to make preparations for any catastrophe that would ensue. Both Grant and the president are also faced with personal problems.

Wilson Tucker, the author of seven mystery novels set in Illinois, used Chicago and Joliet as the settings for *The Year of the Quiet Sun* (1970), a story in which an author and scholar is transported into the year 2000 along with two other members of a research team.

Epilogue — The Norwegian Emigrant Novel in Chicago

Professor Gerald Thorson in 1977 described novels written in Norwegian and set in Chicago. The first of these were *Fram!* ("Forward!") (1882) by Ole Buslett, a Wisconsin author, and *Husmandsgutten* ("The Cotter's Boy") by Hans Anderson Foss, which appeared in serial form in the Iowa *Decorah-posten* begining in 1884. The heroes of both novels come to Chicago from Wisconsin. Buslett's hero, Eivind Fjeld, loses his money to an absconding banker; Foss's hero, Ole Haugen, acquires a fortune by becoming a leading Chicago merchant. In the end both heroes return to Norway.

Although Chicago at the time had the largest concentration of Norwegians in the United States, most of whom had settled in the Wicker Park area and later in the Humboldt Park and Logan Square areas, these books give little indication of life in Chicago nor of the Norwegian community.

Kristofer Janson's *Sara* (1891) is both a romance and a social criticism. In the novel we follow a young Norwegian-American girl from Wisconsin to Chicago, then to Rome, and then back to Chicago, where, successfully married to a wealthy American, she lives in a lakeshore mansion. Along the way, Sara works in a Chicago garment factory, an activity which gives the author an opportunity to criticize the capitalist class.

Alan Saetre's *Farmerkonen Marit Kjølseth's erfaringer i Chicago* ("Farmer Wife Marit Kjølseth's Adventures in Chicago", 1896) also follows its heroine from Wisconsin to Chicago in a somewhat farcical tale. This immensely popular book (24 editions) does not, however, offer much of a picture of life in Chicago. Its success led Gudmund Hagen, editor of *Vesterheimen* ("The Western Home") to publish *Per Kjølseth, eller Manden til Marit* ("Per Kjølseth, or the Husband of Marit", 1903). Most of this novel is set in North Dakota, Washington, D.C. and New York. During a stopover in Chicago, Per is accused of being an anarchist because of his posession of an odorous cheese.

Gulbrand Sether's *Bernt Myrstua* (1920), an autobiographical novel, is set partly in Chicago. When Bernt, the would-be writer, finds Chicago too clamorous for his work, he leaves for Wisconsin.

J. N. Kildahl's *Naar Jesus kommer ind i huset* (1906) is the first to make explicit use of the Norwegian community in Chicago. Kildahl, president of St. Olaf College, had been a pastor in Chicago in the 1890's. But his book (in translation, "When Jesus Enters the Home") is more of a tract than a novel.

Paul O. Stensland og hans hjaelpere eller Milliontyvene i Chicago ("Paul O. Stensland and his Associates, or the Millionaire Thieves in Chicago", 1907), is a fictional version of the misadventures and disappearance (with his bank's money) of a prominent Chicago Norwegian, president of a bank, a member of the Board of Directors of the 1893 Columbian Exposition, and a close friend of Mayor Carter Harrison.

George Taylor Rygh, successor to Kildahl in the Bethlehem Lutheran Church in Chicago, was the author of *Morgenrødens Vinger* ("The Wings of Dawn," 1909), a novel about a Chicago cabinet maker whose first factory is destroyed in the Fire.

Peer Strømme's *Den vonde volde* ("In the Clutches of the Devil," 1910) is the first of the Chicago novels to convey the immigrant experience without excessive didacticism. The novel was first published serially in *Eidsvold,* a literary magazine in Grand Forks, North Dakota. Strømme had been editor of the Chicago *Norden* from 1888 until into the new century. His account of Norwegian bohemians in Chicago owes much to several European Norwegian novels, according to Thorson.[37]

Coda

And so, after one hundred and fifty years of Chicago history and some twelve hundred titles, we come to a stage in the literary history of Chicago.

It is a stage in more ways than one. Just three years ago, the Chicago *Daily News,* indirectly and directly the "seed" of a great many Chicago titles, ceased to publish. All of the "old guard" are gone — in the last year two of the last — Algren and Farrell — have died, and on the day these words are being written, word comes that Meyer Levin is dead in Israel.

But as Algren and Albert Halper said, writing will go on in Chicago. Although Bellow seems to be writing his memoirs, there may be more from him. Petrakis is still a relatively young man. Gwendolyn Brooks still has that fire within her. And surely there'll be many more young black writers. As for theater — well, David Mamet seems to be just getting started.

Some fifteen hundred novels, plays, collections of verse and short fiction and other books have been reviewed in these pages. They've covered the long range of Chicago pre-history and history, beginning with the French explorers and missionaries and continuing through the days of the Fort, the Sanitary Fair, the years of growth, the Civil War, the Fire, the Haymarket Affair, the Columbian Exposition, the development of the "stick house" and the skyscrapers, the coming of age of a Chicago literature — and all of the stirring events of Chicago's second century.

Through the pages of these books have paraded those legendary figures who helped make and corrupt Chicago — C. T. Yerkes, both John Kinzies, Gurdon Saltonstall Hubbard, "Old Hutch," the Armours, Cudahys and Swifts, Abraham Lincoln, Stephen A. Douglas, Al Capone, George Washington Gale Ferris, "Little Egypt," Sally Rand, Clarence Darrow, "Cap" Streeter, the Everleigh Sisters, "Hinky Dink," "The Bath," Samuel Insull, the mayors — "Our Carter", "Long John" Wentworth, "Big Bill" Thompson, Cermak, Daley, Byrne.

The authors of these books have established reputations not only as

Chicago writers but have won national and international fame as well: Fuller, Garland, Ade, Lardner, Dreiser, Ferber, Anderson, Masters, Farrell, Algren, Bellow, Levin, Norris, Sandburg, Hecht, Gunther.

Their books have become Chicago and American classics: *The Cliff-Dwellers, Rose of Dutcher's Coolly, Sister Carrie, The Pit, The Chicago Poems, The Young Manhood of Studs Lonigan, So Big, Show Boat, The Front Page, The Man With the Golden Arm, Herzog, The Old Bunch.*

In their pages we have watched the city's growth from that small settlement around the Fort and John Kinzie's home to its present size, overrunning satellite cities as it went — Kenwood, Hyde Park, Rogers Park, "Streeterville (!)," — until it finally ran up against suburbs that refused to yield their identities or other sovereignities — Evanston, Lake Forest, Oak Park, Hammond. We have seen the movement into and across the city of its ethnic groups — Jews, Blacks, Czechs, Poles, Swedes, Norwegians, Germans, Italians, Russians, Belgians, Dutch, Greeks, American Indians, Irish and Catholics. We have seen the "neighborhoods" — in that special Chicago sense: Hyde Park, Up Town, Pullman, Old Town, Rogers Park, Humboldt Park, Woodlawn, Chinatown, Prairie Avenue, the Gold Coast, Back of the Yards, the Levee — even "The Loop!"

We have seen the myriad of occupations that have helped Chicagoans fulfill their lives — explorers, priests, politicians, merchants, thieves, actors, actresses, gangsters, athletes, ministers, teachers, authors, poets, pimps and prostitutes, journalists, shop girls, factory workers, police, housewives, railroad men, grocers, confidence men, architects.

A long time ago author Frank Norris said there were only three "story cities" in the United States: New York, New Orleans and San Francisco.

Then he proceeded to write one of his best novels, *The Pit* about Chicago!

So here's to Chicago — now not only the "Garden City," the "Windy City," the "I Will" City, but for now and evermore — the "Story City" of America.

Postscript

Three novels about romantically-obsessed teen-age boys came in 1979, 1980 and 1982: Scott Spencer's *Endless Love*, most of which is set in Hyde Park; Thomas Rogers' *At the Shores*, set in Indiana Shores, Indiana; and Steve Tesich's *Summer Crossing*, set in East Chicago. Tesich's novel seems to derive from his earlier autobiographical film, *Four Friends*. Tesich's film and novel focus on a Yugoslavian family, like Tesich himself, immigrants to the Chicago area.

Appendix

Mystery Novels With a Chicago Setting

The following mystery novels which have their settings in Chicago (occasionally only in part) are in addition to those listed or discussed in the earlier chapters of this book. Refer to index for authors or titles of those books. See also the heading "Mystery novels."

The following titles and their authors are *not* listed in the general index. Authors are listed alphabetically — titles are listed alphabetically under authors' names.

Synopses of the books listed below will be found in Thomas Kilpatrick's and Patsy Rose Hoshiko's *Illinois! Illinois!* (1979). Howard Haycraft's *Murder for Pleasure; the Life and Times of the Detective Story* (1941) is an early study of the genre. Russel Nye, in his 1970 *The Unembarrassed Muse,* has a chapter "Murderers and Detectives (244-269)" on the genre. On pp. 428-429 he provides a bibliography of other booklength and journal discussions.

Titles listed below *are* indexed by subject matter in the general index, *i.e.,* Newspaper reporters, Suburbs, Chinatown.

Baker, [Howard] North and Bolton, William. *Dead to the World.* 1944. Mystery begins in Chicago city morgue.

Ballinger, William Sanborn [pseud, Bill S], *The Body Beautiful.* 1949. Chicago showgirl is stabbing victim.

———. *The Body in the Bed.* 1948.

_____. *Portrait in Smoke.* 1950. From Chicago's Stockyards to the North Side, to Oak Park and to Lake Shore Drive in the 1940s.

Barry, Joe [pseud]. See Lake, Joe Barry.

Bloch, Robert. *The Scarf.* 1947. Mystery story writer is murderer.

Brown, Frederic. *The Bloody Moonlight.* 1949.

_____. *Compliments of a Fiend.* 1950.

_____. *Death Has Many Doors.* 1951.

_____. *The Fabulous Clipjoint.* 1947. Young printer and older carnival man become private detectives.

_____. *The Late Lamented.* 1959. Embezzlement.

_____. *Mrs. Murphy's Underpants.* Chicago's racing syndicate.

Browne, Howard. *Halo for Satan.* 1948. By John Evans [pseud].

_____. *Halo in Brass;* A Paul Pine Mystery. 1949. Prostitution, gambling, lesbianism and murder.

_____. *Halo in Blood,* by John Evans [pseud]. 1946. Gambling and murder.

_____. *The Taste of Ashes.* 1957. Blackmail.

Bradley, Mary (Wilhelmina) Hastings. *Nice People Poison.* 1952. Young Chicago attorney solves case.

Charteris, Leslie. "King of the Beggars" in *Call For the Saint* is set in Chicago. 1948.

Clason, Clyde B. *Dragon's Cave, 1939; The Fifth Tumbler,* 1936; *The Purple Parrot,* 1937. All feature a Professor of Roman history who turns detective.

Creasey, John. *Affair for the Baron.* 1967. Partly in Chicago.

Dewey, Thomas B[lanchard]. *As Good as Dead.* 1946. Partly Chicago.

_____. *The Brave, Bad Girls.* Chicago detective.

_____. *Deadline.* 1966. Detective saves man from electric chair.

_____. *Death and Taxes.* 1967. Murder gangland style.

_____. *Don't Cry for Long.* 1964. Politician's rebellious daughter.

_____. *Draw the Curtain Close.* 1947. Murder is cheaper by the dozen.

_____. *The Girl Who Wasn't There.* 1960.

_____. *Handle With Fear . . .* 1951. Murder, fraud and gangster warfare.

_____. *How Hard to Kill.* 1962.

_____. *The King Killers.* 1968.

_____. *The Mean Streets.* 1955. Teen-age gang terrorizes neighborhood.

_____. *Portrait of a Dead Heiress.* 1965. Chicago society.

_____. *Prey For Me.* 1954.

_____. *A Sad Song Singing.* 1963. Missing folk singer.

_____. *You've Got Him Cold.* 1958. Blackmail.

Eberhart, Mignon G[ood]. *The Cases of Susan Dare.* 1934. Six short mystery novels, five set in Chicago.

_____. *Danger in the Dark.* 1936. Murder in a wealthy suburb.

_____. *The Dark Garden.* 1933. Lake Shore estate murder.

_____. *Dead Men's Plans.* 1952. Great Lakes shipping business.

_____. *Deadly is the Diamond . . .* 1958. "The Crimson Paw," one of the four novelettes in this collection, is about a Chicago dog breeder.

_____. *Express to Danger,* in *Five of My Best.* 1949. Murder begins on the El.

_____. *Fair Warning.* 1936. Suburban Chicago estate.

_____. *The Glass Slipper.* 1938. North Side neighborhood.

_____. *The Hangman's Whip.* 1938. Delayed honeymood.

_____. *The House on the Roof.* 1935. Opera singer, resident of penthouse, is slain.

_____. *Postmark Murder.* 1956. Good Chicago setting.

Edgley, Leslie. *The Runaway Pigeon.* 1953. The "pigeon" is a "stool pigeon," an informant.

Edwards, James G. [pseud]. See MacQueen, James William.

Forbes, [Deloris Florine] Stanton. *The Sad Sudden Death of My Fair Lady.* 1971. Murder at the 1933 World's Fair.

Freeman, Martin Joseph. *The Case of the Blind Mouse.* 1935. Chicago radio star is kidnapped and murdered.

_____. *The Scarf on the Scarecrow.* 1938. Murders on rundown suburban estate.

Friend, Oscar Jerome. *The Murder at Avalon Arms.* By Owen Fox Jerome [pseud]. 1931. Gambling.

_____. The Red Kite Clue. 1928.

Fredericks, Ernest Jason. *Lost Friday.* 1959. Elgin, IL.

Garfield, Bryan [Wynne]. *Death Sentence.* 1975. Self-styled judge-executioner's vendetta against street criminals.

Gillian, Michael. *Warrant for a Wanton.* 1952. Man sentenced to die in electric chair proves his own innocence.

Gordon, Mildred, and Gordon, Gordon. *Case File: FBI.* By the Gordons. 1953. FBI in Chicago.

Gruber, Frank. *The Scarlet Feather.* 1948. Murder at a Chicago poultry show.

_____. *Navy Colt, The.* 1941. Book agents charged with murder.

Heed, Rufus. *Ghosts Never Die.* 1954. Murder at a Chicago dinner party.

Herber, William. *The Almost Dead.* 1957. Communist group holds wife of financier for ransom.

_____. *Death Paints a Portrait.* 1958. The art world in Chicago.

_____. *King-Sized Murder.* 1954. Blackmail.

_____. *Live Bait for Murder.* 1955. Crime on a honeymoon.

Herman, Lewis. See Targ, William

Homewood, Harry. *A Matter of Size.* 1975. Chicago newspaper columnist takes on Russian agents and Chicago crime syndicate.

James, Franklin [pseud] see, Godley, Robert

Jerome, Owen Fox [pseud] see Friend, Oscar, Jerome

Johnston, William. *Mrs. Barthelme's Madness.* 1976. Suburban housewife and missing child.

Judson, Clara Ingram. *The Green Ginger Jar.* A Chinatown mystery. 1949.

Keeler, Harry Stephen. *Behind That Mask.* 1930. Young Chicago lawyer.

_____. *The Box From Japan.* 1932. Story begins with freight auction and unclaimed box.

_____. *The Case of the Jeweled Ragpicker.* 1948. Murder case solved thirty years later by carnival worker.

_____. *The Case of the Lavender Gripsack.* 1944. A revision of *The Man With the Wooden Spectacles.* Woman lawyer.

_____. *The Chameleon.* 1939. Escaped homicidal maniac.

_____. *The Face of the Man From Saturn.* 1933. Ex-newspaper reporter becomes amateur detective.

_____. *Find the Clock;* A Detective Mystery of Newspaper Life. 1927. Newspaperman fights competition from other reporters as he tracks down an escaped convict.

_____. *Finger! Finger!.* 1938.

_____. *The Five Silver Buddhas.* 1935.

_____. *The Fourth King.* 1930. Murdered Chicago stock broker.

_____. *The Man With the Crimson Box.* 1940.

_____. *The Man With the Wooden Spectacles.* 1941. Echoes *The Man With the Crimson Box.*

_____. *The Mysterious Mr. I.* 1938.

_____. *The Mystery of the Fiddling Cracksman.* 1934. Mystery involving Chicago author.

_____. *The Sharkskin Book.* 1941.

_____. *Sing Sing Nights.* 1928. Three doomed men in New York's notorious prison recall their Chicago experiences.

_____. *The Skull of the Waltzing Clown.* 1935. Insurance swindle.

_____. *The Spectacles of Mr. Cagliostro.* 1929. Son of Chicago millionaire faces commitment to mental institution.

_____. *Thieves' Nights;* The Chronicles of DeLancey, King of Thieves. 1929.

_____. *The Washington Square Enigma.* 1933.

_____. *The Wonderful Scheme of Mr. Christopher Thorne.* 1936.

Lake, Joe Barry. *The Clean-Up,* by Joe Barry [pseud]. 1947. Organized crime in a Chicago suburb, circa 1920s.

_____. *The Fall Guy,* by Joe Barry [pseud]. 1945.

_____. *The Pay-Off,* by Joe Barry. 1943. WWII Marine vs. Chicago gangsters.

_____. *The Third Degree.* 1943. Newspaper man becomes Army Intelligence agent in Chicago.

Latimer, Jonathan [Wyatt]. *Sinners and Shrouds.* Chicago reporter finds fellow reporter murdered. 1955.

_____. *Headed for a Hearse.* 1935.

_____. *The Lady in the Morgue.* 1936.

_____. *Red Gardenias.* 1939.

Lewin, Michael Z. *The Enemies Within.* 1974.

MacDonald, John D[ann]. *One Fearful Yellow Eye.* 1966.

McGivern, William P[eter]. *Heaven Ran Last.* 1949.

_____. *Very Cold for May.* 1950. Chicago public relations man tries to improve image of industrialist.

McHugh, Jay [pseud]. See MacQueen, James William.

MacQueen, James William. [All the following books except the last one are written under the pseudonym of James G. Edwards, M.D.

____. *Death Among Doctors*. 1942. Chicago hospital.

____. *Death Elects a Mayor.* 1939. Chicago hospital scene of Chicago Mayor's murder.

____. *F Corridor.* 1936. Chicago hospital.

____. *Murder in the Surgery*. 1935.

____. *The Odor of Bitter Almonds*. 1938. Chicago sanitarium.

____. *The Private Pavilion*. 1935. Chicago hospital.

____. *Sex Is Such Fun,* by Jay McHugh, [pseud]. 1937. Chicago suburb.

Maling, Arthur [Gordon]. *Bent Man*. 1975. Jewel thieves.

____. *Decoy.* 1969. Crime syndicate.

____. *Go-Between*. 1970. Son of business tycoon.

Means, Mary, and Sanders, Theodore. *The Beckoning Shadow,* by Denis Scott, [pseud 1946.

Nielsen, Helen (Berniece). *Gold Coast Nocturne*. 1951.

O'Connor, Richard. *The Waiting Game,* by Patrick Wayland, [pseud]. 1965.

Oppenheim, E. Phillips. *The Million Pound Deposit*. 1930.

Ozaki, Milton K. *The Black Dark Murders,* by Robert O. Saber, [pseud]. 1949. Chicago co-eds are murdered.

____. *Case of the Cop's Wife*. 1958.

____. *The Cuckoo Clock*. 1946.

____. *A Fiend in Need*. 1947.

____. *Maid for Murder.* 1955.

____. *Never Say Die*. 1956.

____. *The Scented Flesh,* by Robert O. Saber, [pseud]. 1951. White slave traffic.

____. *Too Young to Die,* by Robert O. Saber, [pseud]. 1954.

Pendleton, Don[ald Eugene]. *The Executioner: Chicago Wipeout*. 1971. Self-styled hitman wages war against Chicago Mafia.

Peters, William. *Blondes Die Young,* by Bill Peters [pseud]. 1952. Show girl is murdered.

Plum, Mary. *Dead Man's Secrets*. 1931.

Pruitt, Alvin. [pseud] see Rose, Alvin Emanuel

Raymond, Clifford Samuel. *The Men on the Dead Man's Chest*. 1930.

Russell, Charlotte Murray. *The Case of the Topaz Flower.* 1939.

____. *Dreadful Reckoning*. 1941. Wealthy Chicago clan.

____. *The Tiny Diamond*. 1937. Chicago University student.

Saber, Robert O. [pseud]. See Ozaki, Milton K.

Sanders, Theodore. See Means, Mary.

Scott, Denis [pseud]. See Means, Mary.

Sinclair, Bertha M (Cowan). [pseud B. M. Bower]. *Fool's Goal*. 1929.

Targ, William and Herman, Lewis. *The Case of Mr. Casady.* (1939) Book collector is murdered.

Thayer, Tiffany. *Thirteen Men* (1931).

Ullman, James Michael. *Lady on Fire* (1968).

____. *The Venus Trap* (1966).

Wayland, Patrick. [pseud] see O'Connor, Richard.

Dime Novels With a Chicago Setting

These books are listed by authors' names where known. Pseudonyms are cross-listed. There are synopses in Thomas Kilpatrick's and Patsy-Rose Hoshiko's annotated bibliography, *Illinois! Illinois!* (1979). Many of these, with a definitive discussion of the genre, are described in more detail in Albert Johannsen's, *The House of Beadle and Adams and its Dime and Nickel Novels* (1950). Charles Bragin published a bibliography of *Dime Novels (1860-1928)* in 1938. There is a fine short discussion of the genre in Russel Nye's 1970 *The Unembarrassed Muse* (chapter Eight, "The Dime Novel Tradition"). In particular, Nye identifies a number of the authors, pointing out, for example, that although there were several authors for the "Nick Carter" novels, Frederick Van Rensselaer Dey claimed to have written about a thousand. (108)

Extensive collections of "nickel" and "dime" novels are in the Albert Johannsen Collection in the Swen-Franklin-Parson Library at the University of Northern Illinois (DeKalb) and in the Children's Literature Research Collection in the Walter Library at the University of Minnesota.

A few other titles have been discussed in preceding chapters. See "Dime novels" in the Index. The titles below are not in the index; they are listed here by authors' names, or else anonymously ("Anon.") where an author is not identified.

Anon. *Caught in Chicago;* or, Bob Brooks Among the World's Fair Crooks. 15 p. 1893.

——. *The Brady's Chicago Crew;* or, Exposing the [Chicago] Board of Trade Crooks. 29 p. 1904.

——. *The Shoe With Three Pegs;* or, Convicted by a Footprint. 31 p. 1886.

Arnold, Allan. *Belle Boyd,* The Girl Detective, A Story of Chicago and the West. One of the few women subjects in this genre. 31 p. 1891.

Bethune, J. G. [pseud]. See Ellis, Edward Sylvester.

Broughton, F. Lusk. *Thugs of Chicago;* or, Old Pinch on the Trail, The. 32 p. 1890.

——. *Jack Breeze, the Chicago Sleuth;* or, The Langdale Case. 42 p. 1887.

——. *A Quarter-Million Burglary;* or, V-Spot and the Cracksmen. 31 p. 1896.

Cobb, Weldon J. *Always on Deck;* or, Making a Start in Life by Archie Van [pseud]. 64 p. 1887. Boy struggles to regain birthright.

"Nick Carter" author. *Compact of Death;* or, Nick Carter's Singed, Hair Clew, The. Chicago about 1905. 28 p. 1905.

——. *The Man and His Price.* (1902, 1927). Lennox Bouton Grey calls this a "romance of adventure," on the "outer fringes of 'literature,'" with a very meagre notion of locale, all related in one sentence paragraphs for "tabloid" minds." (593-595)

——. *Nick Carter's Name at Stake;* or, After the Sunset City Sharpers. 22 p. 1895.

——. *The Pullman Plot;* or, Nick Carter's Chance Clew. 15 p. 1894.

Old Cap Collier author. *The Chamber of Horrors;* or Old, Cap Collier Unearthing the Great Insurance Fraud. 30 p. 1895. Mysterious disappearances at the Columbian Exposition.

——. *Chicago's Greatest Crime;* or, The Most Mysterious Case on Record. Detective seeks sausage maker's missing wife. 30 p. 1898.

_____. *Infanta Eulalia's Jewels;* or, Old Cap Collier Among the Crooks at the World's
Fair. The Infanta was the most distinguished foreign visitor at the Columbian
Exposition. 32 p. 1893.

Demarest, Arthur N. *"Three Fast Widows and Naughty Men;"* A Story of Life in
Chicago. 72 p. 1877.

Ellis, Edward Sylvester. *The Chicago Drummer's Deal;* or, Detective Skid's Diamond
Haul, by J. G. Bethune, [pseud]. 16 p. 1893.

Fenton, Walter. *Old Neversleep, the Government Detective.* 30 p. 1885.

Grant, Major A F [pseud] see Harbaugh, Thomas Chalmers.

Harbaugh, Thomas Chalmers. *Lincoln's Spy; or, The Loyal Detective.* A stirring story
of the plot to burn Chicago. Major A F Grant [pseud] Confederate plot in
Chicago. 23 p. 1886.

_____. *Old Search in Chicago;* or, "Piping" a World's Fair Mystery. Major A F Grant
[pseud] 47 p. 1892.

Howard, Police Capt [pseud]. *Monte, the French Detective in Chicago.* 27 p. 1887.

Ingraham, Prentiss. *The Actor Detective in Chicago;* or, Dick Doom's Flush Hand. 16 p.
1893.

_____. *Dick Doom in Chicago;* or, The Ferret of the Golden Fetters. A Romance of a
mysterious Man-hunt. 16 p. 1896.

_____. *Dick Doom's Big Haul;* or, The Rogue Round-Up in Chicago. A Romance of the
World's Fair City. 15 p. 1893.

_____. *Dick Doom's Ten Strike;* or, The Top Floor Club's Exposé. Dick Doom in "drag!"
16 p. 1893.

_____. *The Gentleman Crook in Chicago;* or, Nick Norcross, the River Rat, Dick Doom's
Shadow Hunt. 16 p. 1893

Merrick, Mark [pseud]. See Rathbone, St. George.

Merritt, Ja[mes] C. *Going Out West;* or, The Fortunes of a Bright Boy. 30 p. 1911. Partly
set in Chicago.

Miller, Warne, M. D. [pseud] See Rathbone, St. George.

Montague, Ja[mes] D. *The Fire Bugs of Chicago.* 13 p. 1897. *Illinois! Illinois!* (item
445, p 196) lists the same title by Walter Fenton.

Morris, Anthony P. *Blank Harley's First Case;* or, "Piping" the "Levee" Gang. 30 p.
1893. The "Levee" was Chicago's notorious vice district.

_____. *El Diablo, The Terror;* or, "Piping" the River Pirates. 44 p. 1892. River pirates on
the Chicago River?

_____. *Old Rafferty's Luck;* or, "Piping" the Anson Case. 40 p. 1886

_____. *Slocum the Ferret and His California Pard;* or, The Tráil of a Ruby Necklace. 29
p. 1895.

_____. *The Fire-Fiends;* or, Hercules, the Hunchback. 32 p. 1887. Story set at the time
of the 1871 Fire.

Morris, Charles. *Dick Dashaway;* or, A Dakota Boy in Chicago. 15 p. 1882.

_____. *Joe, the Chicago Arab;* or, A Boy of the Times. 31 p. 1890. An "Arab" was a boy
who lived on the streets.

_____. *The Secret Service Boy Detective;* or, Tony Blink's First Scoop. 14 p. 1888.

Patten, Gilbert. *Frank Merriwell in Chicago;* or, Masked by Mysteries. 32 p. 1896.

_____. *Frank Merriwell's Speed;* or, Breaking the Chicago Colts, by Burt L. Standish [pseud]. 29 p. 1900. Mix of baseball and crime.

Pinkerton, Allan. "Claude Melnotte as a Detective" in *Claude Melnotte as a Detective* [and other non-Chicago stories]. 1875. Title story takes place in fashionable Chicago hotel. Pinkerton was a member of the famous private security force, organized in Chicago.

_____. *The Detective and the Somnambulist [and] the Murderer and the Fortune Teller.* 1875. Two stories set partially in Chicago.

Rathbone, St. George. *A House of Mystery;* or, Jack Sharp in Chicago by Mark Merrick [pseud]. 46 p. 1884.

_____. *The Mystery of a French Flat;* or, Obed Grimes Strange Case by Warne Miller, [pseud]. 30 p. 1896. World's Columbian Exposition setting.

_____. *Old Forge, the Blacksmith Detective,* by Warne Miller. 30 p. 1894. The Haymarket Affair.

Richards, Gale. *Link Rover in Chicago;* or, Making Things Fairly Hum. 28 p. 1905.

Sims, A. K. *Chicago Charlie's Diamond Dash;* or, Trapping the Tunnel Thieves. A Story of the White City. 31 p. 1893. Murder at the World's Columbian Exposition.

Standish, Burt L. [pseud]. See Patten, Gilbert.

Standish, Hal. *Fred Fearnot and the White Masks;* or, Chasing the Chicago Stranglers. 28 p. 1896. New York banker missing in Chicago!

_____. *Fred Fearnot in Chicago;* or, The Abduction of Evelyn. 32 p. 1899.

Strayer, Ed. *Waldo, the Wizard Detective;* or, A Strange Murder on the Lakes. 32 p. 1897. Murder on a Lake Michigan yacht.

Van, Archie [pseud]. See Cobb, Weldon J.

Wade, Bernard. *Larry Murtaugh's Early Career;* or, The Counterfeiter's Compact. 30 p. 1895.

Winch, Will [pseud]. *Abducted at Midnight;* or, The Dude Detective's First and Last Trail. 1892.

_____. *Kinduke, the Daring;* or, A Midnight Mystery of Chicago. 30 p. 1896. Woman saved from watery grave in Chicago River.

_____. *The Marine Detective;* or, Tracking the Ship-Insurance Swindlers. 1892. Merchant ship disappears in Lake Michigan.

Chapter 1

1. Sandburg, Carl. "Chicago," *Chicago Poems* (1916), 1.
2. Cayton, Horace R. "The Known City," *New Republic* (May, 12, 1947), 30.
3. Farr, Finis. *Chicago* (1973), 402.
4. ___. *Chicago.* (1973), 403-404.
5. Bremer, Frederika. *Homes of the New World* (1853), I, 605.
6. Kipling, Rudyard. "How I Struck Chicago, and How Chicago Struck Me," *From Sea to Sea: Letters of Travel* (1899).
7. Mencken, H. L. "The Literary Capitol of America," *Nation* (London), (April 17, 1920).
8. Peattie, Donald Culross. *A Prairie Grove.* (1938), 16.
9. Beach, Joseph Warren. *American Fiction 1920-1940.* (1942), 7-8.
10. Kinzie, Mrs. John H. *Wau-Bun/The "Early Day" in the Northwest.* (Chicago, 1932), 1x.

Chapter II

1. Field, Eugene. *Culture's Garland* (1887), 239.
2. Hall, Joseph. "Dark Maid of the Illinois, The," *Tales of the Border,* (1835). [Orig. in *The Knickerbocker,* 1833].
3. Russell, Ruth. *Lake Front* (1931), 19.
4. Hudson, Jay William. *Nowhere Else in the World,* (1923), 215-216.
5. Grey, Lennox Bouton. *Chicago and the Great American Novel: A Critical Approach to the American Epic.* Unpublished 1935 University of Chicago Ph.D. dissertation, hereafter referred to as *Grey.* Pp. 39,44.
6. Hubbard, Bela. "The Early Colonization of Detroit," *Michigan Pioneer Collections,* I, 367-368 (1900).
7. Peattie, Donald Culross. *Prairie Grove, A* (1938), 33.
8. Peattie, 16-17.
9. Halle, Louis J., Jr. "The Past of the Prairies," *New York Tribune Books* (April 10, 1938), 4.
10. Smart, Charles Allen, "The Illinois Wilderness," *Saturday Review of Literature* (XVII, April 26, 1938), 5.
11. Kinzie, Juliette. *Wau-Bun, the "Early Day" in the Northwest* (1856). The quotation is from p. 220 of the 1932 edition, edited and with an introduction by Milo Milton Quaife. Dr. Quaife's notes explain or correct many of Mrs. Kinzie's statements. The 1901 Rand McNally edition is also useful for its notes by Mrs. Kinzie's daughter, Nellie Kinzie Gordon. See also, Farr, *Chicago* (1973), 14.
12. Masters, Edgar Lee. *The Great Valley* (1916), 8.
13. Richardson, John *Hardscrabble; or, The Fall of Chicago* (1850), 75-76.
14. Masters, *The Great Valley,* 5.
15. Kinzie, *Wau-Bun,* 233.
16. Cooper, James Fenimore. *The Oak-Openings; or, The Bee-Hunter* (1848). Quoted from pp. 42ff. in 1909 Boston edition.
17. Written in a journal in 1836, but not published until 1844, contrary to Mrs. Kinzie's statements. See footnotes, p. 233, *Wau-Bun,* and Grey, 64-66
18. Grey, 72
19. Grey, 64.
20. Grey, 64-65.
21. Grey, 54.
22. *Sartain's Union Magazine of Literature and Art,* VI, 99.
23. Dust jacket of 1852 edition of *Wau-nan-gee* ...
24. Grey, 64-66.
25. Duncan, Hugh Dalziel. *The Rise of Chicago as a Literary Center from 1885 to 1920.* (1964), 1.
26. *Kinzie, Wau-Bun,* 1ix.

27. Payne, William Morton. "Literary Chicago," *New England Magazine.* (NS, VII), 696.
28. Grey, 59-60.
29. Fuller, Henry Blake. "Address of Mr. Henry Blake Fuller," *The Chicago Public Library 1873-1923 Proceedings* ... (1923), 83-86.
30. Quaife, Milo M. *Chicago and the Old Northwest* (1923), 448-449.
31. Grey, 61.
32. Hurlbut, Henry, in *Chicago Antiquities* (1881). See Currey, J. Seymour, *Chicago, Its History and Its Builders* (1912) I, 76.
33. Kirkland, Joseph. *The Story of Chicago* (1892), I, 59.
34. Duncan, 1. Grey's thesis reinforces this point.
35. Taylor, Benjamin Franklin. *Complete Poetical Works* (1886), 236-237.
36. Duncan, 4.
37. Grey, 94.
38. Duncan, 2. Grey's thesis seems to serve as a model for Duncan's argument.
39. Grey, 96-97. The manufacturer was Richard T. Crane.
40. Parrish, Randall. *When Wilderness Was King, A Tale of the Illinois Country* (1904), 105.
41. Masters, Edgar Lee to Harriet Monroe. Harriet Monroe *A Poet's Life* (1938), 381.
42. Masters, Edgar Lee. "Fort Dearborn," *The Great Valley* (1916), 1-2.
43. Bradley, Mary Hastings. *Old Chicago* (4 vols., 1933). The volume titles are: *When Chicago Was a Frontier: The Fort; When Chicago Was a Town: The Duel; When Chicago Became a City: Debt of Honor; Chicago in the Eyes of the World: Metropolis.*
44. Grey, 63, 65, 114. Farr, Finis. *Chicago* (1973), 23, 33.
45. Published in *Sloan's Garden City Magazine* (1854), and subsequently in six editions.
46. Grey, 110, 111.
47. Grey, 113-114. See also Farr, 23, 33.
48. Kinzie, Juliette. *Mark Logan, Bourgeois* (1887), 171, and *passim.*
49. Grey, 114.
50. Grey, 121.
51. Masters, Edgar Lee. "Emily Brousseau in Church," *The Great Valley* (1916), 39.
52. Advertisement, Chicago *Daily News,* (July 12, 1933), 23.
53. Holt, Alfred Hubbard. *Hubbard's Trail* (1952), 279.
54. Grey, 42, fn. 2. Grey says this story wavers between Joseph Hall's "anti-French mockery" in "The Dark Maid of the Illinois," and Longfellow's "noble invocation" in *The Song of Hiawatha.*
55. Kinzie, *Wau-Bun,* 219. Kinzie says the French used the spelling "Chicagoux."
56. Kirkland, Joseph. *The Story of Chicago* (1892), I, 8-9; O'Brien, Howard Vincent. *All Things Considered* (1948), 23-24; Grey, 42, fn. 2.
57. Kirkland, *The Story of Chicago,* I, 9.
58. Alsberg, Henry G. *The American Guide* (1949), 518.

Chapter III

1. Horton, George. *The Long Straight Road* (1901), 308.
2. Marsh, Fred T., review of *Old Chicago,* New York Times, (April 30, 1933), 6.
3. Lewis, Lloyd, and Smith, Henry Justin, *Chicago/the History of its Reputation* (1929), 60.
4. Lewis and Smith, 118.
5. Lewis, Smith, 118.
6. *Knickerbocker Magazine,* LIX-LXI (beginning April, 1862). Of fourteen Civil War fictional pieces published in 1862, including seven books, three appeared in the *Knickerbocker.* (Grey, 204, fn. 1)
7. *Knickerbocker Magazine,* (January, 1863), 71.
8. Jackson, Helen Marie Fiske Hunt. *Scribner's* (1874), VIII, 213-23, 294-303. Republished in *Saxe Holm's Stories,* Second Series (1878), 1-65.
9. Johnson, Elizabeth Winthrop. *Two Loyal Lovers: A Romance* (1890), 279.

10. Fleming, Herbert E. "The Literary Interests of Chicago," *The American Journal of Sociology* (January, 1906), 378.
11. Fleming, 380-386, 390.
12. Fleming, 381.
13. Fleming, 381.
14. Fleming, 381.
15. Anonymous. *Luke Darrell, the Chicago Newsboy* (1868) v.
16. Grey, 209.
17. These terms for Chicago, plus "Urbs Recondita," ("The Rebuilt City") were coined by Alfred T. Andreas and used in his *History of Chicago* (1884-1886) as titles for the three volumes.
18. Medill, Joseph. Chicago *Tribune* (September 10, 1871). See Lewis and Smith, 118, and Farr, 100. For Mrs. O'Leary's cow, see Lewis and Smith, 122-123. For the Fire, see 123-131, and Farr, 100-109.
19. Farr, 107.
20. Roe, E. P. *Taken Alive and Other Stories* (1883), 19-20.
21. Farr, 107. Farr has a precis of the novel.
22. Pattee, Fred Lewis. *A History of American Literature Since 1870* (1915), 386-387.
23. Hall, Mordaunt. "The Chicago Fire." *New York Times* (March 12, 1925) 17:2.
24. Grey, 213.
25. Grey, 215-216.
26. *Spicy,* 147-148.
27. *Dictionary of National Biography* (1933), X, 556. Grey 213.
28. Grey, 274.
29. *McGovern, John. Daniel Trentworthy, A Tale of the Great Fire at Chicago* (1889), 175-176.
30. Grey, 282.
31. B.R.C. Review of *In Old Chicago.* The New York *Times* (January 7, 1938), 15:2.
32. Asbury, Herbert. *Gem of the Prairies: an Informal History of the Chicago Underworld* (1940) is one source for the information here. See Lewis and Smith and Farr and other sources for confirmation.
33. Field, Eugene. "Sharps and Flats," Chicago *Morning News* (April 4, 1895). See the advertisement for *Life in Chicago* in the end pages of *Chicago After Dark* (1879). See Stead, William T., *If Christ Came to Chicago! . . .* (1894), Chapter 5, p. 10.
34. Grey. 219-220.
35. _____. 316-317.
36. Anonymous. *Suppressed Sensations* (1890), 5-6.
37. Bragin, Charles. *Dime Novels: Bibliography, 1868-1928* New York, 1938: Johannsen, Albert. *The House of Beadle and Adams and Its Dime and Nickel Novels,* Norman, OK, 1950.
38. Kilpatrick, Thomas L. and Hoshiko, Patsy-Rose. *Illinois! Illinois! An Annotated Bibliography of Fiction* (1979).
39. "Outwardly respectable but notorious predecessor of the Chicago Press Club" which was founded by Franc Bangs Wilkie in 1880. See Grey, 330, and Andreas, III, 705.
40. *Illinois! Illinois!,* item 554, p. 240-241.
41. Dreiser, Theodore. *The Titan* (1914), 399-400.
42. Grey, 323
43. Shumaker, Arthur W. *A History of Indiana Literature* (1962), 324.
44. Draper, John S. *Shams, or Uncle Ben's Experiences With Hypocrites . . .* (1887? 1898), 267.
45. Duncan, 19, 20. Duncan says that "the writer in Chicago could not base his work on an existing indigenous literary tradition. The tradition was not there; it had to be created. Some way of looking at the urban Chicago experience [was necessary]."
46. Duncan, 21, in part.

Chapter IV

1. Mayer, Harold M. and Wade, Richard C. *Chicago/Growth of a Metropolis* (1969), 117, and numerous other sources.
2. Lewis and Smith, 137-138.
3. Lewis and Smith, 136.
4. Fleming, 500-503; Mott, Frank L. *A History of American Magazines,* Vol. III, p. 53.
5. Fleming, 514-515.
6. Fleming, 516.
7. Halper, Albert. *This is Chicago* (1952), 472.
8. _____. 474.
9. Grey, 171.
10. Taylor, Benj. F. *Theophilus Trent/Old Times in the Oak Openings* (1887), 107.
11. Farr, 63.
12. Thompson, Slason, *Way Back When* (1931).
13. Field, Eugene. *Culture's Garland* ... (1887), 1.
14. Fleming, 514.
15. Field, 168.
16. Field, Eugene, *The House* ... (1896).
17. Fleming, 517.
18. Read, Opie. *The Colossus* (1893), 87-88.
19. Grey, 131; Lewis and Smith, 275-276.
20. Blake, Faye M. *The Strike in the American Novel* (1972), 18.
21. McMichael, George. *Journey to Obscurity* (1965), 57-65. The story appeared in *Lippincott's Magazine* (1878), XXII.
22. Carter, Everett. "The Haymarket Affair in Literature," *American Quarterly* (1950) 270-278. Carter does not list Charlotte Teller's *The Cage* (1907).
23. _____. 271-273.
24. Howells' correspondence on the Haymarket Affair is in *Life and Letters* of William Dean Howells, ed. Mildred Howells (1928) 398-403, Vol. 1.
25. Carter, 275.
26. _____. 275.
27. Carter concentrates on MacKaye, Howells, Herrick, Frank Harris, and Howard Fast. He also ignores *Lake Front.*
28. Harris, Frank. *The Bomb* [American ed.] 1909, Foreword.
29. Russell, Ruth. *Lake Front* (1931) 209.
30. Grey, 423.
31. Carter, 278.
32. *Roderick Leaster, Rodger Latimer's Mistake, With the Procession, Chicago's Black Sheep, The Gospel of Freedom,* and *Differences* all stressed the value of "emotional adjustment" over "material relief" after the institution of Hull House. Grey, 602.
33. Newberry, Julia, diary, June 9, 1869. Farr, 89.
34. Lewis, Lloyd, and Henry Justin Smith. *Chicago: The History of Its Reputation* (1929) 76.
35. Kilpatrick, item 272, p. 127.
36. _____. Item 776, p. 327.
37. Kirkland, Joseph. *Zury: the Meanest Man in Spring County* (1887) Preface.
38. _____. "Realism Versus Other Isms." *The Dial,* XIV, 160 (February 16, 1893) 99.
39. _____. *Zury* ..., Preface. This "Preface" was not reprinted in a 1956 University of Illinois Press edition.
40. Garland, Hamlin. "Zury, The Meanest Man in Spring County," *Boston Evening Transcript* (Monday, May 16, 1887).
41. Lewis and Smith. 55-57.
42. Kirkland, Joseph. *The McVeys* (1888) "Introductory," 1.

43. Henson, Clyde E. *Joseph Kirkland* (1962) 25.
44. Smith, Rebecca Washington. "The Civil War and Its Aftermath in American Fiction, 1861-1899." (Unpublished University of Chicago dissertation, 1932) p. 64-69. Cited in Grey, 204, fn. 1.
45. Grey, 335.

Chapter V

1. F.P.A. (Franklin P. Adams), *The Chicago Sun Book Week* (September 19, 1943) 3.
2. Payne, William Morton, "Chicago's Higher Evolution," *The Dial* (1892) XIII, 205-206.
3. Garland, Hamlin, *Crumbling Idols* (1894) *passim.*
4. Sommers, Lillian. *Jerome Leaster of Roderick Leaster & Co.* (1890), 14-15.
5. Lewis and Smith, 203.
6. Blake, Faye M. *The Strike in the American Novel* (1972) 15, 57, passim.
7. ———. 25.
8. Garland, Hamlin. *A Member of the Third House* (1892), Quoted in Grey, 446-447, fn. 2.
9. Blake, 218.
10. Anonymous. *The Beginnings: A Romance of Chicago As It Might Be* (1893), 107-108.
11. Blake, 73.
12. Other tract novels — Phelps, Corwin, *An Ideal Republic, or, A Way Out of the Fog* (1896); Hall, E. J., *Masters of Men* (ca. 1890-1895); Granville, Austin, *The Fallen Race* (with an introduction by Opie Read) 1892.
13. Mott, Frank Luther. *Golden Multitudes* (1947), 170.
14. Hofstadter, Richard. *Coin's Financial School* (1963), 2.
15. When I checked out one library's "copy," it turned out to be nothing but dust in an envelope, with the book's title on the outside.
16. Farr, 204.
17. Andreas, A. T. *History of Chicago.* Title of Volume III.
18. Farr, 165-169, *passim;* Lewis and Smith, 177-182.
19. Pierce, Bessie L. (ed). *As Others See Chicago* (1933), 385.
20. Lewis and Smith, 178.
21. Grey, 455.
22. Monroe, Harriet. *Valeria; and other poems* (1892), 213.
23. ———. *A Poet's Life* (1938) 99.
24. ———. "The Columbian Ode," *Chosen Poems* (1935), 81. Monroe's account of the writing of the Ode and of the problems she encountered at the Exposition are in *A Poet's Life* (1938), 116-131.
25. *Chicago Tribune* (October 22, 1892). Reported in *A Poet's Life* (1938), 121.
26. Monroe, Harriet. *A Poet's Life* (1938), 131.
27. Kirkland, Joseph, and Carolyn. *The Story of Chicago,* II, 27 (1894).
28. Farr, 179-180.
29. Pady, Donald S. "Thomas Brower Peacock," *Bulletin of Bibliography,* XXVIII, 2 (April-June, 1971), 38.
30. Monroe, Harriet. *Chosen Poems* (1935) viii.
31. Grey, 455-456.
32. Farr, 404.
33. Burnham, Clara Louise. *Sweet Clover* . . . (1894), 410. The quotation was later carved on the wall of the Joseph Bond chapel at the University of Chicago.
34. Grey, 460.
35. Burnett, Frances Hodgson. *Two Little Pilgrims' Progress* . . . (1895), 11-12.
36. Grey, 461.
37. Butterworth, Hezekiah. *Zig Zag Journeys on the Mississippi* . . . (1892), i.
38. ———. *Zig Zag Journeys to the White City* (1894), viii.

39.   Grey, 458-459.

40.   Herrick, Robert. *Waste* (1924), 117.

41.   Barnes, Margaret Ayer. *Years of Grace* (1930), 38.

42.   Grey, 431-432. Farr (193-195) also discusses briefly the implications of Adams' visit to the Exposition. In essence he supports Grey's conclusions. Two other novels of the Exposition are: Charles McClellan Stevens ("Quondam"), *Egyptian Harp Girl/Mystery of the Peristyle* (1894); Thomas and Anna M. Fitch, *Better Days* (1892).

43.   H. B. Milman's *Mr. Lake of Chicago* (1888), one of these one-time books, was modeled, like many others of the late 1880s, on Archibald Clavering Gunter's *Mr. Barnes of New York* (1887), the latter, according to Frank Luther Mott, one of the five best-selling books of the year *(Golden Multitudes* [1947]), 177.

44.   Beach, Edgar R. *Stranded:* . . . (1890), preface.

45.   Grey, 335.

46.   *Illinois! Illinois!* Item 313, p. 145.

47.   Richberg, Eloise O. Randall. *Bunker Hill to Chicago* (1893), 13.

48.   Grey, 334.

49.   Read Opie. *The Colossus* (1893), 121.

50.   Hamill, Pete. "Author Dies shunned by the City He Loved," *Minneapolis Tribune,* (May 14, 1981), 2.

51.   Grey, 512.

52.   _____. 512.

53.   Read, *Judge Elbridge,* 8.

54.   _____. *ibid.,* 190.

55.   Morris, Robert L. *Opie Read, American Humorist* (1965) 161. On the same page Morris reports that Read wrote his best-selling novel, *The Jucklins* (1896) in two weeks.

56.   _____. *ibid.,* 161.

57.   Train, M. *Ray Burton* . . . 23.

58.   _____. *ibid,*41.

59.   _____. *ibid,* 77. See Grey, 284, for a discussion of the significance of the quotations indicated by footnotes 57-59.

61   Garland, Hamlin.

62.   *Illinois! Illinois!* Item 640, p. 274.

63.   _____. Item 311, p. 144.

64.   Grey, 362. The first edition carried the pseudonym of "Robert Dolly Williams."

65.   Grey, 363. The character is "Dr. Gowdy" in *Under the Skylights,* a book which is a *roman à clef.*

66.   Grey, 363. See Keith, Katharine, *The Girl* (1917), and Meeker, Arthur, *Prairie Avenue* (1949).

67.   Other even lesser Chicago books of the time: Verdendorp, Basil (probably the pseudonym of Charles M. Hertig), *The Verdendorps* (1893?), and Kranz, Sigmund, *Street Types of Chicago* (1893).

68.   Upton, George P. *Musical Memories.* From 1869 on, Upton wrote musical reviews and criticism for the *Tribune* under the guise of "Peregrine Pickle."

Chapter VI

1.   Mencken, H. L. Quoted in Smith, Alson J., *Chicago's Left Bank* (1953), 3.

2.   Payne, William Morton. "Literary Chicago," *The New England Magazine.* NS, VII, 683-685.

3.   _____. 684-685.

4.   _____. 694-697.

5.   _____. 699.

6. Fuller, Henry Blake. "The Upward Movement in Chicago," *Atlantic Monthly,* LXXX (1897) 534-547.

7. Anonymous. *The Dial,* XIII (1892) 151, pp. 205-206. The essay was written in response to a London *Times* editorial comment that Chicago "needed to be sweetened by a sense of life that is simultaneously being embellished and refined."

8. Upton, George Putnam. "Music in Chicago," *New England Magazine* (NS, 7:477-494) 493-494.

9. Payne. "Literary Chicago," 685-686.

10. _____. 686.

11. _____. 686.

12. _____. 687.

13. Wiggins, Robert L., quoting Joel Chandler Harris in *Life of Joel Chandler Harris* (1918) 148.

14. Wheaton, Emily [Mrs. Roswell Field]. *The Russells in Chicago. The Ladies Home Journal,* January 1902, pp. 9-10.

15. Brubaker, Robert L. "130 Years of Opera in Chicago." *Chicago History,* VIII, 3 (Fall, 1979) 156 ff.

16. Schlereth, Thomas J. "A Robin's Egg Renaissance: Chicago Culture, 1893-1933." *Chicago History,* VIII, 3, (Fall, 1979) 148. Farr, Finis, *Chicago,* 191, 291.

17. _____. 146.

18. Duncan, Hugh Dalziell. *The Rise of Chicago as a Literary Center From 1885 to 1920: A Sociological Essay in American Culture* (1964) 109.

19. Kramer, Dale. *Chicago Renaissance/The Literary Life in Chicago 1900-1930* (1966) 208-209.

20. Fleming, Herbert E. "The Literary Interests of Chicago." *American Journal of Sociology,* XII, 524 ff.

21. Payne. "Literary Chicago," 685.

22. Fleming. 525.

23. _____. 525.

24. Chatfield-Taylor, Herbert C. *With Edge Tools* (1891) 40.

25. _____. 50-51.

26. _____. *An American Peeress* (1894) 63.

27. _____. *Two Women and a Fool* (1895) 151.

28. Field, Eugene. *Culture's Garland* (1887) 239.

29. Grey, 48.

30. Crawford, Bartholow, Kern, Alexander C., and Needleman, Morris. C. *An Outline-History of American Literature* (1950) 186.

31. Grey, 44.

32. Garland, Hamlin. *A Son of the Middle Border* (1917) 367.

33. _____. *Crumbling Idols* (1894) 147-157.

34. _____. *Daughter of the Middle Border, A* (1921) 2.

35. Monroe, Lucy. *Critic,* XXIII (July 22, 1893) 60; Pizer, Donald, "Summer Campaign in Chicago," *WHR,* XIII (1959) 375-382.

36. Garland, Hamlin, "Literary Emancipation of the West," *The Forum* (XVI, October) 161. See also *Crumbling Idols.*

37. Boyesen, Hjalmar Hjorth. "The Cliff-Dwellers," *Cosmopolitan* (January, 1894) XVI, 373-374.

38. Anonymous, *The Dial* (October 1, 1893) XV, 174-175.

39. Field, Eugene. *Sharps and Flats,* I, 47-51. See also, Holloway, Jean, *Hamlin Garland* (1960) 84-90.

40. Pizer, Donald. *Hamlin Garland's Early Work and Career* (1960) 129.

41. Van Doren, Carl. "Contemporary American Novelists," *Nation,* CXIII (November 23, 1921) 596-597.

42. Garland, Hamlin. *A Daughter of the Middle Border* (1922) 25.

43. Herrick, Robert. *Memoirs of an American Citizen* (1905) 191-192.

44. Fleming, V, 787.

45. *The Chap-Book,* July 15, 1898. The issue had only the cover and a second page of explanation.

46. Burgess, Gelett, quoted in Kramer, Sidney, *A History of Stone & Kimball* ... (1940) 38.

47. J.K., "Who Reads a Chicago Book?" *The Dial* (September 1, 1892) 131; J. M., "Who Reads a Chicago Book?" *The Dial* (September 16, 1892) 194; Waterloo Stanley, "Who Reads a Chicago Book?" *The Dial* (October 1, 1892) 206-207 [all volume XIII]. "J.K.'s" letter complained that Chicagoans "read almost no home productions." "J.M." responded that the cause was the failure of Chicago critics to review "Chicago" books. Waterloo, a well-known Chicago writer of the time, agreed that Chicago literary criticism was of poor quality and that "Chicago" books had attracted the attention of qualified Eastern reviewers and "thousands of people outside Chicago read Chicago books." But the future of the "virile, independent" Chicago literature was good.

48. See, for instance, Edward Wagenknecht's "Utopia Americana," no. 28 in the University of Washington Chapbooks (1929).

49. Morgan, Anna. *My Chicago* (1918) 188.

50. Seymour, Ralph Fletcher. *Some Went This Way* (1945) 69-70. Duffey, Bernard, *The Chicago Renaissance in American Letters* (1954) 51-74. Morgan, Anna, *My Chicago* (1918). There are many other sources.

51. Pilkington, John Jr. *Henry Blake Fuller* (1970) 71.

52. Fuller, Henry Blake. "Pensieri Privati" (1878? 1880?). See Griffin, Constance, *Henry Blake Fuller* (1939) pp. 7 ff., and Bowron, Bernard, "Henry Blake Fuller: A Critical Study" (unpublished Harvard University Ph.D. dissertation, 1948) 506, n. 1.

53. _____. "Howells or James?" Ed. Darrel Abel. *Modern Fiction,* III (Summer, 1957) 159-164.

54. _____. "The Romance of a Middle-Aged Merchant and His Female Private Secretary." *Chicago Tribune* (4 October, 1884) 16. [Unsigned]. Pilkington, John Jr. *Henry Blake Fuller* (1970) 51.

55. _____. *The Cliff-Dwellers* (1893) 242.

56. _____. *The Cliff-Dwellers,* 4-5.

57. _____. *The Cliff-Dwellers,* 226.

58. *Letters of Charles Eliot Norton,* II (1913) 218.

59. Harris, Mark. "Fuller and the American Procession," in *With the Procession* (University of Chicago, 1965) vi.

60. Fuller, Henry Blake. *With the Procession* (1895, 1896) 1-2.

61. See, for instance: Mayer, Harold M. and Wade, Richard C., *Chicago/Growth of a Metropolis* (1969) pp. 124, 133, 134-5, 199, 301, 273.

62. Garland, Hamlin. *Roadside Meetings* (1930) 267-268.

63. Fuller, Henry Blake to Hamlin Garland. Pilkington, John, Jr. *Henry Blake Fuller* (1970) 144.

64. Seymour, Ralph Fletcher. *Some Went This Way* (1945) 144.

65. _____. 144.

66. Pilkington, 148. These lines, however, are not in the first edition of the book in the University of Iowa Library at Iowa City.

67. Seymour, 144-145. Pilkington, 151.

68. Ellis, Elmer. *Mr. Dooley's America: A Life of Finley Peter Dunne* (1941) 49. Duncan, 112.

69. Schaaf, Barbara C. *Mr. Dooley's Chicago* (1977) 341-342. The quotation appeared in the *Chicago Evening Post* July 7, 1894.

70. Shumaker, Arthur W. *A History of Indiana Literature* (1962) 447-448.

71. _____. 449.

72. Kelly, Fred. C. *George Ade, Warmhearted Satirist* (1947) 110.

73. Shumaker, 450, fn, 9.
74. *Farr, Chicago,* 254. Grey, 507.
75. Grey, 508.
76. Shumaker, 453-454. But see Duffey (1954) 19.
77. *Chicago Record* (September 17, 1897). George Ade, *Fables in Slang* (1900) 135-142. Shumaker, 452.
78. Grey, 609.
79. Kelly, *George Ade,* 171.
80. Shumaker, 461-462.
81. Shumaker, 470.
82. Pattee, Fred Lewis. *The New American Literature* (1930) 16-17.
83. Harper, J. Henry. *The House of Harper* (1912) 321. Quoted in Ziff, Larzer, *The American 1890s/Life and Times of a Lost Generation* (1966) 126.

Chapter VII

1. Dell, Floyd. "Chicago in Fiction." *Bookman* (December, 1913) 376-377 [Part II of two parts].
2. Howells, William Dean. "Certain of the Chicago School of Fiction," *The North American Review* (CLXXVI, 558) (May, 1903) 734-746.
3. Duncan, Hugh Dalziell. *The Rise of Chicago as a Literary Center From 1885 to 1920: A Sociological Essay in American Culture* (1964) xvi.
4. Mott, Frank Luther. *A History of American Magazines* (1957) IV, 688.
5. Duffey, Bernard. *The Chicago Renaissance in American Letters (1954)* 101.
6. Norris, Frank. *The Pit/A Story of Chicago* (1902) prefatory statement.
7. _____. "The House With the Blinds," *The Third Circle/A Deal in Wheat* ... (1928) 11 [Works, vol 4].
8. Dell, "Chicago in Fiction," *Bookman* (November, 1913) 270-271.
9. Pattee, Fred Lewis. *New American Literature* (1930) 36.
10. Farr, Finis, *Chicago,* 404.
11. Rose, Lisle. *A Descriptive Catalogue of Economic and Politico-Economic Fiction in the United States, 1902-1909* (Unpublished University of Chicago Ph.D. diss., 1935) 256-260.
12. Doubleday, Page & Co. advertisement, *Publisher's Weekly* (October 15, 1904) 938 quotes to that effect from the *Chicago Record-Herald.*
13. Mott, 686.
14. Kilpatrick, Thomas L. *Illinois! Illinois!* (1979) 286, item 673. "Merriman" was the pseudonym of George T. Richardson and W. D. Quint.
15. Banks, Charles Eugene. *John Dorn, Promoter* (1906) 44-45.
16. Redlick, David E. and Rosemarie. *Literary America/A Chronicle of American Writers From 1607-1952* (1952), 111; Fischer, John, Ed., *The Jungle* (1946) x. Other sources.
17. Grosch, Anthony R. *Social Issues in Early Chicago Novels, Chicago History* (Summer, 1975) IV, 2, 71.
18. Anonymous "The Great John Ganton," *The New York Times* (May 4, 1909) 9:1.
19. Rose, Lisle. *A Descriptive Catalouge of Economic and Politico-Economic Fiction in the United States, 1902-1909* (Unpub. University of Chicago Ph.D. diss., 1935) 36.
20. Anonymous, "Simeon Tetlow's Shadow," *The Nation* (LXXXVIII, 2287) April 29, 1909, 443.
21. _____. 443.
22. Kilpatrick, Thomas, *Illinois! Illinois!* (1979) 160, item 355.
23. Only pages 312-333 are set in Chicago, during a political convention. Lisle Rose, on page 177 of his dissertation, says that "Devlin" is probably modeled on "King" James McManes of Philadelphia (see fn. 19 above).

24. Featured is an Irish boss of the notorious First Ward who loves Mr. Dooley's "dear old Archey Road." (p. 295).

25. Lisle A. Rose. *A Descriptive Catalogue of Economic and Politico-Economic Fiction in the United States, 1902-1909*. (Unpublished University of Chicago diss., 1935.) Chap. 5.

26. Mayer, Harold M., and Wade, Richard C. *Chicago/Growth of a Metropolis* (1969) 160.

27. _____. 160.

28. Lewis, Lloyd and Smith, Henry Justin. *Chicago/The History of Its Reputation* (1929) 234.

29. Grey, 603.

30. Anonymous. *"By Bread Alone."* By J. K. Friedman. *The Athenaeum* (April 26, 1902) 526.

31. Grey, 603.

32. Warren, Maude Radford. *The Land of the Living* (1908) 11, 26, 111.

33. Dell, Floyd, "Chicago in Fiction," 376.

34. Hapgood, Hutchins, *The Spirit of Labor* (1907) 9.

35. Grey, 391, calls it "the Briggs House."

36. Grey, 392.

37. Hapgood, Hutchins. *An Anarchist Woman* (1909) 153.

38. Grey, 495.

39. Mott, Frank Luther. *Golden Multitudes* (1947) 193-197.

40. Grey, 365.

41. Payne, Will, *The Story of Eva* (1901) 96-97.

42. Dreiser, Theodore. *Sister Carrie* (1900) Chapter 2.

43. Dell, Floyd, "Chicago in Fiction," 375.

44. Bourne, Randolph. "Theodore Dreiser," *New Republic* (April 17, 1915) II, 8.

45. Boynton, Percy H. *Some Contemporary Americans* (1924) 127.

46. Bourne, Randolph. "Theodore Dreiser," *New Republic* (April 17, 1915) II, 8; *The Dial* (June 14, 1917) 508.

47. Kazin, Alfred. "Theodore Dreiser: His Education and Ours," *The Stature of Theodore Dreiser* (1955) 158.

48. Maltin, Leonard. *TV Movies 1975 Edition* (1974) 85.

49. Farr, Finis. *Chicago*, 404.

50. Duffey, Bernard. *Chicago Renaissance*, 63.

51. Grey, 544, fn. 3.

52. Howells, William Dean. "Certain of the Chicago School of Fiction," *North American Review* (CLXXVI, 558) 739. Howells also compares Wyatt to Jane Austen.

53. J. C. *"Duchess of Few Clothes," The Reader Magazine*, IV (June, 1904) 110-111.

54. Kilpatrick *Illinois! Illinois!* 180-181, item 411.

55. Andrews, Clarence. *A Literary History of Iowa* (1972) 71.

56. Anonymous, "The Story of a Fibber," *The New York Times* (March 21 1903), 191.

57. Noe, Marcia. *A Critical Biography of Susan Glaspell* (unpublished University of Iowa dissertation, 1976) 31-32.

58. Anonymous. *"The Glory of the Conquered," The New York Times* (March 13, 1909) 14:145; (June 12, 1909) 14:374.

59. Noe, Marcia, 57.

60. Anonymous, "Maroon Tales," *The New York Times* (January 22, 1910) 15:38.

61. Arvin, Newton. "Homage to Robert Herrick," *The New Republic* (March 6, 1935) LXXXII, 93.

62. Herrick, Robert. *The Gospel of Freedom* (1898) 104.

63. Dell, Floyd. "Chicago in Fiction," "Robert Herrick's Chicago," First Paper, *Bookman* (November 1913) 38, 275.

64. Herrick, Robert. *The Common Lot* (1904) 338.

65. Dell, Floyd. "Chicago in Fiction," 274.

66. Herrick, Robert. *Memoirs of an American Citizen* (1905) 95.

67. Herrick, *Memoirs*, 191.

68. Duffey, Bernard. *Chicago Renaissance,* 120.
69. ———. *Chicago Renaissance,* 121.
70. Dell, "Chicago in Fiction," 274.
71. Duffey, Bernard. "Realism and the Genteel in Robert Herrick's Chicago Novels." *WHR* (VI, 3, 1951-52) 269.
72. ———. 270.
73. Wheaton, Emily. *"The Russells in Chicago, Ladies' Home Journal* (December, 1901) 10, 46.
74. Wheaton, *The Russells,* 46.
75. The best account of the "Levee" is in Lloyd Wendt's and Herman Kogan's *Lords of the Levee* (1943), reprinted in 1967 as *Bosses of Lusty Chicago.* See also Herbert Asbury's *The Gem of the Prairie* (1940).
76. *Illinois! Illinois!* Item 386, p. 170.
77. ———. Item 392, p. 172.
78. Kilpatrick, Thomas. *Illinois! Illinois!* 214-215, item 489.
79. Kilpatrick, Thomas, *Illinois! Illinois!* 150, 328.

Chapter VIII

1. Patterson, Joseph Medill. *A Little Brother of the Rich* (1908) 17.
2. Seymour, Ralph Fletcher. *Some Went This Way* (1945) 10, 13.
3. Duncan, Hugh D. *The Rise of Chicago as a Literary Center from 1885-1920: A Sociological Essay in American Culture* (1964) 1, fn. 1, p. 14.
4. Hackett, Francis. *American Rainbow* (1971) 151-152. Hackett also describes many other "Little Room" members.
5. Dedmon, Emmet. *Fabulous Chicago* (1981) 207.
6. Seymour, Ralph Fletcher. 161-162.
7. Browne, Maurice, in *Illinois/A Descriptive and Historical Guide* (1939) 135.
8. Duffey, Bernard. *Chicago Renaissance* (1954) pp. 239 is the source for this quote and for other information here. See also Anna Morgan, *My Chicago* (1918) 44, 69.
9. Glaspell, Susan. *The Road to the Temple* (1926) 248.
10. Glaspell, 218.
11. Monroe, Harriet. *A Poet's Life* (1938) 391-392.
12. Dell, Floyd, in Kramer's *Chicago Renaissance* (1966) 194. Quoted from the *Friday Literary Review* of the *Evening Post.*
13. Kramer, Dale *Chicago Renaissance/The Literary Life in the Midwest 1900-1930* (1966) 195.
14. Glaspell, 218.
15. Hecht, Ben. *A Child of the Century* (1954) 337-338.
16. Morgan, Anna. *My Chicago* (1918) 190-193. Morgan's book records much of the social life of the artists of this period.
17. Hecht, Ben. *A Child of the Century* (1954).
18. Williams, Kenny Jackson. *In the City of Men/Another Story of Chicago* (1974) 184-185. Williams' opinions are echoed by numerous others, including Edgar Lee Masters (*Tale of Chicago,* 341-342), H. L. Mencken and Bernard Duffey.
19. Dell, Floyd. "Joseph Medill Patterson's Chicago. Chicago in Fiction/The Fourth Paper," *Friday Literary Review* of *The Chicago Evening Post* (2/16/1912) 1.
20. Anonymous. "Latest Fiction," *The New York Times Book Review* (June 14, 1914) 269-270.
21. Review of *The Other Side of the Wall,* Boston Transcript, (January 17, 1920) 6.
22. Glaspell, Susan. *The Road to the Temple* (1927) 212.
23. Kramer, Dale *Chicago Renaissance* (1966) 105.
24. ———. 108.
25. Glaspell, *The Road to the Temple,* 181.

26. ———. 212.

27. ———. 213.

28. Hart, John E. "Floyd Dell: Intellectual Vagabond," *Western Humanities Review* (Winter, 1962) XVI, 1, 70.

29. Gardner, Virginia. "A Literary Editor Reminisces: Henry Blackman Sell," *Chicago History* (Fall, 1974) 101-110, *passim*.

30. Lardner, Ring, Jr. *Gullible's Travels* (1916).

31. Maltin, Leonard. ed. *TV Movies* (1974) 10. But see Roger Dooley's *From Scarface to Scarlett* (1981) 403.

32. Meyer, Harold M. and Wade, Richard C. *Chicago/Growth of a Metropolis* (1969) 252.

33. Barnes, Margaret Ayer. *Prevailing Winds,* prefatory note.

34. Dondore, Dorothy. *The Prairie and the Making of Middle America: Four Centuries of Description* (1926) 374.

35. *Illinois! Illinois!* Item 687, p. 288.

36. ———. Item 686, p. 287.

37. Anonymous. *"Dawson, '11: Fortune Hunter,"* *Nation* (96, 2840) 36.

38. Kramer, Dale. *Chicago Renaissance,* 251-252.

39. *Illinois! Illinois!* Item 335, p. 152.

40. *The Dial.* (March 22, 1917) 62:247.

41. Ferber, Edna. *A Peculiar Treasure* (1939) 172.

42. ———. 179.

43. ———. *Cheerful by Request* (1918) 43.

44. ———. *A Peculiar Treasure* (1939) 233.

45. Halper, Albert. *This is Chicago* (1952) 1.

46. ———. 1.

47. Overton, Grant M. *The Women Who Make Our Novels* (1922) 295.

48. Ferber, Edna. *Fanny Herself.* (1917) 138-139.

49. ———. 159.

50. ———. *A Peculiar Treasure* (1939) 223.

51. Wyckoff, Elizabeth Porter. *"The Real Adventure,"* *Publishers' Weekly* (January 15, 1916) 89:190.

52. Two in particular. Dale Kramer's anecdotal *Chicago Renaissance/The Literary Life in the Midwest 1900-1930* (1966), and Bernard Duffey's scholarly *The Chicago Renaissance in American Letters, a Critical History* (1953).

53. Sklar, Robert. "Chicago Renaissance," *Commonweal* (January 6, 1967) 377.

54. Hutchens, John K. "When Poets Looped the Loop," *Saturday Review* (January 28, 1967) 35.

55. Jones, Llewellyn. "Salad Days of Our Literary Life," *The Chicago Sun Book Week* (October 10, 1943) 4.

56. Mencken, H. L. "The Literary Capitol of the United States," *The Nation* (London, April 17, 1920).

57. Sandburg, Carl. *Always the Young Strangers* (1952) 128-129; *Chicago Sun Book Week* (May 16, 1943) 5.

58. Monroe, Harriet. *A Poet's Life,* (1938).

59. Sandburg, Carl.

60. ———. "Mamie," p. 35.

61. ———. "They Will Say," p. 9.

62. ———. *The Chicago Race Riots* (1919). Introduction. A 1969 edition has an introduction by Ralph McGill.

63. Winter, Calvin. "Theodore Dreiser's *Jennie Gerhardt,*" *Bookman* (December, 1911) 433.

64. Maltin, Leonard. *TV Movies* (1975) 291. The New York *Times* praised the film's "laudable sincerity," and Roger Dooley *From Scarface to Scarlett* (1979) called the film a "creditable version of" the novel. (133).

65. Grey, 521-522, lists fictional treatments of Yerkes.
66. Wendt, Lloyd and Herman Kogan. *Bosses in Lusty Chicago* (1967), reprint of *Lords of the Levee* (1943) 221-229.
67. *Sherwood Andersons' Memoirs* (1942) 235. Reported by Duffey, 201.
68. Kramer, *Chicago Renaissance*, 240.
69. Grey, 403.
70. *Illinois! Illinois!* Item 278, p. 130.
71. _____. 130.
72. Grey, 484.
73. *Illinois! Illinois!* Item 276, p. 129.
74. Anderson, Sherwood. *Poor White* (1920) 30-31.
75. _____. "Evening Song," *Mid-American Chants* (1972) 61.
76. Monroe, Harriet. *A Poet's Life/Seventy Years in a Changing World* (1938) 240.
77. _____. 247.
78. _____. 249.
79. Seymour, Ralph Fletcher. *Some Went This Way* (1945) 139-140.
80. _____. 143-144.
81. _____. 140-141. Seymour notes that on the back cover of every issue "was printed Walt Whitman's line, 'To have great poets, there must be great audiences too.'"
82. Duffey, *Chicago Renaissance . . .*, 185, 222.
83. Jones, Llewellyn. "Salad Days of Our Literary Life," *The Chicago Sun Book Week* (October 10, 1943) 4.
84. Reader's of Anderson's autobiography, My Thirty Years War (1930) may get the impression that Clara Laughlin and Floyd Dell were more influential. See p. 54 for Emma Goldman's influence.
85. Kramer, *Chicago Renaissance*, 244-262. Duffey, *Chicago Renaissance in American Letters*, 189-193. Margaret Anderson, *My Thirty Years War* (1930), 174-176.
86. Joost, Nicholas. *The Dial/Years of Transition* (1967) 93, says Waldo left The Dial July 15, 1916. *The Dial* moved to New York July 1, 1918 under Scofield Thayer's aegis.
87. Anonymous. "One Woman's Story," *Bookman* (April 13, 1913) 37:201, 202.
88. Budd, Louis J. *Robert Herrick* (1971) 84, quotes Herrick to this effect.
89a. H. I. B. "Parable or Novel?" *New York Times* (March 2, 1913) 18: 107.
89. Reported in the "Saturday Review of Books and Art," *The New York Times* under the title "Literature in Chicago" (October 13, 1902) 1.
90. Anonymous. *The Dial* (April 1, 1913) 54:306.
91. Mayer, Harold M. and Richard C. Wade. *Chicago/Growth of a Metropolis* (1969), 242, credit W. H. Wright, an early Gary realtor, with this assertion.
92. Middleton, George. "C. T. Jackson's *My Brother's Keeper*," *Bookman* (November, 1910) 303.
93. Grey, 398-399.
94. Austin, Mary. *A Woman of Genius* (1912) 400.
95. Kinzie, Mrs. John H. *Wau-Bun* . . . (1932 edition) 219-220.
96. Farr, Chicago, 257.
97. Duncan, Hugh D. *The Rise of Chicago As a Literary Center,* 90.
98. _____. 71. See also Mark Twain's letter to W. D. Howells in *One Afternoon With Mark Twain,* (George Ade, 1939).
100. Anonymous. *"The Losing Game," Nation* (April 14, 1910) 377.
101. Balmer, Edwin and MacHarg, William. *The Indian Drum* (1917) 4.
102. Anonymous. "Cecily," *Boston Transcript* (November 4, 1916) 6.
103. Tobenkin, Elias. *Witte Arrives* (1916) 128.
104. Anonymous. "Notes on New Books," *The Dial* (April 19, 1919) 424.
105. Anonymous. "The Eternal Sophomore," *Nation* (February 22, 1919) 108, 2799, p. 285.

106. Hedges, M. H. *Iron City*. Bourne is quoted on the dust jacket.
107. Anonymous. "*Iron City*," "New Books" (1920) 695.

Chapter IX

1. Plum, Mary. *The Killing of Judge McFarlane* (1930) 1.
2. Wendt, Lloyd and Herman Kogan. *Bosses in Lusty Chicago,* (1967) 339.
3. Sullivan, Edward D. *Rattling the Cup on Chicago Crime* (1929) 82-89. Neither the *New York Times* nor Burns Mantle document Miss Winter's history in New York City.
4. Neville, Marion. "The Spectator," *Chicago Sun Book Week* (November 1, 1942), 22. *NUC pre-1956 Imprints* lists neither.
5. Neville, Marion. *Chicago Sun Book Week* (11-1-42) 22.
6. Kehr, Dave. "Screening the Past," *Chicago* (November, 1981) 220.
7. Maltin, Leonard, editor. *TV Movies 1975 Edition* (1974) 487.
8. Reviewed in New York *Daily News,* June 4, 1975; *Newsweek,* June 16, 1976; *New York Times,* June 4, 1975; *Time,* June 16, 1975.
9. Mantle, Burns. "The Plays and Their Authors," *Best Plays of 1926-27* (1927) 354.
10. *New York Times* (January 5, 1928) p. 33, col. 1.
11, *New York Times.* "Defiant Over *The Racket*," (January 6, 1928) p. 27, col. 2.
12. Mantle, Burns. Best Plays of 1927-28 (1928). "The Plays and Their Authors," 384.
13. Mantle, Burns. *Best Plays of 1927-1928* (1928) v.
14. Harris, Jed. Introduction to *The Front Page* (1928) n.p.
15. ———. Introduction (n. p.).
16. "R. M. L." "*The Front Page*," *The New Republic* (September 5, 1928) 73.
17. Kael, Pauline. *The Citizen Kane Book* (1974) 27.
18. Dooley, Roger. *From Scarface to Scarlett/American Films in the 1930s* (1981) 257.
19. Atkinson, J. Brooks. "*The Front Page*," *The New York Times* (August 26, 1928) VII:1:1.
20. Kehr, Dave. "Screening the Past," *Chicago* (November, 1981) 220.
21. Dooley, Roger, 258.
22. Kael, Pauline, 61.
23. Dooley, Roger, 265.
24. The Authors. Epilogue, *The Front Page* (1928) n.p.
25. Harris, Jed. Introduction, n. p.
26. *National Union Catalog* Pre-1956 Imprints. Vol. 237, 535.
27. Walt, Charles. *Love in Chicago* (1929) Dedication, n. p.
28. Asbury, Herbert. "Rise and Fall of a Crime King," *New York Herald Tribune Books* (June 2, 1929) XI, 7.
29. Dooley, Roger. *From Scarface to Scarlett,* 289.
30. *Illinois! Illinois!* Item 1133, p. 433.
31. Ferber, Edna. *A Peculiar Treasure* (1939) 247.
32. ———. 261.
33. ———. 262.
34. Hackett, Francis. "*The Girls*," *The New Republic* (29:158) January 4, 1922. The book was also reviewed favorably by Heywood Broun in *The Bookman* and by Louise Maunsell Field in *The New York Times*. Reviews in *The Dial* and *The Boston Transcript* were less favorable.
35. Nathan, Robert. "A Novel in Black and White," *Literary Review* (October 22, 1921) 99.
36. Ross, Mary. "Hard Life and High Times of Edna Ferber," *New York Herald Tribune Books* (February 5, 1939) 1.
37. Ferber, *A Peculiar Treasure,* 283.
38. ———. 289. I can find no record of a production of *Minick* in Chicago at that time.
39. Dooley, Roger. *From Scarface to Scarlett,* 541.
40. Ferber, *A Peculiar Treasure.* 247, 276.

41. *So Big* ran in serial form in *Woman's Home Companion* in 1923, as *Selina,* which makes my statement more emphatic.

42. Towne, Charles Hanson. "Edna Ferber Answers Her Critics," *Literary Digest International Book Review* (April, 1924) 344-345.

43. Roger Dooley (*From Scarface to Scarlett*) likes the second version, Leonard Maltin (*TV Movies*) the third.

44. Ferber. *A Peculiar Treasure,* 304.

45. Kronenberger, Louis. "*Show Boat* is High Romance," *New York Times Book Review* (August 22, 1926) 5.

46. Grey, 238-239.

47. Anonymous. "*Skeeters Kirby,*" *New York Times Book Review* (March 4, 1923) 14, 16.

48. Anonymous. "Romance, Reality and Revolt in New Novels," *Literary Digest International Book Review* (April, 1923) 53.

49. _____. 53.

50. Anonymous. *New York Times Book Review* (March 4, 1923) 14.

51. L. L. "The Dance of Life," *Nation* (September 12, 1923) 117-270.

52. Anonymous. "Yellow IS Black," *Independent* (May 13, 1922) 108:3816.

53. Lovett, Robert Morss. "*Homely Lilla,*" *Dial* (May 23, 1923) 75:513.

54. Krutch, Joseph Wood. "Mr. Herrick's Return," *Nation,* CXVI, (February 14, 1923) 190.

55. Duffey, Bernard. *Chicago Renaissance,* 115.

56. Herrick's literary ideas are best presented in: "The Background of the American Novel," *Yale Review* III (1914) 213-233; "The American Novel, " *Yale Review,* III (April 1914) 419-437; "In General," *Nation,* CXIII (7 December, 1921) 658-569; "Let Us Talk About Unpleasant Things," *Harper's,* CLXV (October, 1932) 598-604.

57. Morris, Lloyd. "Mr. Herrick Arraigns His Fellow Americans," *Literary Digest International Book Review* (May, 1924) 466.

58. _____. 466.

59. Van Doren, Carl. "Forty Years in the Wilderness," *The New Republic* (April 23, 1924) 235.

60. Hutchison, Percy A. "That World Within the College," *New York Times Book Review* (May 2, 1926) 7; Buxbaum, Katherine. "*Chimes,*" *International Book Review* (June, 1926) 452.

61. _____. 452.

62. [Flanigan, Zoe.] *Grey Towers* (1923) Unpaged prefatory note.

63. Anonymous. "*The Professor's House,*" *The Nation & The Athenaeum* (December 19, 1925) 440.

64. Canby, Henry Seidel. "A Novel of the Soul," *Saturday Review of Literature* (September 26, 1925) 150-151.

65. Krutch, Joseph Wood. "Second Best," *The Nation* (121, 3142) 336; Harper, Moses. "Americans All," *The New Republic* (September 16, 1925) 105, 106.

66. Newman, M. W. "*So Long, Chicago,*" *Chicago Daily News* (Final edition, Saturday March 4, 1978) 2, 3, 5, 6, 8.

67. Hecht, Ben. *Child of the Century* (1954). Caption on photo of Henry Justin Smith ff. p. 36.

68. Anonymous. "*Poor Devil,*" *New York Herald Tribune Books* (October 27, 1929) 24.

69, Anonymous. *Book Review Digest* (1922) 496.

70. Anonymous. "In the Huxley Manner," *New York Times Review of Books* (February 27, 1927) 8.

71. Gunther, John. *The Golden Fleece* (1929) 152-154.

72. Kunitz, Stanley J., and Haycraft, Howard. *Twentieth Century Authors* (1942) 819.

73. The phrase comes from Henry Justin Smith's *Deadlines*; it was also used by R. H. Andrews in this *A Corner of Chicago* (1963).

74. Hecht, Ben. *A Thousand and One Afternoons in Chicago,* preface.

75. _____. Preface.

76. Hecht, Ben. *Erik Dorn* (1963) 77-78.

77.   Algren, Nelson. Introduction to *Erik Dorn* (1963) ix.
78.   Grey, Lennox Bouton. 244-245.
79.   Anonymous. *"Jake,"* *New York Times Book and Magazine* (May 8, 1921) 22.
80.   _____. 22.
81.   Anonymous. "A Tribal Chronicle," *New York Times Book and Magazine* (December 4, 1921) 8.
82.   *Illinois! Illinois!*, 425, item 1108.
83.   _____. Item 1234, p. 468.
84.   _____. Item 868, p. 356.
85.   Butcher, Fanny. "First Channon Novel Gives New View of Chicago," *Chicago Tribune* (July 27, 1929) 7.
86.   Synon, Mary. *The Good Red Bricks* (1929) 81.
87.   Hall, Mordaunt. "Miss Swanson's First Talker." *New York Times* (November 2, 1929) 14:6.
88.   *Illinois! Illinois!* Item 822, 343-344.
89.   Adams, Franklin P. "Et Haec Olim Meminisse Juvabit," *Chicago Sun Book Week* (September 19, 1943) 3.
90.   Farr, Finis. See also Meeker, Arthur, "Birdie," *Chicago With Love* (1955) 177-192.
91.   Fuller, Henry B. "The Smith Family Populates a Western Novel," *Literary Digest International Book Review* (September 25, 1925) 663.
92.   In *Chicago With Love* (1955, 191) Meeker says that "Birdie" Fairbank was at work on a novel "which promised in many ways to be her best." After her husband died, the book was "laid away unfinished; she had no heart to write."
93.   Anonymous. *"The Invisible Gods,"* *Literary Digest International Book Review* (September 25, 1925) 663.
94.   Lovett, Robert Morss. "Workers in Metal," *New Republic* (December 7, 1921) 48-49. Lovett reviewed Charles G. Norris' *Brass* in the same article.
95.   Nevins, Allan, "A Family Chronicle," *Saturday Review of Literature* (November 13, 1926) 3:294.
96.   Anonymous. "Mr. Riesenberg Rebuilds His Novel of Publicity," *New York Times Review of Books* (February 12, 1928) 5.
97.   Bates, Ernest Sutherland. "The Realism of Business," *Saturday Review of Literature* (December 4, 1926) 3:336. Hellman, Lillian F. "Stale Sweepings," *New York Herald Tribune Books* (April 1, 1928) 15.
98.   Lohrke, Eugene. "A 'Serious' Hero," *New York Herald Tribune Books* (October 16, 1927) 17.
99.   Gale, Zona. "The Story of a Jew Who Married a Christian," *Literary Digest International Book Review* (May, 1925) 375.
100. Anonymous. *"The White Girl,"* *New York Times Book Review* (January 20, 1929) 8.
101. G. H. *Springfield* [MA] *Republican* (May 28, 1928) 6.
101a. Larson, Nella. *Passing* (1929) 97. Grey, 667.
101b. Seabrook, W. B. *Saturday Review of Literature* (May 18, 1929) 5:1017.
102. Coblentz, Stanton A. "Conflicting Characters," *Literary Review* (December 2, 1922) 260.
103. Dale, Virginia. "The Season in Chicago," *The Best Plays of 1927-28,* Burns Mantle, ed. 18. (1928) 18.
104. Burroughs, Edgar Rice. *The Mucker* (1921) 74.
105. *Illinois! Illinois!* 287, item 677.
106. Goetzinger, Clara Palmer. *Smouldering Flames* (1928) 12.
107. _____. 9.
108. Anderson, Sherwood. *Horses and Men* (1923) 139-140.
109. _____. 289.
110. _____.
111. _____. 235.
112. _____. xii.

113. Anonymous. "Nowhere Else in the World," New York Times Book and Magazine (October 28, 1923) 8.
114. Hudson, Jay William. Nowhere Else in the World (1923) 381.
115. Tomlinson, David O. Dictionary of American Biography Supplement Seven (1981) 239.
116. Marshall, James. Ordeal By Glory (1927) 288.
117. Anonymous. "Into Middle Age," New York Times Book Review (October 2, 1928) 16, 18.
118. Anonymous. "Winslow, Thyra Samter," Book Review Digest (1923) 467, col. 2.
119. Ferber, Edna. International Book Review (February, 1923) 19.
120. Newman, Frances. New York Herald Tribune Books (March 21, 1926) 6.
121. ———. 6.
122. Hansen, Harry. Midwest Portraits/A Book of Memories and Friendships (1923) 63.
123. Nye, Russel. The Unembarrassed Muse/The Popular Arts in America (1970) 320.
124. "Chicago," as it is copyrighted varies from this version. The fourth line reads: "The folks who visit all wanna settle down." The ninth line reads: "You come along and bring your wife." The writer has known the printed version since the 1920s, and never knew of the other version until 1982.
125. Van Doren, Mark. Nation (June 18, 1924) 118:712.
126. Guiterman, Arthur. Outlook (May 28, 1924) 137:157.
127. Dow, Dorothy. "Black Babylon," Black Babylon (1924) 11-20.
128. ———. 11.
129. Anonymous. "Poet Masters Tunes His Lyre to Nuptial Key?" [Chicago Tribune?].
130. "Amy's Corner," Democrat-Reader (October 23, 1947).
131. Lewis, Edwin Herbert, Ph.D. University of Chicago Poems (1923) 1.
132. ———. 27.
133. Lechlitner, Ruth. "Wind, Rain and Flame," New York Herald Tribune Books (December 4, 1927).
134. Dillon, George. "Twilight in a Tower," (from Boy in the Wind, 1927) This Is Chicago, ed. Albert Halper (1952) 42.
135. Lovett, Robert Morss. "Boy in the Wind," The Dial (April, 1928) 84:339, 342.
136. Borrows, Marjorie, comp. Pulitzer Prize Poems (1941) 176.
137. Kramer, Dale. 310.
138. Kramer, Dale. 335.
139. Kramer, Dale. 335. Jay Robert Nash revived the Chicago Literary Times in the early 1960s.
140. Kramer, Dale. 335.
141. Dedmon, Emmett. Fabulous Chicago (1981) 274.
143. Kehr, Dave. "Screening the Past," Chicago (November, 1981) 176.
144. Kehr, Dave. 176.
145. Kehr, Dave. 176.
146. Kehr, Dave. 177.
147. Kehr, Dave. 177.
148. Hall, Mordaunt. "The Girl From Chicago, New York Times (December 20, 1927) 33:2.

Chapter X

1. Andrus, Louise. Though Time Be Fleet (1937), Foreword.
2. Figures are taken from annual reports in Publisher's Weekly.
3. Sullivan, Edward D. Rattling the Cup on Chicago Crime (1929). Quoted in "The Lowdown on Chicago" by W. R. Burnett, New York Herald-Tribune Books (August 25, 1929) 4.
4. Burnett, W. R. "The Lowdown on Chicago," New York Herald-Tribune Books (August 25, 1929) p. 4.
5. Kehr, Dave. "Screening the Past," Chicago (November, 1981) 177, 219.
6. Lait, Jack. Put on the Spot (1930) 207.

7.   Tobenkin, Elias. *In the Dark* (1931) 153-154.

8.   Dooley, Roger. *From Scarface to Scarlett* (1981) 291.

9.   ———. 295-296. Kehr, 220.

10.   Kehr, 219.

11.   Dooley, 592, *passim*.

12.   Feld, Rose C. "The Liberals." *New York Times Book Review* (September 11, 1938) 2.

13.   ——— 2.

14.   Grey, 654-655.

15.   Fairbank, Janet Ayer and Barnes, Margaret Ayer. *The Alleged Great Aunt* (1935) Foreword.

16.   Starrett, Charles Vincent Emerson.

17.   Grey, 655.

17.   Butcher, Fanny. "Pens Charming Story of Bride," *Chicago Daily Tribune* (July 13, 1935) p. 6.

19.   Engle, Paul. "America Remembers," *American Song (1934) 91*.

20.   Adams, J. Donald. "A New Voice in American Poetry," *New York Times* (July 29, 1934) *Books*, p. 1. Whipple, Leon. "Variations on an American Theme," *Survey Graphic* (October, 1934) 510.

21.   Cowley, Malcolm. "Eagle Orator," *New Republic* (August 29, 1934) 80:79. Tate, Allen. *The New Republic* (October 10, 1934, 245).

22.   Benét, Stephen Vincent. *American Song* (1934) dust jacket. Benét's brother, William Rose Benét, in his *Saturday Review of Literature* column, The Phoenix Nest (April 11, 1936, p. 18) also found much to praise in the book.

23.   Monroe, Harriet. "Chicago, 1933," *Poetry* (June, 1933) 147.

24.   Reigelman, Milton M. *The Midland/A Venture in Literary Regionalism* (Iowa City, 1975).

25.   Boynton, H. W. "Somebody in Boots," *New York Times Books* (April 7, 1935) 6.

26.   Redman, Ben Ray. "Two Novels: $2,000," *The Saturday Review of Literature* (May 4, 1935) 18.

27.   ———. 18.

28.   *Wilson Bulletin for Librarians* (April, 1935) 402, 404.

29.   Rutenber, Ralph D., Jr. "Foundrymen and Bosses," *New Republic* (September 19, 1934) 165-166.

30.   *Illinois! Illinois!* Item 495, p. 217. *Chicago Side Show* has only 22 pages.

31.   Calverton, V. F. "This Negro," *The Nation* (August 16, 1930) 131, 3396, 157-158.

32.   Marsh, Fred T. "A Brilliant First Novel in *The Opening of a Door*," *New York Times Book Review* (August 16, 1931) 4.

33.   Kazin, Alfred. *"Give Us This Day,"* *New York Herald Tribune Books* (May 17, 1936) 12.

34.   Farrell, James T. "Between Two Wars," *Saturday Review of Literature* (March 13, 1937) 5.

35.   Goldberg, Isaac. "A Jewish Prize Novel," *Saturday Review of Literature* (January 29, 1938) 17.

36.   Kazin, Alfred. "Odyssey of the Twenties," *New York Herald Tribune Books* (July 23, 1939) 4.

37.   Ferber, Edna. *A Peculiar Treasure* (1939) 294-295.

38.   *Illinois! Illinois!* Item 1124, p. 430.

39.   Anonymous. "The Story of a City," *Saturday Review of Literature* (October 17, 1931) 8:206.

40.   Grey, 159.

41.   Masters, Edgar Lee. *The Tale of Chicago* (1933) 339-340.

42.   Shea, Agatha L. "Tale of Prairie Adventure . . ." *Chicago Tribune* (October 22, 1932) 8.

43.   For instances, see Ben Hecht, *Child of the Century*, p. 217, and Dale Kramer, *Chicago Renaissance*, p. 259.

44.   Dawson, Margaret Cheney. "A Sentimental Bodenheim," *New York Herald Tribune Books* (June 1, 1930) 4.

45. Anonymous. "The Rise of Elsa Potter," *New York Herald Tribune Books* (August 21, 1932) 6.

46. Jones, Howard Mumford. "Willa Cather Returns to the Middle West," *Saturday Review of Literature* (August 3, 1935) 7.

47. ———. 7.

48. Lengel, William C. *Candles in the Wind* (1937) Introduction.

49. *Illinois! Illinois!* Item 783, p. 332.

50. ———. Item 1004, p. 396.

51. ———. Item 320, p. 147.

52. Rukeyser, Muriel. "A Prize Novel," *New York Herald Tribune Books* (October 4, 1931) 20.

53. Grey, 669.

54. ———. 669. *A Man and a Woman* (1931) pp. 50, 75, 60.

55. Anonymous. "A Man and a Woman," *Chicago Daily Tribune* (March 21, 1931) 19.

56. Herrick, Robert. Dust jacket of *The End of Desire* (1932).

57. Anonymous. "*The End of Desire*," *New York Times Book Reviews* (January 10, 1932).

58. See, for instance Fanny Butcher's "Critic Praises Chicago Novel by Chicagoan," *Chicago Daily Tribune* (January 25, 1930) 9.

59. Winslow, Thyra Samter. "Even Chicago Has a Heart," *New York Herald Tribune Books* (September 7, 1930) 2.

61. ———. 2.

62. *Illinois! Illinois!* Item 855, p. 354.

63. Field, Louise Maunsell. "The Other Woman," *New York Times Book Review* (April 25, 1937) 21, 23. Field, alone of the book's critics, noted that the novel was originally published serially in two parts, each with a different title.

64. Anonymous. "Iron Man," *New York Times Review of Books* (January 5, 1930) 6.

65. *Illinois! Illinois!* Item 800, 337-338. Also published as *Glamor; a novel about ten million dollars,* and *If I Had a Million.*

66. Dooley, Roger. *From Scarface to Scarlett* (1979) 34-35, 400-401.

67. DeVoto, Bernard. "Streamline Version of Harold Bell Wright," *Saturday Review of Literature* (March 30, 1935) 581.

68. Anonymous. "*Green Light,*" *New York Times Book Review* (March 17, 1935) 20.

69. Butcher, Fanny. "Years of Grace," *Chicago Daily Tribune* (June 28, 1930) 12. Ms. Butcher was a friend of Mrs. Barnes and her sister.

70. Barnes, Margaret Ayer. *Years of Grace* (1930).

71. Lowrie, Rebecca. "The Piera Clan," *Satuday Review of Literature,* (September 17, 1931) 106.

72. Anonymous. "A Co-ed College," *New York Times Book Review* (August 3, 1930) 7.

73. Marsh, Fred T. "Harvard and Boston Adrift," *New York Times Book Review* (September 30, 1934) 6.

74. *Saturday Review of Literature* (November 21, 1936) 24; *New York Herald Tribune Books* (October 11, 1936) 12; *New York Times Book Review* (October 11, 1936) 7.

75. For instance Charlotte Moody, "Two Novels of College Life," *Saturday Review of Literature* (June 5, 1937) 12.

76. Van Gelder, Robert. "An Interview With Mr. James T. Farrell," *New York Times Book Review* (May 17, 1942) pp. 2, 17.

77. Canby, Henry Seidel. "James T. Farrell's Indelible Portraits," *Saturday Review of Literature* (December 7, 1935) 7.

78. Algren, Nelson. "New Chicago Cantos," *Saturday Review of Literature* (November 14, 1953) 29.

79. Branch, Edgar M. *James T. Farrell* (1971) 107.

80. A. C. B., "Calico Shoes and Other Stories," *Saturday Review of Literature* (October 27, 1934) 250.

81. Hilliard, Celia. "Sophistication Sells/*Esquire's* Chicago Success Story," *Chicago* (May, 1980) 134-140.
82. Dooley, Roger, *From Scarface to Scarlett* (1981) 124.

Chapter XI

1. Algren, Nelson. *Chicago: City on the Make* (1961) 58-59.
2. *Illinois! Illinois!* Item 873, p. 359.
3. Dean, Charlotte. "Growing Pains," *New York Times Book Review* (May 2, 1943), 8; Ross, Mary, *"Yesterday's Children" New York Herald Tribune Weekly Book Review* (May 2, 1943) VIII, 10.
4. Bellow, Saul. "Starting Out in Chicago," *American Scholar* (Winter 1974-1975) 44, 1, 71.
5. ———. 72.
6. Wilson, Edmund. "Books," *New Yorker* (April 1, 1944) 20:78.
7. ———. 78.
8. Aldridge, John W. "Saul Bellow at 60: A Turn to the Mystical," *Saturday Review* (September 6, 1975) 22.
9. Trilling, Diana. "Fiction in Review," *Nation* (December 13, 1947) 653-654.
10. *Illinois! Illinois!* Item 658, p. 280.
11. *Illinois! Illinois!* Item 716, p. 304.
12. Smith, Alson J. *The Left Bank of Chicago* (1953) 250-251.
13. ———. 251.
14. Fuller, Edmund. "Scene: Chicago, 1885-96, *Saturday Review* (April 30, 1949) 14.
15. Anonymous. "Chicago, Chicago, a Calendar, 1981." Apple Almanacs, July 8.
16. *Illinois! Illinois!* Item 796, p. 336.
17. Thanet, Octave (Alice French). "Communists and Capitalists; A Sketch From Life," *Knitters in the Sun (1887)* 173 ff.
18. Levin, Meyer. *In Search* (1950) 141-142.
19. Strauss, Harold. "Citizens," *New York Times Book Review* (March 3, 1940) 2.
20. Smith, Alson J. *Chicago's Left Bank* (1935) 244-245.
21. Strauss, Harold. "At Sutton & Co.," *New York Times Book Review* (October 11, 1942) 7.
22. Appel, Benjamin. "The Refinery People," *Saturday Review* (February 20, 1943).
24. Sugrue, Thomas. "Confused Liberal," *New York Times Review of Books* (August 22, 1943) 4-5; Rothman, N. L. "Shock of Discovery," *Saturday Review* (October 9, 1943) 46; Feld, Rose "Grand Crossing," *New York Herald Tribune Weekly Book Review* (August 29, 1943) VIII, 3.
25. Match, Richard. "'By the Way He Acts,'" *New York Herald Tribune Weekly Book Review* (November 7, 1948) 20.
26. *Illinois! Illinois!* Item 1173, 445-446.
27. ———. Item 1172, 445.
28. Field, Louise Maunsell. "Aunt Jessie," *New York Times Book Review* (February 22, 1940) 22; Benét, Rosemary C. "Holt," *Saturday Review of Literature* (August 15, 1942) 11.
29. Sullivan, Richard. "Merging of Boyhood and Manhood," *New York Times Book Reviews* (April 8, 1945) 3. Hay, Sara Henderson, "The Magnetism of the Opposites," *Saturday Review of Literature* (April 7, 1945) 9.
30. Smith, Alson J. *Chicago's Left Bank* (1953) 245.
31. Bell, Lisle. "Two Kinds of Women," *New York Herald Tribune Weekly Book Review* (March 16, 1947) VII, 10.
32. *Illinois! Illinois!* Item 1550, 569.
33. ———. Item 1143, pp 436-437.
34. Daniels, Jonathan. "Nostalgic Picture of a City Summertime," *Saturday Review* (August 18, 1945) 28.

35. Conroy, Jack. "Name and Nativity Made a Social Misfit of Johnny," *Chicago Sun Book Week* (August 5, 1945) 5.

36. Kogan, Alice. "On Chicago's Northwest Side," *Chicago Sun Book Week* (March 16, 1947) 2.

37. Jack, Peter Munro. "Native Son," *New York Times Book Review* (March 3, 1940) 2, 20.

39. Cayton, Horace. "Negro Migrants in City," *Chicago Sun Book Week* (March 23, 1947) 2; Pratt, Theodore. "Ed Tyler," *New York Times Book Reviews* (March 23, 1947) 18.

40. Moran, Peggy. "Craig Rice's Chicago: Breezy, Boozey, Bribery, But Beautiful" (unpublished, 1982).

41. _____.

42. Crother, Bosley, Review of *The Underworld Story* (1950) *New York Times* (July 27, 1950) 29:4.

43. H. H. T. Review of *Mrs. O'Malley and Mr. Malone* (1951) *New York Times* (February 23, 1951) 33:2.

44. *Illinois! Illinois!* Item 1084, p. 419.

45. Kehr, Dave. "Screening the Past," *Chicago* (November, 1981) 222.

46. Kehr, Dave, 226. The film *That's Entertainment* (1974) shows "New York Street" and makes this point also.

47. Motley, Willard. *Knock on Any Door* (1947).

48. Cayton, Horace R. "The Known City," *New Republic* (May 12, 1947) 30.

49. Cowley, Malcolm. "Chicago Poem," *New Republic* (May 4, 1942) 613-614.

50. Woodburn, John. "People of the Abyss," *New York Times Review of Books* (February 2, 1947) 2.

51. _____. 2.

52. Algren, Nelson. *Chicago: City on the Make* (1961) 22. Algren makes a similar point in *Conversations With Nelson Algren.*

53. Webster, Harvey Curtis. "Chicago Poems of Distinction," *Chicago Sun Book Week* (April 20, 1947) 4.

54. Nelson, Starr. "Social Comment in Poetry," *Saturday Review of Literature* (January 19, 1946) 15.

55. Lechlitner, Ruth. "Lone Songs," *New York Herald Tribune Weekly Book Review* (September 25, 1949) VII, 44.

56. Brooks, Gwendolyn, "The Anniad," *Annie Allen* (1950).

57. *Illinois! Illinois!* Item 875, p. 360.

58. _____. Item 876, p. 360.

59. _____. Item 867, pp. 357-358.

60. Smith, Alson J. *Chicago's Left Bank* (1953) 243.

61. _____. 243.

Chapter XII

1. Saxton, Alexander. *The Great Midland* (1948) 49-50.

2. Derleth, August. "New Dubkin Book is No 'White Lady,'" *Chicago Sunday Tribune* (September 13, 1953) 6.

3. *Illinois! Illinois!* Item 702, p. 298.

4. Hass, Victor P. "Rich Humor, Deep Sorrow in New Novel," *Chicago Sunday Tribune* (February 19, 1950) 11.

5. *Illinois! Illinois!* Item 778, p. 328.

6. Grossman, Ron. "Literary Geography," *Chicago* (March, 1980) 141.

7. Algren, Nelson. "Jungle of Tenements," *Saturday Review* (June 6, 1953) 16. Ottley, Roi, "Men Before Being Boys; Powerful Story of a 'Gang,'" *Chicago Sunday Tribune* (June 28, 1953) 4.

8. Hughes, Langston. "Harlem," in *Montage of a Dream Deferred* (1951) p. 71.

9. Wagenknecht, Edward. "Noble Novel of a Chicago Family's Life," *Chicago Sunday Tribune* (September 17, 1956) 3.
10. *Illinois! Illinois!* Item 966, p. 385.
11. *Illinois! Illinois!* Item 965, pp. 384-385.
12. ———. Item 850, p. 353.
13. ———. Item 1394, p. 518.
14. Bullock, Florence Haxton, "Ample Tale of a Big Chicago Family," *New York Herald Tribune Book Review* (April 27, 1952) 4.
15. Butcher, Fanny. "Vigor, Tenderness, Pioneer Spirit in 'The Chicago Story,'" *Chicago Tribune Magazine of Books* (April 27, 1952) 4.
16. Millstein, Gilbert. "Pent-Up Hatreds," *New York Times Book Review* (August 17, 1958) 23.
17. ———. 23; Curley, Thomas F. "Ordered Argot," *Commonweal* (August 20, 1958) 523; Phelps, Robert. "Sharp Eye and Nimble Pen," *New York Herald Tribune Books* (August 17, 1958) 3.
18. Curley, 523.
19. *Illinois! Illinois!* Item 1522, p. 561.
20. Rehder, Jesse. "Encounter With a Genius," *New York Times Book Reviews* (April 13, 1958) 41.
21. Motley, Willard. *We Fished All Night* (1951) preface.
22. Cronin, Robert. "Motley's Study of Futility," *Chicago Sunday Tribune* (November 25, 1951) 19.
23. Swados, Harvey. "Angry Novel," *Nation* (December 29, 1951) 173:572.
24. Redding, J. Saunders. "Mr. Motley's Chicago, Big and Grim," *New York Herald Tribune Book Reviews* (November 25, 1951) 8.
25. ———. 8.
26. Dempsey, David. "Skid Row Revisited," *New York Times Book Reviews* (August 10, 1958) 18.
27. Geismar, Maxwell. "Mr. Motley Again in Darkest Chicago," *New York Herald Tribune Book Reviews* (August 17, 1958) 4. Algren, Nelson. "Epitaph Writ in Syrup," *Nation* (August 16, 1958) 187:78. Hicks, Granvile. "Art and Reality," *Saturday Review* (August 9, 1958) 41:11. Algren, Nelson: Motley Novel Tackles the Dope Problem," *Chicago Sunday Tribune* (August 17, 1958) Books, 1.
28. Algren, 1.
29. Dressler, David. "Mobsters Eat High," *Saturday Review* (June 2, 1951) 13; Hass, Victor P., "Burnett's New Novel is No Little Caesar," *Chicago Tribune* (June 3, 1951) 5.
30. Lynch, John A. "Chicago Chase," *Commonweal* (August 27, 1954) 60:518; J. S. "Man on the Lam,"*Saturday Review* (August 21, 1954) 37:38; Sandoe, James. "A Refreshing Anti-Hero," *Herald Tribune Book Review* (August 15, 1954) 8.
31. Levin, Meyer. *In Search* [autobiography] (1950) 26-28; *Compulsion* (1956) Foreword.
32. Atkinson, Brooks, *New York Times* (October 25, 1957) 21:1; (November 3, 1957) 11:1:1.
33. Levin, Meyer. *Compulsion* [drama] 1959, Foreword.
34. Newman, M. W. "So Long, Chicago," *Chicago Daily News* (March 4, 1978) 5.
35. Particularly in an interview with reporters, after a lecture at the University of Iowa in the spring of 1981.
36. *Illinois! Illinois!* Item 1280, p. 483.
37. Algren, Nelson. *Chicago: City on the Make* (1951) 13.
38. ———. 15.
39. 116-117.

Chapter XIII

1. Halper, Albert. *This Is Chicago* (1952) Foreword, viii.
2. Algren, Nelson. *Chicago: City on the Make* (1961) 23.
3. *Illinois! Illinois!* Item 1228, p. 466.
4. _____. *Item 1518, p. 559.*
5. Maltin, Leonard. *TV Movies* (1975) 256.
6. *Illinois! Illinois!* Item 1494, p. 550.
7. Brown, Frank London. "McDougall," in Edward Margolies, ed. *A Native Sons' Reader* (1970) 287.
9. *Illinois! Illinois!* Item   , p. 134.
10. _____. Item 874, p. 360.
11. _____. Item 1078, pp. 416-417.
12. _____. Item 1069, p. 414.
13. Anonymous. *Time* (June 15, 1962) 79:86.
14. *Illinois! Illinois!* Item 1311, p. 492.
15. Coleman, Alexander. "Darwin in Reverse," *New York Times Book Review* (January 10, 1965) 26.
16. *Illinois! Illinois!* Item 1440, p. 532.
17. Blakesley, Richard. "Front Office Intrigue in TV Network," *Chicago Sunday Tribune* (October 19, 1958) 3.
18. Cassill, R. Verlin. "A Magic Square of Self-destruction," *Book World* (October 26, 1969) 3.
19. *Illinois! Illinois!* Item 821, p. 2343.
20. Maltin, Leonard. *TV Movies* (1975) 201.
21. _____. 408.
22. Wagoner, David. *Staying Alive* (1966) 17. Originally published in *Southern Review.*

Chapter XIV

1. Bloch, Robert. *American Gothic* (1974) 184.
2. Newman, M. W. "So Long, Chicago" *Chicago Daily News* (March 4, 1978) 5.
3. *Illinois! Illinois!* Item 1306, p. 490.
4. Racher, Peter M. "Algren's Iowa days were not golden," *Des Moines* [Iowa] *Register* May 11, 1981) 3A.
5. Vonnegut, Kurt, interview, reported by Peter M. Racher, *ibid.*
6. Racher, Peter M. *ibid.*
7. Algren, Nelson. Reported by Pete Hamill in the *Minneapolis Tribune* (May 13, 1981) and other sources.
8. Hamill, Pete. "Author dies shunned by city he loved." *Minneapolis Tribune* (and other sources) May 13, 1981.
9. Barnes, Clive. "Plot Trial's Theatrical Character Stressed," *New York Times* (May 26, 1970) 33:1.
10. *Illinois! Illinois!* Item 1445, 533.
11. Fair, Ronald L. *World of Nothing* (1970) 80.
12. _____. "Author's Note [n.p.n.] *We Can't Breathe* 1972.
13. Fair, Ronald L. *Excerpts* (1975) 10.
14. *Illinois! Illinois!* Item 1374, p. 511.
15. _____. Item 1408, p. 522.
16. _____. Item 1391, p. 517.
17. _____. Item 1395, p. 518.
18. _____. Item 342, p. 155.
19. Stade, George. "Tracking Down a Predatory Prey," *New York Times Book Reviews* (June 23, 1974) 6.
20. Powers, John R. *The Last Catholic in America* (1973) 80.

22. Advertisement, back cover, Popular Library edition, *The Unoriginal Sinner and the Ice-Cream God* (1977).
23. *Illinois! Illinois!* Item 1448, p. 534-535.
24. ———. Item 1449, p. 535.
25. Anonymous. "Windy City," *Kirkus Reviews* (April-June, 1979) (May 15, 1979) 598.
26. McEvoy, J. P. "Sunny Boy," *Saturday Evening Post* (April 30, 1938) 8-9, 42-44, contains the best statement of Guest's philosophies.
27. Leonard, William. "*Boss* is half fun, half dull," *Chicago Tribune* (May 26, 1973) 1:10.
28. Winer, Linda. "Dillinger: Rough, Tough, Empty," *Chicago Tribune* (January 26, 1979) 3:3.
29. Terry, Clifford. "At Work and Plays With David Mamet," *Chicago Tribune Magazine* (May 8, 1977) 16.
30. Simon, John. "Permanents and Transients," *New York* (May 14, 1979) 75.
31. Winer, Linda. "A Mamet Stage Marathon Races Toward a Dead End," *Chicago Tribune* (November 27, 1977) 4.
32. Edgar Lansbury, quoted in "At Work and Plays With David Mamet," by Clifford Terry. *Chicago Tribune Magazine* (May 8, 1977) 16.
33. Blei, Norbert. "A Chicago Classic," *Chicago* (April, 1980) 128.
34. Gordon, Eleanor. "Poets and Poems of the City," *Chicago* (March, 1980) 120.
35. ———. 122.
36. Gross, Alan. "The Architect" *Chicago* (February, 1982) 92-96.
37. Thorson, Gerald. "Norwegian Emigrant Novels Set in America," *Mid-America IV* (East Lansing, Michigan, 1977) 74-88.

Abandoned Woman, An 182

Account Overdue See *The Gifted*

Ace Chisholm and the Works 317-318

Achievement of Luther Trant, The 157

Adamant, a Quarterly of Beautiful Verse 260

Adams, Franklin P. (F.P.A.) 52, 90, 92, 191

Adams, Frederick Upham (Grizzly) 90

Adams, Harrison (pseud.) See St. George Rathbone

Adams, Henry 60

Adams, J. Donald 227

Adams, James Truslow 18

Adam's Rib (film) 214

Addams, Jane 46, 69, 84, 104, 105, 109, 112, 120, 256, 306, 314, 344

"Address of Mr. Henry Blake Fuller" fn. 29, chap. II

Ade, George 2, 36, 40, 51, 68, 90-93, 94, 95, 102, 112, 113, 126, 132, 155, 162, 180, 213, 214, 220, 249, 347

Adler, David 159, 246

Adventure (magazine) 200

Adventures of Augie March, The 305, 339

Adversary in the House 268

Advertising business in Chicago 194, 244

Aestheticism 74-75, 78, 125ff

Affair of Doctors, An 333

"After the Ball" 63

Against Fate: A True Story 35

Against Odds: A Romance of the Midway Plaisance 61

Age of Innocence, The (play) 260

Airport (novel and film) 319

Al Capone (novel) 304

Al Capone (film) 304

Albert, Bessie 47

Alderman's Wife, The 105

Aldis, Dorothy [Keeley] 125, 128, 243, 244

Aldis, Mary 85, 127, 128, 145

Aldridge, John W 266, 305

Alger, Horatio 26, 27, 42, 49, 123, 138, 295

Algren, Nelson 67, 185, 229-231, 258, 262, 283, 288, 297, 301, 302, 306, 307, 321, 326, 333, 346, 347

Alienation of author from society, 5

"Alibi Ike" (story) 137

Alibi Ike (film) 137

Alice Ann 195

Alice in Wonderland 61

"All-American boy" 102

All Quiet on the Western Front (Remarque) 24

All the Year Round 244

"All Things Considered" 132

Allee, Marjorie Hill 256, 286

Alleged Great-Aunt, The 225

Allen, Geneva and James 331

Allen, Lizzie 57

Allen, Steve 337

Aloneness 305

Alsberg, Henry 20

Altgeld, John Peter 45, 55, 122, 202, 205, 268

Altman, Robert 323

Alton, IL 189

Altrocchi, Julia Cooley

Amazing Web, The 226

Ambush at Fort Dearborn 15

America 75

"America Remembers" 228

American, The 45, 268

American Academy — Institute of Arts and Letters, The 327

American Acres 254

American Book Award 344

American Buffalo (play) 343

American Fur Company 17

American Dream Girl, An 259

American Family, An 144

American Fiction 1920-1940

American Gothic (Bloch) 332

American Guide, The 20

American Graffiti (film) 331

American Magazine 140, 143

American Mercury 169, 212

American Peeress, An 2, 77

American Railway Union Strike 43, 108

American Scholar, The 305

American Song 228

American Tragedy, An 108, 279

Among Those Present 209

Anarchist Woman, An 109, 255

Anarchists 43-45, 64, 67, 108-109, 144, 145, 154, 185, 206, 345

Anderson, Edward 231

Anderson, Margaret 139, 153, 208, 213, 225

Anderson, Maxwell 214

Anderson, Sherwood 110, 129, 135, 141, 145, 149ff., 162, 180, 202-203, 208, 212, 213, 214, 225, 283, 306, 347

Andersonville 336

Andreas, Alfred T. 18, 96, 191

Andrews, Charles Robert Douglas Hardy 181, 240, 249, 271

Andrews, Robert Hardy — see Andrews, Charles Robert Hardy Douglas

Andrews, R. H. "Shang" 2, 31, 36, 46, 57, 133, 302

Andrus, Louise 231

Angel Arms 205

"Angel of the Stockyards," 314

Angel With a Broom, The 139

Angels Can't Do Better 265

Angle, Paul 288

Animal, The 326

Anisfield-Wolf Award 305

Anna Christie (film) 214

Anne Herrick 242

Annie Allen 286

Anti-collegiate spirit 15

Anti-Semitism 273, 300 See also *A Peculiar Treasure*

Anvil, The 261, 284

Appendix A 315, 324

Apple of the Eye, The 233

Appleton, WI 140, 143, 174, 176

April Harvest 291

April Snow 4, 291

Archer, William 128
"Archey Road" 91
Architect, The 345
Arden Acres 253
Are You Decent? 205
Arena, The (magazine) 79, 109
Aren't You Even Gonna Kiss Me Goodby? 317
Arkansaw Traveler 42
Armageddon 57, 70
Armitrage Trail (pseud.) See Coons, Maurice
Armour, Phillip D. 98, 101, 108
Armour Scientific Academy 92
Armours, The 100, 263, 269, 296, 347
Armstrong, Dwight LeRoy 35, 36
Armstrong, Louis "Satchmo" 270
Arnold, Edward 214
Arnold, Matthew 73
Arnow, Harriette 267
Art
Art for art's sake 146
Art Institute, Chicago 24, 74, 79, 123, 125, 130, 142, 149, 151, 211, 234, 249, 260, 299
Art Palace, Columbian Exposition
Art theater 128
Artie: A Story of the Streets and the Town 92
Artists' world See Studio
Arvin, Newton 117
Asbury, Herbert 149, 170
Aschmann, Helen Tann 313
Ashenhurst, John M 228
Asleep and Awake 65
Associated Press 326
"At The Turn of the Road" 116
Atheism See Robert Ingersoll
Athenaeum Building 84, 125
Atkinson, Brooks 167, 303
Atkinson, Eleanor Stackhouse 16
Atlantic First Award 292, 309
Atlantic Monthly 101, 309

Attic Club 83, 84, 131
Auditorium Building 25, 51, 74, 84, 120, 125
Aunt Jessie 274
Auntie Mame 314
Aurora, IL 159
Austin, Mary 155, 158
Author's League of America 168
Autobiography of a Beggar, The 107
Autobiography of a Thief 109
Autobiography of Jack Woodford, The see Woolfolk, Josiah Pitts
Automatic Capitalists, The 97
Ayres, Lew 248

"B.L.T." See Taylor, Bert Leston
"Babcock, Bernie" 120, 155
"Bachelor-girl" novels 60, 116
Bachelor of the Midway, The 60
"Back of the Yards" (Goodman) (play) 130-131
"Back of the yards" district. See "Canaryville"
Bad Samaritan, The 204
"Bagtime" (column) 341
Bagtime 341
Bagtime (musical play) 341
Bailey, Charles W. II 315
Bailly, Joseph 17
Baird, Edwin 156
Baker, George Pierce 166
Baker, Sherman 276, 298
"Ballad of Ryerson" 210
Ballinger, Bill (pseud.) See Ballinger, William Sanborn
Ballinger, William Sanborn 296
Balmer, Edwin 140, 157-158, 169, 171, 180, 193-194, 201, 214, 226
Balzac, Honoré de 112, 195
Bancroft, Hubert H 63
Bandarlog Press 126
Banditti of the Prairies 33

Banker and the Bear/The Story of a Corner in Lard, The 98
Banks, Charles Eugene 36, 82, 100
Banning, Margaret Culkin 276
"Barkeep Stories" 79
Barnes, John W 286
Barnes, Margaret Ayer 15, 137, 144, 158, 192, 214, 225, 251-253, 260, 263
Barriers Burned Away 2, 27ff., 121, 315
Barriers Burned Away (film) 28
Barron, Elwyn A 49
Barrymore, Lionel 195
Baseball in Chicago 123, 278, 315-316, 321, 325, 341
Basil and Josephine Stories, The 337
"Basket benevolences" 46, 69, 109
Bastard Wench From Chicago, The (film) 322
Bates, Clara Doty 49
Bates, Ernest Sutherland 195
"Bath, The" See Coughlin, "Bathhouse John"
Baum, L Frank 84, 126
Beach, Edgar Rice 64, 105
Beach, Joseph Warren 4
Beach Umbrella, The 330
Beadle and Adams 32
Bean Eaters 305
Bear for the FBI, A 320-311
Bears, Chicago 322
"Beast in the Jungle, The" 113
Beauty's Peril; or, The Girl From Macoupin 36
Beaver Trail 19
Bech-Meyer, Nico 55
Beck, Robert (Iceberg Slim) 331
Beckoning Waters, The 291
Beef, Iron and Wine 133
Beer Baron, The See *Song of the Eagle, The*
Beery, Wallace 214
Beggars Can Choose 189
Beginners, The 198-199

Beginning: A Romance of Chicago As It Might Be, The 55
Behold a Cry 255, 280
Beiderbecke, Bix 270
Bein, Albert 169
Belasco, David 257-258
Believe My Love 314
Belushi, Jim 340
Belushi, John 340
Bell, Lisle 276
Bellamy, Edward 54
Bellow, Saul 263, 264, 265, 266, 288, 290, 301, 305, 307, 308, 324, 339, 346, 347
Benchly, Alexandra Jane 321
Benét, Stephen Vincent 229
Benjamin Franklin Citation 309
Bennett, James O'Donnell 136
Bergen, Candice 340
"Bernard Carr" 258
"Bernard Clare" 258
Bernard Clare 258
Bernt Myrstua 346
Berryman, John 324
Bertram Cope's Year 89
Bessie Cotter 224-225
Best American Plays of 1926 164
Best American Plays of 1927-28 166
Best American Short Stories of 1917 141-142
Best Policy, The 101
Better Days see fn. 42, chap V.
Beyond the Black Ocean 120
Big Business Girl 240
Big Business Girl (film) 240
Big Midget Murders, The 281
Big Wheel, The 63, 332
Bigot, Mary see Healy, Mary Bigot
Bigotry 174
Bill and Brocky; A Story of Boy Life in Chicago . . . 65
Bingham, Elizabeth 130

Biograph Theater 30, 285, 341
Bisno, Beatrice 236-237
Black, Margaret Horton Potter See, Potter, Margaret Horton
Black Babylon 209
Black Cat Club, The 121
"Black city" 53, 56, 57, 82
Black Crook, The 173
Black Partridge 11ff., 191
Black Partridge, or the Fall of Fort Dearborn 15
Blackguard 186
Blackrobe 240
Blacks in Chicago 33, 69, 74, 92, 121, 148, 156, 167, 178, 198, 199, 210, 211, 233, 270, 273, 279-280, 285, 290, 293, 304-305, 309-310, 311-312, 325, 328ff., 340, 343, 347
Blake, (Atkinson Pratt), Eleanor 243
Blake, Emily Calvin 191
Blake, Faye M 43
Bland, Alden 280
Bleacher Bums (musical play) 341
Blessed is the Man 235
Blind Man's Eyes, The 157
Blind Mice (play) 234
Bloch, Robert 332
Blondell, Joan 240
Blood of the Lamb 314, 317
Blossom, Henry Martyn 69
"Blue Blood" 176
Blue Door, The 225
Blue in Chicago (short stories) 338
Blues Brothers, The 340
Board of Trade 35, 57, 70, 97, 98, 122, 123, 195, 196, 197
Boarding House Blues 259
Bodenheim, Maxwell "Bogie" 130, 141, 145, 186, 210, 212, 214, 240
Body Politic 342
Bogart, Humphrey 285

Bohemianism 31, 53, 81, 90, 124, 143, 149, 153, 161, 180, 185, 191, 193, 203, 208, 212, 250, 259, 337, 346
Bohemians (nationality) 62, 105, 262, 278, 312, 347
Bolanyo 84
Bomb, The 44-45
Bombardier, The 328
Bombeck, Erma 335
Bond, The 109, 188
Bondage of Ballinger, The 113
"Boodling," "boodlers" 28, 68, 97, 148
Book and Play Club 213
Book of the Fair, The 63
Book of the Month Club selection 248, 269, 279, 338
Book of Verses, A 84
Book Review See *New York Herald (and Tribune)*
Bookfellows 231
Bookman, The 143, 210
"Booksellers' Row" 39
Boosterism 20, 76
Booth, Emma Scarr 65
Borden, Mary 186, 190
Boring, Charles O 57
"Boss," political 29, 103-105, 155
Boss 341
Boss (play) 341
Boss, The 105
Bosses in Lusty Chicago 149
Boston, compared with Chicago 3, 35, 39, 66, 78, 94, 100, 117, 255, 323
Boston Transcript, The 143
"Bottle of Milk for Mother, A" 284
Bourget, Paul 53, 57
Bourne, Randolph 111-112, 161
Boy in the Wind 211
Boy Scouts of America 335
Boy Trouble 297
Boyce (Harrison), Neith 109, 188
Boyce, W D 39
Boyd, Thomas 187
"Boyd, Woodward" See Shane, Peggy

Boylan, Malcolm Stuart 295
Boyle, Kay 320
Bradford Masters 276
Bradley, Mary Hastings 15, 17, 19, 22, 29, 139, 239, 247
Bradley, Van Allen 323
Brady's Chicago Clew ... 122
Branch, Edward 260
Brand for the Burning, A 314
Brand New Life, A 260
Brande, Dorothea (Thompson) 244
Brandy in the Wilderness 322
Brashler, William 333
Brass 193
Brass Knuckles 344
Breath of Scandal (novel) 193
Breath of Scandal, The (film) 158
Breathe the Air Again 273
Brecht, Bertold 168
Briary-Bush, The 201
Bride and the Pennant ..., The 123
Bridgeport 10
Bright Land, The 239
Britany, emigrants from   see *Give Us This Day*
British   See English
Britt, Sappho Henderson (pseud) See Woolfolk, Josiah Pitts
Broadway 209, 222, 303, 333, 342
Broadway (play) 168
Broken Lance, The 114, 115
Broken Necks ... 184
Bronson, Charles 306
Bronzeville Boys and Girls 305
Brooks, Gwendolyn 264, 285, 293, 304-305, 306, 307, 324, 346
Bross, William "Deacon" 38, 41
Brower, James W 123
Brown, Frank London 293, 294, 311-212
Brown, Frederic 281
Brown, Helen Dawes 35
Brown, Joe E 136

Brown, Judge Henry 12, 13
Brown, Karl 224
Browne, Charles Francis 85
Browne, Francis Fisher 25, 39-40, 73, 153
Browne, Maurice 128-129, 145, 151, 166, 208
Browne, Waldo 153
Browning, Robert 39, 72
Brunner, Bernard 310, 326, 329-330
Bryan, William Jennings 56, 108
Bryant, McKinley 223
Bryer, Jackson R 336
Buck, Pearl S(ydenstricker) 300
Buck ... 160
"Bucket-shops" 157
Budd, Lillian 4, 291
Buddenbrooks 195
Budlong Woods 340
"Buffer, The" (play) 130
"Bughouse Square" 300, 332
Bull Moose Party 192
Bulwer-Lytton, Edward 215
Bunker Hill to Chicago 66
Bunyan, John 61
Burdette, Robert Jones 90
Burgess, Gelett 83
Burglar's Fate and the Detective, The 33
Burgoyne, Leon E 15
Burn, Killer, Burn 309
Burnett, Carol 168
Burnett, Frances Hodgson 61
Burnett, W(illiam) R(iley) 166, 169, 220, 221, 222, 248, 263, 264, 302
Burnham, Clara Louise Root 2, 60-61, 72, 139, 332
Burnham, David W 151, 194, 247
Burns, Walter Nobel 221
Burritt Durand 33, 155
Burroughs, Edgar Rice 200-201
Burroughs, Rev J C 73
Burroughs, William 328
Busch, Niven 29
Bushnell, William H 17

business man or baron 29, 36, 45, 66, 85, 96-97, 99-100, 101, 155, 157, 160, 162, 182, 192ff., 199, 200, 243, 252, 263, 277, 317
"Business romance" at turn of century 14, 15
Business Widow, The 166
business woman 100, 243
business world vs social world   See, also Chicago genteelism
Buslett, Ole 346
But Death Runs Faster 281
But the Patient Died 281
But Who Wakes the Bugler 287
Butcher, Fanny 132, 227, 241, 251, 297
Butler, Ellis Parker 90
Butler, Samuel 177
Butler University 166
Buttered Side Down 141
Butterfly, The 82
Butterworth, Hezekiah 61
By a Hair's Breadth 34
By Bread Alone 106
Bynner, Witter 209
Byrd Flam in Town ... 36
Byrne, Jane 347
Byrne, Baby, Byrne 342

C.V.C. Murders, The 171
Caan, James 340
Cabell, James Branch 296
Cable, George Washington 79
Caesar and Cleopatra 128
Cage, The 44, 108, 110
Cagney, James 222, 224, 262, 323
Cahill, Holger 196
Cain — Abel 236
Caldecott Award 63
Caldwell, Lewis A H 280
Calico Shoes 259
Call Northside 777 (film) 282-283
Calmer, Ned 337
Calumet City 298
Calumet "K" 107
Camp Douglas 24, 51, 191, 300

Camp Grant, IL 137

Campbell, Gladys 153

Camus 320

Can All This Grandeur Perish? 259

Canadians in Chicago 233

"Canaryville" 130, 176, 190, 283, 347

Canby, Henry Seidel 179, 180, 258

Canby, Vincent 338

Candida 128

Candles in the Wind 243

"Cantata" (Harriet Monroe) 58

"Capitalists and Communists; A Sketch From Life" 43

Capone, Al(phonse, Scarface) 3, 30, 164, 169, 212, 221, 222, 285, 304, 321, 323, 338, 347

"Captain John Whistler " 16, 149

Captain of Company K, The 24, 49-50

Cardwell, Ruth 231

career women See also women in business, "bachelor girl" novels 187, 242, 243

Carl Almendinger's Office ... 23

Carleton, Will 23

Carmen 136

Carnegie, Andrew 43, 49

Carr, Clark Ezra 96, 197

Carrie (film) 112

Carroll, Charles 338

Carroll, Loren 221

Carruth, Hayden 315, 324

Carse, Robert 291

Carter, Everett 43-45

Carter, John Stewart 317

Carter, Rubin "Hurricane" 327

Carvillo, Ramino 342

Cary, Lucian 136, 145, 206

Casady, Constance 231

Case and the Girl, The 170

Case Book of Jimmy Lavender, The 225

Casey, Robert J. 181, 226

Cashman, John 332

Caspary, Vera 197, 234-235, 252, 263, 296, 313

Cassill, R Verlin 320

Cather, Willa 127, 155, 158, 162, 176, 180, 242

Catherwood, Mary Hartwell 8, 14, 15, 21, 35, 78, 79, 81, 290

Catholic Sentinel, The 335

Catholics in Chicago 132, 277, 292, 314, 335, 337, 343, 347

Cayton, Horace R 1, 283

Cecily and the Wide World 159, 255

Censorship, of Chicago literature 222 in Chicago 166

Century of Progress Exposition 17, 20, 61, 63, 219, 227ff., 238, 324

Century World's Fair Book For Boys and Girls 61

Cermak, Anton (Tony) 262, 282, 347

"Certain of the Chicago School of Fiction" 113

Chamales, Tom T 293

Chameleon, The 116

Chance, Frank L 123

Chandler, Jeff 248

Chandler, St. Lawrence 103

Channon, Henry 189, 247

Chap-Book 51, 69, 82-84, 94, 152

Chappell, Fred A 65

Charisse, Cyd 306

Charlatans, The 115, 127

Charles Scribner's Sons 41

Charley and Eva Roberts' Home in the West 35

Charley Manning 254

Charlie Flowers and the Melody Gardens 336

Châtelaine of La Trinité, The 3, 72, 85

Chatfield-Taylor, Hobart C[hatfield] 2, 36, 49, 75-76, 145, 152

Chaucer, Geoffrey 61

Checkers, A Hard-Luck Story 69

Cheerful by Request 141, 171

Chekhov, Anton 258, 327

Chernoff, Maxine 344

Chester 48

Chevalier of Pensi Vani, The 3, 72, 85

"Chicago" (Sandburg) 146, 310, 323

Chicago (Carroll) 338

Chicago (Farr) 149

Chicago (film) 165

Chicago (magazine) see, also, *Chicago Magazine, The* 163, 165

Chicago (musical comedy) 165

Chicago (name) 19-20

Chicago (play) 164-165, 194

Chicago After Dark 31

Chicago After Midnight (film) 168, 217

Chicago American 166

"Chicago: An Obituary" 212-213

Chicago and the Great American Novel ... 2

Chicago as a literary center 81

Chicago, attitudes toward 3, 98, 108-109, 111, 113, 117-118, 119-120, 134, 135, 143, 150, 153-154, 155, 160-161, 190, 203, 204, 208, 215, 220, 238, 308, 327, 328-329. See also "Black City"

Chicago by Day and Night ... 62

Chicago Calling (film) 306

"Chicago, Chicago" (song) 209

Chicago: City on the Make 306

Chicago Club 127

Chicago.Confidential 302

Chicago Confidential (film) 302

"Chicago Conspiracy" 328

Chicago Daily News 41, 68, 79, 90, 133, 135, 148, 180, 183, 184, 189, 225-226, 236, 240, 304, 306, 324, 325-326, 347

Chicago Deadline (film) 287

"Chicago Hamlet, A" 202

Chicago Historical Society 1, 11, 17, 25, 123, 173, 191
Chicago in 1812: The Massacre of Fort Dearborn 14
Chicago in Tears and Smiles 48
Chicago International Exposition 521
Chicago Inter-Ocean 56, 136
Chicago Kid, The (1935 film) 224
Chicago, Kid, The (1969) film 322
Chicago Ledger, The 39
Chicago Literary Club 73
Chicago Literary Times 212
Chicago Magazine, The 72
Chicago: Narrative of a City 313
Chicago Naturalistic Novel, 1930-1966, The 2
"Chicago: 1933" 229
Chicago Opera House 149, 231
Chicago Plan 151
Chicago Plant: or Chicago in 1970 70
Chicago Poems 146, 285, 348
Chicago Post 91
Chicago Press Club 43, fn. 39, chap 3, 70
Chicago Public Schools 158
Chicago Renaissance in American Letters, The 2
Chicago Renaissance/The Literary Life in the Midwest 2
Chicago Review 286
Chicago River 9, 10, 19, 64, 92, 172, 189, 225, 254, 261, 291
Chicago Sanitary Fairs 28, 66, 347
"Chicago School of Fiction" 112, 124, 140, 284
Chicago 70 (play) 327-328
Chicago Side-Show 233
Chicago Story, The 296-297
Chicago Street Gazette 57
Chicago Sun-Times 323, 341
Chicago Symphony Orchestra 74
Chicago Syndicate (film) 302

Chicago/The History of its Reputation 184
Chicago Theater Society 128
Chicago Tribune 16, 23, 25, 30, 34, 38, 42, 49, 56, 58, 70, 85, 102, 104, 115, 135-136, 139, 141, 158, 164, 166, 167-169, 195, 201, 205, 227, 238, 245, 260, 297, 316, 317, 320, 341, 342
Chicago Tribune Souvenir Glimpses of the World's Fair . . . 63
"Chicago to Nemakagon Lake" 344
Chicago University 73
Chicago, University of 2, 35, 44, 89, 105-106, 111, 112, 116-117, 123, 139
Chicago, University of Poetry Club   See Poetry Club
Chicago Women's Medical College 313
Chicago WPA Writers' Project (See also Illinois Federal Writers' Project) 284, 339
Chicago's Black Sheep and Bonnie McCleary's Friends 69, 110
Chicago's Greatest Crime See Appendix
"Chicago's higher evolution See Genteelism, Chicago
"Chikagou and Tonika" 20
Child of the Century, A 167
Childhood and Other Neighborhoods 344
Children of the Market Place 177, 197
Childsplay 314
Chimes 179
Chimmie Fadden 68
Chimmie Fadden Out West, A Sequel . . . 68
Chinatown 34, 68, 226, 249, 347
Chinn, Laurence 314
Chocolate or Vanilla 250
Chosen Country 296
Christ in Chicago 200

Christ in Concrete 273
Christian Messenger 23
Christmas Mystery, A 57
Christofero Columbo 59
Chronicle, Chicago 90
Chronicle novels See "three-generation" novels
Church and Goodman 23
Churchill, William 247
Churchill, Winston 162
Chute, The 232, 272
Cicero, IL 30
"Cinderella" 141, 171, 295
"Cinemania" 229
Citadel, The 155
Citizens 272
City Dogs 333
City of Purple Dreams, The 156
City of Purple Dreams, The (film) 156
City of Wonders 61
City That Never Sleeps, The (film) 302
Civil War, The 23ff., 30, 51, 73, 96, 100, 192, 267, 300, 336, 347
Clarence Allen, the Hypnotic Boy Journalist 126
Clark, Christopher 294
Clark, Herma Naomi 238, 260
Clark Street 163, 164, 207, 301, 322
Clarke, Cyril John 229
Clark's Field 153
Clarkson, Ralph 84
Clason, Clyde B. 226
Class Ring 297
"Classified" 287
Classified (film) 287
Claw and Fang . . . 155
Clemens, Samuel Langhorne (Mark Twain) 126
Cleveland, President Grover 90
Clever Sister, The 276
Cliff-Dwellers, The 86-87, 88, 127, 348
Cliff-Dwellers, The (club) 126ff., 153
Close of the Day, The 121

Clubs, literary and art (See Cliff-Dwellers, Little room, White-Chapel, Schlogl's) 52, 72ff., 125ff.
Cobb, Weldon J 62
Coffins For Two 225
Cohen, Lester 194-195
Coin's Financial School 56
Colby College 100
Coleman, Alexander 316
Coleman, Alta May 241
College Humor-Doubleday Doran Prize 245, 255
College life, novels of 115ff., 179, 180
Collier's Weekly 104, 221
Colorado 81, 82, 158
Colosimo, "Big Jim" 30, 163-164, 233, 304
Colossus, The 42, 66
Columbian Exposition, see World's Columbian Exposition
"Columbian Ode, The" 58, 148, 260
"Columbian Ode/An Ode of Greeting" 59, 63
Columbus, Christopher 57, 82, 325
Comedies All (plays) 130
Comic strip in Chicago 217-218
Comiskey, Charles A 123
Command the Morning 300
Common Lot, The 118, 127
"Communists and Capitalists: A Sketch from Life" 271
Compact of Death; or, Nick Carter's Singed Hair Clew 122
Compare These Dead! 281
Complete Poetical Works (B F Taylor) 14
Compulsion 138, 236, 303, 345
Compulsion (play) 303
Compulsion (film) 303
Concrete Wilderness, The 322
"Condominium, The" 337, 340
Coney Island (film) 304

Confessions of a Club Woman, The 122
"Congo, The" 153, 208
Connie Bell, M.D. 313
Conrad, Joseph 258
Conroy, Jack 261, 278, 283
"Consider the Lilies" 176
Contemporary American Authors 287
Continental Divide (film) 340
Convention 315
Conversations With Nelson Algren 317
Cook, Elisha 130
Cook, George Cram 116, 129, 132, 134, 145, 171, 209, 213
Cooke, Marjorie Benton 85, 154
Cooley High (film) 331
Coolidge, Calvin 232
Coons, Maurice 304
Cooper, James Fenimore 12, 216
Copper 282
"Copperheads" 23, 24
Corbett, Elizabeth 159, 254, 255, 263, 264, 267
Corbett, James 136
Corcoran, Charles 240
Cormack, Bartlett 166
Corner in Wheat, A (film) 157
"Corner in wheat" 31
Corner of Chicago, A 240
Coronet 251
Corpse Steps Out, The 281
Corrington, John William 328
Corrothers, James David 121
Cortlands of Washington Square, The 4, 192, 239
Cosmopolitan (magazine) 80
"Cotter's Boy, The" See *Husmandsgutten*
Couffer, Jack 322
Coughlin, "Bathhouse John" 30, 97, 109, 149, 164, 176, 185, 225, 238, 347
Coulter, Cyrus 330, 344
Counterclockwise 321
Country Joe See [McDonald], Country Joe
Covici, Pascal 131

Covici-Friede, Covici-McGee 131, 146, 168, 212
Cowdrey, Robert H 32, 54
Cowley, Malcolm 228-229, 248, 284
Crackerjack Marines, The 300
Craig, Randolph Walker see Rice, Craig
Crane, Stephen 48, 258
Cranky-Ann, the Street Walker ... 31
Crawford, Joan 223
Creative Writing 286
Crime and Punishment 311
Crimson Cloak, The 209
Crimson Love ... 48
Criticism, literary 133ff.
Criticism and Fiction 80
Cromie, Robert Allen 30
Cronin, Dr H P 34, 90, Appendix
Crosby, Bing 164, 323
Crosby Opera House 22, 33, 74, 191
Cross, Marquette see Marquette Cross
Crother, Bosley 282
Crowley, Mary C 61
Crumbling Idols 80, 83
Crump, Paul 309
Crystal Icycle, The 246
Cub Scouts of America 335
Cubism 146
"Cubs," Chicago 136, 215, 224-225, 333, 341
Cudahys, the 196, 347
Cugat, Xavier 302
Culture's Garland ... 41, 94
Cuppy, William (Will) Jacob 116-117
Current (magazine) 79, 86
Currey, Margery (Mrs. Floyd Dell) 145, 149, 208
Curtain for Crime, A 281
Curtis, Cyrus 100, 143
Curtis, Wardon Allan 121
Cutie; a Warm Mama 186
Cutter (film) 340
Cyrano de Bergerac 42
Czechs see Bohemians

Dadism 146, 240
Daily Crescent, Appleton 140
Daily Record, Chicago 42
Dale, Virginia 267-268
Dalesacres 254
Daley, Richard 3, 338, 341, 344, 347
Dali, Salvador 295
Dam, The 251, 265
Damien: Omen II (film) 340
Damrosch, Walter 74
Dan Gunn, the Man From Mauston 36
Dana, Charles A 41
Dance, Fools, Dance (film) 223
Danger, Keep Out 272
Dangerous Business 194
Dangerous Woman and Other Stories, A 259
Dangling Man 265-266, 305
Daniel Trentworthy . . . 28, 29, 53, 54, 64
Daphne's in Love 189
Dark Garden, The 226
Dark Hazard 248
Dark Laughter 203
"Dark Maid of Illinois, The" 6-7
Dark Princess: a Romance 197
Darren, James 302
Darrow, Clarence S 108, 109, 122, 153, 169, 183, 208, 213, 224, 230, 262, 306, 345, 347
Darwin, Charles 39, 200, 316
Daughter of a Republican, The 120
Davenport, Iowa 40, 65, 116, 134, 202, 249, 270
David Lockwin: The People's Idol 42
Davieson, Sarah 47
Davis, Clyde Brion 287
Davis, George 233
Dawn O'Hara . . . 140
Dawson '11 — Fortune Hunter 138
Day, Kingsley 341
Day of Fortune 196
Deaconess Stories 106
Dead Man Inside 225

Dean Man's Secret 228
Deadlines . . . 181
Deal in Wheat, A see Norris, Frank
Dean, Ella Wood 161
"Dear Julia—" 238
"Dear Midnight of Love" 149
Dearborn, Henry 9
Dearborn Theater 70
Death For an Angel 281
Death of a Young Man, The 204, 205
Death of the Detective, The 332-333
Debs, Eugene V 108, 109, 268
Debt of Honor see *Old Chicago*
Decade of Short Stories 286
December 337
Decorah-posten 346
Dedmon, Emmett 128, fn, 214
Dee, Ruby 294
DeHavilland, Olivia 137
DeKalb, IL 340
Dell, Floyd 84, 89, 98-99, 111, 116, 117, 118, 119, 128, 129, 132, 134, 141, 145, 150, 171, 188, 201, 208, 209, 213, 241, 249
Democratic Convention, 1968 3
Den vonde volde 347
Dennis, Charles H 135
Denny and the Dumb Cluck 249
Denslow, W W 126
Denver, CO 41, 82
Department stores 35, 42, 66, 87, 115, 132, 147, 196, 281, 299, 313
Depression, 1930s 192, 223, 225, 227, 229ff., 238, 243, 245, 247, 253, 259, 262, 264, 265, 273, 277, 279ff., 284, 290, 292, 305, 310, 313, 314, 337, 339, 341
Derek, John 285
Derleth, August 291
Des Plaines River 251, 254, 265
Des Plaines Street see Haymarket Affair

Detective as fictional character 36 see Appendix
Detroit 11, 248, 267
Detroit Free Press 34
Detroit International Airport 319
Dever, Joseph 292
Devil's Stocking, The 327
DeVoto, Bernard 235, 255
Devout Bluebeard, A 122
DeVries, Peter 262, 265, 287, 314, 324, 336
Dial, The 13, 25, 39, 41, 49, 51, 74, 79, 84, 90, 125, 143, 146, 154, 159, 160, 211, 212
Dickens, Charles 55
Dickson, John 344
diDonato, Pietro 272
Dies, Edward Jerome 98
Differences 110
Dilettantism 71, 73, 76, 78, 81, 125 ff., 155, 247
Dill Pickle Club 212
Dill Pickler, The 212
Dillinger, John 30, 236, 285, 294, 341
Dillinger (film) 285
Dillinger (play) 341
Dillon, George 153, 211, 212
"Dime Novels" 32, 62, see Appendix
Dinehart, Alan 195
Dinglefest Theater Company 340
"Dinner Party, The" 251
Dishonored Lady, The (play) 260
Dissertations by Mr. Dooley 91
Diversey 169, 336
Divorce of Marcia Moore, The 276
"Dixie Dugan" 248
Do Black Patent Leather Shoes Really Reflect Up? 334ff.
Do Black Patent Leather Shoes Really Reflect Up? (musical play) 335
Dobler, Bruce 338
Doc Horne . . . 92
Dr. Caldwell: . . . 47
Dr. Bryson 121

Doctoraw, E L 345

Dodd Mead Intercollegiate Literary Fellowship 267

Dodd Mead Librarian Prize 300

Dogberry Bunch, The 35

Doggett, Mrs. Kate 73

Dog-racing 248

Doherty, Edward J 136

Doll House, The (play) 158

Dollmaker, The 267

Dondore, Dorothy 137

Donelson, Kathryn 64

Donnelly, Joseph P 240

Donnelly, R R 23

Donnelly, R R and Sons 18, 42

Donohue, H E F   316, 317, 318

Don't Look and It Won't Hurt 336

"Dooley, Mr." 91, 120-121, 181

Dooley, Roger 167-168, 170, 174, 222

Dorinda 268

Dos Passos, John 296, 312

Dostoievsky, Fyodor 183

Doubleday Doran See College Humor — Doubeday Doran Prize Novel

Doughty, Frances Worchester 122

Douglas, Amanda M 18, 96

Douglas, Lloyd C 250, 286, 347

Douglas, Stephen A 23, 51, 177, 239

Douglas, Mrs. Stephen A 317

Dow, Dorothy 209-210

Drago, Harry Sinclair 191

Dragons Drive You 230

Draper, John S 36

Dream of Kings, A 309

Dream of Kings, A (film) 309

Dreaming Tree, The 345

"Dregs" (play) 130

Dreiser, Theodore 2, 36, 37, 51, 92, 108, 110-111, 113, 129, 145, 147ff., 162, 180, 188, 202, 204, 214, 215, 270, 279, 283, 345, 347

Dresser, Paul 190

Drexel Avenue 279

Driven From Sea to Sea 74

Driver, John Merritte 114

Dubkin, Leonard 291

DuBois, William Edward Burghardt 197

Duchess of Few Clothes, The 114

Duck Variations, The 342-343

Duel, The see *(Old Chicago)*

Duff, Herbert B 34, 48

Duff, P[aul] J[ames] 34, 47-48

Duffey, Bernard 2, 97, 119

Du Jardin, Rosamond Neal 245, 297, 313

Duke Herring 186

Duke of Cameron Avenue, The 105

"Duke of Gas, The" see *The Money Captain*

Duke Steps Out, The 206

Duluth, MN 275

Duncan, Hugh Dalziell 2, 13, 15, 75, 96, 156

Dunne, Finley Peter 40, 51, 90-91, 93, 94, 95, 113, 133, 136, 180, 281

Dunne, Irene 176

Dunne Family, The 260

Duryea, Dan 306

du Sable, Du Saible see Sable, Point du

Dutch in Chicago 172, 175, 347

Dutton, E P Prize Novel 246

Dutton, R L 305

Dybek, Stuart 344

Dyke Darrel, The Railroad Dectective ... 33

Dynasty: A Novel ... 291

Eagle in the Air 311

Earl of Chicago, The 224

Earl of Chicago, The (film) 224

Early Summer 267

Earth 261

East of Eden 195-196

East of Midnight 295

Eastland 213

Eastman, Max 273

Ebb, Fred 165

Ebel, Camille Layer 312

Eberhart, Mignon G 226, Appendix

Ebony 293

Eckersall, Walter 135

Eckert, Allan W 345

Economist, Chicago 90

"Ed Lanson" 259

"Eddie Ryan" 259, 334

Eddy, Arthur Jerome 101, 296

Edgewater Beach Hotel 130

Edna His Wife 253

Edison, Thomas A 42

Education 160, 161, 178, 242, 340 See also Novels of College Life

Education of Ernest Wilmerding 110, 200

Education of Henry Adams 63-64

Edwards, James G, M D See MacQueen, James W

Edwards, S W 310

Eggleston, Edward 51

Egyptian Harp Girl see fn. 42, chap V

Eidsvold 347

8 Faces at 3 281

1887 Literary Congress 51

"1812," the Story of the War of 1812 ... 16

1835 Chicago Powwow 17

Eighth Day, The 318

Eklund, Jane [Ball] 276-277

El Goes South 246

"Eldest, The" 141, 142

Eldest, The (play) 171

Elegant Eighties, The 238

Elkin, Stanley 337, 340

Ellen Rogers 259

Ellis, Edward Sylvester See Gordon, Col H R

Ellis, Elmer 91

Ellison, [Earl] Jerome 250, 265

Ellsworth, Col Elmer 23-24

Elsie Dinsmore at the World's Fair 61

Emerson, Ralph Waldo 3

End of Desire, The 245

End of Mr. Garment, The 226

Endless Road, The 299

Engle, Paul 228, 324

English in the Chicago area 10, 78

English, Professors of (See Lee, Linn, Herrick, Lovett, Bellow) 124, 215, 316

English Review 40

Ensign Ronan; A Story of Fort Dearborn 15

Environment (film) 214

Epic of America 18

Epic of Chicago 18

Epistolary novels 99-100, 136, 203

Erik Dorn 184

Esquire 183, 236, 261

Essanay Film Studios 214

Eustace Chisholm and the Works 318

Evangeline 65

Evans, John [pseud] see Browne, Howard

Evanston, IL 64, 82, 131, 141, 144, 163, 243, 300, 314, 318, 319, 347

Even in Laughter 231

Evening American, Chicago 108

Evening Post, Chicago 90, 91, 104, 126, 134, 145, 149, 213

Evening World, New York 161-162

Everleigh Sisters 30, 176, 302, 347

Everett, Henry L 55

Every One His Own Way 112

Evvie 313

Ewing, Annamarie 270

Excerpts 329

Expert, The (film) 174, 286

Eye for an Eye, An 108

"F.P.A. See Adams, Franklin P

"Fable of Sister Mae . . ." 93

"Fables in slang" 92

Fables in Slang 68, 92-93

Fabulous Bastard from Chicago, The 322

Fabulous Kid from Chicago, The 322

Face in the Stone, The 292

Face of Night, The 310

Face of Time, The 258

Fair, Ronald L 310, 328

Fairbank, Janet Ayer 4, 15, 137, 144, 158, 191-193, 214, 239, 251, 263

Fairbank, Kellogg "Ked" 137, 192

Faith and the Good Thing 330-331

Fallen Race, The see fn. 12, V

Falling 337

Fame is the Name of the Game (film) 287

Family Pictures 305

Fanny Herself 142-143, 173, 201, 232

Fantazius Mallare 212

Far Away Music, The 275

Far Down, The 255

Far From the Madding Crowd 49

Farm, Field and Fireside 56

"Farm Hand" 234

"Farmer in the Dell" 172, 174, 287

Farmerkonen Marit Kjølseth's erfaringer in Chicago 346

"Farmer Wife Marit Kjølseth's Adventure in Chicago" 346

Farr, Finis 1, 2, 3, 60, 99, 149

Farrar, John 241

Farrell, James T 2, 51, 148, 229, 236, 255, 257ff., 261, 263, 264, 272, 283, 284, 286, 290, 294, 301, 306, 307, 308, 309, 324, 346, 347

Farson, Negley 189

Fast, Howard 45, 268

Father and Son 258

Father Goose, His Book 126

Faulkner, William 234, 298, 316, 327

"Faun-in-the-city" See Dell, Floyd

"Fay, Felix" 90, 134-135, 202

Faye, Alice 28-30

Faye's Folly 267

Fearing, Kenneth Flexner 204-205

Fearing, Lillian Blanche 65, 72

Fearnot, Fred 32

Federal Theater Program, 1930s 229, 236

Federal Writers Program, 1930s 229-230, 279, see Chicago WPA Writers Program

Felicity 115

Felix Fay 134-135

Fellow Mortals 247

Ferber, Edna 10, 24, 34, 132, 133, 140-143, 144, 158, 171-177, 184, 191, 201, 207, 211, 232, 237, 249, 270, 287, 305, 306, 347

Ferris, George Washington Gale 63, 347

Ficke, Arthur Davison 129, 145, 153, 208

Fiddler, Robert 341

Fidelia 180

Field, Eugene 30, 40, 41, 49, 51, 58, 70, 72, 75, 77, 80, 82, 90, 92, 93, 94, 115, 162, 180, 194

Field, Louise Maunsell 274

Field, Marshall 28, 43, 98, 142

Field, Marshall IV 263, 326

Field, Roswell 85, 113

Field, Mrs. Roswell 74, 120

Field Museum 25

Fields, Vina 87

Fields, W C 169, 249

57th Street Studios 180, 204

Figaro 82

Figaro Fiction 82

Films as drama 5

Film industry and Chicago 214, 339

Films, gangster, see Gangster in Chicago fiction and films

Financier, The 148

Find the Motive 213

Fine Arts Building 84

Finley, Martha 61

Finney (film) 332

Fire, Chicago 3, 5, 17, 18, 20, 23, 25, 26ff., 30, 33, 40, 43, 46, 65, 66, 70, 72, 74, 76, 85, 91, 173, 188, 191, 192, 194, 225, 252, 270, 306, 312, 313, 347
Fire, Columbian Exposition 61
Fire, Iroquois Theater 121, 247
Fire, Peshtigo, Wisconsin 30
Fire of Spring, The 114
Fireweed 227
First Ward See Coughlin, "Bathhouse John"
Fisher, Dorothy Canfield 237
Fisher, Fred 208
Fisher, Vardis 256
Fitzgerald, F Scott 121, 137, 180, 258, 337
Fitch, Thomas and Anna M fn. 42, chap V
Flail, The 160
Flame of Happiness, The 180
Flanagan, Zoe 179
"Flapper" 203
Flaubert, Gustave 111-112
Flavin, Martin 275
Fleming, Herbert E 25ff., 39-41, 82, 286
Fleming, Robert Edward 2
Fletcher, John Gould 127
Flinn, John J 61
Flower, B O 79
Flower, Elliott 101, 104, 121
Flower, Mrs. Luch 104
Flowering Stone, The 212
Flynn, Errol 250
Foiled by a Lawyer . . . 32
Folded Leaf, The 275
Football, professional and amateur 92, 322, 325-326, 339
For Her Daily Bread 46, 69
Foran, Martin A 32
Ford, Corey 296
"Ford, Webster" See Masters, Edgar Lee
Forerunner, The 109
Forest and Stream (magazine) 82
Forge, The 153, 212
Forrest, Leon 330

Fort, The see *Old Chicago*
Fort Crèvecoeur 7, 78
Fort Dearborn 3, 9-13, 17, 78, 149, 173, 191, 239, 306, 347
"Fort Dearborn" Masters 9, 10, 16, 149
"Fort Dearborn: Chicago" Taylor 14
Fort St. Louis 7, 78
Fort Sheridan 133, 300
Fortnightly Club 73
Fortune Machine, The 339
Forum Theater 340
"Forward!" see *Fram!*
"Forward young woman" see "new woman"
Fosse, Bob 165
Foundry, The 232, 273
Four Friends 340
"Four-Leafed Clover, The" 24
Four's a Crowd (film) 168
Fourth Postman, The 268
Fourth King, The 226
Fox, Fanny Ferber 250
Fox, Mary Virginia 15
Fox River 226
Foy, Eddie 121
Fram! 346
Frances a la Mode 299
Frances by Starlight 299
Franciosa, Tony 287
"Frank Merriwell series" 32
Frank Merriwell in Chicago 32
Frank Merriwell's Speed 32
Frankie and Johnny 244
Franks, Bobby 30, 302
Frederick, John Towner 229, 279
Free Born 238
"Free Love" 109, 146
Freeman, Martin Joseph 226
French, The 3, 6-8, 14, 238, 271, 312, 347
French, Alice (Octave Thanet) 43, 46, 108, 117, 144
Friday Club of Chicago 228
Friday Literary Review See *Evening Post*, Chicago
Friedman, Israel Kahn 34, 36, 85, 106, 109

Friedman, Richard 344
Friend, Oscar Jerome 226
Friends of American Writers 213, 309
Friends of Literature 309
"From A-Z" 116
From Side Streets and Boulevards . . . 66
From the Old World to the New . . . 56
Front Page (play) 136, 166-168, 213, 348
Front Page, The (film) 5, 167-169
Fuessle, Newton A 160, 193
Fugitive 231
Fugitive Love 189
Full Fathom Five 317
Fuller, Henry Blake 2, 3, 5, 13, 31, 49, 51, 70, 72, 74, 81, 84, 85-89, 95, 126, 128, 145, 152, 162, 192, 213, 255, 347
Fuller, Iola 290
Fury, The 340

Gable, Clark 223, 236, 324
Gaily, Gaily 167, 322
Gaily, Gaily (film) 186, 322
Gaines, Diana 295, 315
Galati, Frank 340
Gale, Zona 169, 196
Galena, IL 50, 239, 322
Galesburg, IL 146, 207
Galsworthy, John 128, 187
Gambler/A Story of Chicago Life, The 33, 67
"Gamblers' Alley" 34, 175
Game Time 331
gangster as literary figure 162, 163ff., 189, 220ff., 231, 236, 238, 240, 241, 246, 270, 278, 283, 285, 295, 298, 306, 321, 322-323, 332
Gangster Girl (film) 221
Ganton & Co.: A Story of Chicago . . . 101, 296
Garfield, John 282
Gargoyles 184, 185

Garland, Hamlin 3, 12, 39, 41, 50, 51, 54, 68, 75, 78-81, 84, 85, 88, 89, 94, 95, 126, 132, 145, 194, 213, 347
"Garlic Creek" 10, 19
Garrick Theater 321
Gary, IN 154, 278
Gas-House McGinty 259
Gasoline Alley (comic strip) 217
Gault, William Campbell 326
Gay Nineties, The 52
"Gay Old Dog, The" 142, 287
Gay Old Dog (film) 142, 287
Geismar, Maxwell 301
Gem of the Prairie, The 25, 149, 170
Gene Krupa Story (film) 271
"General William Booth Enters Heaven" 153
Geneva, IL 33
"Genius," The 127, 149
"Genteelism," Chicago 51, 71-73, 78, 79, 112, 119, 124, 125, 143, 145
Gentle Julia (film) 214
Gentle Tyrants, The 312
Gentleman From Chicago, The 332
George, Henry 54, 114, 156
Georgie May 240
"Georgy Porgy, Prodigy" 209
Geraldine Bradshaw 294-295
Gerhardt's Children 338
German Opera Company 74
Germans in Chicago 24, 30, 40, 105, 133, 139, 160, 234, 328, 337, 347
Gerson, Noel Bertram 326
Gerstenberg, Alice 85, 125, 130, 155
Ghetto, Chicago 31, 46, 56, 127, 137, 236, 294
Ghetto, The 283
Ghosts (Ibsen) 113, 114
Gibbons, Floyd 136
Gibson, Hoot 217
Gide, Andre 320
Gifted, The 296
"Gigolo" 173, 287
Gigolo (film) 287
Gilded Torch, The 290

Gingerich, Arnold 261
Ginsberg, Allen 327
Girl, The 160
Girl From Chicago, The (film) 216
Girl from Macoupin, The see *Beauty's Peril . . .*
Girl Happy (film) 322
Girl of Chicago, A 110
Girl Who Lived in the Woods, The 127, 154
"Girl Who Went Right, The" 141
Girlhood in Chicago 317
Girls, The 10, 24, 172-173, 174, 175, 176, 191, 213, 270
Gissing, George 195
Give Us This Day 235
Givins, Robert C[artwright] 47
Glaspell, Susan 116, 128, 129, 132, 134, 141, 145, 158, 171, 198, 201, 213, 257
Glenna Loved It! . . . 342
Glory of the Conquered/ . . . The 116
Glory of the Hummingbird, The 336
Glyn, Elinor 154
Go Naked in the World 293
Go Now in Darkness 310
God Bless This Child 331
God of Might 196
Goddard College 342
Goetzinger, Clara Palmer 202
Going Down Fast 321
"Going to Market" 234
Gold Brick, The 104
Gold Coast 125, 127, 128, 137, 139, 144, 202, 300, 347
Gold Coast and the Slums, The 283
Gold Shod 193
Golden Box, The (film) 340
Golden Children, The 329
Golden Fleece, The 183
Golden Grain 234, 267
Golden Ladder, The 102
Golden Watch, The 297-298
Goldie Green 187
Goldman, Emma 106, 153
Goldstein (film) 321

Goldstein, Shelly 342
Gooch, Fani Pusey 48
Good Housekeeping (magazine) 199, 210
Good Is For Angels 294
Good Red Bricks, The 190
Goodbye, Columbus 315
Goodman, Kenneth Sawyer 128, 130
Goodman Memorial Theater 128, 130, 199, 260, 343
Goose Island 69
Gordon, Col. H R [pseud] 15
Gospel of Freedom, The 117, 161
Gothic element in Chicago novels 53
"Gowdy, Dr." see fn. 65, chap. V
Grable, Betty 306
Grabo, Carl 245
Grace Hickox's Studios 130
Graduate, The 295
Graham, Marie 122
Grand Crossing 237, 283
Grand Hotel (film) 114
"Grand Old Man" see Stagg, Amos Alonzo
Grand Portage 254
Grant Cary 168
Grant Park 241, 316
Granville, Austyn (see fn. 12, V) 57
Grape Dealer's Daughter, The (film) 339
Grapes of Wrath 265
Graustark 102, 113
"Gray wolves" 104
Grayson, Kathryn 176
Grease (musical play) 289, 290
Grease (film) 290 fn.
Grease II (film) 290 fn.
Great Bear, The 194-195
Great Chicago Fire, The 30
Great Chicago Fire, 1871, The 30
The Great Cronin Mystery . . . 34
Great Divide, The 93
"Great Grim Lincoln, The" 209
Great Hotel Murder, The 226

Great John Ganton, The (play) 101

Great Lakes 291

Great Midland, The 273, 280

Great Tradition, The 256, 286

Great Valley, The 16, 18, 149

Great Wheel, The 63

Greater English Club 213

Greeks in Chicago 138, 292, 293, 308, 309, 347

Green, Paul 279

Green, Rose Basile 255

Green Jade Hand, The 226

Green Light 250, 286

Green Light (film) 350

Green Valley 140

Greene, Bob 340

Greenlee, Sam 317

Greenwich Village 171, 193, 213, 240

Grey, Lennox Bouton 2, 8, 12, 14, 15, 19, 20, 26, 27, 28, 29, 44, 45, 60, 61, 62, 64, 66, 70, 77, 85, 107, 109, 110, 150, 155, 161, 176, 186, 197, 225

"Grey city" see University of Chicago

Grey plague, 20th century's 315

Grey Towers 179

Griffith, David Wark 157

Grosch, Anthony R 101

Gross, Samuel Eberly 42

Grotesques 129

Grouch at the Game 93

Growing Dawn, The 209

Gruber, Frank 281

Guardian Angel and Other Stories 211

Guest, Eddie 339

Guest, Judith 320, 339

Guggenheim Award 211, 333

Guiterman, Arthur 209

Guillotine Party 259

Gullible's Travels 136

Gulliver's Travels 61

Gunsaulus, Dr. W F 41, 72

Gunter, Archibald Clevering see fn. 43, chap. V

Gunther, John 132, 180, 182, 214, 347

Gurdon S Hubbard 18

Gus the Bus and Evelyn ... 133

Guthrie, Arlo 328

Guys and Dolls 164

Haas, Joseph L 331

HAB Theory, The 345

Hackett, Alice Payne 43

Hackett, Francis 124, 126, 128, 132, 133-134, 145, 173, 213

Hagen, Gudmund 346

Hailey, Arthur 319, 333

Haldeman-Julius Publications 185, 194

Half Portions 171-172

Hall, E. J. see fn. 12, chap. V

Hall, Grace D 235

Hall, Joseph 6-8, 77

Hall, Mordaunt 217

Halligan's Illustrated World's Fair 82

Halper, Albert 40, 51, 142, 205, 229, 232-233, 234-235, 263, 264, 273, 277, 287, 297-298, 306, 307, 346

Halsted Street 29, 43, 46, 56, 105, 160

Ham, Roswell G [ray], Jr 296

Hamill, Pete 67, 327

Hamilton, Harry Raymond 18

Hamilton, Henry E 18

Hammond, IN 298 fn., 347

Hammond, Percy 136

Hand's of Clay; a Great City's Half ... 105

Handsome Cyril ... 126

Handsome Heart, The 287

Hansberry, Lorraine 294

Hansen, Harry 2, 132, 134, 135, 145, 179, 181, 207ff., 241, 249

Hanson, Harvey 331

Hapgood, Hutchins 69, 108, 155, 188

Hapgood, Mrs Hutchins see Boyce, Neith

Happy Average, The 104

Happy End (musical play) 169

Happy Families 319

Harding, Ann 252

"Hardscrabble" see Bridgeport 10

Hardscrabble; or, The Fall of Chicago 10, 12, 48

Hardy, Thomas 49

Harlow, Jean 248

Harper, William Rainey 194

Harper and Brothers 284

Harper Prize Novel 233, 275

Harper's Monthly 94

Harris, Frank 44-45

Harris, Jed 168

Harris, Joel Chandler 42

Harris, Mark 87

Harris, Phil 307

Harrison, Carter W 64, 346, 347

Harrison, William 320

Harte, Bret 38, 75, 81, 301

Harvard University 64, 87, 100, 108, 188, 255, 273

Harvest (Horton) (play) 169

Harvest, The (Levin) 344

Harvey, William H "Coin" 56, 146

Hasimaier, Jerry 342

Haver, Phyllis 165

Hawks, Howard 168

Hawthorne, Julian 75

Hawthorne, Nathaniel 3, 75

Hayes, Laura 60

Haymarket Affair 23, 33, 43ff., 53, 66, 109, 118, 144, 154, 155, 200, 205, 271-272, 306, 313, 327, 347

"Haymarket Affair in Literature, The" 43-45

Haymarket: Footnote to a Bombing 44

Hazard of New Fortunes, A 44-45

Hazenplug, Frank 84

He Ran All the Way 282

He Ran All the Way (film) 282

Head of Apollo, The 255

Head, Cloyd 129

Head, Franklin 126

Headly, Glenne 340

Heald, Captain 11

Healer, The 153

Healy, George Peter Alexander 46

Healy, Mary Bigot 15, 46, 190

Healy, Paul F 317

Hearst, William Randolph 108

Hearst's Cosmopolitan (magazine) 205

Heart of Silence, The 318

"Hearts" (play) 130

Hearts Undaunted 16

Hecht, Ben 51, 128, 129, 131, 132, 135, 136, 140, 164, 165, 166-168, 181, 184, 208, 212, 213, 214, 216, 217, 221, 223, 236, 240, 283, 306, 322

Hedges, M H 161

Heights and Depths 26

Hellman, Lillian 196

Hell's Highroad (film) 215

Hemingway, Ernest 180, 247, 273, 327, 344

Henrici's 238

Henry, O (see Porter, William Sidney)

Henry, Mrs Rebecca 237-238

Henry is Twenty 144

Her Infinite Variety 103

Herald, Chicago 90, 104, 164

Herbst, Josephine 267, 270

Herman, Lewis 226

Heroes for Sale (film) 262

Herrick, Robert 3, 31, 44-45, 51, 63, 95, 108, 109, 113, 117-119, 132, 134, 153-154, 161, 162, 178-179, 180, 204, 214, 245, 246, 255, 265-266, 295

"Herring for my Uncle, A" 234

Hertig, Charles M 71, fn. 67, chap V

Herzog 305, 348

Hey, Jewboy 319

Heyer, Rachel G 20

Heywood, "Big Bill" 108

Hicks, Granville 301

Hidden Faith . . ., The 68

Hidden Fire 298

Higher Animals, The 316, 318

Hillman, Sidney 236

"Hillport" see "Mount Royal"

The Hind and the Panther 61

Hinrichsen, Steen 212

His Girl Friday (film) 168

History of Chicago, (Kirkland) 48-49

History of Chicago, The (Andreas) 18, 96

History of Illinois 12, 13

Hobbledehoy's Hero 338

Hoffman, Abbie 327-328

Hoffman, Judge Julius 328

Hog Butcher 310

"Hog butcher" School of Literature 146

Hoge, Alice Albright 317

Holbrook, Amelia Weed 68

Holden, Martha R 62

Holley, Marietta 62

Hollywood 215-216, 220, 224, 244, 268, 283, 286, 299, 315, 322, 342

Holm, Saxe, pseud. see Jackson, Helen Hunt

Holme, Frank 126

Holmes, Oliver Wendell 75

Holt, Alfred Hubbard 18

Holt, Isabella 187, 248, 274

"Home Fires" 251

"Home Girl" 173

Homecoming 134

Homely Lilla 178

Homosexuality 89, 317-318

Honeyfogling Time 267-268

Honky (film) 311

Honor Divided 235

Honorable John Hale . . . 268

Hoover, Paul 344

Horan, Kenneth [O'Donnell] 241-244

Hopkins, Mark 116

horse racing 224

Horses and Men 202-203

Horton, George 121

Horton, Kate 169

Hoshiko, Patsy Rose see *Illinois! Illinois!*

Hot Stuff . . . 48

"Hotel, The" 152

Hough, Emerson 82, 85, 126, 139

House, The [Allee] 286

House, The: An Episode . . . (Field) 41

House Across the River, The 254

House on the North Shore, The 115

How Bob and I Kept House . . . 47

Howard, Elizabeth 268

Howard, Fred [Steven] 336

Howells, William Dean 44-45, 85, 88, 89, 92, 94, 95, 113, 117, 153

Howey, Walter 136, 167-168

Howland, Bette 338

Hoyt, Helen 127

Hubbard, Gurdon S, partial autobiography 17, 18, 19

Hubbard, Gurdon Saltonstall 4, 17ff., 99, 194, 296, 347

Hubbard's Trail 18

Hudson, Jay William 7, 203-204

Hughes, Howard 295

Hughes, Langston 233, 294

Hughes, Thomas 39

Hull, General 11

Hull House 46, 56, 69, 84, 106, 108, 109, 110, 120, 127, 128, see also Addams, Jane

Hull House Magazine 284

Hull House Theater 127-128

Human Note, A 103

Humboldt Park 345, 347

Humboldt's Gift 305

Humpty-Dumpty 185

Hungarians in Chicago 24, 176

Hungry Men 231

Hunky Johnny 278

Hunt, Barbara 287

Hurlbut, Henry M 14

Hurst, Fannie 237

Husmandsgutten 346

Hutchens, John K 145

Hutchens, Paul 224

Hutcheson, Frank 79, 90

Hutchinson, Benjamin P "Old Hutch" 98

Hutchison, Percy A 179

Hyde Park 60, 187, 230, 347

Hyman, Elaine 129

I, Jerry, Take Thee Joan 245
I Lived This Story 255
I Love You, Irene 336
I Loved a Woman (film) 231, 263
Ibsen, Henrik 113, 114, 128, 159
Ice Before Killing 280
Iceberg Slim [pseud] see Beck, Robert
Icepick ... 338
Ideal Republic, An ... (see fn. 12, chap. V)
Idle Hands 193
"Idyll of the Shops" (play) 130
"If Christ Came to Chicago" 56
If Christ Came to Chicago ... 34, 56-57, 123
If I Had a Million (film) 249
If the Devil Came to Chicago 57
If the Heart Be Hasty 320
Illini, The 96, 98, 197
Illinois Federal Writer's Project see Chicago Writer's Project
Illinois! Illinois! ... 32
Illinois State Legislature 197
Illinois State Penitentiary, Chicago 337
Illinois, University of 230, 309
"Imagism" 146
In a Wild Sanctuary 320
In Babel 93
In His Steps 110
In Old Chicago (film) 28, 29, 30
In Reckless Ecstasy 146
In Search 272
In the City by the Lake 65
In the City of Men: Another Story of Chicago 2
"In the Clutches of the Devil" 347
In the Dark (Richberg) 138
In the Dark (Tobenkin) 222
In the Land of the Morning 309
In the Mecca 305
In the Name of Love (film) 215

In Town, and Other Conversations 137, 191, 251
Incidents and Events in the Life of Gurdon S. Hubbard 18
Indian Drum 157
"Indian Summer" 196
Indiana 36, 89, 91, 100, 113, 118, 126, 147, 161, 166, 215, 268, 271, 275, 336
Indians, The 3, 95, 128 fn., 157, 191, 291, 312
Infatuation: and Other Stores ... 185
Informer, The (film) 310
Ingersoll, Robert 45, 46, 53, 82, 92
Innocents, The 198-199
Instead of the Thorn 139
Instruct My Sorrows 274
Insull, Samuel 3, 30, 230, 231, 239, 247, 298, 347
International Correspondence School 194
International Writers' Workshop (Iowa) 228
Inter-Ocean, Chicago 135, 160, 187
inter-racial marriage 329-330
Into Your Tent I'll Creep 336
Invisible Gods, The 193
Invitation to Live 286
Iowa 33, 36, 40, 43, 50, 78, 82, 90, 109, 114, 139, 141, 150, 171, 199, 202, 207, 228, 229, 268, 275, 336, 337
Iowa City, Iowa 315, 326
Iowa School of Letters Award 330
Iowa, University of 228, 270, 315, 326
Irene 164
Irish in Chicago 63, 66, 79, 91, 93, 104, 107, 126, 137, 254, 257ff., 283, 292, 328, 336, 347
Irish Mollie; or a Gambler's Fate ... 31
Irish Mollie, the Queen ... 31
Irish Players 129
Iron City 161

Iron Heel, The 123-124
Iron Man 248
Iron Man (film) 248
Iron Pastoral, The 285
Irvine, St. John 128
It Happened on Rush Street 336
"It Passes By" 128
Italian-American Novel, The 235
Italians in Chicago 105, 235, 281, 283, 329, 347
It's a Wonderful Word 186
It's Different for a Woman 297
It's Not Far, But I Don't Know the Way 321
It's Not My Problem 244
Ives, Burl 301

J. Devlin — Boss 103
Jack, Peter Munro 279
Jack and Jill Theatre 130
Jackroller, The 283
Jackson, Charles Tenney 154
Jackson, Helen Hunt 24
Jackson, Margaret Weymouth 189, 242
Jackson Park 51, 54, 58ff., 63, 194
Jack-the-Ripper 90
Jacques Marquette S J, 1637-1675 240
Jade Green Cats, The 243
Jake 186
James, Bertha Ten Eyck 153
James, Franklin [pseud] see Godley, Robert
James, Henry 2, 85, 113
James, Jesse 34
James, Marquis 136
James T Farrell 260
Jane Addams, a Biography 112
Jane Cable 102
Janson, Kristofer 346
Jaynes, Clare [pseud] 266, 274, 299
Jazz 267, 270-271, 304
Jazz; and Other Stories ... 185
Jean Christophe 196
Jefferson Award 343
Jelley, Symmes M 32

Jenifer, Laurence Mark 282
Jenks, Tudor 61
Jennie Fowler 242
Jennie Gerhardt 148
Jennie Gerhardt (film) 148
Jenny (play) 260
"Jerome" 328
Jerome Leaster of Roderick Leaster & Co 53, 69, 155
Jerry Bleeker; . . . 47
Jerry the Dreamer 89-90
Jesse James in Chicago 34
Jewish Publication Society of America 237
Jews in Chicago 105, 140-143, 156, 159, 197, 198, 207, 232, 234, 235, 236, 266, 277, 278, 283, 291-292, 297-298, 305, 319, 328, 336, 338, 347
"Jim" 75
Joan Kennedy 189
John Crerar Library 25
John Dorn, Promoter 100, 127, 157
John Kinzie, the Father of Chicago 16
Johnson, Charles [Richard] 330-331
Johnson, Curt 338
Johnson, Elizabeth Winthrop 24
Johnson, Fenton 151
Johnson, Hilding 167
Johnson, Martyn 128
Joliet, IL 345
Joliet, Louis 6
Jones, Allan 176
Jones, Jack 326
Jones, Fernando 191
Jones, Howard Mumford 242
Jones, Jenifer 112
Jones, Llewellyn 85, 141, 145, 153, 209, 241
Joseph Greer and his Daughter 198
Josslyn 181
Journalism in Chicago 131ff., 159, 166, 181ff., 204, 249, 322
Journey Home 250
Journey in the Dark 275
Joy of Working, The 132

Joyce, James 153, 316
Jucklins, The fn. 55, chap V
Judge, The 34
Judge Elbridge 67
Judgement Day 258
Judith 259
Judson, Clara Ingram 62, 195
Jungle, The 101, 109, 130, 159, 232
Just Folks 110, 137
Juveniles, books for 196

Kael, Pauline 167, 168
Kalamazoo, MI 140, 174
Kane's World 319
Kansas 35, 84, 110, 121, 192, 203, 233
Kantor, MacKinlay 169, 229, 246, 262, 263, 336
Kapustkans 286
Karlins, Marvin 321
Kaufman, George M 174
Kazin, Alfred 112, 235, 237
Keeban 171
Keel, Howard 176
Keeler, Harry Stephen 226
Keenan, Henry Francis 40
Kehr, Dave 165, 167, 215, 283
Keith, Katherine 15, 70, 160, 246
Kelly, Regina Z[immerman] 19
Kelmscott Press 84
Kenna, Michael, (Hinky Dink) 30, 109, 149, 164, 176, 185, 225, 238, 347
Kennedy, Adam 336, 337
Kennedy, Howard Hogue see Woolfolk, Josiah Pitts
Kennedy, Louise Mabie 158
Kennedy, Mark 293
Kennedy, Robert 322
Kent, Mona 271
Kenton, Edna 209
Kenwood 347
Kenyon, William Asbury 35
Kerouac, Jack 318
Kerr, Charles H and Company 55, 146
Keyes, Evelyn 248
"Keyhole Eye, The" 317
Kildahl, J N 346
Killer in the Kitchen 281

Killing of Judge McFarlane, The 228
Kilpatrick, Thomas L 47, 65, 100, 150, 155, 238
Kimball, H Ingalls 42, 77, 80, 83, 84
King, Charles 55
Kinzie, Eleanor Lytle 16
Kinzie, Mrs. John H (Juliette) 4, 10ff., 51, 72, 186, 306
Kinzie, John H, Jr 10ff., 347
Kinzie, John H, Sr 4, 9, 10ff., 30, 343
Kinzie, Mrs John H, Sr 10ff.
Kipling, Rudyard 3, 162, 306
Kirk, Hyland C 61
Kirkland, Mrs Carolyn 12, 48, 49
Kirkland, Joseph 12, 14, 20, 24, 28, 48ff., 51, 59, 65, 66, 72, 78, 79, 112, 191
Kiss and Kill 281
Knebel, Fletcher 315
Knickerbocker Magazine, The 23
Knife and the Needle, The 315
Knight, John S 326
"Knights of Labor" 150
Knock on Any Door (novel) 283-284
Knock on Any Door (film) 284
Knocked for a Loop 281
Knopf, A A 165
Knox College 207
Koch, Joanne 44
Kogan, Herman 30, 149, 289
Komroff, Manuel 251
Korean War 332
Kramer, Dale 2, 75, 134, 149, 212, 213
Krautter, Elisa (Bialk) 250
Kremlin, The 316
Krupa, Gene 270
Krutch, Joseph Wood 178, 179
Kuehl, John 336
Kurtz, Ann 312

Ladies and Gents 234
Ladies Home Journal (magazine) 74, 120, 317
Ladies in the Parlor 225
Ladd, Allen 287

Lady Elgin, The 19
"Lady or the Tiger, The" 75
Lady Windermere's Fan 76
Lady's Western Magazine 25
Laemmle, Carl 214
Laflin, Louis E, Jr 199
Laird and Lee 123
Lait, Jack 123, 133, 163, 221, 302
Lake Forest, IL 2, 154, 228, 248, 332, 337, 339, 344, 347
Lake Front 7, 45, 238
Lake Michigan 6, 68, 90, 96, 151, 157, 158, 194, 245, 252, 280, 298, 332, 339
Lake Shore Drive 120, 137, 139, 202, 296, 340
Lakeside Library 39
Lakeside Monthly (magazine) 25, 39
Lakeville: or Substance and Shadow 46, 190
Lalime, Jean 9, 30
Lally, John Patrick 242
Lamb, Martha Joan 15, 23, 28
Lamensdorf, Leonard 319
Lampe, Keith 328
Land is Ours, This 19, 268
Land of Plenty, The 312
Land of Strangers 291
Land of the Living, The 107
Land Poor; A Chicago Parable 47
Landers, Ann 314
Landlooker, The 30
Lane, Abbe 302
Lane, Gertrude Battles 175
Lane, Mark 327
Langworthy Family, The 255
LaPlante, Laura 176
Lardner, Ringgold (Ring) Jr 94, 135, 136, 141, 204, 213, 220, 306, 335, 347
Larson, Nella 197
La Salle, Robert Cavalier, Sieur de 6, 9, 16, 20, 77-78, 290
La Salle Street 6, 77, 290
La Salle: The Life and Times ... 290
Last Carousel, The 327

Last Catholic in America, The 334
Last Doorbell, The 281
Last Man is Out, The 321
Last of the Badmen (film) 307
"Latchkeys" (play) 131
Late Show 337
Latimer, Margery [pseud] See Toomer, Mrs. Jean
Latimore, Jonathan (Wyatt) 226
Latino Chicago (play) 342
Laughlin, Clara Elizabeth 110, 115, 126, 137, 160, 209
Laura 313
Lawd Today 310
Lawrence, Catherine 266-267
Lawson, Don[ald Elmer] 314
Lawson, Robert 63, 332
Lawson, Victor F 41, 180, 326
Lawson, W B 34, 181
Lawyer Manton of Chicago; ... 33
Lazarus, Emma 105
LaZebnik, Ken 341
Lazy Laughter 187
Le Jemlys [pseud] see Jelley, Symmes M
Leacock, Philip 302
League of Nations 255
Lean Twilight 205-206
Leather Duke, The 281
Leatherstocking Tales 216
Lechlitner, Ruth 211
Lee, Jeannette Barbour Perry 102, 138, 156
Left Bank of Chicago, The 269
Left Front 261
Legend of a Lady; The Story of Rita Martin 271
Lehr und Wehr Verein 150
Leiter, Joseph 98
Lemmon, Jack 168
Lengel, William Charles 242
Lenihan, Winifred 234
Leopold, Nathan 30, 108, 183, 203, 224, 236, 303-304
Lesemann, Maurice 211
Let No Man Write My Epitaph 284, 301
Let No Man Write My Epitaph (film) 301-302

Let's Re-Elect FDR (play) 260
Letter to Einstein Beginning Dear Albert 344
Letters From a Self-made Merchant to his Son 99-100, 101, 296
Letters From a Son to his Self-Made Father 100
Letting Go 315
"Levee, The" 121, 302, 347
Levin, Meyer 138, 181, 183, 214, 236, 244, 245, 260, 261, 263, 272, 273, 283, 288, 303, 306, 344, 346, 347
Levinson, Helen Poetry Prize 147
Levinson, Salmon O 147
Lewis, Alfred Henry 90
Lewis, Edwin Herbert 110, 160, 204, 210
Lewis, Janet 153
Lewis, Lloyd 23, 132, 181, 184
Lewis Sinclair 176, 180, 201, 243
Leyendecker, J C 84
Libbey, Laura Jean 136
Library, Chicago Public 25, 72, 342
Library Journal 293
Life (magazine) 276, 314
Life Adventure, The 259
Life for a Life, A 153
Life in the Theater, A (play) 342
Life With Father 275
Life's Greatest Game (film) 215
Light a Little Lamp 314
Light From Arcturus 227
Light of Other Days 255
Lightning (film) 215
Lights Are Bright, The 158
Lincoln, IL 297
Lincoln, Abraham 23, 26, 33, 49, 107, 155, 177, 191, 192, 209, 229, 239, 310, 347
Lincoln-Douglas debates 23
Lindsay, Vachel 127, 145, 149, 153, 208, 210
Line Between, The 233
"Line o' Type or Two, A" 115

Lines Short and Long 88
Lingle, Jake 30, 223
Linn, James Weber 112, 116, 255, 256, 265-266
Link Rover in Chicago; . . . 124
Lion at my Heart 292
Lippman, Walter 148, 188
Lipton, Georgianna see Rice, Craig
Literary Budget, The (magazine) 25, 70
Literary capitol of the United States 3, 124, 145, 204
"Literary Capitol of America, The" 162
Literary clubs see Clubs, literary
Literary Congress, World's Columbian Exposition 79
Literary Digest, The 143
Literary Life (magazine) 75
Literary societies see Clubs, literary
Literary Times, Chicago 240
Literature, Chicago, themes in 29, 119, 220, 238, 246, 264, 290, 309
Literature of place 4
"Litere" See Somers, Lillian
Little, Richard Henry 131, 136
Little Big Man 295
"Little Blue Books" 185
"Little Boy Blue" 75, 181
Little Brother of the Rich, A 115
Little Caesar (novel) 166, 169, 213, 222, 248, 302
Little Casesar (film) 166, 169, 221-222, 261
Little Dreaming, A 150
"Little Egypt" 60, 347
Little Egypt (film) 62-63
Little Gate 270
Little Girl in Old Chicago, A 18, 96
Little Girl Next Door, The (film) 214
Little Hell — Big Heaven 274
Little Lord Fauntleroy 61

"Little" magazines in Chicago 82, 261, 286
Little Men, Big World 302
Little Miss Dee 113
Little Night Music, A 287
Little People 272
"Little Renault, The" 78
Little Review, The 153, 208
"Little room" 83, 84-85
Little Room, The 84, 126ff.
Little Theater, Chicago 127ff, 145, 151, 154, 155, 162, 208, 212, 228
"Live From Second City" 342
Living Quarters 338
Local color literature 41
Lloyd, Demarest 153
Loeb, Richard See Loeb, Leopold
Logan, General 191
Logan Square 346
London 46, 56, 90, 162, 328, 332
London, Jack 123
Lone Canoe (play) 342
Lonely for the Future 259
Long Straight Road, The 121, 127
Longfellow, Henry Wadsworth 65
Looking Backward 54
Looking for Mr. Goodbar (film) 340
Loon Feather 290
Loop, Chicago 3, 141, 217, 248, 281-282, 283, 347
"Loop Hound, The" 141
Lord, Edna 314
Lord, William S 82
Lords of Flatbush see *Cooley High*
Lords of the Levee 149
Lore, Phillips [pseud] see Smith, Terrence Lore
Lorimer, George Horace 90, 96, 99-100, 136, 143
Los Angeles 166, 214
Losing Game, The 157
Lost City 212
Lost violin; They Came From Bohemia, The 62
Lotta Embury's Career 139
Loughborough, Jean 60

Loux, Dubois H 96, 312
Love and Mrs. Sargent 314
Love in Chicago 169
Love Legend, The 187
Love Letters: . . .48
Love Nest and Other Stories, The 204
Love Without Money 189
Love's Dilemmas 119
Love's Purple 161
Lovett, Robert Morss 108, 119, 175, 178, 193, 211, 265-266
Lowell, Amy 127
Lowell, James Russell 75
"Lower half, The" 34, 36, 53, 93 105ff., 137, 173-174, 222, 230, 231, 232, 272, 284, 313-314
Lowrie, Rebecca 252
Luck in Disguise 47
Lucky Number, The 34, 106
Lucky Stiff, The 281
Lucy Gayheart 242
Luke Darrell, the Chicago Newsboy 26
Luke Walton or the Chicago Newsboy 26
Luisitania 131
Lyceumite, The (magazine) 146
Lynch, Lawrence L [pseud] See Van DeVenter, Emma Murdock

MacArthur, Charles 132, 136, 140, 166-168, 186, 220
McClurg, A C and Co 39, 41, 137
McConaughy, J W 105
McCord, Joseph 246
McCormicks, the 44-45, 263, 317
McCormick Hall 315
McCutcheon, George Barr 36, 91, 92, 102, 113, 115, 126, 180, 213, 214
McCutcheon, John Tinney 90, 91, 102, 122, 126, 135, 138, 180, 195, 214
[McDonald], Country Joe 327
McDougall, Ella 66, 68
"McDougall" 312

McDougall Street Theater 171

McDowell, Mary 314

McEvoy, J[oseph] P[atrick] 248

McFadden, Bernard 276

McGee, Billy 131

McGivern, William P[eter] 281

McGovern, Jon 28, 33, 43, 66, 70, 155

McGrady, Father Thomas 120

McGrath, Lieutenant Tom 282

McHarg, William 157-158, 201

McHugh, Jay see MacQueen, James W

McIlvaine, Caroline M 18

McIntyre, John T 104

McKay, Allis 244

MacKaye, Steele 43-45

Macmillan Publishing Co 284

MacNeil, Claudia 294

McPhaul, Jack 283

MacQueen, James William 226, 281, Appendix

McVeys, The 49-50, 65

Machine Gun Kelly (film) 307

"Madame Bovary, American" 154

Maeterlinck, Maurice 128

Magazines, literary 24ff., 39ff., 75, 127

Magic City 228

Magnificent Obsession 113

Mail order business 142, 232, 300

Main Road, The 138

Main Street 201

Main-Travelled Roads 83

Maloff Saul 319

Maltin, Leonard 137, 165, 322, 323

Mama Black Widow 331

Mame (musical play, film) 314

Mamet, David 342-343, 346

"Mamie" 147

Man and a Woman, A 245

Man in the Middle, The 302

Man Next Door, The 139

Man of Property 187

Man of Purpose, The 201

Man of the Hour, The 108, 117, 144

Man Who Dared, The (film) 262

Man With the Golden Arm, The (novel) 285, 348

Man With the Golden Arm, The (film) 5, 285, 347

Man With the Iron Hand, The 7

Manacle and Bracelet; ... 33

Manet, Edouard 75

Manhattan Melodrama (film) 235

Mankiewiez, Herman J 216

Manners, J Hartley 101

"Man's Story, A" 202

Mansfield, Richard 210

Mantle, Burns 136, 164, 166

Marching Men 110, 150

Marina Towers 301

Marines, United States 300

Marion, Francis 223

Mark Logan, The Bourgeois 14, 17

Mark Twain   see Clemens, Samuel Langhorne

Markey, Gene 167

Maroon Tales 117

Marquette, Pere Jacques 6, 7, 16, 78, 239, 240

Marquette Cross 7, 77

Marriotts and the Powells, The 187, 220

Marry in Anger 295

Marsh, Fred T 255

Marshall, James 205

Marshall, Sidney 280

Marva Collins Story, The (film) 340

Marxist-Socialist philosophy 236

Mary North 110

Mary Wollaston 198

Masefield, John 128

Mason, Amelia Gere 49

Mason City, IA 276

Mason, Edith 107

Massacre, Fort Dearborn 11ff., 26, 43

"Massacre Tree" 14

Masselink, Ben 300

Masters, Edgar Lee 9, 10, 15, 16, 17, 18, 21, 84, 89, 129, 135, 145, 149-150, 176-178, 197, 209, 210, 213, 239, 283, 306, 347

Masters of Men (see fn. 12, chap. V)

Matson, Norman 197

"Matter of Time, A" 311

Matthau, Walter 168

Matriarch, The 233

Mature, Victor 306

Maud Martha 293

Maupassant, Henri de 111-112

Maxfield Parrish "blue" 84

Maxwell, William 275

May, Earl Chapin 239

Maybe Next Year 278

Mayer, Jane [see Clare Jaynes, pseud] 299

Means, Elizabeth Farnsworth 8

Meat packing in Chicago 19, 26, 77, 99-100, 101, 118, 231, 250-251, 262, 269, 296, 310 see also "Porkopolis"

Mediator, The 212

Medill, Joseph 38, 41, 56, 317

Medium Cool (film) 322

Meeker, Arthur, Jr 2, 70, 264, 269-270, 275, 288, 306, 307

Meighan, Thomas 166

Me-Ka-tai-me-she-Kia-Kiak, or Black Hawk ... 12

Member of the Third House, A 54

Memoirs of an American Citizen, The 44-45, 118-119, 296

Mencken, H[enry] L 3, 71, 93, 94, 145, 162, 204, 213

Menjou, Adolphe 165, 167

"Menu, The" (play) 130

Merchant Prince of Cornville, The (play) 42

Meredith, George 154

Merger, The 320

Merlanti, Ernest G 235

Merriman, Charles Eustace [pseud for George T. Richardson and W. D. Quint] 100
Merrymakers in Chicago . . . 195
Merwin, Samuel 97, 100, 107, 144, 155, 187, 317
"Merwin-Webster" 97
Metropolis, The see Old Chicago
Meyer, Lucy Jane Rider 106, 110
Michigan 40, 90, 100, 135, 169, 182, 205, 214, 219, 227, 229, 244, 333
Michigan, University of 261
Michigan Avenue as a fine arts center 74ff., 125ff.
"Michigan Water" 324
Mickey One (film) 322
Mid-American Chants 151
Midas Touch, The 292
Middle class 237, 254
Middleman, The 333
Midland, The (magazine) 229
Midnight and Percy Jones 226
Midwest Portraits: a Book of Friendships and Memories 2, 208, 249
Midwestern Expression, A see Earth
"Milk Bottles" 202-203
Millay, Edna St. Vincent 210
Miller, Arthur 342
Miller, Francesca Falk 16, 270
Millett, Fred B 287
Mills of Mammon, The 123
Mills of Man, The 104
Milman, H. B. see fn. 43, chap. V
Milton, John 152
Milwaukee, WI 140
Milwaukee Journal, The 140
Minick (play) 174
Minnesota 215, 229
Miracle Mile 46
Mirage 177
Mirage of the Many, The 57

Mirror, The 177
Mirror, Mirror on the Wall 271
Miscegnation 198
Miscellaneous Poems (Kenyon) 271
Miss Mordeck's Father 48
Missouri, University of 204
Mr. Achilles 138, 156
"Mr. and Mrs. Fixit" 205
Mr. Barnes of New York see fn. 43, chap V
Mr. Blandings Builds His Dream House 41
"Mr. Dooley" 136
Mr. Dooley at His Best 91
Mr. Dooley in the Hearts of his Countrymen 91
Mr. Dooley in Peace and War 91
Mr. Dooley on Making a Will . . . 91
Mr. Dooley Says 91
Mr. Dooley's America 91
Mr. Dooley's Opinions 91
Mr. Dooley's Philosophy 91
Mr. Lake of Chicago see fn. 43, chap. V
Mister Noodle, An Extravaganza 249
Mr. Salt 97
Mr. Weld Retires 249
Mrs. Mahoney of the Tenements 110
Mrs. O'Malley and Mr. Malone (film) 282
Mitch Miller 177
Mitchell, Bradford 20
Mix, Tom 214
Mixed Doubles (play) 199
Moby Dick 23
Modern Instance, A 88
Moline, IL 43
Molloy, Paul 316
Money Captain, The 97, 148
Money Magic 80-81
Money Makers, The . . . 40
Money, Money, Money 298, 318
Monroe, Harriet 16, 49, 58ff., 72, 79, 128, 129, 136, 141, 145, 146, 148, 149, 151-153, 155, 208, 214, 225, 228-229, 241, 260

Monroe, Lucy 79, 84, 261
Montana Kid, The (film) 217
Montgomery, Louise 110
Montgomery, Richard R 123
Montgomery, Robert 224
Montgomery-Ward Co 142
Montross, Lois Seyster 195, 209, 243
Montross, Lynn 35, 195-196
Moody, Dwight L 106
Moody, Minnie Hite 227, 256
Moody, William Vaughn 93, 153
Moody, Mrs. William Vaughn 152
Moon-Calf 90, 134-135, 201
Moore, Colleen 175, 214
Moore, Ward 273
Moran, Bugs 220
Moran, Peggy 281
More, Donald Lloyd 338
More Quick Curtains (plays) 130
Moreau, Pierre "The Mole" 30
Morgan, Al[bert Edward] 328
Morgan, Anna 84-85, 128, 130, 131
Morgan, Helen 176
Morgan Park 310
Morgenrødens Vinger 347
Morning News, Chicago 91
Morris, Henry O 55
Morris, Ira 296-297
Morris, Lloyd 179
Morris, William 84
Morse, Linda 327
Morte D'Urban 314
Mortimer, Lee 302
Mother Goose in Prose 84
"Mother Knows Best" 287
Mother Knows Best 176
Mother Knows Best (film) 177, 287
Motley, Willard 264, 283, 288, 300, 307, 333
Mott, Frank Luther 43
Moulton, Louise Chandler 75
Mount Parnassus 134
Mount Royal 254
"Mount Royal" 254, 267
Moyer, Charles 108
Mucker, The 200-201
Mudgett, Herman W "Dr." 30

Mueller, Lisa 344
Munchausen, Baron 92
Mundis, Jerrold [J] 338
Muni, Paul 223
Murder at the World's Fair 228
Murder in the Fog 171
Muscatine, IA 270
"Muscular Christian hero" 36, 143
Museum of Science and Industry 63, 214
Music in the Streets 234
"My Aunt Daisy" 234
My Bodyguard (film) 340
My Brother's Keeper 154
My Chicago 84
My Days of Anger 258
My Invincible Aunt 244
My Kingdom for a Hearse 281
My Uncle and Miss Elizabeth 276
Mysteries of Chicago 31
Mysterious Disappearance of Helen St. Vincent, The 61
Mysterious Waye . . .221
Mystery novels 170ff., 199, 225ff., 264, Appendix
Mystery of Paul Chadwick 33
Myth Maker, The 311

Naar Jesus kommer ind i huset 346
Naked Soul of Iceberg Slim, The 331
Nan Thursday 268
Naperville, IL 47, 275
"Narrative of the Massacre, The" 11ff.
Narcissus 255
Narrowing Wind, The 266-267
Nash, Ogden 323
Nathan, George Jean 165, 212
Nathan, Robert 173
Nation (London) 177
Nation, The 103, 143, 233, 338
National Book Award 309
National Guard, Illinois 295, 311

National Union Catalog 214
Native Son 279-280, 310
Native Son (The Biography of a Young American) (play) 279-280, 343
Naturalism, literary 81, 108, 253
Nausea 260
Navy Pier 300
"Near a Park" 209
Nearing, Scott 238
Nebraska 127, 155, 158, 162, 176, 180, 227, 241, 242, 286
Nedra 102
Need to Hold Still, The 344
Negro (see Blacks, Chicago)
Neighborhoods, Chicago 5, 193-194, 328, 347
Nellie Bloom and Other Stories 211
Nelson, Battling 136
Neon Wilderness, The 284
Ness, Elliott 321
Nesting Ground, The 324
Never Come Morning 284
Never Give All 188
Nevins, Allen 179
New and Selected Poems (Wagoner) 323-324
New Anvil, The 261
New Axis . . . 335
New England Attitudes toward Chicago 60, 66, 70, 192, 255
New England Magazine, The 71-72
"New Greek Town" 292
New Hampshire, University of 333
New Horizons see *Creative Writing*
New Men for Old 132
New Mr. Howerson, The 57, 110
New Orleans 348
"New primitives" 248
New Republic 119, 143, 167, 211, 232
"New woman" see also "bachelor girl" 31, 36, 46, 155, 161, 188
New Year's Eve/1929 260

New York City 3, 22, 28, 39, 46, 57, 68, 95, 107, 153, 168, 176, 186, 190, 192, 196, 198, 201, 206, 212, 214, 215, 217, 222, 235, 236, 261, 263, 270, 293, 294, 303, 305, 315, 328, 336, 347
New York Dramatic Critics Award 294, 343
"New York Street" (film setting) 283
New York Times 28, 101, 110, 116, 143, 164, 166, 168, 177, 217, 233-234, 265, 282, 338, 341
New Yorker 168, 266, 271, 333
Newberry, Julia 46
Newberry Award 63
Newberry Library 25, 46, 55, 301, 336
Newman, Charles [Hamilton] 335
Newsboys 26
Newton, Charles 169
Nichols, Edward J 272, 278
Nicholson, Meredith 162
"Nick Carter" 32, 122, Appendix
Nietschean superman hero 100, 107
Night Studies 344
Nightmare in Chicago (film) 323
Nims, John Frederick 285, 286
1941 O Henry Stories 284
1919 race riots 147, 148, 155, 234, 237, 280
1968 Democratic Convention 322, 327-328, 339
1929 stock market crash 241, 247, 250
No Place Like Home 333
No Place to Go (film) 175
No Star is Lost 258
No Stranger to my Heart 243
No Woman Knows (film) 143
Noble savage, gangster as 216, 223
Nobody Ever Stands on the Evening Express (play) 342

Nobody's Perfect 338
Norden, Chicago 347
Norma Ashe 257
Norris, [Benjamin] Frank-[lin] 2, 3, 31, 94, 95, 98-99, 117, 162, 347, 348
Norris, Charles G 193
Norris, Hoke 321
North, Jessica Nelson 153, 214, 253
North, Sterling 153, 181, 212, 214, 242, 253, 257, 261
North American Review, The 95, 113
North Shore 115, 120, 122, 138, 182, 188, 241, 263, 297, 313, 317, 333
North Side 3, 4, 5, 40, 46, 120, 139, 144, 169, 188, 191, 194, 199, 214, 235, 244, 247, 251, 268, 269, 280, 283, 284, 285, 291, 293, 296, 332, 334, 341
Northeastern Illinois University 333
Northern Illinois University 340
"Northwest Conspiracy of 1864" 24
Northwestern University 77, 119, 135, 144, 151, 158, 180, 234, 250, 255, 300, 305, 332, 333, 338
Norton, Charles Eliot 81, 87
Norton, F S [pseud] see Cowdrey, Robert
Norwegians in Chicago 189, 197, 225, 345ff., 347
Not on the Screen 89
Not Without Laughter 233
Nothing But the Night 303
Novak, Kim 285
Nowhere Else in the World 7-8, 203
Nuptial Flight 177

O'Canaan! 237
O Henry see Porter, William Sidney
Oak-Openings; or, The Bee Hunter see fn. 16, chap. II
Oak Park 205, 296, 347

Oates, Joyce Carol 335
O'Banion, Dion 164, 223
"Obie" 343
O'Brien, Edward J 142
O'Brien, Howard Vincent 20, 127, 131, 132, 181, 241
O'Brien, Pat 167
Observations of Mr Dooley 91
Oconomowoc, WI 247
Octave Thanet [pseud] see French, Alice
Octopus, The 98
Ode as a literary form 59
Odyssey of Kostas Volakis, The 308-309
Ogden, William B 13
O'Hara, John 265, 271
Ohio 90, 103, 145, 148, 203, 219, 254
"Old Billy at the World's Fair" 82
Old Bunch, The 236, 245, 303, 348
Old Callahan Place, The 255
"Old Cap Collier" 32, 122, Appendix
Old Chicago 17, 22, 29, 239
Old Gorgon Graham 99-100, 101
"Old Greek Town" 292
"Old Hutch" see Hutchinson, Benjamin P
"Old King Brady" 122
"Old Man Minick" 174, 249, 286
"Old Man River" 176
"Old Man's Story, The 64
Old New York 22
Old Town 310, 347
Old Woman, The 129
O'Leary, Big Jim 30
O'Leary family 22, 26ff.
Oliver, King 270
Olivier, Laurence 252
Olsen, Tillie 337
Olson, Elder 153
On Fortune's Road 97
"On the Banks of the Wabash" 190
On the Shore 234
On the Spot (novel) 221
On the Spot (play) 221 fn.
On the Stairs 88

On What Strange Stuff 250
Once Again in Chicago 227
Once in a Blue Moon 210
One Basket 287
One Crystal and a Mother 188
One Girl Found 241
"130 Years of Opera in Chicago" 74
One of the McIntyres 68
One of Us 163
One Schoolma'am Less 68
$1,000 a Week 239
"One Thousand and One Afternoons" 184
One Thousand and One Afternoons in Chicago 184
1001 Afternoons in New York 184
One-Way Ride, The 221
One Woman 226
One Woman's Life 44-45, 153
O'Neill, Danny 257ff.
O'Neill, Eugene 108, 109, 171, 188, 214, 312
Ongon 96, 113
"Only a Bird in a Gilded Cage" 209
Only Gift, The 276-277
Only Love Lasts 246
Opening of a Door, The 233
Opera 33, 74, 155, 171, 199, 231, 298
Opera Murders, The 171
Orchestra Hall 24-25, 74, 127
Ordeal by Glory 205
Ordinary People (novel) 31, 320, 338-339
Ordinary People (film) 338-339
Organic Theater of Chicago 341
Origin of the Species 200
Osborn, Catherine B 321
Oshkosh, WI 214
"Other Chicago, The" 324
Other Side . . . , The 32
Other Side of the Wall, The 133
"Other Story, The" 198
Other Story, The 198
Ottumwa, IA 140, 174
Ouilmette 10
Our Very Best People 220

Outlook (magazine) 110
Outsider, The 293
Owls' Club, The 33
Own Your Own Home 136

P.A.L., A Novel of the American Scene see *Red Horses*
Paderewski, Ignace 74
Painted Scene, The 144, 205
Pal Joey (book, play, film) 271
Palette and Chisel Club 125
Palmer, Potter 28, 173, 269
Palmer, Mrs. Potter [Bertha Honoré] 36, 45, 62, 75, 173, 227
Palmer House 36, 155
Palmolive Building 261
Pamela 202
Panic of 1857   23
Panic of 1893   56
Panic of 1873   23, 192
Panic of 1907   107
"Pa-pa-ma-ta-be" See Hubbard, Gurdon Saltonstall
Papier, Judith Barnard 319
Pappas, Irene 309
Paradise City 247
Pareau, Pete 90
Paris, France 39, 46, 62, 111, 315
Paris Was Another Time 259
Parish, John Carl 7, 21
Parker, Dorothy 210
Parker, Sir Gilbert 42
Parker, Mary Moncure 110
Parkman, Francis 78
Parlement of Foules 61
Parrish, Maxfield 84
Parrish, Randall 15, 20, 170
Parrish, Robert Harkness 276
Parsons, Alice Beal 224
Partisan Review, The 261
Party Girl (film) 307
"Pasquale's Picture" 86
Passage From Home 278
Passing 197
Passing Show, The 128
Passionate Pilgrim, The 144
Past and Present of Solomon Sorge, The 319

Pater, Walter 204
Pattee, Fred Lewis 27, 99
Pattern of Three 247
Patterson, Eleanor "Cissy" [Gyzicka] 136
Patterson, Joseph Medill 115, 132, 136, 161, 162
Patti 74
Paul Kovar or Anarchy 43-44
Paul O Stensland og hans hjaelpere eller Milliontyvene i Chicago 346
Paul O Stensland and his Associates . . . 346
Payne, Philip 104, 114
Payne, Will 31, 89-90, 95, 96-97, 111, 113, 131, 148, 157, 198
Payne, William Morton 13, 40, 70-72, 73, 75, 85, 90, 213
Peacock, Thomas Brower 59, 63
Pearce, John Irving 156
Peattie, Donald Culross 4, 8-9, 34, 254, 291
Peattie, Elia Wilkinson 35, 35, 84, 85, 110, 136, 139
Peattie, Louise Redfield 231, 254
Peattie, Robert Burns 136
Peck, Richard 336
Pecking Order 293
Peculiar Treasure, A 143, 174
Peewee 201-202
Peggy From Paris 93
Pelham, Laura Dainty 127-128
Pendy 312
Pennant for the Kremlin, A 316
"Penny Divers, The" 234
Penny Philanthropist, The 110, 137, 160
Penrod 199
People's Program . . . 55
Per Kjølseth, eller Manden til Marit 346
Per Kjølseth, or the Husband of Marit 346
Pere Goriot 321
"Peregrine Pickle" see Upton, George P

Pericles on 31st Street 309
Personna 93
Personality Plus 141
Pestalozzi-Froebel Teachers College 305
Petrakis, Harry Mark 292, 308-309, 324, 346
Pflaum, Melanie 312
Phelon, William A, Jr 68
Phelps, Corwin fn 12, chap V
Phi Beta Kappa 166, 261
Philadelphia Centennial Exposition (1876) 60, 62, 227
Philistine 94
Philistinism 71-72, 73
Phillip, Quentin Morrow 277
Phillips, Leon 299
Philopena 199
Phoenix, AZ 126
Phyllis Anne 188
Physical Culture 344
"Pianissimo revolt" 94
Pickled Poodles, The 282
Pictorial Review, The (magazine) 199
Picture Frames 206
Picture of Dorian Gray, The 76
Piercy, Marge 321
Pilgrim's Progress 61
Pimp, the Story of My Life 321
Pink Marsh: A Story of the Streets . . . 92, 156
Pinkerton, A Frank 33, Appendix
Pinkerton, Alan 28, 33, 122
Pinkertons, The 31, 32, 33
Pioneer, The 50
Piper's Tune, The 246
Pippins and Cheese 84
Pit, The 2, 98, 127, 295, 320, 347, 348
Pizer, Donald 78, 80
Place to Stand, A 324
Plagemann, Bentz 318
Playboy Building 261
Players' Workshop 129, 130
Playshop Theater 130
Playwrights, Chicago 129ff., 167-169, see also Edna Ferber

Plum, Mary 163, 226, 228, Appendix
Plunger/A Tale of the Wheat Pit, The 98
Poe, Edgar Allen 3, 258
Poet and the Rent, The (play) 342
Poet Laureate, Illinois 305
Poet Laureate, Kansas 59, 63
Poetry: A Magazine of Verse 145, 146, 149, 151-153, 162, 186, 210, 211, 212, 213, 228-229, 253, 260, 280, 286, 288, 305, 324
Poetry Club, University of Chicago 211
Poetry Lovers of America 213
Poetry of Observations 35
Poet's Life, A 151, 260
Poitier, Sydney 294
Police, Chicago 120-121, 130-131, 166, 282
Policeman Flynn 121
Policeman's Love-Hungry Daughter, The ... 185
Policy King, The 280
Polish in Chicago 137, 195, 234, 250, 283, 284, 300, 328-329, 332, 333, 347
Politician, The 107
Politicians, Chicago 298, See also "Boodlers," 300-301
Politics, Chicago 103, 300, 306
"Poliuto" see Wilkie, Franc Bangs
Pollard, J Percival 82
Poole, Dr W F 49
Poolroom 224
Poor Devil 181
Poor People 106
Poor White 150
"Porkopolis" 19, 26, 41, 72, 99-100, 296-297 see also Chicago as a Meat Packing Center
Porter, Eleanor H 136
Porter, Gene Stratton 136
Porter, William Sydney (O Henry) 35, 93, 133, 140, 206, 309
Portia Faces Life 171

Portrait in Smoke 296
Portugese in Chicago 234
Postgate, John W[illiam] 33
"Pot Boiler, The" (play) 130
Potter, Margaret Horton 15, 70, 102, 114
Powell, Paul 338
Powell, William 235
Power and the Glory, The (film) 263
Powers, J[ames] E[arl] 314
Powers, John R 333-335
Practically Seventeen 297
Prairie Avenue 11, 26, 70, 111, 237, 251, 269, 280
Prairie Avenue 2, 14, 269, 347
Prairie Farmer ... (magazine) 23
Prairie Fire ... 17
Prairie Folks 83
Prairie Grove, A 4, 8-9, 21, 254
Prairie Pirates, The 239
Prairie Voices: A Literary History of Chicago ... 2
Pravda 316
Precipice, The 10, 139
Pre-Raphaelite Brotherhood 210
Presley, Elvis 322
Press Club, Chicago 42, 69
Preston, Keith 13
Prevailing Winds 251
Price of a Party, The 158
Princeton University 107
Prisoner Ate a Hearty Breakfast, The 250, 265
Prizefighting 190, 248
Probation officers 137
Profane Earth 196
Professor's House, The 180
Progress and Poverty 156
Prohibition 140, 155, 162, 163, 170, 220, 222, 223, 237, 240, 304
Proletariat novelists 232, 267, 272, 336
Prologue (film) 340
Promise Keeper, The ... 335
Promised Land, The (play) 164
Prostitution 31, 46, 65, 109, 185, 224-225, 313, 322

Protection 221
Proud Lady 109, 188
Proust, Marcel 276
Provincetown, MA 171, 213
Provincetown Players 129, 131
Provincialism in literature 4
Pruitt, Alan [pseud] See Rose, Alvin Emanuel
Pryor, Judge Roger A 43-44
Public Enemy, The (film) 222, 261
Puerto Ricans in Chicago 329
Pulitzer, Joseph 59
Pulitzer Prizes 137, 174, 175-176, 211, 251, 275, 286, 336
Pullman, IL 45, 54, 106, 347
Pullman Company, The 55
Pullman, George M 11, 54, 91, 106
Pullman Strike 23, 55, 91, 106, 108, 182, 268, 269
Puppet Booth, The 128
Purdue, University of 91, 102
Purdy, James 318
Puritanism 2, 26, 76, 256, 309
Pursuit of Happiness, The 319
Purvis, Melvin 341
"Push," Chicago 22, 61
Put on the Spot 221
Putnam, Samuel 212-213, 264
Pygmalion-Galatea theme 250, 286
"Pyramus and Thisbe" 139

Quad-Cities, Iowa-Illinois 108, 145 See also Moline, IL
Quaife, Milo M 13
Quaint Crippen; Commercial Traveler 68
Quammen, David 330
Quick, Herbert 54, 114
Quick Curtains (plays) 130
Quinlan, Sterling 320
Quinn, Anthony 309
Quint, W. D. see Charles E. Merriman [pseud]
"Quondam" see Stevens, Charles McClellan

"Race, The" 234
Race riots, 1919 See 1919 race riots
Racket, The (play) 166, 213
Racket, The (film) 166
"Rackets" 31, 302
Radical, The 107
Radio 248, 268, 271, 281
Ragged Edge, The 104
Rago, Henry 324
Ragtime 345
"Railroad fiction" 36, 42, 66
Railroad strike of 1877   43
Railroads 42, 54, 68, 98, 102, 107, 151, 161, 198, 237-238, 263, 273, 295
Rainbow (film) 214
Raisin in the Sun, A (play) 294
Raisin in the Sun, A (film) 294
Rand, Ayn 182
Rand, Sally 63, 347
Rand McNally & Co 17, 23, 42
Rapp, William Jourdan 224
Rascoe, Burton 135, 136, 167, 241
"Rat Pack" 323
Rathbone, St George 60
Ravinia Summer Opera Festival 199
Ravinia Workshop (theater) 130
Ray Burton, A Chicago Tale 68
Raymond, Clifford Samuel 220, 268
Raymond, Evelyn Hunt 15
Rayne, Martha Louise 35
Rayner, William 332
Rea, Margaret Lucile Paine 281
Read, Opie 36, 43, 49, 66, 70, 82, 84, 91, 110, 213
Reade, Charles 28
Reagan, Mrs. Ronald 175
Reagan, President Ronald 342
Real Adventure, The 143, 159
Real Issue, The 84
Realism, Literary 48, 51, 53, 78-81, 124, 145, 283, 294, 301

Rebellion 132, 161
Record, Chicago 126
Record-Herald, Chicago 93, 137, 146, 154
Red Badge of Courage, The 48
Redbook (Red Book) (magazine) 136, 158, 230
Red Carnelian, The see *Red Is For Murder*
Red Flag; or, The Anarchists ... 43
Red Horses 194
Red Is For Murder 281
Red Pavilion, The 183
Redding, J Saunders 301
Redford, Robert 340
Reed, Donna 287
Reed, H V 25
Reed, John 153, 188
Reed, Myrtle 15
Reedy, Marion 177
Reef, The 296
Reformer, The 110
Reilly, Patricia 240
Remarkable Mr Pennypacker, The 48
Remember the Day 244
Renaissance, American 3, 23
Renaissance, Chicago 3, 20, 36, 63, 70, 89, 129, 134, 143, 144ff., 161, 185, 186, 193, 208, 212, 227, 238, 240, 241, 260, 274, 280
Report From Part One 305
Reporter 183
Reporter, newspaper 39, 48, 55, 68, 89ff., 132-133, 144, 167-169, 181ff., 188, 192, 233, 287
Republic Steel "Massacre" 272
Repudiation of the city   see City, repudiation of
Rescued From Fiery Death 121
Restless Age, The 195
Restless Corpse, The 281
Resurrection City 322
Resurrection Rock 201
Reunion (play) 343
Revenge of the Space Pandas, The ... (play) 342

Review of Reviews 56
Revolt from the village theme 115, 202, 203
Revolt of the Brutes ... 61
Revolutionary War 196
Reynolds, Katharine 140
Rhoda 199
Rice, Craig 281
Rice Theater 14, 74
Rich Man, Poor Man 192-193
Richards, Gale 124
Richardson, George T See Merriman, Charles E [pseud]
Richardson, Major John 10, 13, 48, 78
Richardson, Merrick A 69, 110
Richberg, Donald 66, 138, 201
Richberg, Eloise O Randall 66
Richer Harvest, The 254
Richert, William 317
"Rickard's Daughter" 209
Rickett, Francess 333
Riddle of the Yellow Zuri, The 226
Riesenberg, Felix 194
Right Murder, The 281
Right of Way, The 42
Riley, James Whitcomb 51, 75, 80
Riot 305
Rise of Chicago as a Literary Center ... 2
Rise of Elsa Potter, The 242
Rise of Silas Lapham, The 88
River, Walter Leslie 204, 205
Rivera, Chiquita 165
Rivers of Eros, The 330
Rivers Run Together 328
Riverview Amusement Park 300, 310
Road Between, The 258
Road to the Temple, The 128
Roadhouse Nights 221
Roast Beef Medium 141
Robards, Jason 323
Roberta 65
Roberts, Edith [Elizabeth Kneiple] 274, 276
Roberts, Elizabeth Madox 153, 211

Roberts, John Hawley 255

Robertson, Donald 128

Robin and the Seven Hoods (film) 323

"Robin's Egg Renaissance: Chicago Culture . . . , A" 74

Robinson, Edward G 166, 221, 231, 262

Robinson, Rose 311

Rock 290, 299

Rockefeller Grant for Writing 333

Rockford, IL 105, 224

Rodger Latimer's Mistake 64, 69

Roe, E P 2, 27-28, 29, 72, 121, 315

Roe, Edward R[eynolds] 47

Roeburt, John 304

Rodgers and Hart 271

Roger Gresham 119

Roger Touhy, Gangster (film) 285

Rogers, Ginger 165

Rogers Park 246, 347

Rogers, Thomas 319

Rollins, William 273

Rollo Johnson, The Boy Inventor . . . 126

Roman á clef 106, 155, 159, 179, 201, 249, 258, 320

"Romance of a Middle-Aged Merchant . . ." 85

Romance of Dollard 78

Romance of Fire 224

Romantic realism 253

Romantic Woman, The 186, 190

Romanticism 77, 78, 79, 124, 137ff., 145

Romany Club 130

Romeo and Juliet 66, 320

Ronan, Ensign George 15

Roosevelt, Franklin Delano 260, 262, 265, 272

Root, George F, Dr 139

Rootabaga Stories 207

Rosaire, Forest

Rosa's Confession, a Realistic Romance . . . 48

Rose, Alvin Emanuel 281

Rose and the Ogre 269

"Rose for Emily, A" 234

Rose of Dutcher's Coolly 80-81, 83, 89-90, 138, 140, 147, 157, 348

Rosehill Cemetery 66

Rosen, Alan 340

Rosenfeld, Isaac 278

Rosenwald Fund, The 301

Ross, Sam 279, 282, 291-292, 295, 339

Rostand, Edmund 42

Roth, Philip 315

Roxie Hart (film) 165

Royko, Mike 327, 340

"Rube" in Chicago see also "Rural vs. city" 35

Ruben, Jerry 328

"Ruby" 329

Rukeyser, Muriel 245

Rural vs. City life 35, 36, 66, 81 see also City, repudiation of, and Revolt from the village theme

"Rush Street Philosopher, The" 336

Russell, Charlotte Murray 226

Russell, Lillian 136

Russell, Raymond [pseud] see Fearing, Lillian Blanche

Russell, Rosalind 168

Russell, Ruth 7, 45

Russells in Chicago, The 74, 120

Russians in Chicago 155, 156, 235, 291-292, 312, 347

Ruth Middleton 268

Ruth of the U S A 140

"Rydell High School" 290

Ryerson, Martin Antoine 210

Rygh, George Taylor 347

Sable, Jean Baptiste Point (Point Sable, Point-au-Sable, de Sable, du Saible) 3, 9, 19

"Sabine Farm, The" 41

Sacco and Vanzetti 205

"Sade Iverson" see Peattie, Elia W

Saetre, Alan 346

Sag Harbor, NY 67, 237

St John, Adela Rogers 317

St John, James Allen 200

St John, Jill 287

St Louis, MO 22, 123, 194, 309

St Nicholas Theater Company 342

St Olaf College 346

St Paul, MN 187, 336

St Valentine's Day "massacre" 30, 223, 304, 323

St Valentine's Day Massacre, The (film) 323

Sainted Sisters, The (play and film) 250

Saints' and Sinners' Corner 41, 75, 82

Sale, Chic 174-175

Samantha at the Centennial 62

Samantha at the World's Fair 62

San Francisco, CA 83, 166, 214, 348

Sandburg, Carl 29, 51, 71, 132, 135, 140, 145ff., 180, 181, 185, 207-208, 212, 283, 284, 287, 305, 306, 310, 323, 347

Sanders, Daphne see Rice, Craig

Sanders, Ed 328

Sands, The 270

"Sands, The" 46, 64

Sanger, Margaret 188

Sara 346

Saracen Club 73

Sarah Thornton 242

Sarett, Lew 135, 213, 229

Sartain's Union Magazine . . . 12, 20

Sartre, Jean Paul 266

Sattey, Helen R[owland] 300

Saturday Afternoon 241

Saturday Evening Post 90, 96, 99, 107, 136, 143

Saturday Review of Literature, The (Saturday Review) 194, 198, 211, 305

Saul Bellow 305

"Saul Bellow at 60" 305

Saxe Holm's Stories 24
Saxton, Alexander Plaisted 273, 280, 283
Sayre, Gordon [pseud] see Woolfolk, Josiah Pitts
Scaffold, The 336
Scanlan, Agnes Leonard 26
"Scarface" see Capone, Al
Scarface (novel) 304
Scarface (film) 167, 222, 223
Scarface Mob, The (film) 321
Scarred Chin, The 198
Schaeffer, Susan Fromberg 337
Schiller, Cecily 278
Schlogl's Round Table 70, 135, 208, 249
Schulte, Francis H 79
Schulte Company, F. H. 54
Schultz, Alan Breuer 242
Schwimmer, Walter 336
Scopes Trial 108
Scott, G C 54
Scott, Henry E 35, 105
Scottsboro Trial 108
Scouting (magazine) 335
Screaming Mimi, The 281
Seale, Bobby 328
Searches and Seizures (novel) 337
Searches and Seizures (film) 340
Second City 342
Second Generation, The 112
Secret Six, The (film and novel) 223
Secret Toll, The 170
Seekers, The 69
Seely, Herman Gastrell 139
Segal, George 323
Seifert, Shirley 317
Seiffert, Marjorie 129, 145, 229
Seldens in Chicago; . . ., The 47
Selected Poems (Brooks) 305
Self-made man 29, 89, 99-100
Self-Made Man's Wife; The Letters to Her Son . . . 100
"Selina" 175
Sell, Henry Blackman 132, 134, 135, 181

Senator's Lady, The 317
Sentimentalism 137ff.
Seth & Bill & Mr. Quarles and Me 332
Sether, Gulbrand 346
Settlement workers and houses 69, see also Hull House
Settlers, The 344
Seven Against the Years 257
Sex is Such Fun 226
Sexual Perversity in Chicago (play) 343
Seymour, Charles 90
Seymour, Ralph Fletcher 84, 88, 89, 125, 127, 139, 152
Shackleford, H K 43
"Shadow, The" 65
Shadow Across the Campus 300
Shadow Before, The 273
Shadow Men, The 138
Shadow of Victory: A Romance . . ., The 15
Shadowed by Three 31
Shadowed to Europe: A Chicago Detective . . . 32
Shame of a Nation, The (film) 223
Shams, or, Uncle Ben's Experiences . . . 36
Shane, Peggy 187
Shapiro, Karl 288, 305
Shards of Gods 328
"Sharps and Flats" 41, 77, 80, 92
Shaw, Clifford 283
Shaw, George Bernard 44, 128, 154
"Shaw-nee-aw-kee" see Kinzie, John Sr
"Sheaf for Chicago, A" 324
Sheean, Vincent 181, 211
Sheldon, Charles M 110
Sheldon, Edward Brewster 105
Shelia 311
Shelley, Percy Bysshe 90
Shenton, Edward 205-206
Sherburne, James 328
Sheridan, General Phil 191

Sheridan Road Mystery, The 170
Sherrods, The 113, 115, 127
Shield of Silence, The 226
Shifting for Himself . . . 123
Shining Trail, The 290
"Shirtsleeves to Shirtsleeves" 251
"Shooting of John Dillinger Outside the Biograph . . ." 324
Short Line War, The 97
Short stories see Friedman, Kahn, Ferber, Fairbank, Webster, Anderson, Lardner, W. Smith, L. Montross, Toomer, Halper, McEvoy, Tuthill, F F Fox, M A Barnes, Farrell, Algren, Petrakis, Coulter, Powers, Dybek, Hecht, Ade, Roe, Herrick, Winslow
Show Boat (novel) 34, 175-176, 348
Show Boat (musical play) 176
Show Boat (film) 176
Show Business 206-207
Shumaker, Arthur W Fn. II, 42 and p. 93
Side Lights on Darkest Chicago 34
Sideshows of a Big City . . . 249
Sidewalks Are Free, The 291-292, 295
Siegel, Sam 319
Silence of History, The 259
Silver Eagle, The 220
Silver Inkwell, The 287
"Silverman, The" See Kinzie, John Sr
Simeon Tetlow's Shadow 102-103
Simmons, Dr Geoffrey S 333
Simon and Schuster 303
Simon, John 343
Sinatra, Frank 271, 285, 323
Sinclair, Harold 250
Sinclair, Upton 101, 132, 232
Singing Heart, The 140

The Sinister Sex ... 185
Sister Carrie 81, 108, 111, 112, 115, 132, 138, 140, 147, 148, 155, 201, 270, 348
Six Days to Sunday 326
Sixty Seconds 186
Skeeters Kirby 177, 193
Skid Row 301, 310
Skipworth, Alison 249
Sklar, Robert 145
Sklovsky, Max 291
Slabs of the Sunburnt West 207-208
"Slave Girl, The" 65
Slaves of Success 104
Sloan's Garden City Magazine 25
Slovaks in Chicago see Bohemians
Smart, David A 261
Smart Money (film) 262
Smith, Alson J 269, 272, 275, 288, 297
Smith, Elbert H 12
Smith, Frederika Shumway 269
Smith, Harry B 49
Smith, Henry Justin 131, 133, 135, 180, 184, 185, 214, 223, 240, 326
Smith, Mark 333
Smith, Terence Lore 331-332
Smith, Wallace 205, 224-225
Smiths, The 192-193, 295
Smouldering Flames 202
Smucker, Barbara C 312
Snake Pit, The 297, 321
"Snickelfritz" 90
Snivig C Trebor [pseud] see Givins, Robert C
So Big (novel) 171, 175-176, 177, 213, 287, 348
So Big (film) 175
Social Lion, The 70
Social Settlements see Settlement workers
Socialism 144, 145
Society of Midland Authors 213, 309
Solberg, Gunard 311
Soldier's Field 300
Solo 270, 304
Solomon's Palace 339

"Some Great Moments in Sloppy Scouting" 335
Some Like It Hot 281
Some Went This Way 127
Somebody Else's Wife 337
Somebody in Boots 230, 231, 284
Someday, Boy 279
Sometime 245
Somewhere the Tempest Fell 267, 270
Sommers, Lillian 46, 53, 109, 155
Son of the City; ... A 139
Song of the Eagle, The (film) 223
Song of the Lark, The 127, 155, 158
Songs and Satires 149
Songs of the Soil 150
Sons of the Fathers 272, 277
"Sophy-As-She-Might-Have-Been" 141
Soul of Anne Rutledge, The 155
Sound and the Fury, The 298
Sound of a City 259
South Dakota 50, 55, 188, 241
South Federal Street 321
South Side, Chicago 2, 5, 24, 49, 118, 129, 148, 166, 172, 237, 248, 257, 269, 278, 292, 293, 294, 298, 317, 321, 329-330, 335, 336, 340
South Water Market, old 151, 171, 175, 227
Spaniards in Chicago 329
Spanish-American War 23, 100, 102, 231, 312
Spearman, Frank Hamilton 121
Spellbound 186
Spicy, A Novel 28, 53
Spiderweb Clues 170
Spiegel, Clara see Clare Jaynes, pseud
Spirit of an Illinois Town ... 78
Spirit of Labor, The 69, 109
Spirit of the Ghetto, The 109
Spirit of the Lower North Side, The 209

Spoilsmen, The 104
Spook Who Sat by the Door, The 311
Spoon River Anthology, The 89, 149, 177, 201
Spoor, George 214
Sporting Youth 223
Springfield, IL 149, 202
Squirrels (play) 342
Stack, Robert 321
Stagg, Amos Alonzo 117, 300
Standish, Burt L [pseud] see Patten, Gilbert
Stanger, Wesley 121
Stanwyck, Barbara 175
Starrett, Vincent 181, 209, 212, 214, 225-226, 229
"Starting Out in Chicago" 305
State Street 209-210
Stateville Prison 190, 201, 224, 282
Staying Alive 324
Stead, William T 21, 34, 56, 123
Steichen, Edward 146
Steichen, Lillian (Mrs. Carl Sandburg) 146
Steiger, Rod 304
Steinbeck, John 265
Stelmark/A Family Recollection 309
Stephen Vincent Benét Narrative Poetry Award 313
Stern, Karl 313
Stern, Lucile 292
Steuber, William 30
Stevens, Charles McClellan 61, fn. 42, chap V
Stevens, Grant Eugene 122
Stevens, Thomas Wood 130
Stewart, Charles David 160
Stewart, James 282
Sting, The (book) 340
Sting, The (film) 340
Stock market crash of 1929 182
Stockton, Frank R 75
Stockyards, Union 101, 123, 130, 142, 161, 204, 238, 245, 297, 313-314
Stolen Husband, The 241

Stolen Laces, The . . . 33

Stone & Kimball 42, 77, 80, 83, 84

Stone, Fred 175

Stone, Herbert S 82-84, 131, 154

Stone, Herbert S & Company 69, 92, 97, 121

Stone, Irving 268

Stone, Lewis 214

Stone, Melville E 41, 82, 84, 180, 326

Stony Island Avenue 146, 149, 208

"Stories of the Streets and Town" 92

Story (magazine) 284

Story From Pullmantown, A 55

Story of Ab, The 43, 84

Story of Chicago, The (Kirkland) 20, 49

Story of Chicago, The (Atkinson) 16

Story of Eva, The 111, 140

Story of Pullman, The 55

Story of Tonty, The 78

Staight 344

Stranded: A Story of the Garden City 64

Strange Adventures of Mr Middleton, The 121

Strange Case of Eric Marotte . . . 156

Strange Interlude 166

Street, Ada and Julian 18, 194

Street in Bronzeville, A 285

Street Types of Chicago fn 67, chap V

Streeter (musical play) 340

Streeter, George Wellington "Cap" 270, 340-341, 347

"Streeterville" 270, 341, 347

Strømme, Peer 346

"Strenuous Lad's Library, The" 126

Stribling, T S 200

Strindberg, [Johan] August 129

String of Amber Beads, A 62

Strobel, Marion 15, 209, 210, 211, 213, 241, 247, 264, 280

Strong, Edmund C 33

Strong-man hero See Nietschean strong-man hero, "Muscular Christian" hero

Stryk, Lucian 324

Stuart, Jesse 228-229

Stuckey, Sterling 311

Studio, The (magazine) 82

Studio world, Chicago 125ff., 143, 145

Studs Lonigan trilogy see *Young Lonigan* . . .

Sturm, Justin 204

Suburbs, Chicago, literature of 140, 157, 187, 200, 225, 253-254, 267-268, 273, 297, 313, 317

"Sudden Sixties, The" 173

Suicide 320

Sullivan 287

Sullivan, Louis 344

Summer's Outing, A 64

Sun Maid, a Story of Fort Dearborn, The 15

Sunday Heroes, The 326

Sunday, Billy 209

Suppressed Sensations 31

Surbridge, Agnes 122

Swados, Harvey 301

"Swallow-tail culture" 73

Swanson, Gloria 190, 214

Swanson, H W 240

Swedes in Chicago 242, 262, 266-267, 291, 299, 347

Sweepings (novel) 194

Sweepings (film) 195

Sweet Adeline (film) 215

Sweet Clover, A Romance of the White City 2, 60, 63, 72, 232

Swerling, Jo 164

"Swift Walker" see Gurdon Saltonstall Hubbard

Swift Walker; A True Story . . . 19

Swifts, The 263, 296, 347

Swing, David 49

Sylvia's in Town 242

Synge, John Millington 129

Synon, Mary 190

T. R. Baskin (film) 340

Taft, Lorado 81, 84, 126, 131

Taft, Oren, Jr. 128

Taft, Zulime (Mrs. Hamlin Garland) 81

Tale of Chicago, The 239

Tales From Town's Topics 62

Tales of Chicago Streets 185

Tales of Darkest America 151

Tales of the Border 6-8

Tall, Dark and Handsome (film) 285

Tame Surrender, A . . . 55

Tanner, Edward Everett 314

Targ, William 226

Tarkington, [Newton] Booth 3, 158, 159, 162, 199, 214

Tarzan the Ape Man 201

Tasker Martin 295

Tate, Allen 228-229

Tattlings of a Retired Politician 122

Taylor, Benjamin Franklin 14, 25, 40, 72

Taylor, Bert Leston (B.L.T.) 115, 136, 141, 162

Taylor, Ellen DuPois 188

Taylor, Laurette 101

Taylor, Robert 306

Tebbel, John 290

Technocrat, The 297

Tecumseh 11, 191

Television 320, 337, 342

Tell No Man 317

Teller, Charlotte 44, 108

Temperamental Henry 144, 317

Ten Men of Money Island 54

Ten One-Act Plays 130

Tender is the Night 121, 137

Tennyson, Alfred Lord 39, 212

Terkel, Studs 327

Terms of Conquest, The 181

Terrell, John Upton 290

Thalberg, Irving 173

Thanet, Octave [pseud] see French, Alice

That Boy Bob; . . . 123
That Royle Girl (novel) 169
That Royle Girl (film) 169
"That's Marriage" 141
Thayer, Tiffany 226
Theatrical fiction 66, 114-115, 143, 155, 180, 188, 190, 206, 207
Their Own Apartment 227
Thelma 296
Theophilus Trent: . . . 40
Theory of the Leisure Class, The 65
There is a Tree More Ancient Than Eden 330
These Are the Times 266
Thicker Than Water 234, 252
Thief (film) 340
Thief Who Came to Dinner, The 331-332
Third Owl, The 226
Third Weaver, The 191
Thirteenth District, The 103
Thirty 132
30 (film) 322
This is Chicago 306
This is my Body 205, 211
This Land is Ours 19, 268
This Marriage 274
This Our Exile 247
This Side of Paradise 179
This Was Life 256
Thom, Robert 303
Thomas, Theodore 23, 74, 84, 120, 158
Thompson, Kathleen 342
Thompson, Maurice 75
Thompson, Slason 41, 75
Thompson, William "Big Bill" 39, 262, 282, 347
Thompson's Restaurants 300
Thoreau, Henry 3
Thorne, Paul and Mabel 170
Thoroughbred, The 144
Thorson, Gerald 346, 347
Those About Trench 110, 160
Though Time be Fleet 231
Thousand and One Nights, The 122
Three-generation novel 144, 173, 176, 193, 238, 252
Three Girls in a Flat 60
Three Girls Lost (novel) 241

Three Girls Lost (film) 241
Three Priests 292
Threshold, The 154
Through Dooms of Love 313
Thunderbolt, The 182
Thurber, Alwyn M 68
Thurston, Louise M 35
Tides 18, 194
Tietjens, Eunice 152, 186, 209
Tiger 242
Time (magazine) 315
Time at Her Heels 243
Time Travelers, The (film) 30
Times, Chicago 31, 40
Tin Sword 295
"Tinker to Evers to Chance" 123
Titan, The 129, 148, 220
To Walk the Line 330
To Whom It May Concern 259
Tobenkin, Elias 159, 196, 222
"Toby" tent shows 36
Today (TV show) 328
Toledo, OH 90, 103
Tolstoi, Lev Nikolayevich 111-112
Tomboy and the Champ (film) 321
Tomlinson, David 204
Tomorrow's Bread 236-237
Tonty (Tonti) 20, 77-78
Toomer, Mrs Jean 205, 210
Toronto, Canada 332
Toronto Workshop Company 328
Torrio, Johnny 30, 164, 304
Touched With Fire 290
Towers Along the Grass 184
Towers With Ivy 256
Townsend, Edward Waterman 68
Toyland 332
Trail, Armitage [pseud] see Coons, Maurice
Train, M 68
Train Boy, The 26
Tramp in Society, A 54
"Tramp, Tramp, Tramp" 139
Treat, Roger 299
Treat 'Em Rough; . . . 137
Trebor, Snivig C [pseud] see Givins, Robert C

Tree has Roots, The 256
Trend (magazine) 286
Trespasser, The (novel) 190-191
Trespasser, The (film) 190-191
Trial of Helen McCleod, The 224
Trilling, Diana 267
Trimmed, Lamp, The 127
Trodden Gold 182
Trojan Women, The 184
Trotti, Lamar 29
True Love, a Comedy . . . 113, 189
Trumbull, Logan "Steve" 164
Trumbull Park 293, 294, 311
Tucker, Wilson 345
Tuesday to Bed 276
Tully, Jim 224-225
Tupper, Edith Session 34
Turmoil, The 159
Turn of the Balance, The 104
Turpin, Waters E 237
Tuthill, Jack
Twelve Great Stories 259
Twenty Years at Hull House 69
27th Ride, The 223
Two College Girls 35
Two Little Pilgrims' Progress . . . 61
Two Loyal Lovers: A Romance 24
Two Women and a Fool 75, 77
Tycoon in Chicago 97, 103, 301

Ulysses 153
Uncertain Voyage 247
Uncle Bob and Aunt Becky's Strange Adventures . . . 123
Uncle Ben's Experiences With Hypocrites . . . 36
Uncle Jeremiah and Family at the Great Fair: . . . 61
Uncle Tom's Cabin 159
"Under dog" see "Lower half"
Under the Skylights 70, 81, 127
Underground Railroad 275

Underworld, Chicago 302 see
also Gangsters in Chi-
cago literature
Underworld (film) 164, 216
Underworld Story, The (film)
282
Uneasy Years 295
Union Park 234
Union Square 205, 232
Unions, labor 101, 107, 132,
150, 238
Universe of Time, A 259
University of Chicago Poems
210
Unlovely Sin; and Other
Stories . . ., The 185
Unmarried Father, An 188
Unoriginal Sinner and the
Ice-Cream God, The 334
Unpaid Piper, The 187
Unquenched Desire 155
"Unseen, The" (play) 130
Untouchables, The (TV
series) 311
Unwritten Will, The; . . . 47
"Uplift" movement see Gen-
teelism, Chicago
"Upstage" (play) 130
Upton, George Putnam 41,
70, 72-73
Up Town 347
"Upward movement, Chica-
go" see Genteelism,
Chicago
"Upward Movement in Chi-
cago, The" (Fuller) 72,
74
"Urbs in Horto" 1, 25, 26, 55
"Urbs Incinerata" 26
"Urbs Recondita" Fn. 2, Chap
II
U. S. A 296, 312
Utopia TV Store 344
Utopian novels in Chicago 52,
54ff., 61, 154, 201, 233,
Contrasted with Col-
umbian Exposition
novels 60

Vale of Laughter, The 318
Valley of Enna and Other
Poems . . . 209

Van Deventer, Emma Mur-
doch 32, 61
Van Doren, Carl 81, 179
Van Doren, Mark 209
Van Peebles, Marvin 310-311
Van Vechten, Carl, 198
Van Volkenburg, Ellen (Mrs
Maurice Browne)
Vanguard Press 257
Veblen, Thorsten 64, 208
Vedder, John K 281
Vendetta 331
Venney, Michael [pseud] see
Rice, Craig
Verdendorps, The 71, fn 67,
Chap V
Verdon, Gwen 165
"Veritism" See "Realism,"
Garland, Hamlin
Vesterheimen 346
Victoria, Queen 39
Victoria Hotel 344
Viet Nam 309
Village Voice 343
Villon, Francois 327
"Virgin and the Dynamo,
The" 63
Virtuous Girl, A 240
Visioning, The 116, 201
Visions of the Dusk 151
Visit to Pay, A 248
Voice of the Seven Sparrows,
The 226
Volstead Act see Prohibition
vom Strande, Wilhelm 48
von Sternberg, Josef 163
von Tilzer, Harry 209
Vonnegut, Kurt 327
Voyage of Pere Marquette, The
8
Vynne, Harold R[ichard] 48,
62

Wabash Avenue (film) 306
Wacker Drive 151, 172
Wade, Richard C footnotes 1,
Chap IV
Wagenknecht, Edward 295
Wagoner, David 298, 302, 324
Waiting for the Signal 55
Wake, The 337
Walcott, Arthur see William
Churchill

Walden 23
Walgreen, Charles Rudolph
256
Walk on the Wild Side, A
(novel) See Somebody
in Boots
Walk on the Wild Side (film)
230
Walker, Mildred 227
"Walking delegate" 107, 108
Walks About Chicago 40
Wallace, Edgar 221
Walling, William English 108
Walsh, William Thomas 57
Walt, Charles [pseud] see
Bein, Albert
Walter Sherwood's Probation
26
War of 1812 10
Ward, David S 339
Ward, Florence [Jeannette
Baier] 140, 180, 188,
245, 254
Ward, Mary Jane 248, 256,
288, 297, 321
Warner, Charles Dudley 75
Warner Brothers 263, 283
Warren, Maude Radford 107,
138, 188
Warwick, LaMar 265
Washburne, Marion Foster
115
Washington, D C 3, 106, 155,
229
Washington, George, biog-
raphy of 28
Washington Brown, Farmer
35
Washington Park 69
Washington's Farewell
Address 277
Washington Square Players
129
Washington Times-Herald
317
Waste 63, 127, 178
Water Engine, The (play) 343
Water Tower 336
Water Tower Plaza 270
Waterloo, Stanley 43, 57, 70,
75, 84
Waterman, Margaret 321
Watkins, Maurine 164-166

Watseka 18, 19

Watson, Carrie 57

Wau-Bun/The "Early Day" in the Northwest 4, 13ff., 51, 64, 72, 186

Waukegan, IL 342

Wau-Nan-Gee; or, The Massacre at Chicago; . . . 12

Wave, The 212, 225

Waves of Night and Other Stories, The 309

Wax Apple, The 248

Way, W Irving 84

Way and Williams 84

Way Back When Fn. 12, Chapter IV

Way of All Flesh, The 177, 215

Way of All Flesh, The (film) 216

Wayne, John 306

We Accept With Pleasure 235, 255

We Are Betrayed 256

We Are Incredible 211

We Can't Breathe 329

We Fished All Night 300

"We, The O'Learys" 29

We Who Died Last Night 277

Web of Life, The 118

Weber and Fields 141

Webster, Henry Kitchell 85, 98, 105, 107, 131, 141, 143ff., 159, 198-199, 205, 214, 225

Wedding, A (film) 340

Wedding Present (film) 168

Weill, Kurt 168

Weismuller, Johnny 200

Wells, H G 154, 162

Wellman, William 165

Welton, Arthur Dorman 223, 249

Wendt, Lloyd 149, 288

Wentworth, Edward Chichester 110, 199-200, 209

Wentworth "Long John" 32, 347

West, William W 323

West Madison Street 283

West Side 4, 40, 105, 108, 120, 139, 144, 153-154, 171, 172, 190, 201, 234, 236, 261, 283, 297-298, 321, 332, 340

Westcott, Glenway 153, 211, 233

"Western Association of Writers" 79

"Western Home, The," 345

Western Monthly 25

Westward Passage (novel) 252

Westward Passage (film) 252

Weverka, Robert 339

Wexler, Haskell 322

Wharton, Edith 2, 22

What Time Collects 260

What's The Big Hurry? 298

Wheaton, Emil see Mrs. Roswell Field

Wheeler, Keith 296

Wheeler, Preserved [pseud] See McDougall, Ellen

When Boyhood Dreams Come True 259

"When Chicago Was Young" 238, 260

When Chicago Was Young (play) 260

"When Jesus Enters the Home," 346

When Mother Wore a Bell Skirt . . . 238

When Time Was Born 259

When Time was Running Red 259

When Time was Young 259

When the Wind Blows 299

When Wilderness Was King . . . 15

Wherever I Choose 244

Whip Hand: A Tale of the Pine Country, The 100

Whipple, Leon 228

Whistler, James Abbott McNeill 9

Whistler, Captain John 9, 16, 17

White, Betty 255

White, Hervey 69, 110

White, William Allen 84, 92

"White City" 51, 53, 54, 56, 57ff.

"White City and the Black, The" 53, 86

White City Chips 62

White Girl, The 196-197, 234

White Lightning 204

White Sox, Chicago 224-225

Whitechapel Club 90, 131

Whitehead, Ralph 69

Whiting, IN 154, 272

White Sox, Chicago 316

Whitlock, Brand 90, 103

Whitman, Walt 3, 244

Whitmore, Stanford 270, 304

Whitney, Phyllis A[yame] 281, 287

Who is the Next? 225

Who Killed Cap Cronin? 34

Who Killed the Pie Man? 332

"Who Reads a Chicago Book" 84 see also fn 47, chap VI

Whole World is Watching, The 328

Wicked City 122

Wicked Nell, a Gay Girl of the Town 2, 31

Wicker Park 346

Wickware, Francis Sill 276

Widdemer, Margaret 127

Widow From Chicago, The (film) 216, 221

Wiggins, Robert L 73

Wigwam in the City 312

Wilcox, Ella Wheeler 75

Wild Boys of the Road (film) 230

Wild Onion 221

Wild Season 345

Wild Willie, Wide Receiver 326

Wild Wine 245

Wilde, Oscar 44, 76

Wilder, Billy 168

Wilder Thornton 318

"Wildwood, Nellie" [pseud] for Elizabeth Farnsworth Means

Wilful Heiress, A 65

Wilkie, Franc Bangs 33, 40, 67

Wilkinson, Elia see Peattie, Elia Wilkinson

Williams, Brock 224

Williams, Charles 92

Williams, Chauncey 84
Williams, Francis Churchill 103
Williams, Kenny Jackson 2, 132
Williams, Kirby 171
Williams, Margaret and Robert 286
Williams, Wilber Herschel 123, 195
Willingham, Calder 294-295
Will-O-the-Wisp 209
Wilson, James Grant 72
Wilsons, The 296
Winchell, Walter 321
Windfall: a Novel About Ten Million Dollars 249
Winds Over the Campus 256
"Windy City" 3, 31, 98, 124, 146, passim
Windy City (Ross) 339
"Windy City, The" (Sandburg) 207-208
Windy McPherson's Son 150
Wine of Astonishment, The 139
Winer, Linda 342, 343
Winesburg, Ohio 212
Wingèd Victory, A 90, 110, 119, 127, 175
"Wings of Dawn, The" 347
Winnetka, IL 19, 247, 298, 331-332
Winninger, Charles 176
Winslow, Thyra Samter 206-207
Winter, Dale 164, 166
"Winter Evening" 234
"Winter Solstice" 343
Winters, Shelley 302
Winters, Yvor 153
Wirth, Louis 283
Wisconsin 30, 50, 80-81, 89, 100, 102, 111, 112, 138, 141, 142, 171, 185, 203, 227, 233, 247, 276, 281, 312, 346
Wisconsin, University of 80, 160, 205, 206
Wisdom's Gate 253
Wise, Winifred E[sther] 19, 299
With Edge Tools 76

With the Procession 87-88
Within This Present 253
Witte Arrives 159-160
Wizard of Oz, The 84, 126
WJZ 169
Wolf, Edwin, 2nd 237
Wolf, The 98
Wolf Point; An Adventure in History 291
Wolheim, Louis 166
Wolves Against the Moon 17, 21, 268, 313
Woman, role of, in Chicago 13, 62, 66, 80-81, 95, 102, 138, 160-161, 194, 240ff.
Woman About Town 244
Woman in Red (film) 263
Woman in revolt 143
Woman of Fashion, A 241
Woman of Genius, A 155
Woman That's Good, The . . . 62
Woman's Club 73
Woman's Devotion; or, The Mixed Marriage . . . 33
Woman's Duplicity; . . . 48
Woman's Home Companion (magazine) 175
Women in business see Career Women
Women May Learn 245
Women vs men authors 64, 186
Women's Christian Temperance Union 163
Wonder Hat, and Other One Act Plays, The 130
Wonderland 335
Wong, Anna May fn., 222
Woodburn, John 284
Woodford, Jack [pseud] See Woolfolk, Josiah Pitts
Woodlawn 347
Woods, The (play) 343
Woolfolk, Josiah Pitts 213
Working man see Unions
Works Progress Administration 305
World, New York 28, 59
World Changes, The (film) 262, 263
World I Never Made, A 258

"World of Nothing" 328-329
World of Nothing 328-329
World War I 130, 133, 136, 140, 144, 172, 178, 179, 182, 189, 193, 199, 202, 213, 222, 223, 224, 231, 232, 236, 237, 247, 262, 269, 273, 277, 278, 280, 313
World War II 232, 263, 264-266, 267, 270, 273, 274, 277, 279, 284, 286, 287, 290, 292, 293, 296, 299, 300, 305, 312, 314, 318, 328, 336, 338
World's Columbian Exposition 2, 3, 22, 32, 36, 43, 53, 54ff., 66, 78, 79, 82, 87, 91, 94, 119, 129, 146, 148, 178, 179, 208, 214, 227, 228, 230, 247, 251, 269, 270, 306, 312, 325, 332, 346, 347
World's Fair Murders 228
World's Fair Mystery, A 62
Wren, Percival Christopher 221
Wright, Frank Lloyd 345
Wright, Harold Bell 136
Wright, John Stephen 23
Wright, Richard 229, 261, 264, 279-280, 283, 284, 293, 306, 310, 311
Wrigley, Philip 316
Wrigley Building 283
Wrigley Field 341
Writers' Workshop, University of Iowa 228
Wrong Murder, The 281
Wuthering Heights 186
Wyatt, Edith Franklin 112, 162, 193
Wyman, Jane 175
Wylie, Philip 226
"Wynken, Blynken and Nod" 181
Wynne, Madeline Yale 84

Yaffe, James 298, 303
Yale University 115, 169, 342
Yandell, Enid 60
Year of the Quiet Sun, The 345

Year of the White Trees, The 299

Years of Grace 63, 137, 251-252

Yeats, William Butler 153

Yellow Book, The 82-83

Yellow Contraband (film) 216

Yerkes, Charles Tyson 30, 58, 103, 120, 148, 347

Yesterday's Children 265

Yesterday's Love 259

Yet Other Waters 258

Yexter, William J 47

"Yippie" movement 327-328

Yonnondio From the Thirties, . . . 337

Yoseloff, Martin 276

You Know Me, Al 136

Young, Loretta 240

Young & Fair 313

Young Dillinger (film) 8

Young Lonigan: A Boyhood in Chicago Streets 2, 257

Young Manhood of Studs Lonigan, The 2, 257, 348

Young Phillips, Reporter 223

Young Runaway, The (film) 321

Your Life Lies Before You 249

Zabel, Morton Dauwen 260

Zanuck, Darryl 29

Zara, Louis 19, 214, 235, 268, 286, 288, 306

Zelma, the Mystic; . . . 68

Ziegfield, Florenz 176

Ziegler, Elsie Reif 292, 314

Zig Zag Journeys in the White City 61

Zig Zag Journeys on the Mississippi . . . 61

Zipline, River Park 338

Zorbaugh, Harvey W 283

Zouave Cadets 23-24, 191

Z-Papers, The 333

Zukor, Adolph 214

Zury: The Meanest Man in Spring County 49-50